FRANK DUFFY
SECOND VICE-PRES.

WILLIAM GREEN
THIRD VICE-PRES.

JAMES DUNCAN
FIRST VICE-PRES.

T. A. RICKERT
FOURTH VICE-PRES.

FRANK MORRISON
SECRETARY

DANIEL J. TOBIN
TREASURER

SAMUEL GOMPERS
PRESIDENT

JACOB FISCHER
FIFTH VICE-PRES.

MATTHEW WOLL
SIXTH VICE-PRES.

MARTIN F. RYAN
SEVENTH VICE-PRES.

JAMES WILSON
EIGHTH VICE-PRES.

1924
EXECUTIVE COUNCIL *of the*
AMERICAN FEDERATION *of* LABOR

PEU 124

THE FIRST EXECUTIVE BODY OF THE FEDERATION (1881). THEN KNOWN AS ITS
LEGISLATIVE COMMITTEE.

SAMUEL GOMPERS   W. H. FOSTER
CHAS. F. BURGMAN   RICHARD POWERS   ALEX. C. RANKIN

AMERICAN
FEDERATION OF
LABOR

—

HISTORY, ENCYCLOPEDIA
REFERENCE BOOK

PREPARED AND PUBLISHED BY AUTHORITY OF THE
1916 AND 1917 CONVENTIONS

VOLUME II

FRANK MORRISON
Secretary

SAMUEL GOMPERS
President

GREENWOOD PRESS, PUBLISHERS
WESTPORT, CONNECTICUT

Library of Congress Cataloging in Publication Data

American Federation of Labor.
  American Federation of Labor.

  Reprint of the ed. published by the American Federa-
tion of Labor, Washington.
  Includes index.
  1. American Federation of Labor--History.
HD8055.A5A196 1977   331.88'32'0973   77-3562
ISBN 0-8371-9568-3

Originally published in 1924 by American Federation of
Labor, Washington, D.C.

Reprinted with the permission of American Federation of
Labor and Congress of Industrial Organizations.

Reprinted in 1977 by Greenwood Press, Inc.

Library of Congress catalog card number 77-3562

ISBN 0-8371-9568-3 (set)
ISBN 0-8371-9570-5 (Vol. II)

Printed in the United States of America

FOREWORD

*T*HIS *is the second volume of the American Federation of Labor History, Encyclopedia, Reference Book. It contains a brief statement of all important matters considered and acted upon by the American Federation of Labor conventions held in 1919, 1920, 1921, 1922, and 1923.*

The first volume of the book was devoted to the proceedings of the various conventions from 1881 to 1918, both inclusive. The present volume follows the same method used in preparing the first. It would be well to repeat portions of the foreword in the first volume, as follows:

> *The many questions considered have been compiled and published in encyclopedia form. This has developed a ready reference book and will be of great assistance not only to the officers and members, but to all who seek to know the principles upon which our trade union movement is founded and the wonderful successes achieved. Those who desire information in detail can readily refer to the conventions proceedings, as the work is also a bibliography.*

> *While each subject is briefly treated the intention has been not to omit anything that will prevent a thorough understanding of every principle. The rule followed was to use the official language of the convention. The belief was that it should be an American Federation of Labor book, not the work of any individual or group of individuals. The real authors are the delegates to conventions, extracts from whose resolutions and speeches are printed literally but in condensed form. It is the American Federation of Labor officially talking to you as you read, not an individual author. Every delegate who presented a proposition, discussed any issue, or in any way left the impress of his thoughts on the trade union movement will recognize the results of his work in the book. Only the names are omitted, making all the delegates equally responsible for the magnificent growth and victories gained by the labor movement.*

The labor movement of no other country has ever published such a complete history. It requires only a moment to find the action of an American Federation of Labor convention on any question pertaining to labor.

WILLIAM C. ROBERTS,
Compiler.

HISTORICAL

DURING the last five years the American labor movement passed through a most severe test, but it has come out of the struggle stronger than ever and with the determination to maintain the principles which have brought it success since the organization of the American Federation of Labor in 1881.

This second volume of the History, Encyclopedia and Reference Book containing the proceedings of the five American Federation of Labor conventions since the armistice gives briefly an amazing array of victories notwithstanding the intensive struggle for industrial democracy forced upon the organized wage earners. The determination of certain interests to establish autocracy in industry, conceived during the war, was let loose in all its fury as soon as the armistice was declared.

From March 4, 1919, until March 4, 1923, Congress was controlled by the nation's leading reactionaries who cheerfully aided those antagonistic to labor in propaganda intended to dishearten or discourage the wage earners so they would desert their unions. This sentiment in the ruling powers of congress was so great that bitter and unjust arraignment of labor was the rule.

Bills were presented providing for compulsory labor; for the deportation of foreign-born citizens who engaged in strikes; for taking the police power from the states and placing it in the hands of the federal courts; for legalizing judicial kidnapping; for the admission of 50,000 coolies into Hawaii under bond; prohibiting picketing in labor disputes; making cessations of work in the coal industry unlawful conspiracies and providing for a labor board to fix wages of miners similar to the railroad labor board; discontinuing publication of the Department of Labor *Monthly Labor Review*; relieving the well-to-do from taxation and placing the burden upon those least able to bear it by the establishment of a sales tax; authorizing a ship subsidy; providing for a merchant marine naval reserve service which could be used to break strikes; repealing the clause in the seamen's act permitting seamen to leave vessels in safe harbor; making those engaged in industrial disputes guilty of sedition; providing a penalty of $10,000 fine or imprisonment not exceeding ten years or both for any official of a trade union to advise any person employed in production or operation of any mines or agency of interstate commerce to quit such employment; making travel by water more dangerous by limiting the number of life boats, rafts and life preservers on vessels to 25 per cent, thus leaving 75 per cent of the passengers and crews aboard without means of safety in times of danger, and compelling seamen to work a twelve-hour day. They were all defeated.

Many other bills of lesser moment but all attacks on the normal activities of the wage earners were introduced. Labor had to confine its efforts to an endeavor to defeat the obnoxious measures. It was of no use to attempt to pass remedial legislation.

There also appeared a wave of inspired antagonism to labor throughout the United States and some of the state legislatures enacted legislation that aroused the workers. In Kansas, a compulsory labor law was enacted. Its originator attempted to have other states enact similar laws, but he failed. Later the supreme court declared certain sections of that law unconstitutional. Another state enacted a law permitting voluntary organizations to be sued. In fact many attacks on labor were written into bills and presented in some of the states. But labor was alert and succeeded in defeating the most dangerous of them.

After the armistice the antagonists of labor who had launched a campaign for the so-called "open shop" raised millions of dollars for the purpose of establishing autocracy in industry. Through their influence these bills had been presented. At the same time the Federal Reserve Board raised re-discount rates and refused to loan money on absolutely good collateral. The result would deflate labor and also the farmers. But labor refused to be deflated. It so aroused the wage earners and all just-minded citizens that during the elections of 1922 through the activities of the American Federation of Labor a sufficient number of members of the United States senate and house of representatives were elected to halt the drive against labor. The farmers had been deflated until it hurt so grievously that they joined with labor in many of the congressional districts and voted against enemies of labor and the people and in favor of friends of labor and the people.

The non-partisan policy which brought about these results proved its worth during the first five-month session of the sixty-eighth congress when a real step was taken toward controlling immigration and a proposed amendment to the constitution of the United States to protect child life was submitted to the states for ratification.

The conspiracy to deflate labor and the farmers was met with an aggressiveness on the part of labor that was unequaled in the labor history of any country. A concerted attack, probably under a "gentlemen's agreement," was made upon the textile workers, the mine workers, the railroad shopmen, the granite cutters, the printing trades and many others. Orders were given to reduce wages as much as 22 per cent. But the wage earners refused to accept these reductions and ceased work practically as a unit. The controversies lasted for months but finally labor was successful in defeating the plots to reduce wages. Agreements were made and practically all the strikers returned to work. The railroad shopmen were attacked by the executive and judicial branches of the United States, the attorney general injecting himself into the controversy and brazingly declaring that he intended to use all the forces of the government to protect the so-called labor board created by congress and preserve the so-called open shop. Nevertheless the railroad shopmen won.

An era of prosperity then set in and the president of the American Federation of Labor declared that he did not know of any other reason for the great increase in business industrially than the successful prevention of the reductions in wages. It gave the wage earners greater purchasing power which resulted in unusual prosperity.

For many years the American Federation of Labor urged the enactment of laws both by the state legislatures and the federal congress prohibiting the issuance of injunctions in labor disputes. It finally secured the enactment by congress of what is known as the Clayton act, which declared "that labor is not a commodity or article of commerce" and provided for trial by jury in contempt cases. Some federal judges make their own laws, and if there are any laws on the statute books that will interfere with their decisions they declare them unconstitutional. Consequently here and there judges would refuse to consider the Clayton act in making decisions and some of them declared portions of it unconstitutional.

Members of congress are not elected because they know anything about industry or commerce. The great majority of them are lawyers, many of whom are elected through the influence of certain interests. Therefore some of them conceive many kinds of sumptuary legislation, and especially that which would repress the normal activities of labor and of our people generally. It is a continual struggle to prevent the enactment of sumptuary laws.

In the supreme court's decision declaring unconstitutional the Kansas Court of Industrial Relations act which provided for compulsory arbitration the judges were unanimous in saying:

> It has never been supposed since the adoption of the constitution that the business of the butcher, or the baker, the tailor, the wood chopper, the mining operator or the miner was clothed in such a public interest that the price of his product or his wages could be fixed by state regulation.

In the decision declaring the woman's minimum wage law for the District of Columbia unconstitutional the supreme court held:

> The statute now under consideration is attacked upon the ground that it authorized an unconstitutional interference with the freedom of

contract included within the guaranties of the due process clause of the fifth amendment. That the right to contract about one's affairs is a part of the liberty of the individual protected by this clause is settled by the decisions of this court and is no longer open to question. Within this liberty are contracts of employment of labor. In making such contracts, generally speaking, the parties have an equal right to obtain from each other the best terms they can as the result of private bargaining.

This means that congress or the state legislatures can not enact any law providing for compulsory labor. The minimum wage law was secured by labor to protect women in industry.

But there is a lack of belief that the supreme court will maintain its position under all cases. It has not made a record for consistency only so far as it is expected to favor property as against the human equation. This is fully borne out by a statement in the minimum wage law decision as follows:

> This court, by an unbroken line of decisions from Chief Justice Marshall to the present time has steadily adhered to the rule that every possible presumption is in favor of the validity of an act of congress until overcome beyond a rational doubt.

Then while three members of the supreme court declared that the minimum wage law was constitutional five of the members said it was unconstitutional. The ninth member could not serve as he had appeared in favor of such laws when a practicing attorney. The child labor law was declared unconstitutional by a vote of five to four. It was the five to four decisions that impelled the American labor movement to demand that some check be placed on the assumed powers of the supreme court.

The 1922 convention declared in favor of an amendment to the federal constitution providing that if congress by a two-thirds vote repasses a law declared unconstitutional by the supreme court it shall become the law of the land. Each house of congress is a check on the other. The president, having the power of veto, is a check upon congress, congress is a check upon the president because it can pass a law over a veto by a two-thirds vote. But the supreme court is an autocracy. It is a law unto itself. A petit jury of twelve men must be unanimous in any verdict they bring in. But one of the members of the supreme court can override the 531 members of congress and the president of the United States. Members of the supreme court are appointed for political or for other reasons which are kept secret. There are no appointments more carefully scanned by the financial interests and big business than members of the supreme court.

The history of the American Federation of Labor has demonstrated that voluntary organizations can be kept together by giving each autonomy where compulsion would destroy. The strength of the American labor movement is in its democracy. It is organized similar to the government of the United States. The local unions were organized into international unions. These local unions formed city and state central bodies. The national and international unions organized the American Federation of Labor. The latter has no power other than that conceded by the conventions of the American Federation of Labor. It has federal and local trade unions directly affiliated and has the same power over them as national and international unions over their respective local unions.

Conventions of the American Federation of Labor are the most democratic of any organizations in the world. Every resolution submitted is referred to a committee, reported back to the convention and acted upon. Nothing is suppressed. Every delegate has the right to voice his approval or disapproval of any legislation or other matter proposed. While a rule exists in all conventions that speeches shall be limited to ten minutes, this is seldom enforced by the chair. There has not been an executive session since 1893, which was the only one ever held.

One of the outstanding victories of the American Federation of Labor was the defeat of the scheme to destroy the Department of Labor. The organic law which created the Department of Labor states that it is "to foster, promote and develop the welfare of the wage earners of the United States, to improve their working conditions and to advance their opportunities for profitable employment." The intention was to divide the department into various bureaus and place most of their functions in a proposed "department of welfare."

The 1921 convention of the American Federation of Labor pledged itself "to support any plan which had for its purpose the bringing about of the disarmament of all nations to the farthest extent consistent for the preservation of law and order throughout the world." Three weeks after the adjournment of that convention, the president of the United States approached Great Britain, France, Italy and Japan with inquiries as to whether it would be agreeable to them to participate in such a conference, which would also consider all Pacific and far east problems. The conference was opened armistice day that year and a step was taken to bring about peaceful relations between nations.

The question of education was one of the leading issues in the last five years as it had been since the organization of the American Federation of Labor. Pamphlets were issued ("Labor and Education" and "Education for All") which contain the official progressive declarations on that subject. This makes easily available labor's position on education and adds to the effectiveness of labor's contributions to educational progress.

Colleges, universities, public high schools and other institutions of learning have included many phases of the labor question in their debates. Whenever material concerning labor questions was obtained from the American Federation of Labor the team supporting the contentions of the wage earners generally won. A number of employers' associations had flooded these institutions with anti-labor literature, but it was so antagonistic to those who work for wages that the American Federation of Labor was appealed to for its side of the various questions.

Labor realizes that it must keep in touch with all the educational institutions in order that the students may know the truth about the important issues that arise. The reports of the legislative committee of the American Federation of Labor are sent to them in a circular entitled "What Congress is Doing or Not Doing."

It is not generally known that six million of the twenty million children of school age are absent daily from school. Education has been left to the states. When the selective draft came it was found that 25 per cent of the young men between 21 and 31 could not read or write the English language. Labor, therefore, is contending for a Department of Education. What the states refuse to do the nation for self-protection must do.

A most insidious campaign to break down the protective laws for women in industry has been waged for several years. The scheme is to secure an amendment to the constitution of the United States providing "equal rights" for women. Should it be adopted all laws limiting the hours of labor, maternity laws, mother's pension laws and all other laws enacted in the interest of women would be made null and void. But owing to the opposition of the American Federation of Labor the plan was defeated in a number of states as well as in the sixty-eighth congress.

Most friendly relations exist between the farmers and labor. They have worked together to secure remedial legislation. Whenever farmer measures are introduced in congress and hearings are held representatives of the American Federation of Labor appear before the various committees and urge practical constructive legislation for the farmers. No bill is advocated but the committees are told that the American Federation of Labor will stand behind any practical legislation upon which the farmers themselves will agree or that congress enacts for the benefit of the farmers.

The same amicable understanding exists between the American Federation of Labor and the American Legion. Representatives of the American Legion attend the conventions of the American Federation of Labor and the president of the American Federation of Labor or a representative whom he may select attends and addresses conventions of the American Legion. Labor supported all bills providing for adjusted compensation for former service men as it believed that in failing to enact such legislation our nation would stigmatize itself as ungrateful to those who offered the supreme sacrifice in order that the United States and the entire world should maintain their political liberty.

During the war more than 4,000,000 young men were taken out of industry.

Still there was a sufficient number of men and women in the United States to supply all things necessary for a successful war and at the same time for the civilian population. Yet no sooner did our boys return to their homes than an intensive agitation began for unrestricted immigration. Some of the advocates of letting down the immigration gates admitted that their purpose was to flood the labor market so there would be so many men for each job that wages could be reduced. Finally, through the efforts of labor and all loyal citizens an immigration law was enacted limiting the number that could enter this country to 3 per cent of the foreign born population of any nationality now in the United States. Still this admitted too many immigrants. Then a law limiting the number to 2 per cent was enacted. This provided a non-quota clause which would permit the wives of immigrants and their unmarried children under 18 years of age to come into this country. The object of this was twofold. In the first place labor believes that an immigrant should be permitted to have his family with him. Next if the family of an immigrant remains in the old country he would have to send money there for its support. It is much better for this money to be spent in this country than to be sent to a foreign country. Two foreign governments opposed this law because they wanted, they said, the immigrants to send their money to those countries to help recuperate them. Labor believes that if the money sent to foreign countries was of such benefit to them it would be of as great a benefit to the United States.

After the supreme court had declared unconstitutional two laws for the protection of child life it was found necessary to amend the constitution to empower congress to enact such legislation. During the sixty-eighth congress the following proposed amendment was adopted and sent to the states for ratification:

SECTION 1. The congress shall have power to limit, regulate, and prohibit the labor of persons under eighteen years of age.

SEC. 2. The power of the several states is unimpaired by this article except that the operation of state laws shall be suspended to the extent necessary to give effect to legislation enacted by the congress.

By the authority given congress it can prohibit the labor of children up to a certain age and then limit or regulate the labor of children between that age and eighteen years. Opponents of child labor legislation seek to defeat the amendment by claiming that the labor of all children under eighteen years of age will be prohibited. That age was fixed in order to meet conditions that may arise in the next twenty, fifty or a hundred years. It would not then be necessary to seek another change in the constitution.

For several years after the armistice the communists who were directed from Moscow endeavored to disrupt local unions in order that the American Federation of Labor could be destroyed. Destroying the American Federation of Labor was preliminary to overturning our government. But owing to the solidarity and steadfastness to the principles so long followed by the American Federation of Labor this plot so far has been defeated.

Then came another movement to organize the fascisti fashioned after that headed by the Italian dictator. The latter had said that liberty was dead and that he has stepped over its decomposed body. Fascismo has no place in our republic and strong efforts have been made to stop its growth.

Another organization known as the "Minute Men" appeared in the middle west, its organizer declaring for the so-called open shop. In fact, its organizer advocated a plank in one of the old party platforms declaring in favor of the "open shop." But he could not find a sufficient number of disloyal American citizens who would approve of his un-American idea.

Another enemy of the American Federation of Labor was exposed. This was the Federated Press. It professes loyalty to the trade union movement while at the same time the poison pens of its representatives applaud all those who are "boring from within." The 1923 convention declared that no agency "could serve communism and at the same time serve American trade unionism."

The universal establishment of the forty-four-hour week in the printing industry is one of the great advancements of labor. It also demonstrated that employers who make agreements and then break them must abide by the consequences. The victory in the printing trades will be a warning to other associations of employers that contracts are sacred documents and can not be made "scraps of paper" at will.

For many years legislative representatives in Washington of the various labor organizations worked alone. They did good work for their own organizations but could not always keep informed of proposed legislation affecting other organizations. In 1921, the president of the American Federation of Labor called a meeting of all legislative representatives located in Washington and formed an organization known as the "Conference Committee of Trade Union Legislative Representatives." Meetings are held monthly or more often during sessions of congress. This permits the exchange of information regarding legislation that has been of incalculable benefit. Any legislative representative coming to Washington to represent a national or international union or any labor organization automatically becomes a member of the conference committee. When matters of serious import are being heard before committees of congress or if there is to be a vote taken in either house the members of the committee work together to bring about satisfactory results.

The American Federation of Labor information and publicity service has made it possible for the rank and file in every union to learn what is going on in labor circles in the western hemisphere as well as the rest of the world. This feature was introduced in 1920 because the daily newspapers and other publications made it a practice to misrepresent labor. There also was a great increase in circulars and letters sent to national and international unions, state and city central bodies and local unions containing information regarding the labor movement. These activities bring all organizations nearer together and keep them informed on all matters it is absolutely necessary to know.

A legal information bureau was created in 1922 to collect data and judicial decisions on the rights of labor and to give advice on methods of procedure in time of court proceedings against labor.

Aid given the wage earners of Mexico brought about the great change for the better in their economic condition. The American Federation of Labor had a most powerful influence with the presidents of Mexico and aided in preventing the United States declaring war against that country. This resulted in most friendly relations between the Mexican and American labor movements as well as the loyal citizens of the two countries.

In November, 1919, the Pan-American Federation of Labor was launched through the efforts of the American Federation of Labor. This has brought about more friendly relations between the United States and the Latin republics. It proved the connecting link between the labor movements of North and South America. In 1922 the American Federation of Labor convention declared that it was the duty of the American labor movement to inspire the workers of Pan-America to organize along economic lines and affiliate to the Pan-American Federation of Labor.

Mexican wage earners made phenomenal gains in organization and in June, 1924, it was reported that the membership was nearly a million. The Obregon government had guaranteed free speech, free press and free assemblage. It had also divided up the land, and banditry had practically ceased. The country was making enormous strides and progress when a candidate for the presidency started a revolution. This was suppressed in a few months.

The Panamans have a national organization known as the Panama Federation of Labor with about 3,000 members. In Nicarauga organization work is in progress. The president of Nicaragua is trying to bring about better economic conditions and is having the support of the American Federation of Labor Labor in South American countries is also organizing to a greater extent than ever and all aid and comfort possible is being given by the American Federation of Labor and Pan-American Federation of Labor.

Every effort is being made to change the organic law of Porto Rico so that the people of that country will elect their governor instead of being appointed by the president of the United States. The advancement of the people of Porto

Rico has been phenomenal since becoming a possession of the United States. Labor is organized and is represented in the Porto Rican legislature by strong representatives. The Portland convention directed the Executive Council to also investigate conditions in the Virgin Islands, which had appealed to congress for civil government.

When it was learned that a super-power congress was to be held in London some time in 1924, and it was found that no arrangements had been made for labor to be represented, the president of the American Federation of Labor took steps to secure representation for labor on the American cooperating committee and corresponded with the representatives of labor in England urging them to take similar action. American labor was given representation.

No greater field for human advancement could be conceived than that connected with super-power. Through inter-connection with attending economies electric power and light may be supplied at cheaper rates. Inter-connection and long distance transmission make it possible to develop power plants at or near the mines thus reducing materially the amount of coal to be transported. Carried out to its logical conclusion super-power would revolutionize manufacturing, farming and every other industry.

Because of the conduct of the International Federation of Trade Unions and the intolerable rules and regulations set up for the government and conduct of that organization the American Federation of Labor has been unable to participate in the deliberations of that organization. The objections are:

1. That its new constitution completely abrogated the principle of complete autonomy for each national trade union federation.

2. That through the issuance of appeals and proclamations the executive body of the International Federation of Trade Unions had committed the federation to a revolutionary principle to which the American Federation of Labor is and always has been uncompromisingly opposed and to which no labor movement guided by democratic ideals could give approval.

3. That a system of dues had been adopted which would place upon the American Federation of Labor a heavy and unbearable expense.

After the adoption of the new constitution the International Federation of Trade Unions by a majority vote declared for a general strike by all affiliated trade union federations on May Day, 1920, for the overthrow of constituted government and the establishment of a socialist form of government. The American Federation of Labor could not endorse such a movement. The International Federation of Trade Unions was informed that the American Federation of Labor would not reaffiliate to that body until its constitution would guarantee the complete autonomy of each national trade union federation and a more equitable per capita tax be decided upon.

The federal law providing for the rehabilitation of civilians disabled in industry was secured through the efforts of the American Federation of Labor. In the past many thousands of wage earners were injured while at work who could not return to their former employment. Many of them were thrown upon the mercy of the public and were placed in charitable institutions or lived upon individual charity. Under this law, however, while many thousands could not possibly have returned to their former employment they were rehabilitated so that they could engage in some other occupation and become an asset instead of a liability to the nation.

Woman suffrage for which labor had contended since 1890 became a fact on the adoption of the 19th amendment to the constitution in 1920.

Encouragement for thrift has been one of the activities of the American Federation of Labor. In 1921, it condemned those who were swindling the public with fraudulent and worthless stocks and securities and urged the wage earners and people generally to purchase government securities. Agitation to have laws enacted that would discourage the sale of fraudulent stocks and bonds was entered into with much success.

The year 1921 was a year of unexampled struggle and difficulty. A great part of the effort of the movement was on the defensive, but it was a successfu l defense. The progress of those who sought to destroy freedom through the annihiliation of the organizations was checked. In 1922 the struggle was also bitter but all efforts to destroy the labor movement were successfully resisted. During those two years unemployment was acute but the policy and thought of the labor movement became more and more the policy of the nation. When industry began to thrive the policies of the labor movement continued to be the leading force of the nation's progress. That was inevitable. For the objective of the labor movement is to make the right to life, liberty and the pursuit of happiness material, moral and spiritual facts for every person.

One of the disturbing features of the campaign to destroy the labor organizations was the introduction in a number of state legislatures of bills providing for the compulsory incorporation of trade unions. The originators believed that if trade unions were incorporated they could more successfully injure them and in time entirely annihilate them. But labor was wide awake and fought such legislation to its defeat.

The American Federation of Labor believes that in the future many organizations will determine that in order to take care of all their members it will be necessary to inaugurate the six-hour day. Assistance in the fullest degree is pledged to any organization seeking to establish a shorter workday that will provide such employment. The question of seeking a six-hour day is left to the various organizations to determine, but those that do will have the fullest assistance of the American Federation of Labor

No one law ever enacted by congress or the several states has proved of such value as that providing compensation for persons injured in the course of their employment. The American Federation of Labor believes that industry should pay the cost of caring for the injured and protecting the heirs of those killed in industry. It also maintains that the compensation should be paid out of a state fund and that private compensation insurance should be prohibited.

Trade unions were the result of oppression that brought hunger, poverty and misery. From slaves to serfs to employes has taken centuries of struggle. The desire of our people for a better life, true liberty and greater happiness is being gratified more and more through the economic power of the trade unions. Their principles have been so vital that they have stood as a rock of Gibraltar in resisting all attempts to overthrow them. Although it required many centuries to bring about a recognition of the rights of the wage earners they are now so well established that no one questions the right of labor to organize. The American Federation of Labor has led the labor movements of the world in the economic advancement of labor and the people generally. It believes in evolution not revolution, and in the years to come will continue to bring about greater and greater advancement.

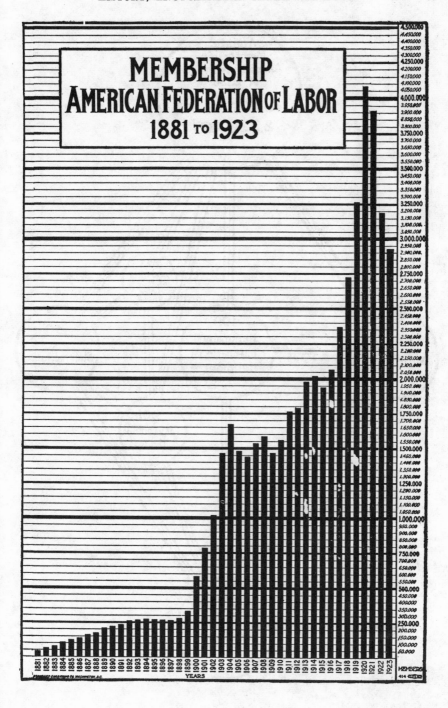

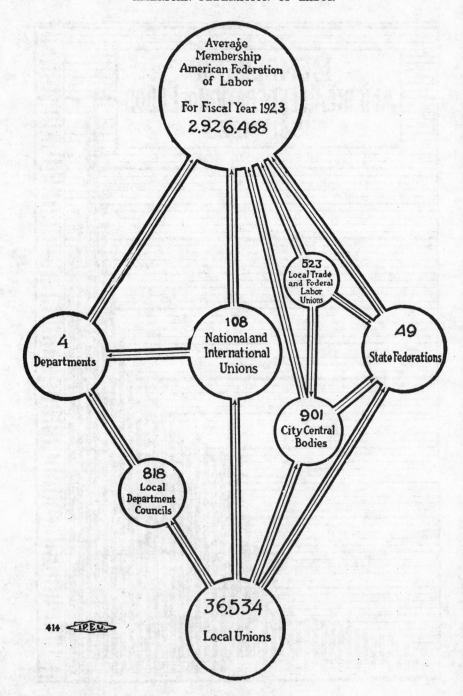

414 I.P.E.U.

ENCYCLOPEDIA.

*A*LL *the important subjects considered by the American Federation of Labor from 1919 to 1923, both inclusive, are contained in this encyclopedia. The original language in which the subjects were clothed is used in order that there can be no dispute in regard to the intentions of the conventions of the American Federation of Labor. The year in which action was taken and the page on which it can be found in the printed proceedings are also given.*

Acetylene Welding—(1919, p. 461) Reaffirmed decision of 1916 that "acetylene welding" is a process and an "acetylene welder" is a tool which can no more come under the exclusive jurisdiction of any one trade or calling than can the hammer or the saw.

Afel—(1919, pp. 207-284-349) The United States Shipping Board had offered to name a vessel for the A. F. of L. and requested the president of the A. F. of L. to make the selection. He chose "Afel." The launching took place June 28, 1919, at the Hog Island Shipyard. The vessel is 7,500 tons deadweight, steel, cargo carrying and oil burning. A committee of the union men employed in the shipyard had charge of the launching and the ceremonies in connection therewith. The officers of all national and international unions and central bodies were invited to be present. The only badge of admission to the launching, which was sponsored by a woman delegate to the A. F. of L. convention, was a union card.

A. F. of L. Advancement—(1919, p. 163) No question of great national policy or of great national interest is decided today without a contribution of thought and viewpoint by the labor movement. The war brought to the nation and to the labor movement questions more vital and more involved than we had known prior to the war. The coming of peace in nowise lessens the magnitude of the issues that must be dealt with. The A. F. of L., however, may face the future and its problems with a confidence born of severe trial and with an increased membership and unity of purpose. The labor movement, representing the great productive forces of society, is an indispensable part not only of society's productive processes, but of society's intellectual, political and sociological processes. It is essential that in order to take fullest advantage of the opportunities that lie just ahead and to assume our full share of responsibility, every possible energy should be bent toward increasing the strength of the labor movement through organization. Satisfying as has been the progress made in the year just closed, a vast amount of work in this direction remains to be done. The greater our strength, the better will our movement be equipped to accomplish the great work that is at hand for the coming year. Now, more than ever, the thought of the world is directed toward the achievement of progress and the establishment of higher ideals. The inspiration for this trend of events has been the product of the labor movement and

the labor movement must continue to lead in this direction.

(1920, p. 213) We have closed a year of complex experiences. Our Federation has gained in strength and influence and it has made during the year a record of achievement that must be a source of pride to every member. Human relations are always disturbed by great wars a d must undergo a period of reconstruction d rearrangement following great wars. We have been passing through such a period of reconstruction and rearrangement; indeed w are still in the midst of it. In reviewing the work of the year we can say with confidence and truth that the efforts of the organized labor movement have been the means of withstanding the tide of reaction and the means of lightening the burdens of our country. We have given true expression to the demand of the masses of our people for progress, for the enlargement of the sphere of human life and for the development of the splendor of our democracy and its institutions of liberty, freedom and justice. The splendid efforts of the organized workers of America have been devoted to the cause of humanity in peace as they were in war and in the years before the war. Our movement for humanity has gained in influence and effectiveness in proportion as it has gained in strength of numbers. Our problems will not be lessened during the year to come. Policies to meet issues of the gravest and most far-reaching importance must be shaped. But viewing the past and the splendid statesmanship and accomplishments of our movement, we are confident of its future wisdom and ability. We call upon the movement to be vigilant in defense of the principles of liberty, freedom and justice, to increase its strength everywhere and to face every task with confidence, fortified in the consciousness that the struggle for humanity and the rights of humanity must triumph over all obstacles. Now for the Five Million Mark!

(1921, p. 151) We have told the story of the year. It is a magnificent record of dignified, militant struggle. The road has been rough and its way has been marked by deceit and treachery among the forces of power and reaction. We are justified in expressing a great pride in the work of the year, but we shall miss the whole lesson and import of the story if we do not use it as a guide to the future. Each year we pause to recount the chapters, not for the sake of the past, but for the sake of the future. The book of yesterday is closed. Let us not dwell lovingly upon its pages, but let us look at them merely for what service they render in preparing us for tomorrow. It has been a year of tense and bitter strife. It has been a year full of preparation for the future. Our closing word to the men and women of the convention and of our great movement everywhere is: Forward, now, for better, fuller lives, for more light in the lives and work of our people, for more of democratic conduct in the work of our great country, for more of justice and freedom for all! Our slogan is organization, our cause is humanity.

(1923, pp. 136-262) The year's work is representative of the labor movement. The work accomplished has been made possible by the close cooperation of the organizations affiliated to the A. F. of L. and their members. With a spiritual consecration to the principles and aspirations of the labor movement, there has been a generous and wholehearted response to every appeal and suggestion. The work of the year demonstrates the constant forward movement of our wage earners; it expresses their beliefs and interprets their aspirations in terms of the common good; it shows that where there is an organized will to improve labor's condition there is also an organized constructive and progressive way. The trade union movement is not static. It meets new conditions as they arise. It does today the work which the conditions of today make imperative for the protection of labor and the safeguarding of the public interest in its highest conception. Standing firmly on the principle of representative democracy, the trade union movement seeks complete freedom for the workers through democratic representative institutions. It knows no race, no creed, no party, no sex, and no sects. It recognizes that united labor stands, divided labor falls. It affirms, and acts upon the affirmation, that the workers have the power to obtain complete freedom through the organization and effective use of their economic power—the power to produce wealth and render service in every branch of industry, agriculture, and commerce. Therefore, for the coming year we urge unceasing efforts in the work of agitation, education, organization, federation and unification. (P. 156) Despite hostile propaganda of the most vicious character, the normal growth of the A. F. of L. has been maintained. Abnormal growth during the war period is not at all a fair barometer and can be safely discounted in measuring our growth, and we find the average normal growth of about 50,000 members per year to have been easily maintained during all the years of our existence. The stability and virility of the A. F. of L. was never more in evidence than at present and clearly indicates the aggressive determination of its membership to carry on its noble work of uplifting the human race by enabling it to carry forward its battle for human liberties and the rights of those who toil.

A. F. of L., Appreciation of—(1923, p. 338) The following was read to the convention: "Greetings from the Portland Grade Teachers' Association to President Samuel Gompers and the A. F. of L., in sincere appreciation of what that body has done under his leadership to improve the status of women in industry, to protect the children of America from too early entry into industrial life, and to support and encourage progress in education."

A. F. of L., Attacks on—(1921, p. 286) Communication from Washington Central Labor Union: "Attempts are being made through a part of the press of the country, with the assistance of organizations of employers and others, to disrupt organized labor and more especially the A. F. of L. It appears that a part of this plan is to first destroy labor's chosen leaders through a vicious propaganda by issues and questions being injected into our economic life that are secondary to the purposes for which we are organized. In conformity with this plan of destruction, attacks are being made upon the president of the A. F. of L., with a view to destroying his usefulness in the minds of the workers of this country. We, the delegates to the Washington Central Labor Union, deplore and condemn this attempted destruction of the A. F. of L. and resent the attempt of outsiders, no matter in what walk of life they may be, to choose our leaders for us."

A. F. of L. a Voluntary Organization—(1922, p. 266) The A. F. of L. being a voluntary organization without police powers can not very well use compulsory methods to gain its ends, nor can it ask affiliated organizations to do that which it can not do itself.

A. F. of L. Building—(1919, p. 69) Receipts, $73,286.35; expenses, $73,284.01. Balance on hand April 13, 1919, $2.34. Amount due on loans April 30, 1919, $72,500. The offices in the American Federation of Labor Building, and particularly the Executive Council room, have been utilized for conferences of representatives of labor organizations and representatives of foreign countries and of the public. The prestige and dignity which our building has given to our country and our cause have been of great importance and advantage. (P. 361) The wisdom and good business judgment in constructing and maintaining a fitting office building for the A. F. of L. at Washington, D. C., is ably manifested in the report of the trustees having directed this business enterprise of our movement. From a general viewpoint this structure is a splendid monument to the constant development and uninterrupted progress of the American labor movement. It fittingly symbolizes the permanent and indestructible character of the American trade union movement. From a financial point of view the submitted report clearly demonstrates that this venture is not alone self-sustaining, but is designed to liquidate the financial obligation it is carrying within a comparatively brief period of time. While never intended as a profit-making undertaking, we have every reason to conclude that this project is profitable to our movement and its cause from every point of observation.

(1920, p. 62) Receipts, $103,281.05; expenses, $102,065.87. Balance on hand April 30, 1920, $1,215.18.

(1921, p. 55) Receipts, $29,006.20; expenses, $25,863.75. Balance on hand April 30, 1921, $3,142.45.

(1922, p. 32) Receipts, $30,859.69; expenses, $24,086.74. (Pp. 137-479) From year to year, three men have been selected to act as trustees of the A. F. of L. building. Their appointments have been made simultaneously and their terms of office expire simultaneously. To avoid the possibility of the building being without any trustee at any time, should the three trustees simultaneously resign or be unable to serve for any cause whatever, in the future the trustees of the A. F. of L. Building shall be chosen for one, two and three years respectively so that there shall always be two trustees in office, and the E. C. shall at the expiration of the terms of the trustees in their respective order elect for three years a successor for the trustee whose term shall expire.

(1923, p. 30) Receipts, $41,599.48; expenses, $32,433.12. Balance on hand August 31, 1923, $9.166.36.

A. F. of L. Committees—(1919, p. 341) To the charge that "committees selected by the A. F. of L. conventions are not representative since they are composed exclusively of the officers of national and international unions, while the delegates who represent the central bodies have no voice in determining the character of committee reports, thus creating an official caste in the labor movement," the convention declared: "The allegation contained in the resolution is untrue, as the committees of this and preceding conventions have contained delegates representing state federations of labor and central labor unions."

A. F. of L. Finances—(1922, p. 168) The president said: "You have heard read in this convention this morning and in the presence of visitors and a corps of newspaper men the report of the financial transactions of the A. F. of L. during the past year. Every dollar received and expended by and for the A. F. of L. and the labor movement has been laid bare and will be printed in the proceedings of the A. F. of L., so that those who may want to look for the good, or, if they can find, to look for the bad—it is all there. I challenge comparison with our open methods in taking the whole world into our confidence. I challenge the open shoppers, the chambers of commerce and the boards of trade and all the other capitalistic organizations to make such a clean showing as is made by the A. F. of L."

A. F. of L. Membership—(1922, p. 167) Notwithstanding the widespread industrial depression and the vicious attacks on organized labor by hostile forces, there has been no material reduction in the normal membership of the A. F. of L. It should be remembered that abnormal war conditions caused an unusually rapid growth of membership in recent years, and we now find that the A. F. of L. is coming through the present period of readjustment in good shape, with a membership considerably in advance of that which would have been attained had the growth followed the usual normal upward trend. The smaller per capita tax receipts for the past fiscal year do not necessarily indicate a corresponding decrease in members. Per capita tax payments represent only the members who are at work. Therefore, the difference in the per capita tax receipts is merely a reflect of the industrial depression and consequent unemployment of thousands of wage earners. To have maintained practically unimpaired its numerical strength in the face of the trying period we have gone through is a most eloquent testimonial to the virility and stability of the A. F. of L. and indicates the high purpose of its membership to carry on the battle for human rights and liberties.

A. F. of L. Officers, Appreciation of— (1919, p. 390) A careful review and unbiased observation of all the activities and accomplishments of the American labor movement, demonstrates conclusively that our movement is the peer of all organized efforts to protect and defend the rights of man and to bring into being a better life, greater happiness and a larger degree of justice and democracy. The trade union movement in its broadest terms is the effort of men to live the lives of men. It is the systematic struggle of the masses to attain more leisure and larger economic resources. It is the conceived movement for self and others directed against oppression in every form. It is a constant recognition of the fact that men and women of the mine, the shop, the mill, the factory, are men and women—not cattle or articles of commerce. It is a movement of protest against all conditions that tend toward the degradation of humanity. All our successes and achievements are not attributable solely to one man or set of men, and without the united support of all organized wage earners little progress would have been realized. We appreciate the value of keen, intelligent, loyal and devoted leadership, which qualities have been clearly and abundantly manifested on all occasions by the president of our federation. This convention therefore declares its appreciation in behalf of the workers of America for the loyal, devoted, self-sacrificing and extremely helpful services contributed by President Gompers to our movement, to our nation, and to all lovers of freedom, justice and democracy, and to express to him our deep and heartfelt sympathy for the great sorrow and loss which he experienced during the past year and for the unfortunate injury to which he was subjected in the recent past. To the secretary, the treasurer and all members of the Executive Council, the convention likewise extends expressions of sincere appreciation for the great and valuable services rendered and for the helpful manner in which they have at all times responded to the tasks imposed and duties required. The services performed by all the officers of the A. F. of L. accentuates the fact that our movement is founded on a love that gladly sacrifices for the common good and that the force of our movement lies in the attempt to bring into established order the idea of human development which has animated sages and prophets of all ages.

A. F. of L. Officers, Responsibilities of—(1920, p. 373) We would respectfully call attention to the magnitude of the task imposed on the officers of the A. F. of L. during the year just passed. The unusual amount of work mapped out for the officers and the Executive Council by the convention of June, 1919, was greatly augmented by reason of the many unforeseen but tremendously important questions which arose during the year; especially is this true because of the efforts of the reactionary elements in the various legislative bodies and the manifestations of hostility to labor coming from sources of influence and power. In addition to these a large number of emergency problems were presented incident to industrial disturbances, calling for advice or action on the part of the Executive Council. The tremendous labor thus necessitated has been met with such unremitting devotion to the interests of the workers and the cause which finds its expression in the A. F. of L. as justifies this convention expressing its appreciation of the work done by these men on whom is laid the trust of guarding at all times the American labor movement from attacks of enemies, either within or without.

(1921, p. 409) We wish to call attention to the enormous amout of work devolving upon the Executive Council of the A. F. of

L. during the last year. Not only has this group of earnest, sincere workers been unusually occupied with the important affairs of their own organizations but they have been called upon to handle not only the routine but a great many emergency questions of unusual seriousness. In addition to this was the large amount of effort required to carry out the recommendations and attend to the matters referred to the Executive Council by the Montreal convention. We wish to call the attention of the delegates to the fact that the expanding labor movement of America, which is reflected in the report of the secretary to this convention, proportionately increases the duties and responsibilities of the executive officers and the Executive Council of the A. F. of L. Especially has this been illustrated by the inordinate demands made upon the time of the president of the A. F. of L., who is now required to be almost protean in order that he may meet the many requests and attend to the many duties that fall upon him because of his position. The fact that these men have so faithfully devoted themselves to the carrying out of instructions and to furthering the interests of all workers is recognized by this convention, which again wishes to repeat the admonition made for the last several years that the officers of national and international unions, as well as delegates to this convention, show something more of consideration for the Executive Council of the federation, and that they do not infringe upon the time and patience of the federation officers and the council by presenting matters that could well be attended to without bringing them to the convention. This is not because of any disinclination on the part of the men who look after the immense amount of detail work which is involved in the proper carrying out of the purposes and designs of the American labor movement, but only as a matter of justice and that they may not be hampered because of being required to give time to matters whose importance does not warrant the attention now demanded from the Executive Council of the A. F. of L.

A. F. of L., Policy of—(1921, p. 193) A. F. of L. president's reply to fraternal delegates: "There are some who would solve all the problems of the universe with the turning of a hand or the twinkling of an eye. Human problems are not solved in that manner; it takes time, and time makes more converts, was the declaration of a wonderful philosopher nearly two hundred years ago—time to understand ourselves, time to make others understand; and he who undertakes to resolve that all the problems of the world shall be solved over night, providing it doesn't rain the following morning, will find a flood in his way, much to his being disconcerted. It is the tremendous task of the human race to bear the trouble and the travail accompanying the development and the struggle for human justice and human freedom; and every gain which we secure for the toiling masses and the masses of the people brings them just that gain and that step nearer the greatest goal of idealism. A noted physician has declared that you can tell the death rate of the babies in our country by the thickness and volume of the pay envelopes of the working people. We are not limited in any of the activities which we may seek to employ for the protection and for the promotion of the rights and the interests of the great masses of the toilers

of America. We have been with you and with all the allied democratic nations in the war, and to the extent of time that we were in it we made our full contribution. We have not done anything which we find it necessary to boast of and we have no cause to hang our heads in shame. The pity of it all was that when the crucial time came there were some of those who had made flamboyant declarations who failed at the crucial hour. What I am to say in the next minute or two is upon my own responsibility, and no one had been consulted about it either as being in my mind or as my expression. I hold that the organized labor movement of Germany failed at the critical hour. It is true that if the labor movement of that country had taken the situation in hand it might have meant the destruction of a few thousand, it might have caused the incarceration of many thousands; but if that had occurred it would have stopped the war. The failure of men to act when the time has arrived, when action is essential, is faithlessness to the common cause. I have nothing in my heart that can be intimated or suggested of feelings of antipathy toward the German people, toward the German labor movement, toward their attempt to conduct a great republican form of government. It can not be driven out of the minds of peoples who have lost young men of their flesh and blood, fallen in defense of this great common cause, to maintain some degree of a self-determination in a democratic form of government. You know, gentlemen, fraternal delegates, that the American labor movement has made its contribution to that great cause, and as one you know also that I have tried to do my full duty in the critical circumstances in which we are all placed; and the fact that at the peace table wisdom did not prevail, I think that most men who have given the subject thought quite agree with that judgment. But it is always hindsight that is so much superior to the foresight, and in the frame of mind in which the people were it was not difficult to understand that they wanted to penalize Germany in some way. We know that the representatives of democracy make mistakes, and that is the peanlty we pay for having democracies—but we have the right to make a mistake rather than to yield to the dictation of some emperor, kaiser, or king. If we want a democracy we must pay the penalty for the mistakes to which democracies are subject. When over in Europe and during the war, I made a number of addresses. I remember that on one occasion a reference was made to the fact that the great storehouse of the world was in the confines of the United States of America, that moneys were being sent over to us, that in time we would become the creditor nation of the world. And I am free to say, this to you on my own responsibility, that I am not so proud that we are the creditor nation of the world. I would rather that the credit should be on a standard of the whole world. But I did say, at the time: "You are singing our praises you are glorifying the institutions of the American republic, you are saying our men are noble and altruistic. I hope that when the war is closed and it is an established fact that the United States is the creditor nation of the world, I wonder whether you will love us as much then as you do now?" As a matter of fact, being composed of humans, we haven't an overweening love for our creditors. All that we can do is as a country to make our contributions toward the establishment of some ties that shall bind us in a common effort to maintain industrial peace. There has not been a movement in the United States or in any other country for the maintenance and perpetuity of international peace of which the A. F. of L. has not been a stout defender. It is this travail, this trouble, this unsettled state of mind, this nervous tension that the war has invoked in everyone of us wherever we are located that does not give most of us the opportunity of clear-minded, well-balanced judgment and expression. The world is topsy-turvy still. In the American labor movement, as in the bona fide labor movements of other countries, there has been an effort to make genuine proposals, constructive proposals of a widespread, deep foundation, and high hopes of a reconstruction plan which the enemies of labor have too little understood to grasp and have had too much of a greedy hand and an itching palm to endeavor to put into practice. We want you to believe, fraternal delegates, that whatever comes the A. F. of L. and its constituent bodies will stand firm for the right, and for the practical application of the principles of right and of justice. Before our enemies, no matter whom they may be, we stand erect, not like the old-time toiler with bent back and receding forehead the man typified by the picture and the poem, 'The Man with the Hoe.' We stand erect as humans, as democrats in the best sense of that term, as sovereign citizens, as wage earners, producers of wealth, asking no favors, yielding nothing but what is right, and determined not to be deprived of any right and privilege to which the humblest citizen of our country is entitled under the constitution and declaration of independence. We want no dictatorship of any kind; we want the recognition of the principle of equality before the law and equality of opportunity. We want neither dictatorship from the bottom nor from the top. We will work out the solution of the problems in meeting them, so that each problem may be met and overcome; and we will find that new problems are continually arising to confront us; but with the solution of any problem today we would be better able to meet and solve the problems of tomorrow, and tomorrow, and tomorrow's tomorrow. Our movement is conducted in its practices clean, open and above board; nothing to hide and nothing to fear. We shall meet a year hence better prepared to meet the problems of the then coming year. Our membership, the great rank and file of organized labor, is looking forward to the proceedings of this convention in the hope that it may be guided by judgment and practicability to accomplish results in the interests of the wage earners and the people of America. And the unorganized, voiceless, unable to express themselves, for they have no method of expression, they, too, are looking with longing eyes for the time when they may ally themselves with us and stand shoulder to shoulder with us; and going down into the lowest abyss of misery and despair help to raise those in the mire up to the standard of the toilers of our country, organized, unafraid, with the highest ideals for the attainment of that brighter and better day of which philosophers have dreamed and poets have sung. The toiling masses of the world all time have had to bear the brunt of the battle, and we must carry on that struggle until the time when

man shall be the brother to man and a' that."

A. F. of L., Progress of—(1923, p. 247) The following telegram from the Secretary of Labor was read: "Organized labor in America is entitled to sincere congratulations on the progress which is marked by this annual convention of the federation. Under wise and sane leadership the trade union movement is going steadily forward, fostering the welfare of the man who toils and bettering the conditions under which he works. The world is alive with new theories, new political and economic nostrums which may mislead the unwary with their glitter. In Europe nations have come close to ruin through these theories. In one great European nation a mere handful of men control the destinies of one of the greatest populations numerically in the world. Two other countries are under absolute dictatorships and a third is fast approaching the same condition. In these nations economic conditions are in a chaos, millions of men are walking the streets seeking employment and those who are able to find work are recompensed by a mere subsistence wage. It is to the eternal credit of the American trade union movement that the false notions of the old world have been unable to obtain a foothold in this country. Here the working man is in demand, jobs are plentiful and wages are at the peak. Here, too, labor has its full share in government. In America labor is well represented in public office, federal, state, county, city and town. Let us hope that the American trade union movement will go forward on the same safe and sane road which it has followed in the past, seeking always the ultimate best for the man who toils. This road leads to the maintenance of the pay envelope of the American workman as the largest and most profitable in the world and to the maintenance of production in American industry at its highest. Great tasks lie before American labor. The devastating evil of child labor must be eliminated from American industry. The million children who toil must be freed from the grasp of the taskmasters. American labor must no longer compete with American childhood. More and more we are coming to a realization of the mutuality of interests between the men who manage industry and the men whose labor makes industry possible. We must do all we can to foster the principle of mediation and conciliation in industrial disputes, substituting the settlement of the council table for the settlement by force. Above all we mut devote ourselves to the intelleetual development of the man who works in order that he may be able intelligently to perform his task and to produce the machinery which will ultimately shoulder the mere drudgery of production. Under his direction American labor can look back upon a great past. It faces a great future."

Agricultural Conference, President's— (1922, p. 92) On January 23, 1922, there was convened in Washington by the secretary of agriculture, acting for the president, a national conference on agricultural problems. Labor was represented in this conference by one delegate, the president of the A. F. of L. In this conference, called to deal with most vital issues, there was but one representative to speak for all the workers and but a small minority to speak for all the actual farmers of the country. Control of the conference was in the hands of a group of railroad representatives, trust magnates, financiers and anti-labor employers. This dominating group immediately made clear its purpose to put the conference on record in favor of wage reductions. Throughout the entire conference the railroad representatives and their friends fought to secure adoption of declarations in condemnation of railroad workers, asserting that only reductions in railroad wages could produce reductions in freight rates. The conference was in the hands of profiteers and exploiters from the start to the finish. The purpose served by the labor representative was to write continually into the record protests against the assertions made by the representatives of railroads and big business and to use the conference as a platform from which to address the public in opposition to the interests that controlled the conference. Constructive effort was impossible and no constructive result was achieved. A detailed report of the work of the labor representative in the Agricultural Conference was published in the *American Federationist* for March, 1922.

Aliens—(1921, p. 414) During the Great War restrictions providing that aliens could not be employed in navy yards and arsenals were withdrawn and many subjects of foreign countries, some not eligible for citizenship, received the benefit of such employment. After the war this rule acted as a detriment to American citizens. It is therefore declared that all employes of a race eligible for citzenship and who fail to qualify be summarily dismissed from the service of the navy and war departments, and the rules of the civil service commission in vogue before the war requiring applicants for employment in the government service to be American citizens be rigidly enforced.

Aliens, Surveillance for—(1922, p. 101) Under guise of a naturalization bill a measure has been introduced in congress that is most dangerous. It provides for the registration of aliens upon landing in this country and until they become citizens of the United States they will be under strict surveillance in their homes, in their employment and as to their political and social activities. Before its introduction the newspapers of the country pointed out the value of the proposed legislation. It was purported to be for the purpose of creating a "new federal bureau of recreation to make better and happier all of the workers of the country and to absorb more quickly into American life the immigrants from other countries coming to our shores for sanctuary." Every immigrant must register each year wherever he is. Advocates of the bill defend this provision by saying that the requirement is not in order to "spy upon him, but in order to be sure of his safety and in order to educate him." Public school officials are to supervise the aliens and the said supervisors must see that their behavior has been proper in every way. Throughout the bill can be found constant threats of imprisonment, cancellation of naturalization papers and deportation if immigrants do not walk the straight line marked out by the supervisors. Any alien who has become a citizen can have his citizenship taken away and be deported. In times of industrial disputes, therefore, foreign born workers would face imprisonment and cancellation of naturalization papers and deportation. This is not overdrawn. Only a few weeks ago a judge in Pittsburgh refused to naturalize a number of miners because they were on strike. (p. 327) The A. F. of L. denounces this legislative absurdity which carries espionage and spying to a point that is repugnant to Americans because it does violence to our cherished ideals of freedom and liberty and equality before the law.

Amalgamation of Craft Unions—(1923, p. 266) In defeating several resolutions favoring amalgamation of craft unions the A. F. of L. declares: All these resolutions carry with them the imputation that the A. F. of L. is confined to "craft" unions. and that it uncompromisingly resents recognition of any organization that resembles or approximates an industrial form. An examination of the roster of the affiliated organizations of the A. F. of L. disproves that false imputation and stigmatizes those who would advance such untruths either as being ignorant or deliberate frauds. Again, these so-called "amalgamation" proposals carry with them the implication that affiliated "crafts" unions can not cooperate, federate or amalgamate because of some fancied power of resistance alleged to be exercised by the A. F. of L. Again, an examination of the records of the A. F. of L. brands such implication as false and untrue. It is not, however, so much the false implications and imputations involved in these so-called "amalgamation" resolutions that should move us to renewed vigor and drastic action as it is the motives of the prime movers who are continually urging these proposals upon the councils of labor. Demonstrative proof is overwhelming that those who are constantly at work dividing the organized workers on abstract discussions of forms of organization and spreading the poison of suspicion against the officers of trade unions have never been loyal trade unionists and have always antagonized the trade union movement. In addition, the self-acclaimed "amalgamationists" are not bent on amalgamation, but upon the disruption and destruction of the organized labor movement of America. In this they serve well the employers who would again assume complete mastery over the destinies of the wage earners. The purpose and aim of these destructionists, as well as their standing within our communities, is no less savory than that of private detectives who would sell the soul of their fellow man for the jingle of gold. In the religious world such men are excommunicated. In the political world such men are ostracized from society, if not treated more severly through the operation of laws relating to treason. In the industrial world, we have tolerated them altogether too freely. These sinister agents, propagandists and destructionists of a foreign foe to our American institutions, should be singled out wherever found and the light of day be thrown upon their nefarious work. Likewise, employers, frenzied in their blindness for wealth and gold, and who, for the moment, find encouragement and hope and give passive if not active support to this and similar movements which seek to distract attention and divide labor's forces, may well hesitate. They should realize that to destroy the evolutionary processes of progress, advancement and application of the ideals of democracy and of the golden rule in all relations of mankind is but to hasten revolutionary tendencies with all that these great social revulsions impress so tragically upon humankind. The trade autonomy declarations of the 1901 convention are therefor reaffirmed.

American Federationist Index—(1923, pp. 130-254) The first volume of the analytical index of the *American Federationist* is approaching completion. It is designed as a guide both to labor's progress during the thirty years since the magazine was first published and to the activities of the trade unionists and the trade unions without whom labor's achievements would have been impossible.

American Legion—(1921, pp. 277-404) Member of the Executive Council requested to attend the national convention of the American Legion to convey to that organization greetings from the A. F. of L., to the end that the relations between these two great organizations now so happily established may be the more closely cemented and made permanent to the advantage of all the members of each of these patriotic societies.

1922, (pp. 137-164-285) The most friendly relations exist between the American Federation of Labor and the American Legion. Frequent conferences have been held between representatives of the two organizations on matters of interest to both. In legislative matters it has been found that the two organizations are working in complete harmony. (p. 360) Surely these two great American organizations, having so large a membership in common, should be friendly forces, cooperating for the enrichment of the common life, and the development of a high quality of enlightened citizenship, characterized by breadth of view, public spirit and tolerance. There should be conferences from time to time between the organizations of labor and the American Legion in every city in which there are legion posts established, for the purpose of removing any misunderstandings that might arise. Where the policies of the two organizations are at variance, as is the case in certain important aspects of the educational field, such conferences, local and national, may bring adjustment through better mutual understanding.

(1923, p. 63) The relations between the A. F. of L. and the American Legion have continued during the year to be cordial and helpful. Pursuant to the instructions of the last A. F. of L. convention the president of the A. F. of L. attended and addressed the last annual convention of the American Legion held in New Orleans in October, 1922. The A. F. of L. and the American Legion cooperated in the observance of American Education Week, December 3 to 9, 1922, and in hundreds of communities throughout the country committees appointed jointly by the two organizations served in the development of the programs. We recommend continuance of the friendly and cooperative relations which have been so beneficial in the past not only to the members of the two organizations directly involved but to our citizenship in general. (p. 249) The invitation extended to the national commander of the American Legion to address the convention of the A. F. of L. is approved, and that in the spirit of reciprocity, cordiality and as evidence of our sincere desire for mutual helpfulness that the president of the A. F. of L. be authorized to accept the kind invitation extended to him and to convey these fraternal greetings and expressions of helpful consideration in person to the coming convention of the American Legion. (p. 140) Resolution adopted by the American Legion state executive committee meeting, Portland, Oregon, Saturday, September 29, 1923, and sent to A. F. of L.: "The history of the rela-

tions between the American Legion and organized labor in Oregon has been one of sincere cooperation and mutual understanding at all times. It has been our experience that, in all things affecting national welfare, national unity, and national protection, we are in common accord. The American Legion of Oregon, speaking by its executive committee now in session, therefore takes this opportunity to extend its greetings and its cordial welcome to the members of your distinguished organization."

American Legion, Rifles for—(1920, p. 119) A bill providing for the loaning of not to exceed ten obsolete or condemned rifles to each post of the American Legion for use by them in connection with the funeral ceremonies of deceased soldiers, sailors and marines, passed both Houses and was signed by the president. Blank cartridges are to be sold the American Legion posts at cost price plus expense of packing and transportation.

American Steel Foundries vs. Tri-City Central Trades Council—(1922, pp. 43-372) This case was first argued in January, 1919. It was re-argued October 15, 1920, again re-argued October 4 and 5, 1921, and finally decided on December 5, 1921, by the United States supreme court. This was an injunction proceeding instituted by the American Steel Foundries, a New Jersey corporation, against the Tri-City Central Trades Council and the individual and collective members thereof to enjoin them from carrying on what was alleged to have been a conspiracy to prevent the American Steel Foundries Company from obtaining and retaining skilled workers to operate its plants at Granite City. The Tri-City Trades Council admitted the use of peaceful persuasion but denied threats of injury or commission of violence. However, a very broad restraining order followed by a like final decree which prevented the use of persuasion and that of picketing at or near the premises of the company or on the streets leading to the premises of the company. An appeal was taken from this order to the United States circuit court of appeals. This appellate court struck out the word "persuasion" wherever it occurred and inserted therein the words "in a threatening manner." Thus the wording was changed but the substance remained. The United States supreme court reviewed the evidence and the decree at length. The first proposition of law decided by the United States supreme court was that section 20, the labor provisions of the Clayton act, which was passed when the case was pending in the court of appeals controlled the disposition of this case, even though the acts had heretofore taken place. By this method of reasoning the United States supreme court created for itself the opportunity of passing judgment upon this section of the Clayton act, treating it as in force, notwithstanding the Duplex decision and as declaratory of what had been the past practice always. The supreme court, in reviewing this section of the Clayton law, held that the object of the congress in enacting this section was to reconcile the rights of the employer in his business and in the access of his employes to his place of business and egress therefrom, with the right of employes, either present, or recent or expectant employes to use peaceful and lawful means to induce present or prospective employes to join their trade union. The supreme court held, however, that in effect, section 20 of the Clayton law, did not apply.

and therefore did not constitute a legal defense, if, in the attempts at persuasion or the inducing of employes to join the trade unions, methods were adopted which, however lawful they might be in their announced purposes, might inevitably lead to intimidation. By judicial declaration the supreme court amended section 20 of the Clayton act by making the motive as well as possible consequences a part of this section of the law. Thus by judicial construction the heart was taken out of section 20 and the effectiveness of this provision of the law was totally destroyed. While the United States supreme court held that all workers have the right to free passage through the streets consistent with the rights of others, nevertheless, three or four groups of workers made up from some four to twelve men in a group, each union interested having several representatives within that group, might lead to assaults and violence. The court considered it was idle to talk of peaceful communication under such conditions and, therefore, held such picketing was unlawful. The supreme court of the United States expressed the belief that it was its recognized duty to have every regard for the congressional intention manifested by the enactment of the Clayton law, and to the principles of existing laws. It believed, however, and so ruled that each case must turn upon its own merits and circumstances. In this case the United States supreme court said that the strikers and their sympathizers should be limited to one representative for each point of egress and ingress in the plant or place of business; that all others be enjoined from congregating at the plant or in the neighborhood; that the appeals of these single representatives should not be abusive or threatening; that they should not approach individuals together but singly and that they should not obstruct an unwilling listener by importunate following or talking. While this was not laid down as a set rule, but only as one which should apply to this case, the court did rule, however, that this was a question for the judgment of the chancellor who heard the witnesses, familiarized himself with the place and observed the tendencies to disturbance and conflict, and that, "the purpose should be to prevent the inevitable intimidation of the presence of groups of pickets, but to allow missionaries." In reaching this decision, the supreme court either demonstrated its misconception of industrial disputes or knowingly closed its eyes to the dangers surrounding union men who would peacefully solicit the membership and support of non-union workers. While every protection is afforded to the employer and safety is made the predominating element for the ingress and egress of non-union workmen and while the right of persuasion is hesitatingly admitted, no protection or safety is afforded to the union workmen or sympathizers who would dare singly to approach groups of non-union workers for the purpose of communicating with them. In other words, every conceivable protection is given the non-union workers but no protection whatever is accorded the union worker in the exercise of his rights against the assaults of the employers' hirelings and violent methods of promoting discord. To protect the union workmen as well was the real intent of congress, yet by subtle interpretation the supreme court of the United States has twisted a legislative enactment intended for the protection of Labor to one

of direct injury to Labor. In this case the supreme court declined to follow the case of the Iron Molders' Union vs. The Allis Chalmers Company, and refused to accept the modification made by the court below. In this Allis Chalmers case the injunction issued by Judge Sanborn was so sweeping in its terms and violative of the constitutional rights and guarantees of citizens that when the subject was directed to Theodore Roosevelt who was then president of the United States, he denounced it as a judicial interference with the inalienable rights of labor and as a partisan inclination toward the rights of employers. Chief Justice Taft who was then a member of the cabinet agreed with the president that the injunction was of too sweeping a nature and at the suggestion of Mr. Taft, the distinguished lawyer, Frederick A. Judson, of St. Louis, now deceased, who was a classmate of Mr. Taft at Yale and by Mr. Taft made his alternate on the War Labor Board, was retained as counsel who argued the case for the molders. As a result, this injunction was modified so as to permit peaceful picketing, the courts saying: "The right to persuade new men to quit or decline employment is of little worth unless the strikers may ascertain who are the men that their late employer has persuaded or is attempting to persuade, to accept employment," and that "provisions of persuasion and picketing, as such, should not be included in the decree." Evidently, what Mr. Taft believed right and just as a member of the president's cabinet, he now finds improper as chief justice of the United States supreme court. Two points of great importance stand out in this decision of the United States supreme court; one is the full recognition that under certain circumstances the effect of the labor sections of the Clayton act in conjunction with existing principles of law is not to be entirely remitted to the actions of the immediate employes and the immediate employer but that other members of a union acting with them ought to be accorded like rights. This may be regarded to some degree a modification of the law as laid down in the Duplex Printing Company case decided over a year ago, though it must be admitted that in this confusion of legal decision the lower courts will accept that point of view which best serves their purpose. The other important position taken by the United States supreme court is that it is entirely proper for a court in equity to supervise the details of picketing. In effect, this decision gives regulative authority over our industrial relations and thus through the injunctive process, the protection of our courts has been extended in a manner never contemplated by our constitution, based upon a philosophy that is so ill-founded that it can not in the long run commend itself to the judgment of mankind. Then, too, this decision illustrates with what ease our judiciary may alter legislative pronouncements intended to safeguard the rights of labor into instruments of oppression and depression. Mr. Justice Brandies concurred in the substance of the opinion and in the judgment of the court. Justice Clarke dissented.

Anti-trust Law—(1920, p. 114) Every so often an attempt is made either in the senate or house to eliminate the provision prohibiting the use of any of the appropriation for the department of justice in prosecuting labor or farmer organizations under the anti-trust act. (P. 361) Executive Council directed to continue its watchfulness to prevent the elimination of that provision.

(1921, p. 396) Executive Council was directed to consider the question of either asking for a rehearing of the decision declaring unconstitutional the provision of the Sherman anti-trust act, which exempted labor organizations from coming under the law, or the enactment of a new law which would be constitutional.

(1922, pp. 108-340) S. 3385, by Senator Edge, provides for the regulation of trades associations. It is to weaken the provisions of the "anti-trust" act but carefully prohibits any of the benefits being gained by labor by exempting labor organizations. Senator Edge introduced S. J. Res. 188 to appoint a committee to investigate existing conditions of industry and commerce in the United States for the purpose of recommending to congress such legislation if any as may be deemed best, to revive industry and to define the rights and limitations of cooperative organizations as distinguished from illicit combinations in restraint of trade. It is presumed that those back of the bill who are continually threatened by the anti-trust act desire a twilight zone in which they will feel safe in any combination they may enter into for the purpose of fixing prices in order to make larger profits. The hearings will be used as propaganda to educate the public into the belief that the profiteers in our country are much abused by the stringency of the "anti-trust" law. Labor believes that the anti-trust law should be repealed, as it is used almost entirely in the prosecution of trade unions which it was said when the law was enacted would not be subject to its provisions. Strenuous objections should be raised if any attempt is made to still further amend the "anti-trust" act to the detriment of labor and the farmers. (p. 373) The following proposals are approved: "An act repealing the Sherman anti-trust law which was intended by congress to prevent illegal combinations in restraint of trade, commonly known as "trusts," but through judicial misinterpretation and perversion has been repeatedly and mainly invoked to deprive the toiling masses of their natural and normal rights. A law which will make more definite and effective the intention of congress in enacting sections 6, 19 and 20 of the Clayton act, which were manifestly ignored or overridden by the court."

(1923, p. 92)—The Sherman anti-trust law and the several supplemental laws predicated upon this law have all been designed to restrain the combining and merging of industrial and commercial groups for the purpose of monopoly and the arbitrary fixing of prices through monopolistic control or restraint of trade. At the time of the enactment of the Sherman law the development of large corporate and associated enterprise was in the making. It was to prevent this further development that the Sherman anti-trust law was enacted. But this law was impotent in the face of the industrial and commercial developments and by decisions of the United States supreme court within the last few years its restraining influence has been annulled for all practical purposes. At the time of the enactment of the Sherman law considerable apprehension was expressed by the organized workers that the anti-combination features of this law would be used by our courts to stifle and destroy trade union organizations and activities. Despite the fact that assurances were given

that no such restraint was contemplated or embraced in this law the same judicial body that freed organized capital from the operation of the Sherman law arbitrarily included labor and labor organizations under its restrictive features. It was hoped that the subsequent enactment of the Clayton law with its labor provisions, declaring that labor was not a commodity or article of commerce would free the workers and their trade unions from these repressive limitations. It was likewise believed that the curtailment placed upon the power of the courts to invade the rights of the workers when engaged in industrial disputes with employers would safeguard the wage earners in their natural freedom and constitutional guarantees to freedom of speech—of conduct, and of assembly. But again the United States supreme court injected itself and by adroit construction and interpretation reversed the judgment of congress and again gave life to repressive legal measures calculated to strengthen the arm of employers when in conflict with the wage earners. (p. 275) The original Sherman anti-trust law was conceived and designed merely to restrain large capitalistic combinations and not to disturb trade unions. Subsequently, the law was altered by judicial interpretation to exclude to all practical intents and purposes the capitalistic combinations originally intended to be checked and to bring trade and labor unions under its repressive features. Attempts were made to correct the result of this presumptuous power of the judiciary. The Clayton law, with its labor sections, was enacted as supplemental to the Sherman anti-trust law. But again the U. S. supreme court has so restricted its labor provisions as to render this law useless for the purposes intended. It is clearly evident that the Sherman anti-trust law and all other legislation related to and of a similar character can not check industrial developments and tendencies and that such laws only furnish added opportunities to repress the trade union movement. Legislative demands are in the making which contemplate the wiping out of these repressive laws together with all suppressive decisions predicated on this sort of legislation.

Arbitration, Compulsory—(1920, pp. 114-361) Executive Council was directed to continue to oppose a bill presented in congress providing for the investigation of all disputes and controversies "threatening the operation of the government," "intercourse between states," or the "distribution of the necessaries of life." Fines and imprisonment are the penalties for calling a strike or lockout while the commission is making an investigation of all labor disputes. The commission is to be named by the president and is empowered to adopt rules of procedure similar to those of the federal courts. After making its investigation the commission shall report what will end the dispute or whether a legislative remedy is required. The bill does not speak of the railroads or interstate commerce as applied to the transportation lines. It applies to any "operation of the government." The construction of ships, buildings, hauling of mail by teamsters; in fact, any employe of the government or of a contractor or subcontractor would come under its provisions in times of controversy. It could be construed by unjust judges as applying to any trade or calling.

(1921, pp. 113-313) The A. F. of L. has on many previous occasions expressed clearly its irrevocable opposition to compulsory arbitration, which is in a large sense included in the "compulsory investigation" of labor disputes. This great organization has from its birth steadfastly championed voluntary arbitration as a method for arriving at the settlement of all disputes or differences which can not be composed by conciliation or mediation, but it never has and does not now consent to the doctrine of compulsion. Compulsory investigation is as repugnant to the concept of freedom for which the federation stands, as is the dogma of compulsory arbitration. We condemn without reservation any measure looking to the end as provided in H. R. 9062.

Austrian Relief—(1920, pp. 169-474) The people of Vienna, Austria, have suffered intense poverty and misery. Indeed, they were in a state of famine. Although authentic investigations were made and reports received as to conditions prevailing there, they are indescribable in their horror. We were appealed to for aid in succoring the famished people of Vienna. Instead, however, of making the appeal particularly to the working people of America, we joined with all other agencies which had the machinery and the facilities, not only to solicit and obtain contributions, but to transform them into the materials to satisfy the wants of the ill-fated people of Vienna and vicinity. Reports coming to us are in grateful acknowledgment of the valuable and effective assistance rendered. In addition, America's workers joined with every effort to alleviate the tremendous distress obtaining among the peoples of Serbia, Armenia and various other lands where the people were suffering.

Baker-Gompers Agreement—(1919, p. 383) The so-called Baker-Gompers agreement consummated on June 19, 1917, was intended as a war measure only. The period in which it was expected to serve has passed, also the institution that functioned in its affairs has automatically dissolved. Therefore this thirty-ninth annual convention of the A. F. of L. will consider the aforesaid agreement null, void and in every way canceled on or before July 1, 1919.

Banking, Currency and Credits—(1921, p. 398) Our present system of credits is tending to centralize more and more a dominating control over the industrial, agricultural and commercial life of the nation, rendering more and more subordinate the freedom of the activities of the industrial workers and farmers. This system of credit is made possible largely through the accumulation of the savings of the great mass of the workers in banks and the collecting of large funds by insurance companies, mutual and otherwise. It is believed the funds thus collected and accumulated and our present credit system have been used to crush and destroy the trade union movement and impoverish the workers as well as the farmers.

(1922, pp. 88-338) Inquiring into the question of the extent to which bankers may dominate industrial enterprises and commercial activities, it is found that the banking system in the U. S. as everywhere else, can be said to dominate industry and commerce in the sense that industrialists and merchants frequently need the capital which is loaned by the banks. Practically every product is sold on credit from thirty to ninety days and in some cases six months. Necessarily almost every concern at sometime or other is required to establish credit facilities or be at least able to discount bills receivable.

Because of these business requirements a bank may make or break a business concern by the granting or refusing of credit in time of stress or during dull seasons, or off-seasons, for seasonable goods and by refusing to discount commercial papers. It is urged, however, that because banking is very largely competitive, their interests divergent and, at times conflicting, and because it is difficult to assume precisely similar ideas on the part of each competitor, it is difficult, if not inconceivable, to describe exactly the form of domination the bankers might wield over industries and commerce. Despite the claims of divergencies and conflicts of interest and the difficulty of adopting precisely similar ideas among bankers because of the spirit of competition, bankers are in a position, nevertheless, to exert, and they do exert, much influence over the business policies of concerns which require large amounts of capital and which are not financially strong. This is especially true of investment banks. Commercial banks can not so readily interest themselves about the operating policies of concerns to which they make small loans until they get into financial difficulty. There is, however, the existence of unfair practices where bankers are on boards of industrial enterprises and where captains of industry are on boards of banks in that a position of preference with respect to banking opportunities is accorded such concerns. The development of interlocking directorates likewise tends to, and does, induce an artificial control as well as provides preferential positions for the interested groups and thereby enlarges the scope of their influence and control. Thus it was made evident in a hearing before the railway labor board that the railroads are controlled by a group of twelve New York banks, trust companies and insurance companies, dominated by J. P. Morgan & Company; that the J. P. Morgan Company control at least fifteen financial institutions; that J. P. Morgan and allied financial interests control at least twenty-four coal mining companies and coal railroads. Practically twenty-five men are the instrument of this and an even wider control. This same group of twelve financial institutions at the same time has interlocking directors with at least twenty of the leading railroad equipment companies. It is evident, therefore, that banks do have a powerful direct and indirect influence and control over the industrial and commercial activities of our people. It is equally evident that an effort should be made to secure a complete divorcement between related financial and industrial and commercial enterprises. We are not prepared at this time to submit a definite program because of the complexity of the problem involved, but the E. C. is authorized to give this subject further consideration and attention and to take such action as may be helpful in having this financial stranglehold removed from the throat of our industrial and commercial life. Particular emphasis was laid upon the investigation of the control and influence of banks over the industrial relations policies that might be enforced upon employers in their dealings with wage earners. Bankers, generally speaking, have been opposed to the trade union movement. Unquestionably, too, the hostile attitude of manufacturers, associations, merchants' organizations and trade associations, has largely influenced the policies of banks in their dealings with firms that express a sympathetic and encouraging attitude toward trade unions. Investigation has disclosed the fact that in a number of cities banking institutions have used their banking facilities to compel employers to assume an attitude toward trade unions which would weaken if not destroy the organizations of the wage earners. In some instances this control over banking facilities has been used to enforce a reduction of wages; in other cases to further the so-called "open shop" or "American plan" idea, while in other cases both these repressive objectives were the ends sought. However, the initiative and source of influence over the use of deposits and funds in banks and the use of banking facilities in fighting organized labor do not always rest with the banks. Indeed, the banks are as much subject to the influence of manufacturers, merchants and trade associations as the individual merchant and manufacturer are subject to the bank's influence and control. Investigation has demonstrated that in a number of cities chambers of commerce, manufacturers' associations, so-called citizens' committees and other varying forms of associations dominated by business men have exercised their collective influence and association with banking institutions to compel employers, who desired to deal fairly with the trade unions, to alter their course and to assume a hostile attitude toward the organizations of the wage earners. Thus, employers have been threatened not alone with curtailment of trade facilities but obstacles have been placed in their way in securing proper credit with which to purchase the necessary raw material. Likewise, threats have been made to call in loans or to deny further loans or to "freeze" credits unless industrial relations policies and employment conditions prescribed by these associations of manufacturers or merchants are complied with. Example upon example might be cited to bear out the finding that banking facilities are being used to destroy the trade union movement and to impoverish the workers through the savings deposited by the workers into our banking institutions. How to meet this situation is a difficult, though not hopeless, task. It has been suggested that to prevent this unjust and unwarranted discrimination of banking and credit facilities, the government should undertake to establish competing government banks throughout the large industrial cities and farming communities and thus bring into play in our banking system a factor that will destroy this menacing control over moneys and credits by a comparatively few, and transform the use of money and credit to serve the needs of all the people instead of proving merely an instrument of exploitation and repression. It has been urged likewise that our postal savings bank system be made more liberal, that the amount of its deposits be enlarged and that the rate of interest be increased. While our investigation has not proceeded sufficiently far either to approve or disapprove the encouragement of government banks to compete with private banking institutions or whether adequate laws might be proposed to prevent a continuance of the dangerous practices to which attention has been directed, we urge that the facilties of the postal savings bank be enlarged and that the rate of interest be increased as well as the amount of permissible deposits be enlarged. Another proposal urged is that of encouraging trade unions to engage in banking institutions.

It would seem that trade unions with a large accumulation of funds might profitably invest these funds in their own banks and attract to themselves the savings deposits of their members and of their sympathizers and friends in general. However, not many trade unions would seem to be organized so as to permit them to enter into the banking business. Where the accumulation of funds is subject to constant withdrawals and use in defense of strikes or lockouts, and for the payment of other benefits, it is difficult to conceive how a trade union might strengthen itself by converting its funds into the working capital of a bank. Then, too, if trade unions are to venture into the banking business, the urgency for the incorporation of trade unions may become more pronounced and make the bringing of a suit against them and the seizure or impounding of their funds more easy of accomplishment. Trade unions could as easily enter into the banking business as they could undertake to operate a factory, a printing office, or any other business enterprise. But where they so enter the business world they abandon the primary purpose of the trade union; and if such business ventures do succeed, those who participate in their control and share in their gains are shareholders and in the final analysis the benefits derived will be in the form of stock dividends. This is especially true of the banking business as wage earners could not be expected to receive greater interests for deposits or to borrow money on better terms than they might secure at other banks. The management of a union bank would be held to as strict accountability as any other banking institution, and the membership would not consent to the acceptance of undue assumption of risks or imprudent venturing of union funds. Under these circumstances, it is difficult to note how this proposal could alter the attitude of the present banking institutions. There are several banks instituted or encouraged by trade unions. Doubtless the experience that may be had by these institutions will indicate the advisability and desirability of encouraging trade unions to enter this field of business venture. While we believe trade union banks are possible, we believe that such ventures should be considered with caution and be approached with extreme care. In connection with this, attention is directed to the action of the last convention of the A. F. of L., at which time cooperative banks and credit unions were approved and the form of legislation enacted on this subject by the commonwealth of Massachusetts recommended for adoption in every state legislature. While the subject of control of banking facilities by bankers and manufacturers and commercial groups to destroy the effectiveness of trade unions and to suppress the workers is one involved in many complex difficulties and impossible of regulation by law, we are not without a strong weapon of defense or retaliation. Those familiar with banking urge that successful banking depends upon the ability to secure and maintain deposits five times equal to the capital invested. This would indicate that the life and success of a banking institution depend upon a minority fraction of deposits placed with such institutions. Since the manufacturing and commercial associations have been using their organized strength to influence banking policies by reason of their use of banking institutions, the trade union movement is equally justified to use the organized power of trade unions to so influence the savings of its members and friends and of trade unions deposited with any banking institution hostile to the workers' interests in the same manner as do the manufacturers and merchants. If the boycott method may be freely used by employers against the borrowers at banks through a denial of banking facilities, the boycott may also be used by labor against the bankers who encourage or who submit to this sort of dictation. Since the banking facilities have come to be used as a weapon for industrial mastery by employers, the savings and deposits of the wage earners in banks must be so controlled by the workers as to protect fully the wage earners interest in this contest, for the firm éstablishment and full maintenance of their rights in industry and commerce. The wide scope and effectiveness of this recommendation is fully understood but the choice is not of our making. Every international and local trade union is urged therefore to direct the attention of the A. F. of L. to any instance or to any banking institution that uses or is influenced to use its banking facilities to oppose, weaken or destroy the trade union movement or to interpose its power and influence into industrial relations affairs so that the Executive Council may investigate each complaint and if no adjustment is reached, then to publish the facts ascertained in its investigation and to call upon all trade unions, wage earners, their friends and sympathizers to place their deposits with banking institutions that will not venture into trades disputes and that will serve all the people in an impartial and just manner. It is particularly recommended that because of the vast consequences involved in this proposal that the power and authority involved shall be exercised solely by the A. F. of L. and its Executive Council and by no other division or branch of the American labor movement.

Stabilizing the Unit of Money—(p. 91) Unquestionably the whole question of inflation and deflation and their avoidance is becoming of increasing importance throughout the world. Every group in our political, social, industrial and commercial organism is affected by the expansion and contraction of our currencies and credits. The lessening of cylical variations in business activity is but another approach to the solution only from a different point of view. The problem, however, is not domestic but world wide. It is of the highest importance that the monetary systems of all countries that play an important part in international trade shall have a common standard of value and that that standard be of a stabilized purchasing monetary unit in order that international trade may be encouraged and exchange rates may be made stable. Whether the problem is one of stabilizing the purchasing power and value of the dollar or of stabilizing the price of commodities, it is one of such proportions that consideration should be given it by the U. S. government through congress. Every influence and interest in our national life should rise above selfishness to a spirit of promoting the future welfare of all and to that end should cooperate with the national government in finding a proper solution to this most urgent need of our time— a more stable medium or method of exchange. (P. 338) Executive Council directed to make a study of the question of establishing a central bank at Washington, D. C., together with

such branch banks as occasion may demand or opportunity afford.

(1923, p. 44) Unquestionably, there is a growing desire on the part of the trade unions and their members to enter into the business of pooling their funds and savings to attract to themselves the additional earning power of their moneys and to balance the credit power now exercised by employing interests. Practically twenty-three labor banks are either doing business or are about ready for business. In addition about twenty more such banks are now in the process of organization. Practically each of these institutions while fundamentally directed to the same purpose varies in some degree either in form of organization or in policies to be pursued and methods to be adopted. It must be apparent, therefore, that any attempt to coordinate the activites of these labor banking institutions through a central bank situated in Washington, D. C., presents practical as well as legal and financial obstacles. In addition, any attempt to interfere with the definite policies and form of organization of existing and prospective institutions will be resented and prove harmful. If there is to be coordination and cooperation of effort between these banking institutions of trade unions such a relationship can only come by future development arising out of a further experience and better understanding of those engaged in these banking activities. We can not pass from the discussion of banking without once more calling attention to the vital question of credit. Banking and credit are as inseparable as life and air. We have said in previous reports that while credit is the life blood of modern business it is not now administered in such a way as to serve primarily the needs of production. Credit as now administered too often increases unearned incomes at the expense of earned incomes and constitutes a burden upon necessary industry. We have pointed out the ideal of credit administration through a public agency. We feel constrained to point out that no appreciable progress toward that end has been recorded, but we can not but feel gratified at the great interest aroused by our analysis and our proposal. Through the growing number of labor banks some progress toward the ideal may be made. Most progress consists of a compromise between conditions and the ideal. Labor banks are much nearer to the masses of the people than are the institutions of what is commonly called Wall Street; and they are more responsive to fundamental needs. As banks, we look upon these institutions as helpful, even though they constitute no remedy. They may force remedies for some of the more glaringly inexcusable exploitations of the banking and financial world. If, through the development of relations between labor banks on sound lines, there can come into being a credit administration in the interests of productive effort, in the interests of true human progress, in the interests of service to society we shall have reason to look upon labor banking as having the character of a truly fundamental step in advance. If there is hope to be seen in the development of labor banking institutions we feel that it must be through the development of a great agency for the constructive administration of credit. (p. 269) The A. F. of L. is against the formation of promiscuous and ill-matured banking institutions conducted by labor. No greater disaster could come to existing

¹abor banking institutions than the failure of one or more ill-considered and badly managed institutions of this character. In this as in all other tendencies the development of labor banks presents a fertile field to those who would exploit and commercialize the hopes and aspirations sought to be realized through institutions of this character. It is, therefore, all the more essential and important that the greatest possible degree of care and caution be exercised by those contemplating investing their funds or savings in the formation of labor banks. Labor banking institutions can not possibly operate as a remedy for economic injustice and industrial unrighteousness. That they can be made helpful supplemental agencies to the trade union movement can not be successfully controverted. That there may be developed through these labor banking institutions an administration of credits in the interest of productive effort, in the interest of true human progress and of service to society, is also hopefully anticipated. Because of this supplemental aid and by reason of the influence that may be manifested in the control of our credit administration the organized workers are urged to give favorable consideration and preference to such labor banking institutions as upon investigation by them are found to be established on sound principles and managed along well established and proper lines. The A. F. of L. is against the possibility and practicability of the A. F. of L. instituting or causing to be instituted a central labor bank at Washington, D. C. Such an institution or arrangement must of necessity arise out of the experience and willingness of existing labor banking institutions.

Banking, Protection for Unlawful— (1922, pp. 107-339) Alarmed by the attacks on the federal reserve system and banking institutions generally their defenders in the house have introduced two bills to punish those who criticize banking institutions. They are known as H. R. 11217 and H. R. 296. Progressive members of the house are fighting the bills, which, if they become laws, would prohibit free speech and free press. The recent denunciations of the increases in the salaries paid by the federal reserve bank of New York would be a misdemeanor and any member of congress who advocated a measure for the protection of the people from illegal banking acts could be fined $5,000, imprisoned for five years or both. The bills are in line with many others that are simply to protect the privileged few from criticism of their acts.

Banks, Cooperative, Credit Unions— (1920, p. 396) Executive Council directed to investigate the advisability of urging the enactment of laws by the nation and by the individual states that will permit of the organization of cooperative or peoples' banks and of credit unions, along the lines of laws heretofore enacted by the states of Massachusetts, New York, Rhode Island, North Carolina, South Carolina, Texas, Oregon, Utah and Wisconsin.

(1921, p. 111-373) There is no essential difference between cooperative banks and credit unions except that the former are on a much larger scale. Cooperative banks loan money to their members on real estate or on shares held by them. Credit unions are governed by virtually the same laws. There is no doubt that both of them are incentives to thrift. The members of both are made up of individuals, not of unions; that is,

individuals who belong to labor organizations do not join them as union men. They are merely associations of citizens who either are employed in a certain factory (in the case of credit unions) or are residents of the place where the cooperative banks are established and are people generally of some means (in the case of cooperative banks). Laws governing cooperative banks and credit unions are virtually the same in various states. The Massachusetts statutes provide for agreement of association on the part of twenty or more persons for the purpose of forming a cooperative bank to accumulate savings of its members in fixed periodical installments and loaning such accumulation to them. Provisions are made for certificate of incorporation, adoption of by-laws and to all intents and purposes such a bank becomes a corporation with all the powers and privileges and subject to all the duties, restrictions and liabilities set forth in the general laws of the state having to do with corporations. The capital to be accumulated by such a cooperative bank is unlimited and is divided into shares of the ultimate value of $200 each. No person is allowed to hold more than forty unmatured shares nor more than ten matured shares in any one such bank, but any person may hold both unmatured and matured shares up to the specified amount. These banks may consolidate upon compliance with certain regulations. The laws relative to credit unions in Massachusetts provide that when seven or more people in the commonwealth associate themselves by agreement for the purpose of accumulating and investing the savings of its members and making loans to members for provident purposes, they may become a corporation by the consent of the board of bank incorporation and upon complying with the law. Credit unions receive the savings of their members in payment for shares or on deposit. They lend to their members at reasonable rates, or invest the funds they accumulate in accordance with certain provisions. (p. 373) Refused to indorse a proposition that the various unions of the A. F. of L. establish a central bank, providing the capital therefor by a direct assessment of a nominal sum against each one of their members, and that then the surplus and other funds of the locals and the grand lodge be there deposited; that these banks then affiliate, and jointly establish local banks for the common use and benefit of all these orders, where their combined membership is large enough to justify. Instead the report of the Executive Council on cooperative banks and credit unions was indorsed. (pp. 389-397) Refused to create a new department of the A. F. of L. to establish in each and every city chartered national banks as rapidly as assessments and profits warrant.

Banks, Postal Savings—(1922, pp. 111-354) A bill has been introduced in congress to increase the utility of the postal savings banks by encouraging savings among the people and to secure the largest returns consistent with adequate security. It provides that the deposits shall be invested in bonds of the U. S. bought on the open market at the lowest possible obtainable price and that no ·other investment of the funds shall be made. The balance of the funds with the exception of a working reserve shall be loaned at the highest obtainable rate of interest in the following manner: Preference shall be given to small loans over large loans; to short-time loans over long-time loans; loans adequately .secured by readily marketable collateral over loans on real estate or other less readily marketable security. The board, which would be composed of all members of the president's cabinet shall fix the rate of interest to be charged on loans, the profit and security of the depositors being the basis of whatever decision is made. Evidence was submitted to the committee on banking and currency of the house that if this bill became a law the government could pay 4 per cent instead of 2 per cent on deposits. (p. 325) The A. F. of L. favors an increase in the rate of interest paid by postal savings banks to at least 3 per cent to be paid quarterly on balances; that accounts should be with the U. S. post office department, thus allowing deposits and withdrawals anywhere; that joint accounts where either of survivors may draw; accounts for minors of any age by parents or guardians and accounts for organizations.

Blair Report—(1919, p. 323) Senator Blair, one of the earliest men in political public life to manifest his sympathy for the workers and to incorporate it into a helpful action introduced and had passed in the U. S. senate a resolution authorizing and directing the committee on labor and education to make an investigation of economic and industrial conditions. The report made by this committee was never fully published and the four volumes that were published are now almost out of print. This report and the interesting facts set forth therein make a valuable contribution to the history and industrial condition at that time. The A. F. of L. herewith petitions the U. S. senate to order a reprint of this report and such other papers, documents and memorandum now in the possession of senate custodians or ex-senator Blair. The president of the A. F. of L. stated that while the edition of the document referred to was almost entirely out of print, he had managed to secure a copy and had it on file in the office of the A. F. of L. He stated further, that there was no copy in the Library of Congress and none available in the document room of either the house of representatives or the United States senate.

Bolshevists Made by Congress—(1920, p. 102) No more just arraignment of congress has been uttered than that of the president of of the A. F. of L. in a hearing before the committee on interstate and foreign commerce of the house. He was protesting against the plan of compulsory arbitration proposed by a member of the interstate commerce commission, and he declared that congress was tying the hands of labor in fighting boleshevism and anarchy. He said: "You are the greatest breeders of bolshevism. It is such legislation as this that encourages the growth of the I. W. W.'s and bolshe-viks. That is what you are doing, gentlemen. You are giving them the means to undermine the American Federation of Labor. Already they and the bolsheviks are saying to the workers, 'that is what you get for return of your loyalty and patriotism during the war.'"

Bonus and Stop-Watch Systems—(1921, p. 119) When the army appropriation bill for the fiscal year 1921 was before the house it was discovered that the clause prohibiting the use of the bonus and stop-watch systems had been omitted from the measure. On motion the clause was restored to the bill. Another attempt to strike out the provision was defeated by a vote of 177 to 47.

Bonus for Federal Employes—(1919, p. 132) For the fiscal year ending June 30,

1919, the federal employes were granted an increase of $120, beyond their statutory salaries. They asked that the increase be $360 for the fiscal year ending June 30, 1920. This was refused by the house committee on appropriations, which reported in favor of the former sum, $120. On January 18, by a vote of 202 in favor, 79 opposed, 149 not voting, Representative Nolan of California secured the adoption of an amendment increasing the $120 to $240, which sum remained through all stages of the passage of the bill. This additional compensation is effective only for the year ending June 30, 1920, and it does not apply to railroad or postal employes, or to persons whose basic wages or salaries have been increased more than $200 since June 30, 1918, or who entered the service since that date. (Pp. 135-329) According to the language of the $240 increase clause carried in this year's legislative appropriation act, a comparatively small number of the employes in the navy yards and arsenals will receive it unless the departments choose to exercise their discretion in the employes favor, as the bill gives them the right to do. In that respect the bill is worded the same as the $120 increase clause. An effort was made to have this clause so amended that it would give employes in the navy yards and arsenals the benefit of the $240 increase in case they had not received during this fiscal year an increase aggregating over $200. They have received an increase of 64 cents per day, which for 313 working days amounts to $200.32, and this would bar them from participation in the increase, excepting through departmental discretion. An attempt to amend the bill so as to make absolutely certain that the men in the navy yards and arsenals receive the $240 increase failed. A second attempt to assure these employes the $240 was made by an amendment offered to the general deficiency bill, but this bill failed of passage.

(1920, p. 107) After the war began, and rather than institute an inquiry into the wages of employes of the government, a general bonus was granted. This amounted at first to $120 per year and later was increased to $240. This year the employes asked for an increase of the bonus. When the legislative, executive, and judicial appropriation bill was under consideration, a point of order was raised against the bonus, the claim being made that it was new legislation. The appropriation was therefore omitted from the bill. When the bill reached the senate the committee on appropriations recommended that the bonus be reinstated for another year. This was approved. The house agreed to the amendment and the bonus was therefore retained. (p. 479) The A. F. of L. appreciates the temporary relief rendered public employes by the granting of this bonus, but is opposed to this system, and desires to express the hope that the wages of public employes will be increased to an amount which will make unnecessary the granting of a bonus.

(1921, p. 114) In the legislative, executive, and judicial appropriation bill in the sixty-sixth congress, the provision for a bonus of $240 for federal and district employes was stricken out on a point of order. The bill was then sent to the senate where the bonus provision was restored. The senate also incorporated in the bill the provision that the employes of the navy yards, arsenals, and women's bureau should receive the bonus. The house agreed to all the amendments of the senate except that referring to the employes of the navy yards, arsenals and women's bureau. The objection to granting the bonus to the navy yard and arsenal employes was said to be based on the fact that a wage board determines their wages. Under the law employes of the navy yard and arsenal receive the prevailing rate of wages in their respective districts. The wage board in fixing rates subtracted the $240 bonus which it was believed congress would grant them. Congress, however, refused to give them the bonus and their wages were therefore reduced. Efforts will be made in the sixty-seventh congress to have this great injustice remedied.

(1923, p. 89) When the question of a bonus of $240 to government employes for the fiscal year ending June 30, 1923, was under consideration in congress an attempt was made to reduce it to $180. There had been delay in taking up the bonus question, Chairman Madden of the appropriations committee of the house stating that it was not included in the sundry civil appropriation bill because it was possible that the reclassification bill would pass and there would be no need of the bonus. The federal employes accepted this promise in good faith, but when Chairman Madden reported the bill providing for the bonus of 1923, the amount was fixed at the lower figure. Vigorous protest was made by the A. F. of L. and the organizations of federal employes. Representative Lehlbach moved to strike out $180 and insert $240. This was adopted. (P. 359) It is heartening to note that under the operation of the classification act, which becomes effective July 1, 1924, the annual fight for a continuation of the bonus for federal and District of Columbia employes will no longer be necessary. Hereafter, under the provisions of the classification act, the bonus will be part of the base pay. It is gratifying to note that the long fight for the adoption of the principles embodied in the classification act is nearing a successful end. The Executive Council and the organized government employes affected by this long-sought legislative reform are commended for achieving substantial results from a congress that was reluctant to heed labor's wishes. Having won the legislative fight, organized labor must now watch carefully the administration of the classification act so that the intent of congress is not nullified by restrictive or reactionary interpretations.

Budget System—(1919, p. 358) The A. F. of L. gives its approval of the principle of a federal budget system to efficiently administer the financial affairs of our government, and the Executive Council is authorized and directed to investigate the federal budget systems proposed and to approve and support that budget system, which in its judgment, is best designed and devised to safeguard the interests of the workers and all our people, and calculated to minimize our national expenditures without interfering or retarding the legitimate and helpful activities of our national government.

(1920, p. 121) The house passed a budget bill which provided for the appointment of a director and assistant director to whom all departments, bureaus, boards or other establishments of the government, except the legislative branch and the supreme court, should furnish information in regard to the powers, duties, activities, organizations and financial transactions and objects of their respective offices. An annual estimate of expenses of all departments was to be submitted by the president to this board, which would pass such sum as seemed to the director

to be necessary. The senate substituted a bill which provided for a commissioner and two assistants, attorneys and professional experts. Budget legislation failed.

(1921, p. 108) None of the bills presented in the sixty-sixth congress contemplated a true budget system. The only change from the present system would be the creation of a new bureau which might gradually become an efficiency bureau and add to the expense of government without accomplishing the purposes intended by law. Unless a law creating a budget system can be enacted that will place the responsibility for the amount of the appropriations and the taxes levied it would be ineffective. (P. 312) Since the convention met a law has been enacted for the creation of a budget bureau, to be maintained in the treasury department and under the direction of a comptroller general and assistant comptroller general to be appointed by the president. All department and bureau heads will be required to report to the budget bureau concerning the needs of the several departments and bureaus of the government. The budget bureau also will be in touch with the ways and means committee of the house of representatives, which is the agency through which the revenue of the country is raised by taxation. It is thus expected to keep a closer relation between the income and outgo of the government. Responsibility for both the collection of taxes and the expenditure of moneys is by this measure placed directly on the executive, who has the power of veto over the budget or any item contained therein; hitherto, the president has been able to evade any responsibility for extravagance or wastefulness in any department of the government because of the archaic method of making appropriations and the loose and irresponsible conduct of the various administrative departments and bureaus of the government in the expenditure of money beyond the sums appropriated. While economy is justifiable, it is a crippling niggardliness when followed in the making of appropriations for welfare, humanitarian, or scientific work, or for work that would conserve the health and safety of the great mass of the working people. Neither should false economy impair the efficiency of the government and its departments. The budget law in its present form is not perfect by any means, but it is a long step in the right direction, and as time will bring to the fore all of the present defects, the law will undoubtedly be amended from time to time.

(1922, p. 108) The bill providing for a bureau of the budget became a law. The bureau has developed into a bureau of efficiency. Thousands of employes have been discharged, wages reduced and the employes of the government kept in a continual state of demoralization. The arbitrary actions of the director of the budget and the assumption of power that he was never intended to wield has resulted in a revulsion of feeling in congress. And it is freely stated that if anyone would introduce an amendment to the law weakening the powers of the director or even going so far as to repeal the entire law it would find a sufficient number of friends to insure its passage. (P. 326) It is unfortunate that the incompetent administration of the budget system has reacted unfavorably against this unworthy innovation intended to improve governmental methods of transacting business. Budget administrators have prostituted the high purpose of the budget system by using it for political propaganda. The Executive Council is directed to use its earnest efforts to correct the glaring administrative defects which are operating to the disadvantage of the present budget system.

Burleson—(1919, p. 345) President Wilson in his message to congress made this declaration: "The question which stands at the front of all others, in every country amidst the present great awakening is the question of labor. The object of all reform in this essential matter must be the genuine democratization of industry, based upon a full recognition of those who work, in whatever rank, to participate in some organic way in every decision which directly affects their welfare or the part they play in industry." Burleson's archaic and autocratic attitude has resulted in a demoralized service, discontented and resentful employes, confused and choked industrial processes, and a people wrathful and indignant at a long series of administrative blunders; therefore the A. F. of L. in convention assembled, speaking directely for four millions organized wage earners and firm in the belief that this reflects the sentiments of the vast majority of the American people, requests President Wilson to remove Postmaster General Burleson from office. (p. 430) The United States postal service was created and designed to perform a great public service and promote the public good and was not intended as a money-making institution or profit-making venture. Under the maladministration of Postmaster General Burleson, these original and helpful purposes of our postal service have been perverted by a mad desire to subordinate public service, humane treatment of employes, and a just, fair and indiscriminatory charge for the delivery of second-class mail to the realization of a profit-showing ledger sheet. The treatment accorded employes of the service is archaic and despotic unswervingly imperialistic, Prussianistic and in complete opposition to the ideals, hopes and aspirations represented by America. Therefore, this convention petitions the president of these U. S. in the interests of the many thousands of public employes and in the interest of the public dependent on an efficient postal service to select as a new postmaster general a man sympathetic to the original intent and purposes of this great service and one who is in harmony with the newer concepts of the rights of labor and the rights of a free people so eloquently expressed by the president on so many occasions.

(1920, p. 111) Postmaster General Burleson, in his report to the 66th congress protested against any wage increases to postal workers "as manifestly unjust." He renewed his request for legislation that would prohibit postal employes from affiliating with the A. F of L. and from exercising their fundamental right of direct petition to congress. No heed was paid to the postmaster general's archaic recommendations. Despite the fact that the Atlantic City convention of the A. F. of L. unanimously adopted a resolution requesting the removal of Postmaster General Burleson from office the postal workers are still under the domination of this obviously unfit official whose administration of the high office he holds is distasteful to the American people and at variance with modern industrial methods.

Burleson Retreats—(1919, p. 307) The postmaster general issued an order that all employes of the telephone companies who engaged in a strike for twenty-four hours would be dismissed from the employ of the government. A committee was appointed to go to Washington and confer with the postmaster general. The committee reported that the postmaster general had withdrawn the order and signed a complete reversal in part as follows: "Order No. 3209. Employes of telephone companies shall have the right to bargain as individuals or collectively through committees or their representatives chosen by them to act for them. Where prior to government control a company dealt with representatives chosen by the employes to act for them who were not in the employ of the company, they shall hereafter do so. The telephone companies shall designate one or more of its officials who shall be authorized to deal with such individuals or representatives in matters of better conditions of labor, hours of employment, compensation or grievances, and such matters must be taken up for consideration within five days after presentation. Such employes shall have the right to organize or to affiliate with organizations that seem to them best calculated to serve their interest, and no employe shall be discharged, demoted or otherwise discriminated against because of membership in any such organization, as prescribed in bulletin No. 9, issued by me, dated October 2, 1918. In case of dismissal, demotion or undesirable transfer of employes where no real cause is shown by company for said dismissal, demotion or undesirable transfer, it shall be considered that discrimination was practiced, and upon such finding the employe shall be reinstated to former position with full pay for time lost or shall be reimbursed for any loss sustained by reason of demotion or transfer."

Burnett, John L.—(1919, pp. 121-389) We desire here formally to express labor's appreciation of Representative John L. Burnett's staunch championship and advocacy of labor's fight for the restriction of immigration and recognition of the principle which the labor movement has considered advisable and in the interests of the people generally.

Burns Detective Agency—(1920, p. 350) The secretary reported: "I have here a letter which contains the information that the merchants and business men of Montreal are being solicited by a canvasser representing the Burns Detective Agency who claims to be publishing a book with inside information about what goes on in the convention of the A. F. of L. This is to be furnished for fifty dollars a copy. I want to call the attention of the delegates and the public to the fact that the conventions are open, that there are no secret proceedings, and it is not necessary for the merchants or business men of Montreal to pay fifty dollars for such a book."

Canada and A. F. of L.—(1920, p. 6) In response to the addresses of welcome the president of the A. F. of L. said: "May I say this to you as representative gentlemen of the government of the dominion, of the province, of the city and of labor, that we heard some apprehension as to whether our convention would be welcomed in Montreal. Indeed, there came percolating to us hints and indiscretions that it would be better that the A. F. of L. Executive Council would decide upon some other city than Montreal, some other country than Canada. There were some of us who had a degree of misgivings upon coming to Montreal or to

Canada at all in this year, 1920, by reason of the fact that the presidential and congressional campaign and elections are to occur in the United States this year. But when these hints and intimations were conveyed that it might not be well to come to Canada, perhaps, like the forbidden fruit, it whetted our appetites, and we made up our minds if there were no legal objections that we would come to Canada. And so we decided to come to Canada, notwithstanding the fact that the Executive Council exercised a great responsibility and took upon itself in the name of labor, in the name of international good will, to even change the date of the convention so that we are here a week earlier than the constitution of the federation provides. In other words, we made up our minds to put it to the test, and we have the abiding faith that our confidence was well placed. And if ever a body of organized workers were justified in their work and their choice, then the judgment of the people, the right-thinking people, of the Dominion of Canada was with this movement for justice and right, your words of welcome from all quarters justifies our action and we are well rewarded. There is no body of men outside of Canada who have quite so good a will toward the people and the Dominion of Canada as the A. F. of L. There is not anything within the borders of your dominion which the people of the United States covet. There is not a sentiment of nationality and humanity within the breasts and the minds of the dominion people which the A. F. of L. will fail to second. Politically the organized labor movement of Canada is as independent of the United States as the United States is independent of Canada. The autonomy of the workers and of the citizenship of Canada is just as safe from our hands as ours is from theirs. Industrially and economically we are largely bound to each other. We can not help ourselves. Even if we wanted to be separated we could not be separated. Our interests, the protection of our lives, of our standards, of our welfare are all involved, one with the other, and interwoven. And the men and women of Canada are determined, as the men and women of labor of the United States have decided, that industrially our interests are one and we propose to act as one. It may not be generally known, or rather it may not be known absolutely by all, that in the United States we also have our political divisions and subdivisions. The A. F. of L. has not attempted to interfere in the political affairs of any state within the United States. That jurisdiction belongs to the state federations. Is it not imaginable, then, that what we would not do and would not dare do in the United States towards the states we would attempt to do in the Dominion of Canada? It is entirely preposterous. My hat off for the men and women of this dominion who love it for its worth, for its history and for its hopes for the future. I have been to very many parts of this wonderful dominion, and I doubt that there is any territory on the face of the glove that is richer in all that will make life worth living than this dominion. I know its people to a considerable extent, and I know they are virile and strong, and full of grit, and full of hope, and full of aspirations for the development of Canada in order that its people shall hold its place in the front ranks of the progressive nations of the world. May I say this, that having read authenticated statements, made by some who presumed to know the conditions and the relations of the labor movement between the United States and that of Canada, and the assertion that the only use for which the working people in the international labor movement of Canada were affiliated with their trade unions or with the A. F. of L. was to fleece the working people of Canada out of their money, that moneys are sent to the United States in tremendous sums and very little comes back to Canada. Prompted by that misstatement, of which I was then only partially aware, I undertook to communicate with the officers of all international unions, asking them for the exact figures of the payments by the organized labor movement of Canada, by the international trades unions, and the expenditures for all purposes made for the men and women of the organized labor movement of the dominion. The responses which I received are incorporated in the report which the Executive Council of the A. F. of L. will have the honor to submit to this convention, and will show that $200,000 more in the past year was transmitted to and expended for the labor movement of Canada than was received from the organizations of labor in Canada. I feel that the matter was referred to in one of the addresses of the gentlemen who have spoken to us this morning that I could not escape the opportunity and the desire to put the subject before you, perhaps a bit prematurely, but I hope with some effect and to the ascertainment of the truth. I want to refer also to a misunderstanding that has gone forth among some of the people of Canada, and I have reference to the word 'international.' They have tried to confuse the word 'international' in our trade union movement with the internationale of some parts of Europe. I don't know that there is any body of men anywhere so out of harmony with that so-called internationale as the A. F. of L. But we surely can not call the United Brotherhood of Carpenters and Joiners of America for instance, a national organization, because it has a large number of members in the Dominion of Canada. And we recognize the Dominion of Canada as an independent nation, at least independent of the United States, and if we want to have the affiliations with and from our Canadian fellow trade unionists we can not have a national trade union movement, it must be international. What is true of the carpenters is true of the coal miners, it is true of the printing trades, it is true of my own trade, the Cigar Makers' International Union of America, and it is true of nearly every other organization of workers."

Canadian Trades and Labor Congress— (1919, pp. 160-379) The trade union movement of Canada and of the affiliated local and international unions in the Dominion of Canada are passing through the trying ordeal of conflicting emotions, passions and moods through which every permanent institution is subjected at some time or other. While old doctrines and theories, tried and found wanting, are again seeking dominance in Canada, we are confident that out of this clash, turmoi and confusion the trade union movement will emerge stronger, more powerful and influential than ever before in that its soundness and validity will not only have been clearly demonstrated, but that the forces arrayed against the legitimate trade union movement and its activities will have been weakened, if not destroyed. It is not sufficient, however, that we should remain calm and quiescent in this hour of trial; it is our duty to assert ourselves and help in this period of stress by advice, counsel and active assistance of the older and more experienced leadership of staple organizations of the wage earners. The convention therefore believes that the suggestion for a readjustment of the method of financial contributions in behalf of directly affiliated local unions with the Canadian Trades and Labor Congress is well directed. All affiliated international unions should consider following a similar procedure and that no time should be lost to give proper advice and counsel to their respective membership in Canadian local unions either by communication or personal visitation and by calling their attention to the dangers lurking behind the appeals which are so alluringly made to them and which will divide the wage-earners into separate movements and destroy the effectiveness of their organized forces.

Canadian Trades and Labor Congress Enjoined—(1921, p. 171) In December, 1920, the executive of the Trades and Labor Congress of Canada, notified the Canadian Brotherhood of Railroad Employes of the cancellation of their charter. This organization has been affiliated to the Trades and Labor Congress of Canada since December, 1917, and its membership chiefly includes those eligible for membership in the Brotherhood of Railway Clerks, Freight Handlers, Express and Station Employes, International Brotherhood of Teamsters, Chauffeurs, Stablemen and Helpers, Hotel and Restaurant Employes International Alliance and Bartenders International League (dining car service), the Amalgamated Association of Street and Electric Railway Employes of America, United Brotherhood of Maintenace of Way Employes and Railway Shop Laborers, International Brotherhood of Firemen and Oilers, etc. Immediate action was taken by the Canadian Brotherhood of Railroad Employes to apply to the courts for an injunction restraining the executive of the Trades and Labor Congress to carry into execution this revocation of their charter and decision has been rendered by the courts in favor of the Canadian Brotherhood Railway Employes. Briefly, the grounds of the decision were that the executive of the Trades and Labor Congress have no distinct power, under their constitution, to revoke the charter of any affiliated union of this kind. Further, if they had such a power that the executive council could not take action unless they were in session assembled, and further that before such action could be taken the organization involved would have to be notified of distinct charges and given an opportunity of being present to defend itself. It will be necessary at the forthcoming convention of the Trades and Labor Congress to amend the constitution in such a manner as to allow of the full carrying out of the policies accepted by the Trades and Labor Congress of Canada since 1902 of holding in affiliation only such organizations as are not in conflict with those chartered by the A. F. of L.

Canadian Labor Movement—(1919, p. 181) The marked increase in Canadian trade union membership recorded in 1917 was surpassed in 1918, and indicates a rapidity of growth, probably without precedent in the history of organized labor of the Dominion. At the end of 1913 trade union members in Canada numbered 175,799. The two following years showed a decline of 32,456, reducing the membership to 143,343. In 1916, although there was a loss of 41 local branches, the membership figures showed a gain of 17,064, increasing the total to 160,407. The year 1917 showed the substantial increase of 44,223 members, bringing the total to 204,630, comprised in 1,974 local branches, a gain in branches for the year of 132. At the close of 1918, the membership for all classes of trade unions in Canada, was 248,887, comprised in 2,274 branch unions, a total increase for the year of 44,257 in membership and 300 in local branches. There are 96 international organizations having one or more local branches in Canada, and between them they comprise 1,897 of the branch unions in the dominion, an increase of 195 over the number recorded in 1917. The total international membership at the close of the year 1918 was 201,432, a gain of 36,536. The local unions of the international organizations are distributed throughout the nine provinces as follows: Ontario, 820; Quebec, 277; British Columbia, 224; Alberta, 181; Manitoba, 127; Saskatchewan, 112; New Brunswick, 78; Nova Scotia, 75; and Prince Edward Island, 3. In addition to the international organizations having branches in the dominion there are thirteen bodies classed as non-internationals, who have between them 332 local branches, with a combined membership of 37,928, an increase for 1918 of 88 branches and 5,585 members. The local branches of the non-international organizations are located as follows: Ontario, 103; Quebec, 58; Nova Scotia, 52; Alberta, 27; Manitoba, 24; British Columbia, 23; Saskatchewan, 19; New Brunswick, 10; and Prince Edward Island, 3. Apart from unions having either international or non-international affiliations there are 45 independent units in the dominion, 27 of which have reported a membership of 9,527, a gain of 2,136 as compared with the reported membership from 28 independent units which were in existence in 1917. The majority of these independent units are located in the provinces of Quebec, and some of them are of a semi-religious character. Of the 45 independent bodies in the dominion, 31 are located in Quebec, which province shows an increase of 12 in this class of organization. In September, 1918, a convention of "national" unions of the province of Quebec was held, 27 unions being represented. Officers were elected, and it was decided to hold another convention in the city of Three Rivers in 1919, when the question of forming a federation of "national" unions would be considered. The remainder of the 45 independent unions were located as follows: British Columbia, 5; Ontario, 3; New Brunswick and Manitoba, 2 each; Nova Scotia and Prince Edward Island, one each. The past two years have also demonstrated the possibility of organizing the women workers and in the machine and textile industries important progress has been made in bringing women into the ranks of the organized workers. The enfranchisement of women by the dominion parliament and in the majority of the provinces of Canada has made it all the more necessary that the women should be organized industrially as well as politically. With their knowledge of industrial conditions and the need for improvement in these conditions it is being made easier to convince the women workers of the need of organization, and special efforts will have to be made to enlist the services of capable women organizers to bring more of the women toilers into the ranks of organized labor.

(1920, p. 205) Because of charges made in Canada by persons outside the labor movement to the effect that the Canadian labor movement is being "fleeced" through its affiliation with the American labor movement and that much money is sent out of Canada while little is returned; the president of the A. F. of L. instituted an inquiry into the whole question and issued a questionnaire to all national and international unions, including the railroad brotherhoods, which are unaffiliated to the A. F. of L. The returns cover almost the entire field and show clearly that a far larger sum is returned to Canada for expenditure there by the various international unions than is received from Canadian members in the form of dues and assessments. Incomplete returns show $617,324.19 received from Canadian members by international unions in the last year. There was sent into Canada $553,695.90 for various benefit purposes and $282,018.50 for salaries to officers and organizers in Canada. The total amount of money sent into Canada for expenditure in Canada was for the year $835,714.40 or $218,390.21 above the amount received from Canada. The half dozen organizations from which reports have not been received could not materially alter the situation. The American labor movement is a movement for the advancement of the interests of the workers. While politically the labor movement of Canada is as independent of the American labor movement as is the Canadian citizenship and the citizenship of the United States, yet the industrial relations between Canadian members and members in the United States has always been a relation unaffected by the border line. The figures are produced in this instance in order that a charge originating outside of our movement may be effectively answered from within and in order that its falsity may be thoroughly understood by all. (p. 229) Nothwithstanding the strenuous efforts which have been made during the past year by secessionists and others to undermine the strength of the international trade union movement, there was an increase in membership. Ninety-nine international organizations have now branches in Canada and these report an aggregate membership of 260,247 as compared with 201,432 last year, a gain during the year of 58,815. The number of local unions was increased by 412, there being at the present time 2,309 local branches of the international unions. In addition to the 260,247 members of international unions other forms of combination amongst the workers, including independent, national unions, national catholic unions and the one big union claim among them an aggregate membership of 100,000. These figures, however, lack corroboration though it would be unwise to underestimate the activities displayed by these bodies in retarding the organization of the workers of the dominion into international organizations.

(1922, p. 155) The report of membership submitted to the last convention of the Trades and Labor Congress of Canada showed a slight increase over that of the preceding year. It has not been possible, however, to maintain this favorable position up to the present time, the decline in membership caused by the long period of unemployment having manifested itself in Canada to a marked degree during the past several months. The campaign against international trade unions is being vigorously waged from many quarters. A portion of the press lose no opportunity to urge workers to sever their connections with international unions. The Quebec pro-

1609A—2

vincial legislature passed a resolution last session with the same object, and during the discussion the prime minister and others announced the probability of definite legislation next session to bring this about in that province. The problems with which workers in nearly all countries are faced are demanding our daily attention and include immigration, unemployment relief, protection against sickness, accidents and destitution i n old age, broadening of educational facilities and, in general, the creating of opportunity for the social and industrial development of every worker.

Canal Zone Investigation—(1923, p. 281) The president of the A. F. of L. is hereby instructed to proceed to the Canal Zone at the earliest convenient date, accompanied by such officials and attaches of the A. F. of L. as he may deem necessary, to make an investigation which, upon his return, will enable him to forcefully and properly lay before President Coolidge the deplorable conditions of the employes on the Canal Zone.

Cancer—(1921, p. 306) Address by president of American Society for Control of Cancer: "The message I bring to you in a most authentic way is one of hope regarding this terrible disease, cancer. After the age of forty years one person in ten dies in this country of cancer. At this time one woman in eight and one man in twelve is the rate. Eighty-five thousand people die annually in the United States from cancer. It is our belief that the majority of these deaths are needless, that they might be prevented. If the condition should be treated earlier in its stages the mortality should be comparatively small. Contrary to the usual belief, cancer is not hereditary, it is not transmitted from father or mother to the children, but it is so dreadfully common that hardly a family is without it. However, it is a comfort to be able to say that it is not hereditary. Cancer is not contagious, it is not transmitted from one person to another. We know of no instance in which the physician or surgeon or nurse has taken cancer, so to speak, from a patient. Further, cancer is not in the beginning a blood disease, it is purely local; it is only in the late stages when it becomes generalized that it enters the blood system. Again, cancer is not a disgrace and should never be thought of in that way. It is only a terrible misfortune. Almost all cancer begins at a local point of irritation. Let me illustrate that by the familiar cancer of the lower lip in men. It begins generally after the age of 35 years, and it increases in frequency from that age up. Cancer of the lip begins as a local sore, a local irritation: a scab forms and falls off, another forms and falls off, and the cycle is repeated until it becomes very dangerous. A man who is in this situation should at once consult competent medical authority. I come before you with no panacea, no cure whatever; I simply say to you when you notice a sore of the kind I have described, go at once and get advice. Eight thousand women die yearly in this country from cancer of the breast. There should be almost no deaths from this source among women. Whenever a woman, especially beyond thirty or thirty-five years, notices a small beginning lump she must go at once and seek advice. She must not delay. It is at first purely local and is very easily cured at that stage. Cancer at the beginning is painless—please remember that. I often feel that it would be very much better if it were painful. It is only in the advanced and incurable stage that it becomes painful. The average person today unfortunately delays seeking advice until the expiration of ten or twelve months, and it is the task of the educational society which I have the honor to represent, to endeavor by such talks as these to reduce that period as nearly as possible to one day. Again another source. There are no less than 30,000 deaths yearly from cancer of the stomach. It is more frequent in men than in women and generally begins at the age of 35 to 40. The pain is earlier in cancer of the stomach. The earliest symptoms are indigestion, nausea, and together with these a loss of weight. There is what we call the pre-cancerous stage in all of these conditions, and in the stomach that is very, very frequently ulcer of the stomach. When a man or woman notices a pain in the stomach, dyspepsia, loss of weight and strength, let him go at once and seek advice. Moles, especially these black moles, not infrequently develop into cancer, especially on irritation. All of these little irritable places on the face or body may cause cancer, and if you are in that condition, go at once and have it taken care of. We are hopeful that within the next ten years the death rate from this terrible malady will have been greatly diminished."

Cash in Lieu of Vacations—(1919, p. 133) Bill to give navy yard employes permission to accept cash in lieu of their present grant of thirty days leave per year with pay was defeated through the opposition of the A. F. of L.

Central Bodies, Affiliation to—(1923, p. 340) On the matter of affiliation of local unions of national and international unions with central bodies and state federations of labor, while we feel that it is desirable, advisable and necessary that they should do so, we doubt whether the best results would be obtained through an effort on the part A. F. of L. to bring about that end by compulsion. In fact, the A. F. of L. is a voluntary association of national and international unions and can not take unto itself compulsory features in dealing with these national and international unions even by "recommendations."

Central Bodies, Authority of—(1919, p. 447) No Central Labor Union, or other central body of delegates, shall have the authority or power to order any organization, affiliated with such central labor union, or other central labor body, on strike or to take a strike vote, where such organization has a national organization, until the proper authorities of such national or international organizations have been consulted and agreed to such action. A violation of this law shall be sufficient cause for the Executive Council to revoke the charter.—(Sec. 5, Ar. XI, Constitution A. F. of L.)

Central Bodies, Representation in— (1919, p. 446) Executive Council directed to investigate the present form of representation and election of delegates to central bodies.

(1920, p. 204) Executive Council reported: "In the interest of fair representation and fair distribution of authority the minimum number of delegates to which any one local union should be entitled in central bodies should be 3, leaving it discretionary with central bodies to fix the maximum number of delegates at less than 8 and to any figure that local conditions and experience have demonstrated to be most efficient and helpful." (p. 436) Convention made the minimum 2 and the maxi-

mum 10. The matter was again referred to the Executive Council with definite instructions to establish a graduated basis of representation to govern central and state bodies.

(1921, p. 133) Executive Committee reported a basis of representation as follows: Locals having less than 50 members, 2 delegates; from 50 to 100, 4; 100 to 250, 6; 250 to 500, 8; 500 or more, 10. (p. 430) Law committee approved of the recommendation, but the convention again referred the matter to the Executive Council for further investigation and report to the next convention.

(1922, p. 300) The A. F. of L. adopted the following basis of representation of local unions to central bodies: Local unions having 50 members, 2 delegates; 100, 3; 250, 4; 500, 5; for each additional 500 or majority fraction thereof, 1 delegate.

Charity, Contributions for (1922, p. 473) It is most regrettable that there will be many families who will be in want on Christmas day for the necessaries of life. Many children will miss the greatest pleasure of childhood by finding empty stockings hanging on the mantelpiece or about the stove when they awake on Christmas morning. Hardly anything causes more sorrow than the failure of Santa Claus to make his annual visit,—and the cause is the fact that the real Santa Claus is out of employment. But the A. F. of L. always has discouraged the pleadings for donations and contributions from business men, even to allay hunger. No local union has ever been known to refuse to give aid and comfort to a member and his family in times of dire need. The camaraderie developed through association in a trade union movement has proved a wonderful impetus and a wonderful incentive to those who have to help those who have not. Members of trade unions should care for their own needy fellow workers. To receive gifts from those outside of the organizations of labor would be accepting charity. Whatever is given by the unions or union men to those in dire need is the exemplification of the brotherhood of man.

Child Labor—(1919, p. 110) After many years of agitation, the congress attempted to regulate child labor throughout the nation by the enactment of public statute No. 249 of the 64th congress, approved September 1, 1916, which provided that no producer should ship or deliver for shipment in interstate or foreign commerce any article or product of any mine or quarry in the production of which children under the age of 16 years had been employed, or the product of any mill, cannery, workshop, factory or manufacturing establishment in which children under the age of 14 years had been employed, or children over the age of 14 years had been permitted to work more than eight hours in any one day, or more than six days in any week, or after seven in the evening or before six in the morning. On June 3, 1918, the supreme court declared this law unconstitutional by a vote of 5 to 4. The court held that the congress had gone beyond its powers in attempting to exclude from interstate commerce a product not in itself evil. This law, the court said, prohibits instead of regulates, which latter is the power given to congress by the constitution. On July 12 the war labor policies board outlined as a national policy that contractors doing work for any of the government departments should not directly or indirectly employ child labor contrary to the provisions contained in the act adopted by congress and declared unconstitutional by the court. The secretary of labor was made responsible for the enforcement of a contract clause to that effect, to be inserted in all government contracts. By direction of the secretary of labor a conference was called to discuss permanent child labor legislation, which met on August 21. There were present representatives of the A. F. of L., National Child Labor Committee, Women's Trade Union League, National Consumers' League, and various governmental officials who had helped to formulate or enforce the act of September 1, 1916. After numerous meetings and much discussion, a new child labor bill was agreed upon which proposed to levy an excise tax upon the products of any mill, cannery, workshop, factory or manufacturing establishment in which children under the age of 14 years had been employed, or children between the ages of 14 and 16 years had been employed for more than eight hours in any one day or more than six days in any one week. This plan was changed by the senate, which placed an excise tax upon the net incomes of establishments employing child labor instead upon the products of those establishments, with the enforcement of the provision of the act resting primarily with the commissioner of internal revenue instead of the department of labor. The bill became a law. On May 2, 1919, Federal Judge James E. Boyd, of Greensboro, N. C., held the provisions of this latest child labor act unconstitutional. This is the same honorable judge who enjoys the distinction of being the first to discover the unconstitutionality of the previous act. His decision, according to the newspapers, is based upon the assumption that congress was trying to do by indirection what it has no constitutional power to do directly. Whether or not this is true, congress through the power of taxation has repeatedly accomplished ends which it could not reach directly. The tax on oleomargarine was placed deliberately in the first instance with intent to destroy the industry for the benefit of the farmers. The phosphorous match industry was destroyed, and was intended to be destroyed by a tax. And the whole structure of high protection was camouflaged by the title "to raise revenue," when the distinct purpose, in hundreds of instances, was to prevent or diminish importation of certain goods or articles, and thus prevent to that extent the raising of revenue. The supreme court of the United States has refrained heretofore from inquiring into the motives of Congress in passing legislation, particularly tax legislation, but this judge of a lower court does not hesitate to enter into such an inquiry, notwithstanding the fact that the supreme court has refrained. What the final result will be when Judge Boyd's swift decision reaches the court of last resort can be only conjecture, but the promptness of the delivery of this decision raised a query as to whether it was written in advance of the presentation of the case, and by whom. While the lower court decided adversely on the child labor law, yet the case is pending before the supreme court of the United States. We hope and expect that that court will declare the law to be constitutional. Pending decision by the supreme court the officers of the internal revenue service have decided that the purport of the law as declared by the congress and signed by the president shall be in effect and will remain in effect subject to decision by the supreme court of the United States.

(1920, p. 100) While congress refused to pass a resolution favoring a constitutional amendment prohibiting child labor, the 10 per cent tax provided for in the revenue act of 1918 has been of great benefit in discouraging the evil. Reports of the internal revenue department show there has been a great falling off in the employment of child labor. The supreme court has not yet given its opinion on the appeal fron the decision of Judge Boyd, of Lindsboro, N. C., that the law is unconstitutional. (p. 460) Unhappily any adequate curb on the exploiters of childhood is still lacking, but the comparative effectiveness of the 10 per cent tax amendment in the revenue act of 1918, more than justifies the vigorous effort of the A. F. of L. in the campaign for its enactment. A nation may fairly be judged by its treatment of its children.

(1921, p. 110) No action was taken by congress on resolutions providing for a constitutional amendment permitting the passage of laws prohibiting child labor. Child labor, however, is being continuously eliminated because of the 10 per cent tax provided in the internal revenue act of 1918. The 66th congress gave no attention to the protection of children being exploited in industry. It was a question that did not appeal to those who controlled the politics of either house. It is hoped that the 67th congress will show a more humane spirit and be willing to pass a resolution providing for a constitutional amendment permitting congress to protect children under 18 years of age. (p. 315) We approve of the efforts of the Executive Council to secure adequate protection of the childhood of the couutry through legislation and a constitutional amendment on the subject of child labor, and direct that there be no relaxation in these efforts. The welfare of the nation as a whole is so vitally involved, that children must not be left unprotected in states with unawakened consciences which are backward in this respect.

(1922, p. 5) June 14, Flag Day was set aside to consider the decision of the supreme court of the United States declaring the excise tax on net profits on employers of child labor unconstitutional. (pp. 33-104-169) As far back as 1881, in the first constitution adopted by the A. F. of L., the American labor movement declared: "We are in favor of the passage of laws in the several states forbidding the employment of children under the age of 14 in any capacity, under penalty of imprisonment." Then the A. F. of L. believed, as now, that of the many injustices and wrongs growing out of our modern industrial system, none is no grievous or so inexcusable as that of the employment of young and innocent children who are forced to toil for the sustenance of life when they should be in the schoolroom, the playground or the home, developing their physical, mental and moral well-being. In those earlier days the effort made to take the children out of the factories and place them into the schoolrooms was looked upon as an undue interference with "individual" right. It was then believed that little children were the sole property of fathers and mothers and that their little bodies might be freely sold in our industrial life for financial gain. Humane considerations finally prevailed, and a number of states enacted laws preventing the employment of child labor and requiring children of tender years to attend schools. Unfortunately, however, the same consideration was not given to the life and well-being of little children in some of our states. To remedy this evil, federal legislation was proposed and enacted prohibiting the transportation of goods from one state to another when such articles or commodities of trade were manufactured or produced by child labor. On September 1, 1916, the first federal child labor law was enacted. No sooner did it become a law than deliberate attacks were made upon it. First, the attempt was made in the United States congress to postpone its enforcement for one year after the conclusion of the war, while an injunction was also sought in the federal courts before Judge James E. Boyd, of the western district of North Carolina, to restrain the enforcement of the law on the ground that it was an interference with state rights. Ultimately, this case reached the supreme court of the United States. On June 3, 1918, the United States supreme court, by one of its famous five to four decisions, declared this legislative effort to stop the national commercializing of child life an unconstitutional intereference with state rights. In the meantime national interest was centered upon the artificial coloring of butter and oleomargarine. In order to discourage, if not to prohibit, the transportation of oleomargarine from one state to another, congress used the taxing powers of the federal government and enacted a law requiring the manufacturers of oleomargarine to pay 10 cents a pound tax for the use of coloring matter in oleomargarine. The phosphorous match industry was likewise destroyed, and it was deliberately intended that it should be destroyed by a prohibitive tax. Legislation of this character having been held to be constitutional, it was believed that the same principle might be invoked to discourage the employment of child labor and thus prevent the commercializing of the little bodies of children in interstate commerce. Accordingly, congress enacted another child labor law (approved February 29, 1919), which placed a tax of 10 per cent on the net incomes of establishments employing children under 14 years of age, or those between 14 and 16 years of age for more than eight hours in any one day or more than six days in any one week. This humane law was attacked and again Judge Boyd, of the western district of North Carolina, restrained its enforcement. The United States supreme court rendered a decision May 16, 1922, declaring the law unconstitutional in that it attempted to do by indirection that which the United States supreme court held in the first case could not be done directly, viz., interfere with state rights. The supreme court also indulged in a learned discussion as to when a tax is an excise tax and when a tax is not an excise tax and finally concluded by holding that in this particular case congress had not levied an excise tax but a regulative and prohibitive tax and that, therefore, congress acted outside of its constitutional authority as a legislative body. After analyzing the principal features of the law and its operation, Chief Justice Taft, who announced the decision in behalf of the supreme court, said: "In the light of these features of the act, a court must be blind not to see that the so-called tax is imposed to stop the employment of children within the age limits prescribed," and then, as if to temper the harshness of its rulings, it added that the court must perform its duty "even though it requires us to refuse to give effect to legislation designed to promote the highest good." Perhaps one of the remarkable features connected with this decision of the United States supreme court is the fact that the first child labor law decision was by the bare majority of one—a five to four decision, while this later decision had only one dissenting opinion, that of Justice Clark. It would, therefore, seem that the supreme court of today is by far more legalistic and less humane in its attitude and temperament than was the supreme court of 1918. By this decision of the supreme court we find our nation and its people once more confronted with a legal bewilderment wherein animal life and inanimate objects receive greater consideration than the life and welfare of children. According to prior decisions, congress may prevent the shipment of lottery tickets, phosphorous matches, baled hay and other things from one state to another. It may tax bank notes out of existence and use its legislative authority to protect trees and cattle. But by this decision, it must keep its hands off when the health and life and well-being of the nation's children are concerned. We protest most emphatically against such unjust and inhumane decisions. We realize that our protest, in so far, as the supreme court is concerned, will fall on deaf ears. However, we address our protest to congress and urge that it immediately approve and endorse a constitutional amendment to undo the harm the supreme court has done to the youth of our land. We also urge that renewed energy be displayed in the several states for the enactment of effective child labor laws and we urge that a nation-wide appeal be immediately directed to every man and woman throughout our land who has a heart and soul and conscience, to promote the welfare of the nation's children and to unite in the purpose of conserving child life and to protect it against selfish greed and brutual avarice. (p. 373) The A. F. of L. urges congress to enact "a child labor law which will overcome the objections raised by the United States supreme court to the laws heretofore passed by congress and nullified by the court.

(1923, p. 34) The A. F. of L., since its inception in 1881, has persistently advocated laws prohibiting child labor. It repeatedly has declared that the children should be in the school or playground and not in the factory. Through the influence of the A. F. of L. many states have adopted child labor laws. Congress has enacted two laws prohibiting the work of children, but the supreme court in each case declared them unconstitutional. Immediately after the second decision of the supreme court in May, 1922, the president of the A. F. of L. called a meeting of representatives of prominent national organizations of women and men which organized the Permanent Conference for the Abolition of Child Labor. It was held June 1, 1922. The Executive Council brought the matter to the attention of the Cincinnati convention and upon this recommendation the convention decided that Flag Day, June 14, 1922, be set aside and observed by the convention to permit labor to express its protest against the legal difficulties placed in the way of protecting child life. The addresses delivered received wide publicity and awakened the consciences of those who up to that time had been apathetic in their duty in the preservation of child life. Thereafter the voice of the people became so loud and insistent that members of congress took heed and twenty-eight bills for the protection of child life were introduced in the two houses, twenty-six of them providing for amendments to the constitution. July 6 1922, a subcommittee met in New York to draft a proposed constitutional amendment to present to a subsequent meeting of the Permanent Conference for the Abolition of Child Labor. After several meetings of the permanent conference the following draft of a proposed amendment to the constitution was adopted: "The congress shall have power to limit or prohibit the labor of persons under eighteen years of age and power is also reserved to the several states to limit or prohibit such labor in any way which does not lessen any limitation of such labor or the extent of any prohibition thereof by congress. The power vested in the congress by this article shall be additional to and not a limitation on the powers elsewhere vested in the congress by the constitution with respect to such labor." It was not until February 24, 1923, that the senate judiciary committee reported on the various amendments to the constitution that had been submitted to the senate. The committee recommended the following: "The congress shall have power concurrent with that of the several states to limit or prohibit the labor of persons under the age of eighteen years." The same proposed amendment was reported favorably to the house. Despite all efforts to have the resolutions passed congress adjourned without taking action. Immediately after adjournment of congress the president of the A. F. of L. called a meeting of the Permanent Conference for the Abolition of Child Labor, of which he is chairman, and it was unanimously agreed that an intensive campaign should be launched immediately to have congress pass a joint resolution proposing an amendment to the constitution for the protection of persons under eighteen years of age. The amendment presented by the judiciary committee of the senate was acceptable to the permanent conference. The words "persons under eighteen years of age" were used because of the difference of opinion as to whom the word "children" applied. After several conferences an appeal was prepared for distribution throughout the nation. It was signed by seventeen of the most prominent national organizations of women and men in the country as follows. American Federation of Labor, Federal Council of the Churches of Christ in America, General Federation of Women's Clubs, Girls' Friendly Society in America, National Child Labor Committee, National Congress of Mothers and Parent-Teacher Associations, National Consumers' League, National Council of Jewish Women, National Council of Women, Inc., National Education Association, National Federation of Teachers, National Federation of Business and Professional Women's Clubs, National League of Women Voters, National Woman's Christian Temperance Union, National Women's Trade Union League, Service Star Legion, Young Woman's Christian Association. The agitation for the child labor amendment should be taken up by every state and city central body and local union in the United States. National and international unions are requested to secure copies of the leaflet from the A. F. of L. and distribute them among their local unions. There is great opposition to child labor legislation in certain districts in the United States. This applies to the textile industry, the beet sugar industry and portions of the south. The convention is urged to take strong ground in demanding the necessary legislation for the protection of child life. (P. 244) It is but natural that the A. F. of L. should lead in this great humanitarian

movement for the protection of child life and child labor. The economic and social status of American working men and women enables them to understand most clearly how important and vital to the nation and organized labor is the conservation and protection of child life. This purpose can not be attained if employers are permitted to profit by the exploitation of little children in the mills, mines and factories of our country. The first congress of labor held in the United States after the decision of the supreme court which declared the child labor law unconstitutional made the following declaration in favor of an amendment to the constitution of the United States: "An amendment prohibiting the labor of children under the age of 16 years in any mine, mill, factory, workshop or other industrial or mercantile establishment, and conferring upon congress the power to raise the minimum age below which children shall not be permitted to work, and to enforce the provisions of the proposed amendment by appropriate legislation." Since the adoption of this declaration by the Cincinnati convention of the A. F. of L., held in June, 1922, the report of the Executive Council shows that diligent, unceasing efforts have been put forth by it for carrying out the intention and purpose of this expression of organized labor. It is remarkable that within the limited space of one year such splendid work has been done in arousing public interest that this constitutional amendment was proposed and received the approval of the committees of both houses of the congress of the United States. All organizations affiliated with the A. F. of L. are urged to call upon their representatives in the house and senate of the United States demanding their support of the proposed constitutional amendment.

Chile—(1919, p. 191) The following appeared on a diploma sent to the President of the A. F. of L. from the Chilean Federation of Labor: "I am sending by this mail to you a special diploma sent by the Chilean Federation of Labor to the A. F. of L., and I would like to receive some special thought from you, Mr. Gompers, toward the Chilean organized labor because I expect to leave this country within two or three months. In the name of the Chilean Federation of Labor I may say that not only the government of the nation have the right to increase their relationships, not only the industrial men or business men need to work in order to get a better understanding between them and through the international trade, but also the people of the nations must work in order to increase its friendships and to cultivate a true sympathy to each other. I think the people of modern democracy are in special conditions for working together by the betterment of the human being. I hope, Mr. Gompers, that not will be so far the day when the A. F. of L. following its policy of international character through the world, send to South America some special commission and I assure you that the Chilean organized labor should receive the American labor mission with all kinds of attentions and greetings of sympathy and welcome. I think the diplomacy of the government does not represent truly the sentiment of the peoples so we must work for our own interest and for the welfare of the working classes. I would like to receive a letter from you, Mr. Gompers, with your opinion about this matter."

Chinese-Japanese Exclusion—(1920, p. p. 375) American citizens protest against oriental coolie immigration, and the ground for their protest is rooted in the cheap standard of living and the ability of the coolie worker to live on less. Exclusion legislation has been established as an American policy, therefore we ask of congress: First, cancellation of the "gentlemen's agreement"; second, exclusion of "picture brides" by action of our government; third, absolute exclusion of Japanese, with other Asiatics, as immigrants; fourth, confirmation and legalization of the principal that Asiatics shall be forever barred from American citizenship; fifth, amendment of Sec. 1 of Art. XIV, of the federal constitution, providing that no child born in the United States of Asiatic or Oriental parents shall be eligible to American citizenship unless both parents are eligible for such citizenship; therefore, we petition the house of representatives and the United States senate, and the president of the United States in behalf of this legislation.

(1921, p. 129) A national organization is actively at work carrying on an extensive propaganda for amendments to the Chinese exclusion act and a number of similar organizations have been formed to supplement this campaign. In a letter sent broadcast to employers, the chairman of the National Agricultural and Industrial Development Committee on the pretense of fighting bolshevism and the like said: "These raids of the reds, communists, and the I. W. W.'s emphasize the desirability of bringing into this country hereafter a class of labor that does not organize, has no foolish notions of six-hour days or five-day weeks, and does not wish to upset our present form of government. The raising of the ban on Chinese labor will, we believe, go far to solve the problem of our present danger." The Western States Agricultural Development Committee is engaged in a similar campaign. A like campaign has been started in Hawaii. In that country where the greater number of the inhabitants are Japanese, labor employed on plantations is paid about 77 cents per day. When an increase was demanded and denied many of these workers left the country. It was then that the sugar planters advocated the admission of 30,000 Chinese, both for the purpose of breaking the strike as well as to retain the low wage standard. Within the past year complaints have been received that the Japanese are encroaching upon the work of the men employed in the shipbuilding industry on the Pacific coast. Many local unions have passed resolutions calling upon congress to extend the Chinese exclusion act to cover all orientals. This subject was brought to the attention of members of congress and the request was made for a definite statement as to the number of Japanese workers employed in the shipyards on the Pacific coast. About this time California senators and representatives were also urged by the secretary of state not to take any drastic action against Japanese immigration pending negotiations with the Japanese government. The senators and congressmen agreed to withhold any action, thus permitting the government to enter into negotiations looking to an agreement with Japan on the question of immigration including "picture brides" now coming into the United States. Up to the present time no agreement has been reached on this subject and no legislation has been considered pending these negotiations. Be-

cause of the extensive campaign again to open wide the gates to orientals, by reason of the unjust criticism directed against the attitude of the A. F. of L. on this question and on account of the strained relations which exist at this time between Japan and our government, the Executive Council deemed it essential that a careful survey be made of the immigration and land laws and policies which now prevail in Japan and China. This investigation discloses that in 1899 Japan promulgated a new set of immigration laws. These laws prohibited the immigration of laborers from all countries to any part of the Japanese empire with the exception of the treaty ports, which are Kobe, Yokohama, Tokyo, Ozaka, Nagasaki, Hakodate. While at the present time there are by lack of enforcement some European laborers working in Japan, they are very few in numbers. Under no conditions are Chinese laborers admitted into Japan except by special permit. Alien laborers are forbidden to engage in any kind of manual labor such as agriculture, fishing, mining, engineering, architecture, manufacture, carriage and vehicle pulling, stevedore and other miscellaneous work. Aliens of all classes are also forbidden to become promoters of political meetings or to become members of a political party. Then, too, aliens are prohibited from engaging in the organization of banks. Aliens are forbidden to construct railways, or to engage in the carrying trade (coasting trade) between native ports. They are not permitted to become brokers in exchange; or to engage in mining and placer mining, or to fish or hunt in the territorial seas of Japan. Neither may aliens nor any firms with which aliens may be connected or in which they may be interested as partners or shareholders manufacture gun powder or explosives. Individual foreigners are not allowed to own land in any part of the empire. Foreigners may own land by forming a company, the company being required to register under the imperial laws of Japan. In that way these companies may enjoy perpetual leases over lots of land in the former foreign settlements in the open ports which were leased by the government to aliens in the early days of the opening of the country to foreign trade. However, these leases have been taken largely over by Japanese. Foreigners may also lease land for industrial or residential purposes, but no agricultural lands can be leased under any circumstances. If a Japanese subject for any reason loses his nationality and becomes an alien he at once loses his rights to land ownership and in the latter case he must transfer all his property rights to Japanese. The foregoing clearly evidence the amazing facts that the Japanese immigration and land laws are as strict as those of any nation in the world and much more so than are the laws of many of the nations. In the face of the above facts Japan does not come into court with clean hands when she objects to the land laws passed by the state of California or when she protests against the inclusion of Japanese in the exclusion of all orientals from this country. Japan has left no stone unturned in her anxiety to protect her subjects against supposed injurious competition or to prevent the operation of any influence whatsoever upon their domestic, national and international policies, conduct or relations from the peoples of other nations. If she takes this right unto herself, how can she deny the same right to any other nation?

The citizens of California are justified in viewing with alarm and apprehension the results of the Japanese invasion in that state. The Japanese colonize together and have gradually driven out American citizens from the most fertile farm lands in the state. They already have under cultivation 92 per cent of the celery, 89 per cent of the asparagus, 79 per cent of the onions, 76 per cent of the tomatoes, 66 per cent of the cantaloupes, 79 per cent of seeds, etc. They undersell the American farmer because of their low standards of living. Not only have they acquired large areas of agricultural lands but they are gradually getting into the trades. The "gentlemen's agreement" has proven to be a failure because the Japanese in a cunning and stealthy manner have outwitted the intent of the law. In 1918, 11,143 new arrivals came to America in spite of the fact that the above agreement is supposed to exclude all except diplomats, merchants and legitimate students. In California alone there are over 100,000 Japanese. This peril is not only a serious condition for California but it is a positive menace to our entire nation. The A. F. of L. is fully justified in taking a firm stand to do away with the "gentlemen's agreement" and in its place inaugurate a definite policy calling for total exclusion of Japanese with all other orientals. We should also go on record as favoring any legislation of the above character that may be presented in congress by the California delegation in the senate and house of representatives. The Chinese immigration laws absolutely prohibit Japanese of any class from entering the country except by special permit. This practically bars not only laborers but students, business men, travellers, etc., from entering the country except for a very short period of time. Unquestionably, the workers of different races, colors, or nationalities throughout the world have a common interest in their respective countries. It is only by furthering that common interest that we can obtain the true objective of the labor movements the world over. While the methods of industrial and commercial enterprise, the supply of raw materials and of capital may have an equalizing tendency between nations, the interchange of viewpoints and the establishing of friendly relationship between workers of the various nations are of far greater importance and tend more readily and effectively to cement the peoples of all nations in a peaceful concord. Today, our people are confronted not alone with the possibility of greater competition with oriental labor and manufacture; they are also facing the development of tendencies leading to the possible dangers of war. No one recognizes more fully than do the American workers the burdens and sacrifices entailed in a contest between nations. We have just emerged from a war out of which it is hoped that the opportunity for future wars would be lessened to the lowest possible degree, if not foreclosed for all time to come. We are confident that the Japanese workers are equally desirous for continued peace as are the American wage earners. We feel sure that the workers of Japan would welcome whatever influence might be set at work to prevent a possible clash between the peoples of Japan and our country. Limited, suppressed and tyrannied, the opportunity of these workers for protest is rendered almost voiceless and the American labor movement is looked to in the hope that existing industrial, commercial and financial differences and difficulties may not be molded into tendencies leading to international conflict. (P. 339) The legislature of Hawaii in furtherance of the conspiracy to degrade American labor has adopted a resolution appealing to congress to permit the immigration of Chinese into the island. A national organization of the enemies of labor and the people of this country have been working secretly for several years to break down the Chinese exclusion laws of the United States. There are said to be 500 Chinese coolies a month smuggled into the United States with or without the connivance of the government or its agents. The people of the United States should awaken to the dangers threatened by the influx of a race that can not be assimilated and will be a curse instead of a benefit to the nation. The A. F. of L., condemns this most despicable conspiracy to break down American standards in order that a few of the enemies of labor and the people may profit from the labor of Chinese coolies to the detriment of all honest employers. We call upon congress to indignantly refuse the appeal of the Hawaiian legislature in the interests of the sugar planters to modify or amend in any manner whatever the laws that were enacted after years of agitation to forever exclude the Chinese. The Executive Council is hereby directed to oppose by every means in its power any attempt to change the exclusion laws so that they would permit the admission of a single Chinaman to enter the United States and its possessions under any circumstances or excuse whatever. (p. 341) The Chinese exclusion act should be enlarged and extended so as to permanently exclude from the United States and its insular territory all classes of Asiatics other than those exempted by the present terms of that act.

(1922, pp. 95-322) It was generally believed that the question of admitting Chinese coolies to the United States or its territories had been settled for all time. It was believed that no American would urge congress to pass a measure that would break down the Chinese exclusion law. But this was before the people of the mainland had heard of the sugar planters of Hawaii and their tactics. For several years, however, a secretly organized agitation had been carried on to permit the admission of Chinese to the United States and it reached a climax when its advocates began to work openly. The first public move was made May 14, 1921, when the vice-president laid before the senate a concurrent resolution adopted by the Hawaiian legislature asking permission to import coolie labor into Hawaii to work on the sugar plantations. It was claimed that there was a shortage of labor. On June 20 the delegate from the territory of Hawaii introduced H. J. Resolution 158, which provided for the admission to the territory of Hawaii of 50,000 of "such aliens otherwise inadmissible" as may be necessary to meet the "emergency existing in the shortage of agricultural labor." The committee on immigration of the house on July 7 after hearing the protests of labor refused to approve of the resolution. Notwithstanding this action, later the same day the Hawaiian delegate presented House Joint Resolution 171. The chairman of the immigration committee sent out a call for a meeting, which approved the bill. The new bill went further than the old as it would admit Chinese coolies to work at any occupation. The chairman, however, did not report the bill, as the president of the A. F.

of L. had learned of the action and asked him for a conference. The president of the A. F. of L. in the conference charged that if the bill became a law it would be a crime not only against labor but against the American people, and insisted that it be recommitted to the committee and hearings held. He questioned the manner of its introduction and approval by the committee and denounced the evident intention of those handling the bill to jam it through the house and then the senate. A conference was held in New York early last year to consider the sugar situation. The question of the admission of Chinese coolies into Hawaii was referred to and the representatives of the sugar interests in that territory urged the mainland sugar interests not to oppose it. They give this advice: "Don't interfere with the enactment of a law permitting Chinese coolies to come into Hawaii. It is the entering wedge; if we get them, you will have no trouble to get them in the United States." There is no doubt about this statement, as representatives of the sugar interests of the United States told of the incident to the committee on immigration of the house. Members of the emergency labor commission in discussing the desires of the Hawaiian sugar planters stated that they only wanted the Chinese coolies five years, when they would be deported; or, if they became wise to American ways too soon they could be deported at any time. Evidence was presented that not only would the thirteenth amendment to the constitution of the United States be violated, but that every law pertaining to the exclusion of Chinese coolies and the literacy test in the immigration law would be repealed if the bill became a law. The president of the A. F. of L. in concluding his statement before the committee, said: "I call your attention to the fact that it is not wise to take the heart and spirit out of America's workers. It is not wise to lead them into a position of fear, anguish and anger where no loyal support comes, because no voluntary loyal support comes to a government that uses oppression and suppression." The desire of the sugar planters for Chinese coolies was because the Japanese working for them had demanded a sufficient wage upon which they could live. They had been receiving 77 cents a day and quit work rather than to continue at that rate. This was in January, 1920. After the laborers had called off their strike the sugar planters raised the wages to $1 a day In November last the sugar planters reduced the wages of men from $30 to $26 a month and the women from $22.50 to $19.50. The Filipino Labor Union made an unavailing protest. (p. 322) Congress urged to hereafter deny admission, as immigrants and permanent residents, to all aliens who are ineligible to citizenship under the laws of the United States.

(1923, pp. 83-355) There is no shortage of labor in Hawaii, according to those in close touch with the situation, and the importation of coolie labor therefore can be viewed as an unwarranted assault upon the Chinese immigration restriction principle. For any importation of coolie labor into Hawaii carries with it the potential danger that it may be extended to the United States. We reaffirm the position of the A. F. of L. in firm opposition to any change of immigration policy as applied to Asiatic labor. . . . We again urge congress to hereafter deny admission, as immigrants and permanent residents, to all aliens who are ineligible to citizenship under the laws of the United States.

Church and Labor—(1923, p. 221) Reply of the president of the A. F. of L. to an address of a representative of the Portland Council of Churches. "Sometimes we may be crude in our expression. After all, it is an unfolding of the conscience and a better understanding of our mission in life. The proclamation of the Executive Council must have the first consideration of the material things of life, for without them we can not aspire to the higher and the better things. It is most gratifying to us to know that the churches of America are coming nearer to this great humanitarian movement of the workers, and I am free to say to you that it is gratifying to us to know that we are coming nearer to the idealism of the churches. In the convention of the A. F. of L. in 1893, held in Chicago, there were not less than 3,000,000 of America's workers unemployed, and in the city of Chicago, where we were meeting, there were men lying on the stone flooring of the corridor of the city hall, in whose chamber we were holding our sessions, and on the iron steps which we had to descend from the chamber to the level floor there were men lying on each step. There was no other shelter for them. and we had to tread our way carefully lest we would trample upon some part of the human form of an unemployed hungry worker. I remember that at that convention a delegation of clergymen came to us and delivered an address. It was more of a patronizing, academic expression of sympathy than any offer of helpfulness, and as the presiding officer of that convention I could not help an expression of resentment of that spirit. I called attention to the fact that America's workers resented the idea of being talked down to; we wanted to be spoken to and respected in the spirit of brotherhood. We wanted them, as we want now, the help of every good man and woman in furthering this great cause in which we are engaged. I am free to say, and I gladly express the truth, that the churches of America and their splendid men have come forward and have performed yeoman work in this great cause in which we are laboring. On behalf of this convention, permit me to say to you, gentlemen, that I thank you for your coming and for the message which you have brought to us."

Civil Service Appeal Board—(1919, p. 351, 1920, p. 422) The federal civil service laws are defective in not making provision for granting employes the right to appeal from the judgment of officials in disciplinary cases involving demotion or dismissal. Lodging arbitrary power in the hands of officials frequently results in injustices being inflicted upon employes and tends toward the up-building of a bureaucracy in our government institutions. The Executive Council is directed to cooperate with the representatives of affiliated organizations of civil service employes in securing the enactment of legislation granting civil service employes the right to a hearing and to an appeal from the judgment of officials in cases involving demotion or dismissal.

(1921, pp. 114-299-374) The creation of a United States civil service board of adjustments to constitute a court of appeals for employes in the classified civil service is proposed in H. R. 207. Grievances or controversies growing out of interpretations of salary laws and other disputes are to be handled by committees of the employes up to and including the chief officials of the bureau or department concerned. When an adjustment can not be made the chairman of the committee of employes shall refer the matter to the chief executive officers of the organization of employers having jurisdiction and if approved then the chief official of the bureau or department shall refer the matter to the board of adjustments. Another bill introduced provides that no person in the classified civil service shall be removed therefrom except for such cause as will promote the efficiency of the service and after a fair trial.

(1922, p. 352) We stand for a real merit system in public service, entrance to be determined by practical tests, tenure of place to be based on merit, promotion to higher positions among other elements to include promotion from the ranks, this to be determined within practical bounds by fitness, temperament and seniority.

Civil Service Employes, Hearings for— (1920, p. 422) The A. F. of L. directs the Executive Council to cooperate with the representatives of affiliated organizations of civil service employes in securing the enactment of legislation granting civil service employes the right to a hearing and to an appeal from the judgment of officials in cases involving demotion or dismissal.

Civil Service Merit System— (1923, p. 304) The A. F. of L. hereby records its opposition to any weakening of the civil service merit system through the creation by law or otherwise of a preferred group, believing as we do that legislation creating class distinctions and preferences, especially based upon military service, is not consonant with the ideals of this nation, whose founders declared against the military being superior to the civil power and for the equality of opportunity for all men.

Coal Fields Investigation— (1921, pp. 117-329) A resolution was introduced in congress directing the committee on education and labor to investigate the conditions in the coal fields of Logan, McDowell, Mercer, and Mingo counties, West Virginia. The object was to ascertain the causes of unrest and to find constructive measures to remove such causes. Among other things it provided that the committee should investigate whether the calling in of federal troops in the various fields was justified; whether armed guards and other armed forces had been maintained or paid for by private individuals or organizations; and whether citizens of the United States had been arrested, tried, or convicted contrary to or in violation of the constitution or the laws of the United States. (p. 195) The secretary was directed to wire all United States senators urging them to vote for the resolution.

Coal Price Control— (1921, pp. 108-373) S. 4828 contained so many dangerous provisions that it caused much concern. While ostensibly to curb profiteering it contained clauses that would endanger the economic interests of the miners and other workers in the coal industry. The federal trade commission was empowered to carry out the purposes of the proposed act. It could decide whether the price of coal was too high. If the commission determined that the supply of coal was threatened the president could declare an emergency. This power was given the president: "The president is hereby authorized, in any such emergency, to deal in coal, at reasonable prices, and to control the production, movement, and distribution of

coal in such manner and to such extent as he shall deem necessary and essential to the protection of the public health." Under the proposed law the federal trade commission was given authority to investigate the activities of all organizations "having to do with the coal industry or trade, whether national or local, regardless of the purposes for which organized or existing." Section 11 provided that "the secretary of labor shall investigate from time to time the wages, output per person, working conditions, terms of employment and the living expenses of miners and other workmen employed in mines from which coal is transported in commerce in order that such information may be available at times of general readjustment of wage contracts in the coal industry." This would give the government power to regulate the living conditions of the workers in the coal industry. It could set a standard by law and the law would be most difficult to change no matter how unjust it might be.

(1922, pp. 103-340) A bill introduced in the senate provided for the establishment of a board in the coal mining industry "to adjust disputes and stabilize conditions of production." The provisions of the act are similar to the labor clauses in the transportation act, which created the railroad labor board that has proved so inimical to the interests of the railroad employes. It also guarantees the right of women to work in coal mines, a practice which was abolished in England in 1837. (pp. 104-340) The A. F. of L. believes that the public is entitled to adequate and accurate information which will include all the items connected with the labor costs of mining coal, including the coal operators' overhead expenses, the freight costs, the costs added by the middleman acting between the operator and the retailer the cost to the retailer and the prices charged by these dealers.

Cold Storage— (1920, p. 107) Owners of cold storage warehouses have had nothing to fear from Congress. Several bills have been introduced to regulate cold storage warehouses, but they have gone the way of all other bills in the interest of the people, into the pigeon holes.

Collective Bargaining— (1920, pp. 115-462) The principle of collective bargaining stands on its own merits, and should require no mandate of statutory law. But where judges by the arbitrary use of the injunction hamper or prevent collective bargaining, that un-American practice should be inhibited by law. And there are certain groups of employes, notably of public employes, whom the public through legislation may properly protect in the exercise of collective bargaining. But, in general the spirit of democracy in industry would best develop through better mutual understanding and voluntary relationships between employer and employe.

(1921, p. 267) It is the sense of the A. F. of L. that every effort should be exerted to organize and educate all wage earners, allowing each and every man and woman who is a part of the A. F. of L. at this time, or who may hereafter become identified with the organization an equal opportunity to enjoy the benefits that accrue through collective bargaining. (Pp. 129-311) We urge the setting up of conference boards of organized workers and employers thoroughly voluntary in character and in thorough accord with our trade union organization, as means of promoting the democracy of industry through development of cooperative effort. We point out to employers the fact that industry, which is the life-blood of our civilization, can not be made the plaything and the pawn of a few who by chance today hold control. Industry is the thing by which all must live, and it must be given the opportunity to function at its best. This points the way to the proper democratization of industry as distinguished from the so-called "shop union" form of organization. We wish to distinctly emphasize the necessity for workers being at all times free to voice their views and opinions, to adjust their differences, remedy their wrongs, and remove their causes for grievance through avenues and agencies of the legitimate trades union. A great cloud of deception has been raised and the public mind greatly befuddled through exploitation of the so-called "shop union" idea, in which the workers in a particular establishment are supposed to have a share in the direction of the affairs of that establishment, especially as regards the conditions and terms of their employment. The intrinsic weakness of such a plan is found in the fact that it restricts representation on shop committees or whatever form or method of expression is adapted to the employes of that particular shop or establishment, thus denying to them the benefit that will ensue from communication with others who are similarly situated and whose interests are common. The trades union movement is the best known agency for the expression of the desires and conservatism of the interests of the workers. Common employment breeds common habits of thought as well as of effort, and common interests must find common outlet, and this is not to be secured under conditions which set up between groups of workers the artificial barrier of what pay roll their names appear upon. Collective bargaining and all the variuous activities for which a trade union properly is formed, and to the legitimate carrying out of which it devotes its existence, may only be given their full and beneficial application when the dealings between employer and employed rest on the full recognition of the trades union as the one proper and efficient instrument for the expression of the needs of its members. Democracy in industry can only be successfully founded on right relations between the workers and the managers, and these relations will not exist until the trades union is recognized as the basic unit and not the group as limited by the single shop or establishment.

College, Harvard—(1922, p. 361) It has been stated in the public press that Harvard College contemplates placing a restriction upon admission based on religious and racial grounds, which would lend strength to the all too prevalent forces of racial and religious bigotry, and especially to anti-Semitism. The A. F. of L. expresses its unqualified disapproval of any departure from true liberal tradition, and condemns as utterly un-American any policy which may deny to any racial or religious groups equal opportunities for education and advancement.

College, Labor—(1923, p. 261) Every member of organized labor needs to have a thorough knowledge of the ethics of trade unionism, economics, and history. We can best carry out the spirit of this resolution if all the affiliated labor unions in the A. F. of L. will actively cooperate on the program as outlined by your committee in connection with the Workers' Education Bureau of America.

Colorado Industrial Commission—(1920, p. 117) The twentieth general assembly of the Colorado state legislature in 1915 enacted the industrial commission law, popularly known as the "can't strike law," through the influence of the Rockefeller interests. It was modeled after the famous Lemieux act of Canada, though much more drastic, as the Lemieux act only applies to public utilities, whereas the Colorado law applies to all industries. It provides that no strike can be called for thirty days after the industrial commission has investigated the dispute and has rendered a decision which can be delayed and which in some cases has taken five months. The wage workers of Colorado, realizing the drastic provisions of the law, as it greatly conflicts with the bill of rights of the Colorado state constitution and with the constitution of the United States decided to ignore its provisions with a view of testing its constitutionality. In this they were unsuccessful. The law enforcement powers of the state were undoubtedly fearful that it would be declared unconstitutional by the supreme court, and prevented the carrying of the case up to that tribunal. They preferred to use it as a club over the workers and always stopped short of testing the law (P. 386) The Executive Council directed to continue aid in bringing about the repeal of the law.

(1922, p. 54) The Colorado industrial commission law was enacted in 1915 and went into effect July 15 of that year. In a little over six years Denver has experienced a continuous succession of strikes. Over 90 per cent of the members of organized labor throughout the state is opposed to this law. It, too, has proven a failure. The convention of the A. F. of L. ever since 1915 has expressed itself in opposition to its unwarranted and unconstitutional provisions. The fact that the law itself was ineffective prompted the employing interests of that state further to amend this law. In 1921 it was amended to give the industrial commission jurisdiction to investigate, hear and determine controversies in all industries and to use whatever time was necessary in the commission's discretion to render a finding or award. In addition, there was enacted a mandatory injunction law by which the industrial commission could invoke the injunction process and thus compel employers and employes to hold all industrial conditions in status quo pending the hearing and findings which the industrial commission might give whenever it felt so inclined. With these additional powers the industrial commission immediately sought to suppress and depress the organized protest, hopes, and aspirations of the wages earners of Colorado. Two cases came before the commission during the past year which demonstrated not only the impracticability, but the gross partiality shown in the enforcement of this law. In October, 1921, when nation-wide notice was given by the employers in the packing house industry that they intended to reduce the wages of the workers in that industry, a referendum vote was taken by the members of the Amalgamated Meat Cutters and Butcher Workmen on the question of accepting or resisting the proposed wage reduction, the result of which demonstrated that the workmen almost unanimously were against acceptance of the reduction. On December 1, 1921, the reduction was put into effect. In Denver, as well as in other cities, the employes of the five big packing houses resisted the wage reduction by giving up their employment. The industrial commission, by reason of the amended act of 1921, went into Judge Morrey's court and obtained a mandatory injunction against District President McCreash, all the officers and twenty-one members of local Union 641 of the Amalgamated Meat Cutters and Butcher Workmen, enjoining them from longer continuing this strike and demanding that the strike be called off and that the conditions restored as they existed before December 1. This injunction named the employers as well as the employes. The employers failed to restore the wages as they existed prior to December 1. On December 10 a citation was issued against President McCreash and others directing them to appear to answer why they should not be held for contempt of court. This citation also contained the names of employers. The employers, however, were not required to come into court nor were they ever molested. District President McCreash, with all the officers and a number of the members (thirty-three in all) were found guilty of contempt of court and were sentenced to jail from one to sixty days for violating the injunction. Nothing was done with the employers, but the workers were compelled to serve their terms in jail. The plea was made on behalf of the workers that the industrial laws in question were unconstitutional. While the court ruled that the law was unconstitutional by including all industries, it nevertheless permitted the iniquitous mandatory injunction law to stand. The second case developed about the 1st of December when the employers in the photo-engraving industry of Denver gave notice to the local photo-engravers' union that on January 1, 1922, the wages of its members would be reduced approximately 15 per cent. The local photo-engravers, in keeping with the requirement of law, filed a notice with the industrial commission as a protest against the reduction. The employers, however, did not comply with the law and merely notified the commission of the proposed reduction. The commission did not at once assume jurisdiction in the photo-engravers' case. The latter part of December the employers posted notices in the shops of the reduction stating that the same would go into effect on January 1. The commission then gave notice to employers and employes not to change working conditions until it had first held a hearing and rendered an award. January 10 was set as the date for the hearing. The employers ignored the commission, changed the working conditions and reduced the wages on January 1. Following this action in a newspaper interview the commission gave out the statement that it would immediately start court proceedings against the employers for ignoring the commission by reducing wages before an award was rendered. However, nothing was done. The local employers paid no attention whatever to the law and reduced the wages. The local photo-engravers refused to work longer. They left their employment on January 10, after they had become convinced that the industrial commission would not compel the employers to observe the law. When the hearing was had on January 10, the local photo-engravers' union appeared in court, but their employers remained away. In spite of all that had occurred, the industrial commission rendered an award that the employers were justified in reducing wages. It was clearly evident that the commission did not dare humiliate the employers by sending them to jail. No, it preferred to humiliate itself. In the case of the photo-engravers, the action of the employing photo-engravers in ignoring the law was justified by the industrial commission. The representatives of the packing house employes were charged with the same offense and were sent to jail. It is thus evident that this is but another form of class-biased instruments of law that can be made to serve the financial interests of employers and deprive the workers of their constitutional rights. This for m of legislation is not only unfair and unconstitutional, but has become equally as obnoxious and dangerous as the Kansas law. Under it the industrial commission may prolong its investigation and hearings indefinitely in cases where the workers are involved and it may render an immediate award where employers defy its powers or where the interests of employers are concerned. In addition, it gives legislative approval to the mandatory injunction process and through this grant of extended equity jurisdiction enables the courts of Colorado to regulate industrial relations and through contempt proceedings throw aside all the safeguards with which the individual citizen is surrounded when charged with wrong-doing by the state and wherein the state has become the prosecutor. Such legislation can find its equal only in the inquisitorial bodies of the dark ages when justice was measured by the position and influence of those coming before the courts and when men were slaves and serfs and not free men. Surely, the patience of man is being sorely tried. In the interest of freedom and equality of opportunity and for the purpose of perpetuating the principles of democracy, this convention should express itself in no uncertain terms against these unconstitutional and unwarranted tendencies to establish an economic and industrial autocracy in our land. (P. 486) The experience had with the Colorado industrial commission law demonstrates even more clearly the real viciousness and futility of legislation of this character. Instead of making for peace and tranquility, it necessarily aggravates and intensifies industrial conflicts.

Communist Delegate Unseated—(1923, pp. 257-258) The delegate from the Silver Bow Trades and Labor Council of Butte, Mont., was unseated for announcing himself a communist.

Community Service—(1922, p. 456) Directed the Executive Council to investigate the community service movement and to give such information and advice to Central Labor Unions as in its judgment is justified.

(1923, p. 124) Modern industrial processes are so highly specialized as to produce an unfortunate psychological effect upon the wage earners. Increasingly psychologists are calling attention to this important fact. They point out that which is so well known by the workers; that is, the deterioration of nervous force and health and crushing the creative instinct. While progress has been made within industry to improve this condition of affairs, further improvement may be made by the workers during their offtime engaging in activities which will give opportunity for self-expression, for satisfying the creative instincts and which will revitalize them generally. Much can be done by the trade union movement in dealing with the leisure time of the wage workers in such ways as to bring about these desirable ends. The field of recreational work has grown wonderfully in the last few years. It is much richer and more varied than in former years. The national organization known as the community service, a non-commercial body, the outgrowth of the war camp community service, is in the field to help promote in every section of the country programs for meeting the leisure time needs of the people. The president of the A. F. of L. is an honorary member of the board of directors of the community service, while the New York City representative of the A. F. of L. is an active member. The chief aim of the community service is to help cities and towns everywhere in the United States by means of trained field service to provide facilities, public and private, for meeting the leisure time recreational needs of all the people. It seeks to secure more parks and playgrounds, more community centers with opportunities for dramatic, music, and art expression, larger use of the schools, promotion of neighborhood organization for wholesome social life, etc., and the end it purposes to achieve is to overcome the evil psychological effects of machine industry, promote health and happiness, prevent misuse of leisure time, provide a chance for under-privileged youth, and neutralize the rush and strain of the present day civilization. (P. 240) We pledge our moral support to the leisure time, recreational and educational work of the community which has as its purpose the helping of cities and towns to provide adequate physical education in the schools, greater park and playground facilities and athletic fields, more community centers with opportunities for educational, musical, dramatic and art expression, and for neighborhood social gatherings. We also urge all international unions, central labor bodies, and local unions to take the initiative or cooperate with other civic bodies in the furthering of community recreation programs, cooperate with the workers of the Playground and Recreation Association of America and with public recreation officials, invite speakers from that association to their annual and other meetings, and open their official publications to articles on subjects pertaining to this general field of activity.

Compulsory Labor Legislation—(1920, p. 373) The A. F. of L. declares unyielding opposition to any legislation which would establish a condition under which workmen may not quit their employment singly or collectively whenever their terms of employment or conditions of labor become unsatisfactory.

(1920, pp. 109-385) Convention commended Executive Council for its zeal in combatting the unfair and discriminatory efforts on the part of the enemies of labor in the senate to have repressive compulsory labor laws enacted.

(1921, p. 115) Three bills providing for the punishment of participants in strikes that would interfere with interstate commerce failed of passage in the 66th congress. S. 4204, by Senator Poindexter, was slipped through the senate, however, by a trick when only two other senators were present (King and Smoot). When the bill had been reached on the calendar Senator Poindexter moved that it be considered. Several amendments were made and it was passed by the three senators. By some unknown means even the *Congressional Record* failed to record the names of those who made the various motions. Friends of labor attempted to enter the senate chamber, but were stopped and engaged in conversation so they could not learn what was before the body. Legislative representatives of the A. F. of L. immediately informed these friends of labor of the trick. Senator La Follette hurried to the senate and moved to reconsider. Later in the session, during the absence of Senator LaFollette, Senator Poindexter moved to take the bill from the calendar and pass it. Senator Gronna objected. The action of Senator Poindexter created much criticism and friends of labor in the senate forced him to agree not to attempt to bring up the bill until notice had been given to those who were opposed to its passage. This prevented the bill from again being considered.

(1922, pp. 109-340) Senator Poindexter again introduced his compulsory labor bill in the 67th congress, but it was not considered.

(1923, p. 86) Several bills were presented to congress prohibiting employes in interstate commerce from ceasing work to better their condition. Senator Spencer in S. 3889 proposed to establish a "federal court of conciliation," although nothing in the bill would suggest conciliation. It provided: "That the court shall have jurisdiction to hear and determine controversies or disputes affecting the operation of interstate commerce as may be brought before it, and to enforce its decisions and findings as the judgment of other federal courts are enforced." Senator Spencer was emphatic in this statement: "If you don't take this law you will take something else, for there is going to be a law passed by congress that will forever end strikes in controversies between employers and employes in the railroad, mining, and probably the electrical and oil industries." December 8, 1922, President Harding in a message to congress, which he personally read, called attention to the "inefficiency of power to enforce decisions of the railroad labor board." He said: "The substitution of a labor division in the interstate commerce commission made up from its membership, to hear and decide disputes relating to wages and working conditions which have failed of adjustment by proper committees created by the railroads and their employes, offers a more effective plan. Public interest demands that ample power shall be conferred upon the labor tribunal, whether it is the present board or the suggested substitute, to require its rulings to be accepted by both parties to a disputed question." He added: "Therefore the lawful power for the enforcement of decisions is necessary to sustain the majesty of government and to administer to the public welfare." Notwithstanding the efforts of unfair employers' associations to have compulsory labor legislation enacted there was no action on the bills presented.

Conferences, A. F. of L., *Dec. 13, 1919*)— (1920, pp. 63-383) October 28, 1919, the Executive Council, together with the executive heads of the four railroad brotherhoods issued to the officers of the national and international unions and to representative farmers' organizations a call for a conference to be held in Washington on December 13. This conference was made necessary by the critical period in which labor found itself with relation to the affairs of the country in general, and the problems of reconstruction in particular. The conference adopted a declaration entitled "Labor, Its Grievances, Protest and Demands.

Feb. 23-24, 1921—(1921, p. 56) Because of the general situation confronting the labor movement and threatening its effectiveness, if not its existence, in a most serious manner, the president of the A. F. of L. called together on December 29, 1920, a number of officials of trade unions and friends of the labor movement for a discussion of the entire subject. After a survey of various movements aiming at the destruction of the trade union movement and the destruction of standards of labor, by the A. F. of L., it was decided to recommend the advisability of a conference of officials and representatives of national and international unions affiliated to the A. F. of L. It also was the recommendation that a special effort should be made to more thoroughly organize the dissemination of information about the trade union movement and its work in order that there might be a more thoroughly informed state of public opinion in relation to questions affecting the welfare of the workers. The Executive Council directed the president to summon a conference of officials and representatives of national and international trade unions to be held in Washington on February 23d. After thorough consideration of all of the issues involved and of an expression of the views of practically all of the delegates, a declaration was adopted February 24, setting forth labor's position and declaring its unalterable determination to resist with all possible strength the efforts of the enemies of labor to undermine and destroy our movement. This declaration was entitled "The Challenge Accepted." (P. 307) The convention indorsed the declarations as follows: We recommend the careful perusal of this important document because of the clarity of statement contained therein in setting forth as it does, succinctly and emphatically, the attitude of the trade unions of America. The courageous assertion of the distinct and definite program of the trade union movement as opposed to the destructive plan contemplated by the opponents of the trade unions is one that must impress all who give it attention. The vital principles and laudable purposes of the A. F. of L. and those international and national trade unions affiliated with it are set out in the conclusions of this conference report.

Conferences, Presidential, Industrial— (1920 pp. 81-383) Two conference summoned by President Wilson sought to find a remedy for industrial unrest and neither succeeded. The first of these conferences was convened on October 6, 1919, in the Pan-American Union Building, in the city of Washington, and continued in session for about a month. This conference was composed of delegates grouped under three headings representing labor, the public, and employers. Various propositions were submitted to the conference for its consideration by the various delegations and individuals. Early in the conference the labor group presented the following program as its contribution to the constructive thought of the conference: "This conference of representatives of the public, the employers and business men, and of labor, called by the president of the United States, hereby declares in favor of the following:

1. The right of wage earners to organize in trade and labor unions for the protection and promotion of their rights, interests and welfare. 2. The right of wage earners to bargain collectively through trade and labor unions with employers regarding wages, hours of labor, and relations and conditions of employment. 3. The right of wage earners to be represented by representatives of their own choosing in negotiations and adjustments with employers in respect to wages, hours of labor, and relations and conditions of employment. 4. The right of freedom of speech, of the press and of assemblage, all being responsible for their utterance and actions. 5. The right of employers to organize into associations or groups to bargain collectively through their chosen representatives in respect to wages, hours of labor and relations and conditions of employment. 6. The hours of labor should not exceed eight hours per day. One day of rest in each week should be observed, preferably Sunday, half-holiday on Saturday should be encouraged. Overtime beyond the established hours of labor should be discouraged, but when absolutely necessary should be paid for at a rate of not less than time and one-half time. 7. The right of all wage earners, skilled and unskilled, to a living wage is hereby declared, which minimum wage shall insure the workers and their families to live in health and comfort in accord with the concepts and standards of American life. 8. Women should receive the same pay as men for eqʻal work performed. Women workers should not be permitted to perform tasks disproportionate to their physical strength or which tend to impair their potential motherhood and prevent the continuation of a nation of strong, healthy, sturdy and intelligent men and women. 9. The services of children less than 16 years of age for private gain should be prohibited. 10. To secure a greater share of consideration and cooperation to the workers in all matters affecting the industry in which they are engaged to secure and assure continuously improved industrial relations between employers and workers and to safeguard the rights and principles hereinbefore declared, as well as to advance conditions generally, a method should be provided for the systematic review of industrial relations and conditions by those directly concerned in each industry. To this end, there should be established by agreement between the organized workers and associated employers in each industry a national conference board consisting of an equal number of representatives of employers and workers, having due regard to the various sections of the industry and the various classes of workmen engaged, to have for its object the consideration of all subjects affecting the progress and well-being of the trade, to promote efficiency of production from the viewpoint of those engaged in the industry and to protect life and limb, as well as safeguard and promote the rights of all concerned within the industry. With a further view of providing means for carrying out this policy the federal government, through its department of labor, should encourage and promote the formation of national conference boards in the several industries where they do not already exist. To still further encourage the establishment of these national conference boards in each industry, these conference boards should be urged whenever required, to meet jointly to consider any proposed legislation affecting industries in order that employers and workers may voluntarily adopt and establish such conditions as are needful, and may also counsel and advise with the government in all industrial matters wherever needful legislation is required. The federal government should also undertake to extend the functions of the department of labor to ascertain and provide adequate information and advice to the several national conference boards on all matters affecting the life, health and general welfare of the wage earners within such industry. 11. The flow of immigration should at no time exceed the nation's ability to assimilate and Americanize the immigrants coming to our shores, and at no

time shall immigration be permitted when there exists an abnormal condition of employment. By reason of existing conditions we urge that all immigration into the United States be prohibited at least until two years after peace shall have been declared.'' The labor delegation also introduced a resolution that "each group comprising this conference select two of its number and these six so selected to constitute a committee to which shall be referred existing differences between the workers and employers in the steel industry for adjudication and settlement. Pending the findings of this committee this conference requests the workers involved in this strike to return to work and the employers to reinstate them in their former positions." Almost at the outset of the conference it was recognized that collective bargaining was the first principle upon which agreement should be reached. Upon this question the conference spent the remaining period of its life and broke up unable to reach an agreement. In an effort to systematize its work the conference appointed a general committee of fifteen members, five from each group, to consider and report upon the various propositions submitted. The members of the public group in this committee of fifteen submitted the following resolution on collective bargaining with the assent of the labor delegation: "The right of wage-earners to organize in trade and labor unions, to bargain collectively, to be represented by representatives of their own choosing in negotiations and adjustments with employers in respect to wages, hours of labor and relations and conditions of employment is recognized. This must not be understood as limiting the right of any wage-earners to refrain from joining any organization or to deal directly with his employer if he so chooses." The labor delegation made every possible effort to meet the wishes of the other delegations in the matter of form and construction of this resolution and it underwent as many as a half dozen changes before hope was finally abandoned. The employers' delegation would not accept any resolution on collective bargaining unless it was so worded as to be anti-trade union in spirit and to provide encouragement and support for company unions. The position of the employers in the conference was throughout a position of anti-unionism, a position of enmity and antagonism to trade union efforts and organization, a position of opposition to the one great constructive agency which offers to the working people their hope of a better future and a greater measure of industrial freedom. They sought continually to find a way to secure approval of the conference for various forms of shop and company organizations and the viewpoint which they sought constantly to inject was the viewpoint of the shop and the individual plant instead of the viewpoint of the industry as contemplated by the A. F. of L. and its affiliated organizations. Clearly the solicitude of the employers for shop organizations and company unions was because they constitute a device for defeating the workers, for organizing them away from each other in small, weak groups and rendering them practically powerless before the employers. Through debate in open session and through committee meetings lasting many days the employers stubbornly resisted every attempt at conciliation and it was this position of

obstinacy in defense of vested rights that led finally to the dramatic disruption of the conference with the departure of the labor delegation from the hall. The defense of the labor position and the attack upon those who sought to perpetuate unfreedom and autocratic control in industry constituted a battle that will go down in history as one of the remarkable episodes of the industrial conflict. The defense of the labor position was marked frequently by passages of brilliancy that have been seldom equalled. For its revelation of the position of the employers and for its value as an expression of labor thought, the following extract from one of the addresses delivered by the president of the A. F. of L., as the leader of the labor delegation on the question of relative rights of Labor and capital as the employers sought to outline them, deserves to find place in the permanent record: "We can not prevent a reduction or check the imposition of an inferior condition upon the organized workers of America, without at the same time checking that same or worse imposition upon the unorganized. There is not a law that we can ask from the United States, there is not a law that we can ask from any of the states, or from any of our municipalities, for the protection and promotion of the rights and interest of organized workers that will not apply equally to every unorganized worker. We speak in the name of labor, organized and unorganized. We speak for labor, the inarticulate, the powerless, the timid, the dominated worker, under duress, we protest that we speak in his name. We hear the term used, the struggle between capital and labor, and that is implied in the statement which I have just mentioned. The struggle between capital and labor. What is capital? Capital consists of tables —these tables and these chairs, these chandeliers, clothes, steel, clothing, boots, shoes, pork, hides and cattle, machinery, wool, sugar, oil, anything that can be brought to your mind relative to the very things that I have mentioned is encompassed in the term "capital"—dead things, inanimate things, material things, things which can be sold and bought, things which are subject to barter and sale; capital invested for the production of still more capital, more inanimate things, material things. And what is labor? Labor is the men and the women, erroneously and intentionally coined in the terminology as labor. It is laborers, workers, human beings, men and women and children, and when it comes to the question of determing what is of greater importance as to men and women and little children, and dollars and things, the soul of mankind goes out to men and women and children, rather than to capital—the regulation of capital, the material things of life, and the regulation of men and women and children. If the old concept of labor and capital had prevailed, we should still find our children of tender age, going into the mines and working underground for twelve, fourteen and sixteen hours a day. If the old concept of labor and capital still prevailed, you would find children in the textile mills of America working twelve, fourteen and sixteen hours a day. If the old concept of labor and capital still prevailed in this year of strife, you would find as of old that women would be in the coal mines giving birth to children, the parentage of which they knew nothing." The labor delegation went into the conference determined to contribute its full share of thought and effort toward the solution of the problems with which the conference was asked by the president to deal. It worked through the long and trying period with all the patience as its command, in the face of most serious difficulties. It remained in the conference until the last possible moment, departing only after the employers by their vote against genuine collective bargaining made it impossible for labor to remain. In a final effort to secure agreement the labor delegation submitted to the conference a resolution so drafted as to insure as far as possible its acceptance. The resolution thus submitted follows: "The right of wage-earners to organize without discrimination, to bargain collectively to be represented by representatives of their own choosing in negotiations and adjustment with employers in respect to wages hours of labor and relations and conditions of employment is recognized." The vote in the conference was by the group system, each group casting one vote. Under the rules no resolution could be adopted except by unanimous vote. The employers, maintaining their position of defense of the shop organization and the company union voted against the resolution providing for collective bargaining through trade unions and through representatives freely chosen by the workers. Thus, though both the labor representatives and the representatives of the public voted for the resolution, it was defeated. With the right of collective bargaining through trade unions defeated and the basis for all further conference removed by the action of the employers' representatives, labor could no longer remain a party to the conference. The labor delegation, therefore, left the conference hall as a unit. The delegates composing the public group held one more session in which a report to the president was drafted. In an effort to retrieve the failure of the first presidential conference, President Wilson summoned a second industrial conference on January 12, 1920. The composition of this conference was entirely different from that of the first conference. No effort was made to secure representative groups, but on the contrary only one group was selected. This was done without any reference to representation for the labor movement and there was no such representation. It remained in session for more than a month, during which time it summoned many witnesses, among whom was the president of the A. F. of L. It undoubtedly gave deep study to the industrial problems confronting the nation and on March 21 made public its report to the president. It can not be disputed that the commission was entirely sincere in its efforts and that it sought earnestly to produce a document that would be of value in the nation's industrial life. Regardless of that, however, the work of the commission was a failure. It proceeded without a proper knowledge of the history of the trade union movement, without a proper understanding of its needs and desires and without an adequate appreciation of the philosophy and psychology. The conference devised a vast mass of machinery composed of a national industrial board and regional and local conference boards and boards of inquiry. The conference recommended that this machinery be made operative by law. The report of the commission is subject to two criticisms of the most serious character. The first of these is that the report seeks to lay upon

the industrial world an intricate structure artificially imposed by force of law. The second is that it seeks to give encouragement and permanency to the various forms of company unions and shop organizations and various forms of so-called employe representation, whose chief merit is that they serve the purposes of the employers by organizing the workers away from each other. It would seem that the conference must to a certain extent have had in mind in drafting its plan the establishment of the Whitley councils. In England, however, the plan under which the Whitley councils are operated rests upon trade union organization and demands trade union organization as a prior condition. The report of the president's second industrial conference lays down no such foundation and establishes no such condition. Its misunderstanding of the character and purpose of the trade union movement in this connection is amply illustrated by the following paragraph from the report: "Employe representation organizes the relations of employer and employe so that they regularly come together to deal with their common interests. It is operating successfully under union agreements, in organized shops. It is operating in non-union shops and it is operating in shops where union and non-union men work side by side. In plants working under union agreement, it adds to collective bargaining an agency of cooperation within the plant. It is itself an agency of collective bargaining and cooperation where union agreements do not obtain." The commission seemed to view the problems of industry from the viewpoint of the single shop instead of from the viewpoint of industries. The character of American industry in its present stage of development and the work of the American trade union movement is ample proof of the fallacy of such a viewpoint. At the time this report is drafted no effort has been made to secure action in congress toward setting up the machinery outlined by the president's conference. Your E. C. is, however, of the firm opinion that should an effort be made, Labor must exert every influence to encompass its defeat. Regardless of how excellent may have been the intentions of the members of the conference the principles which the report seeks to establish in the law are in many respects actually pernicious and in no respect do they serve the needs of the workers. The machinery established by the trade union movement itself out of the day to day experience of years of struggle is superior in every respect to that which it is sought to create under the report of the president's conference. The machinery now in operation is machinery created through strife and struggle in contact with life and conditions and shaped to meet the actual needs of service in the field. The machinery devised by the president's commission is constructed in the seclusion of the secret council chamber, entirely out of contact with the life for which it was designed and entirely unfittedly for the needs of that life.

Congress, Filbustering in—(1919, p. 109) The failure of congress to function at critical times could be avoided by reasonable amendments to the rules of procedure, such as: A stated date after which no new bills should be introduced except those which contain an element of emergency; each committee required to hold hearings and report within a reasonable time, say 30 days after receipt, on all measures referred to it; each measure not of an urgent nature to take its place on the calendar and be acted upon in order; each speaker to confine himself strictly to the subject under discussion and be given a reasonable time limit; a proper method of cloture. An illustration of the need of some provision similar to the one last above suggested is found on page 5104 of the *Congressional Record*, March 3, 1919. With final adjournment due on the following day, and the calendar loaded with essential measures—appropriation and other important bills—the Chair stated the pending question to be on the bill to reclaim lands for homes for the returning soldiers, whereupon Senator Sherman arose and said: "On that I will take the floor, and, in pursuance of the immemorial custom, I will proceed to talk about something else," and he occupied hours of time, 11 pages of the *Record*, and about 17,000 words in discussion of the peace league and other matters not at that time before the senate. The bill for homesteads for soldiers was heard of no more. Much valuable legislation might have been enacted in those precious last hours of the dying Congress had not the 96 senators been compelled by discredited rules, or lack of rules, to waste time while the senator from Illinois thus flagrantly violated the primary elemental rules of parliamentary procedure. (P. 362) As the power and influence of the workers are constantly growing and extending more subtle and more indirect methods and procedures are adopted and followed by hostile legislators in controverting this power and influence of labor in the legislative halls of our states and nation. Parliamentary procedure, originally intended to clarify issues, expedite their fair and intelligent consideration and to reach an early conclusion, has been diverted into an instrument of confusion, evasion, and delay. Legislative measures are apparently favored with knowledge beforehand that ultimate technical parliamentary objections will be invoked to prevent the enactment of such measure into law and thus the public mind is confused as to the real purpose and intent of our legislators. Failure of congress to enact the several legislative proposals into law is not alone a matter of deep regret. This practice of delay and evasion is a matter for severe criticism and condemnation. We view the action of congress in adjourning without making adequate provisions and appropriations for the continuance of the several needful departments of the government under the control of the department of labor, nothing less than a deliberate attempt to promote the well-being of the few and influential to the detriment of the welfare of the great mass of our people. We hold that the time is here to direct the light of day into the nooks and crooks of the dark halls and chambers of congress and remove the angelic cloak by which these misinterpreters of public good shroud their acts of deviltry. The rules of parliamentary procedure of congress are antiquated, ill-designed, and are not used to prove helpful in giving expression to the manifested will of the people. We hold they are used and designated almost exclusively to protect the interests of the possessors of the wealth of our nation. We direct that congress be memorialized to make all the required changes in congressional procedure to facilitate and properly care for the legislative needs of the people.

Congress and Reaction—(1922, p. 114) More than 400 bills have been introduced in the 67th congress which directly or indirectly affect Labor. Ninety per cent of them are inimical to the interests of Labor and the people. The astonishing feature of this, however, is that few of them ever get beyond the committee stage while many are not even given hearings except for propaganda purposes. Most of these bills were presented to carry out pledges to the enemies of labor, but the effect has been to create an atmosphere of the most reactionary nature in everything done or proposed in the capitol. The result has been that 99 per cent of the work done by labor in congress has been to defeat pernicious legislation. There is little sentiment in favor of beneficial legislation. This is so apparent that the statement is often made that if the United States capitol could be transported to the England of the fifteenth century half the members of congress would be "to the manner born." The idea seems to prevail that the outcome of the 1920 elctions means that every liberty of the people can be taken away provided some individual or group of individuals representing the privileged few desire it for their own especial benefit. Constructive legslation is taboo. The fact is that since March 4, 1919, the country' has run itself. In considering legislation only those things that will give some political friend or friends something for nothing are considered. (P. 486) There are at least 50 congressional districts in this country, now represented by men who are not in accord with our legislative program and who are generally hostile to our objectives, from which trade unionists migh be elected. A labor group of 50 trade unionist in the next congress, together with those friends whose support we can depend upon would insure a more sympathetic consideration of those measures touching the lives of the workers than has been accorded legislation of this character by the present congress.

(1923, p. 81) The 67th congress will find an unenviable place in history. Reaction and incompetence, backed apparently by no other thought than personal and partisan political advantage, made it impotent to remedy any of the evils troubling the people of our country. A group of reactionaries seemed to act upon the idea that their sole duty was to draw up bills that would take away guaranteed rights from the people or place further burdens of taxation upon them. Over 20,000 bills were introduced in the senate and house, some 400 of which affected Labor directly or indirectly. After March 1, 1921, efforts were made to pay campaign pledges by introducing compulsory labor and other bills intended to degrade American standards. In fact, it was soon realized that if any remedial legislation was passed by congress it would be a miracle. The whole power and influence of labor was therefore forced to protect itself from vicious legislation instead of endeavoring to secure remedial legislation. There was little legislation enacted during the congress that would benefit the mass of the people. The time was taken up in trying to carry out political pledges by subsidizing private ship owners, in advancing "thou shalt not" legislation, taking the police power away from the states and placing it in the federal courts, and in making our money more easy to counterfeit by displacing old and tried employes in the bureau of engraving and printing. The only consolation labor has is that while it did not obtain the remedial legislation that it sought it prevented the passage of many reactionary measures. (P. 357) We are heartened by the knowledge that the overwhelming repudiation of this congress by an outraged people will bring into the 68th congress a greatly changed personnel from whom better results are confidently expected.

Conscription—(1923, p. 88) The A. F. of L. is of the firm belief there is a desire to force conscription upon Labor in peace times as well as in times of war. This first came to light September 21, 1922, when Representative Johnson of South Dakota introduced a joint resolution (H. J. Res. 384), proposing an amendment to the constitution of the United States, as follows: "That in the event of a declaration of war by the United States of America against any foreign government or other common enemy the congress shall provide for the conscription of every citizen and of all money, industries, and property of whatsoever nature necessary to the prosecution thereof and shall limit the profits for the use of such moneys, industries, and property." Labor entered no objections to the joint resolution as it not only conscripted labor, but also "all money, industries, and property of whatsoever nature necessary to the prosecution" of war. Besides, such conscription could not occur until after a declaration of war by the United States. But opposition immediately arose from the financial interests and big corporations. They insisted it was all right to conscript labor but they would not stand for the conscription of money, industries, and property even in war time. Then it was discovered that it was not necessary to have a constitutional amendment and Representative Johnson presented a bill (H. R. 13201) December 6, 1922, "to provide for the national security and defense." This provided that "in the event of a national emergency," which does not necessarily mean war, the president would be authorized to draft into the service of the United States all persons necessary without exemption on account of industrial occupation. No other interpretation could be placed upon such a bill than that it would mean there could be conscription in peace times. Section 2 of the bill provided that only in case of war the president would have power to determine material resources over which government control would be necessary to the successful termination of such a conflict. Previous to the introduction of this subject in congress a representative of the war college visited the offices of the American Federation of Labor and asked what stand Labor would take on the question of conscription. December 8, President Harding in a message which he read to congress said: "The proposed survey of a plan to draft all the resources of the republic, human and material, for national defense may well have your approval." Under such a law as that proposed when a war would end there is doubt but that conscription of labor would be extended into peace times. That the reactionary group that is controlling the destinies of the United States at the present time are determined if they can to turn progress backward and adopt the policies of the old imperial autocratic and militaristic governments is immediately evident by this species of proposed legislation. The convention should take a firm stand on the conscription proposal. (P. 280) The law of self-preservation implies and requires the use of such force and service as may repel the enemy without and conserve the life within. But to apply principles applicable only to war and to conscript the service of free men unconditional upon a like conscription of property of whatever kind or form is to deify property and to materialize humanity. To apply such principles to a condition or state so vaguely phrased as to enable the conscription of man "in the event of a national emergency " and not to define clearly what is meant by a "national emergency " is to make property the master of man and to make the free citizen the slave of the state.

Conservatory of Music—(1919, pp. 113-428) Bills were introduced in congress for the establishment of a National Conservatory of Music to be owned and managed by the government, with branches in other cities, but they failed of passage. (1920, pp. 120-462) Bills for a National Conservatory of Music met with the same fate.

Constabulary and Militia, State—(1922 p. 343) The A. F. of L. demands that the principle of reduction of armament and of military force be applied, not only to nations, to prevent their warring on each other, but even more stringently to such forms of military organization as are most frequently used against the toilers of our country namely the state constabulary and the state militia.

Constitutional Amendments, U. S.—(1919, p. 355) A proposed amendment to the United States constitution providing that on petition of 500,000 citizens it would be mandatory on the secretary of state to submit an amendment to popular vote was referred to the Executive Council for further examination and investigation with instructions to give careful consideration to any other measures of a similar nature which may be introduced in congress.

(1921, p. 121) Article V of the constitution of the United States provides that amendments thereto shall be initiated either by congress or the legislatures of two-thirds of the states and must be ratified by the legislatures of three-fourths of the states to become part of the constitution. H. J. Res. 12 and H. J. Res. 29 seek to amend Article V of the constitution by proposing that ratification shall be by three-fourths of the people of the states instead of the legislatures of the states. H. J. 21 provides that the people of two-thirds of the states by a referendum of the electors can call a convention for initiating amendments to the constitution which will be valid if ratified by the people of three-fourths of the several states. (P. 325) Experience has proved the necessity from time to time of adapting our fundamental law to changed conditions of national life as is evidenced by the large number of amendments to the U. S. constitution already adopted. We believe the present method of amendment is so excessively difficult as to be undemocratic. Resolutions now before congress for the modification of the method of amendment are steps in the right direction.

Constitutional Rights—(1921, p. 119) A bill introduced in congress but not considered provided for the protection of citizens in the exercise of certain rights and immunities guaranteed and secured by the constitution of the U. S. Such a law would prevent similar occurrences to those arising in Pennsylvania during the steel strike when meetings were broken up and the participants fined or sent to jail.

Contracts, Observance of—(1922, p. 36-262) We feel it of some public importance to report that in an unusual number of instances during the year great organizations of employers have willfully and deliberately repudiated their contracts and broken their pledges to the workers. Whether this is an indication of a growing immorality in the business of the world we are unable to say but we believe it nevertheless to be a fact of profound social importance and worthy of deep study. If the agreements of great organizations of employers are not to be regarded as pledges it will mean that we have come upon a new development which will have to be taken into account in future relations with employers. As instances of breach of contract on the part of employers we cite the following cases: The organized mine owners repudiated their agreement with the United Mine Workers of America compelling the mine workers to cease work. This agreement provided that prior to its expiration representatives of mine workers and mine owners should meet in conference for the purpose of negotiating a new agreement. The mine owners flatly refused to enter into such a conference thus making a new agreement impossible. For the most part the attitude of the mine owners was one of simple disregard for the pledge which they had made. Such excuses as were offered were entirely without value. Their transparency was so obvious that the mine owners soon ceased making excuses. Packing house employers likewise were guilty of violation of agreements made with the workers and it was these violations that led to the necessity for a cessation of work in the packing industry. The Interntional Ladies' Garment Workers were compelled to resort to cessation of work for a like reason. Employers refused to abide by the terms of the contract which they had signed. The contest going on in the printing industry among employers and the printing trades unions, involves a contemptuous disregard and flagrant violation of an agreement by employers and their associations which they had previously urged upon the printing trades for acceptance. This agreement provided for the observance of the eight-hour day and half-holiday—four-hour day on Saturday to become effective May 1, 1921. From the time this national agreement was approved to May 1, 1921, every intervening agreement entered into between local employers and local printing trades unions was made with a full knowledge and understanding of the national agreement that on May 1, 1921, the forty-four-hour week would be observed as the law of the printing industry. By this procedure, all those employers who were not directly associated with the employers' organizations who had entered into this national agreement, indirectly became bound to its terms, conditions and requirements. Regardless of this national agreement, supplemented by these direct and implied local agreements, when May 1, 1921, arrived, the printing trades' employers disregarded and deliberately violated their agreements and the printing trades unions were forced either to strike to compel their employers to observe these contracts or else humiliatingly submit to the dishonorable and contract-breaking dictum of their employers. Quite apart from the struggle to enforce the forty-four-hour week the International Photo-Engravers' Union became involved in a national lockout on January 3, 1922, in an attempt on the part of employers in that craft to increase the working week of the photo-engravers from forty-four to forty-eight hours and in addition, to reduce the wages of all its members at least $5 a week. The photo-engravers were locked out throughout the country on January 3 but after having been out for a period

ranging from one and a half weeks to two weeks, the employers resumed restoration of wages and the forty-four-hour week. Employers in the granite cutting industry are among those who have followed most arbitrary and autocratic policies during the year. The greater portion of the membership of the Granite Cutters' International Association of America is either locked out or on strike because of the refusal of the employers in that industry to meet with representatives of the workers for the negotiation of a new trade agreement. The old agreement expired on April 1, 1922, but a portion of the membership in California has been locked out since early in May, 1921. In the textile industry the conduct of employers was particularly at fault and indicated an unusual greed. The workers in that industry previously had accepted a wage reduction of 22 per cent and it was because the employers sought to enforce an additional reduction of 20 per cent that the workers ceased work as the only means of resistance. As in every case the workers in the textile industry have stood their ground and while the suspension of work still exists the ranks of the strikers are unbroken and the determination to resist injustice is as great as it was at the outset. We have recorded here only those violations of agreements by employers which are of national importance. There have been many other employers who have violated local agreements. We feel that we should point out the vital necessity for scrupulous observance of all contracts and agreements on the part of employers as well as the workers. Labor has been ever most scrupulous in this regard and has urged always the necessity for keeping inviolate every pledge. There have been but few instances where organizations of the workers have repudiated their agreements. There have been many most serious cases where employers have been guilty of such repudiation. This is particularly true in regard to employers during the year just closed. Labor can not afford, however, to tarnish even in the slightest degree its record of integrity and honor. Labor standards must be the highest. They must be unassailable, always. Moreover, if agreements are not kept, agreements must soon lose their value. The pledge of labor has been highly regarded because the pledges of labor have been made to be kept. There must be no deviation from this honorable policy and where there is deviation, and therefore dishonor, the movement must find effective methods for expression of its disapprobation. We know of no similar period of time in which there have. been so many wanton violations of contract on the part of great organizations of employers. We submit that it is a vital essential that there be a return of good faith in industry, a return to standards of morality which will restore the pledges of men to their true and proper meaning. If it is impossible to have faith in pledges given, then the entire industrial structure will be undermined and those who are engaged in productive labor will find themselves confronted with a problem more serious than any which has arisen since the development of modern industry.

(1923, pp. 63-208) We present here a resume of a few of the more important of the strikes that have taken place since our last convention. We call particular attention to the record of contracts and agreements broken by organizations of employers and we urge upon them everywhere the most serious consideration of the deplorable condition thus portrayed. For purposes of this report we present here only the essential facts in relation to each case. Those who desire a more detailed record of these important struggles and victories are referred to the October, 1923, issue of the *American Federationist*.

Miners—Among the important struggles won by labor during the year was the strike of the mine workers. The responsibility for the coal strike of 1922 plainly rested with the coal operators. The operators of the central competitive field were obligated by agreement to meet with the representatives of the United Mine Workers for the purpose of attempting to negotiate a new agreement before the expiration of the old contract, which terminated on March 31, 1922. This the operator refused to do. In addition, the operators declared their intention of forcing wage reductions and establishing the non-union shop in the coal industry. The United Mine Workers of America suspended work when the wage contract expired on March 31, 1922, declaring that they would not accept wage reductions, and, moreover, that they would not return to work until the coal operators met with them in joint conference and negotiated a reasonably satisfactory contract. In August and September, the coal operators, meeting with the representatives of the United Mine Workers of America, renewed the old agreement without any reduction in wages. It was a victory of great moral and material value to the organized labor movement of our time and country. The strike of the anthracite mine workers during the summer of 1922 was for the purpose of resisting a reduction in wages. The present struggle of the mine workers is for an increase in wages, improved conditions of employment and complete acceptance of the principle and purpose of collective bargaining.

Granite Cutters—Employers in the granite cutting industry were among those who continued their arbitrary policies until the solidarity of the granite cutters made a settlement imperative. On June 1, 1921, the Granite Manufacturers' Association of California locked out the California members of the Granite Cutters' International Association of America, repudiating a collective bargain that did not expire until August 1, 1921. Granite manufacturers throughout the country followed the lead of the California manufacturers and either locked out union granite cutters or refused to meet with representatives of the workers to negotiate new agreements for those which expired on April 1, 1922. The unity and aggressiveness of the organized granite workers broke down the resistance of the employers so that by the middle of 1923 agreements had been signed unionizing practically the entire industry with the exception of California. The granite cutters have not only maintained the forty-four-hour week, but in some localities have secured the five-day work week, with $8 per day as the minimum rate.

Ladies' Garment Workers—As a result of cessation of work the International Ladies' Garment Workers' Union reduced the working week in the dress and waist industry from 44 to 40 hours. Employers have not hesitated to make use of the injunction process in disputes with the garment workers. Justice Martin, of Montreal, Canada, not only enjoined the Montreal Garment Workers' Union from striking against a certain employer, but also assessed damages against the union to idemnify the employer to the amount of the difference between the cost of manufacturing garments with strikebreakers and with his regular employes on strike. If necessary, it is the purpose of the Garment Workers' Union to appeal this case to the Privy Council of the House of Lords.

Textile Industries—In the New England textile industry the employers not only sought to impose a wage cut of twenty per cent in addition to a previous one of twenty-two and one-fourth per cent, but also to lengthen the working week from 48 to 54 hours. Under the leadership of the United Textile Workers of America the textile workers ceased work for ten months and resumed with the wage rate in effect prior to the twenty per cent reduction. The forty-eight-hour week was also maintained for most of the industry. The labor movement gave such solid financial support to the Textile Workers' Union that close to one million dollars was disbursed in maintaining the strike.

Typographical Union—The contest in the printing industry is another example of employer violation of an agreement previously urged upon the printing trades for acceptance This agreement provided for the forty-four-hour week on May 1, 1921. From the time the printing industry employers' associations entered into this national agreement, agreements between local employers and local printing trades unions were made with full information that under the national agreement the forty-four-hour week would be operative in the printing industry on May 1, 1921. Therefore, all employers not directly associated with employers who were parties to this national agreement became indirectly bound to its terms. Regardless of this national agreement, and its direct and indirect local application, the printing trades employers refused to apply the forty-four-hour week, thus disregarding and violating their agreements. The International Typographical Union declared the strike to compel employers to observe their contracts.

Contracts Should be Respected—(1921, p. 267) Convention refused to approve a resolution providing that in all contracts entered into by all crafts with their employers there shall be a clause inserted whereby each craft can render such assistance as is needed by any and all crafts, when called upon to do so, without violating its contract. That there shall be given a specified date, stipulated by our national and international unions, that all future contracts made and entered into by organized labor shall expire at the same time.

Convention City—(1923, pp. 37-348) Each convention decides in what city the next convention of the A. F. of L. shall be held. In every case when a city is proposed we are promised that it has the right kind of a hall, printing facilities and that hotels will not raise rates, but very often find that these promises are not carried out. When conditions are not satisfactory or excessive rates exacted, it should be possible to change the meeting place. Therefore the following words are added to Section 1 of Article III of the constitution: "But if the proper convention arrangements or reasonable hotel accommodations can not be secured in that city, the Executive Council may change the place of meeting."

Conventions, Dates for Holding—(1923, pp. 37-349) "The convention of the federation shall meet annually at 10.00 a. m. on the first Monday in October, at such place as the delegates have selected at the preceding convention, except during the years when a presidential election occurs, when the convention in those years shall be held beginning the third Monday of November."

Convention Proceedings—(1923, p. 325) The Executive Council was requested to present a plan to condense and improve the printed minutes of the conventions of the A. F. of L., thereby making the record more definite, attractive and pleasing to peruse.

Conventions, State Federations—(1921, p. 426) Refused to amend the constitution to provide that each state federation of labor hold its convention not less than thirty days nor more than ninety days prior to the state elections for political officers. This was deemed unnecessary, as the state federations have the power to change the dates of their conventions to suit themselves.

Convict Labor—(1919, pp. 131-471) A bill drafted by the A. F. of L. and the National Committee on Prison Labor and having the approval of the secretary of labor contained the provisions: "That the products of prison labor transported into any state or territory for use or sale shall be subject to the operation and effect of the laws of such state or territory to the same extent and in the same manner as though such goods had been produced in such state or territory." It failed of passage.

(1920, p. 108) A bill was introduced in congress providing that the products of prison labor transported into any state or territory for use or sale shall be subject to the operation and effect of the laws of such state or territory to the same extent and in the same manner as though such goods had been produced in such state or territory. This provision is the most important that could be adopted. Under present conditions a state may subject its own prison-made goods to such regulation as will prevent their competing with free labor and at the same time give humane conditions to the prisoners. But should such a state do that, goods made by prison labor under the worst possible conditions could come in from another state and compete with free labor in the open market. The only advantage of such legislation would accrue to the contractors who produced prison goods under bad conditions in other states, giving them the advantage of the market of that state. (P. 479) All state federations of labor urged to give every assistance in securing an adequate federal convict labor law.

(1921, pp. 132-419) We indorse the fight that has been waged nationally and in the various states against the vicious prison contract system and urge still greater effort to bring about the universal application of the state system of paying the prevailing wage of the vicinity, with reasonable deduction for board and upkeep, to convicts employed in the production and manufacture of commodities that come in competition with the products of free labor. Every state federation of labor should see that the governor of its state appoints a commission, as was done in New York state, to investigate the prisons and that it is represented on the commission and that the example of New York State Federation of Labor in working out a constructive program be followed. Care should be exercised by the state federations of labor when advocating the enactment of prison labor laws within their respective states to obtain all necessary information from the A. F. of L. and the National Committee on Prisons and Prison

Labor with a view to having the principle underlying all laws as uniform as possible in the several states. The support of the state branches should be given to the bill now in congress introduced by the A. F. of L. to provide for the employment of prisoners for state use and prohibit the transportation in interstate commerce of convict goods manufactured and destined for the competitive market.

(1922, pp. 104-326; 1923, p. 90) The agitation against prison contract labor is spreading over the country. The General Council of the Federation of Women's Clubs adopted a resolution in its meeting at Atlanta, Ga., declaring "that the evils of the prison system can be traced to profiteering on the prisoners by business interests." Conforming to our own federation's declarations it went on record favoring the employing of prisoners in the production of commodities for use and consumption by state institutions, departments and public works under state control. Many other organizations have begun to realize the menace of contract prison labor and are advocating its abolishment. Every effort will be made in the sixty-eighth congress to secure this most important remedial legislation. (P. 356) The Executive Council is instructed to call a conference of the representatives of the affiliated trade unions affected by the competition of convict labor with the view of devising effective means of abolishing this menace. (P. 356) In the average penitentiary where the contract system is in force, the prisoners have the choice of but one or two industries, regardless of what their previous calling may have been. The largest of these is the shirt making industry, the second largest, the binder twine industry, and another large one, the making of brooms Ninety-two per cent of the states which deal in the contract system provide that none of the products made in the prisons shall be sold within the boundaries of the states making the contract.

Cooperation—(1919, p. 145) The 1917 convention when considering the report of the special committee on cooperation directed "that every local trade union under the jurisdiction of the A. F. of L. be requested to contribute the sum of one dollar in order to establish successfully the federation bureau for promoting and advancing the cause of true cooperation in the United States and Canada." That convention also authorized the president of the A. F. of L. to appoint for a period of one year a qualified trade unionist as lecturer and adviser on a broad plan of cooperation. It was reported to the St. Paul convention that the fund created under authority and the plan authorized by the Buffalo convention had not reached sufficient proportions for the appointment of a cooperative lecturer and adviser. The fund at this time amounts to only $2,383.03. We urge that all affiliated national and international organizations and central bodies take this matter under consideration and promptly send in their contributions to the secretary of the A. F. of L. (P. 317) Since there is a special committee on cooperation this convention merely reaffirms its belief in the untold possibilities in the cooperative movement of benefit to organized labor and the public generally. It endorses the request of the Executive Council that all affiliated national and international organizations and central labor bodies take up the matter of the contributions requested by the Buffalo convention. In order that the funds now in the hands of the secretary may be made immediately useful for the purpose of furthering the cooperative movement, the cooperative fund is hereby made available for the use of the committee on cooperation in the manner that in the judgment of that committee will best serve the interests of the cooperative movement.

(1920 p. 176) Reaffirmed indorsement of the Rochdale cooperative system. The workers recognize clearly that if they establish and operate their own retail and wholesale stores honestly and efficiently, patronizing them loyally, they will reduce the cost of living at least to the degree that the private retail merchant and middleman have been profiteering upon them. In the cooperative movement we shall find a practical solution of many of the material ills afflicting the human family and their cure by peaceful methods. Among the many benefits which are to be expected as a result of the operation of their own wholesale and productive enterprises on a cooperative basis by the workers, will be enjoyed not only the utmost degree of material saving which they shall be able to effect through the institutions they operate, but they will also give a practical demonstration of the extent to which the business and employing interests who operate private enterprises for selfish personal gain are using the powers at their command for the exploitation of the masses; and (perhaps of even greater importance) they will be able to demonstrate conclusively to the workers the extent to which these vested interests are disregarding their own obligations as regards the public interest and their duties to humanity in general. (P. 463) A new contribution of $1.00 or more is hereby requested from every local trade union in the jurisdiction of the A. F. of L. for the promotion of the cooperative movement under the direction of that bureau subject to the approval or disapproval of the Executive Council.

(1921, p. 144) The cooperative movement from several angles is sufficiently serious to warrant the suggestion that the A. F. of L. take a decisive position at this time. There are more genuine cooperative movements properly functioning today than ever before in the history of the movement in our own country. There are also said to be more spurious concerns operating under the guise of cooperation than ever before. Vast sums of money have been collected, diverted or misappropriated under the name of the cooperative movement. It is claimed that a certain association ostensibly promoting cooperation has 1,100 organizers on its payroll, all of whom are making an easy living and piling up fortunes for the promoters. Under the circumstances and in view of the bitter and hostile machinations of profiteering exploiters and the enemies of the true cooperative movement, we hold the A. F. of L. can not afford to retire from the cooperative movement at this time, and we are moreover of the opinion that we can not afford to withdraw until we have by at least one year's effort endeavored to place before our members and all others interested in the cooperative movement the true facts and a clear understanding of the fundamentals of the true cooperative movement and of the dangers of allowing speculative movements traveling under the guise of honest practical cooperation. (P. 316) The A. F. of L. Bureau of Cooperative Societies is made a permanent committee under the direction of the Executive Council. The warning against those who

unsuccessfully exploit the cooperative idea for private profit, or for the purpose of discrediting the genuine cooperative movement under the Rochdale plan, is , particularly timely. In this period of universal profiteering it is particularly necessary that the workers be educated to the necessity of ,mobilizing their collective power, not only as producers, but also as consumers. A representative will be placed in the field who is well informed on cooperation, utilizing the present cooperative fund to be supplemented in any feasible way as may be necessary. The question of instituting an exhaustive investigation of self-constituted "cooperative" societies that are not conducted in accordance with the fundamental principles of the bona fide Rochdale cooperative movement was indorsed.

(1921, p. 129) It is with some hesitancy that we approach the proposal to lend the credit of the government to any commercial enterprise that is essentially competitive in its nature and whose operation would tend to decrease or check the income of those enterprises whose existence is necessary to that of the government from which assistance is sought for the proposed "cooperatives." The fundamental principles of business should apply here as elsewhere. Cooperative institutions should stand on their merits, and require capital and management equally with private ventures. Subsidies or subventions of any kind are inherently dangerous and when resorted to must be jealously safeguarded or they inevitably become destructive. The Executive Council is directed to consider, and report to the convention the questions of government capitalization of cooperative enterprises and the control of credit, capital being placed in the hands of a public agency to be administered by voluntary and cooperative methods.

Cooperation, Committee on—(1919, pp. 129-318) The committee on cooperation authorized to be appointed by the Buffalo convention in 1917 and continued by the convention in St. Paul in 1918, is hereby further continued and is authorized to represent the A. F. of L. to consider and to pass upon such plans for cooperation, that may be submitted and to cooperate in carrying such plans into effect so far as is deemed advisable to carry out such cooperative plans that in their judgment will benefit the wage earner and the community; the cooperative fund shall be made available for the use of the committee on cooperation in the manner that in the judgment of that committee will best serve the interests of the cooperative movement.

Cooperative Stores—(1920, p. 120) A bill was presented in congress providing for the incorporation of the cooperative associations of the District of Columbia, one of which has been organized on the Rochdale system. (P. 464) Reports were made that at a meeting held in Chicago having under consideration the subject of cooperation, those in authority there were not only disinclined but determinedly opposed to having the union label of any trade union upon the product of its members. In other words, to them the question of a label of a cooperative society was sufficient, without regard to the union label and the label and union whose members performed the work and created the products. The information was conveyed that the conference having that subject in charge declined, in the first instance, to endorse such a principle, but that later, through some method the matter was imposed upon the delegates to that conference and against their will. It was agreed to strike out the words "union label" and substitute the words "union made," simply as a means of covering up products furnished by members of company unions and not in any sense union made products. The Union Label Trades Department felt very keenly on the subject and its affiliated members believed that they ought to be given some consideration in connection with any cooperative plan or arrangement that might be arrived at.

(1921, p. 121) The bill providing for the incorporation of cooperative associations in the District of Columbia was not given consideration by the sixty-sixth congress.

Coronado Coal Company vs. Miners— (1919, pp. 100-362) A year ago the convention of the A. F. of L. was advised of the great danger involved in this case and that by the final affirmation of this judgment, the right to strike was not only outlawed, but that the right of the workers to combine and to bargain collectively were likewise seriously attacked. Attention was directed to the fact that this assault and encroachment on the right of trial by jury was a flagrant disregard of constitutional safeguards to the freedom of action guaranteed our people. It was a dangerous principle which the court had invoked to attack the funds of trade unions, to jeopardize the savings of the wage earners, and thus ultimately destroy the virility and aggressiveness of the trade union movement. We are now advised that the appeal of the United Mine Workers in the district court has been in vain and that the misjudgment of the lower court has been affirmed. While the United Mine Workers of America are preparing an appeal to the supreme court of the United States, and while this case is not predicated on the Clayton act, but is being tried under the terms of the Sherman anti-trust law before labor organizations were exempted from its restrictive regulations; it is, nevertheless, important to note that the tendency of the employing interests today is to hold trade unions responsible financially for whatever alleged ill-advised or wrongful act any one of its members or sympathizers may commit, inadvertently or by design, on the theory that the trade union movement is obligated to discipline and to direct the conduct of all its members. Our administration of law presents indeed a mass of inconsistencies and contradictions. While organizations of capital are encouraged and protected, combinations of workers are constantly attacked. While employers may unite and combine against workers and against the buying public. the right of the workers to resist encroachments and to right admitted wrongs is constantly being interfered with. While nations laud the instrument of boycott to force recalcitrant nations to observe international rules and ethics, yet when labor attempts to punish a recalcitrant employer by this same weapon we find its path one of embarrassment and obstruction. Whenever an officer of an incorporated financial, industrial or commercial enterprise exceeds the power specifically delegated to him, the courts declare his act ultra-vires and the company is absolved from all responsibility. But when a labor man at a trade union meeting makes ill-advised utterances, even when such utterances are condemned by those in authority, then the union and its members may nevertheless be robbed of their funds and savings. Such is the awkward contradiction in our administrative law of today. It was the spirit of the jurisprudence of slavery which forbade the slaves the opportunity to read to defend themselves, and so it is the jurisprudence of employers of today to contrive doctrines which deny the workers a full opportunity of defense. The time has passed, however, when our courts should be longer permitted to devise legal doctrines and design local fictions by which to deny the wage earners equal rights and privileges before the law.

(1921, pp. 75-373) The Coronado case against the United Mine Workers of America, District No. 21 of the mine workers and others was brought originally about eight years ago. After a legal history not necessary to be detailed, it resulted in a judgment which was affirmed in the circuit court of appeals for the eighth circuit in favor of the plaintiffs for $625,000, being treble damages under the Sherman act. In brief the defendants including the United Mine Workers of America, District No. 21, United Mine Workers of America and twenty-seven local unions were held liable for acts of alleged violence which had been committed in Arkansas against some seven mines, although the United Mine Workers and District No. 21 had no connection with any of these alleged acts. The international organization was held responsible because of having failed to discipline the members of local unions or of District No. 21 and on scarcely better grounds was District No. 21 held liable. From such decision as stated, an appeal was taken to the supreme court of the United States and a writ of certiorari asked. The case was argued in December and no decision up to the preparation of this report has yet been announced. The substantial fact is that if the decision below is sustained any international body may be held liable on the scantiest suggestion of evidence for the misconduct of individuals not directed by them and of whose methods they may have no knowledge and be without special means of inquiry. For the first time and erroneously, we believe, a court has held labor organizations directly responsible as if they were incorporated bodies. Irrespective of any discussion upon the merits we will anticipate that the United States supreme court will find it necessary to sustain the appeal for this among other reasons which have their technical as well as legal force. But if a different view is taken by the supreme court of the United States no international labor organization may consider itself safe irrespective of any precautions it may take and irrespective of its innocence of even technical wrongdoing, at least until the federal law has been changed. It is therefore in the power and in the hands of the United States supreme court to decided whether the United Mine Workers of America and all other voluntary organizations of workers are unlawful organizations and whether it will be unlawful to belong to them, and simply because of membership therein their members be subject to civil and criminal laws. It will also determine whether any employer or groups of employers doing business with a national or international union are violating the laws. If the court determines that every agreement held by national or international unions with employers is unlawful, this decision will, unless remedied by law, make it impossible for the wage earners of America to organize for their protection and the promotion of their rights and interests upon the constructive basis as the labor movement of America now exists. In that event collective bargaining will be unlawful. Suits will be begun in every state where coal is mined. The operators who have had contracts with the United Mine Workers may sue this organization for damages sustained while strikes have been in progress. Already the coal operators of several states have refused to operate the machinery of the agreement for the collection of assessments to aid the strikers in West Virginia and other state. Other cases have been brought against the United Mine Workers of America, based upon the same grounds as those involved in the Coronado case. One of these is the suit of the Pennsylvania Mining Company. Through this persecution, under the guise of prosecution, the funds of the United Mine Workers of America have been tied up, in perfecting bonds so that the appeal might be made, in the sum of over $1,100,000. Every effort will be made by the A. F. of L. to secure the enactment of a law by congress which will bring relief to the workers from such conditions.

(1922, pp. 58-291) As indicated in previous reports, this case and the decision of the United States supreme court thereon have upset everything that had been commonly understood and accepted to be the law of the land prior to the decision. While the case of the Coronado Coal Company was a case against a trade union, and while the decision therefore necessarily applies in this case to a trade union, it is inevitable that the results should affect not only trade unions but all voluntary associations not incorporated and not formed for profit. This will include the organizations of farmers formed exactly as trade unions are formed, and it will affect a wide variety of other organizations as well. There seems to be no avenue of escape under this decision for any unincorporated association of individuals. Under the doctrine, now for the first time in the history of our republic laid down by the supreme court, every organized unit is liable as such for whatever acts may be performed by individual members or groups of members in violation of law. It has been well said that the decision in this case might properly have been written in a half dozen lines absolving the United Mine Workers of America from guilt and releasing the funds placed in escrow by the treasury of that organization. The point to be decided by the supreme court required only a negative statement absolving certain defendants from liability. It was therefore purely gratuitous on the part of Mr. Chief Justice Taft to go to the extent of writing a decision covering twenty-nine pages in which to lay down not merely a negative finding but what must be in effect positive ruling constituting a decision in anticipation of future cases. Not content with the unwarranted act of rendering a decision in anticipation of a future case, the court went to the astounding extreme of deciding that anticipated case in a manner totally at variance with what has hitherto been the law, which does terrific injustice to the voluntary organization of labor, and which sets up a concept absolutely foreign to everything commonly understood to be contemplated, not only by the statute law of our land, but by the constitution itself. The decision is essentially on a par with the decision in the famous Taff-Vale case in England, which is cited by Chief Justice Taft in the present decision. In fact, Chief Justice Taft seeks to draw support from the Taff-Vale decision for his own conclusions, for he quotes from Mr. Justice Farwell, who wrote the Taff-Vale decision, as follows: "If the contention of the defendant society were well founded the legislature has authorized the creation of numerous bodies of men capable of owning great wealth and of action by agents with absolutely no responsibility for the wrongs that they may do to other persons by the use of that wealth and the employment of those agents." Justice Taft says that Justice Farwell gave judgment against the union and that the judgment was affirmed by the house of lords. It is singular that Chief Justice Taft does not complete the story, the remainder of which is that the Taff-Vale decision became a great political issue in England and was ultimately reversed; and further, that the British parliament as a direct result of the case passed the trades disputes act which made such decisions forever impossible in the future. The Taff-Vale decision, which Mr. Chief Justice Taft quotes with approval and which is entirely in harmony with his own view in the Coronado case, could not be rendered under English law today. It is astounding that the court should have sought a precedent in ancient and outlawed British court findings, ignoring entirely the modern British law upon which all modern British court decisions have been founded. It will be of interest to read the industrial disputes act, the enactment of which was directly due to the Taff-Vale decision cited by Chief Justice Taft. It is as follows:

British Trades Dispute Act—(p. 292) "An act done in pursuance of an agreement or combination by two or more persons shall, if done in contemplation or furtherance of a trade dispute, not be actionable unless the act if done without any such agreement or combination, would be actionable. It shall be lawful for one or more persons, acting on their own behalf or on behalf of a trade union or of an individual employer or firm in contemplation or furtherance of a trade dispute, to attend at or near a house or place where a person resides or works or carries on business or happens to be, if they so attend merely for the purpose of peacefully persuading any person to work or abstain from working. An act done by a person in contemplation or furtherance of a trade dispute shall not be actionable on the ground only that it induces some other person to break a contract of employment or that it is an interference with the trade, business or employment of some other person or with the right of some other person to dispose of his capital or his labor as he wills. An action against a trade union, whether of workmen or masters, or against any members or officials thereof on behalf of themselves and all other members of the trade union in respect of any tortious act alleged to have been committed by or on behalf of the trade union, shall not be entertained by any court. Nothing in this section shall affect the liability of the trustees of a trade union to be sued in the events provided for by the trade union act, 1871, section 9, except in respect of any tortious act committed by or on behalf of the union in contemplation or in furtherance of a trade dispute." The following quotation from the Coronado decision shows how closely Mr. Taft follows the reasoning of the repealed British decision and how greatly he has depended upon the logic used in that repudiated document n now reversing the established law and practices of the United States: "It would be unfortunate if an organization with as great power as this international union has in the raising of large funds and in directing the conduct of four hundred thousand members in carrying on in a wide territory industrial controversies and strikes out of which unlawful injury to private rights is possible, could assemble its assets to be used therein free from liability for injuries by torts committed in course of such strikes." It may as well be said here that even as the people of England found a way to correct and modernize their high courts and their house of lords in the interest of humanity and progress, so will the people of the United States find a way to correct the supreme court of the United States in the interest of humanity and progress and to correct, also, whatever other institution may stand in the way of the attainment and the exercise of human rights. Mr. Taft finds that trade unions have been recognized as lawful by the Clayton act and by various other acts of congress, and of state legislatures. As a matter of fact, no one had supposed that trade unions were not lawful, although there are some who have entertained the hope that some day some way might be found to declare them not lawful. For a great many years unions have been recognized as lawful organizations having a lawful right to exist, and that lawful existence has not rendered them liable as they are now held to be liable by the decision of Chief Justice Taft. How foreign to the real spirit of the Clayton act the present decision is may be judged by a reading of Section 6 of that act, which follows: "Section 6.— That the labor of a human being is not a commodity or article of commerce. Nothing contained in the anti-trust laws shall be construed to forbid the existence and operation of labor, agricultural or horticultural organizations, instituted for the purposes of mutual help, and not having capital stock or conducted for profit, or to forbid or restrain individual members of such organizations from lawfully carrying out the legitimate objects thereof; nor shall such organizations, or the members thereof, be held or construed to be illegal combinations or conspiracies in restraint of trade, under the anti-trust laws." It will be noted by careful reading of this section that trade unions are considered associations of human beings and not organizations interested in the promoting of commodities or articles of commerce, and also that by this section they are not to be construed as combinations or conspiracies in restraint of trade under the anti-trust laws. If it be true, and the language in this section permits no other construction, that trade unions are declared organizations not in restraint of trade, it is inconceivable how the supreme court could have ruled them to be liable, either under the Sherman or Clayton acts, when as a matter of fact they have been specifically exempted from these laws. Justice Taft by his subtle interpretation and construction has directly charged that trade unions are combinations or conspiracies in restraint of trade, because it is only by this presumption and legal assumption that he can in any way justify the declaration that they are associations embraced in the terms of the Sherman and Clayton acts. In addition the foregoing section 6 of the Clayton act was enacted into law to meet the situation that arose by the decision of the supreme court in the Danbury hatters' case. In that case the members of the union were held by the supreme court to be liable as individuals and as a union. To correct this grievous error of the United States

supreme court and immediately following this decision in the Danbury hatters' case, the congress of the United States enacted the Clayton law which was specifically intended to correct what the courts had done in this case and that future decisions of the courts respect the rights of unions and of union members. Evidently, the United States supreme court does not intend to be bound by the legal enactments of congress and feels itself superior to the judgment of the law-making body of the land. The case which Chief Justice Taft quotes is the decision in the Taff-Vale case which was remedied by the enactment of the trades dispute act. The supreme court of the United States decided adversely to labor in the Danbury hatters' case. The congress rectified that wrong by the enactment of the labor provisions of the Clayton act, part of which has been quoted, but this does not seem to suffice the supreme court of the United States for it sweeps aside the act which congress passed to rectify the wrong done by that court. We may be sure that if trade unions were not lawful and had not a lawful right to exist and to function, it would have been found out a great many years ago. Of course, what every student knows is that in the beginning of the existence of trade unions every possible effort was made, not only by employers but by governments, to make their existence impossible and to prevent their growth. Working people fought through many decades to establish the right of free and lawful existence for trade unions, and Mr. Taft is not giving the world any news in that portion of his decision wherein he finds that unions are lawful organizations. Because there are certain laws on the statute books of the United States and of various individual states in which Mr. Taft finds the existence of trade unions recognized, he says in his decision: "In this state of federal legislation, we think that such organizations are suable in the federal courts for their acts, and that funds accumulated to be expended in conducting strikes are subject to execution in suits for torts committed by such unions in strikes. The fact that the supreme court of Arkansas has since taken a different view in Baskins vs. The United Mine Workers of America, supra, can not under the conformity act operate as a limitation on the federal procedure in this regard." The decision seeks to find justification particularly in the anti-trust law, usually known as the Sherman law. We find Justice Taft in his decision using the following language in reference to that law: "Our conclusion as to the suability of the defendants is confirmed in the case at bar by the words of sections 7 and 8 of the anti-trust law. The persons who may be sued under section 7 includes 'corporations and associations existing under or authorized by the laws of either the United States, or the laws of any of the territories, the laws of any state or the laws of any foreign country'. This language is very broad, and the words given their natural signification certainly include labor unions like these. There are, as has been abundantly shown, associations existing under the laws of the United States, of the territories thereof, and of the states of the union." Of course, the Sherman law was aimed at powerful corporations which were at that period engaging in a frenzy of speculation as well as combination, indulging in an exaggeration of a natural economic process to the great detriment of the masses of the people. Con-

Cerning the intent of congress in passing the Sherman law, Chief Justice Taft says: "Congress was passing drastic legislation to remedy a threatening danger to the public welfare, and did not intend that any person or combination of persons should escape its application. The thought was especially directed against business associations and combinations that were unincorporated to do the things forbidden by the act, but they used language broad enough to include all associations which might violate its provisions recognized by the statutes of the United States or the states or the territories, of foreign countries as lawfully existing and this, of course, includes labor unions, as the legislation referred to shows." The full truth is that congress did not have trade unions at all in mind and was so certain that trade unions would never be brought into court under that law that it felt unnecessary to adopt an amendment specifically to exempt unions from its operation. Such an amendment was suggested and it was only for the reason that congress felt the amendment unnecessary that it declined to adopt it as an addition to the Sherman law. The proposal of an amendment to exempt trade unions from the operation of the Sherman law and the debate on the question, will be found in the *Congressional Record* and in the *American Federationist* for July, 1900, pages 195 to 210. Promises of that sort are, of course, of no avail when the supreme court enters the arena, because the supreme court has a liberty peculiarly its own and is not bound to take cognizance of pledges or interpretations given by others. When the Lever law was enacted during the war, specific pledges were given that the law would not be made to apply to labor; but in this case also, the pledges have meant nothing, for the Lever law has never been made to apply to anyone else. And as a matter of fact, when the packers were being tried under the Lever act, the supreme court of the United States found it convenient to hold the law unconstitutional and to permit the profit makers to escape its penalizing effects. The importance of the present decision lies in what may be its future application. The supreme court expressed regret that the decision could not fall with full force upon the United Mine Workers, but it left little doubt as to what will be its application at the first opportunity. There is much in the following sentences from the decision: "There is nothing to show that the international board ever authorized it, took any part in preparation for it or in its maintenance. Nor did they or their organization ratify it by paying any of the expenses. It came exactly within the definition of a local strike in the constitutions of both the national and the district organizations." The only conclusion that can be drawn from these sentences is that in any strike sanctioned by national or international officials or supported by funds from the national treasury no matter how justified the cause of the strike the national organization as such may be held responsible in damages for whatever act may be held unlawful and which may be committed by individuals about whom the national may have no knowledge or of whose action the national may be entirely uninformed. Many reasons have been advanced as to why the decision should be accepted as just, as to why it will not work injustice. For example, some suggest that inasmuch as unions expect protection against forgery of their labels and of their working cards and protection against theft of their funds, they should expect and accept the position in which they are now placed by the supreme court. The logic of the contention is not good. Unions expect punishment of those who commit crimes. Unions expect that those who forge their labels and their working cards and who steal their money will be punished. Unions do not expect, however, that a half million men will be punished for the unlawful acts of a half dozen. For the crimes of the half dozen there is adequate law and it should be used as it was intended to be used. Unions expect protection against forgery and theft exactly as any other organization or person is protected against similar crimes. They have never sought any extraordinary protection and never will seek any extraordinary protection. The unions have as much right to the protection of the law against forgery and theft as has any individual, and no more. There is no more comparison between this simple protection and the law now laid down by the supreme court than there is between any two extremes. Corporations are organized under the law in order to limit their liabilities. An agent of a corporation committing a crime does not make its shareholders, or even the corporation itself, guilty of having committed that crime. We find almost invariably that what is known in law as the doctrine of ultra vires has been specifically designed to shield corporate entities. Their share holders and security holders, against liability for the irresponsible and unauthorized acts of their agents or officers. A trade union is an unincorporated association of individuals who band together voluntarily for mutual advancement, but not for profit. A member of such an association is not an agent of the association unless it is specifically provided by the association that he shall have the character of agent and the standing of an agent. For a national union of workers to be held responsible for the acts of some of its members or of a local union, no matter how remote, is an injustice, the enormity of which is difficult to comprehend. The supreme court has not only rendered a decision which goes beyond any previous decision of that tribunal in its antagonism and opposition to labor, but it has rendered such a decision when under the law of the land and under the practices hitherto obtaining its decision should have been exactly the reverse. The court has taken an occasion when a brief negative finding was required to issue a positive finding which was not required, which was purely gratuitous and which is of a most far-reaching and damaging character. How eager the supreme court was to inflict injury upon labor is found in the sentence wherein Chief Justice Taft said that it was with "great regret that the court finds itself unable to affirm the decision of the lower courts holding the United Mine Workers liable." Therein we find eagerness to the point of daring. The supreme court's regret that it could not hold the United Mine Workers as a national organization responsible for the alleged acts of a small group of members in a distant state. is comparable to the crocodile tears of the court in regretting that it was forced to declare the child labor law unconstitutional. Almost the court regrets too much. Apparently what the court regrets is the fact that the United Mine Workers of America, as an international union, did not commit the act which Chief Justice Taft has held to be a tortious act, so that they might thereby be deprived of their funds at a time when those funds were most needed by the miners and also to blacken the character of the United Mine Workers as a body of men who would commit criminal acts. The Coronado decision does not stand alone as an indication of what the supreme court has in mind in relation to the organizations of the workers. Within a year the court has handed down four decisions of major importance to the labor movement, and in each of these decisions it has delivered a blow at labor and at the normal, natural constructive progress which the labor movement seeks to achieve within the law. The seats of the mighty are made more secure and the paths of justice for the workers are made more and more impassable. The trade union is an agency of public service. It is a fundamental necessity of an age of collective production. Without it modern industry could not be an ordered process; it would be a fantastic, gruesome jungle, imperfect and in constant danger of complete disintegration and anarchy. Yet, despite this striking fact, so little understood by so many, trade unions are treated by the supreme court and by many employers as if they were impediments in the road to social progress, obstacles to human achievement. The modern trade union movement has marched hand in hand with the development of machine and concentrated production. The roots of both are in the same soil intertwined. The life of both is of equal length. One was made necessary by the other. Modern industrial life could not exist in any large sense without the organizations of labor. There could be only disorganized industry operated by slaves. The labor movement has meant to the workers their only channel through which to find a living interest in production under modern conditions; their only means of dealing with the machine and therefore, their only means of saving some liberty from the grasp of the machine and of those who own the machine. The supreme court can not crush this movement without endangering the foundations of society. The workers will not accept slavery, therefore they will not accept that which makes slavery either likely or possible. They will find a way to preserve those liberties which they have and to gain more as time passes.

(1923 p. 93) The Coronado case against the United Mine Workers of America has a legal history of nine years. It involved the question of holding national and international unions liable for alleged misconduct of individuals not directed by the national and international unions and without the approval of methods used and without knowledge of the misconduct of which complaint is made. There was also involved the question of whether suits may be brought against trade unions or voluntary associations as against incorporated bodies. In this case the U. S. supreme court reversed the action of the lower court and virtually directed a dismissal of the cause. In so doing, however, it created a number of new principles of law not even contemplated by congress and indicated certain applications, all of the highest importance to the future of the labor movement and unquestionably inspired to devise additional repressive measures with which to harass and check the trade union movement. As to the United Mine Workers of America, the central organization, the supreme court found that it had no active participation of any kind in the offenses for which judgment was obtained. As to District

No. 21, the supreme court found that the acts which had been committed by its membership with to some extent the participation of the district organization, were not acts which bore any relation to the Sherman act, interferring as they did merely with the production of coal and not with coal itself as an article of interstate commerce and that the purpose of the actions of the defendants was not to monopolize any part of the interstate commerce. The first great proposition which attracts attention is, stated in substance, that so far at least as its ability or liability to sue or be sued, a labor organization is made to be on substantially the same footing at law as a corporation. This may be regarded as judicial legislation, being at variance as seems to be confessed by the decision itself with the prior holdings of responsible courts and basic conceptions of law. By virtue of this decision a labor organization may be sued directly and its funds, at least such funds as are devoted to strike purposes, may be seized, assuming wrongful acts on the part of individual members of the organization engaged in a strike. Heretofore no direct suit at law for damages has been recognized. There has existed, however, as in the Danbury hatters' case, individual liability on the part of all the members of the union for acts considered objectionable and incident to the purpose of the strike. The important point of the decision in this respect is that while it becomes possible to sue the union directly, the individual liability of the members apparently may continue in the eye of the court, precisely as theretofore. The union became a corporation so far as service of process is concerned. but its members yet remain a partnership in fact, so far as the liability of each for the acts of the other is involved. The effect of the statement contained in the last paragraph is of the highest importance as bearing upon the future conduct of unions. It will not be overlooked that the line between coal as an object and not as an object of interstate commerce, is a very close one and may depend upon slight facts in individual cases, a condition of affairs which will leave the industry largely under the supervision of the courts. Perhaps the same remark, however, may apply to a large number of other objects, with the result of making more manifest the fact that courts rather than the legislatures are the real rulers of the country. Under the principle laid down by the supreme court a new suit has been instituted against the Miners' Union, the outcome of which we are not prepared to forecast. (P. 276) The foregoing reviews the lengths to which our courts have gone to legislate against trade unions and to surround them with repressive legal assumptions and presumptions that could not have been enacted into law through the legislative expression of the government. It is unnecessary to review this case and to dwell at length upon the extensive and repressive features involved in this decision of the U. S. supreme court. While under the former decision the United Mine Workers were absolved from blame, and while at present a new suit has been instituted, the outcome of which is problematical, nevertheless the United States supreme court undertook, by judicial interpretation, to do that which the legislative branch of the government alone has power to do. It is also urged that consideration be given to the preparation of legislative demands which shall annul the pernicious and repressive legal doctrines our courts have adopted without legislative approval.

Cooperatives, Exemption for—(1919, p. 129) We favor an amendment to the federal income tax law by which cooperative societies organized under the "no profit" system will be added to the exemption section of the income tax law; and we direct that every reasonable effort be made to obtain this relief from congress.

Cooperative Societies, A. F. of L. Bureau of—(1922, pp. 68-359) Report of Bureau of Cooperative Societies: We have been mainly concerned with keeping before the membership of the trade union movement the proven methods by which cooperative enterprises have been made successful in our own and older European countries, and while being careful not to commit the A. F. of L. in such a way as to involve it in legal controversy, we have warned the membership regarding organizations that were masquerading under the name of cooperative organizations, which in reality were not cooperative institutions in principle and from the circumstances surrounding their operation your committee were satisfied they could not vouch for the honesty of the men conducting them. We have been helpful in this respect to the extent of saving the membership of the labor movement of our country of thousands, if not millions, of dollars which not only would have been lost to them but which would have also resulted in creating feeling that would have operated against the bona fide cooperative movement. During the year splendid endorsements have been given to us or reiterated by practically all of the religious organizations of the country. As a result of the depression in industry and the deflation of the prices of commodities handled by the cooperative societies in our own and every other country, the material success of cooperative institutions has not been such as to encourage their rapid extension or development during the past year. Nearly all cooperative societies have shown a loss on their books for that period. But, when we realize the reduction in the price of the commodities that they handled and which they had in stock and which in many instances amounted to as much as 25 per cent and that this unavoidable reduction in the value of all of these commodities which they had on hand or which had been contracted for shows as a money loss in their records which had to be made up in saving on the regular business done, we find that in reality there has been no loss so far as the operation of the cooperative societies are concerned although it appears so on their books. This kind of loss has, in our judgment, been greater in private concerns than it was in the cooperative institutions. The fact that so many of our people were idle or were only working partial time has resulted in their being more concerned about the price they were paying for the necessities of life and that fact has operated to stimulate interest in the cooperative movement. Not only has attention been directed to the retail or distributive phase of the cooperative movement but a marked interest has been aroused as to the influence which the cooperative movement might have with reference to standardizing industry and providing a continuity of employment. The action of big financial concerns in deflating the prices of the farmers' crops (their wages) and withholding finances from industry so that by means of the starvation process, wages might be reduced in other industries has also made for an interest in productive and banking cooperative activities as well. The activity of your committee in sending out literature explaining the fundamentals upon which Rochdale cooperation is based, pointing out the success of cooperative banks in ours and other countries, as well as what the introduction of workers' cooperation might mean in industry—employment itself—and at the same time making clear that in order to get the greatest success possible out of cooperative production and banking, consumers' or distributive cooperation should first be mastered, and established, has contributed toward a greater activity along cooperative lines in our country on a basis of more practical methods than ever before. We believe we may safely say that there never has been in the United States such a widespread interest or so clear an understanding of the movement as it will affect the workers beneficially as there is at the present time. We further feel that the A. F. of L. and its Bureau on Cooperative Societies of the A. F. of L. which have been indefatigable in giving advice and sending out literature and correspondence furnishing information and advice and being helpful in every way in this work of furthering real cooperative effort has contributed in very considerable degree to the establishment of better understanding and constructive interest in the cooperative movement and the starting and development of the many additional cooperative enterprises which will result in unlimited benefits to the working people of our country. Practically all of the literature on true cooperation sent out by your committee has been done without cost to the A. F. of L. No charge has been made to the federation for postage, stationery, expenses or lost time of your committee. The secretary has performed all the duties involved in the transaction of his office without compensation. Of the entire expense of the committee for the past fiscal year only $4.33 was charged to and came out of the funds of the A. F. of L. The committee took advantage of the opportunity to call meetings of the committee when the members thereof were at some given time and place on other official business. The chairman and secretary of the bureau, the standing sub-committee, held practically all of their meetings in Chicago and at a time when neither was put to extra expense. Your committee deemed it advisable and necessary to call attention to the productive phase of cooperation. The A. F of L. by resolutions is committed to the policy of first mastering distributive cooperation and under the Rochdale plan. Your committee, while not opposed to productive cooperation, is of the opinion that productive cooperation, can not succeed without being carried forward along well-defined principles and encompassed with safeguards that will avoid the pitfalls that have resulted in about 90 per cent, more or less, failure in productive cooperation in our country. Your committee feels that we should confine our efforts to distributive cooperation until it is thoroughly mastered. However, if efforts in productive cooperation are made it should be undertaken only under conditions that will make an at best difficult task reasonably successful. One of the safeguards that may be depended upon to accomplish this end is and has been in vogue in the German cooperative movement for years. We find that when productive cooperation was first started in Germany and conducted along lines similar to those here and in other places, the effort resulted in one failure after another, in all of which scandal was more or less pronounced. The cooperators of the country then formed what is known as the German National Cooperative Society, with headquarters at Hamburg. This society is not engaged in either distributive or productive cooperation. It is a sort of a clearing house for the cooperative societies of Germany. It in a sense occupied the same position that the A. F. of L. does to its affiliated organizations. The national association foresaw many of the things under the old regime which led to failure and scandal, among which was the fact that in any locally established society factions quickly developed superintendents and foremen who held their jobs at the will of majority factions. To overcome this the German National Cooperative Society provided that superintendents and foremen should be elected by the board of directors of the national association after a genuine civil service examination. This immediately had the effect of putting the productive cooperative societies on the high road to success. A local cooperative society had no authority and could not discharge a superintendent or foreman. The superintendent or foreman who was fair to the society as well as to the workers was sure of his position regardless of factions. Majority factions could not discharge either. If a complaint was made the national board of directors caused an impartial investigation to be made and its action with reference to superintendent or foremen was predicated upon this impartial report. Your committee is firmly of the opinion that some such proviso as this should be adopted in our country, and we are moreover of the opinion that productive cooperation will not be entirely satisfactory until this is done. We have a report of a productive cooperative concern in Germany, employing 600 people, with an up-to-date building, which from a sanitary standpoint compares favorably with the best factories in our country. Every member of this cooperative concern has to be a member of the union of his trade. The union as such, however, had no voice in the management of the cooperative factory. They work the regular union hours, under union conditions, and receive the regular union scale of wages, and make far better wages than the highest prices paid in non-union factories. In this particular factory they not only pay the union scale but in all instances more. Each member has one week's vacation each year with full pay. Every person in this factory is a member of the cooperative society as well as a member of the union. This is one of the most prosperous and best factories in the particular line of work that can be found in all of that country. If a plan similar to the foregoing is adopted it should be inaugurated by and under the control of the actual cooperatives, subject to the restriction specified in the foregoing paragraph. We hold the A. F. of L. Bureau of Cooperative Societies could function as such. We, however, hold that if the A. F. of L. is in favor of such a departure and the establishment of such a movement, a national congress of the representatives of cooperative societies should be called by the president of the A. F. of L., and this congress then should adopt the plan or laws that are to govern, subject to advice and helpfulness of the Bureau of Cooperative Societies and the officials of the A. F. of L. The bona fide cooperative movement, such as the Rochdale system, constitutes in our judgment one of the safety valves for the protection of advancing civilization. The cooperative movement can and will if put into proper force, prevent profiteering and the mulcting of the great mass of the consumers in the necessities of life. It will protect fair wages against profiteering. The unnatural and unholy desire of the get-rich-quick and money-mad profiteers if allowed to run to natural conclusions, will some day lead to an explosion. The cooperative movement is one of the things that can prevent such a catastrophe. The cooperative movement in no wise interferes with the existing order of society economically, commercially, or financially. Neither does it destroy individual activity, hope and ambition, and it is well worth the thoughtful help of all true Americans who believe in the destiny of our country and its attainment by and through the natural activities of individuals, singly or collectively, and without the meddling influences of the state. We are sure that all true friends of labor and humanity will welcome the support of so powerful an influence for good and the day when it will function as it should in the laudable effort to save the mass of producers and consumers from the money-mad profiteers.

(1923, p. 110) Report of the Bureau of Cooperative Societies: "No one can successfully dispute the fact that something is radically wrong with our system of distribution. In a great many cases it cost more to sell manufactured products and agricultural produce than it does to produce them. It is stated that out of every dollar spent for agricultural products the farmer receives only eighteen cents and the other eight-two cents goes to transportation, holding and selling corporations, speculators, profiteers and the merchants. The accumulated wealth of the country, much of which is a gift from the past, is crystalized into great corpora ions which are generally speaking managed by salaried employes. Inventive genius has brought to the front wonderfully improved methods of production and to such an extent syndicated capitalists have had to create extensive selling facilities. This fact in itself has created a condition, in which it costs now, under our really unscientific system of distribution, more to sell than it does to manufacture. That which should naturally go to relief of the great masses in better wages shorter hours and lower prices for the necessities of life is really utilized by syndicated capitalists for their own further enrichment and to bolster up and keep going a system that will ultimately, unless checked, lead to destruction. It lies in the hands of the workers and producers, agriculturally and industrially, to save the enormous criminal waste which is now adding to the cost of living, discomfort and misery of the great burden-bearing masses. Next to our trade union one of the most simple and effective means we have in hand of saving much of this waste for the consumer as well as the producer is the cooperative movement. Through the simple Rochdale cooperative system billions of dollars that now go to further enrich the idle few and the enormous army that make up the unnecessary selling power and force would go to the producers and consumers. The insurance business is some indication of what cooperation can do. In the life insurance companies there is fifty billion dollars involved, eight billions of which amount is cash. Forty million policies are in force. These insurance companies are surrounded by state and national laws to such an extent that they don't fail. They furnish millions of dollars to the company owners and employment to a large army of agents whose sole duty is to sell insurance. An insurance company run under the Rochdale cooperative system would have to predicate its policy on the insurance laws and it could not fail. The enormous cost of maintaining the selling forces and the profits which now go to the private owners of these concerns could and would be turned back to the cooperators in the shape of dividends or to a reserve fund, the possibilities of which are unlimited. We recommend that the president of the A. F. of L. employ the services of at least one member of the legislative committee during the time that congress is not in session for the purpose of explaining and promoting the cooperative movement and furnishing standard literature at cost on the different phases of the Rochdale movement. Your committee, moreover, recommends that the A. F. of L. urge all affiliated central labor unions to establish cooperative bureaus for the purpose of study, to obtain information and to carry forward the preliminary work of education in reference to the bona fide Rochdale cooperative movement." (P. 250) The president of the A. F. of L. is authorized to employ the services of a member of the legislative committee to explain and promote the cooperative movement as suggested.

Courts, Labor and Property—(1922, pp. 38-371) One of the greatest influences of government arrayed against the hopes and aspirations of labor for a better day and a brighter life is that exercised by our courts through the so-called "equity" power. Originally designed to do equity where the common and statute laws failed to provide a full measure of justice, this chancery power of our courts has developed to an extent wherein all legislative enactments are subordinated to the prejudices and philosophic conceptions of our judges and our government of law is fast giving away to a government of judicial discretion. No greater danger confronts the liberties and freedom of the people of our time. Our courts have gradually and constantly usurped the functions of regulating industrial relations generally and of the associated activities of the wage earners in particular. Even legislative enactments intended to limit and curtail this ever growing power of our courts have been swept away by the courts in holding that such exercise of legislative authority is unconstitutional. For the time being men of capital, of influence, of wealth, may rejoice in the ready willingness of our courts to protect and promote the selfish and material interests of employers when in conflict with the personal rights and humane interests of the wage earners. In so doing, however, little thought or no consideration is given the grave problem that is appearing upon our economic and social horizon which manifests itself in the great distrust of our courts that is being aroused and the growing spirit of resentment that is being engendered by this class attitude of our judges. The past year is marked particularly with an increasing hostility of the judiciary toward the effort of wage earners to prevent deterioration of their standards of life and labor to protect and to retain their rights and sovereignty as American free men. Today practically every normal activity of the organized wage earners is subject to judicial restraint though legislatures and an enlightened public judgment have recognized such conduct and activities on the part of the wage earners and of trade unions legal and justifiable.

Thus, we have found our courts declaring unlawful strikes called to enforce payment of dues or of fines or to require the observance of union discipline. Likewise, courts have declared it illegal for workers to strike to prevent the introduction of non-union workers even where the announced intent and purpose have been to destroy the union. It has also been held unlawful to strike in opposition to the signing of individual contracts of employment even though these agreement were directly intended to disorganize the trade union workers. In the great industrial struggle of the past year, as in former years, employers have found our courts ever ready and willing to throw the forces of the state on the side of capital and against that of labor. Courts have ever been ready and anxious to enlarge their equity jurisdiction, conceiving every relation of mankind as embodying a material and property element and thereby disregarding the human element and personal rights involved in all these relations of man. Courts, in the exercise of their equity powers, have been guided, not by law or justice, but by personal whims and prejudices and by political theories and conceptions with which they have not been authorized to deal and which are functions that can only be exercised, within constitutional limitations, by our national government and the legislatures of our several states. The dangers to which organized labor has constantly directed public attention were clearly foreseen by our earlier great statesmen and especially by Thomas Jefferson who, in the early period of our government, expressed the frank opinion and conviction "that the germ of dissolution of our federal government is in the judiciary, an irresponsible body working like gravity, by day and by night, gaining a little today and gaining a little tomorrow, and advancing its noiseless step like a thief over the field of jurisprudence until all shall be usurped." How much stronger would be the utterance of condemnation of our courts were Thomas Jefferson to live in our day and in our time and to note the fulfillment of the dire prediction made in the early period of our great republic. Having been permitted to proceed without hindrance or check, our courts have become so bold that they hesitate no longer in declaring openly that the judiciary of our land represents, not the people but a class interest, or, as expressed by Judge Van Sicklen of the supreme court of (Brooklyn), New York when in issuing an injunction against organized labor he said: "The courts must stand at all times as the representatives of capital, of captains of industry." Having appealed to our legislatures for relief against this ever onward encroachment upon the the rights and liberties of our people and having experienced the attitude of mind of our courts that they will brook no interference by our several state legislatures in their ill-founded efforts to protect and promote property and property rights as against personal rights and human considerations, we recommend that an appeal be made to that higher court of public judgment and that the public conscience be aroused to the great and grave menace which confronts the perpetuity of the constitutional rights and liberties of all our people and as originally conceived by the founders of our republic.

Daylight Saving—(1919, p. 185) Convention refused to approve of a resolution protesting against congress repealing the daylight saving law. (1920, p. 119) Congress passed a bill repealing the daylight saving law, but it was vetoed by the president. The bill was passed over the veto August 20, 1919.

Dead, Tribute to Union—(1923, p. 140) The president: "As has been the custom of the A. F. of L. conventions for several years we will pay silent tribute to our departed members who have died since the last convention. There are quite a number of them who have been fighting in the ranks of labor and in that struggle gave all that was in them to serve. They have fallen in the struggle and have passed to the Great Beyond. In addition, the president of the United States has passed away, and I ask you, the delegates and friends in this convention hall, to arise and remain silent in meditation in honor of the memory of departed men." The request of the president was complied with and the entire audience arose and remained standing in silence with bowed heads for one minute.

Democracy of A. F. of L. Conventions— Closing addresses of the president of the A. F. of L.: (1919, p. 474) "All the committees have made their reports and every resolution, 233 in number covering nearly every field of human thought and human activity in the cause of justice, in the cause of freedom, in the cause of democracy, in the cause of humanity, have been treated by this convention. In addition to the 233 resolutions there was the report of the Executive Council covering a multitude of subjects, the reports of several commissions to Europe, the Commission on Industrial Reconstruction, all of them having received the fullest consideration and toleration by this convention. No delegate who had anything to submit, any thought to contribute, and suggestion or motion to make, has been denied that opportunity. This convention attended by the largest number of delegates in the history of our federation, marks also the increase in the membership of our affiliated unions. Just about three years ago I conceived the idea of adopting somewhat of a catchy phrase that might help to induce the activity of our fellow workers. It was 'Now for the 3,000,000 mark.' The report of this convention shows that the average membership of our affiliated unions for the past year was a little more than three and a quarter million. In the last month of our federation the actual membership on which per capita tax was paid passed the figure of 3,600,000. The railroad brotherhoods have made their application for affiliation to the A. F. of L., and when that is accomplished we will have passed the 4,000,000 mark. It is not necessary until after that affiliation to speak, or to hold out to the alluring gaze of the workers a further mark, but when we have in mind that this convention of the A. F. of L., reaching at this moment the zenith of our growth and our movement, and to know the respect we have instilled into the minds of our fellow workers and our fellow citizens, and into the minds of the workers and the peoples of countries outside our own, and when we have in mind the tremendous achievements of our movement in bringing light into the lives of the toiling masses of our country, when we know of the influence we have exerted even with the comparatively small numbers yet organized, it is the harbinger of hope that, as time goes on, if we are to be true to ourselves and true to each other, true to the fundamental principles and true to the high ideals of our movement, it is enough to inspire any one and all of us to greater activity and greater service. It is a privilege to live and to be permitted to live in this age, contributing so much of service to our fellows now and for all times to come. For myself, I may say to you that I appreciate more than I can tell you in words the courtesy you have extended to me while presiding over the convention. I have endeavored to give the best service that is in me, as all of you have done, I am grateful, I am appreciative, I am sure that it is sufficient cause for mutual gratification and appreciation for all those who were privileged to participate in this convention. And for the year to come, aye, for the years to come, let it be our guiding hope to work for a still greater organization, for the organization of the yet unorganized, the skilled and unskilled men and women, the men and women of whatever color, creed, religion, or any other thought which often divides men. In this hope I express to you the earnest desire that you may return to your respective homes and there carry the message to our fellow workers with whom you may come in contact, in fact or through the influence of others, carry this message of the wonderful work accomplished and the wonderful plan of work in the making, and which we hope will find its fullest fruition and accomplishment for the year and the years to come."

(1920, p. 481) "This completes the work of the convention. Every resolution presented to this convention, every part of the Report of the Executive Council, has received the attention and consideration of this convention. It may have been laborious and arduous for delegates and visitors to this convention; but in a great gathering, such as this convention of the A. F. of L. consisting of 578 men and women, meeting as we are, coming from various centers of the United States and of Canada, to have met here and in twelve days considered the variety of subjects of deep import and great possibilities; with men and women intensely interested with the various subjects discussed; it would be unthinkable that feeling would not be aroused. If all this interest and intensity and purpose shall be translated in a determination of all of us to do, if possible, greater service in the common cause of labor, of justice for all the people of our common countries and our contribution to the peace and good will of the world, we shall have met with great results following, and with it all contribute our share to the world's work and for human progress. During the entire sessions of our convention, notwithstanding the rule that ten minutes should be the limit of addresses, no delegate to this convention who has anything to say—except the chairman—has had his time limited. Every man and every woman who has had a thought to contribute, a view to express upon any subject before the convention, had full opportunity to do so; and it should be a source of great pride to the convention, as it is to me, that it was not necessary at any time to limit any one in the expression of his views in addressing the convention. Notwithstanding some of the incidents which have happened, may I express to you my deep appreciation of the courtesy which you have shown me while presiding and at other times, and to assure you that without your assistance success would not have been possible in the determinations which we have reached. It is my earnest hope, and I feel sure I but faintly express yours, that the coming year may be one of greater progress and success for the cause which we represent. I trust that you may reach your homes in safety and in good health and cheer, and bring the word, despite our shortcomings, despite the things that we may not have been able to do—let us present to the world of labor and to all our people the good things that we have done, the great efforts which we have made; and urge them on, and on, and, as the days go by to bring the goal of human justice and right and peace nearer, and nearer, and nearer; and that in our time we shall have the consciousness that we have tried to do our duty to the very best of our ability."

(1921, p. 472) "Before we finally adjourn this convention I think it is but appropriate to make some few observations. First, let me say that there are no regrets that I think any delegate can justly feel because of the legislation of this convention. Here, assembled as we are in open session every minute of our stay in the convention, subject to the inspection and supervision and criticism of the press and of the public, we have been seen at work intensely interested in the proposals which have been received and considered by the delegates. Every resolution has been examined by the committees and received thoughtful consideration and action by the convention. Sometimes there has occurred debate and discussion in which we have felt deeply and keenly concerned and, like red-blooded men and women, have expressed our opinions and convictions in language that was unmistakable. Credit is due to every man and woman who has been in our convention that, notwithstanding how various and divergent have been the views in general, they have been received in a liberal and most generous fashion. The meetings of the labor movement, in our local unions, in our city central bodies, in our state conventions, in our international unions, and in the great A. F. of L. are the most democratic, open-minded gatherings which are in existence in any part of the world. This labor movement is not a pink tea arrangement; it is a movement dealing with humans, with humanity, with freedom, with liberty and safety, not only for the toiling masses but for all the people of our country and of our kind. We deal today with the questions which confront us and deal, too, with the subjects for the immediate and the distant future to safeguard the rights, the freedom, the justice and the democracy to which the people of our country and our time are entitled. If there were unanimous agreement among our delegates, among the men and women in our movement, there would be no need for our gathering, and out of the conflict of mind and conscience and heart come the better understanding of the problems by which we are confronted; and each one of us doing his or her level best to reach the wisest, most practical and constructive conclusion that shall bring benefit and advantage and happiness and love and fraternity and patriotism among all of us—the love of humanity. And so I may say that though there has been great divergence of opinion, manfully and womanly expressed in terse language, I doubt very much—indeed, I am fully pursuaded—that there is not a more intelligent body of men and women anywhere engaged in the solution of serious problems in which there is a broader intelligence or a plainer expression of that which is in the minds of the delegates than right in the conventions of the American Federation of Labor. May I say that I should very much appreciate, as I know it would contribute a great step forward, if the organizations of labor

in all our cities and towns would fittingly celebrate the coming Labor Day, the first Monday in September? Let us show with pride and satisfaction that our ranks are united in spirit and in fact; that we propose to greet our friends and sympathizers and those who understand us with the friendliest greetings, and that those who are antagonistic to our movement may understand that we will go on in solid phalanx to meet the future face to face. Just prior to our coming to Denver to hold this convention, and a few days after our arrival here, we were received and referred to with sneers and contempt by those who do not know, or, if knowing, are so absolutely hostile that they have closed their minds to reason. This A. F. of L. has met in the open, and at least for the present our conduct has silenced our enemies. We have met and we have completed the business of this convention. When we adjourn and return to our respective homes, and offices, when we meet our fellows, our townsmen and women, when we meet the great public and our respective constituencies, let us carry to them a message of honor and good will and fraternity. Let us endeavor during the coming year to make still greater strides in the onward and upward movement, which is the basic principle upon which the American trade union movement is founded; so that when we meet in 1922 at Cincinnati we shall have a record of achievements for the, right, for the men and women of labor, for the children of our country, that there may be implanted in their hearts and in their minds the thoughts and the ideals for that better day of which the philosophers have dreamed and the poets have sung and the toilers of the world have struggled; that we may be nearer that ideal day when in the full sunshine of midday we can face the world, conscious of the fact that we have done our whole duty."

(1922, p. 500) "It seems appropiate that the president of the A. F. of L. should make some observation regarding our convention which will close in a few minutes. May I say this, that this convention, where the delegates have been working hard, consistent and persistent, and where the discussion has been open and free, where no time has been called upon any delegate who had anything to say, whether on a resolution, a recommendation of the Executive Council in its report or any delegate present, not one has been smothered either in committee or by the convention. Every delegate to this convention has had full opportunity to express himself or herself. I am proud of the work of this convention. The convention has stood firm for right, for justice, for freedom, not only for labor, but for every man, woman, and child in our own America, as well as for those who are struggling in any other part of the world. We have done much. We have brought our faith and our hopes and our aspirations for peace and self-determination among the peoples of the world. We have made our contribution; we have expressed ourselves fundamentally and righteously upon the Russian situation, but for the people of Russia, that wonderful people, American labor has nothing but the sincerest friendship; it has given, and will continue to give, assistance, cooperation, and sympathy toward the development of these people and aid them in their laudable effort for their own reconstruction, and for the expression and hope for self-government among the people of that government so unfortunately situated. None the less have we taken an introspective view of the situation of the United States of America. We are one hundred per cent loyal to the republic of the United States. Were we disloyal or were we indifferent we might allow wrong to prevail without dissent or protest, but being Americans in all our hopes and ideals, it is the bounden duty of loyal thinking and patriotic Americans to find the faults, to take cognizance of the wrongs, to have an understanding of the unjust tendencies which a group of people in our country aim to impose upon the people of our republic. In our actions and declarations respecting wrongs done, injustices imposed upon any group or individuals of the citizenship of the United States, were we not to take cognizance and take our stand for reformation, for right for justice and the perpetuation of the democracy of our republic, we would be untrue to the citizenship we have undertaken. The A. F. of L. will respond to, aye, will anticipate, any demand made for the safety and the perpetuation of our republic. At the same time we shall exercise our judgment and our rights according to the laws and the constitution of the United States of America and attempt to check the imposition of wrong and injustice, and to secure the right to the permanency of this beloved republic of ours."

(1923, p. 274) "This convention, the forty-third in the history of the A. F. of L., is soon to come to a close. We have finished our work. Not a resolution was presented that has not had the consideration of the committee to which it was referred, that was not later reported to this convention and the convention has decided as to its course. I doubt if there is any other group or association in any part of our country or in any other country on the face of the globe where every proposition is given consideration. Any delegate having any proposition to submit knows that it must receive consideration; it can not be smothered by the convention or in any of its committees. This convention, as all previous conventions, has been a full, free, and open forum. Our antagonists may point to an incident in this convention and undertake to deny that statement. The answer to that denial is this: This is a convention of the A. F. of L. The A. F. of L. is made up of trade and labor unions, and any man who is avowedly hostile to the trade and labor unions has no right to try to enter the conventions of the A. F. of L.; he has no more right to have a voice in determining the policies of the A. F. of L. than a pronounced member of the democratic party would have to sit in the conventions of the republican party and shape its policies, or a pronounced republican to sit in the conventions of the democratic party and undertake to shape its decisions. One who is avowedly hostile to the makeup of the American labor movement, one who will in this year of grace 1923 say that the conditions of the American worker have become worse, and worse, and worse, knows, if he hasn't bidden good-bye to his reason, that his statements are false, untrue, and misrepresent the actual conditions. To attempt to besmirch the character, first, of our movement, and, secondly, of our men, is unworthy of even a fair antagonist. Differences of opinion are not only tolerated but invited; but these differences of opinion must be within the labor movement to thresh out as to how best that movement can function, not for its destruction. I am pursuaded fully that the actions and decisions of this convention have been such as to clarify the atmosphere. We have been altogether too tolerant, not in opposition to differences of opinion, but to the

men who have openly avowed and declared that they are boring from within, for the undermining of the principles and policies upon which the A. F. of L. is founded. The men who secretly and in the midnight go out in the woods or forest to plan to destroy, not only the government of our republic, but also the American trade union movement, these men may continue if they will, but they must do so on the outside and not on the inside. I am not sure of this one statement I am about to make, but I have been informed that it is true—and the man who informed me is one I have never known to state what is not true—that the delegate from the Silver Bow Trades and Labor Assembly was not elected, but that he solicited a credential with the understanding that the Silver Bow Trades and Labor Assembly would not have to pay his expenses. In the British Trades Union Congress there was a rule which barred any delegate from attendance at its congresses if the union or the organization that sent him had not paid his expenses. I don't know whether that rule should absolutely obtain in our movement, but I do ask you, my friends and fellow delegates, why should he come to this convention and relieve the Silver Bow Trades and Labor Assembly from paying his expenses as a delegate? From whence comes this plethora of money to pay the expenses of the delegate. The charge and insinuation has been made that our labor men are receiving large salaries. In some instances I think that is quite true. I think the delegates will bear me out when I say that I fought with whatever ability I might have in protest against the increase in salaries of the officers of the A. F. of L. But this may be said on the subject: That everybody who wants to know may know the means by which the officers of the American labor movement receive their income. It is provided in the laws of the organization; no one need inquire from whence the salaries are paid. Is it not a source of proper inquiry to ask by what means and from what source do these men, who come to disrupt our movement, receive their salaries? A few months ago a conference was held in Chicago with representative labor men of that city and of the state. When William Z. Foster referrred to me to give him a clean bill of health as to his conduct, he had the confidence in me that I would give him a clean bill of health, otherwise he would not have asked the question. I told the gathering what he was and who he was and how he had tried to deceive a lot of men in the labor movement, and that I for a time had been deceived by his declarations of loyalty to the labor movement. He then answered that he would throw open the books of his movement. My answer is that it is the general observation that crooks don't keep books. Somehow or other the enemies of our movement take great delight in emphasizing acutely the fact that there has been a diminution in the membership of the A. F. of L., and some of our own trade unionists, in their simplicity, like parrots, repeat the statement. Of course we have lost some members. Has anyone given consideration to the fact that for nearly two years there were from five to five and one-half millions of America's workers unemployed? And assuming that there were from one million and a half to two millions of the union men who were among the five and one-half millions who were unemployed and who could not pay their dues, the unions in turn could not pay their per capita tax to the A. F. of L. for those who were out of work and not earning wages. During the year 1922 there were strikes which covered a period of months, and the men and women in these strikes could not pay dues to their unions, and the unions in turn could not pay per capita tax to the A. F. of L. I would like at this moment if we could know the exact membership of our affiliated unions. Bear in mind that the A. F. of L. counts its membership, not by the exact membership of the unions today or this month, but covering the period of the year previous, an average membership; and in the report made to this convention a period of 16 months is covered, from June, 1922, to September 1, 1923, the period of unemployment, the period of strikes and lockouts involving one and one-half millions of America's workers. The average membership during the period of 16 months is the membership reported to this convention. And yet I say some of our own members will emphasize that we have lost membership and, echoing the maliciously formed terms of our antagonists, take out of the hearts and minds of the union men the confidence they have in the organization, and endeavor to impress them with the idea that the organizations of labor of America are decaying. The same prattling, the same terms that the employers and big business are hurling at our movement. Just a few weeks ago the American Bankers' Association had its annual convention, and they made the same statement that we read in this antagonist press—that the A. F. of L. has lost membership. We have made the morale, the spirit of the membership, move in spite of the drive of every antagonistic employer in our movement, the drive for the so-called open shop, the drive for that treacherously named "American plan," the whole financial interests being thrown in the scale against us, and then, in spite of and in addition thereto, finding in our own ranks people who dare, consciously or unconsciously, drive the heart and soul out of the weak-kneed men. That we haven't lost more, that we have retained the stature and the status of our movement, speaks for it. The confidence, the hope of the toiling masses of our country, bespeaks to us the tribute of honor, of progress, of constructive legislation that shall bring light into the life and the work of the toilers of America. Speaking of the American Bankers' Association. In their last convention they insisted that there must be wage reductions. They said the prices of labor are too high. And then as a remedy they declared that the floodgates of immigration must be opened, and the wages of the men who work and produce wealth must be reduced. I submit that if the proposal to reduce the wages of the working people of America is a remedy, why don't these bankers start in with themselves? I shall not attempt to say that modern banking has not its proper function in our industry and financial life; but I think the service performed by the baker, the carpenter, the bricklayer, the tailor, the plumber and all the rest of us is more important to civilization than that of the banker. The enmity or antagonism of greed and ignorance on the part of that type of men I have just referred to is to be expected, and we can meet them anywhere and beat them anywhere. It is different with the sneak, the one who comes behind you by stealth and stabs you in the back. I believe that the decisions of this convention have and will do many things. I have not the time to enumerate them, but I do believe that it has given notice to all who want to dominate this labor movement, who are not part of it, who are antagonistic to it, to understand that the cleavage has been made, and it will en-

1609A—3

courage our own trade unionists to more clearness of thinking and solidarity of action. It will tell those who are outside that they can come within our fold and receive our cooperation, they in turn to give theirs to us. It will give notice to those who would destroy our movement that this is an American labor movement, a movement of the worker, for the workers and by the workers, and not any so-called intelligencia. Anyone who has a suggestion to make, anyone who has any advice to give, anyone who will help in this great task before us, is most heartily welcome, but when he or they attempt to impose their will upon our movement, we cry a halt. And we have given notice of a halt, and he who does not heed the warning to halt must be swept aside so that we can go on. We have been in session now for nearly two weeks. There has not been a delegate who in that time has desired to speak to this convention but has had the opportunity. One instance in which this did not happen was due to no fault of anyone, I am sure, and it is regrettable, because it is my earnest desire that this shall be continued as a real open forum. In the opening of our convention I took occasion to say that the galleries of this beautiful hall were open to the public and that the newspaper men of the country and of this city were in their places making notes of things which transpired, utterances, declarations, decisions, manners and mannerisms, and all that sort of thing. We may be seen at work, at our best and at our worst. When this convention adjourns, as it will in a few minutes, there will be time for the newspaper men, for the people of Portland, for the people of Oregon, for the people of the country, to make up their minds in the summing up of the total of our work. I am perfectly willing to submit our work and our conduct to their judgment. We shall leave Portland without leaving a bad odor or a bad taste behind us. We have done our work. I feel that we have done it well. We have not reached the age or time of perfection. There occurs to me just a statement made in this convention, "What are we doing and how do we expect to end our movement?" The question was asked: "After you have exerted your constitutional rights, after you have attained your rights, within constitutional lines, what then?" The answer is that we are fighting in our day to make the conditions of the great masses of the people better, and that in so doing we improve the caliber, the intelligence, the virility of the people who are to follow us. I am perfectly willing to see a mile ahead so that when the grand army of labor shall reach that milestone in its progress it may be the better prepared to see the next milestone, visualize that which can not be accomplished in their time, improve the standards of the toilers of their time, so that they in turn again may go on, and on, and on. I am perfectly willing to leave the solution of the far distant future to the future, working along today on the road for that future. Perhaps I may be going too far, and yet I feel sure that I am not when I say on behalf of my associates and myself whom you have honored with a unanimous election for another term, we return our grateful appreciation for the confidence that you have reposed in us. We shall endeavor to serve you and the great mass of labor and the people of our country, contributing something for the alleviation of the misery and for the uplift of all of those who suffer, no matter where they may be, to help in the great work of a better understanding. And you men and women, coming fresh from the organizations you have the honor to represent in this convention, having done and thought and acted likewise, when you return to your homes with safety, may you be greeted with happiness and joy and congratulations upon the work performed by you in this convention; and then when we shall meet, or as many of us as shall meet in the 1924 convention, let us take there the hope and the satisfaction of the year's work well done in the service of labor, in the service of America, in the service of justice, in the service of international accord, in the service toward universal peace, prosperity, progress, and happiness.

Department Delegates, A. F. of L.— (1919, p. 432) The constitution was amended to seat a representative of each department, of the A. F. of L. as a delegate with one vote.

Department of Labor—(1919, pp. 122-374) After many years of agitation and education on the part of organized labor, the federal department of labor was established to deal with those important human relations which grow out of the association of workers and management for production. The organic act thus specifies the purposes of the department: "To foster, promote and develop the welfare of the wage earners of the U. S., to improve their working conditions, and to advance their opportunities for profitable employment." These purposes are essential to national well-being as well as to the development of business organization in accord with sound principles. From year to year we have reported upon and recorded the good work carried on by the department of labor in behalf of the interests and well-being of the wage earners of the country which justifies our advocacy of the department. We appreciate that much more could have been done if the government had given full recognition to the utility of the department and congress had made the necessary appropriations. Although the work of the department of labor affects directly the foundations of organized society, congress from the very first has failed to appropriate sufficient funds for its proper maintenance. Congress instructed the department of labor to perform a humanitarian work of great value to business as well as to wage earners, but has withheld the funds necessary to carry out instructions. By this parsimonious and ill-advised policy congress has for years prevented the department of labor from fully-developing the great usefulness that properly belongs to its functions and field. The 1913 convention of the A. F. of L. instructed the Executive Council and the legislative committee of the A. F. of L. to use every possible means to induce congress to make adequate appropriation for the department of labor. But not until war emergency and war needs demonstrated that national welfare and safety depended upon authorizing the department of labor to develop and make effective national labor policies, was the department of labor given sufficient funds to organize agencies to perform the work which congress instructed it to do in the organic act creating the department. In addition to the national war labor board, one of the principal and essential of these newly created agencies was the employment service. This service had its origin in 1907 when there was created in the bureau of immigration a division of information. This division established a public employment system in connection with the immigration station in New York. It had only the authority granted under the act creating the immigration station in New York and provided solely for the distribution of aliens. The department of labor, with but

meager funds at its command entered into copperative relations with the post office department whereby the country-wide agencies of the latter department were utilized to relieve the labor shortage and more advantageously distribute labor to meet the demands of the harvest season in the wheat-growing states. Early in 1917 an emergency situation arose when the employment service was called upon to locate employment for members of the national guard who had been relieved from service on the Mexican border. Although every department of government was almost immediately provided with funds when congress declared war on April 6, 1917, the employment service of the department of labor did not receive any appropriation until October 6, 1917, six months after war had been declared, and then only $250,000 was appropriated. With this meager appropriation the employment service faced a dilemma of either almost utter failure or the securing of the necessary funds to expand the service to such proportion as would enable it to function adequately in keeping industries supplied with necessary man power. Fortunately, congress had placed in the president's hands a fund of $100,000,000 to be disbursed by him as emergencies arose. From this fund the president turned over to the department of labor on December 5, 1917, for the use of the employment service, $825,000. (P. 374) The purposes of this department are to foster, promote and develop the welfare of the wage earners of our nation and to improve their working conditions and to advance their opportunities for profitable employment. Yet every effort made to attain these ends has been frowned on by congress. While the purposes of the organic act creating this department are broad and comprehensive in principle, congress by technical interpretation and by parliamentary rules and procedure has narrowly circumscribed the functions of this great governmental bureau. No more astounding disregard to the interest and well-being of the workers of our country has been manifested than in the niggardly appropriations which congress has allowed this department to advance the workers' opportunities for profitable employment. Congress in its last appropriation allowed only the sum of $4,171,320 to advance the interests of the workers, who constitute the great majority of the people, while $25,583,205 was contributed to promote the commercial interests, the employing financial speculative interests of our country. Still more astounding is the fact that while only $4,171,320 was allowed to promote profitable employment of the wage earners, $31,691,562 was allowed by congress to promote the interests and advance the value of the possessions of the farming interests of our nation. These figures not only indicate that congress considers money, cattle, and the like of greater value than the welfare and well-being of men, women, and children, but they also present remarkable proof of a subtle political influence at work to dominate and control the destiny of our government and its people. We do not desire to restrict or limit or to interfere with the proper encouragement and development of the agricultural interests of our country, or limit the commercial endeavors of our people, but as expressed by the Executive Council, we do believe that the wage earners of our nation are entitled to equal consideration and to an equal appropriation allowed to all other departments of the government. Efforts should be made to secure adequate appropriations to efficiently maintain all such departments within the department of labor which it deems helpful and needful for the promotion and advancement of the interests of the wage earners.

(1920, p. 102) Since the present congress began its session in May, 1919, there has been a constant endeavor on the part of certain members to keep whittling away at the department of labor. No greater enmity to this department could be shown than the action by the legislative, executive, and judicial committee in its reduction of the appropriation asked by the secretary of labor. He asked for $1,700,000, and the committee slashed it to $1,018,000. On another page of the same bill the appropriation for the department of commerce was $8,377,600. If the present reactionary congressmen are elected to the next congress they will continue to reduce appropriations until the department is made impotent. This charge has been voiced by a number of members of congress. To more effectively destroy its usefulness appropriations were refused for certain bureaus against which members of congress were especially bitter. Bills providing for the establishment of a federal employment service were introduced, but no action was permitted. H. R. 4305, by Representative Nolan; S. 1442 and S. 688, all for that purpose, all lie in the storage plants of the committee on labor of the house and the committee on education and labor of the senate. Every effort of Representative Nolan and his supporters on the house committee to have the bill reported failed. The Steering committee refused to permit its consideration by the house. The only appropriation congress would give the department was in the sundry civil bill. This provided for $400,000. The appropriation of $5,000 asked for the working conditions service of the department failed of passage. This service therefore passed out of existence. Appropriations for the bureau of labor statistics to conduct investigations into the high cost of living were reduced to such figures that the work has been confined to very narrow limits. All appeals to those who support our contention that the department of labor should be made more effective instead of less are met with the answer that the determination to destroy that department is in the minds of the ruling majority of congress. Its leaders refuse to see the great benefits that have been derived from the conciliation division of the department of labor. It was only by intensive agitation and urging by the representatives of the A. F. of L. that the senate finally increased the appropriation for the conciliation division. (P. 385) The service of the department of labor of the government of the U. S. has been of inestimable value to the people of the U. S., no matter what their station or calling in life. It is to be deplored that members of congress should for any reason undertake to hamper in any way the proper activity of a department of the government whose existence is of such great use as this one has proved during the short time it has existed

(1921, p. 146) Efforts are being made to take from the department of labor several of its important bureaus and subsidiary departments and place them under a proposed welfare department. It was through the efforts of the representatives of labor that congress was prevailed upon to create the first bureau of labor statistics. As its name implied, it was merely a bureau of statistics. Later that bureau was changed by act of congress to be a department of labor and its duty and functions were largely of a statistical

character. It was placed as a department under the department of the interior. Later congress abolished the department of labor and substituted the department of commerce and labor. It was during the closing days of the sixty-second congress when congress passed and President Taft, on the fourth of March, 1913, signed the bill by which the present department of labor was created and which provided for a secretary as its chief officer, the secretary automatically becoming a member of the president's cabinet. We declare in no mistaken terms the necessity of retaining in the department of labor all the bureaus and various divisions of work now included and that congress make sufficient appropriations to carry on this work efficiently and proficiently. (P. 308) This is apparently a part of a well-conceived program which has for its end the ultimate extinction of the department of labor as it now exists, to degrade it from its proper importance as a cabinet position and reducing it to that of a bureau, if not altogether extinguishing it. This great purpose has only in part been realized because of the obstacles placed in the way of the department through influences inimical to its design, scanty appropriations, or the total denial of funds preventing full service of the department and hampering materially in the limited effort it has been able to put forth; however, the department of labor has more than justified its creation, and the fact that sinister interests are bent apparently to its destruction is the best possible testimony and evidence as to its value to the workers of America. The Executive Council is instructed and authorized to exert its fullest power to the preservation of the department of labor as a cabinet position under our government, and to prevent the dismemberment of that department by the removal of any of the bureaus that are now functioning properly under the direction of the department of labor. And we urge that the national and international officers lend their assistance to this end that the one cabinet officer, whose function is directly of benefit and importance to the toilers, may not be eliminated. (P. 338) The U. S. employment service, which was of the greatest benefit and assistance during the war and which in the present condition of unemployment would be of equal value in bringing the job to the man and the man to the job if it were allowed to function, was practically eliminated by the refusal of congress to appropriate money for that service. The Executive Council is hereby directed to use its utmost endeavors to defeat any measure that may be now before congress or that may be hereafter introduced for the purpose of weakening or destroying the various bureaus of the department of labor.

(1922, pp. 97-328) The A. F. of L. notes with satisfaction that thus far the attempts of the forces of reaction to scrap the department of labor have been frustrated. It was at the instance of the organized wage earners that the department of labor was first established. All of its varied activities have a direct bearing upon the lives and the welfare of the working people. Its enemies would crush it or emasculate it by dividing its important functions, because they resent the growing recognition by the people of the great contribution to public service by this department of our government, established primarily to meet the needs of the workers.

(1923, p. 85) The two years' fight to prevent the scrapping of the department of labor is in a fair way of being successful. Mr.

Walter F. Brown, representing the president, who is chairman of the joint committee on reorganization of the senate and house, has made a report to the president in which only minor changes are recommended in the present functioning of the department of labor The non-industrial services of the women's and children's bureau will become a part of the department of education and welfare, a proposed new department. While every power of the administration is being used to make friends for the reorganization plan the opposition appears to be so great that it is doubtful if it will pass in the next congress. (P. 279) That efforts should have continued unabated to dismember and weaken if not destroy the work and efficiency of the department of labor, should not occasion surprise. This is practically the only department of the government directly charged with promoting the interests, welfare and well-being of America's wage earners. It is charged with safeguarding the advancement of the human equation in our industrial world, and yet it is given less consideration and is more subject to destructive attacks and tendencies than is any other department of the government. The A. F. of L. urges that labor's demands for a still more efficient and extensive department of labor be impressively submitted to the president of the U. S. and to our national congress.

Department of Labor and Its Secretary— (1919, p. 298) The A. F. of L., from the first year of its existence, when organized in 1881, declared that we desired to have a department of labor in the federal government. After a while a bureau of labor statistics was created, independent of any other governmental department. It made its investigations independently of any other governmental department and its reports direct. There came about a change in which the department of commerce and labor was effected and the bureau of labor statistics was submerged and lost its identity. After several years of further effort we finally secured congressional action which divorced that department so that two new departments were created instead of one—one the department of commerce and the other the department of labor. The first to occupy the position of secretary of the department of labor was Mr. William B. Wilson. Somehow or other in the minds of some of our representatives and senators in congress, there is a notion that there must not be a department of labor exercising functions in the interest of the working masses of our country; and it has been one of the most difficult tasks to get anything like a decent appropriation from congress for the department. It seems as though there has been a policy pursued to starve the department of labor either out of existence or into such a state of weakness that its functions will be of little avail. Outside of the mobilization of the men to be drilled and trained and developed, outside of the departments which furnished the materials and the resources, no department of government gave more real service to the prosecution of the war and the winning of the war than did the department of labor. As a result of this war in which militarism was defeated by the yeomanry of the people of the U. S. and the allied countries, we have reason to believe that the direction cf tne minds of the people of the world will be diverted from military perfection to industrial and humane conditions. As a result of the peace treaty and the league of nations and the

international conferences of labor the activities and the services of the war department and our navy department, as well as the war departments and naval establishments of the world, will become less potent year after year; while on the other hand, the work, the mission of the department of labor in collaborating with the organized labor movement in the functions of that department will enter into all the matters of our everyday lives. The enabling act creating the department of labor is so important in its declarations that it would be well worth while to have them not only read through sometimes but printed and kept in our minds for all time and to suit all occasions. The enabling act creating the department declares that it is the duty of that department to work for the welfare of the wage earning masses of our country. And there is no limit to the ramifications of such activities. As the result of the reports made by the Executive Council of the A. F. of L., this convention resents any attempt to curb or weaken or destroy the department of labor. There are a few men who, no matter how the world will develop, how the mentality of the people will grow, how the yearning for freedom and justice and democracy has grown and has become accentuated and accelerated as a result of the war, will oppose progress. As time goes on the value of the work of the A. F. of L. movement, of the bona fide labor movement of the whole world, will be more and more realized. The constructive work of creating a better public opinion, because we shall constitute largely the public opinion of our respective countries, will go on, it must go on if civilized society can be expected to continue. And we are under obligations to the secretary of labor, the man who never has failed, notwithstanding his great responsibility, as he has declared this afternoon in addressing us as his fellow trade unionists. One of the things against which the criticisms of him have been leveled is that he has refused to deny or repudiate, but, on the contrary, has asserted that notwithstanding any position in life in which he may be placed, he is still, and will continue to be, a thorough trade unionist.

Department of Social Welfare—1921, p. 109) Continuation of the persistent efforts to destroy or to limit the activities of the department of labor was seen in S. 4543, which provided for the establishment of a department of social welfare, the secretary to be a member of the cabinet. It proposed to transfer the following bureaus from the department of labor to the department of social welfare: Children's bureau, women's bureau, bureau of industrial housing and transportation, U. S. employment service, and the U. S. employes' compensation commission. The department of labor was created after many years of agitation by the A. F. of L. Congress has managed gradually to hamper its influence for good. Appropriations for the department of labor have been kept at the lowest figure possible. In fact, the U. S. employment service has been practically abolished through refusal of congress to appropriate funds for its proper functioning. If a bill providing for a department of social welfare becomes a law it will aid the enemies of the department of labor in their determination to destroy it. (P. 307) The A. F. of L. views with great concern this insidious attack upon the existence of the department of labor, which is so vitally related to the cause of the workers of the United States.

The Executive Council is directed to continue its efforts for the preservation intact of the department of labor, which is now threatened with extinction.

Detectives, Industrial Private—(1922, p. 343) There appears a decided effort on the part of certain interests to disrupt organized labor, and one of the methods used is that of the so-called "industrial private detectives." Publicity is perhaps the greatest means to defeat the efforts of these "private detectives;" therefore this convention goes on record as opposed to this type of business being used in industrial problems. We urge the passage of legislation—national, state, and municipal—to the end that this business shall be licensed and regulated, if not prohibited entirely in industrial problems, and that the operatives of the companies be listed and open to public inspection.

Disarmament—(1921, pp. 102-372) The A. F. of L. speaking in the name of the organized workers of our great country has always loyally supported our government. A month before this government made the decisive step whereby it aligned itself on the side of the allies against autocracy and militarism during the great war, the officers of our national and international unions took the solemn pledge "in peace or in war, in stress or in storm, to stand unreservedly by standards of liberty and the safety and preservation of the institutions and ideals of our republic," and labor loyally fulfilled that pledge. It now becomes our duty to call afresh to your minds the declarations of the A. F. of L. on the general subject of disarmament and protest against large standing armies. We have special reference to the two resolutions (Nos. 136 and 163) of the Seattle, 1913, convention. These resolutions dealt with the proposal made by the government of Great Britain that all the powers cease naval construction for a specific period. The labor movements of the several countries, including our own movement, were urged by our movement to prevail upon their respective governments to encourage the movement for international disarmament. Again the 1914 convention declared "that we pledge our support to any plan which has for its purpose the bringing about of the disarmament of all nations to the furthest extent consistent for the preservation of law and order throughout the world." The workers recognize that wrapped up with the safety of this republic are ideals of democracy, a heritage which the masses of the people received from our forefathers who fought that liberty might live in this country—a heritage that is to be maintained and handed down to each generation with undiminished power and usefulness. The labor movement recognizes the value of freedom and it knows that freedom and rights can be maintained only by those willing to assert their claims and to defend their rights. The cause of disarmament and international peace can be promoted by creating and stimulating a public sentiment that will not tolerate waste of life and by establishing international relations understanding and agencies that will constitute insuperable barrier to policies of force and destruction. With humanization, education cultivation, the establishment of the rule of reason, occasions for wars and wars themselves will cease. The working people, the masses of the world population, can end wars if they but have the independence to think and to give their convictions reality by daring to do. For this and many other obvious reasons this convention calls on the government of the U. S. to take the initiative or to cooperate with any other nation or nations for the purpose of a general agreement for disarmament both of the army and naval affairs of the world and that it shall be the duty of the Executive Council to call upon the workers and the people to aid in every way within their power and to have translated into action the sentiments as in this report recommended.

(1922, pp. 87-489) Not more than three weeks after the adjournment of the 1921 convention it was announced that the president of the U. S. had approached Great Britain, France, Italy, and Japan with inquiries as to whether it would be agreeable to them to participate in a conference on limitation of armament and Pacific and far east problems. Formal invitations to such a conference were issued on August 11, 1921, and the conference called to convene on the anniversary of Armistice Day, November 11, 1921, met the following day, November 12. Labor's participation in the effort to insure the success of that conference was two-fold. In accordance with the action of the Denver convention it was "the duty of the Executive Council to call upon the workers and the people to aid in every way within their power to have translated into action the sentiments recommended." At its meeting August 11, 1921, the Executive Council instructed the president of the A. F. of L. to take such action as would best serve to carry out the convention instructions. The A. F. of L. participated in an official capacity in the work of the international conference on the limitation of armament. President Gompers and President Lewis of the United Mine Workers of America, were appointed by President Harding as members of the official advisory commission of the American delegation, in the work of which they participated actively in important capacities. In addition to this, the A. F. of L. made every possible effort to rally the sentiment of the American people in support of the work of the international conference. Pursuant to the instructions of the Executive Council, President Gompers took the initiative in organizing Armistice Day demonstrations throughout the country under the leadership of labor. More than 200 such demonstrations were held. These demonstrations were representative of the entire citizenship, and constituted a powerful force for the success of the conference. In addition to this President Gompers called together about 200 representative men and women from all walks of life in a meeting held in Washington, October 18-19, 1921. At that conference there was organized "The General Committee for the Limitation of Armament," which conducted an active campaign fór the success of the international conference and for the ratification of the treaties negotiated in that conference. A pamphlet entitled "Disarmament," containing the entire record of the efforts of the A. F. of L. in behalf of international peace and disarmament, was prepared under instructions of the Executive Council and was given wide circulation. The president of the A. F. of L. called upon President Harding on July 18, immediately following the issuance of the official call for the conference, presenting to President Harding the question of the wisdom and advisability of appointing a representative of labor as a member of the official American delegation to the international conference. By letter and by cablegram the labor movements of the other participating nations were advised of that action and were earnestly urged to present similar requests to their own governments. American labor was not represented on the official American delegation, but it was represented as has been stated on the official advisory commission, although, it is regrettable to report, no other labor movement was given representation of any character on any of the visiting national delegations or advisory commissions. We desire to record here satisfaction with the work achieved by the international conference on limitation of armament and to express the pride which we .feel in the fact that the U. S. was the initiator of the movement in bringing as much relief as possible to the peoples of the world through practical and immediate reductions in the armaments of the world. It would be idle, of course, to say that the international conference was a complete success and it would be equally idle to expect every such single effort to be a complete success. We feel that the effort did in a most remarkable manner justify our declaration, our efforts, and our expectations. We can not yield to the hope, however, that the danger of international disputes has passed because of the work of the Washington conference. On the contrary, we are strongly of the conviction that if it is permitted to stand by itself the work of the Washington conference will be but a slight contribution toward the stabilization of international relations. Following the conclusion of the international conference on the limitation of armament, an invitation was issued by the allied supreme council to an international conference to be held at Genoa and to be called an economic conference. It was clear that the work of the Washington conference was not, of itself, sufficient to insure lasting international peace; particularly it contributed little, if anything, of immediate value to the economic restoration of the world. Interested primarily in the economic welfare of civilization, your officers publicly expressed the conviction that there should be held, at a suitable time, an international economic conference for the purpose of doing whatever might be found possible to revive the economic life of the world. Speaking in the name of labor a statement was issued by the president of the A. F. of L. expressing the belief that the Genoa conference could not succeed in bringing about econimic revival and further stating that an international economic conference, to be successful, should be summoned by the U. S. to be held in the U. S. under an agenda prepared by the U. S.

Diseases, Venereal—(1919, p. 321) The A. F. of L. heartily endorses the efforts of the U. S. Public Health Service, cooperating with various states, in combattting the spread of venereal diseases. We call upon organized labor to familiarize itself with the government's program of combatting these diseases and to assist in every possible manner the eradication of these scourges of civilization.

Dollar, Stabilizing the—(1919, p. 344) The Executive Council is hereby instructed to make a study of the problem of establishing a dollar of stabilized purchasing power as it may be presented through legislative effort, or otherwise during the year.

Drugs a Menace, Narcotic—(1923, p. 308) We request our government to appeal to Great Britain, Persia, and Turkey, as the principal seats of opium-growing, to cease growing the opium poppy; and to the United Netherlands, Peru, and Bolivia, the principal growers of the cocoa shrub, from which cocaine is made, to cease production of the cocoa shrub, except in such amounts as are strictly necessary for medical and scientific purposes; and call upon China to undertake again the extirpation of the poppy, which she undertook so success-

fully in 1906. The A. F. of L. also appeals to the labor unions of Great Britain, and like organizations in other countries, asking them to urge their respective governments to take adequate action for total suppression of these ruinous drugs, except so far as they can be utilized for strictly medical and scientific purposes; and the president of the A. F. of L. is requested to lay these resolutions before the government at Washington, requesting their transmission through regular channels to the various nations herein named. (P. 366) The A. F. of L. records its gratification of the action of the league of nations opium commission in arranging international conferences looking to the suppression of the production of narcotic drugs; and requests the secretary of state of the U. S. to extend to these conferences on behalf of the people of that nation a cordial invitation to hold their sessions in some city of this country.

Duplex Printing Co. Case—(1921, pp. 74-373) The case of Duplex Printing Press Company vs. Deering, which was decided by the United States supreme court, January 3, 1921, is a great disappointment, because the opinion of the majority members of the court clearly reveals that section 20 of the Clayton act has been emasculated of any protection that labor was supposed to enjoy thereunder. The Duplex Company sought to enjoin officials of the machinists and affiliated unions from interfering with its business by inducing their members not to work for plaintiff or its customers in connection with the setting up of presses made by it. Unlike Hitchman Coal & Coke Company vs. Mitchell, there was no charge that defendants induced employes to break their contracts, nor was it urged in the arguments that defendants threatened acts of violence. The defendants admitted interference with plaintiff's business, but insisted that by the common law of New York and by section 20 of the Clayton act, the facts constituted a justification for this interference with plaintiff's business. Referring to section 20 of the Clayton act, Mr. Justice Brandeis in his dissenting opinion, with whom Mr. Justice Holmes and Mr. Justice Clarke concurred, said: "This statute was the fruit of unceasing agitation which extended over more than 20 years and was designed to equalize before the law the position of workingmen and employer as industrial combatants. Aside from the use of the injunction, the chief source of dissatisfaction with the existing law lay in the doctrine of malicious combination, and, in many parts of the country, in the judicial declarations of the illegality at common law of picketing and persuading others to leave work. The grounds for objection to the latter are obvious. The objection to the doctrine of malicious combinations requires some explanation. By virtue of that doctrine, damage resulting from conduct such as striking or withholding patronage or persuading others to do either, which without more might be damnum absque injuria because the result of trade competition, became actionable when done for a purpose which a judge considered socially or economically harmful and therefore branded as malicious and unlawful. It was objected that, due largely to environment, the social and economic ideas of judges, which thus became translated into law, were prejudicial to a position of equality between workingman and employer; that due to this dependence upon the individual opinion of judges great confusion existed as to what purposes were lawful and what unlawful; and that in any event congress, not the judges, was the body which should declare what public policy in regard to the industrial struggle demands. By 1914, the ideas of the advodates of legislation had fairly crystallized upon the manner in which the inequality and uncertainty of the law should be removed. It was to be done by expressly legalizing certain acts regardless of the effects produced by them upon other persons. As to them congress was to extract the element of injuria from the damages thereby inflicted instead of leaving judges to determine according to their own economic and social views whether the damage inflicted on an employer in an industrial struggle was damnum absque injuria, because an incident of trade competition, or a legal injury, because in their opinion, economically and socially objectionable. This idea was presented to the committees which reported the Clayton act. The resulting law set out certain acts which had previously been held unlawful whenever courts had disapproved of the ends for which they were performed; it then declared that, when these acts were committed in the course of an industrial dispute they should not be held to violate any law of the United States. In other words, the Clayton act substituted the opinion of congress as to the propriety of the purpose for that of differing judges; and thereby it declared that the relations between employers of labor and workingmen were competitive relations, that organized competition was not harmful and that it justified injuries necessarily inflicted in its course. Both the majority and the minority report of the house committee indicates that such was its purpose. If, therefore, the act applies to the case at bar, the acts here complained of can not 'be considered or held to be violations of any law of the United States,' and hence do not violate the Sherman act." As a result of the decisions in this and in the Hitchman case it is undeniable that labor has been unjustly stripped of important rights to which it is under law and right entitled in the federal courts and unless there is some adequate legislative relief it is obvious that certain employers throughout the United States who seek to crush labor will take advantage of those decisions and insist upon the open shop, so-called, which virtually means that labor will be reduced to the same low standard that obtained nearly a century ago; that the lot of the working man will be the same as it was in medieval times, that his wages will be a mere pittance, his hours of labor intolerable, his home a hovel, his clothes rags, his degradation as base as in the days now happily passed.

Education—(1919, pp. 77-431) It is impossible to estimate the influence of education upon the world's civilization. Education must not stifle thought and inquiry, but must awaken the mind concerning the application of natural laws and to a conception of independence and progress. Education must not be for a few but for all our people. While there is an advanced form of public education in many states, there still remains a lack of adequate educational facilities in several states and communities. The welfare of the republic demands that public education should be elevated to the highest degree possible. The government should exercise advisory supervision over public education and where necessary maintain adequate public education through subsidies without giving to the government power to hamper or interfere with the free development of public education by the several states. It is essential that our system of public education should offer the wage earner's children the opportunity for the fullest possible development.

To attain this end state colleges and universities should be developed. It is also important that the industrial education which is being fostered and developed should have for its purpose not so much training for efficiency in industry as training for life in an industrial society. A full understanding must be had of those principles and activities that are the foundation of all productive efforts. Children should not only become familiar with tools and materials, but they should also receive a thorough knowledge of the principles of human control, of force and matter underlying our industrial relations and sciences. The danger that certain commercial and industrial interests may dominate the character of education must be averted by insisting that the workers shall have equal representation on all boards of education or committees having control over vocational studies and training.

(Pp. 112-431) Additional principles which should be incorporated in organized labor's educational policy:

1. With regard to vocational education, the model laws recommended by the Executive Council to the St. Paul Convention, and the principles adopted by that convention, including the endorsement of the unit, as opposed to the dual system of administration, should be re-endorsed. In this connection commendation should be given to the various states which have enacted continuation school laws, and to the labor movement of those states for the part they played in securing such legislation.

2. Hearty support should be given the increasing demand for well considered methods of vocational guidance in our schools.

3. Careful consideration should be given to the simplification of courses of study, especially in the lower grades; but in connection with any movement toward simplification, the committee believes that

4. The upper years of the elementary school should be reorganized to afford diversified training, so that boys and girls who can not go on to higher schools will receive training specifically designed for their needs, and not be compelled as at present to prepare for a role they will never play. These diversified courses should be flexible so that a pupil will be able to transfer from one to another. We must not compel the child to pay the penalty throughout life for a mistaken decision made in childhood. Organized labor should demand and help to secure an expansion and diversification of both elementary and secondary education so that a democratic equality of opportunity for preparations for the callings of their choice may be offered the children of the people.

5. In all courses of study, and particularly in industrial and vocational courses, the privileges and obligations of intelligent citizenship must be taught vigorously and effectively; and at least in all vocational and industrial courses an unbiased industrial history must be taught, which shall include accurate account of the organization of the workers and the results thereof, and shall also include a summary of all legislation, both state and federal, affecting the industries taught.

6. The basic language of instruction in all schools, both public and private, should be the English language, foreign languages to be taught only as subjects in the curriculum.

7. The provision of adequate facilities for the teaching of English to non-English speaking people.

8. The establishment of complete systems

of modern physical education under specially trained instructors.

9. The provision of ample playground facilities as a part of the public school system.

10. Continuous medical and dental inspection throughout the schools.

11. Better enforcement of compulsory educational laws, and the universal establishment of a minimum school-leaving age of 16 years.

12. The extension of a free text-book system to the District of Columbia and such states and communities as have not adopted it.

13. Wider use of the school plant securing increased returns to the community through additional civic, social, and educational services to both adults and children.

14. Public forums should be established in every school where there is sufficient demand, under the direction of the superintendent of schools, working in cooperation with advisory committees, representing the various elements in the community.

15. The educational interests of the children and the future welfare of the state demand a drastic reduction in the prevailing size of classes.

16. In view of the demonstration by war conditions of the industrial and educational value of the metric system the Executive Council is requested to cause an investigation to be made of the advantages of the introduction of the metric system into this country, with a view to determine what further steps, such as congressional action, may be advisable.

17. A thorough going revision upward of the salary schedule of teachers in public schools, normal schools, and universities, to meet the increased cost of living and the growing appreciation of the value to the community and the nation of the teachers' services.

18. The liberal ungrudging reorganizations and increase of school revenues as the only means of maintaining and developing the efficiency of our public schools.

19. In order to secure a more democratic administration of our schools, to develop a spirit of cooperation, and to gain for the community the benefit of the experience and initiative of the teaching body, boards of education and superintendents of schools should confer with committees representing organizations of the teachers' choice in all cases of controversy between school authorities and teachers, and should consider and make official public record of suggestions dealing with the conduct of the schools submitted by the teachers through such committees.

20. Teachers should have tenure of position during efficiency. There should be no dismissals without full public hearings before a commission on which the teachers are fairly represented.

21. In a democracy the primary requirement is a citizenship educated to straightforward, logical thinking, based on facts established by careful sifted evidence. The schools can not develop this essential mental fibre if the pupils are carefully shielded from knowledge of the topics that men and women think about. Secondary only to a citizen's ability to do his own thinking, is his ability to make his influence felt in his group and community by effectively presenting his views to his fellows, and meeting opposition in a spirit of tolerance. This power of effective self-expression and the habits of tolerance, and of intellectual fairness toward opponents,

can not be formed without the discussion of topics that give opportunity for their exercise. Therefore, in order to enable the schools to perform one of their chief functions, preparation for active citizenship, the pupils should be encouraged to discuss under intelligent supervision current events and the problems of citizenship.

22. It is unquestionable that teachers have no right to impose their personal views on pupils. But it is necessary in some quarters to emphasize that neither do school authorities have that right. And it is further necessary to ask this convention to endorse with all its power, the principle that men and women in becoming teachers do not thereby surrender their rights as American citizens, and that inquisitions by school authorities into the personal, religious, political and economic views of teachers is intolerable in a free country, strikes at the very basis of our public school system, and can result only in the development of mental and moral servility, and the stultification of teachers and pupils alike.

23. The right of teachers to affiliate with organized labor is beyond question. And in that connection the right of teachers to hold meetings in school buildings outside of school hours, for the purpose of discussing organization, or of conducting the business of their organization, should not be questioned. Boards of education have no proprietory right in the schools, but are simply trustees for the public, of which the teachers are a part.

24. This convention urges all state and local central bodies to make a committee on education one of their standing committees, where it has not yet been done, and to make vigorous effort to secure adequate representation of organized labor on all boards of education.

25. The achievements of the American Federation of Teachers, in cooperation with the labor movement, during the past year. lead the committee to repeat with greater emphasis the declaration of the St. Paul convention that the most effective guarantee of democracy and of progress in our schools is the affiliation of the teachers of the country with the great democratic force of organized labor, and again to urge the Executive Council of the A. F. of L. and all state and local central bodies give every support to the American Federation of Teachers in the work of organizing the teachers.

(1920, p. 469) The A. F. of L. declares its opposition to the spirit of reaction manifested in a bill passed by the New York legislature but vetoed, providing in brief that no school, class, or course of instruction be conducted without satisfying the regents of the university of the state that the instruction to be given would not be detrimental to public interests. (P. 470) Sections 14 and 25 of the educational platform adopted by the 1919 convention is hereby modified as follows: Section 14. Where there is sufficient demand the school authorities should grant the use of school buildings for public forums, conducted by democratically organized local community groups, responsible under the law for the language used, the topics discussed, and the speakers selected. The democratic method of organization of public forum districts along these lines in Washington, D. C., is commended as a helpful model. Section 25. The most effective guarantee of democracy and progress in the schools is the affiliation of the teachers with the great democratic force of organized labor, which was the pioneer in the agitation for tax-supported public schools in the U. S. in the first half of the last century, and has ever since proved the steadfast friend of public education. The affiliation of the teachers with organized labor is not confined to the U. S. 120,000 out of 140,000 French teachers are so affiliated, as are the great majority of the teachers in Holland. In England the teachers are affiliating with organized labor in constantly increasing numbers. In Australia, particularly in Queensland, the teachers have affiliated. The teachers of the United States and Canada will find vigorous and effective support for progressive educational measures through affiliation with the four and one-half million of organized workers, as has been demonstrated by the growth and achievements of the American Federation of Teachers. The Executive Council of the A. F. of L. and all state and city central labor bodies of the United States and Canada are urged to give every assistance to the American Federation of Teachers in the organization of teachers, and the improvement of the schools.

(1921, p. 327) Educational platform adopted by the 1918 and 1919 conventions reaffirmed.

(1922, p. 368) Additional plank added: "26. The course of study throughout the public schools should be reorganized around social studies, in order that our prospective citizenship may receive adequate preparation for social living." The full influence of the A. F. of L. both nationally and through state and local committees on education will be exerted in support of labor's constructive educational program.

Text Book Investigation—(1922, p. 64) The purpose of the investigation is to determine (1) what agencies and influences are at work attempting to shape the attitude of public school teaching toward fundamental public questions; (2) the nature of the subjects dealing with the broader interests of organized labor, and the extent to which they are being taught; (3) the curricula and text books in use in the teaching of these subjects and the policy of important text-book publishers; (4) conclusions and recommendations.

1. There are numerous agencies attempting to influence public school education. These may be classified into three main groups: (a) Professional associations and official or semi-official agencies directly and regularly concerned with education; (b) philanthropic foundations and societies of long standing founded with educational objects but representing various points of view of those not actively engaged in education; (c) organizations not primarily interested in education but attempting to influence the public schools from their special points of view. The activities of some of these agencies are salutary and result in strengthening and improving the educational system of the country. Such agencies are found largely in groups "a" and "b." Other agencies are neutral in their effect.

2. The subjects in the teaching of which organized labor is primarily interested are civics, economics, history, and industrial history. American history has long been universally taught, though the treatment of it has been changing from a narrow political form to a broader social form in which labor is much more concerned. The other subjects mentioned have recently been introduced into the curricula of the public schools, and the extent of their use is rapidly enlarging. So also is the scope of treatment. A statistical survey of

the present status of these subjects is included in the report.

3. The investigation does not attempt to criticize the text-books in use in these subjects from a narrow point of view which would draw a sharp line between those which are approved and those disapproved. Rather after examination of the best representative texts, it sets up standards of evaluation covering the main points of interest, and grades each text in reference to these standards. Not so much attention is paid to the opinions which a book expresses as to the subjects covered, the adequacy of the treatment, etc. In the case of books giving a one-sided or illiberal treatment of any important subject, mention is made of the fact. But such cases are few. Most of the books given a low grade suffer not from prejudice, but rather from lack of sufficient background and adequate information. Approximately half of the texts in history and civics utterly ignore the labor movement and the subjects of particular interest to labor. However, it is more desirable that the pupil should be given an opportunity to inform himself and to reason about an important matter than that he should be instructed with a hard-and-fast set of precepts, no matter what bias they have. From this point of view, we find only a few really harmful texts and on the other hand, only a few really adequate ones. Publishers are being encouraged and should be further encouraged, to enlarge the scope of treatment in these subjects, and school authorities should be encouraged to use the most adequate texts.

4. The more important recommendations resulting from the investigation follow: "With regard to organizations influencing the public schools, the various bodies of the labor movement should be alert to oppose any effort to limit the independence or dignity of the teaching profession, or to introduce illiberal tendencies into public education. On the other hand, they should encourage and assist the organization of teachers themselves as the best means of raising educational standard. A self-respecting, adequately paid and well informed teaching staff is the best guarantee of an educational system adequate to democracy. Every effort should be put forth to encourage the extension of adequate teaching of civics, industrial history, etc. At the same time measures should be taken to encourage publication and adoption of adequate texts. New text books should be evaluated as published, in accordance with the system here developed, and the results of the evaluation made known by labor bodies to publishers, educational authorities, and teachers." The real importance of these findings consists not only in the evidence of inadequate and biased treatment of social studies, but in the implication to teachers and historians who want practical help in doing their works. It is much more important to know what ought to be done and to prevent future mistakes than it is simply to criticize past achievements.

(1923, pp. 59-245) We believe it advisable at this time to consider certain well-defined tendencies which the labor movement must take into account in its educational program. Maintenance of democratic ideals and sustained progress of a democratic nation are possible only with constantly broadening standards of education. There was never a time when the problems of life were more intricate or more momentous. In world politics we seem to be at the cross-roads— in event of orderly progress we can proceed toward the development of world institutions through which to conduct international affairs and make possible such progress in the industrial arts and intellectual and social culture as even our dreams can not forecast and the alternative road leads to chaos and the waste and futility of continuous war. In national affairs there is in the making the development of fundamental principles to underlie group activity as well as the technical basis for increasingly effective endeavor. The fabric of our social structure is so interwoven that activity is interdependent and by groups instead of individuals separately. In this complexity of social tissue the decision of any industrial issue becomes of far-reaching significance, affecting the welfare of many different elements in industry and society. It is therefore tremendously important that labor make only well-based decisions on all issues and this can be done only with broad and accurate sources of information, for labor holds constructive and decisive relationship to the fundamental problems of living. Experiences of the past in recorded form should be made available for the work of each succeeding day. In addition we must have much more of general knowledge and a more penetrating understanding of the philosophy of life to enable us to discern surely those things which are of permanent value. The provisions for a permanent committee on education signifies the A. F. of L.'s appreciation that labor's educational work requires sustained thought and continuous endeavor. The committee reported as follows:

"In pursuance of the instructions given by the Cincinnati convention conferences were continued with the Workers' Education Bureau to reach agreement upon terms and conditions of cooperation. As the result of two joint meetings an agreement was reported to the Executive Council and approved by us. Under the agreement the Federation is participating in the inauguration of specific educational enterprises for wage earners. The A. F. of L. now forms an integral and organic part of the Bureau. There are affiliated to the Bureau one national federation of labor; 14 national or international unions; 5 state federations of labor; 26 central labor unions and district councils; 8 local unions; 18 workers' educational enterprises; 3 cooperative societies; 3 student associations, making a total of 78. Seven main divisions have thus far developed in the work of the Bureau: The giving of general information on education; educational advice; registry of teachers; publications; cooperative book purchasing; correspondence department; workers' loan library. An editorial committee is developing the Workers' Bookshelf and the Workers' Educational Pamphlet Series. A substantial beginning has already been made and an extensive program of publication developed which includes general texts in the social sciences, literature and natural science and special texts in banking, research, labor biography and a series of studies in basic industries. The greatest care has been exercised to prevent any taint of propaganda from intruding itself into the activities or the literature of the bureau. The Bureau proposes to make its work sustained by working people. Unions and workers participating in educational endeavors should jointly share the expense. Each labor educational enterprise is developed to meet the needs and desires of local wage earners. The courses given have been designed to help wage earners understand the relations

to fellow workers, to the community, to the nation and society as organized internationally. Such understanding must be based upon knowledge of institutions and their historical development. When the whole of life is illumined by interpreting the spiritual life and aspirations which are the generating force, students as workers can approach their problems with the assurance of constructive analysis guided by a unifying philosophy. This is the attitude of mind or function required for sustained progress of the labor movement and hence the necessity of integrating educational work with union activity. In view of the evident importance of educational activity to organized labor we wish to urge upon all labor organizations affiliated to the A. F. of L. that each provide a permanent education committee to deal with the special educational problem of each divisional group and to cooperate in making effective the general educational plans and policies of labor. If each national and international establishes a special co - mittee or agency to direct its educational work and work through cooperating committees in each union; if each central body and state federation take similar action, the labor movement will have the most potential organization in this country which will make labor's voice effective both in policy making, executive work and promoting labor educational enterprises. For under that we may have a basis upon which to estimate progress. Our committee has initiated a survey of educational activity of unions at the present. As soon as the data has been assembled. a report will be made.

The following illustration serves to indicate a need of such organized unity and alertness on the part of organized labor. A notable theme of the speakers at graduating exercises at the close of last school year was the function of the judiciary in our government. As the speakers were practically from outside the workers' ranks the points of view presented were not sympathetic or understanding of labor's struggles. Perhaps no single address makes such a permanent impression on the minds of the group concerned as the commencement address. The situation suggests a strategic undertaking for the coming year. As instructed by the last convention we have endeavored to be helpful in establishing the more general practice of supplying free text books in public schools. This purpose can be achieved only by the collective efforts of all unions. Much remains to be done as is indicated by the following summary: State laws provide for free textbooks in the public schools as indicated: In six states—Delaware, Maryland, Texas, Arizona, California, and Oklahoma—textbooks are furnished free to public school pupils and payment therefor is made from state funds. In Missouri also some funds derived from state sources are available for furnishing free textbooks. In 13 states—Maine, Massachusetts, Montana, Nebraska, Nevada, New Hampshire, New Jersey, Pennsylvania, Rhode Island, South Dakota, Utah, Vermont, and Wyoming—local school authorities are required by law to provide free textbooks for public school pupils. In 19 states—Alabama, Arkansas, Colorado, Connecticut, Idaho, Illinois, Iowa, Kansas, Michigan, Minnesota, Mississippi, Missouri, New York, North Dakota, Ohio, Virginia, Washington, West Virginia, and Wisconsin—local school authorities are specifically permitted by law to provide textbooks for public school pupils.

In a few other states, as in North Carolina, it is permissible to furnish textbooks to poor children. In the preparation of these lists, distinction is not made between elementary and secondary schools, but it may be said in general that most of these laws provide textbooks for secondary pupils as well as for those in elementary schools. The shortening of the time of work, increasing the means of sustenance and the establishment of educational institutions of every kind, open to the wage earners of our land, in the time of leisure afforded them, opportunity to participate in the cultural progress of humanity. Above all things and education of the people, democratic in the true sense of the term must aim to awaken in the child of the most humble wage earner as in the child of the richly born, a lively sense of duty, reverence for the orderly affairs of government, tolerance of those of different faith and thought, a fine national price and a sympathetic international understanding. Moreover, the synthesizing of scientific and aesthetic culture and the various types of educational discipline is indispensible to stability of progress by a civilized people. It is not to be implied that all should have the same educational training or merely be filled with the most possible knowledge, but that instruction or opportunity for individual development be the common possession of all. To have the great mass of the people grounded in scientific discipline is to enable them with most dependable discernment, to estimate the value of knowledge, to esteem the higher learning and to distinguish mere phraseology from fact. Such a unity in scientific and cultural accomplishment is attainable when the highest institutions of learning do excellent work, and their immediate influence extends all along the line downward to the elementary schools. It is, therefore, essential that organized labor shall devote its concern not exclusively to the elementary schools of our land but equally to the colleges and universities which so largely influence the education of the people. Great exertions are necessary for the workers to reach the higher degree of education. It is not alone the youth that requires instruction; the adult worker dismissed from the school and transferred to the workshop needs scientific and aesthetic culture. There is required more than the mere opening access to the highest institutions of learning; there is the needed shortening of the day's work for the language of the scientists and of the masses always remains unintelligible to him to whom leisure to learn is not granted. Through the influence of the organized wage earners under the intelligent and forceful direction of the A. F. of L. much progress has been realized on the attainment of those noble ends, and we are no longer lacking in the effort to bring science and beauty as well as elementary and social culture into the lives of the wage earning groups. The last three conventions of the A. F. of L. have vigorously condemned the so-called Lusk educational bills in New York, and called upon organized labor to urge their repeal and to prevent the enactment of similar measures in other states. We are very glad to report the repeal of the Lusk laws by the last session of the New York legislature after a bitter struggle. Now that this poisonous infection has been removed at its source, we may reasonably expect the failure of other scattered efforts to infringe upon the freedom of teachers as citizens through insult and intimidation. But the labor movement in all the states should remain alert. The report upon social studies in the public schools was transmitted to the Executive Council with recommendations. Such parts of the report as are for general information have been released in pamphlet form, and executive action has already been taken upon such parts as are for administrative guidance. As we have covered a rather wide field of thought in our suggestions it will simplify our suggestions to consider them in concise forms as follows: (1) That the A. F. of L. give increasing stress and thought to developing an increasingly constructive program for our public schools. (2) That permanent education committees be provided in organizations affiliated to the A. F. of L. and their component units. (3) That unions and wage earners cooperate actively in the work of adult education as promoted through our Workers' Education Bureau."

(Pp. 245-249) Committee's report was adopted unanimously.

Educational Systems—(1920, pp. 172-462) The essential foundation of our educational institutions should be such as to make all workers and their children feel that society has done as much as lies in its power to remove all needless and artificial obstacles from their path; that there is no barrier except such as exists in the nature of things between themselves and whatever place in the social organization they are fitted to fill; and more than this, that if they have the capacity and industry, a hand is held out to help them along the path they have chosen. Necessarily the education which should precede that of the workshop should be devoted to the body, to the elevation of the moral faculties and the cultivation of the intelligence and especially to imbuing the mind with a broad and clear view of the laws of that natural world with the components of which the wage earners will have to deal. The development of free public schools, colleges and universities has been one of the important and essential results of cooperative action on the part of the A. F. of L. What has been achieved in this direction is impressive and realized best by those who have lived to see the development of these institutions. While a great advance has been made in general education, there is room for improvement by the greater development of industrial science in our educational system, which, unfortunately, up to the present time, has entered into the school curriculum to only a minor degree. Of increasing importance has been the subject of technical education. Nothing should be left undone to promote that kind of education which will have in view the protection of the industrial development of the country to the uttermost limits consistent with the workers' well-being and the general social welfare. The declaration of the convention of the A. F. of L. of June, 1918, upon this subject, bears repetition, and requires: "The insistence that in all courses of study and particularly in industrial and educational courses an unemasculated industrial history must be taught, which would include an accurate account of the organization of the workers and of the results thereof, and should also include a summary of legislation, both state and federal, affecting the industries taught." The 1919 convention reaffirmed this declaration. Unquestionably the highest division of all science is that which considers living beings, not alone as individuals but as aggregates—that which deals with the relation of living beings one to another—the science which observes men—whose experiments are made by nations, one upon another—whose general propositions are embodied in history and industrial development—whose deductions lead to our happiness or misery—and whose verifications so often come too late. Unfortunately, our entire educational policies have not sufficiently embraced a careful and accurate teaching of the great development which has taken place in our industrial growth and in the principles of the trade union movement. If there be a people which has been busy making history on a great scale—and a most profound history—history which, if it happened to be of Greece or Rome we should study with avidity—it is the American people in the making of industrial history. If there be nations whose prosperity depends absolutely and wholly upon the mastery of its people over the forces of nature, upon their intelligent understanding of and obedience of the laws of the production and distribution of wealth and of the stable equilibrium of the forces of society—it is the United States and Canada. No one will gainsay that the development and influence of industry have played a greater, though perhaps not a more prominent part, than the military and political activities in the growth and development of civilization. No factor has contributed or can contribute more to the comfort, well-being, and opportunities of the masses than the industrial growth and activity of the United States and Canada. Yet we find the history of our nation's development confined almost exclusively to the political changes which have influenced their growth. While it is essential that the theories of political movements should be taught, they are insufficient in themselves and must be supplemented by the theories of industrial relations and a true and accurate conception of political economy. The economists of the past, whose teachings still largely dominate in the educational institutions of our time, have taught and are teaching doctrines which have failed to stand the test of experience and of unbiased investigation. Many of the textbooks used, dealing with industrial problems, have failed completely to state accurately and interpret correctly economic laws and their application to our modern industrial society. As a logical sequence the opinions held and views expressed by the great mass of people in our country upon present industrial problems, have been largely influenced by a false philosophy and an erroneous conception of the laws and principles of political economy and industrial relations. Educators, clergymen, and all men in public life, relying upon these works, have failed in many instances to understand the spirit, purpose, and method of the American trade union movement. Because of the inadequacy and inaccuracy of existing textbooks and because of their failure accurately to interpret labor's efforts and activities there has been created a public sentiment and opinion which has been founded more upon error than upon fact. Those who have undertaken to prepare these textbooks have had little real knowledge of the true economic development of industry in our country. It is therefore evident that the A. F. of L. should undertake the preparation of a statement setting forth sound and accurate economic laws, and the principles, aims, ideals, and aspirations, as well as the philosophy and policies governing the organized labor movement, in textbook fashion. While there are a number of good books to be obtained, dealing with economic and industrial questions, which can prove helpful in correcting the false philosophy which has been perpetuated

from generation to generation, these works are widely scattered and not known to the extent they merit. It would therefore be well if a careful survey were made of all such works now on hand, and that a bibliography be prepared and published which might be circulated among all universities, colleges, public libraries and public schools, as well as among all trade union centers, and that all of these institutions ought to be encouraged to secure these volumes so that they may be available for ready reference at any time by those wishing to give an accurate study to the labor problems. The library and records of the A. F. of L. in themselves present a vast amount of accurate information and data relating to industrial development and industrial relations, and particularly to the influence of the trade union movement in the solving of industrail problems. It is a matter of regret that these works have not been more freely used by all students of industrial questions. Had these records been more fully examined, many of the errors now found in textbooks would have been prevented. There is a great need for textbooks upon industrial questions founded upon accurate, reliable data to be used in our educational institutions. The preparation of such textbooks can be best undertaken, however, by those whose training qualifies them for this duty. Unquestionably, however, there is an obligation resting upon the A. F. of L. to prepare a textbook which would contain a full statement of organized labor's position upon all subjects which form a part of its activities. Such a book, in addition to supplying the necessary information to members of the trade union movement, would likewise serve as the authoritative source from which students and educators might secure the essential information from which to compile elementary and more advanced textbooks dealing with industrial problems. While the educational work which the A. F. of L. has already accomplished and which is contained in such an impressive form in the monthly magazine of the A. F. of L., the American Federationist, in the History Encyclopedea and Reference Book recently issued by the A. F. of L. and the numerous trade union publications and pamphlets, special papers and addresses which have been prepared and delivered by the president of the A. F. of L. and others recognized as qualified to speak for the American trade union movement, all dealing with industrial subjects, has been of invaluable assistance, there exists, nevertheless, the urgent need of supplementing this work by a textbook which shall contain reference to labor's activities, in connection with the public school system collective bargaining, child labor, women in industry, hours of labor, minimum wage rates, political action, union shop, initiative and referendum, equal suffrage, convict labor, health, and workmen's compensation, and all other important activities underlying the philosophy and principles and procedure of the American trade union movement. Such a work should, of necessity, be compiled by a competent unionist thoroughly familiarized by actual experience and contact with the work of the trade union movement, in order to insure the accuracy of all information, data, and conclusions set forth in such a work. Attention is also directed to the fact that there is hardly a branch of industry which does not depend, more or less, directly upon some department of physical science which does not involve for its successful pursuit, reasoning from scientific data. Then, too, those in the higher industrial occupations are most commonly 's elected from the general workers who intelligently grasped the modifications based upon science, which are being constantly introduced into industrial processes. It is interesting to reflect upon the trade guilds and their work in the development of instruction of technical arts of manufacture as well as of organization for those actually employed in workshops who desired to extend and improve their knowledge of the theory and practice of their particular avocation and enlighten themselves upon the principles and laws underlying industrial relations, forces, and influences. It would be helpful if all affiliated international trade unions would therefore be urged to respond to the suggestion of encouraging educational tendencies and opportunities by the preparing of a textbook for the assistance and guidance of its journeymen, helpers, and apprentice members. Such textbooks should include not only the history and development of the particular trade or industry represented, but should also undertake to familiarize its members with the trade developments and problems, the history and development of the trade union movement and the importance of trade union activities in the solving of their peculiar industrial problems. Summarized, your committee recommends for favorable consideration: 1. Including in the school curriculum the teaching of an unemasculated industrial history embracing an accurate account of the organization of the workers and of the results thereof, the teaching of the principles underlying industrial activities and relations, and a summary of legislation, state, and federal, affecting industry. 2. The making of a careful and comprehensive survey and the preparation and distribution of a bibliography of all books, pamphlets and addresses dealing witn industrial and economic problems, which are founded on accurate information, sound principles, and which will prove helpful in removing the false conception of existing theories of industrial, political, and social economy. 3. Encouraging all schools, colleges, universities, libraries, trade union centers, and all institutions of learning to secure copies of the books, pamphlets, and addresses recommended, for use by those interested in securing accurate and reliable information regarding industrial problems. 4. Encouraging textbook writers and publishers to avail themselves of the library and the records of the A. F. of L. upon all subjects dealing with the industrial development and progress, as well as the movement of the wage earners, in the preparation of textbooks on industrial problems and movements. 5. The preparation of a textbook by the A. F. of L. to supplement the existing works of President Gompers and other recognized authorities of the American trade union movement, to be prepared by a competent trade unionist under the direction of the executive officers of the A. F. of L. in cooperation with a special committee for this purpose. 6. Encouraging and assisting affiliated international trade unions in the preparing of textbooks for their membership, dealing with economic laws, the development of their trade and the solving of trade problems, as well as the influence of their trade union activities upon the development of industrial relations.

(1921, p. 104) The convention adopted the following program: 1. It is our belief and conviction that the essential studies and textbooks now used in public schools should be investigated and carefully reviewed. This investigation of textbooks and studies should relate to civics, political economy, and history.

2. We recommend that the textbooks and studies used in the various public schools systems should be secured by the A. F. of L.; these textbooks and studies should then be carefully read and analyzed and the faults of omission or commission should be clearly and fairly indicated. There should be no endorsement given to any particular textbook, in order that the A. F. of L.'s action in this matter can not be subject to unfair criticism or its conclusions used for commercial purposes. 3. The cooperation of the American Federation of Teachers is recommended to ascertain the studies and textbooks used by the various public schools systems and for the purpose of securing copies of these studies and textbooks. 4. We recommend the appointment of a permanent committee on education to cooperate with the executive officers of the A. F. of L. in carrying out the work within its proper sphere of activities as recommended and approved by the Montreal convention. In submitting this recommendation it should be clearly understood that this permanent committee should in no way infringe upon the appointive powers, prerogatives and authority of the executive officers and the Executive Council of the A. F. of L.

Education, Board for Vocational— (1920, p. 112) During February and March certain New York newspapers made vicious attacks upon the board for vocational education, which has charge of the rehabilitation of soldiers and which will have charge of the rehabilitation of cripples in industry if the bill passes. Charges of unnecessary delay, discourtesy to the wounded soldiers, and neglect that amounted almost to brutality were made. Congress ordered an investigation of the charges which extended over several weeks, but nothing serious was proven. (P. 462) The convention congratulates the board on its successful meeting of the charges brought against it. The board is performing an exceedingly valuable service in the rehabilitation of soldiers, and should receive hearty cooperation. In this connection we desire to call attention to the work of the board in the rehabilitation of the victims of accidents in industry or elsewhere. The following 11 states have already availed themselves of the provisions of the act: Rhode Island, New York, New Jersey, Pennsylvania, Virginia, Illinois, Minnesota, North Dakota, Nevada, Oregon, and California. The labor movements of the remaining 37 states should see thau the provisions of the act are accepted by early action of their state legislatures. The full benefits of the act can be obtained in practice only by those states which have workmen's compensation laws. The eight states which still lack compensation laws would find themselves economically compelled to enact such laws, soon after accepting the provisions of the federal law.

Education, Boards of—(1923, p. 249) The A. F. of L. desires that representatives of labor in the various communities regard it as part of their public duty to serve on the local boards of education, or on the boards of trustees of municipal and state universities supported by public funds. These institutions were created to serve all the people, and membership on such boards would insure the fulfillment of this original intention. Furthermore, such action is in entire and complete accord with the long and continuous interesc of American labor in the cause of free public education.

Education Bureau, Workers—(1922, pp. 357-362) With the vast increase in the size and power of organized labor, the education of the adult workers has become one of the fundamental demands of the labor movement. Constant progress is achieved through the increasing intelligence of the rank and file of the membership. The worker must know the relation of the industry in which he works, not only to the labor movement, but also to the structure of our modern society. He must be conscious of the spiritual forces which direct and shape the course of the labor movement and inspire the willingness to stand by the movement. Workers' education is the very basis of a permanent and responsible workers' organization; it must be coordinated with the labor movement and therefore should be regarded as an integral part of the trade union itself. To develop this sense of relationship on the part of the individual worker and quicken this feeling of responsibility on the part of the trade union is part of the function of adult workers' education. In addition, it is becoming increasingly apparent that the character of American democracy depends upon the wisdom and understanding of the adult citizens, and that adult education is not to be regarded as a privilege for a few, nor the concern for a short period of early manhood and womanhood, but is an indispensable part of democratic citizenship and should be universal and lifelong. Adult workers' education gives emphatic support to this principle of democratic government. Indeed, as the president of the A. F. of L. has said: "It may very well be that organized labor, which took such an active part in the establishment of popular education in the U. S., will now take the lead in another movement of vital significance to the cultural development of this country." During the past year the educational committee of the A. F. of L., with the sanction and approval of the Executive Council, entered into a cooperative relationship with the Workers' Education Bureau of America for the promotion of workers' education in the trade union movement in this country. The value of that cooperation was undoubted, but it was felt that closer unity should exist in order to give greater strength and added support to this movement. Accordingly, negotiations were entered into looking to closer affiliation. While these negotiations are still pending, it is confidently expected that within a short period of time the arrangements will be completed whereby this vital service can be placed at the disposal of the American labor movement as an organic part of it. The A. F. of L. directs the Executive Council and the permanent educational committee to continue negotiations with the Workers' Education Bureau of America in the interest of the promotion of the comprehensive scheme of adult workers' education. All international and national unions, all state federations of labor and central bodies are urged to appoint educational committees, one of the fundamental functions of these committees to be the furthering of such a program of adult workers' education.

Education, Department of—(1918, p. 322) Executive Council directed to take measures to secure the creation of a department of Education headed by a cabinet officer.

(1920, pp. 105-460) Companion bills were presented in the senate and house providing for a department of education, the secretary to be a member of the cabinet, and to encourage the states in the promotion and support of education. Representatives of the A. F. of L. pointed out to the joint committee on education and labor of the house and senate that education was the surest and best method of Americanizing both the foreigner and the illiterate natives. (P. 460) Indorsed the department of education bill as revised.

(1921, p. 118) The department of education bill was amended by the addition of the following to section 14: "Provided, that courses of study, plans, and methods for carrying out the purposes and provisions of this act within a state shall be determined by the state and local educational authorities of said state, and this act shall not be construed to require uniformity of courses of study, plans and methods in the several states in order to secure the benefits herein provided." In explanation of this amendment the committee on education reported: "It is thought that this language will more clearly and completely state the purpose and intent of the proviso than the original language used. It was not the purpose of the bill to give the general government power to determine courses of study, or to provide that particular plans and methods of carrying out the purposes and provisons of the bill were to be adopted as a requirement for receiving the appropriations provided. Neither was it intended that any dictation or interference with the public or private school management of any state should be authorized or sanctioned. It is thought that to more clearly negative any such inference in that regard the amendment is justified." The bill passed the house but failed in the senate. It was reintroducee in the 67th congress.

(1922, p. 112) No progress has been made in the creation of a department of education.

Education for All—(1921, pp. 106-324) The 1920 convention (p. 470) directed the Executive Council to compile and publish in pamphlet form the official progressive declarations of the A. F. of L. on the subject of education. The compilation has been made and has been submitted to the permanent committee on education and will be issued in pamphlet form and given wide and general circulation.

(1922, pp. 66-357) The A. F. of L. prepared a pamphlet entitled "Education for All," which is a compilation of the official declarations of the labor movement on education, "in order to make easily available labor's position on education and to add to the effectiveness of labor's contribution to educational progress."

Education, "Open Shop"—(1921, pp. 105-326) An apparently well-organized and systematic campaign has been undertaken by the National Association of Manufacturers to conduct a propaganda in the schools of the country in furtherance of the so-called "open shop." Nothing has been left undone by these interests to mislead the minds of the teachers and students and to prejudice them against the best interests of the workers. Letters and pamphlets have been sent to teachers of economics in the colleges, universities and schools by the manufacturers' associations, supplemented by textbooks containing subjects for debate, all of which are intended to prejudice and mislead those attending our schools and to inculcate the spirit of hostility to the labor movement. This propaganda of prejudice unduly to influence the educational systems of our country has reacted to a large extent upon its promoters. Many letters have been received from students in the colleges, schools, and universities asking for labor's side of this industrial controversy, and every possible effort has been made to correct the erroneous impression that had been created. Students as well as teachers have been furnished with accurate information relating to the industrial questions and every possible assistance has been given them in their studies of economic and industrial problems and principles. Inasmuch as the manufacturers have carried on their campaign for the teaching of false doctrines and erroneous economic principles to such an extent and in such a subtle and plausible form, the A. F. of L. will have prepared pamphlets and literature bearing upon these subjects for distribution to the colleges, universities, and schools. By that method the students as well as the teachers will become fully familiar with the principles underlying the hopes and aspirations of the American workers, and understand that the work of the American labor movement is not confined to the interests of the workers alone, but that its work embraces the improvement and uplift of all our people.

Education of Adult Illiterates—(1919, p.115) A bill presented in congress, providing in substance that the commissioner of education under direction of the secretary of the interior shall devise efficient economic methods for teaching adult illiterates and men and women of meager education in the United States, promote plans for the elimination of illiteracy, and the extension of education among the adult population, and cooperate with state, county, district, and municipal education officers and others in such work was endorsed. (P. 317) The people of the country are realizing now as never before that a democracy must depend primarily upon an educated citizenship for its very life, and that the nation as a whole is under even deeper obligation to the schools than is any section of the nation. In recognition of that fact, the educational bill provides for a federal department of education with a secretary in the president's cabinet, and assigns to the federal government a small proportion of the total cost of our public school system. But recognizing with equal force the value of local initiative and experimentation within the various states, which is an essential part of the genius of our American institutions, the bill safeguards local autonomy, providing that all the educational facilities encouraged by its provisions shall be organized, supervised, and administered exclusively by the legally constituted state and local educational authorities within the several states. We call attention to the effective coordination under one broad agency in a comprehensive measure of all federal educational activities, including Americanization, removal of illiteracy, and physical education, as contrasted with piecemeal, separate treatment of those closely connected subjects.

Education, Part-Time—(1920, p. 469) Model part-time education law for states approved by the 1918 convention reaffirmed. However, even in some of the states which have provided effective legislation, there is an unfortunate tendency to neglect the continuation schools, particularly in the matter of equipment, and too often in the training of teachers. The state of New York has set an example for the country in providing $2,000 scholarships to enable journeymen who have acquired through practical experience the craftsmanship of a trade, to gain through work in normal schools the craftsmanship of teaching.

Education, Physical—(1922, p. 111) H. R. 22, providing for the promotion of physical education through the cooperation by the government with the states, met with very little consideration by the committee on education of the house. The object of the bill is commendable, and with some amendments would make a most desirable law.

Education, Safety for Pupils—(1921, p. 327) The rapid deterioration of school buildings throughout the country, and the use of the deplorable make-shifts for adequate housing for school children, causes this convention to urge organized labor to demand in all communities high standards of cleanliness, attractiveness, sanitation, and safety from fire in all school buildings. And furthermore that building programs be immediately undertaken to remedy the acute congestion caused by the serious shortage of school buildings. The public school must be maintained as a civic model, not permitted to become a symbol of degradation.

Education, Secondary and Collegiate—(1922, pp. 66-357) An invitation was received by the A. F. of L. to send a representative to the session of the commission of collegiate schools of business on correlation of secondary and collegiate education. The sessions disclosed that the commission was thoroughly stirred by such revelations as the fact that of the first 150 freshmen registered in the school of commerce and administration of the University of Chicago in the fall of 1920, 32 per cent had taken no ancient history, 56.66 per cent no medieval history, 59.33 per cent no modern history, 24 per cent no United States history, 86 per cent no English history, 92 per cent no industrial history, 39.33 per cent no civics, 72.66 per cent no economics and 98 per cent no sociology. The freshmen on the average had taken only two and one half years of work in the whole field of social study, and this chiefly history. And what history? About one-quarter had taken no U. S. history, and another quarter only one-half year. As much work had been done in ancient history as in the history of their own country. As preparation for functioning in our industrial society, only one-twelfth had taken any industrial history. Six-tenths offered one-half year's work in civics, one quarter a half year's work in economics, and one-fiftieth a half year of sociology. Similar investigations in the other divisions of the same university showed that the above data were typical of the institution. And in view of the wide geographical distribution of the student body of the University of Chicago, it seems fair to assume that the alarming condition shown applies to our country as a whole. The full significance of this situation can better be appreciated when it is remembered that even the pitiful two and one-half years, on the average, of alleged social studies are mainly offered in the upper years of high school, and are therefore available only to the small proportion of our prospective citizens who complete their high school course. The commission was concerned not nearly so much with the handicap that condition placed on their work in the universities as with the realization that our elementary and secondary schools are so lamentably failing to give to the great bulk of our prospective citizens, whom the colleges would never touch, preparation for social living. The spirit and objectives of the commission are well shown in its declaration that "the organization of social studies in the public schools should be in terms of the purpose of introducing those studies. Their purpose is that of giving our youth an awareness of what it means to live together in organized society, an appreciation of how we do live together, and an understanding of the conditions precedent to living together well, to the end that our youth may develop those ideals, abilities, and tendencies to act which are essential to effective participation in our society. The range of this statement is very broad. For example: the contribution of knowledge and physical environment to our social living are quite as worthy of attention as are the principles of economics or government." Education ought to enable wage earners to get a proper perspective of their relation to society and of mutual obligations. Industry and industrial relations have social implications. The wider the information and education of industrial workers the better equipped they will be to form sound judgments on industrial problems. Discipline in hard thinking and scientific training are a protection against sophistry. Education is a means to better workmanship and better citizenship, as well as to higher manhood. It will tend in freeing the wills of men from the domination of material things and will disclose the ways by which creative intelligence can make material wealth serve the spirit. During the past year the workers' education bureau has urged a cooperative relationship with the committee on education of the A. F. of L. for the purpose of promoting the education and educational facilities of the adult workers. A temporary arrangement was entered pending further conferences to determine if the workers' education bureau can be so reorganized as to warrant the A. F. of L. giving this organization the support and cooperation of the committee on education. As at present constituted this organization can not merit the full support of the A. F. of L. It is, therefore, recommended that in the event the present efforts to overcome existing obstacles fail that the committee on education under the direction of the Executive Council and the president of the A. F.of L., undertake to promote this work under such other arrangements as will serve best the purpose of promoting the education and educational facilities of the adult workers. (P. 357) Special attention is called to the facts here given showing the lamentable inadequacy of the preparation for social living which the schools now afford the great mass of our prospective citizens.

Education, Special Committee On— (1921, pp. 105-324) Made permanent the special committe on education authorized by the 1920 convention which had been directed to cooperate in studying the possibility of coordinating the present educational institutions and activities conducted under the auspices of organized labor; to investigate the strength of the demand for a central labor university which may be developed among the affiliated national unions; to consider the matter of extension courses and scholarships which would make facilities of such an institution of widest service and to consider the practical questions of administration and finance.

Education, Threat to Public (1922, p. 366) In recent years there have been well-authenticated reports that selfish interests are seeking to use the public schools for propaganda purposes, are attempting to censor the utterances of teachers and are undermining the dignity and independence of the teaching profession. Such activities, if the reports are true, strike at the very heart of successful democracy, and tend to tear down the usefulness of the structure of public education which the members of organized labor, in common with other public-spirited citizens, have striven to build up. The trade union movement in the United States has always taken a vital interest in public education and has in many instances throughout the past century been responsible for the extension and strengthening of the educational systems of the country. Prof. F. T. Carlton declares

("Economic Influences upon Educational Progress in the United States, 1820-50," Bulletin of the University of Wisconsin—Vol. IV, 1908): "The vitality of the movement for tax supported schools was derived not from the humanitarian leaders, but from the growing class of wage earners." Not, therefore, chiefly because the reactionary propaganda in question may tend to injure the immediate interests of working men and women, but rather because organized labor is proud of its record as one of the original sponsors of universal public education, and sees the importance to the nation of keeping the wells of truth undefiled, it was found necessary to investigate the truth of these reports, the extent of the damage done, and to inquire in what ways the trade unions may cooperate in the effort to give the youth of the country free and unfettered education which will enable them to cope with the problems of the future.

An obvious and unmistakable danger is that of legislation such as was embodied in the so-called "Lusk Laws" of New York, and is being sought elsewhere. Such legislation, ostensibly directed against "radicalism," requires teachers to take a special oath of allegiance to the constitution of the U. S. and of the state in question, and specifies that a teacher may be dismissed for deficiencies in character or for "disloyalty." "Loyalty tests" are in some cases provided, and espionage is encouraged so that "disloyal" teachers may be reported to the educational authorities. The trade union movement does not expect any teacher to be disloyal to the principle of constitutional government, and it does not believe there is the lightest danger that public school teachers will preach treason or incite to riot, or in any other way abet the forcible overturn of democratic government. To suppose that special laws, not applying to other citizens, are needed to restrain them from doing so is an insult to the teaching profession, and is, in fact, so absurd that we can not but believe the instigators of such legislation had other objects in mind than their announced purpose. And, in fact, the praccal result of such laws is to endanger the independence of teachers in dealing with social problems. Exactly what is "disloyalty" and who is to be the judge? Is it "disloyal" to discuss possible constitutional changes in our form of government? Many narrow-minded politicians would call it so. Is it "disloyal" to tell the truth about vested interests in industry, or to explain the justification of a strike? Many chambers of commerce would call it so. Such laws are not needed to prevent the encouragement of violent revolution, but they do make it possible to prohibit any discussion which does not sanctify the status quo. They open the door to all reactionary powers, which can use them to introduce fear and compulsion into public school teaching, to encourage petty administrative tyranny and espionage and to discourage any form of instruction which might offend the temporarily ruling political machine or commercial interest. Another manifestation of the attempt to restrict public school teaching, which is both manacing and undeniable, is the array of scattered cases throughout the country where teachers or other educational authorities have actually been dismissed or suspended for holding views distasteful to chambers of commerce, security leagues, and the like, or even for joining teachers' unions. There are numerous such cases, which we have canvassed, but which we can not review here in any detail. But, after all, comparatively few states have as yet passed the so-called "loyalty" educational laws, and the number of teachers who have been dismissed or threatened with dismissal on account of their views is small in comparison with the total number. These are important only as extreme symptoms of what is going on elsewhere, in a more unnoticeable and subtle, but nevertheless pervasive and dangerous, way. "These suppressive tendencies," Prof. John Dewey, the noted educational authority, was recently quoted as saying in a public address, "work in a more refined way than laws. The great body of teachers are unaware of their existence. They are felt only through little hints about 'safety,' 'sanity' and 'sobriety,' coming from influential sources. The Lusk laws indicate what can be found all over the country—an attempt to exercise by subtle at times unconscious, movements a restrictive influence upon the teaching body. It is something more than academic freedom that is being menaced. It is moral freedom, the right to think, to imagine. It involves, when it is crushed, a crushing of all that is best in the way of inspiration and ideals for a better order. Our schools are thus facing the greatest crisis they ever faced. Unless they come through it safely, it will be hard, impossible, to get the desired high-mind teachers into the schools. It is not safe to put the education of the young into the hands of a body of officials with coercive powers. They will attempt to shape the minds in conformity with their beliefs. The teachers can prepare the minds for considering the problems of our day so that a better society may be attained only through an awakening of the public." The A. F. of L. reaffirms its traditional position, and recommends that organized labor make every effort to secure the repeal of measures of the type of the "Lusk laws" wherever they have been enacted. (P. 368) Reaffirmed delaration No. 22 adopted by the 1919 convention.

Education, Uniformity in—(1921, p. 419) For the purpose of securing more uniformity of plans for general education and labor legislation and interchange of such information between the various state bodies, the secretary of the A. F. of L. is directed to communicate with the secretaries of all state federations of labor and request that they mail to all other state federations of labor a complete statement of their legislative and educational plans, together with a statement of the results being obtained; also per capita tax being paid by affiliated unions; also stating whether their federation owns and operates labor paper and printing plants, and if not, what methods are being employed to secure publicity for activities and accomplishments of their body.

Education, Vocational—(1920, p. 467) The A. F. of L. again urges upon state federations of labor the necessity for providing, preferably through state legislation, for the appointment of advisory committees to advise with state boards for vocational education and local boards of education in the administration of vocational education, and that these advisory committees include representatives of employers, employes, and the public schools.

Efficiency Bureau—(1922, pp. 106-485) Executive Council, in cooperation with affiliated organizations of government employes, is directed to endeavor to bring about a more satisfactory administration of the United States bureau of efficiency and, if it develops this course is impracticable, then appropriate action be taken to abolish the bureau of efficiency in the interest of greater efficiency in government service.

Efficiency Systems—(1919, p. 121) Through the influence of the A. F. of L. naval appropriation bills have contained a provision which enemies of labor have repeatedly endeavored to have stricken out. It is: "That no part of the appropriations made in this act shall be available for the salary or pay of any officer, manager, superintendent, foreman, or other person having charge of the work of any employe of the United States government while making or causing to be made with a stop watch or other time-measuring device a time study of any job of any such employe between the starting and completion thereof, or of the movements of any such employe while engaged upon such work; nor shall any part of the appropriations made in this act be available to pay any premiums or bonus or cash reward to any employe in addition to his regular wages, except for suggestions resulting in improvements or economy in the operation of any government plant."

(1923, p. 295) In some government establishments, notably the postal service and the bureau of engraving and printing, there have been instituted obnoxious practices, under the guise of "efficiency systems," which are harmful to the workers, and therefore injurious to the service. These "efficiency systems" are devised by so-called experts who have little or no understanding of the practical work over which they assume jurisdiction. Experience has demonstrated in all lines of endeavor that any method of "speeding up" workers beyond their endurance is disastrous to both employer and worker and, particularly, such a policy has no place in government employment, where service and not profit is the motive. The Executive Council is directed to lend every effort in eliminating from government employment these dehumanizing practices which are so harmful to the workers and to the public service. The labor movement, and particularly the affiliated government employes, favor efficient and economical administration in federal activities and prudent expenditure of public funds for labor costs. There is no place in government employment—nor in private employment either—for so-called "efficiency systems,"; designed to speed and harass the worker beyond normal capacity. Copies of these declarations shall be sent to the president of the U. S. and the secretary of the Treasury.

Eight-Hour Law Violators—(1923, p. 304) The federal eight-hour law, enacted in 1868 and amended several times since that date, has been narrowly interpreted and its application confined to but few contracts let by the U. S. government. It was the intention of this law and subsequent amendments to apply to all work done or to be done and all contracts let by the United States government. The officers of the A. F. of L. are hereby directed to cause the present law to be amended, providing for a more general application of the law to contracts let by the United States government.

Elections, Prepare for—(1920, p. 464) We recommend that all trade unionists, whether men or women, where woman suffrage obtains in any degree, be urged to enfranchise themselves by registration, payment of poll tax wherever that out-worn requirement has not yet been repealed, and the meeting of any other required qualification.

Employment Agencies—(1919, p. 428) It is urgently necessary that we guard against unfair treatment by private employment agencies, but the ultimate solution of the private employment agency problem must be the substitution for such agencies of a public employment system with properly coordinated federal, state and local agencies.

Employment Permanent, Government —(1919, p. 391) Refused to declare that civil service should be so extended as to guarantee to all officials and employes of a rank lower than cabinet officers, permanent tenure during efficient service. The adoption of such a law would transfer our government from the representative republican form of government to the bureaucratic form, to which it is opposed. If we continue our present form of government it seems but reasonable that those who are responsible as members of the cabinet should have the right to surround themselves by those of their own selection. Nothing would create a more impossible condition than the election of truly progressive representatives and then to find that the members of the cabinet of that government did not have it in their power to choose their own immediate assistants and representatives. Bear in mind that the adoption of this resolution would approve the establishment of a bureaucratic form of government, such a form of government as would make it absolutely impossible for a cabinet to function successfully. We are opposed to anything tending to fasten upon the American people a bureaucratic form of government.

Employment Service, U. S.—(1919, p. 281) Indorsed bill for the continuation of the United States free employment service. Immediate relief was urged pending the enactment of permanent legislation.

(1920, p. 422) Congress has made no statutory provision for the establishment of a federal employment service, and the present service exists only through appropriation of meager sums secured with difficulty from year to year. The uncertainty of its continued existence renders impossible its full efficiency and adequate development. The A. F. of L. urges Congress immediately to enact the necessary legislation to establish the U. S. employment service as a permanent bureau in the department of labor, with ample appropriation.

(1921, pp. 113-374) The determination of congress to eliminate entirely the United States free employment service was not wholly successful. While it has been reduced to only a skeleton organization because of the refusal of congress to appropriate sufficient funds for its proper functioning the last session appropriated $225,000 for its use. Every effort should be used in the sixty-seventh congress to have a sufficient appropriation made to permit the U. S. employment service to be a benefit to the great army of unemployed of our country. The motive behind the attempt to destroy the service was believed to be political.

(1922, pp. 107-325) Many obstacles have been met in order to secure sufficient appropriations for the proper functioning of the U. S. employment service. After the most active efforts of the legislative representatives of the A. F. of L. an amendment was made in the senate to the deficiency appropriation bill in December which provided for $100,000 for the service. When the bill went to conference the house conferees declared the amendment would have to be stricken out or they would permit the bill to die. Labor insisted that the senate stand by its amendment. Senator Curtis, however, informed the director general of the employment service that the deficiency bill would have to be passed by December 15 and that it would be impossible to amend it before. He contended that as the deficiency bill contained a large appropriation for hospitals for veterans, if a filibuster for the appropriation for the employment service were started, it would endanger the entire appropriation bill. The director general, therefore, withdrew his request for a larger appropriation on the promise that an effort would be made to have the $100,000 appropriated early in January. When H. R. 9458, providing for the relief of the starving people of Russia, was under consideration Senator Ashurst offered a rider appropriating $100,000 for the employment service. This was approved by the senate. When the bill reached the joint conference committee the $100,000 was stricken out and later on the senate concurred in the action. Persistent efforts were continued and when the appropriation bill for the department of labor was passed March 17, 1922, it contained a provision for $225,000 for the employment service.

English Language—(1919, p. 429) Organized labor should continue to do its utmost to secure the universal use of the English language. But to endeavor to have congress to enact a law compelling all societies, fraternal, insurance and others, secret or otherwise, to use the English language, is not only of doubtful advisability but would be clearly unconstitutional.

Equal Rights—(1922, p. 476) The enactment of laws granting the right of suffrage to women does not carry with it in all states all other political rights, and there are on the statute books various laws discriminating against women as to property rights, guardianship rights, naturalization rights and other rights now guaranteed to men. The A. F. of L. hereby declares itself in favor of the removal of all discriminations against women and advocate specific laws to this end. We disapprove and oppose the blanket legislation for this purpose because such legislation is necessarily drawn in general terms which must be subject to judicial construction and therefore place in jeopardy labor laws for women.

(1923, p. 363) Agitation for an "equal rights" constitutional amendment is now being carried on before the several state legislatures. Members of organized labor are urged to vigorously oppose the approval of this objectionable amendment by their respective state legislatures.

Executive Council, Consideration for— (1920, p. 394) We caution the delegates and national and international officers to show more consideration for the Executive Council by settling petty disputes and minor grievances without bringing them as additional burdens to the men whose time is so generously and unstintingly given to the service of the workers. We realize, as this convention must, that the Executive Council does not shirk or evade any of the responsibilities laid upon it, or tasks set before it by the convention, but we also realize that these men are human, and that there is a limit to human capacity for work. The great movement in the direction of a shorter workday is entirely forgotten, apparently, when it comes to referring matters to the Executive Council.

(1922, p. 480) The amount of work laid upon the Executive Council of the A. F. of L. as a result of convention action, and because of the progress of events in the interim between conventions, has grown to enormous proportions. An examination of the report of the Executive Council as a whole will discose the magnitude of its operations and the sequence of its activities, and must impress the careful reader with the thought that the members of the Executive Council are required to put forth such zeal and energy as almost stamps them as supermen. Those who have had dealings, officially or informally, with the officers of the A. F. of L., and with the Executive Council as such are well aware of the unfailing promptness and courtesy with which all requests for assistance in any form are met, as well as the efforts that are put forth to bring together representatives of organizations that are standing apart. The value of such services to the A. F. of L. and its constituent organizations, and through them to the world, is beyond estimation in price. In calling attention to this view of the activities and employment of the officers, and the Executive Council of the A. F. of L., we also desire to call the attention of the delegates to a matter which in the past frequently it has presented to the convention; that is, that a great many cases are brought here for adjudication which well might be disposed of by the parties at interest without troubling the convention. Another tendency that has been noted and which is deplorable is that which leads the convention to refer to the Executive Council many matters that properly should be settled by the delegates. It is not expected that at any time injustice should be done or the door of appeal closed to any, yet it is but fair to all that matters which might be as well disposed of by the convention should be disposed of by the convention and not be sent by reference to the Executive Council, to further burden an already overloaded docket.

Executive Council Report—(1920, p. 422) It is the sense of this convention that the reports of the Executive Council be prepared in ample time to enable the secretary to mail one copy to the address of each delegate whose duplicate credential has been received by the secretary, said copy to be mailed ten days previous to the convening of the convention; delegates failing to present their duplicate credentials within the time that will permit of the secretary conforming to this change, then they to receive their copy of the report at the convention.

Farmers and Labor—(1920, p. 209) It has been the custom of the A. F. of L. to secure cooperation from the organized farmers and to extend cooperation to them in all matter mutually affecting farmers and wage earners. This policy is based upon instructions of long standing given by a vote of the A. F. of L. in conventions. During the year just closed there was increasing harmonious relations with organized farmers, and an increasing understanding of their mutual interest in the great problems confronting the nation. There has been a keen realization among both farmers and wage earners of the fact that they suffer alike from the malpractices, the profiteers and gamblers, and from maladjustments of the machinery by which necessities of life are distributed. They also have a growing appreciation of the fact that farmers, no less than wage earners, suffer from the incompetence of political representatives, and from the unwillingness of those representatives to carry out in their work the wishes of the great masses of the people. During the year representatives of organized farmers have participated with the representatives of organized wage workers in conferences dealing with some of the most vital questions of the year, and with most gratifying results. (P. 393) The Executive Council is directed to continue the development of friendly, harmonious and cooperative relations with the great bona fide body of organized farmers. We take cognizance of the similarity of the position of the farmers and wage workers in their relation to and suffering from the malpractice of profiteers and gamblers.

(1921, pp. 129-308) Under instructions of long standing the Executive Council has pursued a policy of developing cooperation between the trade union movement and the organized farmers on questions of mutual interest. Despite the difficulties in the way of complete accord between the trade union movement and all of the organizations of farmers, due to differences of opinion and policy among the various organizations of farmers, we feel that material progress has been made during the year and we are confident that the prospects for the future are better. It has been possible on a number of occasions during the year to cooperate on important matters with organizations representing the farmers and we feel that this has been to the mutual advantage of the farmers and the workers. The Executive Council is directed to continue the policy that thus far has brought most excellent results. (P. 326) The A. F of L. denounces the intention of the profiteering conspirators to abolish the department of agriculture and pledges its support and that of its 4,500,000 members in any action the farmers may take to protect themselves and their families from their economic foes. The Executive Council is hereby directed to use its utmost endeavors to defeat any measure that may be now before congress or that may be hereafter introduced for the purpose of weakening or destroying the various bureaus of the department of agriculture or the department itself and that the council is instructed to use every proper effort to bring about the strengthening of the department to the end that its great service may be broadened and increased in the interests of the welfare of the farmers and the people of our country. (P. 367) Telegram received from President of Texas Farmers' League: "I feel I am warranted in expressing to you the gratitude of the farmers for the kind words and interest expressed for them by your delegates. It is the hope of the farmer that the day is near at hand when a coalition may be formed between those who toil in the factory and field."

(1922, p. 112) Many bills in the interest of the farmers have been introduced in congress and the representatives of the A. F. of L. have used every effort to have them passed. The interests of Labor and the farmers are so intertwined that when one suffers from bad legislation the other also is affected. It was this knowledge that prompted the representatives of the A. F. of L. to carefully scan every piece of legislation introduced in the interests of the farmers. Every opportunity was used to urge upon congress the necessity for legislation that would encourage the farming industry. (P. 329) The drawing together of the farmers and the organized wage earners these two large groups with so many political and economic contacts, is a portent of larger legislative accomplishments in the future. We recommend a continuance of this policy of cooperating with representatives of the farmers in behalf of legislative measures of mutual interest. (Pp. 112-359) The farmers' cooperative marketing law authorizing the farmers to form associations for collective marketing with immunity from prosecution under the Sherman anti-trust law has been passed. This bill was supported by the A. F. of L.

(1922, pp. 101-479) Through the good work done by Representative John I. Nolan, of California, the scheme of the reactionaries in the house to appropriate money for the department of justice to prosecute (or rather persecute) labor and the farmers under the "anti-trust" act was defeated. For the first time in many years the committee on this appropriation had reported the measure to the house without the clause exempting labor and the farmers from prosecution. Representative Johnson, of Kentucky, submitted an amendment to overcome this intentional oversight. It was a substitute to an amendment made by Representative Denison, of Illinois, which prohibited any of the money. being used to secure injunctions against labor Representative Johnson's substitute was adopted, but when a vote was taken to make it a part of the amendment it was defeated by a viva voce vote. Representatives Johnson and Nolan used every effort to have the substitute adopted, but it failed by a vote of 68 ayes and 175 nays. Representative Mondell had led the fight for the committee, charging that it would be a reflection upon the department of justice to adopt the substitute or amendment. By some parliamentary jugglery the latter had not even been voted on. This aroused Representative Nolan, who declared: "Long before I came to congress, and that was some nine years ago, there was carried in the appropriation bill appropriating money for the department of justice an exemption prohibiting the use of the funds of the department of justice from prosecuting labor organizations and farm organizations under the provisions of the anti-trust law. In 1914, the sixty-third congress passed the Clayton act, amending the Sherman anti-trust law. The appropriations committee of the house at that time did not see fit to wipe out that proviso, and it has been carried in every appropriation bill from that day to this. And it has not been considered a reflection upon preceding attorney generals of the department of justice. And I take issue with the statement of the gentleman from Wyoming that it must be so considered by the widest stretch of the imagination to be a reflection upon the present attorney general or the administration of the department of justice. Let us see what the facts are. Some two years ago the gentleman from Ohio (Mr. Fess) succeeded in committee in having this provision stricken out. I succeeded in getting a roll call in the house proper, and by an overwhelming vote the house defeated the amendment of the gentleman from Ohio (Mr. Fess) and reinstated the very provision that was offered by the gentleman from Kentucky (Mr. Johnson) today. Now, if it is true that after the passage of the Clayton act we continued it, why could we not continue it now after the passage of the Capper-Volstead bill? What assurance have we that the farmer is any more secure under the Capper-Volstead act than the laborer was under the Clayton act?" This scathing rebuke by Representative Nolan had its effect. On April 10 Representative Johnson reintroduced his substitute prohibiting the use of any part of the money appropriated for the prosecution of Labor and the farmers and it was adopted by a vote of 102 yeas to 56 nays. An effort was made to make a record vote, but this failed. (P. 138) During the past year

many conferences have been held by the officials of the A. F. of L. with representatives of the various farmer organizations. These have proved of value as it has given each an opportunity to explain its attitude toward various important questions to be solved. Every opportunity has been taken to impress upon the farmers that labor is interested in their welfare. Whatever injuries the farmer, injures labor and vice versa. The anti-labor publicity agents, however, have gained entrance to the columns of some of the farm journals and they have sought to create friction that would drive a wedge between labor and the farmers. In the president's unemployment conference the farmers voted with labor on all matters directly bearing upon labor movements. The Executive Council is hereby authorized and directed to continue to do what it can in furtherance of such educational work as will acquaint the farmers with the issues that not only affect the wage earners, but the farmers as well.

(1923, pp. 63-324) The efforts of certain interests to drive a wedge between labor and the farmers have not been successful. The most friendly relations exist between the officials of the farmers' organizations and of the A. F. of L. The rank and file of the farmers through the officials of their various organizations are rapidly learning the fact that those who would create enmity between labor and the farmers are their most bitter enemies. Here and there newspapers published in the interest of the farmers are taking a greater interest in labor affairs and are exceedingly active in placing labor's cause before the people. At the same time those farm papers that have usually kept up a continuous denunciation of labor are not so condemnatory as heretofore. Like the daily newspapers farm papers to exist must obtain advertising, and their advertisers in many instances are antagonists of organized labor. To curry favor with such advertisers the farm papers take an anti-labor stand. The publicity bureau of the A. F. of L. should send its "Labor Information" to all the farm papers in the country. Some may use selections from it and those who do not may obtain information heretofore unknown to them. There is no doubt that the earnest efforts that have been made to bring about more friendly relations between labor and the farmers by the A. F. of L. has been of incalculable good and should be continued.

Fascisti Movement—(1923, p. 66) We shall not undertake to deal with the fascisti movement as it has developed and come into power in Italy. We are fully aware of the complexities that surround the situation in Italy and we are not unmindful of the fact that it was largely the threat of one autocracy that helped produce another. We can, however, record our keen disappointment in any gain made by any autocratic movement anywhere. Autocracy can never succeed anywhere except by force and what the world needs most of all is the organization of industrial power and the abandonment of military force. Expenditure of force saps the life blood of industry. What is of immediate concern to us is the effort to organize fascisti groups in the U. S. We denounce this effort as a token of hostility to our democratic institutions and particularly to our American trade union movement. Promotion by a foreign power of a hostile movement on our soil can not be lightly regarded by our movement or by our people in general. No disclaimers from abroad can alter the character of the fascisti nor change the fact that the offspring in America must partake of the nature and purpose of the parent body in Italy. We call upon workers of foreign birth to refrain from joining the fascisti or any similar movement in our country. Foreign workers who come to our shores in good faith come because America offers freedom and opportunity for the individual. To then promote an organization hostile to every institution of American freedom is to trespass on every principle of honesty and to be guilty of conduct which can not be condoned. The Fascisti can not exist in America without the membership and support of workers who have come to America from the birthplace of fascism. There must be no fascisti in our republic and it is the duty of American trade unionism to use every honorable effort to purge the country of this offshoot of European turmoil. Those who can not come to America prepared to find expression for their opinions and requirements through the orderly methods brought into being at such great cost through the establishment of free democratic government are ill-prepared to come at all. The inevitable result of continuance of such efforts as that represented by the organization of fascisti groups in America can lead only to a more determined resolve to bar the doors more tightly to those who abuse the freedom and the institutions of our country. (P. 271) That this movement should find root for growth among our foreign-born people is not surprising. With the advocates of soviet Russia premeating many of the channels of American life, ever conniving to advance the interests of a foreign power among us, it is but an open invitation for like procedures being followed by other powers and influences in other nations. These menacing influences and pernicious practices of both soviet Russia and fascisti Italy within our land are equally subject to condemnation. (P. 272) The A. F. of L. denounces in immeasurable terms the establishment of any form of tyranny either in Italy or any other country under whatsoever name it may be launched; that we protest against any movement having for its purpose the imposition of tyranny or autocracy in America.

Federal Employes' Rights—(1920, p. 480) It is a widely accepted principle that the government as an employer should on its own account and as an example take the lead in establishing just and practical conditions of employment. Under existing conditions there is a notable absence in government employment of any well defined labor policy or any conceded rights or privileges on which the employes may rely as a basis of action. During recent years there are but few rights presumed to be enjoyed by civil service employes that have not been either openly challenged or painfully restricted by one department regulation after another, and a determined effort has been made to deny the right of effective organization and to suspend the right of petition. The industrial conference called by the president after extended investigation and in addressing itself to this subject says: "It is desirable that the utmost liberty of action should be accorded government employes, wholly consistent, however, with the obligations they are under to the state. No objections should be interposed to their associations for mtual protection, the advancement of their interests and the presentation of grievances." This question is of such importance in its effect upon the welfare of the employes and the service as to merit the serious consideration

of political parties and party candidates in the presidential election, now full upon us. Therefore the Executive Council is hereby requested to take such action as it deems practical in bringing the question of government employment to the attention of party leaders and presidential candidates, with a view to emphasizing the urgent need of timely reforms and with the hope of securing some reassuring and definite declaration regarding the rights and privileges of government employes.

Federal Reserve System—(1921, p. 382) There are about 20,000,000 depositors in all the banks which are members of the federal reserve system, and the total deposits of these 20,000,000 Americans aggregate nearly $16,000,000,000. Through the present methods of the federal reserve system, under the present federal reserve board, this money is being used against the best interests of the American people and being largely devoted to the service of the financial and speculative interests, which are exploiting the American people, and hundreds of millions of dollars have been loaned by federal reserve banks to speculative interests and for speculative purposes in New York at interest rates as high as 20 per cent per annum, and often at 30 to 80 per cent, although these member banks secured the people's deposits at 6 per cent. The A. F. of L. demands the prompt enactment by congress of legislation to limit the spread between the rate at which member banks of the federal reserve system secure money and the rate which they are permitted to charge for the use thereof to a percentage to be fixed by congress and not to exceed 1½ per cent; and further demands legislation to prohibit members of the federal reserve system from loaning money for speculative and non-essential purposes, and advocates the prompt creation of a personal rural credit system to help place agriculture, which has suffered a most serious blow through the unnecessary reduction in prices which farmers receive for their products, on a sound basis.

Federal Trade Commission—(1919, p. 469) We the delegates to the A. F. of L. convention affirm our confidence in the federal trade commission and urge that existing vacancies be filled by men of the type of those now serving, whose efforts in exposing the selfish and vicious practices of many of the large corporations of this country have done much to reassure the people that the farmer, wage earners and all consumers are to have a square deal.

(1921, p. 325) The exhaustive expert investigations and constructive work of the federal trade commission have made it outstanding as one of the most valuable activities under government auspices. The sources and nature of the various attacks upon the commission are convincing supplementary proof of the searching character of its studies and of the effectiveness of the remedies it provides.

(1923, p. 275) More recently we find that the federal trade commission, charged with the guiding and administering of the Sherman anti-trust law and the Clayton law, has demonstrated its unfitness to perform the functions delegated to it. Its activities have resulted in no tangible results in so far as large and influential capitalistic combinations are concerned. Indeed, these are thriving more than ever. We do find, however, that the federal trade commission is venturing into a field never intended for it and that it is trespassing upon the relation-

ship between employers and organized workers
in assuming the right and jurisdiction of
passing judgment upon labor contracts, and
which contracts are specifically exempted
under the labor provisions of the Clayton
law. Thus there is developing another sort
of industrial court bent upon destroying the
proper development of and functioning by the
trade union movement.

Federated Press—(1922, p. 362) Executive Council authorized to have an investigation made of the reportorial and news policy
of the Federated Press with the purpose of
learning its accuracy and fairness in the
presentation of labor news.

(1923, p. 130) The Cincinnati convention
authorized the Executive Council to have an
investigation made of the reportorial and news
policy of the Federated Press. The president
of the A. F. of L. was directed to have that
investigation made. He appointed a committee for that purpose. The committee conducted this investigation and reported as
follows: The Federated Press is an incorporated organization of labor publications,
serving at the present time 75 publications,
which are as follows: B. of L. E. Journal,
Eteenpain, Federated Press Bulletin, Gales-
burg Labor News, Illinois Industrial Review,
Labor Advocate (Racine), Labor Herald,
Labor Unity, Laisve, Midwest Labor News,
Milwaukee Leader, Minneapolis Labor Re-
view, New Majority, Ny Tid, Oklahoma
Leader, One Big Union Bulletin, Peoples
Voice, Radnik, Tom Mooney's Monthly,
Toveri, Truth, Tyomies, Voice of Labor,
Volkszeitung, Uj. Elore, Advance, Alba
Nuova, American Railroad Worker, B. C.
Federationist, Cahokia Valley News, Dawn,
Detroit Labor News, Free Voice, Fur Worker,
Headgear Worker, Illinois Miner, Indus-
trialisti, Industrial Solidarity, Industrial Work-
er, Iowa Farm and Labor News, Labor Ad-
vocate (Tacoma), Labor Age, Labor Journal,
Labor Leader, Llano Colonist, Miami Valley
Socialist, Minnesota Union Advocate, Newark
Leader, New York Call, Penvor, Pennsyl-
vania Worker, Plebe, Prosveta, Railroad
Amalgamation Advocate, Seattle Union Record, Searchlight, Spravedlnost, Tri-City Labor News, Vilnis, West Virginia Federationist,
Williamson County Miner, World Tomorrow,
California Oil Worker, Train Dispatcher,
Upholsterers' Journal, Railway Clerk, Electrical Worker, Producers' News, Maritime
Labor Herald. In addition to these newspaper clients the Federated Press service is
furnished to about 200 local unions and central
bodies and to somewhere between 40 and 50
individuals. These take the service mainly
as a means of assiting the Federated Press,
the local unions and central bodies paying
one dollar per week each for the service, the
individuals paying twenty dollars a year, and
having no right to republication of any of the
material in the service. The Federated Press
maintains staff correspondents in Washington,
New York City, Berlin, Moscow, Sydney,
Mexico City, and Chicago; and it has correspondents in other cities in the United States
who are paid space rates. It would be possible to enter into a lenghty and detailed
analysis of the material furnished by the
Federated Press to its various member
publications but this would not be nearly as
illuminating as Mr. Haessler's own statement
of the Federated Press policy. As he stated
it to us the policy of the Federated Press is to
attempt to report the news of all pretending-
to-be factions or wings of the labor movement
and to admit to membership in the Federated

Press publications representing all factions
and wings of the movement. It is regarded
by the Federated Press as desirable that there
should be on the board of directors representatives of all trends of thought in the labor
movement. Having this statement, we endeavored to get from Mr. Haessler a definition
of the term "labor movement" as used by the
Federated Press. We were given to understand that within the meaning of that term
the Federated Press includes all protesting
minorities and that the question of whether
these minorities are revolutionary in character
or not has nothing to do with the case. On
this point Mr. Haessler furnished us with a
copy of a letter which he had written in answer to an inquiry dealing with his policy as
managing editor. The following paragraph
from that letter is illustrative of his attitude as
he states it: "I shall work as managing editor
of the Federated Press as long as I am permitted to carry out my conception of its proper
function, which is, I believe, to be a cooperative
labor news service catering impartially and
cordially to every group in the labor movement. I have tried to cut out the factional
news and reports of internal union strife that
is of no concern to labor as a whole, though
wads of such news come to the desk. I have
tried also to proportion the news so that all
labor elements may have an opening in our
columns if they wish' it." This we believe
to be an accurate presentation of Federated
Press policy, but we can not refrain from
pointing out that the phrase "all labor elements" includes all of the various revolutionary elements outside of the A. F. of L.,
hostile to the A. F. of L., hostile to democratic
principles in general, and in open warfare in an
effort to undermine and destroy the A. F. of L.
It appears furthermore to be the Federated
Press policy to give as much weight and importance to any protesting minority as to the
bona fide trade union movement in the matter
of news. Thus we observed that day after
day the Federated Press carries much more
news in relation to the doings of various protesting minorities than it does in relation to the
activities of the bona fide trade union movement. We observed furthermore that news
stories relating to the trade union movement
are not infrequently handled in such a manner
as to reflect discreditably upon the trade
union movement. It is true that when one
or two of these instances were called to Mr.
Haessler's attention he manifested a desire
to make correction. However that may be,
the fact remains that under the policy of the
Federated Press every agency or organization
which may lay claim to a labor designation is
entitled to representation in the news service
of the Federated Press on a basis of importance
equal to that of the trade union movement.
Every destructive, revolutionary agency finds
a ready entree to the Federated Press service
as long as it makes claim to a labor designation.
The board of directors of the Federated Press
is so composed as to make any policy other
than the one now in force impossible. Without entering into a detailed discussion of the
personnel of the directorate, it is apparent that
a majority of the present directors would in
any test be either hostile to the A. F.
of L. or lukewarm toward it. Among
the directors are W. Z. Foster and Arne
Swabeck, whose philosophy is well known and
with whom a majority of the directors probably will generally be found in sympathy. In
connection with the general policies of the
Federated Press it is worth noting that the
European manager is Mr. Louis Lochner, who,

during the world war, was at the head of the notorious people's council, the head and front of the pacifist propaganda. It is perhaps also worthy of note that general European news, and particularly British news, is supplied to the Federated Press by the London Daily Herald, concerning whose connections with the Soviet authorities there were some months ago most astonishing revelations. It was pointed out to us that A. F. of L. publications might change the policy of the Federated Press by the simple expedient of becoming members in numbers sufficient to outvote the present majority. There are two things to be said about this: First, not less than four-fifths of the present members must vote for the admission of an applicant; and second, even though a sufficient number of editors loyal to the principles of the A. F. of L. should become members of the Federated Press, they would, by so doing, vote themselves into an indebtedness of approximately $48,400, and it is our frank opinion that this would indeed be an unfortunate acquisition. The Federated Press service is sent daily to clients in the form of printed sheets. In addition to the daily printed sheet a monthly bulletin is issued which serves as a house organ. The daily service carries a series of articles under the caption, "Economic News Service," and these are gathered together and printed on a single sheet once a week. In adddition, the Federated Press issues what it calls chain papers, there being at present four of these. In these chain papers one page is reserved for local news of the community for which the paper is issued, while the remaining pages are made up entirely of material carried in the Federated Press service during the week. Samples of all of this material are attached to this report, together with a copy of the by-laws and copies of the monthly bulletin containing the names of clients and the current annual budget which provides for expenditures amounting to $100,000, providing that amount of money can be secured. We found throughout the Federated Press service a continued domination of the news by articles relating to the I. W. W., the so-called amalgamation movement, "political" prisoners, the communist party, the workers' party, the socialist party, and Russian affairs. That is to say, there is a continuous tide flowing through the Federated Press service of a pro-soviet, pro-communist, pro-revolutionary, anti-A. F. of L. character. We found in a long series of issues, under the standing heading, "Labor Trials," a constant repetition of stories about I. W. W. cases, communist cases and the Michigan syndicalist cases. Typical of this column is the issue of May 18, containing under this heading stories about the trial of Ruthenberg in Michigan, a story about political prisoners, and a story about the troubles of the spectacular Upton Sinclair in California. In another issue the column covered I. W. W. cases in Los Angeles and San Francisco; criminal syndicalism cases in Gary, Ill.; and a story from New York about political prisoners. The issue of May 5, 1923, fairly well typifies the general policy of the Federated Press. The columns of the daily service are 14 inches long and there are six columns. Few stories run more than eight inches and any story running from six to eight inches is therefore an important story from the Federated Press point of view. In this issue 40 inches were devoted to various "isms" while the contents of but 10 inches related to real trade union activity. In the same issue there were small items, totalling from six to eight inches, of what might be termed real or bona fide labor news, in addition to the article on economics which in this

case dealt with the Pennsylvania railroad. Among other things in this day's issue was a news story discussing the strike of the Marine Transport Workers, using the name of the International Seamen's Union and the Marine Transport Workers in such a way as to make no proper distinction between the I. W. W. organization and the bona fide crade union. It is true that our instructions confined us to the editorial and news policies of the Federated Press, but the Garland fund had been so much in discussion and had been the basis of a news story in which in our judgment the president of the A. F. of L. received unfair treatment that we deemed it advisable, in view of these and other facts, to make some inquiry in this direction and to include the results in this report. We can not refrain from including here a letter which has some bearing on the situation inasmuch as it was addressed by a member of the board of trustees of the Garland fund to a member of the executive board of the Federated Press who is also a member of the board of trustees of the Garland fund, though neither held these respective positions at the time the letter was written. The letter is as follows: "JUNE 30, 1922. Mr. WM. Z. FOSTER, 118 N. La Salle Street, Chicago, Ill. DEAR BILL FOSTER: Thanks for yours of the 26th. I can't add to what I have said about Costello's relation to the Federated Press. I do wish you could make the effort to straighten things out before you go west—or work on it at long distance, if that can be done. Costello ought to be generous enough to not stand in the way of a really able man taking his place. Can't you persuade him? I am delighted with the prospects and progress of your league. Of course, the future belongs to your bunch. Yours always, ROGER BALDWIN."

It should be explained in relation to the above letter that Mr. Costello was the then managing editor of the Federated Press later succeeded by Mr. Haessler. The last two sentences of the letter of course constitute the most important portion of the letter in connection with this report. They make clear the type of influence wielded by at least two members of the Garland fund which has agreed to give $15,000 to the Federated Press and which has already given a substantial portion of that amount. Taking up again the analysis of Federated Press policy, we find in the issue of May 9, in a story printed under a Washington date line, the following: "European labor is warned by Samuel Gompers not to expect cooperation from organized labor of the United States in general strikes as a means to economic or political advancement." Of course the statement actually issued by the president of the A. F. of L. had to do entirely with general strikes as a means of preventing war and did not deal with strikes in any sense in connection with economic developments. It would be possible to proceed with analysis of a great many of the issues of the Federated Press but there would be, it seems to us, no point to an endless repetition of the same story. An analysis of issue after issue can only lead back to the conclusion that the Federated Press lends itself continuously to the spreading of doctrines subversive of the best interests of the American working people as expressed in the bona fide trade union movement and that this condition is going to continue. The personnel throughout the organization makes this clear and the record of its conduct proves the case beyond any shadow of doubt. We are aware of the fact that a small number of publications purporting to be bona fide trade union publications are members of the Federated Press, subscribe to its service and print it in part or in whole. We make the assertion, however, as emphatically as we may and without qualification, that no publication can follow the policy of the Federated Press as expressed in its daily service and remain loyal to the fundamental principles set up as the standard of constructive trade unionism by the A. F. of L. There should be harmony and united action along constructive lines before we can be entirely successful in the fulfillment of our mission and the attainment of our aim in the labor movement."

(P. 254) We feel that it is important that our trade unions and the labor publications of the country should be fully informed as to the character and pretensions of any organization which seeks to serve news to the labor press and which in so doing seeks to pose as the supporter of organized labor. We believe we should say in this connection that the labor movement does not demand of a labor news service or of any other news service that there be bias or misrepresentation in behalf of trade unionism, and we are glad to note that the special committee does not base its conclusions upon any failure of the Federated Press to show such a bias. But if we do not demand a bias in favor of the trade union movement we can not condone a bias against the trade union movement on the part of any organization that seeks labor's favor and support. We hold that no news service pretending to convey news about the trade union movement can serve the trade union movement and at the same time serve the propaganda of communism. We note that the policy of the Federated Press is represented by its spokesman to be, in the language of the committee, "to report the news of all pretending-to-be factions or wings of the labor movement and to admit to membership in the Federated Press publications representing all factions and wings of the labor movement." The committee represents that it was "given to understand that within the meaning of that term the Federated Press includes all protesting minorities and that the question of whether these minorities are revolutionary or not has nothing to do with the case." The revolutionary character of a portion of the executive board of the Federated Press is obviously and admittedly communist and revolutionary and a large portion of its newspaper clientele is obviously and admittedly of the same character. The trade union movement as represented by the A. F. of L. has so emphatically declared itself upon the whole question of communist and revolutionary dogma and activity that there can be but one course to pursue, either in respect to a news service in which communist propagandists exercise an influence or a determining voice or in respect to any other effort of communist propagandists to invade the trade union movement. The propagandists of communism have but one object in seeking the company of trade unionism and in seeking entree to our movement through its newspaper channels and otherwise. That object is to subvert and destroy the trade unions and to capture the wage earners for revolutionary communism. We are impelled to declare with all of the emphasis at our command that any compromise of whatever nature with either the propagandists or the propaganda of communism is to yield by just that much to the efforts of the propaganda and those propagandists. If there are those that care to

compromise, let us make it clear that they do not speak by authority of the trade union movement, which is uncompromising and unswerving in its hostility to every manifestation of communism and every other revolutionary doctrine, dogma and practice. If the Federated Press chooses to include communist organizations in the category of organizations of labor, our only reply can be that the classification is inaccurate, repugnant and inadmissible. Agencies in whatsoever field they may operate can not serve communism and at the same time serve American trade unionism. We commend the Executive Council for its efforts in causing this investigation to be made and we commend the committee for the obvious restraint manifested in its report and for the fullness with which it has set forth their findings. Upon the basis of these findings this convention adopts the findings as its own and issues warning to the trade union movement in general and to the labor press in particular to be on guard against the insidious encroachment of subversive propaganda either through the Federated Press or any other channel. The Federated Press upon its own record can not hope to have and should not have the support of trade union publications or of trade union organizations.

Federations of Labor, State—(1921, p. 415) All international and national unions are requested to instruct the field representatives and organizers to urge upon all unaffiliated locals the necessity of becoming affiliated with state federations of labor and central labor councils. Instructions to all organizers of the A. F. of L. for similar action were also directed to be made by the Executive Council.

Financial Aid—(1919, pp. 159-468) From time to time it has come to our knowledge, and we have no doubt to the knowledge of other officers in the labor movement, that appeals for financial assistance have been sent out from various sources to the organizations affiliated with the A. F. of L. That the labor unions are recognized for their generosity of response to such appeals is praiseworthy and desirable, but there is another point to be considered and that is that often we have reason to believe that funds thus collected and moneys thus contributed by the men and women of labor are used for purposes other than those set forth in the appeals; used for the advancement of ideas which are in opposition to the underlying principles of the organized labor movement. While we have no desire or intention to suggest that appeals for worthy causes should not be as generously responded to as circumstances may permit, yet we do feel it our duty to recommend that care be exercised to see to it that the funds thus contributed are properly used for the purpose for which the appeal is made.

Fire Prevention—(1920, p. 318) There has been much loss of life, personal injury, and property damage because of fire that could have been avoided by the use of proper fire prevention applicances. The A. F. of L. purposes to aid in securing and enforcing legislation which shall result in the installation of fire prevention devices which will tend to safeguard life, limb, and property, as well as protect the interests of the wage earners and the public generally.

(1922, p. 495) All affiliated organizations instructed to cooperate with the civic officials in their respective cities in all matters that will tend to alleviate the enormous loss of life, labor and material by fire.

(1923, p. 322) The A. F. of L. urges upon all men of labor, organized and unorganized, upon all our citizenship, men and women alike, the greatest care for the avoidance and prevention of fires, and ask all our people to make a continuous effort for fire prevention.

Flag Day—(1921, p. 179) President of the A. F. of L.: "The fourteenth day of June of every year has a peculiar significance for the American people. It was upon that date it was recognized by the congress of the United States that the flag designed and made with the stars and stripes was regarded and accepted and declared as the flag of the republic of the United States. This being the anniversary of the declaration of that flag as America's emblem, and as it has stood, as it has waved in defiance of enemies and to bring comfort and encouragement and hope for freedom and justice in every instance of the existence of our republic, I feel that it is the duty as it is the pleasure of every delegate and visitor to this convention of the A. F. of L. to arise and pay tribute to Old Glory, the flag of the republic." The entire convention arose.

(1922, p. 6) After the playing of the "Star Spangled Banner" by a band, a committee in behalf of the workingmen and women of Cincinnati presented a beautiful silk American flag to the president of the A. F. of L. It was declared by the chairman.' of the committee to be "the most glorious flag that ever was raised in any part of the world, the flag that stands for the noblest institutions in this great country of ours." This poem was recited by an officer of the A. F. of L.:

YOUR FLAG AND MY FLAG.

Your flag and my flag,
   And how it flies today
In your land and my land
   And half a world away!
Rose-red and blood-red
   The stripes forever gleam;
Snow-white and soul-white—
   The good forefathers' dream,
Sky-blue and true-blue with stars to gleam
      aright—
   The gloried guidon of the day, a shelter
      through the night.

Your flag and my flag!
   And, oh, how much it holds—
Your land and my land—
   Secure within its folds!
Your heart and my heart
   Beat quicker at the sight!
Sun-kissed and wind-tossed—
   Red and blue and white,
The one flag—the great flag—the flag for
      me and you—   ,
   Glorified all else beside—the red and white
      and blue!

The president of the A. F. of L. said: It seemed to be the part of understanding that it was most appropriate that this day set apart to celebrate the anniversary of the day upon which the stars and stripes were created, the official flag of the republic of the United States of America and that at no gathering within the confines of the jurisdiction of the United States of America was a service in honor and honoring that flag more appropriate than in the convention of the A. F. of L. And therefore the simple democratic and yet appropriate ceremony so splendidly conducted this morning at the opening session of the third day of the convention, and the morning of that day during which we have decided to discuss the question of the gravest concern to the people of our country not only of today but for all time to come—the safety and the protection of our child life under our starry flag. To me America has more meaning than that of a name. America and the flag which typifies the United States of America typify that which is good and great and noble and sympathetic, making ,for a higher and better understanding of the rights and the protection to which the people of our republic are entitled, standing in the front ranks of civilized nations of the world, battling day after day for the attainment of that great, everlasting time of peace, progress and happiness. To me America is more than a country, more than a continent; it is a name which stands in its best sense as the apotheosis of all that is great and true and free and democratic and humane, and so it gives me pleasure to have taken this simple part in the services which will soon close. May I express my gratitude and appreciation with the presentation by the representatives of the organized labor movement of Cincinnati and vicinity of this flag, the flag of my allegiance, the flag of my idealism which I accept gratefully and shall keep and honor as my guide and guidon to help my fellows so long as life shall remain in me, my fellows of America, my fellows of every clime and of every nation on the face of the globe. The labor movement of our country and of all other countries stands for progress, for protection of the interests and the rights of the masses. There can be no real freedom where labor is enslaved. It is our mission to see to it that the heritage handed down to us by our forefathers of this and of other countries, who have borne the scars of battle, is accepted, and that we take up the struggle where they were compelled to lay it down, be true to them, be true to ourselves and ᴜo the people of our time, and more important than all, to hand down that heritage of freedom to those who shall come after us to bear the burden of their day, to make life and toil better, and better worth the living and the doing. In that spirit, in that thought, with that feeling I express my deep sense of gratitude and declaration of the purpose to serve by the A. F. of L. in the great cause for which our movement was instituted and contends.

Food and Culinary Department—(1920, p. 304) Executive Council directed to call a conference of organizations to learn if there is a desire to form a food and culinary department of the A. F. of L.

(1921, p. 145) Executive Council reported that from reports received from various national and international unions interested it was clearly apparent that the proposal to form a food and culinary department is impracticable of accomplishment.

(1922, p. 471, 1923, p. 325) Action of 1921 convention reaffirmed.

Foreman, Election of—(1919, p. 346) Refused to approve of a declaration that on and after May 1, 1920, the workers in any industry shall have the privilege, and are encouraged to demand the right, to "elect" the foreman under whom they shall work by a majority vote of the entire force of the employes engaged in that industry. The convention declared: "The plan applies not to cooperative enterprise, but to the privately owned and operated industries of this country. We would call your attention to the fact that in the literature which has been circulated upon the question of electing foremen and in the speeches made in trade union meetings upon this same question, the subject does not stop with the election of foremen, because the argument is then made, and it is a logical one, that the election of foreman would be of no value because the foreman would be under the general manager and the board of directors, and if we could only get the trade union movement to commit itself to the election of foremen in industries, it would logically follow that we would have to elect the board of directors and determine who the general manager would be. It is not therefore a trade union proposition."

Forty-Four-Hour Week—(1919, p. 451) The officers of the A. F. of L. are instructed to use their good offices with the secretary of the navy to the end that the forty-four week shall be established in all navy yards; that all piece work shall be abolished, and that no workman shall be required to do any work other than that of the craft under which he is classified.

(1921, p. 422) The A. F. of L. unequivocally endorses the campaign being made by the printing trades unions affiliated with the A. F. of L. to make the 44-hour week universal in the printing industry. The printing trades unions are not at this time striking in an endeavor to secure the 44-hour week; they are on strike for the purpose of enforcing the carrying out of an agreement which the employers made with them at a time when the 44-hour week could have been enforced without a struggle of any kind. We commend the action of the printing trades unions in entering into an agreement with printing office employers to set a date for the inauguration of a shorter work week that would not disturb printing office conditions and would allow printing office employers to complete contracts made under 48 hour agreements previous to the time that the 44-hour week should go into effect. Again we want to join with the printing trades unions in the statement that we are of the opinion that had printing office employers been left free to conduct the business of their own institutions without interference and coercion from employers in other industries there would have been no necessity for a strike to enforce the introduction of the 44-hour work week in the printing offices in this country. We are convinced that the present struggle of the printing trades unions in this country is not a fight against printing office employers but is a struggle against the introduction of what employers please to term an "open" shop condition. We desire to support to the fullest extent the fight being made by printing trades unions to continue the real union shop in industry.

(1922, p. 318) The A. F. of L. emphatically denounces the dishonorable, unwarranted and destructive attitude and action manifested by the printing trades employers and their associations in treating contracts entered into as mere scraps of papers.

Fraternal Delegates—(1921, p. 337) As it is most desirable that the interchange of information between the labor movements of the various countries should be as rapid as possible the fraternal delegates from the A. F. of L. to other countries are directed to make reports immediately on their return to this country. In no case shall the report be delayed more than one month after arrival, and shall be made to the executive council, which will determine the best method of having the information conveyed to the membership generally.

Fraternal Order, A. F. of L.—(1921, p. 426) Refused to make the A. F. of L. a fraternal order as well as a labor organization. The change contemplated the payment of $100 death benefits.

Free Speech, etc., Would Deny—(1921, p. 115) Senator Poindexter introduced in the sixty-seventh congress a bill not only to prevent free speech, free press, and free assemblage, but to take from the states the authority to punish violators of state laws. While ostensibly a bill "to protect the property, processes and agencies of the government of the United States from anarchy and bolshevism" any citizen can on conviction be sent to prison for 40 years, fined $50,000 or hanged, for advocating political, social, or economic changes. Section 2 provides: "Every person who, either orally or by writing, printing, exhibiting, or circulating written or printed words or pictures shall advocate, teach, incite, propose, aid, abet, encourage, or advise the unlawful injury or destruction of private or public property, or the unlawful injury of any person, or the unlawful taking of human life, either as a general principle or in particular instances, whether as a means of affecting political, industrial, social, or economic conditions, or for any other purposes, shall be guilty of a felony, and snall be punished by imprisonment not exceeding 40 years or by fine not exceeding $50,000, or by both such fine and imprisonment." Section 9 provides: "Any person who, by the commission of any act prohibited by this act, shall cause the death of any person, whether such death is brought about directly by the act of such person in the violation of this act, or by any other person incited thereto by such person in the commission of any act prohibited by this act, shall be punished by death." While the proposed law undoubtedly would be declared unconstitutional because it is an invasion of states rights, it demonstrates how far Senator Poindexter is willing to go in his reactionary policies.

Free Speech, Press, Assemblage—(1920, p. 423) There is an unmistakable effort being made by those interests hostile to the labor movement, supported by certain public officials, to deny the rights of free speech and free assembly, so essential to carrying on the work of the A. F. of L., and especially is this tendency pronounced in many of the steel centers of Pennsylvania and the coal fields of Kentucky and West Virginia. The A. F. of L. again declares that the rights of free speech, free press and free assembly are inalienable and beyond the power of any judge, court, legislative body or administrative official to qualify, modify, abrogate, or suspend. (P. 423) The city of Duquesne, Pa., has an ordinance under which the mayor of the city sets aside the guarantees of both state and federal constitutions and prohibits all public meetings either on private property, in halls, or on streets to the A. F. of L. Every effort should be made to have a congressional investigation.

Garnishment of Wages—(1922, p. 113) H. R. 8570 provides for the garnishment of wages of civil employes of the United States. It is a most vicious bill. Section 1 provides that unless there is exemption by state or federal laws the wages of civil employes of the United States, other than officers, shall be subject to garnishment upon any judgment rendered against them in any state or territory. It will be noted that no matter how meager the wages received by the federal employe might be he could be garnisheed in Washington no matter from what city he might come. The further fact that officers of the government would be exempt makes the bill all the more objectionable. So many protests were made that the bill has not been heard from.

Gold Production, To Aid—(1921, p. 110) A bill introduced in the house provides that an excise rate of $10 an ounce be collected on all articles containing gold or gold used for other than monetary purposes, and out of the fund raised $10 shall be paid for each newly produced ounce. The bill seeks to protect the "monetary gold reserve by the maintenance of the normal gold production." Gold is worth $20 an ounce. It is a fixed rate for coinage purposes made by international agreement and no matter whether it costs $5 or $50 an ounce to mine, only $20 can be obtained for gold. The manufacturers, the author of the bill states, obtain the benefit of the fixed price for gold, as the government sells it to the trades at the present monetary price.

Gompers, Samuel—(1922, p. 4) Reply to address of welcome at Cincinnati convention: "In a day like this it is most encouraging to have come from your hearts and minds the expression of hope and the offer of service. The toiling masses of America have few traditions of old, as have the toilers of older countries and older civilizations; but in our own America we have emerged from a condition of servitude to understanding by the great mass of the toilers of America of the sovereignty of the citizenship, of the equality of opportunity which must come to the great toiling masses of America. We do not becloud our minds, nor do we fool ourselves into any fancied security as to the obstacles which have been and are being thrown across our pathway of progress. On the contrary, we understand the designers and those who carry the designs into effect to weaken the spirit or to crush the hopes of American labor for absolute freedom—we understand them and their purpose just as keenly as they do, and we are just as ready, and perhaps much more so. than are the antagonists of the rightful cause and course of the American labor movement. We shall go onward and forward free men as ordained by God and by nature, and as declared in that sacred document, the declaration of independence, and rooted in the constitution of the United States. We are men and women created with certain inalienable rights, the right of life, liberty, and the pursuit of happiness, and we are now more determined than ever that the men of toil shall not be depicted by that wonderful painting, "The Man with the Hoe." And this American labor movement, organized as it is, believes in these great principles enunciated in that world-famed, historic and sacred document; and we are not in a mood to have those rights and those principles guaranteed to us by our constitution taken from us by any subtle reasoning or assumption of power, no matter whence it emanates. I shall not attempt to anticipate the legislation, the proceedings of this convention. I may be permitted to say that these will be told in the report of the Executive Council, which will be submitted to this convention, and by the resolutions introduced or adopted by the convention. But I may take cognizance of just one remark made by his honor, the mayor, which in my judgment—and I think you will agree with me—is the keynote of that which we have to do today. The mayor referred to this gathering as a conference, and if my memory serves me well, he added that conferences are the great distinctive advance which has been made by the human family as against the exercise of force to compel obedience to the will of one. Amen to that and to that declaration. This is a conference or a congress of the chosen representatives of the rank and file of the men and women of toil who are working today in all fields of human industrial activity, and they come here with a mandate and credentials of their constituents to express the views and principles in which they so heartily believe, and the aspirations which they so devoutly aim should be accomplished. We meet here in annual convention for the purpose of arriving at results which shall represent the composite, average view of the toiling masses of America. In our trades unions, in our other labor organizations, in our city central bodies, our state federations, our national and international trade unions, what we ask of employers is that they sit with us around the table, not in any jug-handle movement inaugurated by themselves in which they dominate in fact and in spirit, but to meet in conference with us and there around the table, they as employers and we as workers, the chosen representatives of the workers, to discuss, to ascertain and determine, for some reasonable period at least, and agreement governing the matters which affect both factors of industry, and not forgetting the rights of employers and of business, but having as the most essential consideratiin the human equation in industry. We want conferences. Our adversaries term their antagonistic movement the "open shop," or, cloak it hypocritically, the "American plan," robbing patriotism of its most glorious name to commit a devilish act. There can be no genuine conference between employers and employes unless the employes stand upon an equal footing of responsibility and power, fearless of the lash of unemployment or discharge because of their consistent attitude toward the people they represent. For the first time in the world a conference was held a few months ago in the capital city of our nation, called to discuss a limitation of armaments of the nations of the world. Men and women of this convention, let me call your attention to a fact which may have escaped your notice. At our Denver convention the Executive Council of the A. F. of L., in a report submitted, recommended that the A. F. of L. in convention assembled should call upon the officers of the American government to invite the nations of the world to a conference for the purpose of discussing how far the limitation of armaments could go. And our convention did make that declaration. It was almost a month later when the government of the United States sent its invitations to the nations of the world to attend an international conference in our capital for the limitation of armaments. There were not very good results accomplished, counted with that which still exists, but a beginning has been made, and the consistent course presented by the A. F. of L. for peace and the abolition of international war has been sustained, though to a smaller degree than we hoped by that Washington conference. Some battleships are to be destroyed, some other smaller craft, and a ten years' naval holiday is to be observed. I don't know how many of you are fight fans, but I think those of you who have been at boxing matches know that you have seen just as hard matches among bantams as among heavy weights, and that applies equally to the dreadnaughts as to the little submarine chasers. I think I am doing but scant justice to the claims of organized labor when I say that in every country in the world it has made the greatest contribution toward that purpose "

(1923, p. 201) Reply to addresses of fraternal delegates: "Fraternal delegates from the various organizations to whose addresses we have had the honor to listen, I think I can safely say that your words of encouragement and your message of good will have found a deep lodgment in the hearts and the minds of the delegates to this convention. The information which you have given us is exceedingly interesting; your account of the development of your respective movements has been exceedingly interesting. Several of you who have traversed from your homes to this far northwestern city of the Pacific coast must have a realizing sense of at least one of the problems with which the American labor movement has to contend or deal. Brothers Robinson and Walker, it must have been a compelling understanding when you realized that you are now a greater distance from New York than the distance from your own homes in Scotland and England to New York; that on your travels to Portland since your landing upon the shores of America you have passed through great centers of industry and commerce, of highly developed communities, near several inland seas and over several ranges of mountains; from the Alleghenies to the Rockies. This vast domain of America is a bit different than that of England. In your country you have a people who, many of them, can count their ancestry for centuries as English, as Scotch, as Welsh, as Cornish. In America there are few who can count their genealogy more than a generation or two back, and most of us are of the first nativity in our generation or by acquired citizenship. There is in our country a system of government which it is necessary to thoroughly understand in order that some degree of comparison may be made. When the British parliament meets and enacts a law it is a law of the land. There has been one judge who in his time undertook to annul an act of the British Parliament. He lived but a short time after, and after him no judge or court in England undertook to annul an act of parliament. Whether there is power vested in the courts of our country, as exercised by our courts, it is not necessary at this moment to discuss; but in any event our courts have exercised functions which the history of the United States discloses were never granted or conceded to them. In the government of the United States there is recognized in our constitution three coordinate branches of government—the legislative, the executive, the judicial—and each is supposed to be a balance-check upon the other. In truth and inherently there is no such coordinate power. The legislative branch of our government may, if circumstances warrant, summon to the bar of our congress either or both of the other branches of the government and make them answer to charges, trial, and subject them to impeachment and removal. There is no such power vested in the executive or the judicial branches. In the year of grace 1923 the American citizenship will know how to deal with the assumption of powers of our judiciary, not by the process so summarily invoked a few centuries ago in England, but by the intelligence and the constructive processes of American citizenry. A moment ago I made reference to the different forms of government, as the United States may be compared to that of England. I repeat for emphasis that when your parliament enacts a law it is an act of all England. The federal government of the United States has no such power. Our federal government has and can exercise only such powers as are granted and conceded to it by the several states. Beyond that the federal legislature and the federal government can not go. The laws which affect industry and the exercise of the police powers for the enforcement of such laws are reserved to and by the states. And when we compare the matter of factory laws, laws in the interest of and for the protection of the wage earners, the young and the innocent, we must look to the laws enacted by the states in the United States. But there are two other features to which I think attention might be aptly called. One of them is the make-up of our American citizenship, even in our day. There is a homogeneity among people of England. You are Englishmen, you are Scotchmen, you are Welshmen, but the great sum total of it is that you are in the British Isles. We in the United States were composed of three millions of people at the time of the declaration of independence, and when the government of the republic of the United States was set up. They were Americans from England, from Ireland, from Scotland, from Wales, from Holland, and a few from other countries. Since then we have grown into a population of approximately 110,000,000, and coming from all climes and countries, speaking as many languages and dialects as those who built the tower of Babel. And the worst of it is they continue to speak those languages and to think in their own languages. I desire to submit this thought: No one knows very much better than I do the effect of laws passed by congress or the legislatures of the states; but we are wage earners and we sometimes feel the injustice of the laws passed by these political agencies of state and federal government. I want to ask you men of labor, to turn over in your minds whether it is not a fact that the laws—call them regulations or rules, if you please; I prefer to call them laws—enacted in the offices of our employers do not affect us as wage earners more than any of the laws of the state or of the nation. To have a dominating influence in determining what the laws emanating from the employer's office shall be is of greater importance to the men and women of toil than any law which can be passed by congress or the legislatures of the various states. We have not failed in developing the men of labor who can hold their own in any conference, whether it be economic, political, or sociological. In our movement of America we make no distinction between what we believe to be the interchangeable terms of the trade union movement and the labor movement; ours is a labor movement, conducted by the trade unions of America, and we yield not an inch of activity upon any field for the protection and the promotion of the rights and the interests of the working people and the citizenship of our country to any other body on earth. It would be a most interesting thing to study the difference which exists between the element to which reference has been made, and known under various colors as pink and red and garnet and blue and others of the 57 varieties. The character of the activities of this species of the human in your country and that of the same species in our America are as wide apart as it is possible for humans to be. Their attempt at academic impression upon the labor movement of England is one thing, and the strike-breaking tendencies and activities of that species human in the United States and Canada are of a different type. The seamen and the railroad shopmen, in their recent controversies to protect themselves and their fellows, could a tale unfold that would make the hair stand upon your heads like the quills on the fretful porcupine. If these people were paid by the concentrated interests of the employers of America they could not do their job half as well as they are doing it now. And then another species human—if human they be—is the character of work that aims for the disintegration and destruction of the American labor movement. We will know, and I believe we do now, how to deal with them, too. This movement in America has done so much for American workers, the American people, that there isn't anything that can eliminate it; not the bitter antagonism of employers and big business and high finance, nor of the serpent which is trying to sting us in the heart. It has brought to the life of America's workers a better day; it has given them hope and courage and ability to fight for the right, whatever might betide. It has instilled the spirit of unity and solidarity into the workers, the organized workers and the unorganized, and though the unorganized are not with us in our movement thay are inspirited with the idea and purpose of this labor movement of ours. Reference was made to the movement in England among some of the trade unions to make it easier for men having learned any trade or calling to enter another trade or industry in which the same, or nearly the same, character of work is to be performed, by providing that the membership card of one organization may be accepted in that of another. The A. F. of L. has declared for that principle, and several of our trade unions accept the interchangeable card from one organization to another. There are several of our trade unions that accept the cards of members in good standing in the unions of other countries, so that they can become members of our trade unions without even an initiation fee of any kind. I think that is one of the natural tendencies and developments recognizing the solidarity so necessary to the progress and success of the labor movement. I don't know that what I am going to say upon a particular point is any news. Brother Walker is primarily a representative of the agricultural workers of England, and he referred in his excellent presentation and message to our convention this morning to the fact that two million workers in agriculture and horticulture left the farms and went into other occupations in the cities. It is quite true, but it is also true that, notwithstanding the fact that so many of our workers in agriculture have left the farms, there has been an appreciable increase in the production of agriculture in the United States. I said a few days ago that the trouble with the farmers and the workers in industry in the United States is that they have practically allowed the gentlemen farmers, the trust farmers, the magazine farmers and the political farmers to lead them, and not the mud farmers organized for their own common protection. These interests have played the part such as is portrayed in one of Dickens' books, when he describes two men, stalwart, strong, looking manacingly at each other, and between them a big, corpulent man, with jowls that are hanging over his collar, and he said to one, 'Don't let him get away with it,' and then to the other, 'He is trying to lord it over you,' and they go to it. And while they are fighting each other this great big, suave man rubs his hands, washing them with invisible soap and imperceptible water. And that is the position of the profiteer upon industry and agriculture. I am sure we have been, all of us, not only interested, but greatly gratified at the messages which have come to us from the parliament of labor of Great Britain, from the congress of labor of Canada, from the efforts made by the good women in this trade union league—from all these who are trying to solve the problems of life and labor. It is the mis-

sion of the workers of America, as it is the mission of the workers of our several countries that carry on this work. We have all of us in some degree or another borne the scars of battle, and it falls to us as to the trade union movement everywhere, as the legatees of all the struggles of the human family to lighten the burdens of toil, to make life better worth living, to secure us in our opportunities for progress, to make for the world's betterment, to see to it as best we can to advance the spirit and purpose of national—aye, of international—solidarity, and to make our contribution as best we can. But there is one thing we can not surrender, and that is the right of American organized labor to determine its policy, its methods, consonant with the political, economic and sociological conditions by which we are confronted and surrounded. Consistent with that national autonomy of American labor, we will go the length of anyone, not by mere pronouncement and proclamation, but by the carrying out of the proclamations which we shall issue. Repeating in another way what I said on Monday in part, I prefer, and I believe the American labor movement prefers, to make constructive and reasonable demands, and radical in the determination to carry them through.

Government, Centralization of—(1923, p. 84) S. 1943, by Senator Kellogg, provided "for the better protection of aliens and the enforcement of their treaty rights." Stripping the title and disclosing its intent it provided "for the better protection of aliens if they are strike-breakers, but for their punishment if they are strikers." The principle of this bill was lauded by President Harding in a message to congress on the mining and railroad controversies. The purpose of the proposed law was to permit federal courts to hear and decide cases in which aliens are involved but which the constitution provides come within the police power of the states. Section 4 of the bill provided that to enforce the decisions of the courts in such cases the president of the United States was authorized to use the U. S. marshals and the deputies and if need be the army and navy to prevent wage earners from ceasing work to better their conditions. Senator Kellogg's bill undoubtedly was to make the government of the U. S. a giant strike-breaking agency. Unfair employers contend that the state courts are too near the people and therefore more likely to be just in their decisions than the federal courts. Therefore, they endeavored to give jurisdiction to the federal courts because of their well-known practice of deciding against labor. Representative Edmonds, of Pennsylvania, also submitted a bill (H. R. 12344) providing "for the deportation of aliens who participate in riotous gatherings, and for other purposes." It is well known that innocent men are often arrested and tortured by the "third degree" until they are compelled to confess offenses or crimes of which they are innocent. Other men have been forced to defend themselves in the courts against conspiracies to convict them of crimes of which they know nothing. Therefore, it can easily be deduced that a workmen's meeting can be broken up and any alien participant can be deported through the conniving of police, detective agents, and "agents provocateur" who may be controlled by powerful interests. While ostensibly intended to protect aliens the real object was to give the federal courts the right to assume jurisdiction wherever there is an opportunity to destroy any effort of the workers to protect and advance their rights and interests. The Dyer anti-lynching bill (H. R. 13) had a similar purpose. While labor abhors lynchings, it insists that the federal courts should not be given jurisdiction that would take away the police power of the states, especially when the hidden purpose of such a proposed law is to give the federal courts jurisdiction over industrial disputes in which the workers, as such, find themselves involved. (P. 279) Unquestionably, the real intent and purpose of all such legislative proposals embraces the desire of the employing interests to the development of a supplemental system of law enforcement to enslave further the wage earners to a legal and economic philosophy and practices which would make it extremely dangerous for them to combine to promote their mutual interests. It is a sad commentary upon those urging such legislation that in this madness to strike at the growing power of labor they have no regard or concern for the rights of the several states and by this effort to centralize all powers of government they would libel and slander the administration of all our state governments.

Government Ownership—(1892, p. 39) The A. F. of L. hereby reaffirms its position in favor of government ownership of telegraph and telephone systems and also declares for the government ownership of railroads and transportation.

(1923, p. 368) Amended the declaration of 1892 to read: "government ownership and democratic operation of the railroad systems of the United States."

Greetings to Convention, San Francisco June 8—(1919, p. 360) San Francisco Labor Council sends fraternal greetings and best wishes to the thirty-ninth annual convention of the A. F. of L. May the deliberations and resolves of the delegates bring new strength and will to do what is right and just and may Brother Samuel Gompers, the able and esteemed champion of American labor, be fully restored to health and continue in his work of love and devotion for the cause of all who toil.

Gunmen, West Virginia—(1922, p. 110) Those who have kept posted on the strikes in West Virginia and in Pennsylvania and other states know that private detective agencies furnish gunmen who stir up trouble even riots, in order to break a strike. Under such circumstances wage earners who have ceased work as a protest against unbearable conditions could be sent to jail for 40 years, fined $50,000, or both.

Harvard University—(1923, p. 123) The board of overseers of Harvard University unanimously voted "that in the administration of rules for admission Harvard College maintains its traditional policy of freedom from discrimination on grounds of race or religion." (P. 250) Our institutions of higher learning are an organic part of our national educational effort. They are of the very foundations of our American democratic experiment. As has been said at this convention, "the genius of America consists in our correlation of government by the people with education by the people." In the case of the state universities supported by public funds, this correlation of government by the people with education by the people is the insistent fact. Even our privately endowed institutions are ceasing to be regarded as private institutions save in the source of their income. For the obligation which rests upon the colleges and universities of this country to serve the people and uphold the ideals of the American Commonwealth makes them all public institutions.

Health Insurance—(1919, pp. 144-378) It must be apparent to all who have given this subject serious attention that it is one possessed of great good and at the same time fraught with much danger. Because of the importance of this subject, and by reason of the vast consequences involved, the Executive Council is directed to make further investigation. (1920, pp. 176-387, 1921, pp. 147-310) Similar action.

Hearst Newspapers Condemned—(1921, p. 371) The Hearst newspapers of June 6, 1921, printed what was alleged to be a report of the proceedings of the Chicago Federation of Labor of June 5, in which it was stated, among other things: "Opposition among the rank and file of union labor in Chicago to the re-election of Samuel Gompers as head of the A. F. of L., came to a head yesterday when a meeting of the Chicago body was thrown into an uproar by demands for his ousting. 'Throw Sam Gompers out, throw him out!' shouted delegates from the floor while President Fitzpatrick pounded in vain for order." President Fitzpatrick in a letter to President Gompers denounced the report of the meeting as published in the Hearst newspaper. The convention declared: This is but an example of the propaganda in which the Hearst newspapers are engaged and which has for its purpose the destruction of the organized labor movement of America. The A. F. of L. in convention assembled denounces the malicious misrepresentation, falsehoods and propaganda contained in the report of the proceedings of the Chicago Federation of Labor as printed in the Hearst newspapers. We condemn the practice of those newspapers and other publications which resort to misrepresentation and falsehood.

Hibernians, Ancient Order of—(1923, p. 247) The following resolution was adopted by the state convention of the Ancient Order of Hibernians and was read to the Portland convention: "In accordance with a recommendation of the national convention we pledge our support to organized labor in every movement fostered by it in the interest of humanity and urge that all work performed by our order in the state be given as far as practicable to union labor affiliated with the A. F. of L., and recommend that a copy of this resolution be forwarded to the headquarters of their annual convention now meeting in Portland, and also to the central labor council of Portland."

Hindoos—(1919, p. 358) Directed Executive Council to investigate the exact status of the cases against a number of Hindos who were threatened with deportation.

History, Encyclopedia, Reference Book—(1919, p. 157) The 1916 convention instructed the Executive Council to "have prepared a year-book, which would contain a record of all matters affecting the trade union movement which had occurred during the previous 12 months." The year-book, however, developed into a more elaborate work. A year-book only implies the activities of the A. F. of L. for the year just passed. As this would be the first year-book it was believed it should contain a brief resume of every important action of the thirty-eight conventions. (Pp. 379-474) The problems of labor are admittedly the gravest social and economic problems emerging out of the world's conflict. Quite a number of thoughts, many of them old, but expressed in more modern phraseology, are being advanced for the solution of these complexing and perplexing problems. It is therefore essential that the wage earners of America should have accurate knowledge of the many difficulties which the wage earners have been called on to overcome heretofore. It is still more essential that they should be thoroughly familiar with the methods the

American labor movement has heretofore applied in the solution of the difficulties which have continually presented themselves. In the affairs now confronting our people the American wage earners will be either a bewildered spectator or a conscious director, dependent upon the preference in America of the American mind. We must know the labor movement of America as it has developed in our own country to understand the movements and methods necessary to meet the economic wants and needs of the wage earners of today and tomorrow. We therefore welcome the publishing of the year book by the A. F. of L. and this attempt to supply this knowledge to the American wage earners in a concrete, understandable form. We believe it a splendid guide in the solution of the many problems confronting the wage earners, and that it is a work worthy of the highest commendation. This book should be in the hands of every wage earner, every trade union official, every library—private as well as public—every publication and every student and sympathizer of the labor movement of America. The officers of the A. F. of L. and the officers of affiliated organizations are urged to take adequate steps to the end that this work may enter the home and influence the mind and thought of every wage earner throughout North America.

(1920, pp. 171-387) The "American Federation of Labor History, Encyclopedia and Reference Book" has attracted wide attention. It has proved a wonderful source of agitation to more thoroughly acquaint the people of our nation with the hopes and aspirations of the trade union movement, as it contains practically every important action of the A. F. of L. since its inception in 1881. It has proved of inestimable value to the members of affiliated organizations desiring official knowledge of what has been done, and why, on every question that can arise in the economic and political fields. Many applications for copies of the work have come from foreign countries. High officials of the Japanese government as well as many other public men are studying the American labor movement through the contents of this reference book. The wage earners of Japan who are interested in organizing the workers of that country are using it as a text-book. They desire to organize the labor movement in Japan on the lines followed by the A. F. of L. Every resident of Japan who visits this country to investigate labor conditions secures a copy. Representatives of labor of England, France, and other countries have also sent for copies. It is regrettable, however, that the trade unions of the United States have not interested themselves in the circulation of so valuable and thorough an official history of the American trade union movement. Every local union affiliated to a national or international union or direct to the A. F. of L. should have a copy for its great educational value. There is no question that arises in a local union which can not be answered in the encyclopedia. It tells of the struggles of the labor movement, of the many obstacles and how they were overcome, and presents reasons for the adoption of the policies that have brought the A. F. of L. to its present strength and power for good. Thousands of letters are received at headquarters yearly asking for information. The great majority of these are quickly answered by referring to the book. The underlying principles of the trade union movement require years of study to thoroughly appreciate their value if the knowledge is to be secured by experience, but the encyclopedia takes up every question considered in 38 conventions and explains the position taken on them. This permits the new member of a trade union, when confused as to the reason for certain methods being pursued, to look up the record for the information desired.

(1921, pp. 143-309) The value of the book is splendidly illustrated by the statement of one of the international officers, a delegate to this convention, who reported that wherever in a local union he found the History, Encyclopedia, Reference Book he also found that union doing better work. A more effective recommendation for the book could not be asked. Every local union should have a copy of the work for the use of its members.

(1922, pp. 61-354) The value of the American Federation of Labor History, Encyclopedia, Reference Book as an educator has been demonstrated daily. The copy of the proceedings for the last three years to be added to the work has been prepared and is ready for the printer. It was thought best, however, that as the convention was so soon to be held that the printing be withheld and the action of the Cincinnati convention be added thereto. This would be printed as an appendix to the original book.

(1923, p. 130) The second volume of the A. F. of L. History, Encyclopedia and Reference Book is ready for the printer. It will contain the essential features of the activities of the A. F. of L., its declarations and decisions for the last four years and will make several hundred pages. As the next convention would soon be held it was thought the part of wisdom to delay the printing so as to include the proceedings of the 1923 convention. When printed it will be a valuable addition to the history of the American labor movement. (P. 254) It is satisfying to know that this much-needed volume will soon be available. We feel that there is a sufficient demand for a book of this character among the membership of the trade union movement, and outside of the trade union movement, to warrant the regular annual publication of such a reference book or year-book. An additional volume should be published each year immediately after the conclusion of the annual convention.

Hitchman Coal and Coke Co. Case— (1921, pp. 73-373) In the Hitchman case. the question was presented to the Supreme Court as to whether or not members of a labor union could be enjoined from conspiring to persuade, and persuading, without violence or show of violence, plaintiff's employes, not members of the union, and who were working for plaintiff not for a specified time, but under an agreement not to continue in plaintiff's employment if they joined the union, this agreement being fully known to defendants, secretly to agree to join the union and continue working for plaintiff until enough had agreed to join, so that a strike could be called, and plaintiff be thereby forced to unionize its business of mining coal. This is the essence upon which the Hitchman Coal and Coke Company predicated its case. The Hitchman Company resorted to the practice after the original case had been started of requiring each of its employes to sign employment cards to the following effect:

"I am employed by and work for the Hitchman Coal & Coke Company with the express understanding that I am not a member of the United Mine Workers of America, and will not become so while an employe of the Hitchman Coal & Coke Company; that the Hitchman Coal & Coke Company is run non-union and agreed with me that it will run non-union while I am in its employ. If at any time I am employed by the Hitchman Coal & Coke Company I want to become connected with the United Mine Workers of America or any affiliated organization, I agree to withdraw from the employment of said company, and agree that while I am in the employ of that company I will not make any efforts amongst its employes to bring about the unionizing of that mine against the company's wish. I have either read the above or heard the same read."

The question of the validity and effect of this agreement was largely discussed in the case under consideration and the majority opinion (Justices Brandeis, Holmes, and Clarke dissenting) sustained this contract as a valid one capable of enforcement against any outsider who might interfere with it, a strange part of the situation being that of course it was not enforceable against the party signing it if at any time he saw fit at any moment to quit employment, nor was it at any time enforceable against the coal company which could discharge its employe without a moment's notice. Assuming the contract as valid as we have stated, the Supreme Court maintained the right of the judiciary to restrain any person from urging an employe of the company to break his contract. He might not be solicited to join a trade union while the so-called contract was in existence, the solicitor knowing such fact. Much of the language contained in the case is very broad, as for instance: "Upon all of the facts we are constrained to hold that the purpose entertained by defendants to bring about a strike at plaintiff's mine in order to compel plaintiff, through fear of financial loss, to consent to the unionization of the mine as the lesser evil was an unlawful purpose." Following the literal language of this decision an employer has but to enter into psuedo contracts with his employes and thereafter any attempt to unionize them may be the subject of an injunction. In this case the majority members of the court lost sight of the fact that what the defendants were doing was done in self-defense and not maliciously, and in view of recent decisions throughout the country declaring the right of industrial combatants to push their struggle to the limits of the justification of self-interest, the decision of the majority members of the United States Supreme Court is surprising. Since the employer in the Hitchman case could arbitrarily dismiss an employe any time for the most capricious reason, and had not exacted any agreement by which the employe agreed not to join a labor union, it seems incredible that a court should hold it was improper to lay before such employes the advantages of joining a labor organization. Yet that is what the decision comes to when finally analyzed. As it would not be possible for congress to pass any law which affects intrastate trade or business, it is obvious that both national and state legislation will have to be obtained in order to protect labor adequately.

Hoarding of Food, etc.—(919, p. 329) Executive Council directed to urge congress to enact laws compelling each and every box, barrel, bottle, can, carton or container of such foods, or food products, and each and every article of wearing apparel or article entering the manufacture of wearing apparel, to bear an imprint of the date of its growth, origin, production of manufacture, and if any of such foods, food products, dairy products, wearing apparel or article entering the manufacture thereof, be stored, the date of such storage to be imprinted thereon. It was also urged that a time limit be set within which the aforesaid necessaries shall be offered for sale.

Housing—(1919, p. 383) Each city and town should be authorized and encouraged to build enough houses to meet the needs of its inhabitants, providing with each a tract of land suitable to the locality, and that the federal government participate in the production of a full supply of suitable homes by continuing the Housing Bureau, to aid, encourage, and stimulate the building of dwelling houses. (P. 384) We favor the establishment of a permanent housing bureau for the purpose of providing homes for the workers of this country. A representative of labor should be a member to see that the interests of the workers are fully protected.

(1920, p. 113) Congress failed to create a bureau of housing in the department of labor as urged by the A. F. of L.

(1921, pp. 120-299) Bills providing for the establishment of a bureau in the department of commerce to be known as the building construction and housing bureau were pigeonholed. Another bill providing for the use of money deposited in postal savings banks in the building of homes met with the same fate. The law at present provides that money in postal savings banks be loaned to banks at two and one-half per cent interest. According to the introducer of the latter bill if the government needs money it borrows the same money back and pays six per cent. The bill proposes that the money be loaned to home builders and that the interest rate on the postal savings be increased from two to four per cent. (P. 411) A declaration that all state and local governments should use their taxing powers to relieve the housing shortage was referred to the executive council.

Housing, War—(919, p. 129) Immediately upon the signing of the armistice, November 11, 1918, announcement was made in both houses of congress that large expenditures ought to be curtailed and various projects stopped, in order to save as much money as possible. In the senate the national housing project came up for discussion. During the period of the war $50,000,000 was voted in one bill for the shipping board to enable it to house its employes properly. In May, 1918, congress passed another bill authorizing the housing bureau of the department of labor to expend $60,000,000 for provision of dwellings for workers employed in war activities, in places where there was a scarcity of housing facilities. Of this sum $10,000,000 was to be expended in Washington. There had been delay in the pasage of these bills and further delay occurred before the appropriation became available and actual construction began. When the armistice was signed there were about 80 house building projects under way, some of which were nearing completion, but on many of them not much work had been done. After some criticism in the Senate a subcommittee began an investigation of the housing work which had been undertaken by the bureau. Before the hearings were finished the committee reported the Senate Joint Resolution No. 194, ordering the immediate cessation of work on a large number of dormitories being constructed for the accommodation of war workers on the plaza near the capitol, and construction on all buildings not 75 per cent completed to stop. With but little debate this measure was rushed through the Senate and sent to the house. The A. F. of L., in company with other organizations and individuals, demanded that a public hearing on the bill be held by the house committee on public buildings and grounds, it being be-i eved that the sudden stopping of the housing work was a detriment to many thousands of workers in the war emergency whose services would still be reqired for some time to come. A public hearing was ordered to take place on January 8, at which the completion of the plaza buildings was urged by the representative of the A. F. of L. and the proposition to end construction of all buildings not 75 per cent completed was denounced as unbusinesslike and foolish. The committee was asked to make detailed inquiry and determine the advisability of completing or the abandonment of each project upon its individual merits. The house committee amended senate resolution No. 194 in accordance with these requests and recommended its passage as amended. The bill was not passed, but the secretary of labor continued the housing work along the lines indicated in the bill as amended by the house committee. (P. 329) The Executive Council was directed to have introduced a bill in congress providing that the buildings erected to supply housing facilities by the government should not be permitted to fall into the hands of speculators, but wherever these houses are suitably situated for continued occupancy they should be sold preferably to workers, under moderate rates of payment.

Immigration—(1919, pp. 121-364) Contrary to the propaganda fostered and encouraged by employing interests, the problem confronting our people is not one of emigration but of immigration. While it may be true that during the war all immigration ceased, it is equally true that a number of years will necessarily elapse before the industries of our country will have reabsorbed all the discharged soldiers, sailors, and war workers under conditions of employment commensurate with the more advanced standards of compensation for services rendered. While our immigration laws may be designed to prevent those persons coming to our shores who have little or no faith in our institutions, it is equally essential that our immigration laws are so molded as to prevent unemployment of the workers, which in itself causes so much friction and misery in our industrial relations. We are impressed with the effort made by the Executive Council to prevent the admittance of coolie labor and to avoid the many hardships and difficulties which the admission of coolie labor would necessarily involve. Also favor the approval of legislation for the prohibition of immigration for a fixed number of years and especially during the period of readjustment. (P. 368) Also made to apply to Mexican immigration.

(1920, p. 104) The strongest appeal for immigration made before the house committee was by farmers of Texas who claimed that at certain seasons of the year it was impossible for them to care for and harvest their crops without importing Mexican labor. However, the committee voted not to recommend any legislation. Reports from the border states showed that there was plenty of labor—in fact, a surplus of it at times and the scarcity was only on account of low wages. Owing to the failure of congress to appropriate money to pay the patrol on the Mexican border, many Mexicans, Japanese and Chinese, as well as undesirable natives of other countries, were able to gain illegal entry into the United States. During the war 28,000 Mexicans were admitted to the country to work on farms and only 20,000 returned to their country.

(P. 385) Commended executive officers for having been vigilant and unremitting in combatting the attempts to break down the laws and open the gates to the unskilled workers

who might be attracted hither by the high rate of pay and whose presence might in a short time result in such a congestion of the labor market as would result in great confusion and produce a most unfavorable situation.

(1921, p. 107) The A. F. of L. has repeatedly urged the complete restriction of immigration for at least two years, but approved of the bill which passed the house limiting it for one year. The great increase in unemployment, there being at least 5,000,000 out of work during the early part of 1921, made it imperative that immigration should be restricted as mush as possible. The opponents of bills restricting immigration to any extent whatever are opposing H. R. 4075. They desire to prevent any legislation restricting immigration in order that the country can be flooded with surplus labor. The A. F. of L. should declare for the enactment of a law providing for the fullest limitation and restriction of immigration obtainable. (P. 307) H. R. 4075, as amended by the senate and agreed to in conference, has been enacted into law since the Executive Council's report was written. This measure is not entirely satisfactory, as it does not meet the full requirements of the A. F. of L. It provides for the admission into this country from Europe of aliens to the number of 3 per cent of the foreign born of any nationality now in the U. S., as indicated by the census report of 1910, thus permitting the arrival in America annually of 355,461. The law was passed May 10, 1921, and continues in effect until June 30, 1922. The Executive Council is instructed to continue its efforts to secure the enactment of a law that willl forbid the importation of labor from any country until such time as conditions in our country have become more stabilized, and the relations of life more nearly normal.

(1922, pp. 103-328) The president of the A. F. of L. sent a letter to the members of the immigration committee of the senate in which he urged that immigration should be either absolutely restricted to only blood relatives of foreign born citizens in this country, the 3 per cent law made permanent until conditions called for a change, or, if this were not possible, to extend the expiration of the law until June 30, 1924. The senate followed the last suggestion and amended the house bill making the law expire June 30, 1924. This was agreed to by the house. It also adopted two very important amendments. One of these penalized steamships companies in the sum of $200 for each passenger brought over the quota. The other increased the one-year period which foreigners must live in Canada, Cuba and Mexico before entering the United States to five years. These amendments were urged by the A. F. of L. Reports have been received from the southwest that Mexicans by the carload are passing through New Mexico for the East. These Mexicans come direct from old Mexico and they are being used in railroad work. (P. 322) We urge congress to hereafter deny admission, as immigrants and permanent residents, to all aliens who are ineligible to citizenship under the laws of the United States.

(1923, pp. 39-354) Never in the history of the United States has there been such an insidious agitation for the repeal of all legislation enacted for the protection of the America workers, the American people and American standards. When traced to its hidden lair it is found that the propaganda emanated from the great corporatioins that pay the lowest wages and enjoy the highest protection of any industries in the country. Through the efforts of the Executive Council and our legislative committee the three per cent immigration law which was to expire June 30, 1923, was extended to June 30, 1924. The extension of the immigration law to June 30, 1924, was to avoid, if possible, any legislation by the last regular session of a congress which undoubtedly could not help being repudiated in the following November elections. The wisdom of this procedure was proved in the various attempts made after congress assembled in December and until it adjourned March 4, to enact some legislation that would open the gates to unrestricted immigration. Several bills were introduced which would permit the admission of 50,000 refugees and every influence that could possibly be used to have them passed was brought into play. Sentiment was appealed to. Swarms of people from southern Europe rushed to localities where they would come within the quota if the laws were enacted. Representatives of the Merchant Tailors' Association, the National Association of Manufacturers, the Bethlehem Steel Company and lobbyist J. A. Emery, who thrives on the compensation he receives from labor-baiting employers, were among those who appeared before committees of congress and asked for a law that would permit the admission of hordes of immigrants to this country." The spokesman for the Bethlehem Steel Company said that the company had to pay 36 cents an hour because there was not a sufficient number of immigrants being admitted to the country. He wanted such an excessive number of workers knocking at the gates of employment as to permit the Bethlehem Steel Company as well as all other corporations to fix a rate of wages suitable to the employers. He said that when the workers in the steel industry were receiving only 28 cents an hour thay got along very well because their children were working in factories and other places. Representatives of the American Merchant Tailors' Association said that because of compulsory education laws in the United States boys did not start to learn the tailoring trade until they were at least 14 years of age, while in Europe they began at 9 years of age or under. He wanted unrestricted immigration of skilled tailors. Representative Johnson, chairman of the committee on immigration of the house, presented a bill reducing the quota to two per cent of the number of foreign born individuals of each nationality resident in the United States as determined by the census of 1890. In addition there were to be 400 of each nationality admitted. Under the heading, "Non-Quota Immigrants," the following were to be admitted at any time: "An immigrant who is the husband, wife, father, mother, unmarried minor child, unmarried minor brother or sister, or unmarried minor orphan niece or nephew, of a citizen of the United States who resides therein at the time of the filing of a petition. It also provided in the non-quotas "an immigrant who is a skilled laborer, if labor of like kind unemployed can not be found in this country." The secretary of labor was to determine whether such labor was scarce upon the written application of any person interested. The seamen also objected to the bill on the ground that it would violate the provisions of the seamen's act. Protests were entered by the A. F. of L. and the conference committee of legislative representatives in Washington. Chairman Johnson and Representative Raker appeared before the trade union legislative representatives in the executive chamber of the A. F. of L. building and urged that the bill be approved. Mr. Johnson said that he had worked faithfully to prepare a bill that would be satisfactory and that i it were not supported by labor he was through with immigration legislation. It was agreed that a number of amendments should be submitted to the committee, especially to the non-quota clause, which would permit fraud, and to prevent the direct or indirect repeal of the provisions of the seamen's act. Under the provisions of the Johnson bill almost anyone could come into the country if a friendly citizen would make oath that he was a relative of the immigrant. The house committee on immigration refused to accept the amendments and the bill was reported to the house. Members of the house, however, finding that there were so many loopholes and snares in the bill and that there would be great opposition from labor to its passage, it was not brought to a vote. Congress will have until June 30, 1924, to enact a new immigration bill. As it is expected that the next congress will be more watchful of American interests than the last, there is hope that a proper measure will be passed. The cry is coming from all parts of the country for the Americanization of the foreigner. According to the United States census there are 13,000,000 foreigners in the United States of which 1,500,000 can not speak English and 3,000,000 can not read or write the English language. No better time could a campaign to this end be launched than at present and its success would be made more certain by the complete restriction of immigration. Until the foreigners now in this country are assimilated there can be no success in Americanizing the citizens born in this country. Illiteracy is growing at a rapid rate. The alarming discovery made during the war of the extent of illiteracy in the United States should be a warning to those who now urge the throwing open of our ports to still greater immigration. Congress will be called upon to decide between the greed of unfair employers and the self-preservation of our people.

Immigration and Musicians—(1919, p. 389) In the opinion of the A. F. of L. the term "artists" applies only to such producers in the intellectual field who in their quest for employment are not affected by the element of competition; namely, sculptors, painters, musical composers or virtuosos, and does not apply to musicians who work for wages and who in all else are subjected to and affected by the same conditions as all other wage workers. For these reasons the Executive Council is directed to call the injustice and error of exempting musicians from the operation of the alien contract labor law to the attention of the secretary of labor and request its correction and take all other necessary steps to secure to musicians the protection of the alien contract labor law.

Immigration, Mexican—(1919, p. 385) The A. F. of L. is impressed with the need for safeguarding the interests of American wage earners against unfair competition and discrimination by men of other nations. To avoid international complications, however, care should and must be exercised. We therefore refer to the Executive Council the question of the importation of Mexican laborers and urge the immigration officials to keep close watch over the granting of permits for the importation of alien laborers to the end that the interests of American laborers be safeguarded.

Immigrants, Union Information for— (1919, p. 292) Executive Council requested to investigate advisability of establishing an information bureau, preferably on Ellis Island, for immigrants. (1920, pp. 176-302) Executive Council had given earnest attention to the establishment of a trade union information bureau for immigrants and was directed to continue its efforts.

India—(p. 491) The A. F. of L. stands for self-determination, self-government, justice, freedom, and democracy for all peoples. The A. F. of L. hereby expresses its sympathy for the just struggles and aspirations of the people of India.

India Workers Organizing—(1920, pp. 130-475) The Executive Council received resolutions adopted by the Bombay Mill Hands' first conference, held December 14, 1919. The resolutions contain 27 specifications. In these there is a complete reflection of the condition of the workers in the textile industry in Bombay, and a portrayal of the birth of a new labor movement. The communication from Bombay was published in full in the April, 1920, issue of the *American Federationist*, and for its historical value it is hoped that the delegates to this convention and the officers of the trade union movement will read it. (P. 475) The birth of a new labor movement in India founded upon the principles of constructive trade unionism is gratifying, and justifies the claim that all real economic freedom, justice, and achievement must have its inception in and finally emerge out of the voluntary constructive trade union effort. We see in the splendid start upon which the workers of India are now launched a triumph of industrial justice, freedom, better living and working conditions, and moreover a final realization of the political hopes and aspirations for freedom, democracy and self-government

Industrial Commission Proposed— (1920, p. 118) Several bills presented in congress provided for industrial commissions or conferences between "capital and labor." One of them went so far as to select the names of the participants to be appointed by the president. Objection to this was filed in congress by the president of the A. F. of L. in a telegram sent during the A. F. of L. convention at Atlantic City. This bill and a number of others, which provided for conferences of employers and employes to consider what should be done to eliminate unrest and all other matters of benefit to the country, were refused consideration by the senate and house. The senate adopted a resolution concurring in the call issued by President Wilson for such a conference and this was finally approved by the house.

Industrial Committee of San Francisco—(1923, p. 339) Executive Council directed to continue efforts to have the authorities prosecute the industrial committee of San Francisco, which has by illegal and unlawful means coerced the contractors in these cities who have endeavored to be fair with their employes to refrain from resuming such friendly relations as have heretofore existed between themselves and their employes in the city of San Francisco and vicinity.

Industrialism—(1919, p. 348) Refused to approve of a proposition to change from the craft plan of organizing trade unions to one based on industries or "plant unions," and making all working cards universally interchangeable.

(1921, p. 391) Convention refused to approve of a plan of industrialism which provided that the international unions forego their absolute autonomy to the extent that power to arrange and decide economic programs and policies for the organized workers of North America shall rest in the Executive Council of the A. F. of L., with such restrictions as the judgment and experience of the

workers dictate. (1922, p. 264) Reaffirmed.

Industry's Manifest Duty—(1923, p. 31) We feel that the hour has struck for a pronouncement of the aims of labor that shall more nearly express the full implications of trade unionism than has yet been undertaken in these annual reports. This we have had in mind in the preparation of previous reports, but we have preferred to follow the established practice of the American trade union movement, which is to allow expression of policy and program to proceed naturally from the life and needs of the people, giving voice from time to time only to such proposals and formulations as have been finally shaped out of experiences. Experience continues and is recorded as it unfolds. The recording of experience is perhaps the greatest achievement of all history. We know what the past has given us because the past has given us its records. The record of human experience since the fateful days of 1914 is more intense with the story of rapid development than any other similar period in history. Developments of the most climatic character have raced each other's heels. Trade unionism, as an integral and ever-functioning part of human society, has had its full share of tremendous experiences and it has not failed to observe the experiences of all other functional elements in society. What we have observed is that the period ending with the beginning of the world war found political democracy in its fullest state of development, while the close of that period of overwhelming upheaval marked the opening of the period of intelligent demand and living need for industrial democracy. The close of the war marked for us a turning point in human relations and threw forth in bold relief the inadequacy of existing forms and institutions. Henceforth trade unionism has a larger message and a larger function in society. Henceforth the movement for the organization of the workers into trade unions has a deeper meaning than the mere organization of groups for the advancement of group interests, however vital that function may yet remain. Henceforth the organization of the workers into trade unions must mean the conscious organization of one of the most vital functional elements for enlightened participation in a democracy of industry whose purpose must be the extension of freedom, the enfranchisement of the producer as such, the rescue of indutry from chaos, profiteering and purely individual whim, including individual incapacity, and the rescue of industry also from the domination of incompetent political bodies. The largest freedom of action, the freest play for individual intiative and genius in industry can not be had under the shadow of constant incompetent political interference, meddlesomeness and restriction. Through the muddling conflict of groups who still find it impossible to come together in cooperation we must look to a future that must have its foundation upon cooperation and collaboration. The threat of state invasion of industrial life is real. Powerful groups of earnest and sincere persons constantly seek the extension of state suzerainty over purely industrial fields. Such ignorant encroachments as the Esch-Cummins act, the Kansas court of industrial relations and the Colorado industrial commission act, each a blundering gesture of government acting under the spur of organized propaganda or of political appetite for power, are examples of what all industry has to fear. The continuing clamor for extension of state regulatory powers under the guise of reform and deliverance from evil, can but lead into greater confusion and more hopeless entanglements. Trade unionism must lead the way for true progress, even at the cost of being branded as reactionary by those who do but little save propound formulas based upon utopian thought and devoid of the benefit of experience and of any cognizance of our fundamental social structure, our industrial life or our national characteristics. We advocate organization of all wage earners and of all useful and productive elements. We feel that we shall not labor the point if we review what we have repeatedly said and what all students know, that our national life today is becoming more and more industrial and that the decisions that most vitally affect the intimate daily lives of our people are the decisions that are made in industry, in the workshops and factories, in the mines and mills, in the commercial establishments, on the railroads and in the counting rooms. The decisions that caused more than five million workers to be for months without work were not decisions of congress. The decisions that quickened the wheels and brought men and women back into service were not decisions of congress. Labor now participates more fully in the decisions that shape human life than ever before and more fully in America than in any other nation on earth; but our participation must be gradually brought to completion. The purpose of this is not only the commanding of better wages and better conditions of work, vital as those are and have been. The purpose that now unfolds is broader and nobler and filled with deeper meaning. We have fought our way through the preliminaries, fitting the workers for their greater role by means of the opportunities that have come with the establishment of standards of life and wages befitting American workmen. For the future industry must become something of which we have a national consciousness. It must cease to be a disconnected collection of groups, like states without a union. The future demands an American industry, in which it shall be possible for all to give of their best through the orderly processes of democratic, representative organization. The ruthless drive of purely individual aim and ambition has given America tremendous industrial giants. Great abuse has accompanied great achievement. But what is frequently overlooked is the fact that the ambition to build has been the driving force behind our most remarkable strides. The abuses, terrible and costly as they have been, have been largely coincidental. The ambition to build must be saved; the abuses must be eradicated by means of organization befitting the state of our development and the demands of our time. In no other way can industry continue that growth which is required to satisfy our ever-growing demand for commodities and avoid submersion in a wave of blighting political domination. The functional elements in our national life must fit themselves to work out their own problems, eradicate their abuses and furnish America with an ever-increasing flood of commodities, both necessary and pleasure-giving. Industry alone has the competence and it must demonstrate that competence through organization. The organized functional elements in industry will find easy of solution those problems to which politicians now turn their attention in futility. Industry must organize to govern itself, to impose upon itself tasks and rules and to bring order into its own house. Industry must bring order to itself constructively or it will have an order thrust upon it which would be demoralizing if not fatal. Our people can not live and thrive under the regime

of bureaucracy that threatens unless industry solves its own problems. It was the abuses attendant upon an unregulated natural industrial impulse that brought upon our country that legislative monstrosity known as the Sherman anti-trust law. It is a mistaken zeal on the part of political government, a zeal often encouraged by powers that misinterpret their own role in our industrial life, that burden us with the anachronism known as the injunction. It is a combination of industry's own neglect and of government's effort to function where industry for the moment fails or seems to fail that give us a growing number of boards, commissions, and tribunals to add their weight to the burden of industry. Industry, organized as we urge it must be organized, will begin in truth an era of service, rational, natural development and productivity unmatched by past achievement or fancy. It is not the mission of industrial groups to clash and struggle against each other. Such struggles are the signs and signals of dawning comprehension, the birth pangs of an industrial order attempting through painful experience to find itself and to discover its proper functioning. The true role of industrial groups, however, is to come together, to legislate in peace, to find the way forward in collaboration, to give of their best for the satisfaction of human needs. There must come to industry the orderly functioning that we have been able to develop in our political life. We must find the way to the development of an industrial franchise comparable to our political franchise. There must be developed a sense of responsibility and justice and orderliness. Labor stands ready for participation in this tremendous development. It has long offered conference with all its implications as a substitute for conflict, regarding the folding of arms in idleness only as the last resort in failure of negotiations, signalizing the glaring fact that the industrial destinies of the country have thus far been finally in the hands of one group in the nation's industrial organization. Too frequently the group that controls investment or credit controls the policies of industry. When this occurs industry finds itself guided by the desires of those who seek returns on investment, with little or no regard for any other factor. Modern industry, as we have repeatedly declared and as is conceded by all who understand, functions largely with the assistance of credit. But credit, which is the life blood of productive industry, is continuously purloined for purely exploiting, profiteering speculative and wasteful purposes. It is not infrequently employed for the purpose of withholding commodities from their proper channels in order that inordinate and criminal manipulation and profiteering may take place. Every perversion of the proper functions of industry eventually strikes back at industry and leaves its damaging mark. Industry, as it becomes more intelligently and thoroughly organized and coordinated, as cooperative relations are extended, will in self-defense purge itself of the wrongful, wasteful, uneconomical, anti-social and criminal misuse of credit power. Credit power is one of the most vital powers in the modern world and it arises out of the very existence of the people themselves, being but a token, or guarantee of their ability to use and consume. This power, which arises out of the people, out of the fact that they live and must use commodities, must be stripped of its abuses and administered in accordance with the demands of a normal, rational industrial life in the interests of service and production and not solely or mainly in the interests of profits and perversions of our industrial system. The operation of industry for the dominant purpose of producing private profit has led to a multitude of abuses. It has produced all of the evils of autocracy because it is autocratic. Every factor that enters into the sustenance or operation of industry must be safeguarded and its just reward assured, but there must be an end to final control by any single factor. We have had and must continue to have, until democracy finds its way into industry, abuses for which all producers and all consumers have had to pay through profiteering and privation. The end of such a state of affairs must come at no distant time, or political bureaucracy will gain the ascendancy. And we can not do other than regard such an eventuality as the final mark of incompetency to manage an industrial civilization. Industry must save itself. Industry must find itself. Industry must organize for service, for constructive effort, for orderly continuity, for justice to all who participate. It must bring itself to a realization of its mission and to that end it must organize and come together in deliberative bodies where the full wisdom and experience of all may contribute to final decisions. Much the same lessons that we have learned in our political life—among them the sense of order—must be learned and given effect in our industrial life. Fact must take the place of opinion and selfish interest. To function must be the object, and democratic participation of all who give service must be the mechanism that makes this possible. Industry must realize that it exists to give service to a nation and not to a single master, or to a syndicate of stockholders. We must have an American industrial life, an American industrial order, not a warring group of units, each seeking to be a law unto itself, the while inviting the interference of those whose competence is at best an unknown factor. While we have no wish to offer unasked advice to those who occupy any other field in our productive life, we feel that we may suggest that agriculture, the great life-giving twin of industry, must find its way through to orderliness and justice by adoption of substantially the same methods which we advocate for industry. We fail to find any opportunity for difference in principle. During the past year the relations between industrial workers and productive agriculture have grown tremendously; understanding has been developed everywhere between those who give productive effort in these two great fields. It is our hope that the farmers will continue their work of organization and that we may have and give assistance in pushing forward the program upon which we believe depends our future national well-being and safety. We have sought to set forth a great goal—the goal of America's wage earners— and the salvation of the masses of our people and of our inspiring industrial supremacy. We covet life and the fuller development of life and we therefore demand in behalf of the masses of our people the only course that can make possible the satisfaction of our ambition, the achievement of our ideal and the preservation of our essential liberties. American industry dare not confess incompetence. We call upon all who have eyes to see to join us in a great crusade for industrial democracy as the means to a greater national and individual life and as the means to the preservation of the genius of our people. Industry is the bedrock of modern civilization. We must bring order through organization into that life or suffer it to fall under the dominion of a state bureaucracy which must be destructive alike of freedom for the individual and of progress for industry as a whole. We commit ourselves to greater efforts in the organization of all workers, we urge upon all useful persons the imperative need of organization, and finally, the coming together in working bodies of all organizations through representatives who shall speak for organic groupings. We have long been on the road to this end. We urge no new formula, no new philosophy; we urge only a great consciousness of purpose and a definite aim on the part of all toward its more rapid fulfillment, because the needs of the time make it imperative. (P. 264) The declaration made is not only indisputable in its accuracy of the presentation of trade union philosophy, but that the philosophy contained therein must be the basis of the trade union platform and program in the evolution of our industrial life. The declaration constitutes the one sound foundation of the case for the present order and for a democratic future in our industrial life. The wage earners and the masses of our people are offered a guide by which they may perceive the method and the road by which industrial autocracy may be overcome where it has become rooted and avoided where it has not grown; and they are also offered a guide by which they may know how to avoid the blight of political bureaucracy and unsound "isms." We feel that we are justified in pointing out and that it may serve some purpose to point out that we find in this magnificent expression of labor's philosophy a new and timely explanation of American labor's fundamental reason for the avoidance of entanglement and illusion in the realm of partisan politics. The declaration now under consideration is the product of a trade union movement bent upon intelligent singleness of purpose to function in the world of industry, where the organic life of modern society has its roots and where it finds its sustenance. We have an abiding faith in the ability of industry to develop and erect the methods and machinery for the solution of its own problems. We have faith in its ability to promote and secure justice. We have faith in its ability to develop and give effect to a restraint and a discipline suited to its needs and the needs of humanity and to bring into operation the methods by which it may function most efficiently in the service of mankind. This message is not only the message of trade unionism to the wage earners of our land; it is also the message of trade unionism to every group and every branch of activity in the industrial life of our republic. The wage earners form the preponderant majority of all those engaged usefully in industry, and their need for organization along sound and practical trade union lines is the first requisite. The development of industrial democracy, however, requires that there should be organization throughout every ramification of industry, among all men and women in industry. Democracy in industry requires expression. Agglomerations are bereft of expression because they are unable to develop the channels of expression. We counsel organization everywhere, in order that through organized effort we may develop to its fullest possibilities our magnificent industrial enterprise. Our standards are unquestionably and admittedly the highest in the world. We, as citizens of the U. S. and participants in industry, have a stake in the future of our industry and we have a right and a duty to speak in behalf of the best possible future for ourselves and posterity. We can not too highly commend this brilliant and concise expression of trade union philosophy, and we urge that every opportune and practical method be utilized to disseminate that expression and give it effect in the industrial organization and life of our republic. Humanity must learn to govern itself in industry as it has learned to govern itself in political affairs and to give effect to the same stability and the same guarantees of human freedom and human rights.

Initiative and Referendum—(1919, pp. 130-355) One more state, Massachusetts, was added during the year to those which have finally attained a full measure of government "by the people," through the adoption of the initiative and referendum. This makes 20 states in which the voters may propose and enact laws without the interference of adverse influences.

Initiative and Referendum for Unions—(1919, p. 353) Refused to adopt resolution instructing the Executive Council to, within 90 days, prepare and send to all international unions, a model initiative and referendum provision as a suggested amendment to their various constitutions, such suggested amendment to be drawn in such manner as will make possible the submission of any given proposition to the whole membership of the A. F. of L. simultaneously, and in legal manner; the demand of 5 per cent of the local unions being necessary to invoke the use of this amendment by any international union at given stated periods.

(1920, p. 424) Same resolution defeated.

(1921, p. 428) The resolution if concurred in would interfere in the fundamental rights of international organizations. One of the guarantees given by the A. F. of L. to all international unions is that they should have the right to handle their own affairs and legislate for themselves; that fundamental right can not legally be interfered with. We therefore deem it unnecessary and inadvisable to adopt the resolution.

Injunctions—(1919, pp. 97-361) Nothing is more dangerous to the rights of life, liberty and the pursuit of happiness than to permit any department of government exclusive, absolute and final authority in any matter which directly or indirectly involves or affects the destiny of a people or control over its possessions. Our nation only recently associated itself with other democratic nations of Europe to destroy the hereditary rule of government over the people. Our nation, in association with other nations of free peoples, has just concluded a victorious war for the rights of all peoples to determine their own destinies. While proud of our accomplishments in behalf of peoples of Europe, we have nevertheless been neglectful of sinister influences constantly at work in our body politic, which are slowly but surely sapping the virus of independence from our institutions and are creating an autocracy equal in power and authority to that exercised by the most tyrannical despot ever known to human history. Our nation is founded on the principle that every citizen is a sovereign unto himself and that the powers of government extend only to that degree to which the consent of the governed has been freely, fully and fairly obtained. The governmental authority of our nation has been so divided and designed to prevent the usurping of authority and power by any one department of government not fairly and freely delegated to it by the expressed will of the people. Despite all these precautions to safeguard individual liberty and freedom of action, despite the fact that the early constitutional convention denied the right to our courts to pass on the constitutionality of laws enacted by congress, our courts and judges have been slowly and surely disregarding these restrictions and limitations and now freely and uninterruptedly exercise powers which even the monarchs and kaisers dared not exercise with all their claims to power by inherent divinity. The power of our courts to declare legislation enacted unconstitutional and void is a most flagrant usurpation of power and authority by our courts and is a repudiation and denial of the principle of self-government recognized now as a world doctrine. The continued exercise of this unwarranted power is a blasphemy on the rights and claims of free men of America. This usurpation of power by our courts to subordinate the legislative and executive departments to their will and compel the activities of a free people to their whims and dictates is parralleled and equaled only by the further usurpation of authority by our courts to legislate and punish people in direct defiance of constitutional safeguards to personal liberty and freedom of action. By the issuance of injunctive decrees by our courts, by the restraint they place upon the normal and rightful activities of a free people, by the punishing of free men in the exercise of their constitutional rights without opportunity to a trial by jury, by the removal of safeguards thrown around the individual against extreme and excessive punishments and the denial of an opportunity or executive clemency, our courts have vested themselves with a power greater than any despot ever heretofore possessed. The fate of the sovereignty of American people again hangs in the balance. It is inconceivable that such an autocratic, despotic, and tyrannical power can long remain in a democracy. One or the other must ultimately give way, and we declare that, as wage earners, citizens of a free and democratic republic, we shall stand firmly and conscientiously on our rights as free men and treat all injunctive decrees that invade our personal liberties as unwarranted in fact, unjustified in law and illegal as being in violation of our constitutional safeguards, and accept whatever consequences may follow. Immediate steps should be taken by the Executive Council and by all state organizations for the early enactment of adequate laws to deny the further usurpation of these unwarranted powers by our courts, and that congress be petitioned to impeach all judges from office who may hereafter exercise governmental functions and authority not expressly delegated to them. It is the viewpoint of your committee that the widest possible publicity should be given this subject and that the public mind and conscience should be fully aroused to the dangers confronting the liberties of our people to the end that the judicial autocracy and despotism which has been slowly developing in our midst will come to an early and definite end. (P. 473) Judge Dennis E. Sullivan, of Chicago, sent 32 cigarmakers to jail with fines aggregating $2,875 for picketing a Havana Cigar Company plant. These sentences were imposed notwithstanding the complainant admitted that while picketing the cigarmakers "had done nothing, stopped no one, and had spoken to no one."

(1921, p. 382) The courts in certain jurisdictions, notably in the city of New York, have of late adopted an alarming attitude of antagonism towards organized workers, and have issued numerous sweeping and severe injunctions against labor unions engaged in legitimate struggles to maintain living standards. Such injunctions have in some instances been accompanied by startling reactionary doctrines from the bench, one judge going to the length of proclaiming it to be the duty of the courts "to stand at all times as the representatives of capital" in labor struggles, and another judge reviving a case of 1809 in which workers were convicted of a criminal "conspiracy to raise wages" and holding out the horrible example of an unenlightened age as a legal authority for dealing with organized labor in our day. The A. F. of L. assembled in Denver, Colo., emphatically and solemnly protests against this alarming tendency of the courts, which menaces the very existence of American workers as freemen. We assert that the workers have the inalienable right to work when, for whom, and for what they please and to withhold their work individually or collectively for any reason which they consider sufficient and that to deny them this right means to revive the medieval institution of involuntary servitude; that they have the right to induce their fellow workers to join them in their struggles for economic betterment and to quit work for hostile employers; that the employer has no property right in labor, as labor is neither a commodity nor an article of commerce. We call upon all affiliated organizations, particularly upon all central bodies in the larger industrial communities, to inaugurate energetic campaigns against the ever-growing abuse of injunctions in labor disputes and to conduct such campaigns through meetings, publications and other avenues of publicity earnestly and unceasingly until the intolerable practice is abandoned by legislative relief or otherwise. ((P. 429) All trade unions and their officers of Ohio County, West Virginia, were enjoined on the application of the Building Employers' Association. The convention directed that the enjoined trade unions and their officers should disregard any injunctions that invaded the rights of the workers of this country in the lawful performance of the functions of the trade union movement.

(1922, p. 48) Considered from every point of view, and in the light of a varied and most extensive experience, the injunction process as used by the courts of our land in industrial disputes, is not an instrument of equity, but a weapon of oppression. Through its unwarranted uses and flagrant abuses the courts of equity have become the courts of the rich, the protectors of property and of property rights, and have disregarded the human aspirations and personal rights of the workers. By this system of personal government, statutory enactments by our legislators have been swept aside and judge-made law has taken their places. Practically all the decisions of our courts in industrial disputes arising out of the issuance of injunctions are founded upon the legal point of view that the labor power of a human being is property, and that as such it can be bought and sold, contracted for and treated as an ordinary commodity. This conception is philosophically and economically unsound and is unwarranted in law. It is of modern origin in its application to industrial disputes, not having been seriously contended for until the adoption of the thirteenth amendment to the constitution of the United States with which it is in direct opposition. This legal conception of labor power, taken in connection with anti-combination and anti-conspiracy doctrines, is the cornerstone upon which the equity power of our courts in industrial affairs is founded and which threaten the complete destruction of the ideals of American liberty and American freedom. Prior to the adoption of the thirteenth amendment, it was not neces-

sary to divide the labor power of a human being from the person in whom it is inherent. Absolute ownership of a person necessarily carried with it absolute ownership of the labor power. Contracts to labor enforceable by imprisonment under the master and servant laws, operated in the same way. The person was bought or raised as a slave, he was contracted for if not a slave; in either case he was a labor power that was desired and obtained. After the adoption of the thirteenth amendment the employer found it desirable to find some way of maintaining his grip on the labor power, and so through anti-conspiracy laws, and anti-combination laws and the misuse of the equity power of our courts, the employer did, through the advice of attorneys and prompted by the speculative theory of pseudo-political economists, set about to treat labor power as property, separate and distinct from the person, notwithstanding the fact that the labor power of a human being is the most personal of all things, and so absolutely inherent in the person that it grows with his growth, diminishes in sickness and with age, and passes away at death. As a matter of fact, in cases dealing with disputes between business men and organizations of labor, the courts clearly establish the fact that in similar cases there is one rule for workers and another rule for employers. A case in point is that involving boycott by a citizens' alliance at St. Paul, Minn., of the firm of Delaney Brothers, plumbers, because Delaney Brothers refused to put in their window an "open shop" card. Delaney Brothers applied for an injunction to protect them from the boycott instituted by the citizens' alliance, which included practically all of the business men, manufacturers and bankers'-associations of St. Paul. The court refused to protect Delaney Brothers from the boycott and thus sustained the right of business organizations to use the boycott. In refusing to grant the injunction, the court said in part: "If an act be lawful—one that the party has a legal right to do—the fact that he may be actuated by an improper motive does not render it unlawful. . . . It was lawful for any one of the defendants to sever business relations with the plaintiffs, therefore, it was lawful for two or more of them." Continuing, the court quoted the following decision of Judge Cooley: "It is a part of every man's civil rights that he be left at liberty to refuse business relations with any person whomsoever, whether the refusal rests upon reason, or is the result of whim, caprice, prejudice, or malice, with his reasons, neither the public nor third persons have any concern." In the Pennsylvania case of Cote vs. Murphy the employers' right to boycott again was upheld. From the decision in that case the following is taken: "A combination of employers preventing dealers in the supply used by such employers from selling to an employer who was not a member of their combination and who had consented to the demand of employes, by informing such dealer that no member of the combination would buy from them if they sold to such employer, is not illegal or unlawful, nor does it amount to coercion." There are many other court decisions of this kind, but those quoted are sufficient to establish the point that there is a clear bias in favor of property. Under the decision of the United States supreme court in the case of Truax vs. Corrigan it is doubtful if labor may secure proper legislative redress against the abuses of the equity powers in the form of legislation expressed in the labor sections of the Clayton law. In this instance the

United States supreme court has held this
form or remedial legislation unconstitutional.
In the Tri-City Central Trades Council case
the supreme court has practically taken the
life blood out of section 20 of the Clayton law.
Regardless of whatever legislation has been
secured to protect the workers, when in contest with employers, against the unwarranted
and unconstitutional infringement of their
rights and liberties by our equity courts and
through the process of injunction, all such
legislative checks have been swept aside or
perverted by judicial interpretation and construction. Organized labor, it would seem,
is thus forced to the only alternative of resisting
this judicial encroachment upon the constitutional rights and freedom of America's workers
by the course outlined at a number of previous
conventions of the A. F. of L. and most impressively comprehended in the declaration of the
Atlantic City, 1919, convention. The course
outlined seems to offer the only possibility
of relief from the unconstitutional use of the
writ of injunction. Any other course not
only offers no relief but involves either a
tacit recognition of the right of courts to issue
such injunctions or a long and formidable
struggle through the courts while the workers
everywhere continue to suffer fron the penalties and judgments arbitrarily inflicted by
an arrogant judiciary in the exercise of the
powers which have been usurped and for which
there is no constitutional or lawful justification.
It is also urged that a special effort be made
to get into the public mind the clear conception
of the fact that the power of labor is inherent
in the individual, that it can not be separated
from him and that it can not be treated either
in legislative or in judicial decisions as property without treating the individual as property. With this thoroughly understood, we
shall be in a position to compel our courts to
maintain the validity of those principles
necessary to preserve American freedom and
equal opportunity, or else to secure judges who
will serve human needs and aspirations and
who will not be slaves to precedents. In addition every organization should immediately
advise the officers of the A. F. of L. of each
and every complaint filed against the trade
unions in our equity courts and any attempt
made to secure an injunction against the lawful
activities of trade unions, first, to enable the
officers of the A. F. of L. to extend such advice and helpful suggestions as may present
themselves, and secondly, to enable the A. F.
of L. to compile the injunctions that have
been issued against labor and thus present
forcibly to the public mind the constantly
growing and ever-increasing encroachment of
our equity courts upon the rights of labor
and the trespass upon the constitutional safeguards of the liberties of all our people. Then,
too, it is becoming more apparent each day
that anti-conspiracy and anti-combination
laws dealing with industrial relations do not
operate as a deterrent to monopoly. Rather,
that these ancient doctrines aid in the formation of monopolistic enterprises and monopolistic control of capital and serve only the
purpose of preventing the workers from organizing efficiently and from functioning in
such a manner as will enable the workers to
exercise an effectual voice and vote in determining their terms and conditions of employment and in securing their full share in
the rewards of industrial activities. Efforts
should be made, therefore, to modify or annul
these ancient doctrines so as to safeguard to
the workers, not alone their individual, but
their collective or group rights and liberties
as well and more nearly establish a system of

law that will accord to all an equal opportunity in the pursuit of life, liberty, and happiness. (P. 488) Reaffirmed previous action
on injunctions.

(1923, p. 94) The modern and extensive
use of the writ of injunction especially as
used in labor disputes is revolutionary and
destructive. The injunction writ was designed when popular government was unknown and at a time it was difficult to enact
such laws as would permit a speedy and adequate adjustment of controversies subject to
legal determination. Thus it is said that
equity in law in "the application of right and
justice to the legal adjustment of differences
when the law by reason of its universality
is different," or "that system of jurisprudence
which comprehends every matter of law for
which the law provided no remedy." Thus
conceived it must be apparent, with the development of popular government and the
ready opportunities to provide by legislative
enactment for whatever legal deficiency that
may present itself at any time that either the
injunction writ has outlived its usefulness or
that our legislative system of enacting laws
has failed in the functions assigned to it. In-
dicative and demonstrative of the unwarrantable use of the injunction writ in labor disputes is the fact that in England, from whence
are imported this extra legal devise, the equity
power is limited to property and then only
where there is no remedy at law. In England the injunction writ is not permissible
in labor disputes. While the constitution
confers equity power upon the courts in the
same way that it is made their duty to issue
the writ of habeas corpus and to insure trial by
jury this equity power was so limited and defined by English authorities that our courts
could not obtain jurisdiction in labor disputes except by adopting the legal fiction that
labor was a commodity or article of commerce
and that business was property. This is
exactly what our courts have done and by
this legal assumption our courts have vested
themselves with the most oppressive and repressive legal weapon ever devised and designed to hold in subjection those who must
earn their way through life by the sweat of
toil and under the domination of a "master
class." These injunction writs in labor disputes have been issued in even greater and
greater numbers and each succeeding injunction goes further in its repressive features than
the one before. Indeed, this special form of
class legislation by judicial decree is assuming
an enormous proportion and the wage earners
are compelled to suffer under a set of class
laws which apply to no other group within our
government. It is inconceivable that this
form of government by injunction can long
prevail without serious reckoning. As an
American people we have escaped government by the king. We have just emerged
from the world's greatest conflict and glory
in our achievement that we have rid the world
of the most arrogant of all modern autocracies.
And yet what does it gain us if, indeed, we
permit the growing up of a despotic government by the judges. If we are to preserve
this "government of the people, by the people,
and for the people" then any and all usurpations by the judiciary must be as sternly
resisted as usurpations by any king or other
form of executive. Serious attention has
been given this subject in the effort to prepare
an appropriate and all-sufficient legislative
proposal to adequately meet the situation.
Likewise, we had had under consideration
constitutional amendments designed to accomplish the same purpose. It is believed

that some effective measure of redress may be perfected so as to receive consideration at the coming session of congress. Pending remedial redress from this usurped power of our courts and their unconstitutional intrusion upon the rights and liberties of our people, we reaffirm and adhere to former declarations of the A. F. of L. to maintain our natural and constitutional rights and liberties unimpaired. Policies of repression whether practiced by employers alone or in combination with our courts must not be permitted to stifle, check or retard the righteous growth and full development of the American trade union movement. (P. 276) "Government by injunction" is not merely a phrase. It is, unfortunately, an actual state of affairs. Unless the equity powers of our courts are adequately curbed and properly limited we may as well disband with our legislative branch of government and acknowledge openly and freely what is practically in fact—a government, not by law, but by judicial decree. The evils arising out of the unwarranted extension of equity powers of our courts, the complete destruction of every constitutional safeguard by the use of the injunction writ, the complete subserviency of all other branches of government to this ever-expanding and ever-extending power of our courts of equity may well cause all right-thinking people to pause and wonder as to where we are drifting. With our legislative bodies intimidated by the powers wielded by our courts and with little if any opportunity to confine our courts to the sphere of government originally assigned to them by orderly processes of laws, we can only visualize civil resistance and disobedience to any and all judicial decrees which are not founded on legislative enactments and which are permissible under constitutionally delegated authority. We commend the Executive Council for its diligent efforts to meet this ever-growing menace by legislative redress. It is our sincere hope this procedure may afford relief, but this growing cancer in our body politic will continue its destruction of the social and political fiber of our nation unless drastic measures of resistance are adopted and the poison of assumed authority by our equity judges is removed entirely from our judicial system. (P. 305) The attitude of antagonism toward organized workers by the courts in a great many jurisdictions in the U. S., notably in the cities of New York and Chicago, has manifested itself in an ever-growing number of sweeping and severe injunctions against labor unions engaged in legitimate struggles to maintain living standards. The A. F. of L. emphatically and solemnly protest against this alarming practice of the courts which menaces the very existence of American workers as free men.

Injunction by Labor a Snare, Use of— (1922, p. 47) Because of the ever-increasing use of the injunction process by employers engaged in contest with the organized wage earners, and by reason of the great stress our equity courts have laid upon the observance of contracts and the non-interference of contracts by those not directly concerned with industrial relations, it is not surprising that efforts should have been made by some of our trade unions to use the injunction process against employers with whom they have been in conflict. Three cases of this kind developed during the past year and the experience has clearly demonstrated that the judicial system, founded upon the unrestricted power exercised by our judges in their chancery division can never be made fairly and equitably to adjust industrial disputes. Even were this possible such a procedure would not justify the usurped legislative functions exercised by our equity courts through the injunction process. One of the cases instituted in New York City has aroused much interest and discussion. It has been heralded as proof of the alleged falsity of the charges of the workers that our equity courts are open only to employers. In this instance the employers had entered into an agreement with an international union. Before the expiration of the agreement the employers concerned entered into a separate agreement among themselves to violate the agreement they had entered into with this trade union. The union sought an injunction to prevent the violation of their agreement with the union. The court directed that the employers cease this conspiracy and revoke the resolutions which they had adopted which was the act by which the contract with the union had been broken. An appeal has been taken by the employers in this case. The decison of the lower court is now before the higher courts for judicial review and decision. We await with further interest the decision of the higher courts and would not be surprised if the higher court may decide that inasmuch as the cause of the complaint having been removed that the judicial settlement of the issues involved are merely argumentative and that the court is not concerned with the settlement of moot questions. Should this surmise come true there will be then much room for doubt even as to the validity of the injunction in this particular instance. Another case arose in Minneapolis, Minn., where a local union secured a temporary injunction preventing local employers from carrying out an understanding among themselves to violate the agreement they had entered into with this local union. In this case the employers were bound to an agreement with the union running until December 31, 1922. The only question subject to change was that of wages. A method of arbitrating this question was provided. Instead of proceeding in accordance with the agreement the employers locked out the members of this union and violated the agreement. The local union secured a temporary injunction, but upon hearing to make the temporary injunction permanent, it was denied on the ground that the agreement between the local union and their employers lacked "mutuality." This case was identical to the one to which reference was first made as having been instituted by a union in New York City. In both cases the employers conspired to violate and did violate their agreement with the union. In the New York case the court maintained the validity of the agreement; in the Minneapolis case the court found it convenient to avoid compelling the employers to live up to their contract. Instead, the court permitted the employers to continue to violate their agreement merely by finding fault that the agreement was unenforcible because of a minor section in the agreement which had never been questioned before either by the employers or by the local union and had been part of the agreement for many years. The third case which developed during the year was that of an organization in Chicago appealing for an injunction to restrain third parties from interfering with a contractual relationship between employers and local unions. In this case the local union complained that a self-constituted organization of employers and bankers had arrogated to themselves the task of compelling workmen to accept conditions of employment regardless of their own determination and inclination;

that they had conspired with others to interfere with trade and banking facilities of such employers as would not observe the dictum of this self-constituted organization of employers and bankers. The complaint was also made that this combination purposed the destruction of this particular organization. This combination of employers and bankers entered the plea that the local union did not come into court with clean hands. While the court found that the plea of this combination of employers and bankers was a plea of "confession and avoidance," and while they did transgress on the rights of this particular organization and its members, it declined to give any relief to this organizaion, but immediately proceeded to find that the members of this union guilty of violating law in that they were driving other men from work by various acts of violence, and that therefore they were not entitled to relief through the equity courts. In this case the effort made by a local trade union to use the equity courts to enjoin the admitted wrong-doing of this combination of employers and bankers not only failed but the court availed itself of the jurisdiction given to it to prosecute this particular trade union and its members and find them guilty in general terms of criminal acts contrary to all constitutional methods and in violation of every constitutional safeguard to prevent individual citizens from being unjustly charged and convicted of crime. This procedure is one that violates every principle of law and justice and can not be too strongly condemned. These decisions clearly indicate that the use of the injunction process by trade unions does not present to the workers a fair, just, equitable or constitutional method of protecting and safeguarding their rights. Indeed, two of these decisions demonstrate that an appeal by trade unions to the equity courts may be turned conveniently into an instrument against the rights of the workers. It is thus apparent that while equity courts may be open to labor unions, yet the procedure followed, our equity judges once having been given jurisdiction, leaves room for no doubt that the injunction process is a system of judge-made law which violates every constitutional safeguard to life and liberty.

Injunction, Judge Wilkerson's—(1923, p. 67) On September 1. 1922, Attorney General Daugherty obtained from Judge Wilkerson of the U. S. district court, sitting in Chicago, a restraining order against the officers and members of the railway shop trade organizations which was proclaimed far and wide as the most drastic injunction ever issued in a labor dispute, or in any other case. The order was obtained with great secrecy. The attorney general left Washington announcing that he was going to his home town, Columbus, Ohio. When he reached Chicago, he first obtained a private conference with Judge Wilkerson. Then he appeared in open court, the newspapers having been notified of his intention, but no notice being given to the officers of the railway employes department, whose headquarters are in Chicago, nor to any other defendant. He made an inflammatory speech to the court in which he said that "so long and to the extent that I can speak for the government of the U. S. I will use the power of the government of of the U. S. within my power to prevent the labor unions of the country from destroying the open shop," and further said, "when the unions claim the right to dictate to the government and dominate the American people and deprive the American people of the necessities of life, then the government will destroy

the unions, for the government of the U. S. is supreme and must endure." The attorney general presented the order which he had drawn, which was then signed immediately by the court without change. On this short, one-sided hearing, on the basis that the defendants were engaged in a conspiracy against interstate commerce, the court ordered them to refrain from any sort of activity in prosecution of the strike. For example, prohibiting them from "In any manner by letters, printed or other circulars, telegrams, telephones, word of mouth, oral persuasion, or communication, or through interviews published in the newspapers, or other similar acts, encouraging, directing or commanding any person, whether a member of any or either of said labor organizations or associations defendants herein, to abandon the employment of said railway companies, or any of them, or to refrain from entering the service of said railway companies, or any of them." The order also restrains the national officers from "issuing any instructions, or making any requests, public statements or communications to any defendant," or from using the funds of the organizations to promote the doing of the things restrained. In accordance with the provisions of the Clayton act, the order was made effective the full ten days allowed for an order obtained without notice, and a hearing set on the government application for a preliminary injunction for September 11. When the case was called the defendants' attorneys moved that the government bill should be dismissed for the reasons: "First: That the strike was lawful. Second: That the court had no authority to carry on a criminal prosecution denying trial by jury. Third: That the attorney general had sought and obtained the aid of the court upon misrepresentation of facts, and for the unlawful purpose of aiding the efforts of the railway executives to destroy the railway unions as a part of a national campaign for the so-called open shop." After ten days of arguments and the presentation of something like 2,000 affidavits by the government alleging unlawful acts, which mass of evidence it was physically and financially impossible for the defendants to oppose by counter evidence, the court ordered a preliminary injunction on September 25, which was stated to be practically the same as the restraining order, but which was in fact fundamentally different. The basis of the order, shown in the opinion of the court and the terms of the order, marked a new advance of the courts of equity in their usurpation of power to control industrial controversies. In the first place, the court evidently found it impossible to sustain the government contention that the strike was unlawful. The argument was made (which was afterwards sustained by the supreme court in the Pennsylvania railroad case) that the men were not striking against the government or in violation of the law, and that neither employer nor employe were bound to observe the orders of the labor board; that the employers had refused to obey the orders of the labor board prohibiting the contracting out of work in shops, and that the men had refused, as they had a legal right, to accept the wages and rules fixed by the labor board, and to continue in the employment of railroads which themselves refused to obey the orders of the board. Therefore, the court was forced to base the right to an injunction on the claim that the evidence in the government affidavits—which the defendants had not adequate opportunity to controvert—showed the existence of a "nationwide conspiracy to restrain interstate commerce" by unlawful means. There was no evidence presented directly connecting the officers of the organizations with any unlawful acts, but the court held: "These defendants will not be permitted upon the record here, to deny responsibility for these unlawful acts. They will not be permitted to continue acts which, even though they may be peaceable and lawful in themselves, it has been demonstrated, are only part of a program of unlawful conduct and are done for the accomplishment of an unlawful purpose." The result of this opinion of the court is to extend further the outrageous "conspiracy" theory which has grown in favor in the courts so rapidly in the past 25 years. When there is no proof available to show that men are guilty of unlawful acts it has become the favored means of prosecution to allege a "conspiracy." Then under the strange developments of the law of conspiracy, the courts permit the introduction of almost any kind of evidence which may tend to convince the court that the defendants are guilty. The extension of this doctrine from criminal prosecutions to equity cases increases its menace to individual liberty. In a criminal case at least 12 men must be convinced beyond a reasonable doubt by this sort of vague proof, but in an equity case all that is necessary is to present the evidence before a judge, whose mind may be already prejudiced by newspaper reading and his social background, who is all too ready to believe that all labor organizations are combinations of dangerous men, and thus obtain a finding of guilty on vague, remote evidence, which it is most difficult for the defendants to combat. When it is realized that in the government injunction case this evidence of conspiracy consisted of affidavits obtained by railroads from private policemen, strike-breakers, and other persons signing their names to statements drawn up for them by skillful lawyers it will be understood how easy it was for the government to prove a case to the satisfaction of the court. As an example of the evidence used may be cited the affidavit of a superintendent of the Michigan Central Railroad, who swore that a local chairman of one of the unions was responsible for causing the Gary wreck. Yet this chairman was freely walking the streets of Chicago at the time and had never even been arrested. In this case his counter affidavit was presented to the court as evidence of the danger of the court relying on such evidence which in the mass presented it was impossible for the defendants to prove to be false. It appeared, however, that even after finding the defendants guilty of "conspiracy" upon such evidence, the court hesitated to re-issue the outrageous restraining order which has been obtained ex parte. He, therefore, inserted certain phrases in the preliminary injunction which completely changed its effect. First, the phrase "with intent to further said conspiracy" was injected whereby only such acts were prohibited as were done "with intent to further said conspiracy" of which the defendants were found guilty. As the defendants claimed to have no knowledge of any such conspiracy, they were advised by their attorneys to continue in their work in behalf of the organizations, including work in connection with the strike without substantial change. This interpretation of the injunction was made publicly in printed documents issued by the organizations. Yet the conduct of the officials was not questioned by the court or the government and no contempt cases were brought at any time for the enforcement of the injunction. Thereby it has appeared that the preliminary injunction

as finally issued was not intended, nor did it operate to prevent the continuance of the strike or the activities of the organizations in support thereof. What the injunction thus limited amounted to was simply a threatening gesture on the part of the government, which the railway executives might point to in support of their efforts to intimidate and coerce the workers. No greater abuse of governmental power and the powers of the courts has been shown in the history of labor controversies than this swinging of a stuffed club against several hundred thousand men and their sympathizers engaged in a desperate struggle to maintain their economic freedom against a nation-wide combination of employing interests. The preliminary injunction was further qualified by including the following clause which did not appear in the restraining order: "But nothing herein contained shall be construed to prohibit the use of the funds or moneys of any of said labor organizations for any lawful purpose, and nothing contained in this order shall be construed to prohibit the expression of an opinion or argument not intended to aid or encourage the doing of any of the acts hereinbefore enjoined, or not calculated to maintain or prolong a conspiracy to restrain interstate commerce or the transportation of the mails." Perhaps the best commentary on the opinion of the court and the injunction issued is that found in an editorial by Professor Cook of Yale Law School printed in the *Yale Law Journal* for December 1922. Concerning the opinion of the court which purported to be based on "well-settled law," he wrote: "If by 'well-settled' law is meant law settled by decisions of the supreme court of the U. S. in cases directly in point, rather than by quotations culled from opinions in cases only more or less analogous, it is believed that not a single one of these propositions can be regarded as a statement of 'well-settled law.'" After commenting on the conclusions of the court, this writer continues: "To guard against misapprehension it may be well to repeat at this point that it is not the purpose of the foregoing discussion to pass upon the merits or demerits of the rules of law laid down by Judge Wilkerson, but merely to bring out what the writer believes to be the fact, namely, that the case presented to the learned judge was one which required the making of new law; that is, it involved the exercise of the power to legislate, to establish the law for the case in hand. This being so, it is believed that the time has come to ask this question: Is it wise, in cases involving burning economic issues and fundamental human rights, to permit a single federal judge, or a single judge in any court, not merely to decide the 'law' for the first time—necessarily he must do that—but also to use so drastic a remedy as the injunction to enforce his views of what the 'law' is, unless at least we make adequate provision for immediate review by the proper appellate courts—in the federal system by the U. S. supreme court? Cases of this type involve questions of fundamental importance; they are matters upon which intelligent members of the community are divided in opinion; the law is usually not clearly settled. If, as is almost inevitable under the present system, the review by the supreme court comes years later, it is obvious that if that tribunal decides, as it did in the Tri-City case, that the injunction is too sweeping, or perhaps should never have been granted at all, the law as thus established by the highest tribunal in the land is of no practical importance to the defendants who were erroneously prohibited from doing the things they were legally privileged to do.

In other words, the 'law' which actually governs the litigants in these cases is the 'law' of the trial judge, not that of the supreme court. Can we expect the members of labor unions to continue to have confidence in receiving a square deal from our courts if, after a strike has been broken, the union's legitimate power destroyed, and perhaps the union itself disrupted in consequence—all by the decision of a single judge—they are told years later (in the Tri-City case over seven and a half years later) that the injunction which brought these results about denied them rights given to them by law, perhaps expressly congressional statute?'' The foregoing quotation indicates one of several reasons why this case, which is of so much importance and involves such weighty questions, was not appealed by the shop craft organizations. When the case came on for final hearing May 1, the organizations directed their attorneys to withdraw and take no further part in the proceeding. The reasons for this action were set forth in detail in a lengthy letter from the organizations to their counsel. Briefly summarized, they took the position that in the first place their main contention—that the strike was lawful—had been decided in their favor by the U. S. supreme court in the Pennsylvania case decided in February, 1923, wherein it was held that neither employer nor employe was bound to obey the decisions of the labor board. After this decision it became impossible to assume that the supreme court would hold that the strike itself was unlawful. But in order to combat the government evidence concerning illegal acts committed by strikers and sympathizers as proof of a criminal conspiracy, it would have been necessary for the organization to spend between $25,000 and $50,000 preparing evidence and taking depositions, or bringing witnesses from all over the U. S. It was also quite apparent from the opinion of Judge Wilkerson in the preliminary hearing that he would have found a "conspiracy" to exist and it would have been necessary to appeal the case for eventual relief. This would have required the expenditure of another enormous sum to present the record of the testimony of hundreds of witnesses and a printed abstract of this testimony to the supreme court. It was inevitable that in a strike of this magnitude a great many acts of lawlessnes had taken place. With at least 1,500,000 persons intimately concerned with the strike, it would be inevitable that over a period of many months many lawless acts could be shown. It was pointed out that the total indicated in the government testimony, if accepted as true, would not equal the crime record of a city of $1,500,000 inhabitants over a similar period. But if the court was willing to hold that the responsibility for such acts should be ascribed to the organizations, even when there was no proof directly connecting the named defendants with these acts, then it is clear that the court would have little difficulty in finding a basis for upholding the ruling of the trial judge. Meanwhile, the nation-wide strike conditions had disappeared. Thousands of strikers were working again whose testimony would be required to present the defendants' side of the case, thus stirring up antagonisms that had been allayed, causing vast expense and a great deal of individual hardship for no worthwhile result. Also it became apparent during this case that not only had the judge exceeded his authority in attempting to regulate the conduct of people all over the U. S. when his jurisdiction was limited to a section of the state of Illinois, but that other judges would not attempt to enforce his orders in their jurisdiction and that he himself would be unable to extend the authority of his office beyond the territory limits of the northern district of Illinois. All of these considerations decided the railway unions that they would not be warranted in wasting the time, money and strength of the organizations in this litigation. The Wilkerson injunction may provide a precedent for tyrannical abuse of judicial power in other cases. This injunction and the action of the executive officers of the government in procuring it should exhibit clearly to the American people the dangers involved in the increasing powers assumed by the courts to control industrial controversies and furnish power for arguments in support of legislation necessary to prevent further extensions and abuses of such power and to compel the judiciary to render more service in support of constitutional guarantees, of freedom of speech and trial by jury. (P. 273) The Wilkerson injunction is the most infamous restraining order ever conceived or decreed by either a federal or state court and issued at the solicitation of an attorney general who has neither regard for law nor righteousness. Estopped by the labor provision of the Clayton law to restrain labor organizations in the pursuance of a strike, denied authority to use the funds assigned to his department of the government for the prosecu ion of trade unions, and contrary to principles of the equity courts that equity proceedings can not be invoked to prevent the commission of crime, Attorney General Daugherty proceeded nevertheless to disregard all these legislative restrictions in his determined effort to impose the so-called "open shop" policy upon the railway shopmen's unions. Having ventured beyond all reason and anticipating a possible reversal by the higher courts of the original injunction issued by him, Judge Wilkerson shortly thereafter proceeded to correct the original error by introducing a new doctrine of conspiracy. Thus we find our courts ever ready to amend their original error for want of jurisdiction by committing an error more destructive to the liberties of the people and yet sufficient to clothe their illegal acts with the sanction of legality when reviewed by a court of superior position and authority. This injunction, issued by Judge Wilkerson and decreed by him at the solicitation of Attorney General Daugherty, will ever mark the records of our federal judiciary as the greatest monumental assumption of illegal authority ever manifested by any of our judges. That congress should decline to take cognizance of this gross exhibition of miscarriage of justice indicates clearly that no hope of relief may be found in that constitutional check upon the judiciary which the American people have been led to believe was inherent in the power of congress to impeach.

Injunction Legislation, Anti—(1923, p. 89) The action of Attorney General Daugherty in using the prohibited funds appropriated by congress for the department of justice to secure an injunction against the railroad shopmen aroused members of congress and two bills were introduced to specifically forbid such violations in the future. H. R. 12559 by Representative Huddleston of Alabama provided that any officer, agent or employe of the United States who shall wilfully deprive or attempt to deprive any person of his lawful freedom of speech, or press, or of assemblage, or of due process of law, or of any right, privilege, or immunity secured under the constitution of the United States shall have committed malfeasance in office. It declared that the issuance of any illegal injunction or other process not in good faith and with the wilful intent to deprive any person of any lawful right or immunity or to intimidate any person or put him in fear in the exercise thereof shall constitute malfeasance in office. The penalty was removal from office and a fine of $10,000 or imprisonment for a period of not exceeding ten years, or both. H. R. 12622, by Representative Schall, provided for adding to section 15 of the Clayton act the following: "Provided, That the authority hereby voted in said courts and said district attorneys under the direction of the attorney general to institute proceedings in equity to prevent and restrain such violations shall not extend to such peaceful activities and purposes of labor and agricultural organizations as are specified as being exempt from said proceedings in sections 6 and 20 of said act." Appropriation acts for the department of justice contain clauses that the money shall not be used in the prosecution of farmer or labor organizations under the anti-trust act. Nevertheless, the attorney general used these prohibited funds to pay the enormous cost incurred in securing and enforcing the injunction against the railroad shopmen. No action was taken on the bills. (P. 281) When laws within constitutional limitations are enacted for the guidance of man's conduct, it is presumed and required that every one subject to such laws shall adhere to them or else meet with such measures of discipline and punishment as may be prescribed. If our nation is to set a good example to this essential requirement of government, then surely those charged with administrative authority should be required to adhere more rigidly to this fundamental necessity. It is, therefore, with exceedingly great regret that we note in the Executive Council's report, under the caption "Anti-Injunction Bills," that Attorney General Daugherty, in his zeal and anxiety to enforce upon the railroad workers of the United States what he chose to call the "open shop" and to break the shopmen's strike, should have been permitted to draw upon the moneys of the U. S. government, to which he had no right. We are at a loss to know whether this unlawful expenditure of money can now be recovered. It is quite clear, however, why Attorney General Daugherty was so persistent to secure a favorable judgment from Judge Wilkerson so that his illegal conduct might be graced by the cloak of a judicial decree.

Injunctions, Model Law Against— (1921, pp. 77-373) The labor conference held February 23-24, 1921, to consider decisions of the supreme court that were inimical to labor unanimously approved the following bill for a model law and all state federations of labor were urged to secure its passage by their respective legislatures: "Be it enacted by the senate and house of representatives of the United States of America in congress assembled, That it shall not be unlawful for working men and women to organize themselves into or carry on labor unions and to persuade or induce others to join with them for the purpose of regulating the hours of labor, or regulating the wages, or otherwise bettering the condition of the members of such organizations, or doing any act in pursuance thereof not forbidden by law if done by a single individual. Labor unions and the individual members thereof shall not be liable in damages

for the unlawful acts of their officers or of other members thereof unless they shall have personally aided, counselled and advised the same.

"Section 2. No restraining order or injunction shall be granted by any court of the United States or any judge or judges thereof in any case involving or growing out of a dispute concerning terms of employment or conditions of labor which shall prohibit any person or persons, whether singly or in concert, from terminating any relation or contract of employment or from ceasing to perform any work or labor; or from recommending, advising, inducing, or pursuading others so to do; or from attending at any place where any person or persons might lawfully be for the purpose of obtaining or communicating information; or from inducing or pursuading any person to work or to abstain from work; or from ceasing to patronize any person, firm or corporation; or from recommending, advising, inducing, or persuading others so to do; or from paying, or giving to, or withholding from any person engaged in such dispute any strike benefits or other moneys or things of value; or from doing any act or thing which might lawfully be done in the absence of such dispute by a single individual. The acts specified herein shall not be construed or held to be illegal or unlawful in any court of the United States.

"Section 3. No person shall be indicted, prosecuted, or tried in any court of the United States for entering into or participating in any arrangement, agreement, or combination made with a view of joint action for the purpose of regulating the number of hours of labor, or regulating wages, or bettering the condition of working men and women, or for any act done in pursuance thereof unless such act is in itself forbidden by law if done by a single individual.

"Section 4. All acts of parts of acts inconsistent herewith are hereby repealed."

In the proposal to exert extraordinary efforts to have the foregoing legislative measure enacted into law in every state of the union as well as by our national government, it is not the intent to subordinate the expressions and relief declared for by the labor conference held in Washington as above noted. In addition to declaring for legislative redress this conference likewise declared for the elimination of all anti-conspiracy laws and doctrines as well as all legal fictions designed to prohibit and restrain combinations of wealth, but which in reality have only served the purpose of restricting and prohibiting the organizations of wage earners in their voluntary and normal activities to improve their conditions of work and to promote their standards of life.

Insurance Agents— (1919, p. 389) The question of organizing insurance agents should first be investigated by the Executive Council as to the advisablity and feasibility of such an organization and it is hereby authorized to take such action as its investigation may warrant.

Insurance, Group— (1923, p. 327) Group insurance has made phenomenal progress during recent years and is being used by unfair employers as a means of alienating the affiliation of wage earners from their respective trade unions under the cloak of philanthropy and the plea of paternalism. It is believed that group insurance is subject to efficient use by trade unions, not alone to combat the misuse of these devices by unfair employers, but to give added strength and stability to the trade union movement. There are many trade unions carrying on insurance or death benefit features of some kind and character, and a number of them have provided for group insurance. The president of the A. F. of L. is hereby authorized to conduct an investigation of all forms of insurance and death benefit systems now provided by national and international unions; that this investigation include group insurance plans and other insurance features used by employers to provide insurance for their employes.

Insurance. Strike—(1921, p. 391) The Executive Council was directed to take under consideration the strike insurance being offered by insurance companies, and if it be deemed advisable, to have a congressional investigation.

Intelligence Test—(1923, pp. 111-250) During the year we have observed carefully the progress of the movement to introduce mental tests, commonly known as intelligence tests, in industrial plants. These tests are more properly known as psychological tests. The world war brought the intelligence test to prominence, although much had been done over a term of years prior to that time to develop the intelligence test. This work, however, had been done mainly among school, college, and university students. We have given close and careful study to the question and have consulted not only trade unionists, officials of trade unions and the laymen, but we have called into consultation the men who stand highest in the professional field in the development and application of the intelligence test. There is, we find, a tendency toward introduction of such tests in industrial establishments, some of which have large and carefully equipped departments for engaging employes on that basis. We find ourselves by no means able to agree with all of the claims of those who seek to measure human ability, adaptability and general fitness by such tests, though they have a use and a value. As was the case in connection with the old Taylor stop-watch system, hailed by employers as a device of perfection and finally discredited and all but abandoned as the result of labor's analysis, the intelligence test is, in our opinion, a device that may and undoubtedly will be abused in many cases where it is applied under the sole direction of employers or those retained by employers. It lends itself, where improperly used, to discrimination against wage earners and to the humiliation of wage earners. The fact is that, if it were desired, it would be possible for a group of employers to utilize the intelligence test as the vehicle for the most infamous kind of blacklist—doubly infamous because the worker would be blacklisted on an alleged basis of scientific finding. The full implications of such an effort can easily be imagined. We are of the opinion that the men who have done most in the direction of research and development in the field under consideration here are scientific men of the highest standing and integrity and that it is their purpose to confer upon humanity an agency of helpfulness. Our misgivings are in the direction of employer domination in the application of the intelligence test in employment relations. For the present we find nothing to be done except the maintenance of vigilance the careful observation and study of the uses of the intelligence test and wherever possible the demanding of labor participation in directing the uses to which such tests are put in employment relations.

International Federation of Trade Unions—(1919, p. 419) As the Amsterdam conference was to be held in May, represen-

tatives of the A. F. of L. could not be present because of the convention of the A. F. of L. being held in June. The date was changed to July 25. The convention voted that two delegates be sent to the conference, one of them to be the president of the A. F. of L.

(1920, pp. 131-475) When the A. F. of L. became affiliated with the world's labor movement in 1910 it was known as the International Secretariat, the name of which, however, was changed on the motion of the American delegate in 1913 in the Zurich, Switzerland, convention, to the International Federation of Trade Unions, and has so remained and is now known as such. It should be noted that up to the convention of 1919 the Amsterdam conference required a unanimous vote of all trade union national centers represented to adopt a motion that was fundamentally declaratory in character, and limited attendance to two delegates from each trade union center. This wise provision held inviolate the fundamental principles upon which the A. F. of L. is founded—"complete autonomy"—and preserved the fundamental rights of self-government of the labor movement of each country. Its activities were necessarily and we hold rightfully limited to an exchange of experiences, hopes, ideals, aspirations, dissemination of knowledge in a broader and common interest of the world's producing masses, leaving it free, however, for each country fortified with the knowledge and experience of others, to work out its own internal affairs in its own way. This plan required only a small nominal per capita tax. The system of voting has been changed from two votes for each country represented to one vote for 250,000 members; or less to each national trade union center a majority vote will adopt any motion submitted; that the per capita tax is increased to one-half cent per member per annum, which would bring our financial obligations up to about $20,000 per year for fixed charges. This does not include expenses of sending delegates, or other expenses which the International Federation of Trade Unions is privileged to incur; it increases the representation from a minimum of two delegates to a maximum of ten delegates from each country represented. In connection with this entire subject the letter of Mr. Appleton, president, International Federation of Trade Unions, and the proclamation to which his communication refers should be read. It will be noted that the circular issued by the Bureau of the International Federation of Trade Unions over the protest of President Appleton, among other things, says: "Down with the reaction. Up with socialism." And again, take particular note that the manifesto called for a May Day demonstration—a general strike to achieve the overthrow of constituted government and the establishment of a socialist form of government. The issuance of the foregoing circular was in direct violation of all rules of procedure. It in substance was a demand for a May Day strike of the workers of the world to establish socialism by the use of our economic power—the strike. The question of our continued affiliation with any international federation of trade unions is referred to the Executive Council, and we suggest for its consideration the following: a. Industrial activities on the economic field of endeavor. b. Self-determination on all political matters. c. The abolition of all authority of the bureau and the management committee, except instructions issued by the regular convention of the International Federation of Trade Unions. d. The abolition of the bulletin and the substitution of a quarterly newsletter limited to the actual matters of interest to and concerning trade union activity, and that this newsletter to be edited by the president and sent only to the executive officers of affiliated trade union centers who may print it in their official journals or otherwise as may suit their own desires and convenience. e. Voting, except on roll call, to be limited to an equal number of votes based upon the country having the least number of delegates, i. e., if America has two delegates no other country shall cast more than two votes. f. No decisions to be regarded as conclusive unless the same has been adopted by unanimous vote. g. Per capita tax to be reduced to a point that will permit the federation to function on lines consistent with the foregoing principles. h. The Executive Council to use its foremost endeavors to secure a compliance with these principles, and to hold itself in readiness at all times to lend full strength and influence of the American trade union movement to reestablish the International Federation of Trade Unions movement.

(1920, pp. 166-477) By authority of the Executive Council, President Gompers on May 21, 1919, addressed to Messrs. Bowerman, Oudegeest, and Jouhaux identical invitations to the International Federation of Trade Unions to meet in the city of Washington in October, 1919, at about the time when the International Labor Conference was to be held as provided by the covenant of the league of nations. Plans for the meeting of the International Federation of Trade Unions in some European city in July were thereupon abandoned and the invitation of the A. F. of L. was accepted. It was decided that the delegates representing the A. F. of L. in the meeting of the International Federation of Trade Unions should be the members of the Executive Council. The question of the affiliation of the A. F. of L. with the International Federation of Trade Unions was brought before the Executive Council. It was the decision of the Executive Council that an effort should be made by the federation delegates to have the per capita tax reduced and that the question of continuing in affiliation be referred to this convention of the A. F. of L. The meeting of the International Federation of Trade Unions was convened in the Executive Council chamber of the A. F. of L. Building on the evening of Wednesday, October 29, President W. A. Appleton presiding; President Gompers, Vice-President Woll and Secretary Morrison represented the A. F. of L. at that meeting. The subject of principal concern in the meeting was the international labor conference under the terms of the treaty of peace, then in session. During the course of the meeting the president of the A. F. of L. made a statement of which the following is a part: "One particular reason why I rise to address you is that the newspapers of Washington and other cities within the past week have published the statement that I have opposed the admission of the German and Austrian delegates to the International Labor Conference. Let me say that ever since my return from the Amsterdam meeting, I have busied myself in the effort to secure the admission of the delegates from Germany and Austria. I have busied myself, as I say, with the officials of the government of the U. S. and the peace commissioner at Paris. In addition, Mr. Barnes of the British War Cabinet sent me cablegrams through the American Embassy and which were received by me. I replied to these cablegrams in which I said

substantially that unless German and Austrian delegates are admitted to the international labor conference at Washington the conference would be a failure in advance. I have here copies of the cablegrams received and the cablegrams sent by me and I am going to ask without reading them that they be made part of the record of this gathering in order that there may be no misunderstanding as to where the A. F. of L. and its president have stood upon the admission of the delegates from Germany and Austria. In addition, let me say that in order to facilitate and bring about the admission of the German and Austrian delegates, I sent to M. Fontaine, chairman of the organizing committee and the secretary general of the international labor commission, which met at Paris, a cablegram asking him to convoke a meeting at Paris or London as he might determine, for conference with Mr. Barnes, so that the commission as a commission could prevail upon the supreme council of the peace negotiations at Paris that its attitude might be changed and consent given that the German and Austrian delegates be admitted. As a member of the organizing committee, I have been in conference with the committee for four consecutive days and at that committee meeting here in the office we decided that no permanent organization should be established in the international conference, no permanent officers should be elected until after the decision of the conference that the German and Austrian delegates shall be admitted. They are not here that is not the fault of the conference. So much for that. I am in entire accord that we should do everything within our power to influence the international labor conference to go to the fullest limits of what can be done. What can not be officially declared within the terms of the call may be recommended to the next international labor conference, but I do not think that it is wise or practical on our part to declare that the conference must do thus and so outside of the authority of that conference. So far as the A. F. of L. not being represented at the conference, that is explainable. The American government has not yet ratified the treaty and is therefore not a party to the society or the league of nations and the draft covenant. I have just been informed that the conference and the organizing committee have decided to invite the representative of the A. F. of L. to be there, although not as an official delegate. Now I have that under consideration and more than likely we shall accept and one of us be represented there, but we are placed in the peculiar position that the president is not authorized to appoint, the government of the United States is not authorized to appoint, a delegation of governmental representatives, the representatives of employers and the representatives of the workers because the treaty is not ratified. It is lamentable, it is more than regrettable, but it is a fact and we can not change it. That is not our fault. We have politicians in the United States and I assume you gentlemen and ladies also have some politicians in your own country. I think I have heard of such in other countries than the United States who are playing for partisan politics." It was the decision of the Executive Council in regard to the question of affiliation that an effort should be made by the Federation delegates to have the per capita tax reduced and that the question of continuing in affiliation be referred to this convention of the A. F. of L. In accord with this decision President Gompers wrote on December 29 to President Appleton of the

International Federation of Trade Unions, saying in part: "If the contributions are reduced one-half of the present provisions it should be put in the money value of the English pound. England and the United States can not be asked to contribute a certain stipend when the value of the money of each country is of three to five times the value of the money of Germany, Austria, France and other countries. The A. F. of L. is anxious to be part of the International Federation of Trade Unions. We want the world solidarity of labor endeavoring to work out world labor problems to be of assistance to each other, and the Executive Council of the A. F. of L. feels strongly that unless the situation be clearly met and the solution reached, instead of having a seriously conducted movement in the interest and for the promotion of the welfare of the workers of all countries, much injury will come. I fully concur in the view you express that we maintain our present membership in the International Federation and endeavor to extend its purpose, power and influence upon a more modest program than to exclude not only England and the United States, but make it impossible for the smaller countries also to pay a contribution." In the Amsterdam conference it was decided by the committee having the matter in charge to recommend that the amount of per capita tax be equivalent to 1 cent American money per member per year. Delegate Tobin objected to this amount because we believed it was not necessary to levy so large an amount to carry on the work of the international federation. The committee, however, by a majority vote decided to recommend to the conference the per capita tax of 1 cent per member per year. In the conference itself, after a considerable discussion, the per capita tax was finally fixed at one-half of 1 cent per member per year. In conferences held during the time of the meeting of the International Federation of Trade Unions in Washington in October, 1919, the question of per capita tax was considered and the representatives of the A. F. of L. expressed the viewpoint that the amount fixed by the Amsterdam conference was excessive. At its meeting of February 24-March 3, the Executive Council had under discussion the action of the Amsterdam conference in regard to per capita tax, and instructed President Gompers to enter into correspondence with W. A. Appleton, president of the International Federation of Trade Unions, and to say that we can not affiliate upon the basis of payment as provided in Holland, but that the A. F. of L. is willing to begin its contributions upon the basis of one-fourth of 1 cent per member per year. At the same meeting, the Executive Council instructed President Gompers to correspond with President Appleton of the International Federation, to learn the indebtedness of the International Federation in order that the A. F. of L. might pay its proportion. President Gompers was further authorized to pay as the A. F. of L.'s share not more than $500 and that this sum be transmitted to the International Federation of Trade Unions upon the basis proposed by the A. F. of L., which is one-half of the amount set by the Amsterdam conference, and that the regular per capita tax be not transmitted until such time as the bureau agrees to this proposition. Accordingly on March 11 President Gompers forwarded to J. Oudegeest, secretary of the International Federation of Trade Unions of Amsterdam, a draft in the sum of $400 with the statement that it was "the contribution of the A. F. of L. toward the past indebtedness

of the A. F. of L. to the old I. F. of L. which ceased to exist last summer at Amsterdam, Holland." It was further set forth that the Executive Council "expressed the belief that during the war and for some period thereafter the A. F. of L. was not part of the International Federation of Labor and therefore the above amount, $400, is sent to in part meet the obligations incurred during the period of our affiliation."

(1921, p. 78) Final determination of the question of affiliation to the International Federation of Trade Unions was 'eft to the Executive Council by the Montreal convention. That convention called attention to the excessive tax which it was proposed to levy against the A. F. of L., violation of rules by the Bureau of International Federation of Trade Unions at Amsterdam and the denial of national autonomy, and in addition set forth a number of suggestions which the council was asked to bear in mind in connection with consideration of the subject. The council was asked to use its best endeavors to secure compliance with the suggestions of the convention and in the event of compliance to be in readiness to give full support to the International Federation of Trade Unions. The Executive Council and the officers of the A. F. of L. made every possible effort to secure a compliance with the viewpoint of the A. F. of L., but to no avail. There was an extended correspondence in relation to the question of national autonomy, the question of dues and the question of the authority of the bureau at Amsterdam to issue proclamations and pronunciamentos without authority. Finally and with great reluctance the Executive Council at its meeting in Washington, February 22-March 4, took final action on the question of affiliation, the decision being that until the International Federation of Trade Unions so alters its course as to remove the objections of the A. F. of L., affiliation is impossible. This decision was communicated to the officers of the International Federation of Trade Unions at Amsterdam. (P. 439) We find that the executives of the International Federation of Trades Unions have committed the International Federation of Trades Unions to principles and to policies which are accurately described by our Executive Council as revolutionary, contrary to the policies and the philosophy of our movement, and in conflict with the pronouncement of the Montreal convention of the A. F. of L. We find that while the constitution of the International Federation of Trade Unions may seem to guarantee national autonomy, while it may be interpreted so to do, while it even may have been intended to guarantee national autonomy, there is, in fact and practice, no such guarantee. The A. F. of L. representatives who attended the congress in Amsterdam at which the International Federation of Trades Unions was organized, were inclined to believe in the integrity of intention of the delegates of other countries and were inclined to accept in good faith the provision which the constitution of the International Federation of Trades Unions condemns. American labor has waited patiently, willing at all times to have faith until faith was destroyed. It has been the hope that autonomy might be had under the present constitution. Time has been unkind to the construction which the executives of the International Federation of Trades Unions have placed upon the constitution. Because of these constructions the autonomy of national centers does not exist, either in theory or in fact. American labor can not and will not submit to dictation from without. It must and will determine its own course. We note with utter amazement and resentment the action of the Bureau of the International Federation of Trades Unions in addressing official communications to the organizations affiliated to the A. F. of L. when all communications should be addressed to the executive officers of our national trade union center, the A. F. of L. Particularly is this most offensive as it was done immediately preceding the opening of this convention and in disregard of the rights to which our movement is entitled. We are confident that no such attempt would be made by the international bureau nor would it have the temerity to directly address official documents to the unions affiliated with the British Trade Union Congress, the Confederation de General, the French Confederation of Labor, the German Federation of Labor, or to those of any other national trade union center. We particularly approve of the declaration of the Executive Council as follows: "No one can regret more keenly than do the members of the Executive Council, the inability of the A. F. of L. to be of greater service in the field of international relations than it has been during the past year, but there has been no alternative course to pursue." The Executive Council is hereby instructed to continue its negotiations in an effort to have the the laws amended so that the A. F. of L. may have the opportunity of affiliating at the earliest possible date, and that such negotiations be continued in the spirit and principles enunciated in this report and by the Executive Council.

(1922, pp. 85-420) International labor relations during the year have continued with but little change from conditions reported by us to our last convention. Our affiliation with the Pan-American Federation of Labor has continued and our interest in the work of that organization has been most active and, we hope, effective. In so far as our relations with the European labor movements are concerned these have continued to be of the most friendly nature and have continued to demonstrate the essential solidarity of labor internationally. We have been unable, however, to bring about affiliation with the International Federation of Trade Unions, because the governing body of the International Federation of Trade Unions has not yet found its way to making that affiliation possible. Correspondence has continued and is continuing with the view to affiliation and we earnestly hope that it may be possible to bring about affiliation and active participation in the affairs of the International Federation of Trade Unions during the coming year. Three main points of contention have been uppermost in the discussion with the International Federation of Trade Unions and in our most recent communication, dated February 25, 1922, we inquired whether the officers of the International Federation of Trade Unions could not find some way of removing the objections and making possible our early affiliation. The objections which have continued to stand in the way of affiliation are as declared by the Montreal and Denver conventions, as follows: "First. That the new constitution completely abrogated the principle of complete autonomy for each national trade union federation. Second. That through the issuance of appeals and proclamations, the executive body of the international federation had committed the federation to a revolutionary principle to which the A. F.

of L. is and always had been uncompromisingly opposed and to which no labor movement guided by democractic ideals could give approval. Third. That a system of dues had been adopted which would place upon the A. F. of L. a heavy and unbearable expense." In order to make clear the effort which the Executive Council has made to secure removal of these difficulties the following extract from the council's letter of February 25, 1922, to the International Federation of Trade Unions, is quoted: "The A. F. of L. did not set up these objections as reasons for permanently remaining outside of the International Federation of Trade Unions. It set them up as points of difference which it was hoped might be removed in order that affiliation might become possible. It must be stated unequivocally that up to this time there has been no genuine effort on the part of the International Federation of Trade Unions or of its officers to remove these obstacles and no earnest endeavor to compose them. On the contrary, we are now informed, in your letter of January 5, 1922, that the bureau has now fully endorsed the communications previously sent the Executive Council. Furthermore, while abstaining absolutely 'from a course that might have been calculated to remove the differences, the officers of the International Federation of Trade Unions have made the situation still more difficult by directly challenging the autonomy of the A. F. of L. and ignoring its position, responsibility and authority. This it has done by means of communicating directly with our affiliated bodies instead of communicating with the A. F. of L., a practice unheard of in international labor relations. The thought of the International Federation of Trade Unions in communicating directly with affiliated organizations of the A. F. of L. and not with the A. F. of L. direct, was, we are convinced, for the purpose of creating a propaganda among our affiliated organizations for the purpose of endeavoring to force the A. F. of L. to change its policy to suit the purposes of officials in Amsterdam. That this has failed is due solely to the unanimity of opinion in the ranks of American organized labor. However, the A. F. of L. is willing to overlook this breach of good conduct. The sole purpose in calling attention to it here is to bring out the characteristics of the International Federation of Trade Unions under its present official direction, which is certainly not helpful in overcoming existing difficulties. In the matter of the three points of objection originally raised and again set forth in this letter, something remains to be said. As to the first point, that of the abrogation of national autonomy, is it possible that there may be some correction of this evil? Is there a method of safeguarding national autonomy within the International Federation of Trade Unions? We are not unmindful of the fact that your previous communications have been uncomprising in support of the principle and the practice as they have obtained since the organization of the International Federation of Trade Unions at Amsterdam. Nevertheless, we are hopeful that you may find some way of overcoming the objection. Indeed, we feel that it is entirely possible, if the desire of the International Federation for American affiliation is sincere. We are under the necessity of repeating that the A. F. of L. can not agree to any abandonment of complete autonomy and that it can not place itself in a position where it will be in danger of being committed to policies and principles to which it is opposed. We shall be more than glad to learn of some manner of composing this difference. In relation to the second point, that concerning the issuance of proclamations and appeals committing the International Federation and, therefore its affiliated organizations to principles not in accord with those agreed upon, we have yet to learn if it is intended to abandon this practice in Amsterdam. There is no insuperable obstacle raised in point No. 2. It rests with the officers of the International Federation of Trade Unions whether that point is to continue to be a barrier. Its removal is simple and the A. F. of L. is entirely willing to believe whatever declaration on the subject may be made by the responsible officers of the International Federation of Trade Unions. As to point No. 3, that relating to dues, the A. F. of L. still is of the opinion that the burden imposed upon us is too great. It is earnestly desired that some effort be made to remedy this situation in the direction of materially modifying the proposed dues in accordance with our suggestion. There appears to have been no real effort made in Amsterdam to deal with this question and it is proposed that serious consideration be given thereto. Surely the object of the International Federation of Trade Unions can not be to weaken the domestic efforts of the various national centers by placing an excessive strain upon the finances of the national centers. Then, too, there must be some understanding as to the money standard which shall determine and govern the payment of dues as to whether it shall be the English pound, the American dollar, the German mark, or the French franc, so that there will be no undue proportion of taxation between the organizations on account of the varying exchange value of currency used. While our great interest is for an international movement and to bring about the greatest degree of cooperation and solidarity in that movement, yet no one can fail to understand that our first and dominating duty is to our fellow workers and our movement in America." We have had no reply from Amsterdam in response to this most recent communication, although it had been our earnest hope that a reply might be received and that the reply might be of such character that it would make it possible to report to the convention a more immediate prospect for affiliation. We recommend that efforts be continued in the direction of an early affiliation.

(1923, p. 112) There has been no change in the position of the International Federation of Trade Unions in the direction of meeting any of the objections recorded by the A. F. of L. as a bar to our affiliation. The Executive Council is authorized to continue negotiations in the hope that opportunity may yet be had for affiliation with the organized workers of the Old World. We are eager to bring about the reestablishment of fraternal relations as soon as it can be done without the sacrifice or repudiation of principles which the American trade union movement regards as inviolable. (P. 365) The workers overseas in all lands need our counsel. We welcome theirs. We concede the right of their trade union movements to fix their own standard and their own method of development as best suit their own judgment and action, but our trade union movement reserves the right to fix our economic standards, our political

destinies and social status in our own way and in accord with our experience, predicated upon the past, the present and upon our optomistic, hopeful anticipation of a better, brighter and richer life for all workers who give material service. We are eager to bring about the reestablishment of fraternal relations as soon as it can be done without the sacrifice or repudiation of principles which the American trade union movement regards as inviolable. The Executive Council is directed to continue its efforts to urge the International Federation of Trade Unions to remove the barriers at the earliest possible moment that have heretofore, and do now, prevent our affiliation with the organized trade unions affiliated to the International Federation of Trade Unions.

International Labor Conference—(1920, p. 168) Executive Council reported: "On October 29, 1919, the international labor conference convened in Washington in response to an invitation extended by the government of the United States. The United States having failed to ratify the treaty of peace, and therefore not being a member of the league of nations, the government of the United States was not in a position to name representatives to sit in this conference. The provisions of the labor charter in the covenant of the league of nations are that each nation shall be represented in the labor conference by two delegates representing the government, one delegate representing the employers, and one delegate representing labor. In the absence of any delegates named by the United States government the organization committee of the international labor conference determined to invite participation of delegates representing American workers and American employers. In accordance with this decision the A. F. of L. as the representative organization of workers in the United States was invited to name a delegate to participate in the sessions of the conference. The president of the A. F. of L. was appointed by President Wilson, then at Paris, to be one of the two representatives of the United States in the commission to draft a labor convention for international labor legislation under the peace treaty and was elected chairman of that international commission. He aided in formulating the labor draft conventions which became part of the peace treaty under the terms of which the International Labor Conference was held in Washington. The president of the A. F. of L. also served as a member of the organizing committee which organized the Washington conference. Upon being invited to participate in the conference as a delegate and being instructed and authorized by the Executive Council to attend the president of the A. F. of L. did attend the conference during a portion of its sessions. During the time when the establishment of a universal maximum eight-hour workday was under discussion he participated in the debate, delivering a lengthy address on the subject. Despite the honor conferred, realizing the humiliating position of being a delegate to the conference, but being deprived of the right to vote and have a voice in the decision of issues, President Gompers declined to continue as a delegate without the powers of a delegate. The Washington conference by resolution directed the governing body to set up an international commission to study the question of emigration and immigration. The Executive Council had under consideration a letter from the director of the governing body requesting that the A. F. of L. appoint a representative to serve on that commission. The Executive Council feels itself in a most embarrassing position for two reasons: 1. The government of the United States has not yet ratified the treaty of peace and hence is not a party to the league of nations or the international labor conference or the governing body. 2. The experience of the representative of the A. F. of L. in participating in the international labor conference at Washington, where he was entitled by courtesy to participate in the discussions of the conference, yet was denied, and rightfully denied, a vote in that conference. Inasmuch as the situation has not changed, the Executive Council feels that it can not consistently recommend the selection of a representative to participate in the work of a commission on immigration." (P. 475) Approved. (P. 326) Report by the secretary of labor of the outcome of the international labor conference was made a part of the records: "The international labor conference, part of the league of nations, which met in this city October 29, 1919, adopted a resolution requiring the governing body to set up an international commission to study the question of regulating emigration and immigration and that of protecting the interests of wage earners not residing in their own country. The conference decided at the same time that the representation of European states on this commission should be limited to half the total number of its members. The governing body at its meeting in London last March proceeded to give effect to this resolution in accordance with the following principles: '(1) That of equal representation of governments, workers and employers. (2) That of equal representation of European and non-European countries. (3) That of the respective importance of different countries from the point of view of emigration and immigration.' It decided to invite the British government to nominate an independent chairman of the commission, and it allotted to eighteen other countries, among them the United States, seats for government workers and employers representatives. On May 14th I receive a communication from M. Albert Thomas, director of the international labor office suggesting that the United States send representatives to the commission selected in agreement with the most representative organizations of workers and employers, respectively. section 29 of the immigration act of February 5, 1917, reads as follows: 'That the president of the United States is authorized, in the name of the government of the United States, to call, in his discretion, an international conference, to assemble at such point as may be agreed upon, or to send special commissioners to any foreign country, for the purpose of regulating by international agreement, subject to the advice and consent of the senate of the United States, the immigration of aliens to the United States; of providing for the mental, moral, and physical examination of such aliens by American consuls or other officers of the United States government at the ports of embarkation, or elsewhere; of securing the assistance of foreign governments in their own territories to prevent the evasion of the laws of the United States governing immigration to the United States; of entering into such international agreements as may be proper to prevent the immigration of aliens

who, under the laws of the United States, are or may be excluded from entering the United States, and of regulating any matters pertaining to such immigration.' In order to make sure that this law gave the president authority to appoint delegates to this conference, I submitted the law and the correspondence to the solicitor for the department of labor, and have been advised by him that 'it is the judgment of this office, therefore, that the president has authority under section 29 to send representatives of the government to attend a meeting of the international commission to study the question of emigration and immigration." Upon receipt of this opinion I immediately brought it to the attention of the president, recommending that we be represented in this conference not only by the two delegates selected in agreement with the industrial organizations, but also by a direct representative of the government. The president informed me that he would act upon my advice in this matter, and I consequently cabled M. Thomas to the effect that this government is prepared to send three commissioners to attend the international commission to study the question of regulating emigration and immigration in accordance with the terms of section 29 of the immigration law of this country. The expenses of such a commission can be paid from the general immigration fund. I am writing you for the purpose of asking that the A. F. of L. nominate someone to act as a member of this commission with a view to reaching an agreement upon the appointment. The date of the meeting of the commission has not yet been decided upon, but is likely to be two or more months hence."

International Labor Relations—(1919, pp. 80-259) When the armistice was signed on November 11, 1918, American labor was engaged in a constantly increasing effort to produce supplies and munitions of war. Until just a few days before that event, the workers of America had expected that their utmost efforts in war production would be necessary for a considerable period to come in order to insure victory for the democratic cause. The ardor of spirit and unity of purpose of the American working people were unequalled anywhere in the whole world theatre of war. The armistice and the consequent cessation of hostilities found every activity in a state of impatient speed toward victory. Military documents and records and the official statements of national chiefs who were in most intimate touch with affairs on the western front at the hour of the German collapse certify that the very magnitude and ardor of the work being done at home was one of the principal factors in bringing about the precipitous rout of autocracy through the crumbling of the armies. The American labor movement may feel a spirit of pride in having made so magnificent a contribution to the triumph of the cause of the world's democratic peoples. The signing of the armistice and the beginning of peace negotiations reversed the whole impulse of the nation and turned the common thought of the people toward the tremendous task of placing the nation's life once more on a peace basis. Among the workers of America there had been the conviction formed in the beginning of hostilities—a conviction justified by the whole thought and purpose contained in the nation's declaration of war—that the return to a peace basis should not involve merely a readjustment and a return to conditions that were normal prior to the war but should involve true reconstruction in such a manner as to make permanent the democratic advances made during the period of the war, and because of the war, and to insure natural achievement of continued progress. We feel that this thought concerning the reconstruction of our life along fundamental lines is excellently expressed in the report of the special committee on reconstruction which has been approved by us and is submitted as a part of this report. It is our conviction that if reconstruction is to bring to the working people the opportunities for broader and freer lives to which they rightly and justly aspire, the developments and events leading in that direction must be along the lines laid down in the report of the committee on reconstruction. The committee makes no excursion into the perhaps attractive field of abstract and doctrinaire theorizing, but confines itself strictly to a study of those things which are at once possible and practicable, recommending to the nation a course that not only can be pursued but that in logic and justice must be pursued. Until the moment of signing the armistice the activities of the A. F. of L. had been constantly expanding and increasing in breadth and intensity. Not only was every possible effort being expended at home but contact with the working people of other nations was steadily developing out of the necessities of war. In the whole field of allied hostilities there was a tendency toward bringing into closer contact the various peoples engaged in the war against the central powers, in order that at each step there might be complete understanding and sympathy. Prior to the convention of June, 1918, our federation had sent one mission abroad to confer and advise with the labor movements of our allied countries. It also had sent a mission to confer with the labor movement of Mexico. Both of these missions had completed their tasks at the time the 1918 convention was held. The mission that had just returned from Europe recommended and earnestly urged that the president of the A. F. of L. undertake a mission to the labor movements of Europe and that everything possible be done to bring about a closer contact and a better understanding. In the purely industrial field of labor's activity in connection with the war the whole effort of the American labor movement up to the signing of the armistice had been to carry out the spirit of the declaration of March 12, 1917, and the declaration adopted in St. Paul which set forth the doctrine that labor in the workshops at home should take no action that could not be justified to the men on the firing line in France. This same declaration also held that employers at home should be governed by an identical standard. It may be said in truth and with much pride that this standard was generally observed by the workers and that not only could American labor from day to day justify its action to the men who were on the firing line, but that now upon their return they may find a record of effort and achievement on the part of the labor movement toward maintaining the American standard of life that will justify the confidence and trust that were left to us when they departed for France. It was highly advisable at that time, when the German armies were pressing most vigorously upon the allied lines and when great numbers were feeling keenly sheer exhaustion

after four years of terrific struggle, that the invigorating message of hope and cheer from American labor to the workers of Europe be brought to them as effectually and as frequently as possible in order that they might feel the full support and the great effort which America was then so rapidly developing. Accordingly, the Executive Council at its meeting July 23-28, after deliberating on the recommendations of the labor mission to and approved by the June conventon, decided that the president of the A. F. of L. should visit as many of the allied countries as possible and that he be authorized to "take with him such assistants as he may deem necessary to carry on his work." A mission was selected to go to Italy, which had the approval of the Executive Council. Two missions departed for Europe, one with the special object of visiting Italy and conferring at length with the working people of that country. The other mission in addition to an extended tour for the purpose of conferring with the workers of various countries in their home lands, attended an interallied labor conference in London, September, 1918, where it was able to render most valuable service to the cause of labor and of the allies.

(P. 327) The past has gone forever. Autocracy and militarism, we hope, are buried with it. The future is our immediate concern. Ignoring what has gone before except so far as the lessons taught, we shall build along the lines of reason, judgment and the experiences gained. Typifying democracy and its true spirit, the labor movements the world over, if they be true to themselves and to the best interests of the masses for which they speak, must recognize that democracy in its truest sense, and act on the fundamental principles of equality, justice and humanity. All elements of society are necessary for the highest development and greater progress in civilization, economically, socially and politically. The world's war brought to a triumphant conclusion has prepared the world for democracy on the political field. The mere ending of the war, however, has not insured democracy and justice for the workers on the industrial field. It has not materially changed working and living conditions, but it has aroused fresh hope and quickened aspirations and labor's ambitions. It has created the opportunity whereby the workers regardless of abode can, if functioning through trade unions, more readily, more freely and more effectively carry forward the work of securing justice and safeguarding for labor a fuller measure of democracy in industry. It is the first duty of our own trade union movement, and in our judgment it ought to be that of the movement of other countries, to see to it that this opportunity is not destroyed by diverting the minds of the workers or by delving into the alluring realms of unproven speculative theories which judged by experiences are false and destructive in their nature.

(1920, p. 131) International labor relations have continued to increase in complexity and in their demand upon the time and thought of the American labor movment. Since our 1919 convention, the International Federation of Trade Unions has been reconstituted and two meetings have been held at which delegates representing the A. F. of L. have participated. In addition to these, a delegate during the year attended the British Trade Union Congress and a delegate attended the annual meeting of the Canadian Trades and Labor Congress. A delegate attended the international labor congress held under the covenant of the league of nations in Washington as the representative of American labor. The Pan-American Federation of Labor convention also was attended by delegates representing the A. F. of L. In each of these meetings, problems of world importance developed as a result of the war, demanded consideration. The trade union movement may be proud of the manner in which it has met the great issues that have arisen and it may point with lasting pride to the integrity that has characterized every action having to do with the welfare of world humanity in connection with these various conventions and congresses. However much the high idealism of the democratic peoples of the world may be abused or dissipated in some of the world's political and business circles it has held its place in the labor movement. There can not be during the coming year nor probably ever again in our future, a restriction of our interest and activity in relation to the work and the welfare of the rest of the world. Whatever may be our desires, the fact is that the course of events, and the needs of people have woven our destinies into such a relation with the peoples of the world that our attention can not be withdrawn from what is happening in other countries and on other continents. Nearly two years have elapsed since the signing of the armistice which ended the world war. It is a regrettable truth that this period has brought but small degree of settlement of the tremendous problems brought into being by the war. The accident of circumstance has been left to deal with matters that shoud long since have been brought under control of conscious direction. (P. 473) We hold that the principle of self-determination applies industrially as well as politically in the affairs of human kind and of nations. While realizing our obligations to the peoples of every country in the world and anxiously desirous of fulfilling these obligations to the fullest, yet we can not surrender our democracy and freedom to any foreign political rights involving self-government, country or combination of foreign countries. Neither can we nor should we surrender our rights to determine our own policy and to fix our nation's standards on the economic field of human endeavor and achievement.

(1921, p. 78) During the year there has been no decrease in the activity of the A. F. of L. in international labor affairs. Owing to circumstances over which it has no control, however, the A. F. of L., has been unable to participate in some of the conferences and congresses in which it otherwise would have been represented, but it has neglected no proper opportunity to manifest its interest and to exercise its influence. Because of the fact that our government has not acquired membership in the league of nations, the A. F. of L. has been unable to participate in the international labor organization set up by the treaty of peace and because of the conduct of the International Federation of Trade Unions and the intolerable rules and regulations set up for the government and conduct of that organization, fully explained elsewhere in this report, the A. F. of L. has been unable to participate in the deliberations of that organization. Our federation was represented by fraternal delegates in the British Trade Union Congress and delegates representing the A. F. of L. participated in the extremely important convention of the Pan-American Federation of Labor, held in Mexico City.

Ireland—(1919, p. 325) This convention unanimously affirms its well considered conviction that the people of Ireland should have accorded to them the unquestioned right to determine the form of government under which they should live; that the principle of self determination of small nations applies with as much force to the people of Ireland as to any of the new nations recognized by the peace conference; and that the officers of the A. F. of L. be and are hereby instructed to convey immediately the action of this convention to congress and to the president of the U. S., with the request that the convention's acti n be also presented to the peace conference by the American representatives now in Paris. That the senate of the United States earnestly request the American peace commissi n in Versailles to endeavor to secure for Edward deValera, Arthur Griffiths, and Count George Noble Plunkett a hearing before said peace conference, in order that they may present the cause of Ireland. That the congress of the United States recognize the present Irish republic. (P. 302) This cablegram from Dublin to the convention was read: "Natio al Executive Irish Labour Trade Union Congress sends greetings to workers America. Request them use every effort secure that principle for whi h America claimed enter war be made applicable Ireland." (P. 404) Nothing in the league of nations as endorsed by this convention can be construed as denying the right of self-determination and freedom to Ireland as recognized by the vote of this convention on Tuesday, June 17, 1919. (P. 473) This telegram to convention from Philadelphia was read: "On behalf of the Irish nation we beg you to convey to the A. F. of L. our deep appreciation of and gratitude for its unanimous resolution calling for recognition by congress of the republic set up by the Irish people in accordance with the American principle of self-determination now accepted everywhere as a necessary condition for a lasting peace. We have no doubt that the resolution represents the equally unanimous feeling of the many millions of the American workers whom you represent. God save the sister republics. P. McCartan, Envoy, Republic of Ireland; H. J. Boland, Special Envoy, Republic of Ireland."

(1920, p. 399) The A. F. of L. reaffirms its recognition of the Irish Republic, and respectfully request that the military forces of occupation in Ireland be withdr wn from that country, and that the Irish people be accorded the ri ht of self-determination, the same as all other nations recently given their complete freedom as enunciated in the declarations of the president of the U. S., comprising the fourteen points, all of which were solemnly agreed to by the British government and its allies in the recent World War, and that we tender our aid to the people of Ireland in their efforts for freedom to the end that Ireland be permitted to take its place among the free nations of the world. We appeal to the workers of England, Scotland and Wales, and ask that they exert their powerful influence to the end that their government officials, at present in power by the votes of the people of England, Scotland and Wales, immediately withdraw the army of occupation from Ireland, and permit the Irish people to peacefully pursue their lives under the form of government which they have established through laws made by themselves and executed by their duly elected officials.

(1921, pp. 349-353) The policy of Great Britain threatens the peace of the world. Therefore the A. F. of L. reiterates and reaffirms the action of the Montreal convention, supports the Irish people in their struggle for freedom and for recognition of the Irish republic. That copies of these resolutions be sent to the president, vice-president, and members of the cabinet, urging recognition of the Republic of Ireland and urging a protest to be made to Great Britain against the brutual and uncivilized warfare now being conducted in Ireland. That the executive officers of the A. F. of L. be instructed to communicate with all members of Congress urging immediate enactment of legislation necessary to bring about full recognition of the Republic of Ireland. The A. F. of L. request all its affiliated bodies and their local unions to write to the president, the vice-president, members of the cabinet and members of the senate and house of representatives urging immediate recognition of the Republic of Ireland. The A. F. of L. asks the British trades unions and the trades unions in all British colonies and dominions to cooperate in the objects herein set forth. That a special communication be sent immediately by the Executive Council to the British premier, his cabinet and members of parliament protesting against the campaign of violence and destruction in Ireland. That the A. F. of L. expresses its appreciation to the trades unionists of Great Britain for their efforts on behalf of the Irish people; that the A. F. of L. instruct its fraternal delegates to the British Trade Union Congress to visit Ireland and personally convey to the Irish trade unionists our sincere wishes for their success. That our officers be instructed to take up with the trade unions of Great Britain, her colonies and dominions, a proposal to inaugurate a campaign for the trial and punishment of officers and men of the British regular and auxiliary forces guilty of atrocities in Ireland in a manner similar to that in which German officers are now being tried and punished for violation of the rules of warfare in France and Belgium.

(P. 399) Anonymous statements made in the press against the president and Executive Council in reference to their attitude toward Ireland and said to have emanated from manufacturers were answered by the president: "During my entire life, particularly since my connection with the American labor movement, there has never been a time when my sympathies and convictions did not cooperate with the aspirations of the Irish people in Ireland. I was associated in the organized labor movement of our country in the early days when the struggle in Ireland and all over the world was made for home rule. There was not then living a man of prominence in the home rule movement but with whom I was upon most intimate and cordial and cooperative terms. Whenever the occasion required that I should go to Europe I visted Ireland and paid tribute to the martyrs and the heroes and the statesmen of Ireland in defense of their own country. Of course that was practically impossible during the war. These men included Parnell, Davitt, Redmond, and those who held even subordinate positions. I counted it a privilege and an honor to be the representative of the organized labor movement, with others,

in New York upon the first visit of Charles Stewart Parnell to the United States. I think it was at the Buffalo convention of the A. F. of L., when the subject of the recognition of Irish independence as a separate nation and a republic was up for consideration, I took the position that when the Irish people had spoken and voiced their aspirations in any form I would recognize their voice, and not recognize the voice or voices of Irishmen in the United States in preference to the voice of Irishmen in Ireland. The following year we held our convention in Atlantic City, and thereby demonstrated facts in Ireland, presented to our convention, that the Irish people had spoken and declared for a republic there was not one utterance that I can recall in opposition to it from anyone else or from me. And that declaration was made in our convention. Last year the same subject was up for consideration in the Montreal convention and a resolution was adopted reaffirming recognition of the Irish Republic. Immediately after the closing of the Montreal convention, and after a meeting of the Executive Council, by direction I went to San Francisco to lay before the democratic national convention the demands which labor made. Upon my appearance in the committee room where the committee on platform were seated, Mr. Frank P. Walsh was addressing the committee upon the Irish question. I spoke to some of the men who were the associates of Mr. Walsh and asked them whether they thought that I could have an opportunity to say a few words upon that subject. They told me that that was impossible, because the time had all been alloted to Mr. Walsh and two or three others who were to speak briefly. The arrangements for the presentation of that subject were made without the knowledge of my associates or myself, and so there was no opportunity for me to speak. I think it was immediately after Mr. Walsh concluded his argument that I was called, with my associates, to speak upon the demands we proposed to present. After the close of that session I was in the company of Mrs. Andrew J. Gallagher, of San Francisco, and Mr. P. H. McCarthy. I learned from them that Mr. DeValera, the president of the Irish Republic was in San Francisco at his hotel. It was then about 10 o'clock in the evening, and I expressed a desire that they accompany me on a visit to Mr. DeValera. They did accompany me and were in the room when I expressed to him, as well as my memory would serve, the resolution adopted by the Montreal convention. The A. F. of L. elected two fraternal delegates to the British Trades Union Congress, and of these two one was Bro. Timothy Healy. The fraternal delegates from the A. F. of L. to the British Trades Union Congress are the ambassadors of organized labor of America, and, endeavoring to be of assistance to Ambassador Healy, that part of the report of his address prepared with the assistance of the representatives of the A. F. of L. contained that declaration which Brother Healy, as America's labor ambassador to the labor parliament of Great Britain, presented as the declaration adopted in Montreal, and as read by the secretary. When the American Committee for Irish Relief was organized, that committee asked for the use of my name in an appeal to the American people for financial assistance to relieve the sufferers of Ireland. I readily and cordially gave my name, and that name appears upon the committee's letterheads and appeals. There has been no step that I could take other than what is contained in that declaration. To President DeValera I said that the A. F. of L. tendered its aid to the Irish people in their effort for freedom. There is one real charge substantiated against me, and to which I plead guilty—I have not freed Ireland. I challenge any man to show that I have been faithless to any declaration made by the A. F. of L., or that I have proved false to the faith or negligent to any of its directions. When the A. F. of L. has said and declared that policies should be pursued, even if it drove me to jail. I did not falter in the fight or in the faith. I am sure that if the entire conduct of the president of the A. F. of L. had found its initiative in the minds of the delegates to this convention there might not have been the necessity for this explanation. I feel sure that you all know from what source this whole attempt to destroy my character and reputation and standing emanates—no other person than this traitor to America and the cause of freedom and the cause of Ireland, William Randolph Hearst. Did you ever know of a newspaper, or a chain of newspapers, owned by a multi-millionaire that devoted for more than four weeks, every day and twice a day, articles and editorials against a labor man? He has sent out his minions, his hirelings, to get in touch with some who might be gulled, or if not gulled, bought, so that he might say something derogatory to my character. And who did he get to say a word against me and my work and my character and my faithfulness? Who? A grafter of Boston, a shyster lawyer of Washington, one who was caught in the dragnet of the investigation by congress of the National Association of Manufacturers, and whose chief operator was this man Mulhall; a lawyer, formerly a plate printer, repudiated and stigmatized by that magnificent organization as a man unworthy of belief or credit. And who else? Some rag-tag, bob-tailed politician who was eating pap out of the millionaire bag of William Randolph Hearts. Who is there a recognized, respected trade unionist in America who has uttered anything of the character Hearst desired? In addition to the letter that was addressed to me by Mr. John Fitzpatrick of Chicago, I have letters from Henry Abrams, of the Boston Central Labor Union, in which he described the efforts of Hearst to get someone to say something against me; and when anyone has said a word of commendation of my work or my character it has been suppressed. You know that Mr. Fitzpatrick said in his letter that Mr. Hearst had been scurrying his men all through Chicago to get some reputable trade unionist to say something about me, but without success. In every way this traitor to America, this traitor to humanity, this man whose name it is not fit to express with whatever men hold as honorable and moral, has sought to discredit me. You will have noticed, I am sure, that when the resolution presented by Brother Frey and Brother Larger upon Hearst's conduct through his newspapers was considered I vacated the chair and made no utterance and no move of which I am conscious, and yet the resolution was passed by a unanimous vote. Men, I can not help but make mention of this. You know that at several conventions of the A. F. of L. there have been introduced resolutions for the election of the officers by the initiative and referendum. We have held, first,

that most of the organizations have not machinery for anything like a fair conduct for such elections; and, secondly, that there is no opportunity for any aspirant for any office in the A. F. of L. to present his claims satisfactorily and intelligently for the understanding of the great rank and file of our movement. More prescience, more wisdom has been demonstrated in that course of the conventions not to adopt such a system, and if any evidence is wanted as to the utter impracticability and wrong of such a system, the attacks of the Hearst chain of newspapers furnishes the strongest argument in defense. Here a man, wholly unworthy of respect or confidence either as an American or as a human man, this man with his newspapers in many parts of our country from Massachusetts to California, with his millions for his newspaper enterprise, transmitting the manufactured news to all the other newspapers which find it either cheap or convenient to use that concern, with a circulation of these combined newspapers alone of about eight million copies a day, in a drive daily, twice a day, to besmirch the character of a man who has tried to do his full duty to his fellows, and to this country. What kind of an opportunity would such a man have to defend himself to the great rank and file. In the war he was the lickspittle for the kaiser. In the war he was in constant communication with the kaiser's ambassador, Bernstorff. In the war he was engaged with Bola Pasha, with Captain Boy-Ed, with the whole gang of them. And now let me say there are two main things why Hearst does not like me and I will tell you what they are. First, in his rattle brain there germinated an aspiration to be president of the United States, and both in conference with him and with his man, his main representative Ihmsen, he tried to chain me to his mad chariot for the presidency, and to speak the language of the street, 'I could not see him,' and I frankly told him so. During the convention of the International Typographical Union at Washington, Ihmsen and a man now passed away, a union printer whose name I shall not mention, came to me and asked me whether I would not help to arrange a mass meeting in the National Theatre in Washington in furtherance of Hearst's candidacy for the presidency and I told them I would not. He then asked me if the meeting was called would I preside over the meeting, and speak and I said I would not do it. He then said, 'Will you please attend the meeting?' No, I shall find some other and more amusing or interesting engagement to keep. And so whether he had a chance or not for the nomination I do not know, but at least he could not get my assistance. In the American labor movement I have learned the spirit not only of patriotism and of humanity, but I learned the spirit of international brotherhood and making every honest endeavor for its establishment. I believe in the destiny of this western hemisphere and I hold that though we speak of international brotherhood that it is the first duty of the peoples of this western hemisphere to establish the closest relations and bonds of unity and fraternity. In pursuance of that work we have furthered and fostered and nurtured the Pan-American Federation of Labor, and the closest neighbor to us of all of the Latin American republics, is the Republic of Mexico.

The Hearst interests have large land holdings in Mexico and Hearst's thirst for wealth and power has made him declare in the editorial columns of his newspapers the demand that the United States send its military forces into Mexico to plant the American flag there and never take it down. I have no overweening conceit about my power and influence but whatever power and whatever influence I may have I proposed and now propose and will continue to propose that we shall try to see to it that Mexico shall go on undisturbed and not be overrun by the American forces. Whether Hearst believes I have power or influence or not makes very little difference; the fact is that he believes that I am a thorn in his side, that I am an obstacle in his way to overrun the people and the government of Mexico by the forces of our government and our people to annex that land to ours. And so you know at least two of the causes which prompt this uncanny individual, this man who can find no confidence at home or respect elsewhere in the world. He is not even admitted to what his millions would entitle him—the so-called respectable society. He made an attack upon the members of the Executive Council; he made a direct attack upon Frank Morrison, Matthew Woll, James Duncan, because it happened that we did not have the happiness to have been born in the United States. That editorial he published time and time again in different words, all to the same effect, and I wrote a letter in reply. Perhaps it was silly on my part to attempt to say anything that would penetrate the rhinoceros hide of hypocrisy of William Randolph Hearst. But in that letter I called attention to these two facts: When he questioned our loyalty or the right to speak for American labor because he said that we were not born here I answered him by saying something like this: 'I am willing that the government of the United States or the people of the United States shall decide as between you and me as to who was more loyal to the Republic of the United States in its greatest hour of danger.' And I said this, too: 'Bear in mind that in the gravest period of the Revolutionary War for independence the man who gave it heart and spirit was Tom Paine, an Englishman, and that the man convicted as being the greatest traitor to the Revolutionary cause was Benedic Arnold, born in America.' But he did not publish it. And so I did the best I could with the letter and published it in the *American Federationist*. Now, probably I have taken up more time in speaking of this devil incarnate than I ought to have done, but I can not help it. Now I want to return to the subject of the letter for a word or two. I want the A. F. of L., in any of the declarations it makes upon any subject, to be not only strong, vigorous, virile, but dignified. I have tried to avoid any participation in any discussion upon the Irish question until after the election is over. I did not wish to be placed in a position that I wanted to make any explanation of my conduct with a view of winning votes for me. I may say this, that I hold this position, the position of president of the A. F. of L. in such exalted opinion that I would not stoop to even ask a man to vote for me or to support me for any position. This position of president, the representative spokesman, in part at least, of American labor, must before election and after election be able to hold up his head and say to any man Yes or to say to any man No. No man, no organization, has ever received anything at my hand or offered support, not even my own, in preference over any other organization. The men and women who vote for me for president, when they do, will know that I shall do my full duty without regard to the consequences to myself. I shall do my full duty without partiality and with due regard first to the rights, interest and welfare of the labor movement of the great working people and not forgetting the dignity and the strength and the manhood that is represented in the name of the A. F. of L. I can not help but say to you at this moment that in one of Hearst's Chicago papers—and I presume in all of them—it is asserted that I invited James H. Thomas to come over to this convention to defend me. And he was elected delegate last September by the British Trades Union Congress."

(P. 186) J. H. Thomas, fraternal delegate from the British Trades Union Congress made the following answer to the question, "What is the British labor movement doing for Irish freedom?" "Now, so far as the Irish question is concerned, I don't want to go into the history of it only so far as the labor movement is concerned. The labor movement in Great Britain from the first day that it entered politics at all stood for home rule for Ireland. In John Redmond's time, in Michael Davitt's time, in Parnell's time, in O'Connell's time, in all those periods the British labor movement stood for freedom for Ireland and it stands for that today. But do not make the mistake of deceiving the Irish people. I have 20,000 members in Ireland, therefore if I do not know anything about it no one else does. I have those 20,000 members in my own organization because the Irish railway men won't have an Irish railway organization; they prefer an English organization, and they have got it, for they know what good it has done for them. We are divided in about the proportion of fifty-two per cent in the south and forty-eight per cent in the north. There we have what we call the two sections, north and south. Notwithstanding that we have always stood for home rule, because we believe that no government can dictate to a people the form of government those people require. That is quite clear. But equally do not make the mistake of assuming that we have not fought, for we have, and I did more for the hunger strikers to get them released than probably anyone else. I went to Mountjoy Prison when there were 100,000 people on their knees reciting the rosary. Don't assume that I have not sympathy for them, but don't assume that the British labor movement stands for an independent republic. It is only fair that you should know this. They don't. They stand for freedom, with dominion home rule if needs be. In fact, the only limit we put on is that we are not going to have Ireland made a menace from submarine warfare. Now that is exactly the position, and we have fought and fought, but we don't want your movement disrupted because of differences in it. Brother Healy will remember that he was at Portsmouth last year when Mr. McSwiney was on hunger strike. He had then been on hunger strike for nearly thirty days, and I had on my own responsibility seen the government, seen the home secretary, seen Mr. Balfour, and urged the release of McSwiney, because I believed they had no right to make martyrs of men who were fighting for the freedom of their country. Mr. McSwiney's sister came to the Portsmouth conference. I was in the chair, just as your president is, and the chairman of the standing orders committee came to me and said that Miss McSwiney was there and wanted to address the congress. He said that she was in the ante room and was very excited. I said, 'Very well,' and deliberately closed the conference. I do not want to make any secret of what I did. That is one of the charges. I did not tell the delegates why I closed the conference, but said: "You have got on so well with your business that I will give you a couple of hours. Good afternoon.' And they cheered and went out. You are entitled to ask me why I took that unusual course, first denying her the right to state the case and then closing the the convention rather than allow her to do it. It would be pretty dangerous for your movement or for ours to allow every one who comes along, however good the cause, to address the convention. When once the door is opened in that way it will be pretty difficult to close it. That was the first reason. The second was this: Suppose she had addressed the convention. Her demand was that organized labor should withhold their labor and strike for the release of Mr. McSwiney. Suppose she had put it and the congress had refused it. That would undoubtedly have strengthened the hands of the government by saying even the congress was against it? And supposing they had carried it. No one knew better than I did it would have been hypocrisy, because they could never give effect to it. The real trouble is that Ireland has been deceived for so long that she trusts no one today. Ireland has been fed on promises, broken promises, by English statesmen for years, and she does not trust anybody's word today. I was not going to allow a mere resolution to be passed that would have buoyed up the feelings of the people and then deceive them as they have been deceived before. And I equally warn you against trying to create in their mind that you can solve their difficulties because they love you. The Irish people look to you, the Irish people know their friends are here, they know their relatives are here, but they do not understand you at all. And isn't it a cruel thing for people to assume that merely by the passing of a resolution you can solve this problem of a hundred years? We have seven million members, and sixty per cent of the Irish people are in our unions today. Don't forget that sixty per cent of all the workers in Ireland are members of the international unions. Not only have we sympathy, but we have a direct personal interest. We are doing all we can not to disrupt or deceive the Irish people. The position in Ireland today is beyond words, it is indescribable. I took a deputation of Irishmen to Lloyd George, men from both north and south, nearly eleven months ago, and I said to him: 'You may talk about your military, you may talk about your force, but if the streets of Dublin are running with blood tomorrow there will still remain an Irish problem tomorrow. Why not

solve it? You have realized that you have tried everything.' That was eleven months ago. Whilst we in the British movement condemn militarism, don't forget that we condemn the murder and the outrages against policemen and civilians equally as much as we condemn murder by the policemen and soldiers. Neither can be justified. Murder, whether it be of a policeman or by a policeman, of a soldier or by a soldier, can not be justified. Crime begets crime, and the position in Ireland today is due to that fact, plus the unfortunate difference in Ireland itself. We will continue to do our best; we will continue to fight, but we will not allow our movement to be disrupted on any question, no matter what it is. And I would ask our Irish friends in America who feel, God knows, keener than I can say, to believe me when I say it is not quite so easy to judge this question from three thousand miles as we find it at home. And if we have been unable to solve this problem as a labor party at home, all I can say is that I wish you luck in solving it three thousand miles away.

(1922—p. 145) Report made that the instructions of 1921 convention had been carried out.

I. W. W. (1923, p. 333) For several years past, but more especially since the war, there are efforts more and more open to view to destroy the faith of the working people in democratic government, but particularly in the legislative branches thereof. It seems, further, that definite efforts are put forward to either take away or to bring into contempt those very fundamental principles upon which popular government and organizations of mutual aid have been and still are based. These tendencies have received different names in different countries and they are expressing themselves with some variations in different places, but they are substantially the same everywhere. In Russia it is called the dictatorship of the proletariat, in Italy it is the dictatorship of the middle classes, in Bulgaria and Spain it is not so distinct and crystallized, but in each the tendency and the action taken is unmistakable. The movement seems to be gaining great headway in Germany and is there known under different names and promoted by various parties, while here in in the United States it may all be recognized unde the well-known title of the I. W. W. Let us not overlook the fact, however, that there are I. W. W. at the top of our industrial world, and that these are very influential and much more dangerous than the I. W. W. among the working people. The I. W. W. among the working people could not influence the press sufficiently to fill it with gibes and sneers at the lgislative branch of the government, while insidiously extolling both the executive and judicial. If one were to go through the current daily literature, it would be found to be loaded down with propaganda against popular government, but more especially against the legislative branch thereof. The I. W. W. is carrying on extensive propaganda in traveling, printing and speaking at an expense which obviously has not been gathered from actual or prospective members of the cult. Here and there information crops out of money furnished to them. Here and there, we are informed, detective bureaus are guiding them, and it is beyond belief that such is done without ulterior purpose, and when we find the propaganda from above and below to be identical, we have a right to draw conclusions. It is therefore reasonable and we believe legitimate, to asume that a large part of the means with which the propaganda is carried on comes from those who are in sympathy with that propaganda and who have an abundance of means out of which to give. The I. W. W. are not sent into virgin fields, but where the organizers of the bona fide labor movement go, there they are sure to follow, and always for the purpose of destroying the efforts of legitimate unionism. Where there is an effort to improve conditions, they are sure to appear with their stickers, their literature, and their speakers who begin secretly to instill distrust of any movement that would tend toward collective action. Where strong, well organized unions of labor exist and those unions are found to be too cohesive and too well entrenched for a general attack, the I. W. W. appear with their stickers and their propaganda to destroy the faith in the organization, the faith in the officers, and the faith of men in each other. This is accompanied always by the exaltations of the principles laid down in the preamble and constitution of the I. W. W. When confidence is so shaken as to make it possible to use open propaganda, they promptly begin to use it. From open propaganda they go to open scabbing, spreading and exulting in a contemptuous disregard for all skill and of respect for creative work. When they have succeeded in gathering a sufficient number to follow their policy, they begin of their own motion a policy that distinctly tends to destroy the confidence of such members as they have gathered and to destroy hope of any improvement through collective action. When that is done, their work is finished, and they proceed elsewhere. They claim to be an industrial organization, when, as a matter of fact, they are a purely political one, using industrial conditions and industrial facts as a cloak. It is essential for the preservation of our organizations, our labor movement and our form of government that these facts should be carefully investigated, and that reports carrying authority should be made to the American people, but more especially so to the American working people. The Executive Council is instructed to carry on such an investigation and to make from time to time such report thereon as shall be possible, and to the next convention of the A. F. of L. (P. 334) Statement made by representative of the International Seamen's Union: "When the I. W. W. delegate just expelled was in San Francisco last summer he was permitted to speak for the part here the other day, so he dressed for the part there. He spent his time in a clever, covert way in trying to destroy all faith in the trade union movement. When he was through I asked him some questions, and he said of course it was very natural for me to complain, because thay had taken away my organization. Now I am telling you this just because I want you to understand that I am not of the complaining kind, because I believe in the idea that you must never beg bread from your friends or mercy from your enemies. You must live by your own strength or accept death, so I am not speaking here today out of any feeling for the seamen. We are gradually learning to take care of our elves in the matter. I am speaking because I have given some study to this question; I have paid some careful attention to what the I. W. W. are doing, the principles upon which they claim to be based, and the different names they give themselves in different countries, and to me their plain purpose is to de-stroy not only the labor movement of this country, but of the world. The ladder with which the now governing classes mounted the rampart is of no value to them, and so their purpose is to destroy all the freedom and opportunity that labor has attained in the last one hundred years. Thus we see in every country from South Africa to Norway, from the eastern border of Japan to the Ural Mountains, the same tendencies in legislation and in administration. It is the destruction of republican or democratic government, the destruction of freedom of speech, of press, freedom of locomotion, and the right of assemblage. All these things were necessary before; they are not necessary now. So you have in Russia one phase of it, in Bulgaria another, in Italy another, in Spain another, in Germany another, or half a dozen, but the legislative proposition is substantially the same in every country, and that is the discrediting of the legislative branch of the government everywhere. That is the upper strata of this movement. The upper strata furnishes the means to carry on the agitation amongst the lower order, so-called, of society. You can not find anything for which the great employers stand that is not duplicated in the I. W. W. They are utterly opposed to everything; they are utterly opposed to legislation, they are utterly opposed to anything like the union shop, they are for the 'open shop,' and they are for the proposition of issuing to all workers what should properly be called an industrial card. As the employer is utterly and absolutely opposed to any qualification of skill that he is bound to respect, so the I. W. W. stands in exactly the same position, and in their propaganda and in their literature they are advocating not only utter disregard of skill and the free transfer of men from the teamsters to the cooks, and from the cooks to the barbers, ard so on, but they are claiming in their propaganda and in their stump speeches that there is no such animal in the jungle any more as skilled or creative labor. They come through back doors and side doors into your occupation. They absolutely hide their activities until they have aroused sufficient distrust and disturbance in the mental attitude of the men so that they can go farther openly. They begin with their stickers in absolute secrecy, and you can't discover who issued them, you can't discover who put them out. It is an utter impossibility for them to find the means to do what they are doing. The organization is the least expensive, the most effective and the most dangerous strike-breaking organization in this country. It makes no difference whether they work in the east or in the west, it is the same story. It make no differnce whether they are amongst the miners, the longshoremen, or the woodsmen—as one of them said to us in San Francisco: 'We have made it impossible to organize and to function with a union in any semiskilled occupation.' My latest information is that the woodsmen of the Pacific Northwest here, after having been called on four strikes this summer, all for the purpose of getting their prisoners out of jail, so they said, are getting sick of I. W. W. doctrines and policies and they are tearing up their red cards. Whenever they bring about the arrest and trial of some of these men you will find that if the leader is caught in the net with the rest of the men he goes squarely up to the judge and says, 'Your honor, I am guilty.' And His Honor lets him go. Why? I don't need to explain that to you; you know what human life is and I don't need to go any farther on that question. The longshoremen and the seamen have suffered quite materially from these people on this coast. We seamen are gradually working out of it. We expelled some 40 of them from our union; we don't tolerate any of them in it; we know their password so well that I have listened to it half a dozen times at least on this floor and recognized it for what it was. I hope some of them will get up now and dispute what I am saying. As a result of the trouble that we have had, upon the request of the longshoremen's delegates the representatives of that organization and the seamen met here and we have come to an agreement to mutually assist each other in cleaning these people out. It isn't anything that you are particularly interested in, but it shows that not only the seamen, but the longshoremen as well, understand some of the things that they have had trouble with."

A representative of the Longshoremen made the following statement about the I. W. W.: "Our organization was composed largely of men who owned their own homes and who worked in perfect harmony with their employers up until about 18 months ago, when they were suddenly informed that what we term the 'fink hall' would be established. The president of the A. F. of L. has had considerable experience in the past with the 'fink hall,' and through his assistance we were once successful in eliminating that thing from our water front. It is a system of registration giving the most intimate and personal information about a man, with entirely too many questions for any man who believes in the American principles of freedom and liberty, and it llikewise makes up the most perfect system of blacklisting that there is in America today. The longshoremen in this city naturally refused to accept that system and while the employers were still negotiating with a committee from our organization, without any notice, without any warning, an ultimatum was served upon the men on May 1 of last year that this institution would be established. The longshoremen struck against the 'fink hall.' The system they use is this: First they resort to the press, then the police, and in Portland the regular police force was not sufficient, and they employed a small army of extra special policemen. They threw a cordon of police around the 'fink hall,' and when that was not sufficient to break the spirit of the longshoremen they made arrangements with an organization known as Marine Transport Workers No. 510 of the . W. W., with police protection, if you please, and with busses carrying the strike-breakers they lined up in front of this Marine Transport Workers headquarters, at 109 Second Street, Portland, and took six gangs out of there to break the strike of the longshoremen. By reason of the institution of that 'fink hall' in this city, men who had their homes here for 30 years were compelled to leave their families and go elsewhere for employment, and in many instances they were obliged to sell their property. That 'fink hall' carries with a system of blacklisting that has never been equaled any place in the country. I want to say that my colleague who just spoke is the one man on the Pacific coast in the American labor movement who has by word of mouth and by the printed word traced the history of the I. W. W., and anyone who has read that as carefully as I have can easily trace the unholy alliance that exists between certain employers and the I. W. W. I believe that those employers are as guilty and as responsible for the conditions that exist on the Pacific coast and throughout the country as any other one factor, and I

believe the blame should be placed squarely upon the shoulders of those men who are willing to use the I. W. W. to destroy the legitimate American labor movement."

Japan—(1919, p. 418) Fraternal delegate from Japan delivered this address: "We are aware that the lack of knowledge and misunderstanding breed discord and that is the reason why in 1917 we entreated the president of your mighty organization to come over to our country, and again I make the same appeal. I plead with you, Mr. Chairman, that you respond to our appeal, the appeal of the toiling millions of Japan. The word I wish to leave with you, is 'come and see.' Will you send your representatives and let them see with their own eyes the true conditions of Japan and extend your fraternal, helping hands to us and make the Pacific Ocean true to what its name stands for? I know full well the historic bonds of friend ship which exist between the labor organization of Great Britain and the United States, exchanging their fraternal delegates across the Atlantic Ocean year by year. And I believe their contribution toward the promotion of mutual understanding and friendly feeling between the two countries is beyond measure. Why not transplant the seed of same relation which flourish on the shores of the Atlantic to the shores of the Pacific? Our organization is extremely small, but I have full confidence in your fraternal spirit of helpfulness, and I trust that you know the profound significance which the development of the labor organization in Japan will have to the development of the civilization of Asia." Executive Council is directed to develop a correspondence with the representatives of the workers of Japan for the purpose of more clearly expressing the viewpoint of the American trade union movement, the greatest and most effective labor movement in the whole world. There are many reasons why the workers of Japan should be organized in the trade union movement and a better understanding in so far as fundamental principles are concerned had with the workers of America. The Executive Council is also directed to consider the request made for the president of the A. F. of L. to visit Japan if his duties will permit.

Jews, Massacre of—(1919, p. 321) The A. F. of L. records its protest against the massacres and brutalities committed upon the Jewish population of Poland, the Ukraine and other parts of Eastern Europe, and calls upon the government of the United States to use its great offices with all the governments of the world to the end that recurrence of such inhuman deeds is made impossible, and that national minorities in every country in the world are guaranteed full civil and political rights and protection.

Judges, Election of—(1923, p. 292) The United States supreme court has usurped the power to set aside and nullify acts of congress, thus practically setting itself up as the supreme law-making body, instead of a law-interpreting body. The constitution of the U. S. of America specifically places the power to make laws in the hands of congress, the members of which are elected by the people, and therefore responsible to the people for their acts. The members of our federal courts and U. S. supreme court gain their positions by presidential appointment and continue to hold them for the remainder of their natural lives and bear no seeming responsibility for their official acts to the people, placing them above and beyond and out of touch with the wishes of the people. The A. F. of L. petitions the U. S. congress to submit a constitutional amendment providing for the election of all federal judges by a vote of the people, and providing for division of the country into judicial districts based on population and making the term of office for such judges for the period of four years.

Judges, More Idleness for—(1922, pp. 93-339) Representative Walsh, of Massachusetts, who, although young in years as congressmen go, has gained unenviable fame as one of the most reactionary members of the house, introduced H. R. 9103 providing for twenty-one additional district judges of the United States. The bill slipped through the house and was passed by the senate after a most scathing arraignment of federal district courts by Senator Norris. He declared that all federal courts except the supreme court should be abolished; that they simply duplicate the work of the state courts. He called attention to the scandall created by the "midnight judges bill," one hundred and twenty years ago, and flayed the federal courts, declaring that they are for the rich man or the corporation, as they help to tire out the poor complainant in a case. Senator Norris pointed out that judges are picked men whether of the state or federal bench, and that sometimes they were picked by politicians and often mistakes have been made. He said he was not willing to admit nor did he believe that the federal district judges are any better class of men than are the general trial judges of the state. He added: "About the only difference is that in most parts of the country the federal judges work less and receive more pay." Senator Norris, then pointed out that there was a duplication of court procedure, a double set of judicial machinery in every community —two judges, two courthouses, a duplicate set of administrative officials, including marshalls, sheriffs, clerks, and bailiffs, all doing the same kind of work and the taxpayers footing the bill. He continued: "It did not make so much difference years ago until great corporations began to be formed, until business began to be transacted on a large scale of combination, when litigation became important, involving more money. Then the fault in the system began to appear. To my mind, it is a serious problem and one which congress should consider." Senator Norris said he wished he could "cause the American people to think about it, to work it over in their minds and in their hearts and to realize that we have a judicial system that costs too much. Justice is too expensive, so expensive in fact that the poor man can not afford to buy it." He quoted a statement made by Mr. Henry S. Pritchard, President of the Carnegie Foundation in which he said that "the very existence of free government depends upon making the machinery of justice so effective that the citizens of a democracy shall believe in its impartiality and fairness." In that statement, President Pritchard also said: "There never was a time when it was more important to provide machinery that shall be adequate to accomplish in fact that justice at which the law aims and for whose attainment amongst men it was established. It is not enough for the law to intend justice. It must be so administered that for the great body of citizens justice is actually attained. Be the law never so good in theory, uncertain of dilatory administration, through

the present cumbersome or defective machinery, goes far to defeat its aims. The widespread suspicion, that our law fails to secure justice has only too much basis in fact. If this suspicion is allowed to grow unchecked, it will end by poisoning the faith of the people in their own government and in law itself, the very bulwark of justice. . . . . If those who officially represent the law and do not bend their energies and give their best thought to make the administration of justice fair, prompt, and accessible to the humblest citizen, to what group in the body politic may we turn with any hope that this matter will be dealt with wisely and justly?" During the arguments against the bill, Senator Norris quoted Mr. Taft, ex-president of the United States, a federal judge for many years, and now chief justice of the United States supreme court as follows: "Of all the questions that are before the American people I regret not one has more importance than the improvement of the administration of justice. We must make it so that the poor man will have as nearly as possible an equal opportunity in litigating as the rich man, and under present conditions, ashamed as we may be of it, this is not a fact." Senator Norris also quoted Chief Justice Olson of the Chicago Municipal courts who said in 1915: "When litigation is too costly, the result for many persons is a denial of justice. Such denial or partial denial of justice engenders social and commercial friction. The sense of helplessness thus caused incites citizens to take the law into their own hands. It causes crimes of violence. It saps patriotism and destroys civic pride. It arouses jealousy and breeds contempt for law and government." In an address delivered in Chicago, Mr. Lyman Abbott declared: "If ever a time shall come when in this city only the rich man can enjoy law as a doubtful luxury, when the poor who need it most can not have it, when only a golden key will unlock the door to the court room, the seeds of revolution will be sown, the firebrand of revolution will be lighted and put into the hands of men, and they will almost be justified in the revolution which will follow." One provision of the bill provides vhat all the senior circuit judges shall come to Washington once a year and confer with the chief justice of the United States on the judicial situation, reviewing it, talking about it, and agreeing on a plan for the next year. This is a most dangerous proposal. Of this clause, Senator Norris said: "When these judges come to Washington at the expense of the taxpayers, what will they do? They will meet with the chief justice. They will be dined every evening somewhere. They will be run to death with social activities. They will be killed with social favoritisms before they get down to business. That is especially true in respect to the genial chief justice we have, who dines out somewhere every night. I would like to pause right here to say, Mr. President, that I do not believe there is any man who can stick his legs under the tables of the idle rich every night and be fit the next day to sit in judgment upon those who toil. Honest though he may be, he can not get away from the atmosphere that will surround him, and ninety-nine times out of one hundred, it will affect him and get him in the end. . . . I do not believe there can be any doubt but what in the practical workings the annual pilgrimages these judges will make to Washington will have an unfavorable effect upon them and upon the common idea of the common folks as to the courts." To the layment the bringing of all the senior circuit judges to Washington to be dined, and if possible, wined by the lobbyists of the big interests is most dangerous. It will permit those who believe in judge-made laws to sow the seed that will bring about a unanimity of decisions against labor and the people. However, the bill passed congress and was sent to the president.

Judicial Decisions and Decrees—(1923, p. 91) Attempts made by employers, commercial, industrial and financial interests to destroy or to render impotent the trade union movement of America by means fair or foul, legal or illegal, are not alone foolish but are ill-designed in that they give rise to attitudes and tendencies surcharged with extremely harmful consequences to the whole social, economic and political fabric of our country. With the wide-spread of education and the constant growth of the ideals and principles of democracy the workers can not long be kept in legal or industrial subjection or be denied successfully the right of combining to equalize their power, influence and ability with that of corporate enterprise and associate industries. The necessity for mutual defense and the promptings for the advancement of the common good can not be stifled or be suppressed. Those who would understand these truths and human incentives might well refer to and reflect upon the pages of history. The struggle of labor for freedom, equal opportunity and equal rights is indeed a tragic reflection upon humankind and the brightest hope for a better civilization is indicated in the fact that however strong and influential those in midst of us may be and who lay claim to the greater portion of the wealth and possessions of mankind, the hopes of the real toilers of life can not be everlastingly suppressed and repressed. Thus we find that nearly a hundred years ago the employers of England attempted to destroy trade unions. The combination acts of 1799 and 1800 were expressly designed to prevent the workers from combining to increase wages and reduce working hours. Workmen and their leaders were sent to jail and severely punished for their disregard to those anti-social tendencies and laws. But the promptings of labor could not be suppressed; anti-combination laws proved futile against the rising tide of the wage earners for equality of rights with all persons and groups. For many years then public opinion was strongly in favor of suppressing the trade unions. Employers, government officials, journalists and clergymen urged that organizations of workers were dangerous and every possible legal and economic weapon was used to suppress the trade unions. All these repress measures failed and today the right of the workers to organize and to bargain collectively through representatives of their own choosing is no longer challenged but is legally safeguarded in England. In Russia we find quite another example of the folly and danger of a policy of repression. The attitude of the former imperial government toward all movements of the workers was the recognized policy. Imprisonment, banishment and execution were the weapons used. Finally the inevitable occurred. The old regime was swept aside and the industries of Russia all but ruined. Recent

occurrences can not be fairly understood without embracing a remembrance of the decades and centuries of repression and persecution of the masses. Since the World War there has been a marked tendency and highly concentrated effort here to destroy trade unionism by an appeal to suppression and resort to repression in many forms. We are thus confronted with the all-absorbing question of whether, as a people, we shall follow the progressive course, experienced in England, or whether we shall find ourselves thrust into currents of disorder as have manifested in Russia. The more pronounced and most dangerous policies of repression are those having received legislative or judicial sanction and thus constitute governmental policies which must need amendment or repeal. Chief among these repressive laws, legal policies and judicial decrees are the Sherman anti-trust law and similar anti-combination laws, the legality of individual contracts of employment denying the worker the right to join the trade union of his calling and placing the power to penalize the worker into the hands of an irresponsible employer, the continued usurpation by our judges in the exercise of their chancery powers to issue injunctive and mandatory decrees without limitation and regardlews of their constant infringement upon the legislative or lawmaking branch of government and their flagrant trespass upon the powers and rights reserved to the people by our constitutional form of government. (P. 275) This generalization makes clear that underlying the greater number, if not all, of these repressive legislative enactments and judicial decrees is the pernicious doctrine of conspiracy by which perfectly legal acts when engaged in by the individual become illegal when resorted to by two or more in concert. It is by this doctrine that trade unions were first denied the sanction of the law. Now that this sanction can no longer be denied, we find the application of the device of "conspiracy" used to outlaw and render illegal the primary essentials and activities of the trade union movement.

Judicial Kidnapping, Legalizing—(1922, pp. 99-327) Those people who must depend for their knowledge on the newspapers do not realize the rabid reactionary spirit that has completely controlled certain members of congress. As the country grows older it should progress, not go backward. But there are members of the U. S. Senate who do not believe this, and one of them is Senator Nelson, of Minnesota. In April, 1921, he introduced Senate bill 657, which in effect would legalize judicial kidnapping. No hearings were held upon it by the judiciary committee and some of the members knew nothing about the bill until after it had been surreptitiously slipped through the senate on June 6, 1921. In fact no one knew it had passed the senate until it had been reported to the house, and then it was found that it was a very dangerous measure. The intention of the bill is to give any judge in any federal district the right to issue a warrant for the arrest of an indicted person who may live in a far distant state, arrest and transport him to the place of indictment for trial, without giving a hearing on the question of probable cause before being removed from the district of his domicile. Not only a preliminary examination would be prohibited but also the right and opportunity to secure bail and counsel to present the matter to the court. It has been rumored that the purpose of the bill is to make it possible to drag the miners to Indianapolis to appear before Judge Anderson to answer certain indictments. If any attempts were made to arrest the miners under the present law they would have the right of a hearing in the state where they live and undoubtedly could not be taken to Indianapolis. The president of the A. F. of L., after considering the dangers of the bill, wrote a letter to the attorney general protesting in vigorous language against its passage. The former also held a conference with the attorney general in which he pointed out the un-American provisions outlined above. He also sent circular letters to the national and international unions, city and state central bodies, urging them to protest. Representatives of the A. F. of L. interviewed members of the judiciary committee which had the bill under consideration. The bill was refrred to a sub-committee which was not friendly to its passage. This sub-committee requested an opinion from the attorney general as to the constitutionality of the bill. He never publicly answered this question. However, so far as the judiciary committee of the house is concerned, there is no reason to believe that the bill will be approved.

Judicial Usurpation — (1923, p. 95) Keenly alert to the dangers that beset the organized wage earners of our land, appreciative of the ever-increasing tendency of the judiciary to usurp and arrogate to itself constantly greater powers and more extensive authority and conscious of the need for further constitutional safeguards as expressed by the Cincinnati convention of the A. F. of L., consideration was given the following proposed amendment: "An amendment prohibiting the enactment of any law or the making of any judicial determination which would deny the right of the workers of the U. S. and its territories and dependencies to organize for the betterment of their conditions; to deal collecively with employers; to collectively withhold their labor and patronage and induce others to do so." This and like proposals are being considered by other groups and it is the hope that the forces of all those groups may be marshaled into one solid array so that the purpose intended by this proposal and proposals of like character may be formulated into one complete legislative or constitutional program that will end for all time the suppression and repression that is being manifested against the trade union movement on every hand. (P. 277) The A. F. of L. seeks to impress upon all the necessity of using all powers of resistance at our command to correct the evils of which complaint is made.

Jurisdiction of Unions—(1923, p. 328) The A. F. of L. desires to again point out clearly that each national and international organization affiliated with the A. F. of L. has full and final control over its own internal affairs. The jurisdictional rights of each of the several national and international unions have been clearly and specifically outlined in their charters and such charters have been approved, first by the Executive Council and then by the convention of the A. F. of L., and in at least one instance the jurisdictional rights of a national union were approved by the convention of the A. F. of L. before the charter was issued by the Executive Council. No charter can be more exclusive in its nature than those granted by the A. F. of L. to its affiliated organizations, and no charter is more sacred or will be more carefully respected than are these. It is not within the power or province of any affiliated organization to interfere with the discipline of man-

agement or control of its own affairs by another body so chartered from the A. F. of L. Therefore, it would be an unwarranted invasion on the part of this convention to undertake to prescribe by resolution to an affiliated organization the character or qualifications of its membership. We earnestly hope that the several state and city central bodies which are chartered direct by the A. F. of L., and hold their powers and authority from the A. F. of L., give heed to the principle that the "creature can not become greater than the creator," in this regard; that the restrictions placed upon the A. F. of L. lie with added weight on the bodies subordinate so the A. F. of L., and that any invasion by a central labor union or a state federation of labor of the jurisdictional rights of a national or international union is going far beyond the limit set for the subordinate bodies to control them in their action and relations to the A. F. of L.

Kansas Court of Industrial Relations— (1920, p. 88) Report of Executive Council: Kansas, which for many years startled the world with its liberal legislation, has turned reactionary. The legislature of that state has enacted a law providing for a court of industrial relations. It could well be named, "an act to establish involuntary servitude for the workers of Kansas," or "an act to protect the financial interests of the owners of public utilities and all industries at the expense of their employes." But more harmful than all it destroys the right of collective bargaining, the gateway to industrial peace. The law covers practically every industry in the state of Kansas. It affects every person engaged in the work of reparing foodstuffs from their original state to the finished product, every one engaged in the production of clothing or wearing apparel in any stage of the process of converting it into the marketable product, every miner and every woodchopper and every workman engaged in the production of fuel for any purpose. It affects the railroad men. If two or more persons engaged in these occupations refuse to accept an award by the court of industrial relations they must either pay a fine or be sent to the penitentiary. It is a most sweeping law and is in violation of the Thirteenth Amendment of the constitution of the United States. No matter from what unbearable conditions the workers are suffering they must accept them without question if the court of industrial relations so decides. It is a relic of legislation in the fifteenth century establishing autocracy in industry by law. The court is conducted under the rules and regulations of the supreme court of Kansas and has unlimited power to carry out the provisions of the act. The law repeals the act creating the public utility commission of the state of Kansas and gives all its power and more to the court of industrial relations. This court is composed of three judges appointed by the governor. They are given, among other things, full power, authority and jurisdiction to supervise and control all public utilities and common carriers in the state and are empowered to do all that is necessary and convenient for the exercise of such power, authority and jurisdiction. The power of the court is most extraordinary. If there is no law in existence and one is necessary to carry out the provisions of the act the three judges are empowered to make one. Being judges it is natural to assume they are fully conversant with the methods of making laws to suit every case that comes before them. This extraordinary power is provided for in section 26, as follows: "The provisions of this act and all grants of power, authority and jurisdiction herein made to said court of industrial relations shall be liberally construed and all incidental powers necessary to carry into effect the provisions of this act are hereby expressly granted to and conferred upon said court of industrial relations." When the employes of any public utility or of any industry disagree with their employers over wages and working conditions the court of industrial relations is authorized to make an investigation and decision. Whatever decision is made by this court is mandatory. The employes must accept it or go to jail. The operation of the following named employments, industries, public utilities and common carriers is declared to be affected with the public interest and therefore subject to the supervision of the court: (1) The manufacture or preparation of food products whereby, in any stage of the process, substances are being converted, either partially or wholly, from their natural state to a condition to be used as food for human beings; (2) the manufacture of clothing and all manner of wearing apparel in common use by the people of this state whereby, in any stage of the process, natural products are being converted, either partially or wholly, from their natural state to a condition to be used as such clothing and wearing apparel; (3) the mining or production of any substance or material in common use as fuel for domestic, manufacturing, or transportation purposes; (4) the transportation of all food products and articles or substances entering into wearing apparel, or fuel as aforesaid, from the place where produced to the place of manufacture or consumption; (5) all public utilities. According to the provisions of the law the court has full power to settle any labor or other controversy that may arise. The court has arbitrary power of fixing the "working and living conditions, hours of labor, rules and practices, and a reasonable minimum wage, or standard of wages, to conform to the findings of the court in such matters." If either party to an industrial dispute affecting a public utility refuses to obey and be governed by the order of the court it is authorized to bring proceedings in the supreme court of Kansas to compel compliance. While section 17 of the law provides that it does not restrict the right of any individual employe to quit his employment, section 18 can be construed otherwise. It provides: "Any person willfully violating the provisions of this act, or any valid order of said court of industrial relations, shall be deemed guilty of a misdemeanor, and upon conviction thereof in any court of competent jurisdiction of this state shall be punished by a fine of not to exceed $1,000 or by imprisonment in the county jail for a period of not to exceed one year, or by both such fine and imprisonment." This section undoubtedly nullifies section 17. The only qualification in this section is the word "willfully." The courts can construe this word to any meaning. It can therefore be accepted as a fact that an individual can be punished for quitting work because he objects to an order issued by the court of industrial relations. Section 19 provides a heavy penalty for those who violate any order issued by the court. Any officer of a trade union can be fined $5,000 or sentenced to the penitentiary at hard labor for a term of two years, or both, if the members of his organization fail to comply with an award made by the

court of industrial relations. The mere fact that members of a labor organization have refused to work under an award made by the court could be used by judges in sending their officers to the penitentiary. The law establishes involuntary servitude in Kansas. If the court of industrial relations decides that an employer is not making a sufficient profit, notwithstanding that he may have taken contracts upon a cut-throat basis, it can refuse concessions to the employes and they must accept the verdict or go to jail. Section 25 is most remarkable in its provisions. In the event of a dispute over wages it is brought before the court of industrial relations and the findings of the court are retroactive. If the court decides that wages should be reduced the employers are authorized to deduct the difference between the new and the old wages from the earnings of the employes during the time hearings were in progress or from the day the investigation was determined. This may be six months or more. No legislation of the kind was ever suggested, so far as known, by any legislature in the world. If a man has been paid $4 a day and the court says he must work for $3.50 a day, then the company can deduct 50 cents a day from the amount earned from the time the investigation began. The workers who are always near the brink of poverty are forced to spend every cent they earn to live. Just how employers could recover wages paid under such circumstances is impossible to imagine. The workers would not give back the money they had received as wages. The result would be that men would cease work rather than restore to an employer the money that has been previously earned by hard labor. The same mode of procedure in the disputes between public utilities and their employes will be followed in all other industrial disputes. Section 6 of the Clayton act permits the normal activities of labor and farmer organizations. The Kansas industrial law nullifies this act. Already the people of Kansas have begun to see the dangers in the law. The opposition is gradually increasing and it is to be hoped that before another year has passed it will be repealed. Any law to enforce compulsory labor upon our citizenship will be resented by the people and repealed at the behest of their indignation. The Kansas law is unjust, tyrannical and un-American. It was enacted during a time of great hysteria created through the propaganda of the governor of the state of Kansas. Bitter attacks were made on labor. The law gives absolute protection to the public utilities owners. It is believed that they were instrumental in having it enacted in order to receive protection from the state for those utilities that are in financial difficulties." (P. 379) The report of the Executive Council on the Kansas court of industrial relations law should be earnestly studied by the delegates and membership at large. It presents in a compact but impressive way the contents of statutory laws, which are the expression of an effort to deprive the workers of not only their most potent weapon of defense, but of the last line on which they may depend for protection in their struggle to better their condition of living and to secure a more just proportion of the result of their productive effort. Carefully masked behind a screen of so-called industrial optimism involving the shibboleth of "continuous production," these enemies of labor approach the citadel of labor's strength. If it be permitted that by law men are to be forbidden to cease work, singly or in groups, at such time as they by counsel together have determined, is the point beyond which they can no longer going submissive effort, the state of enforced labor becomes not at heory to be discussed but a fact established. The operation of such a law, even under the most generous interpretation, becomes a confiscation of liberty and property and a denial of human rights. In the Kansas law this element is most emphatically exhibited, because the law places the so-called wage court beyond the reach of those who are most directly affected and intimately concerned in its operation, through the fact that the court is the creature of an appointing power in itself beyond approach. So potent and dangerous a weapon should not be trusted in the hands of any man. The, A. F. of L. throughout its history has consistently favored the settlement of wage disputes and conditions of employment by resort to the doctrine of collective bargaining in which the parties agree on terms mutually satisfactory, mediating or conciliating all points at issue, with voluntary arbitration available for the determination of any question arising which can not be adjusted by methods of conciliation or mediation. This organization has consistently, at all times, opposed the policy of compulsory arbitration, and it now again records its opposition to this destructive policy, no matter under what guise it may be presented. The Executive Council is directed to cooperate with the organized labor bodies of the state of Kansas to bring about the repeal of the act.

(1921, pp. 125-329) The Kansas court of industrial relations act is an admitted failure. Although loudly heralded by its author, the governor of Kansas, as an instrument to tie men to their jobs, he has been unable to make the people of Kansas or any other state accept it as a guide in legislation. The law has proved to be not only ineffective in averting cessations of work but has been rejected by all fair-minded citizens as un-American. Although the governor and his satellites traveled far and wide and pleaded with legislators to enact a similar law not a state legislature after analyzing the act would approve of its provisions. From the enactment of the law up to February last, 285 orders were signed by the court granting rate increases to the public service corporations. These increases in rates were most burdensome to the people of the state, especially the farmers, and they began to study the law. It was not long before protests were raised in all parts of the state. Despite the law strikes have been [numerous in Kansas. These occurred in the coal fields, on the railroads and in the packing houses. There were at least twenty strikes, but aside from the president of the Kansas district of the United Mine Workers and three district board members of the miners no attempt was made to punish any of the workers who participated in them. Not only are the workers and the farmers opposed to the law but many employers refuse to recognize it. The president of the Kansas State Federation of Labor in a report on the workings of the law states that the general manager of the McKinley street and interurban railway interests in Kansas has abrogated a contract with the unions and declares that he will make no further agreement. If the court of industrial relations interferes and makes a decision the railway official declared he would appeal the case to the federal courts to test the authority of the industrial court. Another employer, a large coal operator, settled a

strike with the miners in preference to recognizing the court. The industrial court has proven a huge joke and at present is a dead weight around the governor's neck from which he would gladly free himself if it were possible. This he can not do, however, without admitting defeat. Less than fifteen unions recognized the authority of the court, and in not a single instance was any of them satisfied with its award. A bill was drawn by the officers of the Kansas State Federation of Labor to repeal the act, but it was not presented. The failure to present a bill is thus explained: "This failure was not because of the realization of the utter hoplessness of getting it through. The entire force of labor representatives in Topeka who are urging legislation in the interest of labor decided to ignore the court altogether. The reason was that the law had not yet hurt labor, except possibly a few workers who had submitted their cases to the court." In February, W. L. Huggins, presiding judge of the court, endeavored to obtain permission to address a joint session of the legislature. He desired to point out the causes for the failure of the law. The governor succeeded in preventing the joint meeting and Judge Huggins gathered forty-two members of the legislature in his court room and explained the real situation. He declared that the law had proven a failure because the governor had insisted upon using it as a political tool. The judge told how he had spent a whole month of his time going about the country spreading propaganda favoring the court in the interest of Governor Allen and to induce other state legislatures to adopt it. The object, he said, was to secure a more solid backing for the governor from the people of Kansas. He charged also that the court had caused undue expenditure of funds. Under the new law the labor commissioner, the department of labor and the labor welfare commission are placed under the jurisdiction of the court. The activities of the governor in trying to save himself from ignominy because of the failure of the law has brought forth many requests for literature bearing on the Kansas law. Many colleges, universities and high schools have been furnished with literature and from the reports received a majority of those who opposed such a court have won in the debates. In addition to the failure of the law as first constituted the governor himself admitted this when he had a bill introduced and passed by the last Kansas legislature separating the public utilities commission from the jurisdiction of this court of industrial relations. The act now provides that that court has no further jurisdiction over public utilities except as to the question of wages, working conditions and continuity of service. The fact that not a single state has enacted a law similar to that of Kansas is the best evidence of its pernicious character. Its unpopularity among the farmers and employers, as well as labor, is based on not only its impracticability but its denial of the right of collective bargaining and the forcing of the settlement of industrial disputes by litigation. It is predicted by the labor legislative representatives of Kansas that the law will be repealed at the next session of the legislature. Notwithstanding the propaganda in its favor engineered by the governor he has made no headway in gaining friends for the law. Undoubtedly conceived as a means of attracting attention to himself and thereby placing his name in the field as a contestant for the nomination for president of the United States the governor now realizes that instead of making him a candidate the law destroyed whatever consideration might otherwise have been given to his aspiration. Earnest efforts should be made to repeal the law. In the meantime the widest publicity should be given to the fact that the law makes for tyranny, injustice and unfreedom and is inimical to the interests of not only labor but the farmers and the people generally. (P. 379) We unanimously commend the organized workers of Kansas, and particularly the mine workers and their officers of that state, upon whom the brunt of the battle has fallen, for so courageously opposing this law in the face of injunctions and threats of imprisonment by hostile judges; and thereby preventing this objectionable law becoming operative in the state selected for this legislative experiment and thus fighting the battle for the organized workers of the country.

(1922, pp. 52-486) Regardless of the fact that the Kansas court of industrial relations has proven an utter failure, agitation for the enactment of similar laws in other states has not entirely abated. During the past year proposals of a similar character were introduced into several state legislatures. No greater legal fraud has ever been perpetrated on the American people than this attempt to regulate industries and industrial relations by law. The Kansas law has failed completely in compelling men to work when they have willed otherwise. The Kansas law has failed to prevent men from striking when occasion demanded that workers resort to this final means of protest. The Kansas law has failed likewise in compelling employers to observe decisions of the industrial court. As a matter of fact, this legislation has made for greater misunderstanding and friction than ever prevailed heretofore in Kansas. No opportunity has been permitted to pass that the A. F. of L. has not voiced the protest of Labor against this iniquitous and unconstitutional form of legislation. Every effort has been exerted to bring its failings and its un-American provisions and requirements to the attention of the public in general and the workers in particular. Dissatisfaction is manifested against this law not alone by the workers but by large numbers of employers as well who, while sympathetic with the purpose of this law when applied to Labor, now realize fully that it infringes as well upon the rights of the employers and can be made to regulate industry and affect management of industry quite as badly as it has been used to attempt to regulate the functions and aspirations of organized labor. Indeed, it is becoming recognized quite generally that laws such as this are so intimately connected with the whole structure of modern industry as to entail consequences by far more dangerous to the rights and liberties of our people and far more disasterous to public interests than are the alleged evils the proponents seek to correct. During this year the United Mine Workers of America caused legal proceedings to be instituted for the purpose of testing the constitutionality of this law. Governor Allen and the industrial court commissioners instead of meeting squarely the issues raised have attempted to evade this test by attacking the jurisdiction of

the court. Upon the hearing on the motion to dismiss the action instituted by the United Mine Workers, the industrial court commissioners gave scant attention to the jurisdictional question raised, but proceeded in an attempt to justify the Kansas industrial court act under the "police power" of the state and under the plea that to prevent strikes was in the furtherance of the "public welfare." During this argument Judge Pollock asked the Kansas attorney-general whether or not, in his opinion the law-making body of Kansas could, within its power, enact a statute making it a criminal offense for a workman to cease work with or without a time contract. In reply the attorney-general was compelled to admit that any workman could leave his employment any time he saw fit and that the state could not prosecute him therefor, but he added that two or more could not legally agree to quit, or in other words, strike, and especially so if they had time contracts. Thereupon the court said: "Men have the right to quit work when they please and the state is without power to inquire into their reason for doing so." The court having thus indicated its opinion as to the unconstitutionality of the industrial court law, nevertheless it took under consideration the motion having been made questioning its jurisdiction and held that the proceedings of the United Mine Workers had been instituted prematurely and that it could not render a decision upon the constitutionality of the law until such time that the industrial court might undertake to render or might attempt to enforce any of its decisions under the industrial court law. While the court expressed this judgment upon the motion to dismiss this particular proceeding, it nevertheless allowed an extension of time for further hearings upon this question of jurisdiction. In addition, the court stated that if the industrial court would make a wage scale, and arrest one of the miners for non-compliance therewith, that the court would then be empowered to render a decision upon the constitutionality of the law itself. Thus Judge Pollock as well as the United Mine Workers have not only presented the governor of Kansas and the Kansas industrial court with a fair opportunity for them to justify the enactment of this law before the courts, but a direct challenge has been presented to them to come into court and demonstrate the constitutionality of the law under which they would make mere puppets of workmen. Indeed, we find the governor and his nationwide heralded industrial court law confronted with a state-wide strike of the miners who have challenged him and the industrial court to come into court by attempting to interfere with the existing strike. Instead of so doing the governor and the industrial court have declined to interfere with this strike or to meet fairly and squarely the issues raised in the court. By these evasive and delusive tactics they have publicly acknowledged the impotency of this compulsory service law. It is clearly apparent that the governor and his industrial court dare not meet the issue squarely in the courts and that they are but waiting for the development of a situation in which the element of time contracts may be relied on as a defense to bolster up an unworkable, unconstitutional and indefensible piece of legislation. We shall await with further interest the final decision of Judge Pollock as well as watch with special concern the future attitude and actions of the governor and his industrial court, believing in the meantime that the taxpayers of Kansas may find it advisable, desirable and expedient to prevent the further spending of the people's money for the upkeep of an industrial court, which Judge Pollock indicated in his opinion is unconstitutional and which the governor and the industrial court commissioners by their refusal to enforce this law admit is impracticable. In addition to this particular judicial and possible future legal tests of the constitutionality of this law, the wage earners as well as the people generally throughout Kansas have been aroused against this iniquitous form of legislation more than ever and a state-wide movement has been inaugurated by the organized wage earners of Kansas for the early repeal of this law. Perhaps the only purpose this law has served has been to demonstrate again that men value freedom and liberty and that men can not be made to give service long under any form of compulsion. Self-respecting men will do right when equal rights and opportunities are accorded to them.

Duell-Miller Bill—(p. 54) The proposal for a law similar to the Kansas industrial law was introduced in the New York state legislature during its last session. This proposal followed in purpose and intent the Kansas law though it differed in form and in some particulars was even more mischievous and vicious than the Kansas industrial law. The significant feature of this proposal was that all industrial disputes which went beyond the control of the state industrial commissioner and became "a public consequence" should be adjusted by the state supreme court. For this purpose it was proposed that the court might, upon application, enjoin strikes and lockouts and by the action of one of the parties to an industrial dispute, it might fix wages, hours and working conditions and in a special industrial relations term called by the governor it might supervise, direct and control the operations of all businesses, corporations, labor unions or other agencies representing either employers or employes. This proposal undertook also to regulate the procedure that trade unions would be required to follow in reaching decisions affecting their industrial relations. The entire labor movement of New York state was aroused as never before against this most vicious proposal, and the largest protest meeting ever held in the annals of organized labor within that state was held in opposition to the enactment into the law of this proposal. Before a joint session of the committee on labor of the senate and assembly President Gompers and Vice-President Woll voiced the opposition of American labor against this proposal and every influence was sent into motion to defeat this proposed obnoxious legislation. As a result, the Duell-Miller bill received no further consideration and died with the adjournment of the New York state legislature.

(1923, p. 56) When ex-Governor Allen. of Kansas was advocating his industrial court law, the A. F. of L. immediately protested against the creation of a judicial body charged with powers and duties that virtually deprived the American wage earners of their equal rights and opportunities with all other classes and groups of citizens. Throughout the life of the Kansas industrial court law and the campaign to extend this extra judicial

power over industrial relations, the American labor movement made known the dangers involved from an economic as well as social and political point of view. During that period we had much of the interests of the "third" party to every labor contract and the "public wealth and welfare" was never more adroitly exploited than in the campaign of the proponents of ex-Governor Allen's scheme to impose compulsory labor under the pretense of insuring industrial peace by subjection of the workers of America to the whim and lash of his extra-judicial body. Organized labor's attitude was denounced as "un-American" and its leaders were stigmatized as narrow-minded, class-selfish and disregardful for the safety and well being of the American people. Passing through the weird cycle of judicial procedure the Kansas industrial court law formally came for review before the United States supreme court and on June 11, 1923, the supreme court sustained the objections which organized labor had voiced against this law. The United States supreme court did not declare the entire act unconstitutional. By judicial interpretation and construction and by its actual decision it did declare null and void the very life blood of this law as being in conflict with constitutional safeguards. While the decision of the supreme court does not apply to the entire act it does restrict the activities and work of the Kansas court so as to make that court practically inoperative. It likewise restores the right and freedom to the wage earners of Kansas to organize and to bargain collectively in their own way and to stop work collectively whenever they feel themselves justified in so doing. Kansas once again is heading toward freedom and will have attained complete freedom when every vestige of this law, attempting to impose involuntary servitude upon a free people, shall have been wiped off the statute books. In view of the decision of the supreme court the only purpose now being served by the remnants of ex-Governor Allen's law is to provide jobs for his political appointees on this court and to squander the money of the taxpayers of Kansas. Governor Davis of Kansas is to be commended for his effort to annul this law for involuntary servitude and his desire to wipe it out completely now in order to save the money of the taxpayers. While we are gratified that our years of effort and opposition against this form of legislation have not been in vain and while the decision of the United States supreme court gives cause for vindication of labor's attitude, it is difficult nevertheless to agree with the reasoning followed by the supreme court in its decision because the power and authority that are held to be unconstitutional when exercised by the legislature are nevertheless affirmed as constitutional when exercised by the court. Thus the U. S. supreme court has arrogated to itself the right to determine for the people whether a business is public or otherwise. Then, too, it has arrogated to itself the right to declare and prescribe the circumstances under which one man under the freedom of contract doctrine may cease employment, but may not advise others to join with him in the cessation of such employment. The right to free contract, the right to work or not to work, the right to advise or not to advise someone to join with another in the doing of such things marks the boundary line between slavery and freedom. Our courts have altogether too much power, a power self-assumed and self-asserted until we have become a judiciary ruled country. It is not to be found in any of the documents of our nation, but rises out of the srength of the personnel of the court. The stronger always win; hence, the personnel of the supreme court must either be made up of those who interpret democracy as democracy demands, or else the personnel of the other branches of government must be filled with men stronger than the personnel of the supreme court, that the several rights and powers of these coordinate branches which have been unbalanced in favor of the supreme court may again balance equally. Free labor permits of no exception. Whether the same be in public or private service, whether the laborer act as an individual or en masse, any interpretation whether by courts or legislature that denies labor in the singular or plural (fundamental rights do not rest on grammar—those rights were born long before grammar was invented) to work or not to work as he or they will is a contravention of the constitutional guarantee of freedom of contract, a violation of the very first precept of the fundamental right of free men. (P. 270) The decision clearly indicates that only when employers' interests and their welfare are placed in jeopardy do we find the U. S. supreme court concerned in safeguarding the device of contract and in making secure the free and unhampered use of this device to determine human relationships. Thus, quite incidentally, were the rights of the wage earners to freedom of contract safeguarded. Happily, their security carried with it the practical destruction of former Governor Allen's infamous "Can't-strike law."

Ku Klux Klan—(1922, p. 343) The A. F. of L. should not assume to endorse or condemn any organization, fraternity or association of American citizens unless the purpose of such organization is to organize for the purpose of interfering with the rights, opportunities and liberties of wage earners. The A. F. of L. is firmly of the opinion that the administration of the law is vested solely and entirely in the duly elected or appointed officers of the law, and that those who as members of any secret organization assume to usurp the functions properly belonging to legal authorities, invite mob rule and create in men's minds a disrespect for and disregard of duly constituted authority. The A. F. of L. is also of the opinion that it is not conducive to government by law and the maintenance of peaceful and safe conditions in the community to have members of any organization parade the streets so disguised that their identity can not be discovered, when such disguises are adopted for the purpose of inspiring the thought or belief that the disguised individuals represent an invisible government.

(1923, p. 65) During the year the Ku Klux Klan has continued its campaign of terrorism on such a scale that its operations can not be overlooked. This secret organization promotes discord among our people and strife within the ranks of organized labor, seeks to destroy the cherished American principle of religious freedom and tolerance and purposely fosters racial prejudices. The Ku Klux Klan is destructive of that freedom and devotion to the principles of liberty which we regard as the first essential in democratic civilization. The Ku Klux Klan seeks also to take into its own hands the administration of punishment, thus setting itself up as superior to government in the enforcement of law. We know of nothing that could be more intolerable or more hostile to the purposes of organized government or the trade union movement. The issues involved are not new; they are as old as the institution of organized government. The trade union movement of America long since took cognizance of the importance of these issues to labor and in the convention of 1893 unanimously adopted the following resolutions setting forth fundamental principles which can not at any time be discarded or renounced without the destruction of essential liberties. "We deplore the introduction of any sectarian or captious side issues among the working people. Such movements are destined to divide labor's forces and produce bitter antagonisms as they produce religious bigotry, provoke rancorous intolerance, apd divert the working people from working out their own emancipation. That we here and now reaffirm as one of the cardinal principles of the labor movement that the working people must unite and organize, irrespective of creed, color, sex, nationality or politics." We believe that no trade unionist can consistently participate in the activities of the Ku Klux Klan or any similar organization, and we unhesitatingly denounce its efforts to supplant organized government, to promote religious intolerance, racial antagonisms, and bigotry. (P. 270) It was religious intolerance that so impressed the founders of our American government as to cause them to adopt a measure of security for religious tolerance in the organic act of our great republic. So, too, when in the course of time violent differences developed among our people, founded on inequality before the law, there came into existence the fourteenth amendment to the constitution of the U. S., guaranteeing to all our citizens equality before the law and making secure the life, liberty, and property of all citizens, regardless of race, creed or color. Underlying these great charters to security of life and liberty and the pursuit of happiness is the fundamental requirement that this, our government, must be and always shall be a government by consent of the people, freely expressed and uninfluenced or denied by intimidation, fraud, or duress. The American people can not tolerate the threat or the accomplishment of usurpation of the powers of government by any organization or by any group of whatever kind. We feel that the attempted usurpation of power of government by the Ku Klux Klan is of paramount importance to every American. We can not believe that any American, after giving full thought to the purposes and objects sought to be attained by this organization, can either join or condone such a conspiracy. This is not the first instance of attempt at secretly organize minority control of the powers of government. History offers many similar adventures. But nowhere does history offer an adequate justification for them. We prize democracy because it offers oppportunity for the righting of every real wrong and grievance. It offers opportunity for regular and orderly change of government and it offers and guarantees punishment for crime whereof the guilty party shall have been convicted in a court of law. It provides the jury trial for every alleged criminal. Law can not be for one or for a group and it can not be enforced by one or by a group if democracy is to fulfill its mission. It can not tolerate any secret or private usurpation of its functions if it is to live. As trade unionists we must be concerned with every effort to control or pervert the functions of democratic government by or in the interests of any secret group. We need not be concerned with the motives for such efforts at control of government as those exercised by this secret organization. If the motives were of the best the offense would be no less intolerable, for it is the principle with which we are concerned. We are concerned in behalf of the safeguarding of democracy as a living, orderly system of government. The intolerance of the Ku Klux Klan is its stock in trade. By the arousing of blind hatreds it seeks to nerve its adherents on to a policy that falls little short of treason. Through prejudice it attempts to swerve its followers to a course that could not be made attractive to any following by any other means. Religious prejudices and racial hatreds are fostered and developed as a basis upon which to build defiance for government. Our government guarantees religious freedom and it protects every man, of whatever race, against unlawful acts on the part of any other man. These guarantees are not fixed in our constitution and our law for the purpose of being set at naught by any organization or group, secret or otherwise. They are there for the purpose of protecting most cherished human freedom, freedom to think and believe as the individual mind dictates, freedom to be unmolested and unafraid in the orderly pursuits of life. We can not refrain from pointing out the fact that great wars have been fought for the very freedom that the Ku Klux Klan seeks to deny and destroy. Our own U. S. constitution bespeaks the victory for freedom and tolerance, won only after centuries of struggle and sacrifice. The trade union movement, for itself, has always sought to keep its own councils free from either religious or racial bigotry, intolerance and dispute. Any other course would long since have shattered our ranks, if indeed they could ever have been mustered in the beginning. The trade union movement has always been firm in its support of ordered, orderly, democratic government. It has been a pioneer in the establishment of great and fundamental measures of freedom and it can not now condone any movement for their undoing. We have the highest regard for legitimate fraternal organizations and we pay the highest tribute to them for their good works. But the Ku Klux Klan seeks to overthrow laws and to destroy constitutional guarantees which we prize above everything because they constitute the breath of life itself to free men and women. We condemn this secret conspiracy, this hideous and sinister movement that proudly calls itself the "invisible empire," cloaking itself in masks and mummery while it eats at the heart of our institutions. We call upon Americans in general and trade unionists in particular to beware of this menace and to conduct themselves in the open, under the law, and for the preservation of democratic government and democratic institutions. We call upon them to preserve religious freedom and the rights of all men of all races under the law. It is an American duty and a trade union duty of the highest order for trade unionists to shun this conspiracy and to conduct themselves as Americans worthy of a democratic government and worthy of the freedom and the opportunity and the justice which it has made possible and which it guarantees for the future.

Label, Universal Union—(1922, p. 282) Inasmuch as the autonomy of all organizations affiliated with the A. F. of L. is guaranteed them by the constitution of the A. F. of L., this autonomy, including as it does, the ownership and control of union labels, shop or store cards, working buttons and other insignia to indicate that the commodity is made, sold, delivered or otherwise handled by union labor, the A. F. of L. refuses to endorse the universal union label.

Labor and Peace—(1919, p. 83) "Whether in peace or in war the organized labor movement seeks to make all else subordinate to human welfare and human opportunity. The labor movement stands as the defender of this principle and undertakes to protect the wealth-producers against the exorbitant greed of special interests, against profiteering, against exploitation, against the detestable methods of irresponsible greed, against the inhumanity and crime of heartless corporations and employers. Labor demands the right in war times to be the recognized defender of wage earners against the same forces which in former wars have made national necessity an excuse for more ruthless methods."

Labor and Production—(1920, pp. 86-383) Such emphasis has been laid by employers upon the necessity for increased production that we believe a presentation of the trade union point of view in relation to production should be placed before the nation in authoritative manner and that constructive proposals should be laid down. While it is true that there are no great surplus stocks of essential commodities in storage at the present time, it is not true that labor is curtailing production or that it stands in a position of opposition to capacity production. The essential facts of the present industrial situation are these: A large portion of the world's productive machinery was destroyed by the war. Approximately 9,000,000 men were killed and it is estimated that more than 20,000,000 people have died as a consequence of the war. The productive power of this machinery and of these men is lost beyond recall. Large stocks of materials were consumed by the war. In the case of many basic materials war-time consumption was at a forced rate that ate into the peace-time supply to such an extent that normal conditions may not be possible for a considerable time to come. These are definite conditions that can not be changed by thought or theory. They have had their effect upon present-day production. They are responsible for much of the shortage of commodities which we now experience. The evidence in possession of the trade union movement is that workers are today as willing to work as ever, that they are as eager to work as ever and that their productive capacity is as great if not greater than ever. There have been influences at work since the ending of the war which have operated to check production, but these influences are under the control of employers and not of workers. In so far as possible employers hostile to labor have sought to reintroduce autocratic control into industry, making necessary a resistance on the part of the workers. Labor has enunciated the principle that the workers are entitled to an effective voice in the management and control of industry. To a larger degree than ever before, this principle was agreed to by employers during the war. It was found that it produced results of great value in the winning of the war. It made industry more productive. In the 1918 convention, the A. F. of L. laid down principles which, if followed in practice, would result in the maximum effectiveness of industry. It is a fact that where there has been the greatest fulfillment of those principles in practice there has production been at its best and there has labor been most ardent in its efforts and most fully rewarded for its service. Production is a cooperative undertaking. It is at its best when there is the fullest cooperation. Cooperation is voluntary. It is the negative of compulsion or coercion. Slave labor gave way to free labor in the industrial north long before it was obliterated in the south because slave industry could not compete with free industry. It is a curious chapter of industrial history that whereas wage labor in industry was surrounded with great freedom in the beginning of factory production, it lost freedom with the growth of factory production, necessitating a bitter struggle on the part of workers through organization. Today we face a time in which the pressure of a world hunger for necessaries brings to a head the whole struggle for the further extension of freedom, of voluntary effort, of cooperation in industry. Workers do not shirk work where work allows the free expression of life and thought. The hated task is the slave task. The slow worker is the driven worker, the unfree worker, the unconsulted and unconsidered tool of a mechanism. The 1918 convention laid down this principle: "Those contributing to production should have a part in its control." It further concluded that in all large permanent shops a regular arrangement should be provided whereby: "First, a committee of the workers would regularly meet with the shop management to confer over matters of production. Second, such committee could carry, beyond the foreman and the superintendent, to the general manager or to the president, any important grievance which the workers may have with reference to wages, hours, and conditions." In addition to this, the convention declared that: "It is fundamental for efficiency in production that the essentials of teamwork be understood and followed by all. There must be opportunity for intercourse and exchange of viewpoints between workers and managers. It is this machinery for solving industrial problems that is fundamental." We reaffirm those principles.

Labor—There is a widespread misconception of the meaning of the term "labor." Many employers apparently hold that labor power is something that is to be had for the expenditure of money, that it is something apart from conscious life and that it is something to be controlled and utilized by those who hire or direct labor. Labor is the productive power of men and women. It is the exercise of the power of mankind to sustain itself. Labor is the great underlying factor in the existence of human-kind. Of all living organisms mankind alone has the power to use labor effort intelligently. The conception that some can avoid labor and retain the right to direct others who do labor is malicious and wrong. There must be given to each individual a voice in the shaping of his life and this right must extend to the workers in their organized capacity to be exercised through their chosen representatives. Industry today requires these remedial measures: It requires greater democracy in order to give to the workers full voice in assisting in its direction. It requires more intelligent management and acceptance of the principle that production is for use and not for profit alone. It requires full and free acceptance and use of the best that invention has to offer. It requires bold and audacious reconstruction of method and process in the conduct of basic industry. Labor does not oppose introduction of improved methods in industry. It courts and encourages improvements in processes and in machinery. What it will always resist is the introduction of these processes and this machinery at the expense of the workers. There is a knowledge of industry

among the workers in industry of which society has not begun to avail itself. The effort has been to suppress use of that knowledge and to demean those who possess it. The workers know their work as none but the workers can know it. The shoemaker knows his last and the engineer understands the capacity of his engine. The workers are appalled at the waste and ignorance of management, but they are too frequently denied the chance to offer their knowledge for use. They decline to be enslaved by the use of their own knowledge and they can not give of it freely or effectively except as equals in industry, with all of the rights and privileges and with all of the stature and standing of employers. Adoption of the principle of voluntary effort, of full cooperation in industry, will bring to the industrial life of the nation such an impetus that production will cease forever to be a problem in American life. Adoption of the principles we here urge will inevitably result in a rapid decrease of the number of non-producers who at present live by fastening themselves in one useless capacity or another upon the industrial life of the country. Proper absorption of non-producers into useful channels would be but a simple problem. The welfare of the workers must be a paramount consideration. There can be no progress and no gain in production volume if there is not such consideration. But a greater mutuality in industry would insure proper safeguarding of the rights of workers. Only by such methods and under such principles can there be an advance in production which does not penalize the worker for his own industriousness and for his own alertness and inventiveness. Autocratic industry kills incentive. It punishes brilliancy of attainment. It warps the mind and drains the energy from the body. We have repeatedly condemned the principle of autocratic control of industry and we now declare that short of its complete removal from our industrial life there is no industrial salvation and no hope of abundance in our time. We urge the setting up of conference boards of organized workers and employers, thoroughly voluntary in character and in thorough accord with our trade union organizations, as means of promoting the democracy of industry through development of cooperative effort. We point out to employers the fact that industry, which is the life blood of our civilization, can not be made the plaything and the pawn of a few who by chance today hold control. Industry is the thing by which all must live and it must be given the opportunity to function at its best. Labor turn-over is but one of the evils which will disappear in proportion as the workers are given voice in management. This is proven by statistics which show the lowest turn-over in those industries where the workers exercise the most effective voice by reason of the highest degreee of organization. We propose the salvation of industry. We propose the means whereby the world may be fed and clothed and housed and given happiness. We have service to give and if permitted to give freely and on terms of manhood and equality we will give in abundance. *We can not be driven as slaves, but we can give mighty service in a common effort of humankind.*

Labor, Compulsory—(1920, p. 8) The president of the A. F. of L. said: "Any attempt to enforce compulsory labor must be resisted at any cost. I have no fear as to what the results will be. The whole of life is made up of joy and of pain. The development of the human race is that of pain and travail, as well as joy and the glory of achievement, and the one who fails to understand that there is a law of compensation in all the struggles in the life of the people of the world fails to understand the fundamental principle of human development and progress. At least, so long as life shall be with me, and my mind is not impaired, I shall endeavor to stand for the right of labor, the right of men and women who toil to own themselves, unhampered and untrammeled or unowned by any other human being."

Labor Day—(1919, p. 330) Refused to change Labor Day from the first Monday in September to May 1, the following argument being approved: It is rather peculiar to hear a trade unionist get up in our convention and say that our Labor Day was given us by somebody. Labor Day was established in this country, not by a political party, not by politicians, but by organized trade unionists. It is the only Labor Day celebrated anywhere in the world that had its origin and has been maintained by trade unionists. I hope there is no intention on the part of those who favor the resolution to couple up trade unionism with May 1 in Europe, which, while it has always been celebrated by workers in most European countries, has always taken on a more political character than an industrial character. Labor Day, September 1, is the only holiday celebrated by labor anywhere in the world that was established by organized labor working through the trade union movement. The American Labor Day was inaugurated by a parade in New York city of the men of labor, before any law was put on the statute books of the United States or of any of the states affecting Labor Day. The man in whose brain that thought for Labor Day was generated was one of those who helped to found the A. F. of L., the founder and organizer of the United Brotherhood of Carpenters and Joiners of America, a member of the Executive Council of the A. F. of L., the late P. J. McGuire. Later the American labor movement demanded at the hands of Congress and of the legislatures of our various states that the first Monday in September should be made a legal holiday and be known as Labor Day. and if there were politicians who had any connection with the creation of Labor Day as a legal holiday it was the politicians who yielded to the demand of organized labor. In 1889 the A. F. of L. undertook to organize a movement in reference to the 8-hour work day, and the Brotherhood of Carpenters and Joiners made application to the Executive Council to be selected as the organization of labor of America to make the demand, and that organized labor of every industry should morally and financially support that organization in making the fight. That declaration was made. The carpenters were chosen. There was to be an international congress held in Paris in connection with the World's Exposition of that year, and it fell to the president of the A. F. of L. to write a letter to that congress. That letter asked that the congress make some declaration of international sympathy with the American labor movement, and particularly with the carpenters in their general demand for the 8-hour day. I appealed to the Paris conference to hold demonstrations on May 1 in all parts of Europe in sympathy with the carpenters in their movement for the 8-hour day and as a result of the vote a resolution was adopted by that congress in compliance and out of that the May-day celebration resulted in Europe. As a matter of fact, the idea originated here and was carried to Europe. In Germany, Austria, Italy, and

France—it isn't observed at all in Great Britain—when they have a celebration of their labor day, May 1, it is held on Sunday or in the evening. They haven't the temerity or the strength or the independence to take the day for themselves. I question whether we who are the originators of the thought of Labor Day should fall in line and celebrate it at another date than the one we have selected. (1923, p. 262) Reaffirmed.

Labor Day and Labor Day Sunday—(1920, pp. 207-437) The custom, begun a number of years ago, and recently omitted, of cooperating with the churches for observance of Labor Sunday, the day preceding Labor Day, should be once more established. The A. F. of L. took official cognizance of the growing interest of religious denominations in matters affecting the welfare of the workers, when it adopted a resolution at its convention in Toronto, Ontario, Canada, in 1909, urging that the churches of America be requested to devote part of their services to a presentation of the labor question on the Sunday preceding the first Monday in September (Labor Day). Recent utterances pertaining to labor by groups representing religious denominations are indication that the church can not afford to ignore the welfare of the wage earners, the problems that beset them, and the organized labor movement which aims and works to solve them.

(1921, pp. 149-437) We urge everywhere proper and adequate observance of Labor Day, the first Monday in September, and we call attention again to the appropriateness of joining with the various religious denominations in observance of Labor Sunday, the day preceding Labor Day. The observance of these days and the joining in these ceremonies constitutes an inspiration to our movement too valuable to be neglected, and furthermore, constitutes a means of bringing to those who are not in our movement something of its meaning and its ideals and virility. We earnestly urge a more general and earnest observance of these special days as a service to our movement and to our fellow men everywhere.

(1922, pp. 144-361) We urge everywhere proper and dignified observance of Labor Day, the first Monday in September, and we again call attention to the appropriateness of observance of Labor's Sunday, the day preceding Labor Day. It is interesting to note this year in connection with our own Labor Day that the British Trades Union Congress has begun a campaign to secure for the workers of England a legal holiday to be known as Labor Day. We trust that the British trade unionists will be successful in their effort to secure parliamentary action for the establishment of Labor Day in England.

. (1923, pp. 135-259) We urge everywhere an appropriate observance of Labor Day, the first Monday in September, and of Labor's Sunday, the day preceding Labor Day. An appropriate proclamation for Labor Day and Labor Sunday may fittingly be reproduced here. The proclamation follows:

"The labor movement of America demands for all of our people the full benefit of the life-giving forces of our marvelous civilization through constantly increasing wages and improvement of working conditions and through a reasonable and proper reduction in the hours of work. The labor movement of America demands for the wage earners and for all who serve usefully in any capacity, a sound and just economic basis for life and freedom in the fullest meaning of those terms. The labor movement of America has ever had high regard for the development of the ethical and the spiritual in life, realizing the right of all humanity to partake freely of the great satisfaction that comes to enrich life as a result. The labor movement of our country, recognizing the fact that all freedom and all higher development of life, rest upon first providing assurance of the essentials of existence, has first demanded economic justice as a basis for all other things. But the labor movement has always taught that the material is essential to something higher, and that the inspiration of our movement has its deepest springs in something above and beyond the material. The labor movement strives for economic improvement with unrelenting zeal and fidelity because economic improvement is the first fundamental requisite; but it holds out to all mankind a flaming torch lighting the way to a greater fullness of life, to complete realization of the finer and nobler aspirations of the mind and soul. The labor movement fixes as its goal nothing less than the complete richness of life, without limitation of any kind, the attainment of the complete human ideal, in all of its economic, ethical, and spiritual implications. Through the inspiration of our labor movement, the Sunday preceding Labor Day, which is the first Monday in September each year, has come into general national observance as Labor Sunday. On this day it is fitting to give thought to the aspirations of Labor and to find in what way the soul of labor may give thought and expression to its longings. Because of the aims and aspirations here set forth, we hold it fitting that all churches draw close to their altars the soul of labor on the coming Labor Sunday and that the men and women of labor everywhere make special effort to cooperate with the churches and to secure the cooperation of the churches with them, in order that there may be in the churches everywhere on that day a great unison of expression in behalf of a higher, nobler life for the masses of our people; and in order that there may be everywhere a consecration to the cause of human betterment, particularly in those things that lead to ethical and spiritual growth—in those things that give flower and fruit to the great idealism of our labor movement, the embodiment and the expression of the idealism of our people. May Labor Sunday each year bring home to the masses of our people the great good that humanity may yet achieve, the lofty heights to which it may climb, the inspiration and the enrichment to be found in the great American labor movement which is the hope of the millions who toil. We ask also that Labor Day, the great holiday of the toiling masses, dedicated to them and to their cause, be ennobled and enriched by an expression of the same spirit, the same high idealism and purpose, the same uplifting, inspiring search for the fullness of life and the same determination to achieve triumph over all ills and wrongs through our great movement in its ethical and spiritual aspects, as well as through its purely economic operations."

Labor is Not a Commodity—(1908, p. 20) "The ownership of a free man is vested in himself alone. The only reason for the ownership of bondmen or slaves is the ownership of their labor power by their masters. Therefore, it follows that if free men's ownership of themselves involves their labor power, none but themselves are owners of their labor power. Hence, it is essential that the product of a free man is his own. If he by choice or by reason of his environment sells his labor power

to another and is paid a wage in return therefor, this wage is his own. This proposition is so essentially true that it is the underlying idea upon which is based the entire structure of private possession. To question or to attempt to destroy the principle enunciated involves the entire structure of civilized society. The free man's ownership of himself and his labor power implies that he may sell it to another or withhold it; that he may with others similarly situated sell their labor power or withhold it; that no man has even an implied property right in the labor of another; that free men may sell their labor power under stress of their needs, or they may withhold it to obtain more advantageous returns. Any legislation or court construction dealing with the subject of organizations, corporations or trusts which curtail or corner the products of labor, can have no true application to the association of free men in the disposition or withholding of their labor power. The attempt to deny to free men, by injunction or other process, the right of association, the right to withhold their labor power or to induce others to withhold their labor power, whether these men be engaged in an industrial dispute with employers, or whether they be other workmen who have taken the places of those engaged in the original dispute, is an invasion of man's ownership of himself and of his labor power, and is a claim of some form of property right in the workmen who have taken the places of strikers, or men locked out. If the ownership of free men is vested in them and in them alone, they have not only the right to withhold their labor power, but to induce others to make common cause with them, and to withhold theirs that the greatest advantage may accrue to all. It further follows that if free men may avail themselves of the lawful right of withholding their labor power, they have the right to do all lawful things in pursuit of that lawful purpose. And neither court injunctions nor other processes have any proper application to deny to free men these lawful, constitutional, natural and inherent rights. In the disposition of the wages returned from the sale of labor power, man is also his own free agent. All things he may lawfully buy, he may also lawfully abstain from buying. He may purchase from whomsoever he will, or he may give his patronage to another. What he may do with his wages in the form of bestowing or withholding his patronage, he may lawfully agree with others to do. No corporation or company has a vested interest in the patronage of a free man. If this be true, and its truth can not be controverted upon any basis in law, free men may bestow their patronage upon any one or withhold it, or bestow it upon another. And this, too, whether in the first instance the business concern is hostile or friendly. It is true for any good reason, and in the last analysis, for no reason at all. It is not a question as to whether we like or dislike lockouts or strikes, boycotts or blacklists. The courts have declared that lockouts and the blacklists and all that pertain thereto are not unlawful. It is difficult to understand, then, unless there is some conception in the courts of an employer's property right in some form in the laborer or the laborer's patronage, how they stretch their authority, pervert the purpose of the law and undertake by the injunctive process to outlaw either the strike or the boycott. To claim that what one man may lawfully do when done by two or more men becomes unlawful or criminal, is equal to asserting that nought and nought makes two."

Labor, Its Grievances Protest and Demands—(1920, pp. 64-383) Documents of great importance and of great constructive value to the American republic have been given to the world by the American labor movement before and during the period of time covered by the world war. Labor's voice has not been raised in this manner except at those times when democracy had need of an expression of its views and its proposals. Labor has spoken always with a clear purpose and in answer to a real need. History will beyond doubt place above all other expressions of Labor's views those two documents which marked the beginning and the end of the war. On March 12, 1917, the accredited representatives of the national and international trade unions met in the city of Washington and adopted by ananimous vote the now historic declaration of "Labor's Position in Peace or in War." Upon the platform and the principles there laid down Labor conducted itself through the great conflict. On December 13, 1919, nearly three years later, with victory secure and with the problems of peace crying for constructive attention, the representatives of the national and international unions, the railroad brotherhoods and the farmers' organizations once more assembled in Washington for the purpose of giving expression to the best thought of the trade union movement. "Labor, its Grievances, Protest and Demands" was there adopted. It has taken rank with the earlier document as an expression of deep wisdom and high patriotism. It is an expression of the devotion of America's workers to the principles of freedom, democracy and justice, and an evidence of their ability to contribute to the common effort to safeguard those great principles in the American republic. The conference assembled in the Executive Council chamber of the A. F. of L. headquarters building and deliberated upon the issues which confront the nation. The broad views of American citizenship dominated the assemblage and the conclusions were the conclusions of earnest men and women devoted to the progress of humanity and anxious that its acts might be the acts of wisdom and justice at a time when the trials of America and of the world were most sorely perplexing. The complete declaration which was unanimously adopted by the conference, and the signatories thereto, follow: "We speak in the name of millions who work—those who make and use tools—those who furnish the human power necessary for commerce and industry. We speak as part of the nation and of those things of which we have special knowledge. Our welfare and interest are inseparably bound up with the well-being of the nation. We are an integral part of the American people and we are organized to work out the welfare of all. The urgent problems that sorely trouble our nation and vitally affect us as workers make necessary this special consultation. The great victories for human freedom must not have been won in vain. They must serve as the instruments and the inspiration for a greater and nobler freedom for all mankind. Autocratic, political and corporate industrial and financial influences

in our country have sought, and are seeking, to infringe upon and limit the fundamental rights of the wage-earners guaranteed by the constitution of the United States. Powerful forces are seeking more and more aggressively to deny to wage-earners their right to cease work. We denounce these efforts as vicious and destructive of the most previous liberties of our people. The right to cease work—strike—as a final means of enforcing justice from an autocratic control of industry, must be maintained. The autocratic attitude and destructive action of the United States Steel Corporation and its subsidiary branches to oppress the workers by denying them the exercise of their freedom of action, freedom of association, freedom of expression, must give way to a better understanding and relation and to secure the wage earners in the exercise of their rights and liberties as free workers and citizens. We realize fully all that is involved in the exercise of the right to strike, but only by the exercise of that right can industrial autocrats be compelled to abandon their tyranny and give way to the establishment of freedom and justice in industry. American labor sets for itself the task, gladly and proudly assumed, to preserve and perpetuate this standard of justice and measure of liberty. We protest against the attitude and action of the majority of the representatives of the employers in the employers' group who participated in the president's industrial conference October 6-23, 1919. The proposals which the representatives of labor submitted to that conference were conservative, constructive and helpful. They were calculated to establish a working basis for the promotion of better relations between employers and workers—the right to organize, the right to collective bargaining through representatives of the workers' own choosing. The representatives of the public constituted as a group endorsed and voted for that principle. By a small majority the employers' group voted against it, and thus the proposals were defeated and the conference failed. The protection of the rights and interests of wage earners in national, state and municipal service requires for them the right of organization. Since the interests of these workers can be best promoted through legislation and administration, their right to organization and affiliation with the A. F. of L. must at all times be fully safeguarded. The paramount issues that concern all the people of the United States, and in particular the wage earners, are the perversion and the abuse of the writ of injunction and the necessity for full and adequate protection of the voluntary associations of wage earners organized not for profit. Government by injunction has grown out of the perversion of the injunction process. By the misuse of that process workers have been forbidden to do those things which they have a natural and constitutional right to do. The injunction as now used is a revolutionary measure which substitutes government by judicial discretion or bias for government by law. It substitutes a trial by one man, a judge, in his discretion, for a trial by jury. This abuse of the injunctive process undermines and destroys the very foundations of our free institutions. It is subversive of the spirit of a free people working out their destiny in an orderly and rational manner. Because we have reverence for law, because we believe that every citizen must be a guardian of the heritage given us by our fathers who fought for and established freedom and democracy, by every lawful means we must resist the establishment of a practice that would destroy the very spirit of freedom and democracy. Our protest against the abuse of the writ of injunction and its unwarranted application to Labor in the exercise of Labor's normal activities to realize laudible aspirations is a duty we owe to ourselves and to posterity. Formerly injunctions issued in labor disputes were of a prohibitive character. Within the recent past this abuse of the injunction writ has been enlarged to include mandatory orders whereby men have been compelled to do specific things which they have a lawful right to refrain from doing. We declare these abuses in the exercise of the injunction writ are clearly violative of the constitution and that this issue must be determined definitely in accordance with the guarantees of the constitution of the United States. Workers are free citizens, not slaves. They have the constitutional right to cease working. The strike is a protest against autocratic management. To penalize strikes or to make them unlawful is to apply an unwarrantable and destructive method when a constructive one is available. To reduce the necessity for strikes, the cause should be found and removed. The government has a greater obligation in this matter than to use its coercive powers. Legislation which proposes to make strikes unlawful or to compel the wage earners to submit their grievances or aspirations to courts or to governmental agencies, is an invasion of the rights of the wage earners and when enforced makes for industrial serfdom or slavery. We hold that the government should supply information, assistance and counsel, but that it should not attempt by the force of its own power to stifle or to destroy voluntary relations and policies of mutuality between employers and employes. We specifically denounce the anti-strike provisions of the Cummins bill and all similar proposed legislation as un-American, as being vicious in character, and establishing by legislation involuntary servitude. The warning given by Jefferson that the danger of the people of this republic lies in the usurpation by our judiciary of unconstitutional authority, has been fully demonstrated. A judiciary unresponsive to the needs of the time, arrogating to itself powers which neither the constitution nor the purposes of our laws have conferred upon them, demands that at least in our time Americans must insist upon safeguarding their liberties and the spirit of the sacred institutions of our republic. We urge that the judges of our federal courts shall be elected by the people for terms not exceeding six years. We assert that there can not be found in the constitution of the United States or in the discussions of the congress which drafted the constitution any authority for the federal courts of our country to declare unconstitutional any act passed by congress. We call upon the people of our country to demand that the Congress of the United States shall take action for the purpose of preventing the federal courts from continuing the usurpation of such authority. We declare that the voluntary organizations of the workers, organized not for profit, are agencies of human progress and promote justice in industry and trade. Despite legislative declarations that trade unions

do no come under the provisions of anti-trust legislation, courts have not understood and are not now able or willing to understand that the organizations of wage earners are not conspiracies in restraint of trade. We submit that anti-trust legislation has not only been interpreted to serve the purpose of outlawing trade unions, robbing them of their treasuries and the savings of their members and depriving them of their legal and natural rights to the exercise of normal activities, but that it has also failed completely to protect the people against the outrageous machinations of combinations and monopolies. The United Mine Workers of America did all in their power to avert an industrial controversy in the coal industry. The autocratic attitude of the mine owners was responsible for the losses and sufferings entailed. While the miners have returned to the mines and have only now been afforded the opportunity of having their grievances and demands brought to the light of reason, it is our hope that a full measure of justice will be accorded them even at this late date. There is a widespread belief that wages should be fixed on a cost-of-living basis. This idea is pernicious and intolerable. It means putting progress in chains and liberty in fetters. It means fixing a standard of living and a standard of life and liberty which must remain fixed. America's workers can not accept that proposition. They demand a progressively advancing standard of life. They have an abiding faith in a better future for all mankind. They discard and denounce a system of fixing wages solely on the basis of family budgets and bread bills. Workers are entitled not only to a living, but modern society must provide more than what is understood by the term, "a living." It must concede to all workers a fairer reward for their contribution to society, a contribution without which a progressing civilization is impossible. No factor contributes more to industrial unrest and instability than excessive costs of necessaries of life. It is a demonstrated truth that the cost of living has advanced more rapidly than have wages. The claim that increasing wages make necessary increased prices is false. It is intended to throw upon the workers the blame for a process by which all the people have been made to suffer. Labor has been compelled to struggle desperately to keep wages in some measure up to the cost of living. The demand for higher compensation to meet new price levels has made industrial readjustment necessary. Existing high and excessive prices are due to the present inflation of money and credits, to profiteering by those who manufacture, sell and market products, and to burdens levied by middlemen and speculators. We urge: The deflation of currency; prevention of hoarding and unfair price fixing; establishment of cooperative movements operated under the Rochdale system; making accessible all income tax returns and dividend declarations as a direct and truthful means of revealing excessive costs and profits. The ideal of America should be the organization of industry for service and not for profit alone. The stigma of disgrace should attach to every person who profits unduly at the expense of his fellow men. Labor is fully conscious that the world needs things for use and that standards of life can improve only as production for use and consumption increases. Labor is anxious to work out better methods for industry and demands it be assured that increased productivity will be used for service and not alone for profits. Wage earners aspire to be something more than numbers on the books of an industrial plant, something more than attendants of a machine, something more than cogs in an industrial system dominated by machinery owned and operated for profit alone. The workers insist upon being masters of themselves. Labor understands fully that powerful interests today are determined to achieve reaction in industry if possible. They seek to disband or cripple the organizations of workers. They seek to reduce wages and thus lower the standard of living. They seek to keep free from restriction their power to manipulate and fix prices. They seek to destroy the democratic impulse of the workers which is bred into their movement by the democracy of the American republic. Labor must be and is militant in the struggle to combat these sinister influences and tendencies. Labor will not permit a reduction in the standard of living. It will not consent to reaction toward autocratic control. In this it is performing a public service. Only in high-wage countries is productivity in industry greatest. Only in high-wage countries do the people enjoy high standards of living. Low-wage countries present the least degree of productivity and offer to their people only low standards of living and restricted liberties. Autocracy always insists upon restricting the income and the activities of workers. Creative power lies dormant where autocratic management prevails. No employer has a vested right to the good will of his employes. That must be earned, as between men. It can be earned only when management deals with workers as human beings and not as machines. There can not be a full release of productive energy under an autocratic control of industry. There must be a spirit of cooperation and mutuality between employers and workers. We submit that production can be enhanced through the cooperation of management with the trade union agencies which make for order, discipline and productivity. We hold that the organization of wage earners into trade unions and the establishment of collective bargaining are the first steps toward the proper development of our industrial machinery for service. To promote further the production of an adequate supply of the world's needs for use and higher standards of life, we urge that there be established cooperation between the scientists of industry and the representatives of organized workers. Credit is the life blood of modern business. At present under the control of private financiers it is administered, not primarily to serve the needs of production, but the desire of financial agencies to levy a toll upon community activity as high as "the traffic will bear." Credit is inherently social. It should be accorded in proportion to confidence in production possibilities. Credit as now administered does not serve industry but burdens it. It increases unearned incomes at the expense of earned incomes. It is the center of the malevolent forces that corrupt the spirit and purpose of industry. We urge the organization and use of credit to serve production needs and not to increase the incomes and holdings of financiers. Control over credit should be taken from financiers and should be

vested in a public agency, able to administer this power as a public trust in the interests of all the people. Since the government has not worked out a constructive railroad policy, we urge for and on behalf of the railway workers and of the general public, that the railroads be retained under government administration for at least two years after January 1, 1920, in order that a thorough test may be made of governmental operation under normal conditions. The common carriers of this country are the arteries of travel, commerce and industry. Transportation service and rates are intimately bound up with industrial production in all parts of the country. It is essential that a thorough test be given to all phases of railroad control and operation before a definite peace time policy be finally concluded. Never has the world been confronted with a more serious situation. Millions are in want, facing starvation. The children of war-stricken Europe, half fed, under developed, appeal for help. Only with infinite pain, unnecessary loss of life and slowness of result can Europe rebuild her industries, restore her agriculture, and reestablish her commerce, without the help of America. The treaty setting forth the terms of peace has not been ratified by the United States. Boundaries are not fixed. Peoples are uncertain as to their allegiance. Under such conditions exchange and credit have lost voltage and in turn have paralyzed industry. As members of an organized labor movement that has for years maintained fraternal relations with the working people of Europe, we feel that our nation can not with honor and humanity maintain a policy of isolation and disinterestedness from the distress and suffering of the peoples of Europe. Even if the necessity of the peoples of Europe did not have a compelling appeal, the interrelated economic interests of the world would prevent our limiting our attention solely to this hemisphere. The peace treaty includes provisions in an international agreement to prevent war among nations, with all its cruelties and sacrifices of human life, with its burden of indebtedness and taxation; for reduction in standing armies, the diminution of great navies, and the limitation of the production of arms and ammunition. If the senate shall fail to ratify the treaty of Versailles, our nation may be isolated from other countries of the world which at some time might be pitted against us. Such isolation and possibilities would make necessary the creation and maintenance of a large standing army and a greater and more effective navy in order in some degree to protect the republic of the United States from aggression by those countries which were our allies in the great war and which were and are now our friends. In addition, the workers of America have a deep interest and concern in the labor draft convention of the treaty and in its purposes to raise to a higher standard the conditions of life and labor among the peoples of all countries. Its cardinal declarations and provisions are, that labor should not be regarded as a commodity; that the eight-hour day and forty-eight-hour week are standard; that there shall be one day of rest, preferably Sunday, in each week; that child labor shall be abolished, and continuing education for young workers assured; that men and women shall receive equal pay for equal work; that industrial betterments shall be enforced by proper inspection, in which women as well as men shall take part; that wages shall be sufficient to maintain a reasonable standard of living, as this is understood in each time and country, and that employes as well as employers have the right of association for all lawful purposes. The United States is protected by this draft convention in two ways: (1) That the recommendations which international labor conferences under the treaty may recommend may be accepted or rejected by our government; (2) That no recommendation that would set a lower standard for the people of the United States than already exists within our borders can be at any time presented for consideration and action by the United States. To give the united support of our republic and of the allied countries to effective machinery to raise the standard of the workers' condition in backward countries to help humanize industry for the common world weal, is, we insist, a paramount duty which our republic must perform. We insist, for the reasons herein set forth, that it is the immediate duty of the senate to ratify the treaty of Versailles. The American labor movement resents the attempt of reactionaries and autocrats to classify the men and women of Labor with those groups which have nothing in common with its constructive purposes and high ideals, and with the fundamental principles of our country. Those who aim to strike a blow against the legitimate aspirations of the workers in their struggle for freedom and for a higher and a better life must be met and overcome. We call upon all those who contribute service to society in any form to unite in the furtherance of the principles and purposes and for the rectification of the grievances herein set forth. We call especial attention to the fact that there is a great community of interest between all who serve the world. All workers, whether of the city or country, mine or factory, farm or transportation, have a common path to tread and a common goal to gain. The issues herein enumerated require the action of our people upon both the economic and political field. We urge that every practical action be taken by the A. F. of L., with the cooperation of all other organized bodies of workers, farmers and sympathetic, liberty-loving citizens of the United States to carry into effect the principles and purposes set forth in the declarations of this conference. We call upon all to join with us in combating the forces of autocracy, industrial and political, and in the sublime task of ridding the world of the power of those who but debase its processes and corrupt its functions. In all struggles for justice and human freedom, sacrifices have been made. Having made supreme sacrifices to crush militarism and political autocracy in Europe, America's workers will not surrender to political and industrial autocracy at home. In the struggle now before us, we will contest every effort made to fasten tyranny and injustice upon the people of our republic. We are confident that freedom, justice and the opportunity for a better day and a higher life shall be achieved."

Labor Legislation, International Commission on—(1919, p. 20) The commission was composed as follows:

United States of America—Mr. Samuel Gompers, President of the A. F. of L.

Mr. A. N. Hurley, President of the American Shipping Board. (Substitutes: Mr. H. M. Robinson, Mr. J. T. Shotwell.)

British Empire—The Right Honorable G. N. Barnes, M. P., Member of the War Cabinet. (Substitute: Mr. H. B. Butler, C. B., Assistant Secretary, Ministry of Labor.) Sir Malcolm Delevingne, K. C. B., Assistant Under Secretary of State, Home Office.

France—M. Colliard, Minister of Labor. (Substitute: Mr. Arthur Fontaine, Counsellor of State, Director of Labor.) M. Loucheur, Minister of Industrial Reconstruction. (Substitute: M. Leon Jouhaux, General Secretary of the Confederation Generale du Travail.)

Italy—Baron Mayor des Planches, Hon. Ambassador, Commissioner General for Immigration. Mr. Cabrini, Deputy. (Substitute: Mr. Coletti.)

Japan—Mr. Otchiai, Envoy Extraordinary, Minister Plenipotentiary to H. M. The Emperior of Japan at The Hague. Mr. Oka, formerly Director of Commercial and Industrial Affairs at the Ministry of Agriculture and Commerce.

Belgium—Mr. Vandervelde, Minister of Justice and of State. (Substitute: Mr. La Fontaine, Senator.) Mr. Mahaim, Professor at Liege University, Secretary to the Belgian Section of the Association for the Legal Protection of Workmen.

Cuba—Mr. De Bustemante, Professor at Havana University. (Substitute: Mr. Raphael Martinez Ortiz, Minister Plenipotentiary.) Mr. De Blanck, Minister Plenipotentiary.

Poland—Count Zoltowski, Member of the Polish National Committee, afterwards replaced by Mr. Stanislas Patek, Counsellor of the Board of Cessation. (Substitute: Mr. Francois Sokal, Director General of Labor.)

Czecho-Slovak Republic—Mr. Benes, Minister for Foreign Affairs, afterwards replaced by Mr. Rudolph Broz.

(1919, p. 417) The A. F. of L. notes with satisfaction and pride that our president was accorded the high honor of being unanimously chosen by the commission on international labor legislation as its president and we moreover note that much of the constructive and substantial propositions adopted and made a part of the results achieved by the commission on international labor legislation was due to persistency and tenacity and abiding faith in the power and efficacy of the American trade union movement as typified by the A. F. of L. In this work we take note that he was ably assisted by the advice and support of the A. F. of L. delegation to the peace conference.

Labor Legislative Conference Committee—(1922, p. 78) The introduction of so many bills in congress inimical to the interests of labor and the people made it imperative that the legislative agents located in Washington should decide upon uniformity of action. The legislative agents representing the national and international unions, central bodies and local unions, were unaware of many things that were going on in congress. Some of these incidents were of great moment and did not always come to the knowledge of those most vitally interested. At the same time those who knew of such incidents assumed that those most directly interested also had the same information.. So many things occur in congress that it is impossible for any one man or dozen men to keep in touch with everything. Then it was found that when a committee was holding a hearing some legislative agent, because-there was no communication of any kind between the various representatives, would be compelled to give his testimony alone without the moral influence of the presence of the other legislative agents. There was also complaint by the members of congress that their time was taken up by legislative agents who all brought to their attention the same issue. The president of the A. F. of L. called a meeting for May 26, 1921, and an organization was formed to be known as the Conference Committee of Trade Union Legislative Representatives located in Washington. Regular conferences have been held each month and a number of special meetings have been called when serious legislative situations arose. The conference committee has been an invaluable aid in defeating hostile legislation. Because of the unanimity of purpose governing the representatives it has also been successful in advancing meritorious legislation. There are a number of labor legislative representatives in Washington continually during sessions of congress. Then again from time to time national and international unions send their representatives to Washington for the purpose of watching legislation in the interest of their respective organizations. These all automatically become members of the labor legislative conference committee. The officers of the departments of the A. F. of L. are also members. Whenever any matter of importance is discovered or comes to the attention of a legislative representative, not a member of the organization affected, the secretary is immediately informed of the fact. The latter then communicates with the legislative representative interested and gives him the desired information. In this manner it has been possible to check many schemes that have been planned to secure passage of legislation inimical to labor and the people. And it also has been most effective in furthering legislation benefiting labor and the people.

(1923, p. 45) The wisdom of bringing the trade union legislative representatives in Washington together at stated intervals to confer on legislation before congress has been clearly demonstrated. Since the organization of the conference committee of trade union legislation representatives on May 26, 1921, labor has been unusually successful in defeating much pernicious legislation and at the same time has prevented the repeal of remedial legislation. When it is understood that there were over 20,000 bills introduced in the last congress and each had to be thoroughly analyzed the necessity for united effort on the part of the trade union legislative representatives is apparent. From 30 to 40 members attend each meeting and each bill which directly or indirectly affects labor is considered exhaustively. Sometimes there is quite a difference in opinion as to the provisions of a bill and they are thrashed out until whatever action is taken is unanimous. This very fact proves the necessity for such an organization. Before the conference committee was organized the various legislative representatives worked haphazard. Each decided for himself what was best to do. Now when any bill of importance is being considered in congress the legislative representatives work unitedly, thereby gaining results that under the old method could not be accomplished. They visit individual members of the house and senate and attend hearings. The very fact that so many are actively working along the same line has its influence. Whenever representatives of national or in-

ternational unions are sent to Washington to urge legislation of benefit to their respective organizations they automatically become members of the conference committee and receive the unanimous aid of the members. The A. F. of L. desires that the officers of all national and international unions should keep in close touch with the conference committee's work. (P. 358) This committee has already rendered signal service in developing teamwork among the union legislative representatives. Copies of the synopsis of the minutes of meetings of the legislative conference should be sent to the officers of all national and international unions in order that they may be kept informed on legislative activities in Washington.

Labor Memorial Day—(1920, pp. 207-437) Of late there has been a deviation from the original intention to observe the fourth Sunday in May of each year as Labor's Memorial Day, a day upon which the men and women of labor in every section of the country could meet and by appropriate ceremonies pay tribute to the memory of those who have gone before in the great work for humanity. The custom of observing Labor's Memorial Day was first established at the convention of the A. F. of L. held in Norfolk, Va., in 1907. This convention, by vote, fixed the day as the second Sunday in May. Subsequently, at the convention held in Atlanta, Ga., in 1911, this date was changed to the fourth Sunday. Through some error, however, the date became shifted to the third Sunday, and for some recent years the observances have been held on the third, instead of the fourth Sunday. It is the desire of the A. F. of L. that observance should once more be on the proper day, the fourth Sunday of May each year.

(1921, pp. 149-299) We recommend and strongly urge the observance of Memorial Sunday everywhere, and we recommend to the men and women of labor in our movement the thought that the observance of Memorial Sunday constitutes also a yearly renewal of devotion to the principles of our movement on the part of the living, as well as a fitting tribute to those who have passed away.

(1922, pp. 144-361) We again urge and recommend the observance of the fourth Sunday in May as Labor's Memorial Day, in accordance with the action of the convention of 1907. On this day labor everywhere should conduct appropriate ceremonies in tribute to the memory of those whose lives have been given to the struggle for progress and freedom.

(1923, pp. 135-259) We urge continuance of the practice of observing the fourth Sunday in May as Labor's Memorial Day, pursuant to the action of the convention of 1912.

Labor Mission to Europe—(1919, p. 257) Report of labor mission: The St. Paul convention of the A. F. of L. convened during the most crucial period of the stupendous world conflict. After four years of privations and horrors of war a certain degree of pacifism in the European allied countries, no doubt the outgrowth of "war weariness" and encouraged by enemy propaganda, began to cause some apprehension. The report of the A. F. of L. mission just returning to the U. S. with first-hand information from war-ridden Europe, pointed out and stressed the importance of impressing upon the workers of the allied countries American labor's pledge to work, sacrifice and fight until German militarism and autocracy were overwhelmed, and also conveyed an invitation to the president of the A. F. of L. from representative labor and government officials of England, France and

Italy to visit their countries. The convention approved the report, with the result that the president was authorized and instructed to proceed to as many of the allied countries as possible with such assistants as he deemed necessary. Recalling the many expressions of regret because of the impossibility on account of insufficient notice for a delegation of the A. F. of L. to attend the inter-allied conference in London in February, 1918, President Gompers cabled Mr. Arthur Henderson that an A. F. of L. delegation was coming to Europe and could attend an inter-allied conference if one was called. The result was the speedy decision of the joint committees of the labor party and the parliamentary committee of the British Trade Union Congress and the Confederation General du Travail to call an inter-allied conference to be held in London about the middle of September to which the A. F. of L. was invited to send delegates. We were welcomed at the dock by the lord mayor of Liverpool and the U. S. consul, after which we proceeded directly to London. En route, Mr. Gompers prepared the following statement for the press:
"The American Labor Mission has come to Great Britain and expects to go to France and Italy to bring a message of good will, cooperation and determination to the workers of the three countries to aid in strengthening the bonds of unity that we may all stand behind our respective democratic governments to win the war for justice, freedom and democracy."

The conditions which had developed in Great Britain and which were causing both anxiety and hope at the time of our arrival, are herewith submitted from a British viewpoint as expressed in an editorial: "The decisive part which the U. S. is playing in the war would not have been possible without the loyal cooperation of the labor organizations. From the moment that the president adopted an active policy against Germany, they entered heartily into his plans and in every branch of war work they are rendering services of vital importance. The president of the A. F. of L. and several colleagues arrived in London yesterday on a mission to the trade unionists of Great Britain, France and Italy, and we are sure that their enthusiasm and determination will have a stimulating effect. The great majority of the working classes in all the allied countries are sound, but there is also in all of them a small but noisy and troublesome minority of bolsheviks and pacifists who want the war ended on almost any terms. Many of the leaders of this minority are not working men, but professional agitators who are exploiting the workers for their own advantage. In the U. S., however bolshevik principles are energetically repudiated and the American labor mission may do something to stamp them out of the allied countries. Mr. Gompers states that he has come to meet all the accredited representatives of the trades unions to learn their point of view, and also to press upon them the view which prevails in the U. S. There is no wavering on the other side of the Atlantic, no longing for an indecisive peace, no fear of humiliating Germany too much. Mr. Gompers says: 'We are unalterably determined to stand by the position maintained by our republic and that of the allies until the very end—until the war is won'—and he added the assurance that this is the unanimous decision of the organized labor movement, as well as of all ranks of the American people. He agrees

with the president that force to the utmost must be used until Germany acknowledges defeat and submits to conditions which will atone to some extent for her monstrous crimes, and ensure a permanent peace. Mr. Gompers showed wisdom and patriotism in refusing to give any countenance to the proposals made by certain labor leaders in England and France for a conference with the socialists of the central powers to discuss war aims. Such informal negotiations could only create misunderstanding, encourage pacifism, and embarrass the allied governments. So far as the German socialists are concerned, there is no substantial difference between them and the pan-Germans. They have given their rulers constant support throughout the war. They have never condemned the invasion of Belgium nor called for its evacuation. On the contrary, Herr Scheidermann has endorsed the view that Germany, while evacuating Belgium, must retain economic and military control of it; and as regards the compensation for the terrible losses and suffering inflicted upon it, he proposes that it should come out of an international fund, as if all the belligerents were equally responsible—Great Britain, which came to the defense of Belgium, as much as Germany which wantonly invaded and devastated it. The German socialists have also approved of the infamous terms distated to Russia at Brest-Litovsk, and Roumania at Bucharest. Yet, Mr. Arthur Henderson, misled by his friend, Mr. Troelstra, asserted that the German socialists had accepted the labor party's memorandum on war aims. Mr. Troelstra is a tool of Germany and our government acted wisely in refusing to issue passports to labor delegates to meet him in Switzerland. If Mr. Gompers and his colleagues can rid British and French socialism of the bolshevism and pacifism which are enfeebling and corrupting it, they will add to the debt which all the allies owe them for their strenuous support of their government in the great efforts that it is making to hasten victory."

Arriving in London we were met by a number of prominent trade union leaders. The day following we were guests of the British government at an official reception luncheon at which more than one hundred of Great Great Britain's most representative men from all ranks were present. In proposing Mr. Gompers' health, Prime Minister Lloyd George said in part: "My task is to offer welcome to our eminent guests. I do so for two reasons, one is for the country which they come from and which they represent at this moment—a great country, a country cradled in freedom and nurtured in freedom, a country which has been the refuge of millions in many generations who have fled from political and economic servitude in many lands and a country which is true to its great traditions; the protector of freedom in the undertaking which it has taken upon itself to place the whole of its resources at the disposal of this great struggle for liberty, the greatest the world has ever seen. We welcome them for the great country they represent. We salute the flag of their glorious country. We welcome them for their own sakes. They are the official leaders of the great labor community of America. Samuel Gompers is one of the few international names, one of the few names which is as well known in foreign countries as it is in his own country. If I may say so, he is as well known as the Mississippi. I think I may claim him almost as a kindred spirit. He is one of the very few people who approved of me before the war. For me his presence is doubly welcome. He and I had very largely the same ideas. We conceived that we were fighting the same battle, and he and I, when the war came, in the true christian spirit, have forgiven the people who disapproved of us and we are fully prepared to cooperate with them for the attainment of the ideals we have always fought for. He has devoted his life and his great abilities to democratic progress. He is fighting the same battle now in this war as he was fighting before it. It is not that he has changed his mind; it is not that he has changed his direction; it is not that he has altered his purpose; it is not that he has started a new career. He is pursuing the same purpose. He is climbing toward the same ideals. He is struggling for the same aims that he devoted his honorable career to before the war. In this war men of all classes have contributed. They have contributed in sacrifice. They have contributed in suffering. There has been no distinction of class in this land during the war. For all that I say without hesitation that victory in this war (and here I may say Mr. Gompers will agree with me) means more for those earning their bread by the sweat of their brow than any other class." One of our first requests was that arrangements be made to visit the hospital at Dartmouth where a number of wounded American boys from the front were being cared for. The trip was arranged for the day after our arrival. Those wounded boys, able to do so, assembled on the lawn to hear messages of praise and cheer from the members of the mission and to receive American flags, Red Cross packages, cigarettes and so forth, which we brought. We then visited the various wards giving words of sympathy and encouragement from "home." The week of September 1-7 was spent in Derby, where the British Trade Union Congress was in session. In the interim between the adjournment of the Derby conference and the convening of the inter-allied labor and socialist conference, the mission took advantage of the opportunity to visit Scotland. At Edinburgh, the assurance of our coming was conveyed but a few hours prior to our arrival. Yet we found a splendid meeting prepared for us. The president of the Edinburgh trades council was the official speaker, closing the meeting by the submission of a resolution which was unanimously adopted expressing the complete accord of Edinburgh's trade unionists with the war program of the A. F. of L. The inter-allied labor and socialist conference convened at Central Hall, Westminster, London, September 17, 1918. Eighty-two delegates were seated, among whom was the delegation from the A. F. of L.

Inter-Allied Labor Conference—Proposals of A. F. of L. delegates to inter-allied labor conference, London, September 17, 18, 19, 1918: We recognize in this world war the conflict between autocratic and democratic institutions: the contest between the principles of self-development through free institutions and that of arbitrary control of government by groups or individuals for selfish ends. It is therefore essential that the peoples and the governments of all countries should have a full and definite knowledge of the spirit and determination of this inter-allied conference, representative of the workers of our respective countries, with reference to the prosecution of the war. We declare it to be

our unqualified determination to do all that lies within our power to assist our allied countries in the marshalling of all of their resources to the end that the armed forces of the Central Powers may be driven from the soil of the nations which they have invaded and now occupy; and, furthermore, that these armed forces shall be opposed so long as they carry out the orders or respond to the control of the militaristic autocratic governments of the central powers which now threaten the existence of all self-governing people. This conference endorses the 14 points laid down by President Wilson as conditions upon which peace between the belligerent nations may be established and maintained, as follows: "(1) Open covenants of peace openly arrived at, after which there shall be no private international understandings of any kind, but diplomacy shall proceed always frankly and in the public view. (2) Absolute freedom of navigation upon the seas outside territorial waters alike in peace and in war, except as the seas may be closed in whole or in part by international action for the enforcement of international covenants. (3) The removal, so far as possible, of all economic barriers and the establishment of an equality of trade conditions among all the nations consenting to peace and associating itself for its maintenance. (4) Adequate guarantees, given and taken, that national armaments will be reduced to the lowest point consistent with domestic safety. (5) A free, open-minded, and absolutely impartial adjustment of all colonial claims, based upon a strict observance of the principle that in determining all such questions of sovereignty the interests of the populations concerned must have equal weight with the equitable claims of the government whose title is to be determined. (6) The evacuation of all Russian territory, and such a settlement of all questions affecting Russia as will secure the best and freest cooperation of the other nations of the world in obtaining for her an unhampered and unembarrassed opportunity for the independent determination of her own political development and national policy, and assure her of a sincere welcome into the society of free nations under institutions of her own choosing; and more than a welcome assistance also of every kind that she may need and may herself desire. The treatment accorded Russia by her sister nations in the months to come will be the acid test of their good will, of their comprehension of her needs, as distinguished from their own interests, and of their intelligent and unselfish sympathy. (7) Belgium, the whole world will agree, must be evacuated and restored without any attempt to limit the sovereignty which she enjoys in common with all other free nations. No other single act will serve, as this will serve, to restore confidence among the nations in the laws which they have themselves set and determined for the government of their relations with one another. Without this healing act the whole structure and validity of international law is forever impaired. (8) All French territory should be freed and the invaded portions restored, and the wrong done to France by Prussia in 1871 in the matter of Alsace-Lorraine, which has unsettled the peace of the world for nearly 50 years, should be righted in order that peace may once more be made secure in the interest of all. (9) A readjustment of the frontiers of Italy should be effected along clearly recognizable lines of nationality. (10) The peoples of

Austria-Hungary, whose place among the nations we wish to see safeguarded and assured, should be accorded the first opportunity of autonomous development. (11) Roumania, Serbia and Montenegro should be evacuated, the occupied territories restored, Serbia accorded free and secure access to the sea, and the relations of the several Balkan states to one another determined by friendly counsel along historically established lines of allegiance and nationality, and international guarantees of the political and economic independence and territorial integrity of the several Balkan States should be entered into. (12) The Turkish portions of the present Ottoman Empire should be assured a secure sovereignty, but the other nationalities which are now under Turkish rule should be assured an undoubted security of life and an absolutely, unmolested opportunity of autonomous development, and the Dardanelles should be permanently opened as a free passage to the ships and commerce of all nations under international guarantees. (13) An independent Polish State should be erected, which should include the territories inhabited by indisputably Polish populations, which should be assured a free and secure access to the sea, and whose political and economic independence and territorial integrity should be guaranteed by international covenant. (14) A general association of nations must be formed under specific covenants for the purpose of affording mutual guarantees of political independence and territorial integrity to great and small states alike."

The world is requiring tremendous sacrifices of all the peoples. Because of their response in defense of principles of freedom the peoples have earned the right to wipe out all vestiges of the old idea that the government belongs to or constitutes a governing class. In determining issues that will vitally affect the lives and welfare of millions of wage earners, justice requires that they should have direct representation in the agencies authorized to make such decisions. We, therefore, declare that: In the official delegations from each of the belligerent countries which will formulate the peace treaty, the workers should have direct official representation. We declare in favor of a world labor congress to be held at the same time and place as the peace conference that will formulate the peace treaty closing the war. We declare that the following essentially fundamental principles must underlie the peace treaty. A league of the free peoples of the world in a common covenant for genuine and practical cooperation to secure justice and therefore peace in relations between nations. No political or economic restrictions meant to benefit some nations and to cripple or embarrass others. No reprisals based upon purely vindictive purposes, or deliberate desire to injure, but to right manifest wrongs. Recognition of the rights of small nations and of the principle, "No people must be forced under sovereignty under which it does not wish to live." No territorial changes or adjustment of power except in furtherance of the welfare of the peoples affected and in furtherance of world peace. In addition to these basic principles there should be incorporated in the treaty which shall constitute the guide of nations in the new period and conditions into which we enter at the close of the war, the following declarations fundamental to the best

interests of all nations and of vital importance to wage earners. That in law and in practice the principle shall be recognized that the labor of a human being is not a commodity or article of commerce. Involuntary servitude shall not exist except as a punishment for crime whereof the party shall have been duly convicted. The right of free association, free assemblage, free speech and free press shall not be abridged. That the seamen of the merchant marine shall be guaranteed the right of leaving their vessels when the same are in safe harbor. No article or commodity shall be shipped or delivered in international commerce in the production of which children under the age of sixteen years have been employed or permitted to work. It shall be declared that the basic workday in industry and commerce shall not exceed eight hours per day. Trial by jury should be established.

The American delegation was represented upon each of the committees and their activities accomplished so much toward shaping the final policies of the conference that some pacifists and semi-pacifists present asserted that it was "a Gompers conference." It was apparent, however, that the soundness and the righteousness of the policies advocated by the A. F. of L. were the deciding factor. This became especially evident after the American delegation had won its contest to have the conference open to the press. It was the first inter-allied conference since the war began to which the press was admitted. All of the proposals submitted by your representatives were adopted by the conference, though not without considerable effort on their part. In addition to this your representatives were able to prevent the adoption of resolutions which in effect urged the acceptance of a "peace-without-victory" proposal which had just been advanced by Austria. The knowledge that the American trade union movement was united in supporting its government in the winning of the war coupled with the knowledge that the war policy of the A. F. of L. had been adopted by the inter-allied conference unquestionably contributed largely to weakening the morale in enemy countries and hastening the day of their collapse. Upon leaving London Mr. W. H. Buckler, of the American embassy in London, was assigned to our mission and accompanied us during our visit to Belgium, France and Italy. He proved of great assistance in procuring the necessary permits to travel through the battle area and visit the different cities in France and Italy where your mission deemed it advisable that meetings and conferences should be held. After returning to America we learned that Mr. Buckler submitted a report to the American embassy covering the results accomplished by your representatives. We have secured permission to reproduce this report believing that, coming as it did from a representative American who was not a member of our mission, it would indicate more effectively, perhaps, the value of our activities than if we ourselves should endeavor to sum them up. Mr. Buckler's report was as follows: "On September 23, acting under instructions, I started from London with Mr. Gompers and his five colleagues of the American labor mission who were about to visit France and Italy. As to the details of the mission's activities during the two weeks spent in France and the ten days in Italy, Mr. Gompers himself will doubtless give information as soon as he arrives in Washington this week.

I will therefore merely summarize here such impressions as I have been able to gather, respecting the results accomplished by the mission. 1. Honors paid to the mission unique: "As a token of the respect paid to labor and its representatives in European countries the reception everywhere given to this mission was absolutely without precedent. No group of non-official persons has ever before been received with such public honors and high official marks of distinction as were lavished on Mr. Gompers and his colleagues. 2. Direct results achieved: The good effects produced by the mission were party, perhaps mainly, indirect and of a kind not susceptible of being catalogued. Among its direct achievements, however, the following are conspicuous: (a) Proof that organized labor in the U. S. is solidly supporting the government. This was particularly valuable in France and Italy where pacifist labor and socialism have declared in favor of President Wilson's policy. The fact that American labor said 'we support the president and we are with him in pushing the war to complete victory' made it difficult for the pacifists to criticise the American labor attitude, since to do so would have stultified their own claim to being, loyal supporters of the president. The same good effect was produced in England especially during the inter-allied conference which met at Westminster on September 17-19. There can be no doubt that by securing publicity of the proceedings and moving their declaration on war aims, which included an endorsement of the president's '14 points' coupled with the vigorous prosecution of the war, the American delegates forced Henderson, Thomas and other British delegates to assume a vigorous pro-war attitude, and do disassociate themselves from the views of men like Longuet, leader of the French majority socialists. Had Henderson and Thomas not assumed a distinctly anti-pacifist attitude, they would have placed themselves in the foolish position of openly antagonizing Mr. Gompers, the ardent supporter of President Wilson whom Henderson and Thomas are constantly upholding. (b) Attacking the policy of the 'official' Italian socialists and contradicting their misrepresentations of the A. F. of L. In several of the Italian speeches, notably at Rome, Milan and Turin, Mr. Gompers denounced the false statements issued by the 'Avanti' regarding himself and the policy of the A. F. of L. He showed that the 'official' socialists were afraid to meet the American mission at a conference which had been arranged in Turin, and attacked their tyrannical dictation under which the mayor of Milan, the confederazions generale del labore of Milan and three labor representatives in Turin had been compelled to avoid all contact with the mission. Mr. Gompers' speeches received wide publicity through the Italian press. (c) Establishing friendly relations with the French Confederacion General du Travail, with the French socialists, and with the pro-war labor and socialist groups in Italy. The mission made it clear that, while strongly opposed to internationalism of the German type, they look forward eagerly to promoting after the war cordial international relations between all organizations of workingmen which sincerely endeavor to improve the conditions of labor. The mission showed itself ready to confer with all the socialist members of the French chambers or even with the anti-war socialists in Italy. These latter, however,

did not have the courage to face such a meeting. 3. Indirect results achieved: (a) Strengthening the hands of the pro-war socialists and labor men in France and Italy at the critical moment when the possibility of peace came suddenly into view and when firmness among the allies was of special importance. In this respect the mission performed in France and Italy the same function which it had already carried out in England, especially at the inter-allied labor and socialist conference on September 17 to 19, 1918; that is, it gave backbone and encouragement to the pro-war socialist and labor elements which are prepared to back their respective government in insisting upon complete victory over militarism. Signor Bissolati, the socialist member of the Italian cabinet, on three occasions expressed his personal feeling of gratitude to Mr. Gompers and to the mission for having come to Italy at precisely that moment. The same thought was voiced in different ways on many occasions within my hearing and there can be no doubt that although no pacifists may have been actually converted by the mission, its visit had a most valuable effect in upholding the hands of pro-war Italians and in determining doubters to assume a pro-war attitude. It is a remarkable fact that at none of the mass meetings addressed by Mr. Gompers was any dissent expressed among the audience. The only exception was at Turin (the center of Italian pacifism and 'giolittism') where about 1,500 people listened to Mr. Gompers in an open gallery similar to the London 'Burlington Arcade,' because all theaters and halls had been closed on account of the 'grippe.' Even in this audience, to which hostile pacifists might easily have had access, there was only a slight outburst of hissing, which lasted not more than a minute, and the audience, which stood patiently for over an hour closely packed together in the gallery, cheered all the pro-war sentiments uttered by Mr. Gompers and Mr. Frey. It is also remarkable that the official associations were so afraid of the mission that they forebade their supporters, as mentioned above, to have any contact with Mr. Gompers or his colleagues. These facts show with what salutary respect the mission was regarded by pacifist elements in Italy. The news of the first German note, requesting an armistice and intimating an agreement with the president's '14 points' reached Rome at noon on October 6, the very day on which the mission arrived there. From that moment Mr. Gompers devoted an important part of all the speeches which he delivered in Italy to warning the Italian public against showing weakness or undue anxiety for peace. The fact that the mere announcement on October 6 of the German peace move produced strikes and disorder in Milan, Turin and Florence, shows that these warnings of the American mission were much needed. (b) Demonstrating that the attitude of vigorous and militant labor leaders need not necessarily be hostile to the government of their own country. Colonel Grossi, head of the press section of the Italian general staff, remarked to me that in his opinion one of the most permanent and valuable results of the mission would be to show in a striking way to the Italian working man that representatives of labor, who had achieved great victories for the class which they represented, were sufficiently broadminded and statesmanlike to support the government of their country when they believed its policy to be sound. He said that to Italian labor, which was apt to believe only in revolutionaries, iconoclasts and enemies of its own government, this demonstration could not fail to be extremely instructive. (c) Showing that the U. S. government honors the representatives of its labor organizations and regards them as worthy of every official support. The fact that the mission was not only accompanied by a diplomatic agent sent by the embassy in London, but everywhere received the most marked assistance and courtesies from the American diplomatic missions and from representatives of the U. S. Army and U. S. Navy, was doubtless one of the reasons for the honors paid to the mission by foreign governments as described above under the first heading. It had also, however, a wider importance than this as was several times remarked to me by representative Italians. In view of the confidence felt among Italians in the influence of the U. S. Government upon the coming peace settlement, said that it was most valuable to have it thus publicly advertised at the American mission although unofficial, had the fullest approval and backing of the U. S. Government. A favorite device among the Italian pacifists had been to suggest that the mission did not agree with the views of President Wilson and that the fact of this official support was the best means of scotching that lie." I find that the views above expressed, as to the achievements of the mission in France and Italy, resemble those set forth by Captain W. S. Sanders (British officer attached to the mission) in his report to the war cabinet on the visit of the mission to Great Britain. While I have not seen that report, I gathered yesterday in conversation with him that it makes several of the points above outlined. While in Paris en route to Brest to sail for home a cablegram was received from Mr. Arthur Henderson requesting that a conference of the committee appointed by the Inter-Allied Labor and Socialist Conference of September be called. The proposed conference did not materialize, however, on account of the seamen refusing to man the ship upon which Mr. Henderson had secured passage. In each of the countries visited we were welcomed by the highest government officials who extended every possible courtesy. We were upon several sections of every battle front, at times in the front line trenches and under shell fire. However, our mission was to the workers. No opportunity was overlooked to meet and greet them wherever possible. At public meetings and conferences in London, Derby, Edinburgh, Glasgow, Paris, Rome, Milan, Genoa, Venice, and Turin we explained the basic principles and policies of the A. F. of L. and its determination to stand with our government and the allies until victory was achieved for the democracies of the world. The mission believes that it succeeded in accomplishing definite results toward the winning of the war by exposing the sinister fallacies of the pacifists and peace-by-negotiationists, by strengthening the hands of those who were courageously supporting their governments and their armies and by bringing the spirit and purpose of America closer to the minds and the hearts of the citizens and the soldiers of the allied countries. Our convictions as to what was accomplished are strengthened through the assurances given to us by the governments of the allied countries relative to the results which our presence and our activities had accomplished.

Labor Mission to Italy—(1919, p. 186) Immediately after the ship docked at Genoa a delegation came on board to greet the members of our mission representing the Italian government, the American consul at Genoa, the municipal officials, and the representatives of the labor movement of Genoa. After a conference with these joint representatives, your mission immediately issued the following public statement for the sole purpose of making clear to all classes of people in Italy the objects and purpose of our mission: "We have come among the workers and the people of Italy, as duly accredited representatives of the A. F. of L., to bring fraternal greetings and a message of hope and encouragement in the splendid fight the Italian people are making side by side with the people of all the allied countries in this great world's war for democracy and the complete extermination of militarism for all time, to the end that the people of every country the world over, whether great or small, shall be at liberty to work out their own destiny in their own way without interference from any other country. Fighting as we are for these ideals of human liberty, it is proper that we should intermingle with each other during the struggle so we may thoroughly understand each other, and have a full conception of what the workers in all the allied countries are doing to win this war for the liberties of all the people of all the world. We have not come to tell the workers of Italy what they should or should not do. We have not come to you to criticise or find fault with what ever policy you have adopted in the past or you may now have in mind. We have come officially, representing the millions of workers of America, to tell you that these workers are united in their loyalty to America and the democratic ideals upon which our great Republic is founded: that they are loyal to our President, Woodrow Wilson, and the principles for which he stands, and which he has so clearly presented to the whole world, and should anyone come among you claiming to represent the workers of America and tell you anything to the contrary, he is not giving you a true statement of facts. We have come to tell you that all the vast resources of our country are being utilized with but one single object in mind—the winning of the war, and the defeat of militarism. In this great work the millions of workers, for whom we have a right to speak are doing their full share, loyally and willingly. There has been some talk here and there by pacifists and defeatists in some of the allied countries of a peace conference with the enemy countries. We have to assure you that the A. F. of L. is squarely on record against participating in any peace conference with the representatives from Germany and Austria until the existing military despotism that today controls those countries is crushed and wiped out for all time, and then not until they have given full assurance to the rest of the world that never again will they give their support to any militarist government that deliberately violates treaties or seeks to dominate the rest of the world. American workers have pledged themselves to this principle, and if our liberties as a free people and our institutions are to be maintained, there can be and will be no departing from this principle."

Italian Industries—(1919, p. 187) Every member of our mission was thoroughly surprised and deeply impressed with what he saw in the various industrial establishments visited, which were many and varied, beginning with the great Ansaldo Works, previously mentioned, which has branches in a number of cities and employs over 100,000 workers in its various shops—the great Fiat Automobile Works, which is another of the largest industrial establishments in Italy—the great marble quarries of Carrarra where thousands of tons of pure marble are quarried each year—the hat manufacturing center of Allessandria—the Aeroplane Works, of Gilvana, Farina, and the Caproni Brothers—the large rubber works of Perilli and Company which previous to the war employed 3,000 people and had increased its force to 9,000 during the period of the war, as had many other large industrial plants in other lines of industry. To attempt to give a detailed report of all the industrial establishments visited and the many and varied industries investigated would consume too much space in this report. Suffice it to say that whether in the building of locomotives or big guns, or in the manufacture of the delicate work of an aeroplane, or the artistic work in manufacturing the finest porcelain and chinaware, we satisfied ourselves that Italy took second place to no other country in the world in the efficiency of its workers and the modern, up-to-date methods of its manufacturing system. That there is a great future for Italy as an industrial country, is beyond question if it can only get the proper support and cooperation from other countries in supplying it with those materials of which Italy as a country is barren. It must be remembered that Italy is essentially an agricultural country and has practically no coal mines nor mineral deposits of any value, and is therefore severely handicapped in its factories and industries, especially so in the manufacture of metals, particularly necessary during the war, together with the lack of lubricating oils and other fuels to keep alive its industries, let alone the absolute necessity of coaling and oiling its ships, merchant and naval, running its railroads, and the military necessities of transportation of troops and munitions to conduct modern warfare. We found factories and railroads burning wood and lignite, both commodities bringing exorbitant prices. As a result the home life of Italy went without heat, and this condition continued until the United States entered the war and began to partially supply Italy's industrial needs by sending coal, oil, minerals, etc. It is admitted frankly by Italy's foremost statesmen that the lack of these essentials caused grave and heart-breaking periods of depression and anxiety among the Italian people through the several years of warfare. However, at the time your mission visited the various industrial cities, it found the wheels of industry busily humming to the tune of clanging metal and pounding forge hammers, as the workers of Italy, united in the great effort, turned out thousands of moderns guns, shells, motors, airplanes, etc., each worker seeming to feel that he was an integral part of the nation's life during the crisis. In her shipyards we found the same bustling activity, the workers seeming to understand that their individual work was part of a great race between Democracy and Autocracy, and that it depended upon their efforts to turn the tide. Your mission can not speak too highly of the spirit and morale exhibited by the Italian workers we found in the factories and shipyards. We found all the workers, male and female, inspired with the spirit of hope and optimism toward winning the war. They were cheerful at their tasks and in the skilled industries we found the workers and the mechanics equal to any skilled labor in the world.

Cooperation in Italy—(1919, p. 188). Your committee visited scores of workingmen's cooperative societies, and, in fact, it might be said that the industrial life of Italy seems to depend largely upon cooperative organizations. While these cooperatives played an important part in helping the nation to win the war, they were by no means a product of the war itself, inasmuch as the greater part of the cooperatives were in existence many years before the war. Workingmen and their leaders informed us that the war had given the cooperative movement added initiative and strength, as the Italian government lent its cooperation by giving or loaning vast sums of money to the cooperative societies, which, of course, encouraged larger effort and stimulated greater enterprise among the workingmen's societies. In Genoa everything seemed cooperative—the coaling of the ships, the loading and unloading of vessels, and in one immense cooperative shipyard, all the rebuilding and ship repairing of all kinds; in other words, ships that came limping into port, battered and sinking through submarine attacks, were again made seaworthy through cooperative workmen. The building operations of the Italian cooperatives were conducted on such an enormous and amazing scale that one might properly term it "big business." The contracts for buildings of all descriptions, from the largest hospital in the world now being built in the province of Liguria, to the smallest dwelling in the city, are taken by the cooperative building societies. Of course they are taken on a competitive basis, given to the lowest bidder in price and terms, and the cooperatives usually get the lion's share because they can afford to eliminate excess profits, which would ordinarily find its way into the coffers of the middlemen, investors, and development companies. Aside from the actual building operations, all the material used in the construction work is secured on a cooperative basis; stone from cooperative quarries; iron from cooperative foundries and factories; in short, everything used being purchased from cooperative organizations, and in this manner whatever profits were made accrued solely to the worker. Where private or individual ownership controls the factory or industry the workers have their cooperative stores and restaurants connected with the factory where each worker may purchase at cost needed family supplies. In this movement the factory employers contribute to the cooperative establishments. The workers also have their agricultural cooperatives. Your mission visited one in particular at Ravenna. This agricultural cooperative had a membership of 28,000, and in the course of five years it had reclaimed some 4,000 acres of swamp land and had converted useless lands into a wonderful agricultural country, raising tons of produce and thousands of head of sheep and cattle. During the war period they proved that they had given to the government three-quarters of their cattle reserving only the other portion for breeding purposes. Aside from the producing cooperatives and the consuming cooperatives we found in several industrial centers cooperative savings banks, wonderful institutions operated and owned solely by the workers. One of these banks is capitalized at six billion lira. It is one of the powerful financial institutions of the city, and usually supplies the capital whenever a cooperative society, whether a producing or a consuming cooperative, contemplates some big contract.

Italian Humanitarian Society—(1919, p. 188) The humanitarian society is one of the great educational institutions of Italy. We had the pleasure of visiting one of its industrial educational institutes in Milan. They have accomodation for 720 students. We found boys from 14 years of age up to men of all ages, many of the latter being returned wounded soldiers, fitting themselves for many kinds of trades and callings. The Italian government works hand in hand with this society; for instance, for the work performed by any of these returned soldiers while learning a trade, the society pays the government three francs per day per man, and in return the government provides the men's clothes, food and lodging and the balance of any pay the men may earn goes to themselves. Among the wounded soldiers who were learning a trade in this institute, was one soldier who had been wounded ten times and another four times, with both of whom we shook hands. The humanitarian society is performing a wonderful work along industrial educational lines, and especially among the returned soldiers, many of whom have been wounded in such a manner that it is impossible for them to follow their former trade and are therefore compelled to learn a new one. The humanitarian society sees to it that this is accomplished along proper and efficient lines.

Italian Labor Movement—(1919, p. 189) The organized labor movement in Italy contains many peculiar angles. In the first place it is so mixed in with the cooperative movement and in some respects with the political movement, which really means the socialist movement, that they are inseparable. For instance, there is the general confederation of labor, whose platform is cooperative first, political second, defensive third, which really means the economic movement comes last and is subordinate to the other two. Then there is the Italian labor union, which, while it espouses the cause of the cooperative movement, is not nearly so pronounced in its political or socialist policy as the former organization. Then comes the Catholic workmen's society which is absolutely anti-socialistic; it is a very strong organization, both numerically and financially, allows no politics inside its organization, bitterly fights socialism at every point, and while its title is the Catholic workmen's society, its doors are open to non-Catholics, which comprise a good portion of its membership. Between the time we arrived in Genoa and the day we left Italy, we had the opportunity of meeting and talking to hundreds of thousands of Italian working men and women. Sometimes in the large halls or theatres of the cities we visited and more often inside the large industrial establishments employers for an hour or two hours called all their employes together and closed down the establishments to give us an opportunity to address them which we did, through interpreters. We found them very enthusiastic and always ready to lend a willing ear to what the

Americanos, as they called us, had to say. One peculiar feature which we encountered was that in some of these industrial centers the government officials and sometimes the municipal officials would say to us, "Go slow with these people, don't talk too strong with them, there is some anti-war feeling among these workers." We quickly learned, however, that this was only a delusion. Some pacifists had been at work among them but had evidently made little headway in either winning the workers over to pacifism or creating an anti-war feeling among them. This was made very evident by the manner in which they received from us the information as to what was being done by the workers in America to win the war, and their loud and manifest declarations generally ended in raising their right hand above their head and saying, "We Italians do just like Americano!" "We win the war!" We tried in several places, especially in the larger cities, to meet some of those leading officials of the labor movement who were classed as being anti-war or pacifists. We invited them to come on the platforms at the mass meetings we held and discuss their attitude in the open, but we could never succeed in getting them to consent. In one or two instances, they were apparently willing to discuss their anti-war attitude behind closed doors, which, of course, we decidedly objected to; but in some places it would evidently have been impossible to get them to even do this, although we never tested them along this line. It is only fair, however, to say in every place we visited we met some splendid labor men, all of whom earnestly expressed the hope that a bond of closer relationship would endure between the A. F. of L. and the organized labor movement of Italy when the war was over. Some of the principal leaders in the labor movement went so far as to propose that the A. F. of L. place one of its representatives in Italy for the sole purpose of educating the workers, both organized and unorganized, to band themselves together in an organization constructed on the lines of the A. F. of L., and for the further purpose of propagating this doctrine among the organizations already existing in Italy, and that the Italian organizations would be willing to defray all expenses of such a movement.

Italian Immigration—(1919, p. 189) When we arrived in Genoa among those who greeted us and with whom we were invited to confer in that city was the royal commissioner of emigration and several of his principal officers. They expressed the desire that instead of talking too strongly on the war situation, that we devote some of our time speaking on the subject of immigration, as it applied to the Italian immigrant and the conditions surrounding his immigration to America. The members of our mission were a unit in their refusal to comply with this request, making it very clear that such was not the purpose or object of our mission to Italy. This subject was then allowed to drop, and we heard no more of it until we arrived in Rome and met the other labor mission, headed by President Gompers. The royal commissioner of emigration had arranged another conference inviting both missions to be present to discuss emigration matters. We had not had any opportunity to acquaint President Gompers and the rest of the members of the mission of the previous conference in Genoa, but it was very gratifying to all the members of our mission to discover that President Gompers, with his usual keen foresight fully sensed the situation, as did the rest of his colleagues, and took the identical position our mission had taken on this subject of immigration on our arrival in Genoa.

Statement and resolutions submitted at conference with board of emigration: "The members of the board of emigration, representing the Confederazione Generale del Lavoro, la Lega nazionale delle cooperative ei Segretariati laici di assistenza agli emigranti, welcome in the delegates of the A. F. of L., the working class of the United States of America, hoping that the present visit may be a prelude to more organized relations between the working classes and the social laws of every continent. With regard more especially to the state services and work of trades unions in matters of emigration and immigration, it is their wish that the A. F. of L. may have a great influence in public life on the state laws and in each corporation or union in order to get the largest numbers of supporters of the main points of the resolutions approved in the international socialist congress of Stuttgart, 1907, and in the international convention of the labor unions of Christiana on the immigration policy, resolutions based on the following principles:

"A. That exceptional measures of any kind, economical or political, being inefficient and essentially reactionary in their character, or any restriction in free circulation, or the exclusion of individuals belonging to foreign nationalities or races, are not means to eliminate eventual danger by which the emigration and immigration are often a menace to the working classes, while on the contrary it is the duty of the organized working classes to bring the strongest opposition to bear on the frequent depression of their standard of life as consequence of the importation of masses of non-unionist workingmen and prevent the importation or exportation of unorganized labor.

"B. That the difficulties caused in many cases to the working classes by the immigration in masses of unorganized labor, accustomed to a lower standard of life, are not imaginary nor of little consequence, and the inconveniences created by certain kinds of emigration are not to be overlooked; but from the standpoint of the labor solidarity and association, the exclusion of individuals of certain nationalities or races is to be considered an unacceptable measure.

"C. That in countries of immigration the following measures are to be observed: No importation of men under contract labor; legal protection by introducing a normal and common standard of a day's work; minimum of wages; abolition of the sweating system; regulation of work at home; care of sanitary conditions; suppression of the restrictions forbidding to certain nationalities and races the sojourn in country and the advantages of its social, political and economical rights; naturalization made easier; admission of the immigrants in the unions and more especially admission of all the members of the corresponding unions of other countries, if presenting certificates of the union from which they come. In the absence of union regulations, the admission fee of the union of the new country shall be put on the account of the union from which they came—acquisition of rights of help and other benefits in proportion to the fees paid.

"With regard to the above principles and with special reference to the relations between the United States of America and Italy, it is their wish, first, that the principles underlying the Italian social legislation —the equal treatment of laborers, national as well as foreign, by legal protection, by social insurance and so forth, may be accepted in the social legislation of the United States of America and more especially the one referring to the accidents among working men. They also declare that the proposal (1905) of the president of the U. S., included in the act of 1907, for an international congress in matters of emigration (proposal enthusiastically approved by the commissariato di emigrazione in Rome, in its report to parliament, 1907) has been unanimously accepted by the Italian labor organizations and the societies for the assistance to emigrants."

Motions discussed at the meeting held at the office of the Commissioner General of Emigration on October 9, 1918, between the American Labor Delegation and Samuel Gompers, the Board of Emigration and the Board of Labor:

"1. Be it resolved that the A. F. of L. be recommended to give its support to the request made by the Italian people in the U. S. that the Italians who have left the U. S. to join the Italian military forces be freely readmitted in the U. S. after the war, except those who are to be excluded for physical or sanitary reasons.

"2. Be it resolved that the A. F. of L. be recommended to give its support to the request which will be made to the U. S. Government that the contract laborers be admitted in the U. S., provided that they arrive with a contract which has been previously approved by the proper American authorities and that these laborers which arrive with such contracts be not considered undesirable citizens.

"3. Be it resolved that the A. F. of L. be recommended to establish through the proper American authorities special agreements with the office of the commissioner general of emigration with the purpose of organizing a regular service of information on the labor conditions and on the industries which do not need Italian labor and on all other subjects which may be useful to direct, control and employ the Italian emigrants."

After a lengthy conference and all the points both in the statement and in the resolutions had been thoroughly discussed, President Gompers replied on behalf of our labor mission, clearly stating that we could not see our way to endorse the resolution submitted, but that we would agree to receive the resolutions for a future discussion but would not commit ourselves to any of them.

Labor Missions Abroad—(1919, p. 398) The work performed by the missions was of inestimable value to our allies who, after four years of struggle upon the battlefields of Flanders, France and Italy were rapidly approaching a point which would try the souls of the most sturdy and heroic of all mankind. War weary with the ceaseless, merciless contest, they sorely needed the encouragement and assurance that America, with all its vigor and manhood, its resources, industrial, financial and economic, was with them to win the struggle to obtain democracy, freedom and justice. The able manner in which this assurance was conveyed, especially to the war-ridden working masses, had its immediate stimulating effect and brought new hope and courage and a determination to carry forward the battle against autocracy and militarism to a triumphant conclusion. Our missions undoubtedly strengthened the morale of the people of the countries visited and thus made for an earlier victory than would otherwise have been achieved and thereby saved many precious lives and the expenditure of vast sums of money. If they saved the life of only one American citizen their work was not in vain. We congratulate the forethought and judgment of the Executive Council for its prompt action in sending these missions at the psychological moment, and we express our gratification at the able and effective manner ·in which the members of the missions performed their delicate and arduous duties.

Labor Press—(1919, p. 162) Gaining in strength from month to month the official trade union publications of the U. S. are a constantly growing power and influence for human advancement. The service of the official trade union journals to the nation during the war was inestimable. There was no more consistent and right-minded agency of support for our government and our cause in the war than the labor press. With a true understanding of the issues involved, the trade and labor papers gave the cause of democracy unwavering support; at the same time giving the staunchest support to every right of human freedom in the field of industry at home. The labor papers of America form a great chain of sentinels on guard for the cause of mankind throughout the country. Their struggle for existence is frequently a hard one and their path at no time is a rosy one. Every possible support should be given to the labor press in order that it may be strengthened for the still greater work that lies ahead. It is with a sense of pride that we note the marked and constant improvement in the labor papers of the country together with their constantly increasing influence upon the thought and judgment of the nation. The labor press is unified and bound together by the *American Federationist* and the A. F. of L. News Letter. The *American Federationist* provides the labor press with the best thought of the labor movement and the great issues that are constantly facing the workers. Through the News Letter the labor papers are given a weekly service of live news concerning developments and progress in the organized labor field. These two agencies give to the labor press material which is invaluable in strengthening the labor papers and which has done much to help them reach their present high standard. During the war the official publications of the A. F. of L. and the labor press in general were compelled to undergo many unusual hardships. One of the chief of these was the abnormal cost of print paper. Added to this was the limitation placed on the quantity of print paper any one publication might use. The dislocation of business and its consequent influence on advertising revenue was another source of considerable inconvenience to the labor papers. These obstacles, however, were overcome. There has not yet been a return to normal conditions, neither is such a return likely for some time to come. In order that the labor papers may be best equipped to give the largest measure of service to the labor movement under these abnormal conditions, it is doubly the duty of every member of organized labor to give the most hearty support to the labor press of the country and to the publications of the A. F. of L. The great guiding purpose of the whole labor press is one of unselfish service to the labor movement. Everything that adds to the strength and circulation of the labor press adds to the strength and power of the labor movement in its efforts to advance the interests of all working people. We heartily commend the splendid service rendered by the labor press in the past and confidently look for a greater and more distinguished service in the future.

(1920, p. 208) During the year just closed the official trade union journals rendered exceptional service to the labor movement. No class of publications in the U. S. exhibited a finer balance of judgment or pursued a more consistent course in the support of those principles which make for human progress. The year was a most trying and difficult one for many reasons. Questions of great public interest remained unsettled. Private interests and political interests made these questions more difficult of solution or impossible of settlement for the time being. In addition to facing these issues of unusual character and importance, the trade union press faced great difficulties in relation to their supply of white paper. That the labor publications have been enabled to go through the year and with such credit to themselves and with constantly growing strength and influence, is a token of the ability and ingenuity of their publishers. It may not generally be known that there are approximately 300 publications in the U. S. devoted to the cause of organized labor and expressing the viewpoint and policies of the trade union movement. The *American Federationist* has been able during the year to be of material assistance to the union and general press, furnishing to these publications a constant source of leadership in dealing with the momentous questions affecting public policy during the year. It is gratifying to know also that the non-labor daily and periodical press has given much attention to the expression of labor thought as found in the *American Federationist* and has from month to month quoted largely from its columns. The A. F. of L. *News Letter* presenting week by week to the labor press the news of the labor world has continued to serve the movement ably in its sphere. In the *News Letter* the labor press finds a concise presentation of the happenings of the world of labor each week and is thus enabled to present in turn to the readers a reflection of the activities of the workers throughout the nation. In addition to these regular publications the A. F. of L. has by the unusual press of events during the year been under the necessity of publishing a number of pamphlets containing information of national and international importance. In the opinion of the Executive Council, the achievements of the trade union movement as chronicled in the files of the *American Federationist* since its establishment in 1894, should be made available to all who seek to be informed and who are in need of convenient references. For this reason there is being compiled a complete subject and author index of the *American Federationist*. This index is well under way and will be published before the end of the present year. The publishers of standard subject and author indexes to current periodicals have not included the *American Federationist* in their list of indexed periodicals. This has deprived students, writers and all who are engaged in research work, of the valuable information to be found only in the files of the *American Federationist*. Since the *American Federa-*

tionist is on file in nearly all the colleges, universities and public libraries throughout the U. S. and in many of the labor offices throughout America, the index now being prepared will make the material contained in its files available to all.

(1921, p. 142) Demand for pamphlets and leaflets giving the viewpoint of the trade union movement on various phases of its activity has increased remarkably during the year. A number of new pamphlets have been published. We ask all affiliated bodies to bear in mind the publications issued by the A. F. of L. at headquarters and to make the utmost use of them.

(1923, pp. 129-253) The bona fide trade union publications of the United States and Canada have within the past year improved in quality and influence to a degree that is most gratifying. There are in existence more than 300 trade union weekly, semimonthly, and monthly publications. The relationship between the A. F. of L. and the labor press, whether privately owned or whether owned by organizations of labor, has been most helpful and satisfactory. Some of the most thoughtful and valuable journalistic endeavor in America is today to be found in the publications of organized labor. In many cases the labor press finds itself the sole channel for the exposure of wrong and the sole champion of constructive remedy. We urge upon the labor publications the vital need for the extension of circulation at all times and we point out to the labor press the great advantage to be gained by cooperative effort through organization in its own field. Every labor publication should become a part of the bona fide organization of trade union publications in order that there may be derived not only the inspirational benefits of association but in order that there may be had the practical results of mutual helpfulness and of multiplied strength. The mission of the labor press is to spread the truth concerning labor's cause. It is obligated to perform that mission in the most effective manner possible. We call attention to the fact that during the year a number of publications have come into the field asserting that they speak for labor, though their real mission is the destruction of the trade union movement. Some of these publications are privately-owned and represent merely the beliefs of their owners. Others, however, are the organs of an organized propaganda for the destruction of the bona fide labor movement. Every development of this character increases the need for vigilance on the part of the true trade union press. We congratulate the labor press most heartily for its loyal and effective work during the past year. We look forward with confidence to another year of improved service in the cause of the union movement.

Labor Primer, Elementary—(1921, p. 326) The Executive Council is directed to prepare an elementary primer of the labor movement, setting forth the purposes and methods of the A. F. of L., possibly in question and answer form in the interest of clearness and effectiveness.

Labor Review, Monthly—(1922, p. 100) The sundry civil appropriations bill passed by the sixty-sixth congress contained a provision to abolish all printing of publications issued by the various departments of the government after December 1, unless especially ordered continued by congress. This meant the discontinuance of the *Monthly Labor*

Review published by the department of labor. Representative John I. Nolan, of California, immediately introduced a bill providing for the printing of that most necessary publication. Many conferences were held with members of the printing committee, both of the house and the senate, and while no action was taken by congress the printing committee is still permitting the publication of the *Monthly Labor Review* in its original state. While members of the printing committee appear to be friendly to the continued publication of the *Monthly Labor Review*, there is an undercurrent that is evidently trying to bring about its abolishment. On January 4, 1922, Mr. Johnson of Washington, introduced house bill 9726, which proposed to limit the size and number of copies of any publication of any department of the government and provides for strict censorship of anything printed in them. Labor and the farmers both entered vigorous protests and nothing as yet has been done with the bill. However, if it should become a law the joint committee on printing would wield a censorship over all department publications that would destroy their usefulness. Every effort is being made to defeat the conspiracy which has for its purpose the discontinuance of all important governmental publications or their reduction to forty-eight pages with the contents controlled by the joint printing committee. (P. 359) The Executive Council is directed to continue its so far successful efforts to defeat these measures.

Labor, Shortage of—(1923, pp. 136-356) The "shortage of labor" cry is for the purpose of influencing the people of our country to believe that it is necessary to open the immigration gates so that a sufficient number of Chinese coolies, Japanese coolies, Mongolian coolies and all other coolies as well as persons from southern Europe can be brought into the country to break down wage standards. Shortly after the officials of our government admitted that there were at least 3,000,000 unemployed in the country this propaganda was launched. The A. F. of L. and every other organization of loyal American citizens has for years struggled to combat the obstacles in the way of the Americanization of the foreigner as well as of those born in our own country. It has been an uphill fight as the opposition comes from those who are powerful financially and politically and who would sacrifice the welfare of our people in order that they can satisfy their greed for greater and greater fortunes. The contest is between the privileged few and the great mass of our people. While the premeditated propaganda was being sent throughout the states of the shortage of labor 2,000 men and women gathered before the U. S. civil service commission building in Washington in the shadow of the capitol in answer to a call for applicants for laborers and charwomen. Some stood all night to be the first to apply when the office opened. Furthermore the surplus of labor became so acute in Cleveland and other cities that warnings for wage workers not to go to those cities were sent out through the press associations by labor officials of those cities. Reports received by the A. F. of L. show that even now there are thousands unemployed in our country but the giant corporations who are never satisfied unless they have thousands of wage workers clamoring at the gates of their plants for employment care nothing for this. Their one thought is profits and dividends. The A. F. of L.

should demand of the congress legislation that will not permit the breaking down of American standards in the interest of the few. Nor is American labor willing to permit the employers to impose standards of living and work and the normal workday even though there shall be a surplus of labor. To this end the A. F. of L. will launch an intensive campaign to point out to the workers and to those who legislate the great crime that would be committed in permitting hordes of immigrants from Southern Europe or Asia to enter America. Congress will be called upon to make sufficient appropriation to permit the immigration bureau of the department of labor to function. The secretary of labor has claimed 100 foreigners enter the U. S. every day in violation of the immigration laws. This could not occur if sufficient funds were available for carrying out our immigration laws.

Labor Statistics, Bureau of—(1919, p. 322) Realizing that the establishment of stable conditions in business and industries is of the utmost importance at the earliest possible time, the A. F. of L. condemns in strongest terms the efforts of certain employers of labor to construct a basis upon the lower standard of living resulting from curtailed consumption due to high prices of commodities and in response to patriotic appeal. The work of the department of labor, through its bureau of labor statistics, is most highly commended for the great good accomplished in establishing figures which furnish a fair basis to be used in making desired readjustments.

Labor, Tribute to American—(1919, p. 84) A testimonial to the fidelity of American labor to the ideals of labor and of the American democracy that should find a place in the records of the American labor movement was contained in the annual report to the president of the U. S. for the fiscal year ending December 1, 1918, by Josephus Daniels, secretary of the U. S. navy. Secretary Daniels in his report paid to American labor the following tribute:

"The relations between labor and the navy department have been highly satisfactory during the past year. In spite of the general bidding for skilled mechanics, the workmen in our navy yards, with surprisingly few exceptions have remained loyal to the department, and have refused to leave their vitally necessary work in the yards for more lucrative positions elsewhere. In addition, on several occasions when the general relations between capital and labor appeared under the extraordinary conditions created by the war, to have reached a critical stage, the various trades in our navy yards addressed resolutions to the secretary of the navy so clearly defining their belief that the duty of all loyal American workmen lay in securing the maximum production of war materials by combined individual efforts, without regard to selfish considerations of personal betterment, as to have no slight effect in bringing both sides in controversies going on outside the yards to a realization of the need of forgetting their disputes and devoting their energies toward winning the war. Much of this satisfactory condition is due to the loyal cooperation of the heads of the A. F. of L., with whom the department has maintained the friendliest relations and whose wise and patriotic councils have done much to keep such yard workmen as were members of labor organizations keenly alive to a sense of their duty as American

citizens. The department feels it may take some credit to itself for this condition of affairs on account of the principle it has established during the last five years of frank dealing with men of labor and by the rule that any grievance could be brought, without red tape or formality, directly to the attention of the secretary of the navy at any time for investigation or correction. The navy department trusts the men who build and repair ships and make munitions, it believes they trust the department, and that is the whole secret of successful cooperation between employer and employe. The navy has suffered severely in common with all industry through the shortage of labor. It was early seen that men to operate our yards to their greatest capacity could only be secured by further crippling the building of merchant ships—so imperatively needed—and the manufacture of munitions. The policy was established, therefore, of making no demands for more labor beyond what was absolutely necessary for the upkeep of the fleet and a very limited amount of new construction. Even this required a large augmentation of our yard forces; but while at times work has been delayed more than we would have preferred, yet enough men have been found to carry on the absolutely needed requirements of the service."

Labor's Constructive Demands—(1921, p. 127) The trade union movement stands for the preservation and enlargement of fundamental rights and its first demand must be always in behalf of those rights. Combined autocratic powers are making every effort to destroy the freedom of workers to join together in defense of their interests. There may be conflicts that are more spectacular, but there is none upon which, in the long run, human progress will turn with greater effect. When mankind emerged from a state of serfdom and particularly when human energy came to leave the land for the places of industry, the vital thing in human relations was the firm establishment of individual freedom. The right of the individual to comport himself and to contract for himself as a free man was paramount and upon that freedom, won by tremendous effort, our present social order rests. But industry developed. Individual industry gave way, with the discovery of the power of steam and with the invention of machinery and the application of electricity, to an industrial order in which the unit of effort was a group. This change in industry made group action necessary for the protection of individual rights. Today in industry there are few rights of fundamental value to men and women unless those rights are as available to men in groups and associations as to individuals. The right of an individual to quit his work is firmly established. Employers of reactionary character aided by legislators who either do not or will not understand, seek today to make it unlawful for groups of workers to quit their work in unison. The purpose of quitting work is to satisfy some desire on the part of the worker, or to attempt to secure such satisfaction. Modern industry grants no satisfaction to the worker who quits alone. Individual liberty must find its modern counterpart in group liberty. The individual contract, which aimed to exchange equal values between parties of equal standing, must find its modern counterpart in a group contract. There is no mutuality, no equality, in a contract between an individual worker and a billion dollar corporation employing hundreds or thousands of workers. The principle that gave vitality to individual freedom and to the individual contract is dead in modern life unless it also means a like freedom of action to groups of men associated to protect and promote a common interest. The "individual contract" which employes separately are forced to sign as a condition precedent to securing work and by which they must agree not to acquire or retain membership in labor unions, means jobless starvation or acquiescence by the workers under coercion. Such giving up of one's ownership of one's self, his sovereignty and manhood under such conditions is like agreeing with a thug at the point of his gun to give up one's purse and regard that transaction as a contract entered into by the highwayman and his victim. As manipulated by employers for the denial and abrogation of individual rights, under the protection of anti-combination and conspiracy laws, such "individual contract" in industry is one of the most pernicious, subtle and dangerous devices ever used for the oppression of humanity. In our modern industrial civilization, where the individual right and the individual liberty is so largely dependent upon a similar freedom for the group of which the individual is a part, the freedom of the individual is frequently either abridged or denied by a denial of group rights. Anti-conspiracy laws as applied to industrial life, a miserable heritage from a miserable page of the early efforts to crush the aspirations and liberties of working people, must go entirely. They must be removed from the body of law under which we live. The whole issue of freedom today turns upon the question of group rights. Today the rights of the individual, the relations between workers and employers, can be safeguarded and guaranteed only as the rights of the group are equally safeguarded and guaranteed. Those who seek to crush and oppress the workers see this clearly. Through old and new laws and through contractual devices under the protection of these laws they seek to destroy the movement of the workers and to destroy freedom for the workers. We call upon the workers everywhere to resist with every proper activity this new slavery. Our freedom must be complete and all-abounding. Restriction of freedom is abolition of freedom. We call upon this convention and upon the workers everywhere to dedicate themselves again to the struggle for freedom. The aspirations of human life must not be jeopardized by the pressure of an industrial system that has not yet learned how to give its best service or how best to accommodate itself to the growing needs of human life. This demand we place above all others as meriting and requiring our most energetic action everywhere. Freedom must not perish on the altar of either greed or cupidity. In addition we reiterate and reaffirm these principles: Those contributing to production should have a part in its control. It is fundamental for efficiency in production that the essentials of teamwork be understood and followed by all. There must be opportunity for intercourse and exchange of viewpoints between workers and managers. It is this machinery for solving industrial problems that is fundamental. There must be given to each individual a voice in the shaping of his life and this right must extend to the workers in their organized capacity to be exercised through their chosen representatives. Industry today requires greater democracy in order to give to the workers full voice in assisting in this direction. It requires more intelligent management and acceptance of the principle that production is for service and not for profit alone. It requires full and free acceptance and use of the best that invention has to offer. It requires bold and audacious reconstruction of method and process in the conduct of basic industries. Labor does not oppose introduction of improved methods in industry. It courts and encourages improvements in processes and in machinery. What it will always resist is the introduction of these processes and this machinery at the expense of the workers. Proper absorption of non-producers into useful channels. The welfare of the workers must be a paramount consideration. There can be no progress and no gain in production volume if there is not such consideration. But a greater mutuality in industry would insure proper safeguarding of the rights of workers. Only by such methods and under such principles can there be an advance in production which does not penalize the worker for his own industriousness and for his own alertness and inventiveness. Autocratic industry kills incentive. It punishes brilliancy of attainment. It warps the mind and drains the energy from the body. We have repeatedly condemned the principle of autocratic control of industry and we now declare that short of its complete removal from our industrial life there is no salvation and no hope of abundance in our time. We urge the setting up of conference boards of organized workers and employers thoroughly voluntary in character and in thorough accord with our trade union organizations, as means of promoting the democracy of industry through development of cooperative effort. We point out to employers the fact that industry which is the life blood of our civilization, can not be made the plaything and the pawn of a few who by chance today hold control. Industry is the thing by which all must live and it must be given the opportunity to function at its best. Labor turnover is but one of the evils which will disappear in proportion as the workers are given voice in management. This is proven by statistics which show the lowest turn-over in those industries where the workers exercise the most effective voice by reason of the highest degree of organization. Cooperation should be encouraged as an effective means of curbing profiteering. To stimulate rapid development of cooperatives the federal farm loan act should be extended so as to give credit to all properly organized cooperatives, just as credit is now given to individual farmers. Cooperation is no less vital and worthy of support than are the railroads, which were given hundreds of millions of dollars and an area of land equal to New England to facilitate their establishment. There should be legal enactment to protect cooperatives against discrimination by manufacturers and wholesalers. Control of credit capital by those whose chief interest is the cumulation of profits results inevitably in the open door for profiteering. We repeat and emphasize the demand of organized labor that control of credit capital be taken from the hands of private financiers and placed in the hands of a public agency to be administered by voluntary and cooperative methods. We urge that the U. S. department of labor compile and issue monthly statements of the cost of manufacture of those staple articles which form the basis of calculation in fixing the cost of living.

Labor University, National—(1920, p. 465) While organized labor will always place its main dependence for educational facilities upon the public school system, which it has done so much to establish and develop, a university endowed by the A. F. of L. would be as legitimate and have at least as important function as a university the endowment of which came from any other private source. But there are practical questions of administration and finance which will require careful study. The president of the A. F. of L. is instructed to appoint a committee to study the possibility of coordinating the present educational institutions and activities conducted under the auspices of organized labor; to investigate the strength of the demand for a central labor university which may be developed among the affiliated internationl unions; to consider the matter of extension courses and of scholarships, which would make the facilities of such an institution of widest service, and to consider the practial questions of administration and finance.

Labor's Dead, In Honor of—(1920, p. 352) President Gompers: "At this time I think we should follow the practice of years, and in the name of our revered departed, the men and the women in the labor movement of Canada and the U. S., the men and women who have helped in the great cause of human justice, disenthralment and freedom, the delegates to this convention and the friends will arise and remain in silent meditation in honor to the memory of our sacred dead." All the audience arose and remained standing in silence, with bowed heads, for the space of one minute.

Labor's Progress—(1922, p. 153) We have passed through a year of trying experience. We can say with conviction that our movement has given true interpretation to the aspirations of the workers of our country. Constantly confronted with new problems, the labor movement is compelled to hold itself in readiness to shape new policies as new issues arise. It is essentially a movement of progress and it never can be anything else. We point out to the workers of our country, wherever they may be, the supreme necessity of organization in order that the workers may be able to present a constantly growing opposition to those who would despoil the workers and in order that there may be a constantly growing force for constructive effort. The great need of the time for the workers is organization and ever more organization, but more than that, the greatest asset that our country can have and the greatest safeguard that it can have, is a constantly growing, constantly developing enlightened and democratic trade union movement. We urge for the coming year unceasing efforts in the work of organization, federation and unification. It would be improper and unjust not to refer to the splendid cooperation and assistance that have been given by the officers and representatives of the various international unions affiliated to the A. F. of L. This assistance and cooperation have been of the most helpful character and have been given in a spirit of service to our movement. This cooperation and assistance has been one of the great evidences of the solidarity and strength of our movement and we express the hope that a similar spirit of cooperation and mutual

helpfulness in the common cause may prevail during the year to come.

"Lame Ducks" in Congress—(1923, p. 81) With a sense of grim humor, members of congress who have been defeated for reelection and who are "hold-overs," that is, for four months they may sit in and be members of the house or the senate and determine the vote on legislation notwithstanding their repudiation by the people of their respective states or districts, have been dubbed "lame ducks." One of the greatest issues before the people of the U. S. is the menace from legislation enacted by "lame ducks." Although the ship subsidy bill was condemned in every part of the country by people in nearly all walks of life the house passed it by twenty-four majority. Of those voting for the ship subsidy bill in the house seventy-one were "lame ducks," members who had been repudiated by their constituents, and with that vote only was the bill passed by the house. Such a wave of resentment swept over the country that Senator Norris introduced a bill providing that terms of congressmen should expire in December after the election and that a congress of the newly elected representatives be called together in the following January. The bill passed the senate but was pigeonholed in the house. The "misleaders" of the house being "lame ducks" would not permit the bill to be reported for action. It is believed that the next congress will take suitable action to eliminate this incongruous menace to legislation, legislation upon which the people have expressed themselves by their votes. The will of the people as expressed by their votes must be translated into law. (P. 357) We believe that legislation along the line of the Norris bill, which passed the senate in the 67th congress and which provided for the new congress meeting in the January following the election, should be promptly enacted into law.

Leaves of Absence—(1919, p. 355) The A. F. of L. urges upon congress the enactment of legislation which shall provide for the retention of the civil service status by the officers and unions affiliated with the A. F. of L. who are called upon to absent themselves from their official duties and their reinstatement in the service at a salary no less than that received by them at the time such leave of absence is granted. Leaves of absence, either temporary or extended, should be granted the officials of affiliated unions to conduct the work of their organizations without prejudice to their official standing in the government service.

Legal Information Bureau—(1922, p. 398) The Executive Council was authorized to establish a legal bureau for the purpose of collating all laws and judicial decisions on the rights of labor, such bureau to enlist the voluntary assistance and cooperation of lawyers friendly to the cause of labor and experienced in industrial litigation.

(1923, p. 42) The people of America are today a nation overridden and over-burdened by laws and judicial decisions based upon unwritten as well as by statutory laws. In the fiction of the law all men are presumed to know the law, yet no profession has so enlarged its hold upon the people as has the legal profession. We have not only our courts of law, we have also our equity or chancery courts which function without the rules and regulations prescribed by the legislative branch of government, which altogether too often assume to enact special legislation and protect and promote special class interests. Then, too, the power of our courts over the legislative branch of government is constantly increasing. This assumed power has reached such a point that the majority of the law has become the sole expression of judges who assume power and authority not conferred upon them. We have today practically forty-nine different kinds of law—one kind for each state in the union. We have another kind of law for our federal courts, and to this may added a special kind of law for the District of Columbia, making a total of fifty different varieties of law. When we enter the field of equity jurisprudence we find that we have almost as many kinds of laws as we have judges. The fiction underlying our equity jurisprudence is that our equity judges are guided not so much by law as by the spirit of equity presumed to be contained in the King's conscience rephrased to meet the modern conception of the state. Our system and variety of law have become so cumbersome, irksome, confusing and expensive and so perversive of justice that even the most forward-looking and right-thinking lawyers have come to realize the necessity of a restatement of the law so that some semblance of order might be established out of the legal chaos. No section of the law is more uncertain, inequitable and unjust than that relating to industrial relations. This phase of the law presents simply a maze of confusion and pitfalls. Even the highest court in the land seems to be lost and to go groping in the dark when dealing with questions affecting modern industrial conditions and relations. It applies old and worn-out economic and political doctrines to our modern system of production and distribution, and attempts to square the principles of an age of peasantry with our present day development of highly organized industrialism and commercialism. If there is to be a restatement of the law on industrial relations it is of the utmost importance that the various conflicting decisions of the courts be reconciled so far as possible in a manner consistent with the just and equitable demands of the workers. In this work organized labor should be accorded its proper influence and helpful cooperation. Then, too, in the furtherance of new laws and the enactment of new legislation much effort, time and money have been spent by the organized wage earners and sympathetic groups of people only to find later that our courts have placed erroneous constructions or interpretations upon such laws or have declared them unconstitutional. Because of these tendencies and developments the faith of the American wage earners in our political institutions is being shaken. The workers are fast losing the essential respect for and confidence in the American judiciary. Frequently, too, serious questions of law relating to industrial relations have been placed in the care of lawyers who are unfamiliar with the struggles of labor and the fundamentals upon which their struggles are based and the justice for which they are striving. Altogether too often have the results of the workers' long legislative struggles been placed in jeopardy by the employment of legal counsel untrained in industrial relations affairs. At times beneficial labor laws have been questioned in the courts without the A. F. of L. having been advised of such litigation and afforded an opportunity to be helpful in advising for the defense of such laws. Because of these grave situations and by reason of the great beneficent good that may be derived by a coordination of labor's legal defense, the Cincinnati convention authorized the creation of a legal information bureau. In contemplating the establishment of this bureau, the vista of duties to be performed which came to our minds might well cause anyone to hesitate to venture upon an enterprise of such gigantic proportions. Wisely, however, the convention directed that the legal information bureau, at least in its embryo state, should be confined to the purposes of "collating all laws and judicial decisions on the rights of labor, such bureau to enlist the voluntary assistance and cooperation of lawyers friendly to the cause of labor and experienced in industrial litigation." Progress has been made in organizing a voluntary staff of lawyers who are familiar with and competent to handle litigation involving industrial relations affairs. Efforts are also under way to collect all available briefs drawn in labor cases and supplemented by subsequent decisions, these to be kept up to date and indexed. It is the purpose of the legal information bureau to prepare briefs from time to time on all important subjects affecting the rights and interests of labor and also to prepare briefs on all new questions that may arise. It is intended later that the bureau shall secure so far as possible favorable constructions of new legislation and to prepare criticisms of decisions and by publication seek to arouse a public opinion and form a public demand for legislation and judicial decisions helpful and favorable to labor and therefore for the promotion of the common good. The legal information bureau functions only in an advisory capacity; it can not possibly undertake the active defense of labor's rights whenever menaced before the courts. This is a matter entirely within the care of the affiliated unions. It is the purpose of the bureau wherever possible to assist the attorneys selected by the trade unions and then only when the fundamental rights of labor are involved or favorable labor and social legislation is challenged in the courts. To accomplish this purpose, successfully, the full, hearty and complete cooperation of all affiliated unions is essential. (P. 268) Unquestionably, there is a growing need for an efficient and proficient central agency for the collecting and collating of legal decisions and decrees and to disseminate to all affiliated organizations or their legal representatives required and helpful information, in order that the wage earners' rights, interests and prerogatives may at all times be properly defended when challenged in the courts. To undertake an active part in all legal controversies in which the affiliated unions may become involved is not alone undesirable but impracticable. Neither is it desirable or advisable that the guidance of trade union activities, policies and procedures should be placed under the control and influence of those who are trained in the law but who are unfamiliar with trade union problems and who do not bear the responsibility of executive officers charged with the administration of trade union affairs.

Legislation, Committee on—(1921, p. 426) This addition was made to section 3 article III, A. F. of L. constitution: "Committee on legislation to which shall be referred all resolutions pertaining to national legislation." The discretionary power of the chair in referring resolutions is not impaired.

Legislation, Labor—(1919, pp. 108-362) *Summary of labor legislation enacted during portion of second session and all of the third session of the sixty-fifth congress.*

1. Extending the use of the special fund and authorizing acceptance of gifts under the rehabilitation of disabled soldiers' act. (Public no. 279, 65th cong., 3d session.)

2. Commission to fix minimum wage for women and minors in the District of Columbia. (Public, no. 215, 65th cong., 2d session.)

3. To readmit to U. S. after discharge from foreign service aliens in cobelligerent friendly armies. (Public, res. no. 44, 65th cong., 2d session.)

4. Transportation including sleeping-car accommodation to war workers of the U. S. government no longer needed. (Public, no. 246, 65th cong., 3d session.)

5. For the manufacture of cotton fabrics at the Atlanta, Ga., penitentiary to supply the requirements of war and navy departments with tents. etc., for the army. (Public no. 194, 65th cong., 2d session.

6. To enable the president to carry out the price guarantee for the 1918 and 1919 crops of wheat. (Public, no. 348, 65th cong., 3d session.)

7. Revenue act, approved February 24, 1919, provides a 10 per cent tax on income of concerns employing child labor. (Public, no. 254, 65th cong., 3d session.)

8. Legislative, executive and judicial appropriation law carried $184,000 to enforce the child labor provision in revenue law. (Public, no. 314, 65th cong., 3d session.)

9. Government grants $240 temporary increase in compensation to all employes. (Public, no. 314, 65th cong., 3d session.)

10. Bonus of $60 is given to soldiers, sailors and marines at the time of their discharge. (Revenue law, public, no. 254, 65th cong., 3d session.)

11. Allowing persons of army, navy and marine corps, in the present war, to retain uniforms, also to receive 5 cents per mile for railroad fare home. (Public, no. 300, 65th cong., 3d session.)

12. Increase in compensation for postal employes. (Public, no. 299, 65th cong., 3d session.)

13. Provision for commission to reclassify salaries of the government employes. (Public, no. 314, 65th cong., 3d session.)

14. Provision for commission to investigate the salaries of postmasters and employes of the postal service with a view to the reclassification and readjustment of same. (Public, no. 299, 65th cong., 3d session.)

15. Appropriation of $200,000,000 to aid the states in the construction of rural post roads. (Public, no. 299, 65th cong., 3d session.)

(1920, pp. 97-384) *Summary of labor legislation enacted from May 19, 1919, to April 15, 1920, of the sixty-sixth congress.*

1. Appropriation for the rehabilitation of injured soldiers by the vocational education board, $6,000,000. (Public, no. 11, 66th congress.)

2. Appropriation of $8,000,000 for the vocational education board. (Public no. 21, 66th congress.)

3. Deficiency appropriation of $5,000,000 for the vocational education board. (Public, no. 73, 66th congress.)

4. Appropriation of $400,000 for U. S. employment bureau. (Public, no. 21, 66th congress.)

5. Woman suffrage amendment.

6. Increased compensation for employes of the government printing office. (Public, No. 23, 66th congress.)

7. Deficiency appropriation of $263,072.04 for the enforcement of immigration laws. (Public, No. 73, 66th congress.)

8. Rent commission provided for District of Columbia in food control bill. (Public, no. 63, 66th congress.)

9. Postal employes granted $150 increase. (Public res. no. 19, 66th congress.)

10. Increased compensation granted policemen, District of Columbia. (Public, no. 94, 66th congress.)

11. Increased compensation granted fire department employes, District of Columbia. (Public, no. 124, 66th congress.)

12. For the retirement of school teachers in the District of Columbia. (Public, no. 111, 66th congress.)

13. Granting custom inspectors overtime for lading and unlading vessels at night. (Public, no. 131, 66th congress.)

14. Civil service retirement.

(1921, p. 106) *Summary of legislation enacted by the sixty-sixth congress since the report made to the Montreal convention, including portion of the second session, all of the third session and first few days of the sixty-seventh congress.*

Directing war finance corporation to take action for relief of agricultural sections of the country. (Public resolution no. 54.)

1. Lever food control law repeal. (Public resolution no. 64.)

2. Women's bureau—department of labor. (Public. no 259.)

3. Bonus for federal employes, firemen and policemen. (Public, no. 364.)

4. Merchant marine. (Public, no. 161.)

5. Increase in compensation to postal employes. (Public, no. 265.)

6. Retirement for civil service employes. (Public, no. 215.)

7. Vocational rehabilitation of cripples in industry. (Public, no. 236.)

(1922, p. 92) *Summary of legislation enacted by the sixty-seventh congress up to May 1, 1922—laws enacted favorable to labor.*

1. Limiting immigration until June 30, 1922, to 3 per cent of the number of foreign born of any nationality in the United States according to the census of 1910. (Public, no. 5.)

2. Extending the expiration of the 3 per cent immigration law to June 30, 1924.

3. Increasing the number of years to five instead of one that foreigners must live in Canada, Cuba or Mexico before entering the United States.

4. Penalizing steamship companies that bring more than the quota of any nationality provided in the immigration law.

5. Appropriating $5,000,000 for purchase of seed grain and of feed for farmers in crop failure areas of U. S. (Public, no. 177.)

6. For relief of distressed and starving people of Russia. (Public, no. 117.)

7. Authorizing association of producers of agricultural products. (Public, no. 146.)

8. Appropriating $75,000,000 for construction of rural post roads. (Public, no. 87.)

9. Public protection of maternity and infancy. (Public, no. 97.)

10. Establishing veterans' bureau in treasury department. (Public, no. 47.)

11. Increasing force and salaries of patent office employes, etc. (Public, no. 147.)

12. Authorizing extension of time for payment of construction charges on reclamation projects, etc. (Public, no. 185.)

13. Amending act for retirement of employes in classified civil service. (Public, no. 142.)

14. Bringing all persons in classified civil service under retirement act. (Public, no. 182.)

15. Providing that watertenders, oilers and firemen shall work eight hours instead of twelve whether in port or at sea.

16. Appropriation of $225,000 for U. S. employment service of department of labor.

17. Appropriation for women's bureau of department of labor increased from $75,000 to $100,000.

(P. 326) Considering the reactionary attitude of the present congress the officers are congratulated for the excellent showing made. The offensive and defensive legislative activities of the A. F. of L. during the past year have been carried on with extraordinary ability and unusual vigor.

(1923, pp. 79-357) *Summary of legislation from May 1, 1922, to March 4, 1923—favorable legislation enacted.*

1. Providing for the appointment of a commission to investigate questions relative to interestate commerce in coal. (Public, no. 347.)

2. Prohibiting profiteering in coal. (Public, no. 348.)

3. Bonus for federal and district employes of $240 per year for the year ending June 30, 1923. (Public, no. 257.)

4. Forbidding the expenditure of appropriations for the departments of state and justice to prosecute labor and farmers' organizations. (Public, no. 229.)

5. Workmen's compensation for longshoremen. (Public, no. 239.)

6. Extending the federal retirement act to include charwomen, laborers and other employes whether classified or unclassified who are employed on an annual basis and whose pay is less than $600 per annum. (Public, no. 243.)

7. Reclassification act. (Public, no. 516.)

8. Equalizing pensions of retired policemen and firemen of District of Columbia. (Public no. 428.)

9. Bonus for federal and District employes of $240 per year for the year ending June 30, 1924. (Public, no. 544.)

10. Extending compensation for occupational diseases to those receiving them until March 1, 1924. (Public, no. 537.)

11. Prohibiting shipment of filled milk in interstate or foreign commerce. (Public, no. 513.)

12. Extending retirement act to employes 55 years of age or over who shall have served for 15 years and who become involuntarily separated from the government service. (Public, no. 363.)

Legislation, State—(1921, p. 122) Notwithstanding the expenditure of millions of dollars and the activities of practically every organization of employers, financial interests and their paid attorneys, the efforts of the antagonists of labor to secure repressive legislation in the various states failed almost completely. (P. 418) On behalf of the general labor movement of the country we express our sincere appreciation of the valiant fight made by the various state federations of labor against the reactionary and viciously anti-labor elements who controlled most of the state legislatures during the past year, and commend them for the success that attended their efforts in frustrating the enemies of labor in the attempts made to saddle on the wage earners of the various states repressive legislation. Continued support will be given

by the A. F. of L., and we urge still greater support by the national and international unions for the various state bodies.

(1922, pp. 115-457) Notwithstanding the wave of reactionism that has been spread over the country by the enemies of the people they have failed in a great majority of the legislatures to secure the legislation they so much desired. Persistent efforts to have the Kansas court of industrial relations' act copied by other states met with no response. This convincingly proves the fact that the Kansas law which has for its purpose compulsory labor does not commend itself to even those who might be willing to prohibit the normal activities of labor. Representatives of the state federations of labor and city central bodies are to be commended for the practical results obtained in fighting anti-labor measures. In some of the states really beneficial legislation was enacted, but in many of them the real work has been in defeating bad legislation. While in some of the states no remedial legislation was enacted there were no reactionary laws passed.

(1923, pp. 96-226) The wave of reaction, while subsiding, has not yet died. Many laws favored by the workers have been secured and others have been amended to wipe out existing evils. There is now a covert attempt being made to tear down the existing workmen's compensation laws but with little effect. As ever, the real strength of the trade union movement has been shown in its defeat of obnoxious legislation. Some states have recently adopted a law giving the right of a jury trial in certain cases of contempt of court. As fast as these laws have secured the attention of the courts, they have been held to be unconstitutional, as being an invasion upon the duties of one coordinate branch of the government by another. It might be well, therefore, if the strength of labor were devoted to securing constitutional amendments to cure this evil, rather than waste time and useless expenditure of money in costly and futile litigation. As reported last year and as was experienced during the period just ending, several attempts to introduce compulsory labor laws met with failure. The various workmen's compensation laws received a considerable amount of attention by both their friends and enemies. However, the advantage lies with labor, as in most cases inimical legislation was defeated and that extending the laws was passed. Great credit is due to the various state legislative committees for the good work performed during the past year.

Letter Carriers—(1921, p. 337) Directed Executive Council to cooperate with the letter carriers in urging congress to furnish equipment allowances for rural carriers. (1923, p. 227) Reaffirmed.

Liberty Bond Purchases—(1919, p. 70) True to its record of supporting the government in its just cause during the war and in furtherance of that purpose, the A. F. of L. subscribed $10,000 to the fourth liberty loan and $10,000 to the fifth loan, making a total of $50,000 invested in liberty bonds in the United States. In addition, since we reported upon this subject to the St. Paul convention, the purchase of $5,000 of Canadian victory loan bonds has been effected, making a total of $15,000 of victory bonds. It is regrettable that there is no exact record of the amount subscribed by our affiliated organizations and their membership to the various bond issues of the U. S. and the

Canadian government, for beyond doubt millions of dollars have been invested in this way, as well as in war savings stamps.

Libraries, Public Utilities—(1919, p. 319) We believe that public libraries are public utilities and should be owned, controlled and administered directly by the state or city financing such libraries. We believe the present low and inadequate salaries and intolerable working conditions in our public libraries are due to the fact that most of the libraries are under the control of private corporations who are not responsible to the community at large, although they are spending the public's money. Since the right of workers to organize in trade unions and to bargain collectively is recognized and affirmed by the U. S. government this right shall not be denied, abridged or interfered with by the employers of the library. Therefore the A. F. of L. declares in favor of civil service for librarians; that a member of a library union to be elected by the union, be placed upon all committees having in charge library activities in which union labor is asked to cooperate, such as the war service committee of the American Library Associations; that a member of union labor be represented on all boards of trustees for libraries; and we earnestly urge all locals to give all assistance possible towards the organization of these workers.

(1922, p. 496) Reaffirmed.

Lincoln Day—(1922, p. 344) The Executive Council is directed to use every proper influence to secure the enactment of a law making February 12, the anniversary of the birth of Abraham Lincoln, a legal holiday within the District of Columbia.

(1923, p. 89) By direction of the Cincinnati convention a bill was introduced in congress making February 12 a legal holiday for the District of Columbia, to be known as Lincoln Day. Much opposition arose, the contention being that congress has designated only two legal holidays, Labor Day and Mother's Day. Fourth of July, Christmas, New Years and other holidays in the District of Columbia and territories are holidays by general consent and not because of congressional legislation. Notwithstanding this attitude of the leaders of congress there should be no let-up in urging the establishment of Lincoln Day in honor of the memory of our great martyred president, the great emancipator and consistent advocate and defender of the rights, interests and welfare of the common people. Lincoln Day would be a milestone each year in the struggle to maintain that freedom for which he struggled and for which he gave up his life. He represented all that was great in human conduct and the celebration of the anniversary of his birth would be an incentive to the youth of our land as well as all the people to follow the teachings of his life and thereby bring about a higher civilization. (P. 226) This convention reaffirms the declaration of the Cincinnati convention, urging that February 12 be declared a national holiday, to be known as "Lincoln Day," in honor of the Great Emancipator.

Living, High Cost of—(1919, p. 312) In the defense of present high prices, the claim is repeatedly made that wage rates are responsible for this condition. This claim ignores the economic fact that wages are the last cost that is increased and that present wage levels do not equal increased living costs as stated in government reports. The bureau of labor statistics, U. S. department of labor, has reported that the labor cost in the manufacture of one pair of welt shoes is 36.8 cents. (This report is made in bulletin no. 232, May, 1918, on "Wages and hours of labor in the boot and shoe industry: 1907 to 1916." Bulletin no. 232 indicates the low labor cost in production because of specialization and machinery that is not affected by even substantial wage increases. The Executive Council of the A. F. of L. is hereby instructed to select other industries dealing with necessaries of life and urge the proper government officials to conduct inquires similar to that reported in bulletin No. 232.

(1920, pp. 90-91) No single problem has had a greater bearing upon the welfare of the American wage earners in their daily lives during the year just closing, than the cost of living. Recent figures covering the nation as a whole are not available for purposes of comparing increase in the cost of living with the increase in wages, but the last figures of a general nature issued by the U. S. department of labor, bureau of labor statistics, showed that, while since 1913, the average advance in the wages of organized workers was 55 per cent, the average increase in the cost of living was 83.1 per cent. There is no reason to presume that this margin between wages and cost of living has decreased since these figures were issued. There are on the contrary, statistics to show that the margin has materially increased. No statistics are needed to convince us that the increase in the cost of living has been a serious factor in the lives of the great masses of our people, and it is certain that there is no justification of any kind, either in fact or in theory, for the bulk of the burden that has been thrown upon the people in the form of increased prices. In order that there may be something available in the way of definite figures showing the complete lack of reason and the ruthlessness which underlie a great part of the increase in prices of staple commodities, there is submitted here a compilation made from a series of articles published in one of the most reliable daily newspapers in New York City and subsequently used as part of a speech in the U. S. senate, and which, so far as the Executive Council is aware has not been questioned. *Cluett, Peabody & Co.*—Net profits for 1919 were $5,153,129, an increase of 175 per cent over 1918. *International Paper Co.*—Average annual net profits for three-year period, 1916-19 increased 487 per cent over previous period, 1909-15. Aggregate common stock dividend for those three years was $74.15. *May Department Stores Co.*—Net increase in common stock earnings, 1919 over 1915, 174 per cent. *Amoskeag Mfg. Co.*—Net increase in common stock earnings, 1919 over 1917, 811 per cent in spite of decrease in business handled. *United States Rubber Co.*—Net increase in common stock earnings, 1918 over 1916, 43 per cent (1919 figures will show much more). *United Drug Co.*—Net increase in common stock earnings, 1918 over 1916, 148 per cent. *Tobacco Products Corp.*—Net increase in common stock earnings, 1918 over 1914, 1,547 per cent. *United Fruit Co.*—Net increase in common stock earnings, 1919 over 1914, 547 per cent. *Standard Milling Co.*—Net increase in common stock earnings, 1919 over 1913, 196 per cent. *American Linseed Co.*—Net increase in common stock earnings, 1919 over 1916, 780 per cent. *National Enameling & Stamping Co.*—Net increase in common stock earnings, 1916 to 1919, over 1909 to 1915, 1,178 per cent. Increase in average annual earnings for this three-year period 326 per cent, over previous seven-period year period. *General Cigar Co.*—Increase in net income, 1919 over 1917, 84 per cent. *Manhattan Shirt Co.*—Increase in net income, 1919 over 1915, 275 per cent. *American Ice Co.*—Increase in net income, 1919 over 1914, 393 per cent. *Pacific Mills.*—Increase in net income, 1919 over 1915, 218 per cent. *Burns Bros. Co.*—Increase in net income, 1919 over 1916, 72 per cent in spite of the fact that the company sold 75,000 fewer tons of coal in 1919. *American Hide & Leather Co.*—Increase in net income, 1919 over 1914, 265 per cent. *Corn Products Refining Co.*—Increase in common stock earnings, 1919 over 1915, 639 per cent. *Endicott-Johnson Corp.*—Increase in net income, 1919 over 1915, 353 per cent. *Central Leather Co.*—Increase in net income, 1919 over 1918, 103 per cent. Increase in accumulated surplus earnings, 1919 over 1914, 288 per cent. *American Woolen Co.*—Increase in net income, 1918 over 1914, 316 per cent. Net increase in common stock earnings, 531 per cent. The fact is that scarcely a day passes that does not bring to almost every family some item of increase in the cost of living—some addition to the accumulation of burden of conscience-less exploitation. Neither the government nor the employers have brought the light of wisdom to this most serious and pressing problem. The employers have clamored in unison for more production, for greater effort on the part of workers who are already weighted under the double burden of operating the machinery of production and bearing the burden of profiteering placed upon them by exploiting interests. That increased production will not solve the problem is clear, for no amount of increase in production can of itself remove the curse of profit piled upon profit. The answer to 100 per cent profits is not increased production. The answer to robbery is not mere plunder. It is no more true to say that decreased production is responsible for high prices. Neither decreased production nor increases in wages is responsible. These charges made by employers and by the enemies of labor generally are foul aspersions on labor. They have no foundation in fact. They are libels, without cause and without truth. The working people of America, in the U. S. and in Canada, are contributing full service toward the sustenance of the life of our countries. Their great eagerness is to provide for all an ample supply of the necessities and of the happiness of life and they resent with all the intensity of their being the gross injustices that are practiced by those who contribute no useful service but who stand between producer and consumer, grasping in avarice and pyramiding profit upon profit to a point that actually menaces the safety and welfare of our economic and social life. While employers have called for more production as the remedy for high prices, the U. S. government, through the department of justice, has conducted a campaign of stupidity, seeking here and there to pillory some trifling merchant, while permitting the great aggregations of capital upon which the enormous profits have been heaped to escape in the enjoyment of a monumental plunder. The campaign of the department of justice reached the heights of the ridiculous when it solemnly advised the American people to strike a fatal blow at profiteering by buying the cheaper cuts of meat. This would have constituted a voluntary reduction in standards of living. It was developed before a congressional committee that the great packing interests had cooperated in the conduct of this campaign for the purchase of cheaper cuts of meat and it was admitted by a representative of the packers that an increased demand for such cuts would speedily cause the price of them to advance. Finally, the campaign of the department of justice against the high cost of living was abandoned with the announcement that it was too costly. The government has tacitly admitted its inability to provide a remedy for the excessive cost of living. Labor has from the outset foreseen the condition in which the nation finds itself today. It long since laid bare the forces that were at work. It long since set forth remedial measures which, had they been accepted and put into operation, would have saved the republic from an agony that has wrenched at its very mainsprings of life and threatened its very foundations. The documents and declarations of the labor movement furnish an analysis proven correct by time and events. That establishes an understanding of the basis of the evil. We propose and demand enactment of the following specific proposals as constituting a program of remedy, and the only program of remedy that has been placed before the nation: 1. We demand that the government be authorized to buy standard commodities direct from producers and that these commodities be distributed through regular retail channels at a retail price to be fixed by the government. We demand that this power be made use of as a corrective for profiteering and we call attention to the fact that the government has established a precedent for such action in its sales of surplus war supplies. 2. We demand that the federal government through the internal revenue department ascertain the amount of excessive war profits extorted from the American people during the years 1916, 1917, 1918, 1919, and 1920, and that these excessive war profits be taken through its taxing power by the federal government and applied to the extinguishment of the floating debt of the government and to the partial retirement of liberty bonds at par in order that the existing inflated structure of currency and credit may be reduced and that the government may carry out its sacred obligation to the people to maintain its liberty and victory bonds at par. 3. Cooperation should be encouraged as an effective means of curbing profiteering. To stimulate rapid development of cooperatives the federal farm loan act should be extended so as to give credit to all properly organized cooperatives, just as credit is now given to individual farmers. Cooperation is no less vital and worthy of support than are the railroads, which were given hundreds of millions of dollars and an area of land equal to New England to facilitate their establishment. There should be legal enactment to protect cooperatives against discrimination by manufacturers and wholesalers. 4. Control of credit capital by those whose chief interest is the cumulation of profits results inevitably in the open door for profiteering. We repeat and emphasize the demand of organized labor that control of credit capital be taken from the hands of private financiers and placed in the hands of a public agency to be administered by voluntary and cooperative methods. 5. We urge that the U. S. department of labor compile and issue monthly statements of the cost of manufacture of those staple articles which form the basis of calculation in fixing the cost of living. 6. As a means of aiding these and other anti-profiteering measures the federal government should be authorized to establish permanent boards for the prompt investigation of profits and prices. All income and other tax returns should be available for inspection. We do not demand, nor do we desire, a precipitate collapse in prices generally, for in such a collapse there would be the greatest danger of national calamity. The program we have here laid before the nation is constructive and is practical. Because it is constructive and practical, because it contains measures native to American life and American thought, we urge and demand for it the immediate and effective consideration of the people and of the authorities of our country. (P. 384) The attention of the public in general is directed to the statistics showing the enormous profits reaped by corporations, companies and individuals dealing in the necessaries of life. It is difficult to discuss in temperate language the inordinate greed of the profiteer who has so shamelessly swollen his hoard of pelf by looting those at his mercy. The enormous and inexcusable increase in the cost of living is not due to natural conditions. It was inevitable that the intrusion of a war of such stupendous magnitude as that so lately over should have produced a general and almost cataclysmic disturbance of price levels, but when the war was over and products of labor were no longer being poured without stint or regard into the maelstrom of destruction, we might with reason have looked for such readjustment of industrial conditions as would at least have checked the upward flight of the cost of living. At the Atlantic City convention in 1919 the hope was confidently put forward that the peak of high prices had been passed. Experience has proved the contrary. At no point has the advance in wages kept pace with the advance in prices, and however strenuously the worker sought relief, he found himself hopelessly at a disadvantage in the unequal contest. (P. 478) The A. F. of L. favors the widest and fullest publicity as regards the production of and prices of all commodities offered for sale.

(1921, p. 112) Notwithstanding the most persistent urging no sentiment could be developed in the last congress for the investigation of profiteers in the necessaries of life. This encouraged the profiteers to continue their practices without fear of punishment. While wholesale prices decreased retailers continued to charge unreasonable prices. This condition has been most burdensome on the masses of the people, especially because of the large numbers of unemployed. Of all the remedies proposed none are more to be commended than those submitted to President Harding by the federal trade commission. In a report made April 18, 1921, to the president the commission upheld labor's contention that there was no justification for a reduction in wages. The commission held that "the first object should be to increase rather than lessen the purchasing power of the ordinary consumer." It also pointed out that the chief beneficiaries of high prices are the merchants and brokers. In order to force down high prices the commission recommended that it should be authorized by law to continue its efforts to obtain and publish information respecting the ownership, production, distribution, cost, sales and profits in the basic industries more directly affecting the necessaries of life, such as shelter, clothing, food, and fuel. The results of the investigation would be for the information of congress and the promotion of the public welfare. It also recommended the enactment of laws to eliminate unnecessary reconsignments and brokerage operations including gambling in

"futures." There are too many overturns between the producer and consumer, and therefore the recommendation is most practical. If the people are in full possession of all the facts of costs of distribution and the profits made on the necessaries of life public opinion would have a powerful effect in reducing prices, and there would be no necessity of prosecution under the Sherman anti-trust law. The natural development of economic laws can not be checked by legislation. Besides the Sherman anti-trust law has not been a deterrent to profiteering. Its use or rather abuse has been almost exclusively in the persecution of labor. Where corporations have been prosecuted the verdicts have helped them to continue practices which the law was intended to prohibit. The commission also recommended the encouragement of cooperative associations of agricultural producers and cooperative consumers' organizations. This would be most helpful to the farmers, but in order to be of full value to the people it should be extended to the trade unions. The same influences that are injuring the farmers and the purchasing public are also endeavoring to destroy the rights of the workers to better their economic condition. The A. F. of L. therefore believes that publicity for the results of such an investigation as is recommended by the federal trade commission would be a great factor in reducing the cost of living by compelling those who sell the necessaries of life to accept smaller profits. It is also believed that in all legislation providing for the regulation of corporations or monopolies the question of publicity should be incorporated. (P. 325) The exhaustive expert investigations and constrctive work of the federal trade commission have made it outstanding as one of the most valuable activities under government auspices. The sources and nature of the various attacks upon the commission are convincing supplementary proof of the searching character of its studies and of the effectiveness of the remedies it provides. The Executive Council is directed to make every effort to secure: 1. The authorization by law of the continuance of the work of the federal trade commission in obtaining and publishing information respecting the ownership, production, distribution, sales and profits in basic industries, more directly affecting the necessaries of life, such as shelter, clothing, food and fuel, the results of the investigation to be for the information of congress and the promotion of the public welfare. 2. The enactment of laws to limit unnecessary reconsignments and brokerage operations, including gambling in futures. 3. The encouragement of cooperative associations of agricultural producers and cooperative consumeers' organizations. 4. The inclusion of provisions for adequate publicity in all legislation dealing with the regulations of corporations and monopolies.

"Lobbying"—(1921, p. 119) Bills were introduced in the 66th congress intendeed to prohibit anyone from personally approaching a member of congress in favor or disapproval of any proposed legislation. One provides: "That it shall be unlawful for any person or any agent or counsel for any person, firm, company, corporation, or association to attempt to influence any member of congress personally and directly otherwise than by appearing before the regular committees of the congress or subcommittees thereof, or by newspaper publications, public addresses, or by written or printed statements, arguments, or briefs delivered to the members of congress."

Another contains a clause that may and can be interpreted to the injury of labor. The following sentence appears in section 5: "No person acting as such legislative agent shall have any interest in any bill contingent upon its passage." "Any interest" may mean anything, as the language used does not imply a pernicious purpose. The bills suported by the A. F. of L. are for the lercit of not only labor but all the people. Any bill that would improve the social and economic conditions of the workers, and therefore be a benefit to the representatives of the A. F. of L., would make the latter liable under the law to a fine of not less than $500 or more than $5,000 and be debarred from acting as legislative agent or counsel forever after. The bills also provide for the registration of legislative agents. There is no objection to this clause. In fact, it is most desirable. A third bill is a most drastic attempt to prohibit personal appeals to members of congress for or against legislation. These bills are evidences of the extreme reactionary policy of the last congress. Similar bills were introduced in the 67th congress. (P. 315) Congress is supposed to be fundamentally a representative body, and no artificial barriers should be erected between the members of congress and the people of the country.

(1922, p. 114) Efforts to enact a law punishing "lobbying" have been unavailing because of the un-American provisions which provide that a legislaive agent can not personally talk to a member of congress on any measure before that body.

Mailing Privileges, Newspaper—(1920, p. 120) S. 3718 provides that all publications given second-class mailing privileges must be printed in the English language if printed in the continental United States and must be originated and published for the dissemination of information of a public character, and have a legitimate list of subscribers. Trade union publications must be printed in the English language. The mailing rates proposed are: First and second zones, 2 cents a pound; third zone, 3 cents; fourth zone, 4 cents; fifth zone, 5 cents; sixth zone, 6 cents; seventh zone, 7 cents, and eighth zone, 8 cents. (P. 361) Executive Council directed to oppose the zone system. The president of the A. F. of L. said: The A. F. of L. has for years declared for a low rate of postage, a postage of 2 cents on first-class mail, a lower rate than that which obtains in the third-class mail, a low rate ofpostage for parcel post and second-class rates for newspapers and magazines, including trade union journals. The policy of the Federation upon that subject has been emphatically expressed time and again, and it was deemed unnecessary to heap precedent upon percedent, declaration upon declaration, upon a similar matter. But there is one thought, which, with others, I have endeavored to express in regard to the postal system of the United States. Some of the administrators of that great department have always desired to show a surplus, or, if not a surplus, that the department should pay for the service it renders, while others have deplored when there has been a deficit. I have insisted that it was not necessary for any department of our government doing a public service to be self-sustaining. We do not ask that the army of the United States shall be self-sustaining; we do not ask that the navy of the United States shall be self-sustaining, nor the interior department, the state department, nor the treasury department. And why the post office department? We do not even ask in our localities that the school

system shall be self-sustaining. These are great expenditures which the people make through their government, in the interest of the government to be of service to the people, and we should get away from the idea that any one particular department must be self-sustaining or conducted for profit.

Marine Transport Department—(1922, pp. 136-472) The several organizations to be affected by the formation of the Marine Transport Department were consulted as to their wishes in the matter. The A. F. of L. is convinced that the majority of the transportation organizations do not desire the formation of such a department.

Maritime Nation, U. S. A.—(1919, p. 445) The A F. of L. believes our nation should become the leading maritime nation of the world and never should be dependent again upon foreign tonnage, and to that end earnestly urges congress to adopt plans enabling the men employed in the shipyards to be constantly employed.

Maternity and Infancy—(1919, p. 429) The A. F. of L. urges congressional action directing federal cooperation with states in providing funds and in organizing and carrying forward the welfare, medical, nursing and instructional services necessary to secure reasonable care for every mother and young child.

(1921, p. 117) While the senate passed a bill providing for the public protection of maternity and infancy and providing a method of cooperation for the government of the U. S. and the several states, it failed of passage in the house although reported favorably by the committee on interstate and foreign commerce. The bill provides that congress shall be authorized to appropriate annually certain sums to be paid to the several states for promoting the care of maternity and infancy, maternal and infant hygiene and for making such studies, investigations and reports as will further the efficient administration of the proposed act. The children's bureau of the department of labor is charged with the carrying out of the provisions of the act and the chief of the children's bureau is to be the executive officer. It is a most meritorious measure. The 1919 convention of the A. F. of L. urged congress to enact a law such as that contemplated in the bill now before congress. (P. 417) Unanimously endorsed the Sheppard-Towner maternity bill and directed the Executive Council to make every effort and use every available means to the end that this meritorious bill becomes a law.

(1922, pp. 113-326) Congress enacted a law providing for the promotion of the welfare and hygiene of maternity and infancy. Forty-one states have accepted the law.

Meat Packing Monopoly—(1919, p. 127) In a letter to the president July 3, 1918, the federal trade commission reported that it had found an intricate fabric of "monopolies, controls, combinations, conspiracies and restraints." The commission said: "It appears that five great packing concerns of the country—Swift, Armour, Morris, Cudahy, and Wilson—have attained such a dominant position that they control at will the market in which they buy their supplies, the market in which they sell their products, and hold the fortunes of their competitors in their hands. The producer of live stock is at the mercy of these five companies because they control the market and the marketing facilities and, to some extent, the rolling stock which transports the product to the market. The competitors of these five concerns are at their mercy because of the control of the market places, storage facilities, and the refrigerator cars for distribution. The consumer of meat products is at the mercy of these five because both producer and competitor are helpless to bring relief." The commission found that these combinations and monopolies were made possible through the ownership or control of the stockyards, refrigerator and other special cars, warehouses and cold-storage plants. It recommended: 1. That the government acquire, through the railroad administration, all rolling stock used for the transportation of meat animals and that such ownership be declared a government monopoly. 2. That the government acquire, through the railroad administration, the principal and necessary stockyards of the country, to be treated as freight depots and to be operated under such conditions as will insure open, competitive markets, with uniform scale of charges for all services performed, and the acquisition or establishment of such additional yards from time to time as the future development of live-stock production in the United States may require. This to include customary adjuncts of stockyards. 3. That the government acquire, through the railroad administration, all privately owned refrigerator cars and all necessary equipment for their proper operation, and that such ownership be declared a government monopoly. 4. That the federal government acquire such of the branch houses, cold-storage plants, and warehouses as are necessary to provide facilities for the competitive marketing and storage of food products in the principal centers of distribution and consumption. The same to be operated by the government as public markets and storage places under such conditions as will afford an outlet for all manufacturers and handlers of food products on equal terms. Supplementing the marketing and storage facilities thus acquired, the federal government establish, through the railroad administration, at the terminals of all principal points of distribution and consumption, central wholesale markets and storage plants, with facilities open to all upon payment of just and fair charges. (P. 329) The Executive Council was directed to have a measure introduced in congress to prevent the continuation of the monopolistic control over food products exercised by the meat packers.

(1920, p. 112) The fight against the meat packing monopoly began early in the sessions of the 66th congress. During the year, however, the department of justice reached an agreement with the meat packers to the effect that they should divest themselves of ownership in the stockyards within a specified time and refrain from dealing in unrelated food products. This agreement took the force out of the demand for legislation. A bill was prepared by the A. F. of L. and introduced at the end of the long hearings by the house committee on agriculture on the various meat packers' bills, the committee was divided on the question whether or not any legislation should be recommended.

(1921, p. 109) All legislation proposing regulation of the meat packing monopoly was defeated by congress. This was accomplished by juggling by the friends of the packers in the closing days of the 66th session. S. 3944 passed the senate and was sent to the house. The house substituted H. R. 15995, which was said not to be entirely unsatisfactory to the packers. Congress adjourned, however, without action. S. 3944 provides that after two years no packer shall own or control directly or indirectly any stockyards

unless it can be proved that he has been unable to dispose of such ownership, in which case the period can be extended. This makes it possible for the packers to remain in control of the stockyards for an indefinite period, as the burden of divorcing themselves from ownership of stockyards and cars is placed upon the packers. An amendment was presented but defeated providing that the railroads should obtain control of the stockyards within two years. The bill as presented in the senate provided no penalty for non-compliance on the part of the packers with the proposed law. (P. 381) The A. F. of L. endorses and demands immediate enactment by congress of legislation to control the meat packers which shall make mandatory the adoption immediately by the meat packers of a uniform system of accounting to be prescribed by the regulatory or supervising agency created by such legislation; the early acquisition by the railroads of the principal and necessary stockyards and of all refrigerator cars and special equipment cars used for transportation of meat and meat products and perishable food products; and a system of compulsory registration of all packers engaged in the meat packing industry, of stockyard owners and of market agencies and dealers engaged in the business of buying and selling in commerce live stock at a stockyard; and further provide for governmental information and non-financial assistance to cooperative, municipal and other governmental slaughterhouses, packing plants and warehouses.

(1922, pp. 114-326) The law enacted by congress to control the meat packing industry, which was still further weakened by providing that no official engaged by the department of agriculture to administer the act be paid more than $5,000 a year. In criticizing the limiting of salaries to be paid to the officials to $5,000 Senator Kenyon declared on the floor of the senate that it would mean that competent men could not be employed to do the work and that successful enforcement of legislation would be blocked.

Metric System—(1919, p. 431) Executive Council directed to investigate the advantages of the introduction of the metric system into this country with a view to determine what further steps, such as congressional action, may be advised. (1920, p. 118) Investigation among members of congress as to the introduction of the metric system in the United States disclosed much opposition.

Mexico—(1920, p. 125) We have observed during the year just closed a recurrence of the propaganda for intervention in Mexico, which had remained quiescent during the period of the war. It is an established fact that propaganda for intervention in the affairs of our neighboring republic has been of a well-organized and generously financed character. This propaganda has had the assistance of a number of Americans formerly in the service of our government, and it has been energetically fostered by certain of our newspapers. The existence of this propaganda has made it difficult at times for the reading public to understand the exact status of internal events. The propaganda has so interfered with the free flow of accurate news as to become a menace to our international relations with Latin-America. While for the moment the acute danger of intervention in the affairs of Mexico seems to have passed, the danger will never be removed entirely so long as the organized exploiters of the oil, mineral, timber and land values in Mexico continue to conduct a propaganda devised to serve their interests, regardless of its effects upon international peace. We declare our condemnation of propaganda of this character, in the most emphatic terms, and we call upon the people of our country to be at all times warned of its existence and apprehensive of news sources and newspapers known to be colored by its activities. We declare our firm belief in, and unflinching support of, the principle long since enunciated by the American labor movement and the policies enforced by President Wilson, to the end that the Mexican people must work out their destiny in freedom and without menace from more powerful and aggressive forces seeking to advance selfish aims. We see no justification for interference in the affairs of a neighboring republic and we call attention to the harmonious relations which exist between the organized workers of Mexico and the organized workers of the U. S., as exemplified in the report of our delegates to the Pan-American Federation of Labor, submitted to this convention. We call upon our people to be of all possible assistance to the people of Mexico in working out most serious problems under most distressing circumstances. We conceive it to be our province to be of service to the people of Mexico, to make every effort to understand their difficulties and their problems and to work with them in harmony in the solution of problems common to both peoples. We are unalterably opposed to any exercise of force by the United States to satisfy the desires of those Americans whose sole interest in Mexico is the exploitation of its workers, its boundless wealth of oil and minerals. We can conceive of no greater disservice to America, or to the cause of America, than the effort to embroil two peaceful, democratic nations in international difficulties. It may be pointed out that the people of Mexico have not always in their internal affairs been able to express themselves freely and in democratic manner, and it is true that there have been grave interferences with democratic thought and expression in our neighboring republic. The greater and more important truth is, however, that in spite of tremendous obstacles and in spite of difficulties of long standing, the Mexican people have continually striven toward the establishment of democracy, toward the elevation of their standards of living and of their standards of education, and have never willingly consented to the imposition of autocratic power. We conceive it to be the high office of our free and liberty-loving nation to be of assistance to a people who have struggled so valiantly to achieve the liberties and the standards which we enjoy. We commend the course of President Wilson in his conduct of policies toward Mexico, and declare our approval and support of that policy of non-intervention and non-interference, not only in the past, but for the future. (P. 473) Unquestionably the greed of capitalist exploiters is at the bottom of the difficulties between the United States and Mexico. A full understanding of the truth by the people of both countries will frustrate the efforts of greed to embroil the two nations in conflict. Ordinarily we concede to Americans the right to invest in Mexico or in any other country, and, under ordinary circumstances Americans who do not so invest are entitled to the protection of their government. It is an accepted principle that the people of one country who emigrate from it to another are bound by the laws of the country to which they emigrate, and this principle applies equally to those who acquire titles and grants as well as those who engage in business. When there is added to such a condition the fact that much of the land to which certain adventurers obtained possession corruptly and in collusion with the previous governments of Mexico unfaithful to their people, they are not justified in having other nations of which they are citizens protect them in these corrupt practices and holdings. And where American capitalists engage in intrigue and in deliberate defiance of the law of a foreign land in which they invest, we deny that they have any just claim upon the government of the United States for its protection. There has been in the United States, as the Executive Council points out, a persistent campaign to induce intervention in Mexico by the United States. The thought back of the campaign for intervention or annexation is that ill-gotten property of Americans in Mexico will be more secure under an American protectorate or by annexation. We call attention to the unquestionable fact that the issue of intervention in Mexico will be more acute during the immediate future than it has been for some time. There are evidences of a growing determination on the part of many of those interested in Mexican investments to force the issue to a conclusion. Intervention, in one form or another, is urged and one of our great political parties has written into its platform a declaration which clearly means deep sympathy with this demand. The extent of the propaganda for intervention, the powerful backing it enjoys, and the stake of fabulous wealth for which it plays, are clearly brought out in an interesting and instructive expose of the whole situation relating to Mexico published in the June issue of 1920 of the *American Federationist*, which we commend to the attention of those seeking information on the subject. We express our deep sympathy with the Mexican people. Their trial has been severe. Their idealism has been inspiring and their tenacity of purpose in persisting in the struggle toward freedom and justice and a freer opportunity for development and expression has been evidence of a national character that eventually will force Mexico into the ranks of the ordered and orderly and advanced nations of the world. It is with satisfaction that we call attention to the fact that between the working people of the United States and Mexico there has been no misunderstanding, but that on the contrary there has been the most harmonious and complete agreement upon all matters of principle and upon all questions of human progress. They find in mutual effort a common advantage and we point out that while the workers are in harmony there is the best and surest guarantee of international harmony. We urge the Executive Council to make known as widely as possible the position of American organized labor and its understanding of the facts.

(1922, pp. 490-491) Since December, 1920, the present government of Mexico, headed by Hon. Alvaro Obregon, who was elected president by the Mexican people in what was without question the fairest and most truly popular election Mexico has ever had, has been in power and has maintained in that country a degree of public order that compares favorably with the degree of public order maintained in any other country. It is a fact beyond dispute that certain powerful groups of American capitalists have sought and are seeking through all means at their command to shape the policy of the U. S. towards Mexico in such a manner as to bring to American investors the largest possible return from their investments in Mexico without the slightest regard for the needs and the welfare of the Mexican people and the requirements of the Mexican Government for the successful administration of the public affairs and the necessary and proper conservation of the natural resources of the country. The recognition of the government of Mexico by that of our country is absolutely essential for the re-establishment of the cordial and friendly relations that should be the rule between two neighbor republics and their peoples, and inasmuch as the U. S. and Mexico will always be neighbors, the delegates to the forty-second annual convention of the A. F. of L. assembled in Cincinnati, Ohio, do hereby petition the proper authorities of the U. S. that immediate recognition be granted to the government of Mexico, of which Hon. Alvaro Obregon is president.

Migratory Workers—(1923, p. 337) The A. F. of L. directs the attention of the organized workers to a situation which has become increasingly acute. Its distressing features have been intensified by the general disturbance of social and industrial relations incident to the upheaval of affairs following the World War. We refer to the situation of the casual or migratory laborer. The St. Louis convention of 1910 directed the Executive Council to give particular attention to this great mass of unskilled labor and endeavor to perfect the international organization in accordance with the principles of the trade union movement and the laws of the A. F. of L. The Atlanta convention in 1911 reaffirmed this action as did the San Francisco convention in 1915. The Executive Council is directed to call the attention of state federations and city central bodies to the action of the various conventions with the request that steps be taken to carry out the plans then adopted.

Military Training, Compulsory—(1919, pp. 96-327) The war against the militaristic, autocratic machine of Germany would have been waged and won in vain if militarism were to be foisted upon the nations of the world. The treaty of peace ending the war has destroyed the ability of German militarism to menace the peace of the world, and with the demolition of that juggernaut the opportunity for the peoples and nations of the world to live their lives and work out their destinies unafraid is offered. There is, therefore, no longer necessity for large standing armies or for universal or compulsory military service. With the danger of militarism destroyed and the Lague of Nations established there can be no good reason for large standing armies, great navies, or stupendous munition plants, whether governmental or privately owned. We therefore urge upon our fellow workers and fellow citizens, upon the government of our republic and upon the peoples and the nations of the world, that with the coming of security in international peace we should come to a basis of the reduction of the armed forces of the world to a minimum consistent with safety and progress. The views we express upon this subject are not to be construed as opposition to proper physical training; on the contrary, we hold that the workers and the masses of the people should have the fullest and broadest opportunity for the highest physical and mental training. But we do insist that in view of the history of militaristic

propaganda and in view of the present situation and the outlook for the future, that physical training should not be confused with compulsory military service—a service thinly veiled to disguise militarism in its incipiency.

(1920, pp. 110-359) The military committees of the house and senate both proposed to include compulsory military training for all the young men of the country. As the session wore on, however, the enthusiasm for compulsory military training (conscription) receded and nothing was done. (P. 425) The A. F. of L. opposes the introduction of military training into the schools and the establisment of compulsory military service or training as unnecessary, undesirable, and un-American.

(1921, p. 116) Because of the protest made by the president of the A. F. of L. against the clause providing that in case of a "national emergency" labor could be conscripted for employment in industry in times of peace as well as in times of war, all reference to compulsory military training was stricken from the army reorganization bill. In the event of a strike on the railroads or the mines the president could declare a "national emergency" and compel the employes in those industries to remain at work no matter what grievances they might have. A subcommittee of the committee on military affairs of the house was appointed to hold hearings and study the entire question of compulsory military training and report to congress. No report, however, was made. One of the subjects to be investigated was that providing that all men between the ages of 18 and 45 years should be registered in case of a "national emergency" and assigned by the military authorities to either civil occupation or military duty. (P. 390) The A. F. of L. opposed universal compulsory military training, recognizing that the chief purposes of most of those advocating such military training is not to defend our country, but to create a militaristic spirit and to use a large standing army to defeat the purposes and aspirations of labor and of farmers to secure legitimate changes in our economic and industrial system in an orderly way and to improve their own economic status.

Miners and Lever Act—(1920, pp. 181-362) One of the chapters of the labor history of the year of greatest moment to the labor movement is that relating to the controversy between the United Mine Workers of America, the mine operators and the government of the U. S. The facts regarding this controversy are of special and peculiar importance not alone because of the economic issues involved but because of the introduction of the mandatory injunction into the struggle by the attorney general of the U. S. Having in mind the menace of the injunctive process to labor's struggle for a greater freedom and a higher standard of manhood and womanhood, the 1919 convention of the A.. F. of L. declared itself in part as follows: "The fate of the sovereignty of American people again hangs in the balance. It is inconceivable that such an autocratic, despotic and tyrannical power can long remain in a democracy. One or the other must ultimately give way, and your committee believes that this convention should declare that as wage earners, citizens of a free and democratic republic, we shall stand firmly and conscientiously on our rights as free men and treat all injunctive decrees that invade our personal liberties as unwarranted in fact, unjustified in law and illegal as being in violation of our constitutional safeguards, and accept whatever consequences may follow. Immediate steps should be taken by the Executive Council and by all state organizations for the early enactment of adequate laws to deny the further usurpation of these unwarranted powers by our courts, and that congress be petitioned to impeach all judges from office who may hereafter exercise governmental functions and authority not expressly delegated to them." The struggle of the miners, the first phase of which was brought to a climax by the use of the mandatory injunction by the government, began late in July, 1918, when the international officers of the United Mine Workers of America requested of the United States fuel administrator that representatives of the mine workers be given an opportunity to present reasons for a substantial wage increase to the bituminous coal mine workers. This request was followed in the month of August of the same year by a formal demand on the part of the organization for a wage increase. The fuel administrator, refused the request for a hearing and President Wilson, to whom the appeal was taken by the miners for an opportunity to be heard, affirmed the decision of the fuel administrator, after delaying the matter until after the signing of the armistice on November 11, 1918. Subsequent to the signing of the armistice and the cessation of actual hostilities in Europe, the mine workers in common with all others, found that the cost of the necessities of life continued to increase rapidly. Under pressure of this increase in the cost of living, the then president of the United Mine Workers of America, on March 18, 1919, called a general policy meeting of the representatives of the mine workers which was held in Indianapolis. At this meeting his recommendations for the adoption of the policy recommending demands for a six-hour workday, a substantial increase of wages and nationalization of the mines, were adopted and were presumed to constitute the recommendation of the meeting to a national convention of the United Mine Workers of America. It should be noted in connection with the steps taken by the Mine Workers at this time that price restrictions on coal had been lifted by the federal fuel administration on February 1, 1919, and that on July 1, 1919, Fuel Administrator Garfield resigned his position. These two acts served to partially release the mine operators from the provisions of the Lever act, while bringing no similar freedom to the mine workers. The convention of the United Mine Workers was held in Cleveland, Ohio, beginning on September 9, 1919. This convention gave consideration to the previous actions of the policy meeting in Indianapolis in the preceding March and by an overwhelming vote endorsed the wage demands and policies as the program of the organization. These demands were presented by the officers of the United Mine Workers to the coal operators of the central competitive field, embracing western Pennsylvania, Ohio, Indiana and Illinois, at an interstate joint conference which convened in Buffalo, N. Y., on September 26, 1919. It early became evident that the coal operators had no intentions of consummating a wage agreement with the United Mine Workers and the most earnest attempts of its officers were insufficient to negotiate a basic wage scale. The conference in Buffalo continued until October 2, 1919, and a reconvened session was held in Philadelphia from October 9 to 11, inclusive. Conditions in no wise changed and a sine die adjournment of the conference, without an agreement, was had in Philadelphia on October 11. Acting in conformity with instructions of the Cleveland convention, the president and secretary of the international union on October 15, 1919, issued a strike call to all members of the United Mine Workers of America working in the bituminous coal fields, effective at midnight, October 31, 1919. On October 21, 1919, in response to an invitation issued by Secretary of Labor William B. Wilson, the full scale representation of operators and miners met with the secretary of labor in Washington and continued in session until and including October 24. The mine workers' representatives offered to negotiate a wage scale without reservations, but were met with the insistent and reiterated demand of the operators that the strike order of October 15 be withdrawn. In view of the instructions of the miners' convention, the representatives of the miners refused to take this action and the meeting adjourned without progress. On October 25, 1919, President Wilson issued a statement to the country wherein he demanded a recall of the strike order by the United Mine Workers' officials declaring the proposed strike to be "not only unjustifiable but unlawful." This astounding action crystallized tremendous public opinion in opposition to the mine workers and the department of justice instituted injunction proceedings against the United Mine Workers in the federal courts with a view of preventing the strike. On October 31, 1919, Judge Albert B. Anderson of the federal court district in Indianapolis, upon petition of the government, issued a temporary restraining order against the officers of the United Mine Workers. This order sought to restrain them from performing any act in furtherance of the strike and prevented legitimate intercourse with their membership. On November 1, 1919, some 452,000 men ceased work in response to the strike order and in violation of the terms of the injunction. On November 8, 1919, Judge Anderson, sitting in Indianapolis, upon prayer of the government, issued a mandatory writ of injunction wherein the officers of the organization were given 72 hours to rescind the strike order. Upon issuance of the temporary restraining order issued by Judge Anderson on October 31, officers at A. F. of L. headquarters made public the following statement:

"Throughout the period of war and during the nation's time of stress, the miners of America labored patiently, patriotically and arduously in order that the principles of freedom and democracy might triumph over the forces of arbitrary authority, dictatorship and despotism. When the armed hostilities ceased last November the miners found themselves in the paradoxical position where their intensive labors were being used to further enrich the owners of coal mines and merchants dealing in coal by the immediate reduction of the mining of coal. Of course, the mine owners readily conceived that an overabundance of mined coal would seriously disturb the high prices of coal and endanger their large margin of profits. On the other hand, the miners found that with the constantly rising cost of necessities of life and with their income reduced over 50 per cent because of idleness that they had reached the limit of human endurance. Orderly and approved processes were resorted to to negotiate a new understanding with the mine owners and which would enable the miners to work at least five days during each week throughout the entire year and allow them a wage sufficient to enable them to live in decency and free from many of the pressing uncertainties of life. In attempting to negotiate this new understanding and relation the miners found that their plea for continuous employment would destroy the mine owners' arrangement to curtail the mining of coal so as to continue exploiting the public with high and exorbitant prices. The mine owners very cleverly met the issue by appearing willing and anxious to negotiate, but only if the miners would first throw aside the only power at their command to gain a respectful hearing and fair consideration—the decision to strike whenever it was demonstrated fair dealing did not prevail. We are now faced with a coal strike of vast magnitude. The government now proposes to intervene because of a possible coal shortage. Apparently the government is not concerned with the manipulation by the mine owners which has made for the present coal shortage and undue unemployment of the miners for the past 11 months."

Instead of dealing with those responsible for this grave menace to the public welfare, it now proposes to punish those who by force of circumstances have been the victims of the coal barons' exploitations. The miners are now told the war is not over and that all war legislation is still in force and if reports received are correct, the government intends to apply existing war measures not against the owners of the coal mines, but against the coal miners. The government has taken steps to enforce war measures by an injunction and it has restrained the officials of the United Mine Workers from counselling, aiding, or in any way assisting the members of the organization for relief against grievous conditions of life and employment. It is almost inconceivable that a government which is proud of its participation in a great war to liberate suppressed peoples should now undertake to suppress the legitimate aims, hopes and aspirations of a group of its own people. It is still more strange that a nation which may justly be proud of its Abraham Lincoln should now reverse the application of the great truth he enunciated when he said that as between capital and labor, labor should receive first and foremost consideration. The injunction against the United Mine Workers bodes for ill. An injunction of this nature will not prevent the strike—it will not fill the empty stomachs of the miners—it may restrain sane leadership, but will give added strength to unwise counsel and increase bitterness and friction. This injunction can only result in creating new and more disturbing issues which may not be confined solely to the miners. These views were presented to Attorney General Palmer.

On November 5, the following telegram was sent by the president of the A. F. of L. to members of the Executive Council with the exception of William Green, secretary of the United Mine Workers: "In view of critical labor situations in the judgment of Vice-President Woll, Secretary Morrison and myself requiring immediate consideration and action of E. C., under authority of Section 4, Article 6, of Constitution of A. F. of L., I invite the members of the E. C. to meet in A. F. of L. Building at Washington at 10.30 o'clock Sunday morning, November 9, 1919. Members of E. C. are strongly urged to be in attendance." The purpose in not sending a copy of the telegram to Vice-President Green was to avoid causing him unnecessary embarrassment. Labor's view of the use of the injunctive process to which the government had resorted in the case of the mine workers, was conveyed to the attorney general in detail and earnest protest was entered. It was pointed out that the Lever act under which the court proceedings were being brought was not intended to apply to strikes or lockouts and it was urged that the restraining order and the injunction be withdrawn and that the miners be called into conference with the operators and an effort made to negotiate a settlement. In accordance with the summons above quoted, the Executive Council met in Washington on November 9 and formulated its views in a declaration which was then made public. Emphasis was laid upon the menace contained in the introduction of the mandatory injunction into industrial disputes, and the pledges given that the provisions of the Lever act under which Judge Anderson was operating, would not be used in cases of strikes or lockouts, were set forth in detail. The declaration adopted by the Executive Council follows: "The Executive Council of the A. F. of L. called into special session in the city of Washington for the express purpose of considering the coal strike, the conditions which brought on the strike, as well as the court proceedings brought by the government, submit to our fellow citizens and to our fellow workers the following statement: The Executive Council is of the opinion that the officers of the United Mine Workers of America did everything in their power to avert this great industrial controversy. Of all the great industries in our country, there is none so dangerous to human life as the coal industry. The men who go down under the ground to dig coal, so that the domestic and industrial needs of the nation may be supplied, are engaged in work more hazardous than any other employment. Due consideration has never been given to the danger surrounding the coal miners. There is no other class of employment where each individual worker is so isolated and in whose districts there is such a lack of opportunity for social intercourse and enjoyment. The condition of the miner and his family is such that he is practically deprived not only of sunshine and fresh air, but to a certain extent he is deprived of the association and companionship of all other human beings outside of his own particular class who are themselves engaged in the dangerous and unhealthy occupation of coal mining. The miners suffer more than any other workers from periods of compulsory unemployment. Authentic statistics show that the miners have less than 200 days of employment during each year. The wages of the miners, consequently, having to spread over the entire year, are greatly reduced as a result of the non-employment existing in that industry. The high cost of living has presented itself in perhaps a more serious form in isolated mining camps than in large industrial centers. There is usually not the same opportunity for the miners in the mining camps to make their purchases to such advantage as is presented in other localities. Their isolation prevents this. The United Mine Workers in their convention, held during the month of September in the city of Cleveland, adopted a positive declaration demanding improved conditions of employment for the miners. They further instructed the officers to proceed to obtain by negotiations with the operators the working conditions that the convention unanimously adopted. There were almost 2,200 delegates seated in the convention, representing 500,000 organized miners. They further positively and explicitly instructed their officers that unless an agreement was reached on or before the first day of November, 1919, that the resolution of the convention calling for a strike on November 1, 1919, should be communicated to the membership. There was no alternative except for the officers, who are elected by the membership, to carry out the direct instructions of the membership or resign from their positions as officers, in which event chaos and confusion would result. The officers of the Mine Workers, with their scale committee, entered into conferences and discussions with the operators in the city of Buffalo. They stated at the conference that they had full power to negotiate an agreement; in other words, that they had the power to give and take in the conference. The employers refused to make any offer whatever. Later on the miners answered the call of the secretary of labor and further endeavored to reach an agreement, but failed. The officers then proceeded to carry out the instructions of their membership and communicated the results of the failure of negotiations, and by order of the convention the strike automatically took effect November 1, 1919. The machinery which has existed for years and which has been successful in bringing about agreements between the miners and the operators still exists, and they as representatives of the miners were and are ready and willing to enter into negotiations without reservation to reach an agreement. At this time our government interjected itself and applied for an injunction. A temporary restraining order was granted by a federal judge which restrains the officials of the miners from in any way advising their membership on the situation, or contributong any of the moneys of the mine workers to the assistance of the men on strike, also restraining them from discussing, writing or entering into any kind of a conversation with their membership on che strike situation. The government then proceeded to further invade the rights of the miners, not only by restraining the miners, their officers and members from furthering the purpose for which the men contended, but went to further lengths of demanding from the court an order commanding the officers of the miners' union to recall and withdraw the strike notification, and the court complacently complied and issued the order. Never in the history of our country has any such mandatory order been obtained or even applied for by the government or by any person, company or corporation. Both the restraining order and the injunction, in so far as its prohibitory features are concerned, are predicated upon the Lever act, a law enacted by congress for the purpose of preventing speculation and profiteering of the food and fuel supplies of the country. There never was in the minds of the congress in enacting that law or in the mind of the president when he signed it, that the Lever act would be applied to workers in cases of strikes or lockouts. The food controller, Mr. Hoover, specifically so stated. Members of the committee having the bill in charge have in writing declared that it was not in the minds of the committee, and the then attorney general, Mr. Gregory, gave assurance that the government would not apply that law to the workers' effort to obtain improved working conditions. Every assurance from the highest authority of our government was given that the law would not be so applied. In the course of President Wilson's address to the Buffalo convention of the A. F. of L., November, 1917, among other things, he said:

"'While we are fighting for freedom, we must see among other things that labor is free, and that means a number of interesting things. It means not only that we must do what we have declared our purpose to do, see that the conditions of labor are not rendered more onerous by the war, but also that we shall see to it that the instrumentalities by which the conditions of labor are improved are not blocked or checked. That we must do.'

"The autocratic action of our government in these proceedings is of such a nature that it staggers the human mind. In a free country to conceive of a government applying for and obtaining a restraining order prohibiting the officials of a labor organization from contributing their own money for the purpose of procuring food for women and children that might be starving is something that when known will shock the sensibilities of men and will cause resentment. Surely the thousands of men who are lying in France, under the soil, whose blood was offered for the freedom of the world, never dreamed that so shortly afterwards in their own country 450,000 workers endeavoring to better their working conditions, would have the government decide that they were not entitled to the assistance of their fellow men and that their wives and children should starve, by order of the government. It is a well-established principle that the inherent purpose of the injunction processes, where there is no other adequate remedy at law, is for the purpose of protecting property and property rights only, thereby exercising the equity power of the court to prevent immediate and irreparable injury. It was never intended and there is no warrant of the law in all our country to use the injunction power of equity courts to curtail personal rights or regulate personal relations. It was never intended to take the place of government by law by substituting personal and discretionary government. The Lever act provides its own penalties for violators of its provisions. The injunction issued in this case has for its purpose not a trial by court and a jury, but an order of the court predicated upon the assumption that the law might be violated and by which the defendants may be brought before the court for contempt and without any trial by jury. We declare that the proceedings in this case are unwarranted, as they are unparalleled in the history of our country, and we declare that it is an injustice which not only the workers but all liberty-loving Americans will repudiate and demand redress. The citizenship of our country can not afford to permit the establishment or maintenance of a principle which strikes at the very foundation of justice and freedom. To restore the confidence in the institutions of our country and the respect due the courts, this injunction should be withdrawn and the records cleansed from so outrageous a proceeding. By all the facts in the case the miners' strike is justified. We endorse it. We are convinced of the justice of the miners' cause. We pledge to the miners the full support of the A. F. of L. and appeal to the workers and the citizenship of our country to give like endorsement and aid to the men engaged in this momentous struggle."

In addition to the adoption of the statement made public, it was the unanimous decision of those in attendance at the meeting that a circular be issued in the name of the Executive Council of the A. F. of L. to all national and international unions, state federations of labor, city central bodies and local unions, the organizers, and the labor press, calling upon all to give every support to the miners' strike and to the miners' cause. Reconvening on Tuesday, the Executive Council received the information through the press that a conference called by the president of the United Mine Workers of America had, after a session lasting 17 hours, decided that the order of the court be complied with; which was that the strike order of October 15, 1919, be withdrawn. Later the following telegram was received by the president of the A. F. of L.: "Miners' conference met yesterday morning 10 a. m., and remained in session until 4.30 this morning. Sixteen districts expressed their opposition to continuing the strike in defiance of our government with all its civil and military forces arrayed against us and that we should prove again that the mine workers of our country are law-abiding citizens notwithstanding that they feel keenly the wrong perpetrated against them. President Lewis desired me to convey to you the information that under those circumstances it was absolutely necessary in order to save our organization from disruption that he should comply with the order of the court to rescind the strike order. There was no other reason that would have compelled him to take such action." The executive officers of the mine workers' organization on November 11 signed an order rescinding the strike order of October 15. Following the receipt of the telegram the Executive Council formulated the following as the expression of its views: "The Executive Council of the A. F. of L., reviewing his record, expresses the opinion that it was misled by the officers of the United Mine Workers of America and their representatives as to the attitude they would take in the strike and the injunction. The Executive Council declares that in so far as the incident and the fact is concerned the officers of the United Mine Workers of America have dealt with it as their judgment warranted, but in the principles involved by the restraining order and the injunction and the mandatory order in connection therewith the A. F. of L. will proceed as a matter of principle, right and freedom of the workers of America to contest every inch of the ground until freedom shall again be reestablished." Notwithstanding the rescinding order, the strike continued and on December 3, 1919, upon information brought by, government attorneys in the federal court Judge Anderson cited for contempt 84 officers of the United Mine Workers whose arrests followed immediately. Bail in the sum of $10,000 each was required for their appearance in court on December 9. On December 6 the president and secretary of the United Mine Workers went to Washington, upon the solicitation of the government, and a proposal for the settlement of the strike was advanced upon honorable premise. This arrangement provided for an adjudication of the claims of the mine workers by a coal commission, upon which the mine workers would be given representation. It further provided that the commission would asume the powers of the United States fuel administrator and resulted in the elimination of Dr. H. A. Garfield. It further provided for the immediate application of a 14 per cent increase upon all wage schedules. This arrangement was accepted by the representatives of the mine workers in conference in Indianapolis on December 10. Orders were immediately issued for the return of all men to work under

this arrangement and the strike officially terminated. Mining operations were promptly resumed and the coal crisis ended. On December 19, 1919, President Wilson appointed Henry L. Robinson, Rembrandt Peale and John P. White as members of the bituminous coal commission. On January 5 to 7, inclusive, a reconvened session of the international convention was assembled at Columbus, Ohio, and the policy of the officers of the organization in accepting the peace terms proposed by the president was affirmed by a vote of 1,638 delegates in the affirmative to 221 delegates in the negative. On January 12, 1920, the bituminous coal commission commenced its hearings at the American Red Cross Building, Washington, D. C. On March 11, 1920, Messrs. Robinson and Peale, members of the bituminous coal commission, submitted the majority report of the commission to President Wilson. On March 13, 1920, Mr. John P. White submitted his minority report as a member of the bituminous coal commission to President Wilson. On March 23 the president of the United States in a public statement endorsed the findings of the majority members of the bituminous coal commission and addressed a communication to the operators and miners directing them to consummate a wage agreement with the commission's report as its basis. On March 31, 1920, the joint interstate conference of operators and miners assembled in New York and formally signed a wage scale agreement for the central competitive field, extending from April 1, 1920, to March 31, 1922. This agreement provides for an increase of 24 cents per ton upon mining rates throughout the United States, pick and machine mined coal, with a 20 per cent increase in rates paid for yardage and dead work. It further provides for an increase of $1 per day to day workers and monthly men in all classifications. The tonnage rate increase in the central competitive field is the equivalent of 30.7 per cent increase. In the coal producing sections south of the Ohio River, comprising the states of West Virginia, Kentucky, Tennese and Alabama, the increase approximated 45 per cent. In application to the tonnage schedules of the bituminous coal producing districts of the country as a whole the increase is equivalent to 35 per cent. Attention is called to the paramount fact that the action of the court at Indianapolis in introducing the mandatory injunction into the dispute between the miners and the operators leaves before the organized labor movement and the workers of the United States in general an issue which can not be evaded and an issue which can never be settled until it is settled in such a manner as to restore the liberties and the freedom which have been destroyed. So long as it is possible for courts to assume the power and the authority assumed by the federal courts in Indianapolis, so long will it be possible for judges throughout the land to suspend and nullify rights guaranteed in the constitution of the United States, rights without which democracy is crippled and incomplete. The declaration of the convention of 1919 and the determination there expressed is reaffirmed. The rights that have been called into question and which have been abrogated by a federal court must be restored and made safe beyond further attack. The liberties of the people of the United States must be protected no matter what the hazard and no matter what the cost. Upon such rights as those which were called into question by Judge Anderson rest the foundations of the American republic. We further call attention to the betrayal of pledges on the part of those charged with the duty of upholding the law, in connection with the issuance of the injunction against the United Mine Workers. We called attention to a portion of an interview with Representative Lever, the author of the food bill under which the injunction was issued, which appeared in the New York *Times* of May 20, 1917: "Never was such a drastic bill drawn. The president had given his word that it is only a war measure and that it ceases to be in effect when the war is over. It is framed simply to safeguard the nation's food supply for its own use and for whatever we can do for our allies while we are *fighting the war out*." When the bill came up for action, Representative Keating, on behalf of labor, urged an amendment providing that nothing in section 4 should be construed as repealing sections 6 and 20 of the Clayton act. June 22, 1917, this debate was held in the house between Representatives Lever and Keating, as reported by the *Congressional Record*, page 4396:

Mr. Lever: "We do not believe, and the matter was thoroughly discussed in the committee on agriculture, that this section in anywise serves to repeal or amend in the least particular either the Clayton anti-truth act or any other act which deals with the right of men to strike for purposes of increasing their wages or bettering their living conditions. We do not believe that this affects that in the least."

Mr. Keating: "Let us get the issue cleared up. Let us get a concrete case. Suppose that men engaged in work on the railroads of the country—we will say, the telegraph operators on a particular line in this country—decided to strike. Is it the object of the gentlemen, and is it the object of this bill, that the power shall be vested in some one to compel those men to go back to work? Let us face the issue squarely, and if this is not your purpose, why not adopt this amendment?"

Mr. Lever: "I am glad to face the issue squarely. If there were such a combination to strike for the purpose of bettering living conditions or increasing wages there is no purpose in this bill, and there is no authority in this bill, to prevent it."

The following day this statement was made by Representative Keating: "Mr. Chairman, this amendment is the one I offered the other day to section 4 of this bill. At that time I made it apply exclusively to section 4. In its present form it applies to the entire bill. When my amendment was before the house the other day the contention was made that I was seeking to have farmers' organizations and labor organizations exempted from the operation of this bill. I want to impress on the members of the house that I am not seeking any exemption for any class. Neither the farmers nor the members of labor organizations, so far as this amendment is concerned, are granted exemption from the provisions of the bill. The sole object of this amendment is to clarify the bill. The chairman of the committee on agriculture has assured us that it was not the purpose of the framers of the bill to interfere in any way with section 6 and section 20 of the Clayton anti-trust law. Mr. Hoover, who will be called upon to administer this act, in a conference held a week or two ago with representatives of all the great labor organizations of the country, confirmed this view and suggested the amendment which I have offered. On that point the chairman of the committee on agriculture (Mr. Lever) has requested

me to read the following memorandum which he has received from Mr. Hoover: 'Washington, D. C., June 22, 1917. Memorandum for Mr. Lever. The labor representatives are very much exercised over the possible reading of the food control bill to stretch to control of wages, and they suggest that an amendment may be made providing that the labor provisions of the Clayton act should not be affected by the proposed bill. I understand that Mr. Keating proposed this amendment and it was defeated. It appears to me that there is no intention in the bill to interfere and I believe it might silence a great deal of criticism and opposition which might be raised in the senate if this amendment could be undertaken. I do not wish to impose my views upon you, but simply to suggest that as it is not the intention of the bill to regulate wages, it might do no harm to satisfy this element in the community that they are immune from attack.'"

On Monday, August 6, 1917, this statement regarding the right of labor to strike was made in the senate (*Congressional Record*, Monday, August 6, 1917, page 6403): "Mr. Chamberlain (senator in charge of the bill): Mr. President, there is not anything in the act, it seems to me, that would prevent labor organizations from peaceful picketing or the peaceful strike if they see fit to indulge in it; and, while as I said, I did not vote against the senator's amendment, and I do not recall having been with the conferees when it was receded from, I would not have hesitated to do so in conference, because I think it unnecessary. It was insisted upon by the senate conferees for quite a while and finally went out. I really do not know how many days it had been in conference before the senate conferees finally receded. But, Mr. President, I have not any fear that in the administration of the food law anything would be attempted by the president or by the agencies which he has power to create under the act to prevent any labor or other organization from doing in a peaceful way all that they can now do under the Clayton law to protect themselves and their rights without any saving clause in the bill under consideration. It is not necessary in this bill in order to protect rights." Other conferences were had by the president and secretary of the A. F. of L., among them conferences with Secretary of Labor Wilson and the then Attorney General Gregory. In each case the assurances were repeated; the attorney general gave the assurance that he would write to the district attorneys not to construe section 4 as interfering in any way with the normal activities of labor. During the debate in the senate August 8, the following dialogue took place (page 6481, *Congressional Record*):

"Mr. Husting: I voted for the Hollis amendment to the bill, which provided that the provisions of the bill should not be construed to prevent strikes or peaceful picketing or in any way amend or repeal the provisions of the Clayton act. I would not favor the clause striking out this amendment if I thought it had that effect. I do not think it has that effect. I was sufficiently interested, however, in the argument made by the senator from New Hampshire, and by arguments already made upon the legal effect of striking out the Hollis amendment, to inquire from those who will have the administration of this law in their hands as to what construction would be placed upon it by them in the event that it became a law in its present form. I am authorized by the secretary of labor, Mr. Wilson, to say that the administration does not construe this bill as prohibiting strikes and peaceful picketing and will not so construe the bill, and that the department of justice does not so construe the bill and will not so construe the bill."

"Mr. Reed: Will the senator then say to us why the amendment which would have removed any necessity for construction, or any doubt, was stricken out?"

"Mr. Husting: I can not answer that question with authority, but I understand it was stricken out because it was not thought necessary or essential, that it had no effect whatever. I think it would have been wiser to have left it in, but it was stricken out, I understand, upon the argument that it could not legally be construed in that way and that it was surplusage or redundancy."

"Mr. Reed: Has the senator talked with the attorney general?"

"Mr. Husting: I will say that I have not. I have not talked with the attorney general. However, I can say that the secretary of labor advised me that this was the opinion of the administration and the department of justice. He did not give it merely as a matter of belief on his part, but said that he was authorized to so state."

"Mr. Reed: Now may I ask one further question? Suppose that a complaint should be filed in a court of the United States charging a violation of this act, and that the case was lodged in court, and the judge of the court should hold that under the charge made a violation of the law had occurred, is the senator prepared to say to the country that the attorney general has stated that under such circumstances as that he would nullify the law and undertake to control the court?"

"Mr. Husting: Mr. President, I can not say anything further than what I have already said. I do not presume any United States district attorney will prosecute any person under this law contrary to the interpretation placed upon the law itself by a superior officer."

"Mr. Lewis: I am advised that the provisions we placed in the federal trade commission act in the closing days of its consideration to the effect that there shall not be prosecution of farmers' organizations or members thereof or of labor organizations or members thereof for any of the acts to which we particularly addressed ourselves as criminal concerning commercial bodies, would exclude the prosecutions of which the senator from New Hampshire had such a sincere fear."

"Mr. Husting: Mr. President, that is my belief. I will say to the distinguished senator from Illinois, that is my view of it; and not only as it my view, but as I said before, it is the view of the administration, and I am advised is also the view of the department of justice and of every eminent and able attorney on the floor."

That a promise had been made that a separate bill embodying the amendment that the law should not "modify or amend or repeal the Clayton act" is established in the following statement made in the senate August 8, 1917 (page 6482, Congressional Record):

"Mr. Husting: But it appears here from the debate that many senators have taken the view that this measure does not modify, or amend or repeal the Clayton act. So the action of many senators and their votes will be based upon the assumption that it does not so modify amend or repeal that act, and the fact that others do think so will have no other effect than to put their opinion against the opinion of those who believe otherwise. If

there is any division of opinion here upon the question of what effect this proposed legislation will have on the anti-trust laws let a bill be introduced embodying the Hollis amendment and let it go through both houses, as I think it will, without much opposition. Then all uncertainty will be swept away. But notwithstanding that this bill is not exactly as I would have it if I had the writing of it, it is necessary to pass this bill at once."

While the discussion over the Hollis amendment was at its height the supreme court gave an opinion in the case of the Paine Lumber Company vs. Neal. It was held by the court that private individuals could not institute legal proceedings under anti-trust legislation. This encouraged the officials of labor in the belief that the striking out of the Hollis amendment would not work to the injury of labor, as only the government could institute prosecutions and the government had given assurance it would not. And as the president and the attorney general of the United States has said there would be no prosecutions by the department of justice, labor felt safe. In view of the use to which the writ of injunction was put in the case of the miners, and in view of the clear violation of pledges on the part of representatives of the United States government, both legislative and executive, special importance is given to the national non-partisan political campaign now being waged. It is vitally necessary for the preservation of the rights, liberties and freedom of the working people of the United States that no effort be spared to defeat at the polls those who have proven not only their enmity to the interests of the great masses of our people, but their absolute and complete failure to comprehend the welfare of the republic. Few charges more serious than those here raised have been brought against officials in the public life of our country. In this case the workers have been compelled to suffer from disruption of their liberties at the hands of those charged with safeguarding their liberties, and to suffer in addition as the result of the betrayal of pledges solemnly given while our nation was at war and solemnly accepted by a labor movement given heart and soul to the cause in which the nation was struggling, the cause of human freedom, the cause of democracy, the cause of humanity everywhere, in the United States no less than in other countries.

(1921, p. 113) The Lever act, which was used almost exclusively to persecute labor, was repealed by the 66th congress. There was much opposition to its repeal. This was accomplished only after persistent agitation by representatives of the A. F. of L. Within 24 hours after the repeal the United States supreme court declared the Lever act unconstitutional on an appeal instituted by a convicted food profiteer. While originally intended to punish the profiteers it failed of this purpose and was used to prevent the wage earner from seeking adequate wages and improved working conditions.

Miners, Courts, Labor—(1921, pp. 71-373) The workers of America have been forced to defend their rights and to prevent encroachments upon their liberties not alone in the law courts, but also in the equity divisions of the courts. They have been required likewise to meet assaults intended for the weakening and destruction of the trade union movement and the annulment of the right of collective bargaining in the criminal branch of our courts. The most conspicuous examples of these attempts to stigmatize the trade union movement as a criminal conspiracy and to outlaw the right of wage earners to bargain for their services on equitable terms acceptable to themselves are those directed against the United Mine Workers of America. On October 31, 1919, Judge A. B. Anderson of the federal court at Indianapolis, at the suit of Attorney General Palmer, issued an order restraining the officials of the United Mine Workers of America from maintaining a strike which had been previously ordered by the regular biennial convention of the organization. The bill of complaint filed by the government was expressly based on Sec. 4 of the Lever act as authority for the interposition of the government and the court. Upon the hearing a temporary injunction was issued extending the restraining order so as mandatorily to require the officials of the union to recall the strike order. Despite compliance with this decree by the officials who were defendants to the action, many members of the union refused to return to work until the subsequent appointment of the bituminous coal commission, created by President Wilson for the determination of a new wage scale. Before this commission was agreed upon the government filed criminal informations against the officials of the union charging them with disobeying the injunction. Upon the creation of the national bituminous coal commission the government recommended the indefinite postponement of the hearing of these criminal informations, and they have since remained upon the court docket with the defendants under bond. Since then the supreme court of the United States in the profiteering cases, has declared Sec. 4 of the Lever act invalid, and by the act of congress of March 3, 1921, all these war-time measures have been expressly repealed and terminated. On March 11, 1920, the federal grand jury at Indianapolis returned a bill of indictment against the officials of the United Mine Workers and of its district organizations in Indiana, Ohio, Illinois, and western Pennsylvania, including members of its joint scale commission, in which indictment were also included, as defendants, operators of this field who had entered into wage-scale agreements with the union. This indistment was in 18 counts, 13 of which were based on Sec. 4 of the Lever act and the remaining five based on Sec. 9 of that act. Upon a hearing Judge Anderson quashed the counts based upon Sec. 4 on the ground (afterwards sustained in the profiteering cases by the United States supreme court) that the language of the section was too vague and indefinite to define a criminal offense. The remaining five counts of the indictments based on Sec. 9 were sustained and were set for trial November 8, 1920. At this date the further consideration of this indictment was continued indefinitely, and on February 25, 1921, the federal grand jury for the district of Indiana, returned a new indictment in five counts based on Secs. 1 and 2 of the Sherman act. The officials of the miners were again indicted together with the operators of the central competitive field who had met the miners in joint wage-scale conferences. In this indictment the defendants are charged with having conspired together, in their respective groups in their joint wage-scale agreements unduly to restrain trade and to monopolize trade in coal. Motions to quash this indictment have been filed and are now pending. Notwithstanding that the matters alleged in the last indictment cover and include all the matters complained of in the indictment pending under Sec. 9 of the Lever act,

the latter indictment has not been dismissed.

Miners, Injunctions Against—(1922, pp. 40-371) One of the most flagrant abuses of equity power was that manifested by Judge A. B. Anderson in issuing an injunction against the United Mine Workers of America at the request and behest of the mine owners of West Virginia. In the case of the Borderland Coal Co. et al. *vs.* The United Mine Workers, the mine owners of West Virginia not only sought to prevent the unionizing of the mines in West Virginia, but they attempted to secure a blanket injunction covering 62 other mine operators of non-union mines in the Williamson District, W. Va., who had not applied in their own behalf for a like injunction. In this particular case the mine owners of West Virginia not only sought to have Judge Anderson prevent a trespass upon their mining properties or to prevent violation of individual contracts of employments with non-union miners, but the effort was made to annul the collective agreement between the United Mine Workers of America and the operators in the central competitive field and to have the United Mine Workers dissolved or enjoined from functioning on the ground that this trade union is a seditious and otherwise unlawful organization. While Judge Anderson declined to hold the United Mine Workers a seditious organization, he nevertheless declared it unlawful for the United Mine Workers to organize the mine workers of West Virginia. He attempted also to enjoin the continuance of the agreement then existing between the United Mine Workers and the mine owners of the central competitive field. Because a small portion of West Virginia and a small section of the southwestern part of the country had not been organized, Judge Anderson held that an attempt to unionize the West Virginia mines was in effect an effort to monopolize the coal industry and that, therefore, the purpose of the United Mine Workers was an illegal one and that all efforts to that end must be enjoined. This he attempted to do by an injunction. To all intents and purposes this judicial decree was of equal, if not greater, force than a legislative declaration that it is unlawful to organize all wage earners of a certain trade or industry into a trade union and that employers must at all times be assured a non-union market of workmen even though our national congress has declared that labor organizations are lawful institutions and that the wage earners of America may organize without such limitations and restraints as Judge Anderson attempted to impose upon the workers by his personal dictum in this case. Not satisfied with having restrained the United Mine Workers of America, its officers, agents, representatives and members from making lawful union arguments and lawful union speeches to the pool of non-union workers, and not content with trying to prevent them from using lawful persuasion to induce non-union miners to join the unions by openly severing their relations of employment to join the union, not in violation of but in exact and legal accordance with their contracts of employment, Judge Anderson also enjoined the enforcement of the performance of then existing contracts between the operators of union mines and the United Mine Workers in the central competitive field with respect to what is called the "check-off" system. Thus he (Judge Anderson) attempted to do indirectly that which he dared not to do directly; that is, to dissolve the United Mine Workers as a seditious and unlawful organization. It matters little whether Judge Anderson declared the United Mine Workers of America an unlawful organization if the same end would be accomplished equally well by declaring all of its activities and functions as being unlawful. This tragic overreaching of judicial power inflamed the passions of men everywhere throughout the country. Confronted with the possibility of a complete stoppage of mining throughout the land and under circumstances that threatened to impress the entire public mind with the despotic and tyrannical development of the exercise of equity powers by our courts, the appeal of the United Mine Workers of America to the United States court of appeals received immediate attention and action and Judge Anderson's injunction was suspended. The appellate court of the United States, in its decision, confirmed the dangers which organized labor has constantly directed to public attention and which have been permitted to grow without check or hindrance. That court declared that Judge Anderson had gone too far and thereby confirmed the charge that an injudicious and prejudicial temperament governs our courts today in the issuance of injunctions in industrial disputes. Speaking particularly of the contracts then existing between the operators of union mines and the United Mine Workers in the central competitive field and the check-off system declared unlawful by Judge Anderson, the appellate court said:

"So far as the contracts themselves and this record disclose, the check-off is the voluntary assignment of the employe of so much of his wages as may be necessary to meet his union dues and his direction to his employer to pay the amount to the treasurer of his union. In that aspect the contract provision is legal; and quite evidently there are many lawful purposes for which dues may be used. If in truth the bargaining with respect to the contract was not free, if either the employe or the employer put the other under duress, the injured party might have cause to seek cancellation. (But if he had nothing to urge in the way of duress except "economic necessity," he might not succeed.) If in bargaining one of the parties was not free by reason of the greatly preponderant power of the other the legislatures of these central states and the congress might consider whether public interest required or justified the limitation of the otherwise existent freedom of contract by abolishing the check-off as a subject-matter of contract, in similitude to the legislative abolition of truck stores, dangerous appliances, unsanitary working places, exhausting hours, etc., as permissible subject-matters of contract. But appellee is not a party to the contract, is not the attorney of either contracting party, and is not the agency to establish the public welfare. If nothing else should prevent appellee's being given that part of the decree now under consideration, the llack of injury to appellee by the existence of the check-off contracts would suffice. The injury to appellee's property rights in interstate commerce, of which appellee was apprehensive, was that it would be coerced into paying the high costs of production prevalent in the central competitive field and thus be unable to meet, or at least to meet so profitably the existent competition in interstate commerce. As long as appellee is assured, as it now is, that it will have full protection in operating its closed non-union mine and in marketing its coal in interstate commerce without interference, appellee should rather pray that all the elements causing high cost of production in the central competitive field should be maintained. But appellee insists that it is entitled to have the performance of the existent check-off contracts enjoined, because the check-off is the "heart" of the United Mine Workers' organization. Appellee is confusing a series of remote causations with the proximate cause of the injury. The only property that was injured was appellee's freedom in operating its mine and in putting its coal onto cars in West Virginia to be shipped in interstate commerce. The proximate cause of the injury was the described interferences in the Williamson District with appellee's aforesaid right to freedom. Without direct and immediate interfering acts, the desires and intents of the conspirators in the central competitive field would have been innocuous. In the series of causations the check-off provision was undoubtedly one of the elements. Manifestly unless money was collected, the union's executive officers could not send it into West Virginia to aid or promote the interfering acts. But in the same contracts that contain the check-off feature were provisions for the payment of wages and the recognition of the miners as human beings with the physical capacity to labor. On a parity with appellee's contention respecting the check-off element, all the other elements in the series of causation leading up to the proximate cause should also be enjoined. Money could not be sent into West Virginia by the executive officers, unless it was collected from the miner's wages; nor unless the miners earned wages; nor unless the miners were human beings having the capacity to labor. From the record as it now stands we are convinced that the district court committed substantial errors in exercising its judicial discretion in the following particulars: (1) In not confining the grant of relief to appellee; (2) in not limiting the prohibition of the unionization or attempted unionization of appellee's mine to the threatened, direct and immediate interfering acts shown by the bill and affidavits; (3) in not limiting the prohibition of the sending of money into West Virginia to the use thereof in aiding or promoting the interfering acts; and (4) in enjoining the performance of the existent check-off contracts in the central competitive field."

This is but one of the many instances of the injudicious discretion our courts are permitted to exercise through the injunction writ in industrial disputes. The record is replete with class-biased errors committed by our judges in the interests of employers and against the rights and freedom of the wage earners. That in this instance the appellate court reversed Judge Anderson in some of the most drastic provisions of his decree is not a vindication of the injunction process or assurance that the rights and freedom of the wage earners are protected. To the contrary, this decision is but accumulative evidence of the growing arrogance and a greater and more flagrant usurpation of authority by the judiciary of our land.

Judge McClintic's Injunction Against the Miners—(Page 42) In the state of West Virginia there were some 90,000 men engaged in the coal industry. Until the recent national suspension 50,000 of those men were working under trade agreements between the operators and the United Mine Workers' Union; but in the southeastern section of that state about 40,000 miners were situated in isolated communities and held in leash by a system of peonage and bondage which find s its equal only in that condition of affair s which prevailed among the colored race before the emancipation proclamation. In Mingo county, which is one of the counties affected by this condition nearly a year and a half ago the miners joined the United Mine Workers' Union. The next day 168 mines were closed down and the workers locked out because they refused to work unless their right to remain union men was fully recognized. Since that time many outrages have been committed in the homes and upon the persons of the people in that section of the country and nothing was left undone by the operators and their hirelings to brow-beat and dishearten the miners and to force them into a humiliating submission. As is common in many mining communities the homes of the locked-out miners were either owned or controlled by the operators and stores were likewise owned or controlled by them. Unable to break the ranks of the miners in any other way, the miners were refused credit at these stores and eviction proceedings were resorted to in the most inhumane fashion. The miners and their families were thrown out into the streets without food or shelter. To prevent undue misery, suffering, sickness and starvation and to furnish shelter to the miners and their families the United Mine Workers proceeded to lease several acres of ground and to erect tents as well as to provide food and clothing and other essentials of life. Again frustrated in their attempt to discourage the locked-out miners the operators applied to and received from the courts an injunction requiring the miners not to maintain but to destroy the tent colonies; prohibiting the transmission by the officers of the miners' union funds with which food and clothing might be bought. In other words, the officers of the miners' union were to join with the operators in the process of starving the miners and the miners' families into submission. The company selected for this purpose was the Borderland Coal Corporation and Judge R. McClintic of the district court of the United States for the southern district of West Virginia was the one picked out to issue the injunction. This application for an injunction was filed about the same time that injunctions were asked for from Judge Anderson in Indianapolis. Judge Anderson's injunction was vicious to the extreme. However, when it was pointed out to Judge Anderson that his order forbidding the sending of funds to the starving miners of West Virginia could not and would not be complied with, he, Judge Anderson, declined the operators' request to deny the miners food and shelter essential to life. Judge McClintic, however, was not even moved by this consideration. In the injunction he issued against the United Workers he restrained "all the members, agents and representatives of the United Mine Workers' organization, be, and they are hereby, enjoined and restrained from and after the period of 30 days from further maintaining the tent colonies in Mingo county or in the vicinity of the mines of the plaintiffs, and they, the said last-named defendants, are hereby enjoined and restrained from further furnishing to the inhabitants of said tent colonies or to those who may hereafter inhabit the same, any sum or sums of money, orders for money, merchandise, or orders for merchandise, or any other thing of value so as to make possible the continuance of said tent colonies in said Williamson-Thacker coal field in the vicinity of the mines of the plaintiffs, the court finding that the presence of such tent colonies in the vicinity of said mines is a continuing source of menace, threats, intimidation and danger to the persons of the plaintiff's employes and to the plaintiff's properties and business in in-

terstate trade and commerce." In other words, Judge McClintic ruled that it was unlawful to furnish shelter to workers and their families who were without homes; that it was illegal to provide food to the children and women of the locked-out miners, as well as to the miners; that it was unlawful for the locked-out miners and their families to live in any of the houses or tents that might be furnished to them and that these miners could not even legally spend such money, or anything of value, as might be given to them or be earned by them because to permit these miners to live in the vicinity of plaintiff's mines was a continuing source of menace, threats, intimidation and danger to the Borderland's mines, property and commerce." It is almost inconceivable that any court, however hostile it might be toward the workers, would go to such lengths as might cause the illness, starvation and death of children and women in order that business companies might become the absolute masters of those engaged by them as well as those outside of their employ. The United Mine Workers immediately prepared an appeal to the higher courts; and evidently because of fear that the enforcement of the inhumane provisions of this injunction might inflame public sentiment against the injunction process, the circuit court of appeals, fourth district, Richmond, Va., on April 17, 1922, suspended these vicious restraints and continued all other provisions of the injunction issued by Judge McClintic. While hearings have been had on the appeal that the complete injunction be permanently set aside, and while it is possible that the more inhumane provisions of Judge McClintic's injunction will be permanently set aside, this injunction of Judge McClintic's presents conclusive evidence that the injunction as used in industrial disputes is devoid of all sense of fairness and decency and that our courts of equity can be turned conveniently into instruments of the greatest iniquity whenever it will best serve the interests of soulless corporations and a mad desire for wealth.

Miners, Refuse Thanks to—(1920, p. 118) While the services of the wage workers of our country during the war have been forgotten, it should not be overlooked that Representative Goodykoontz presented a resolution in congress thanking the mine workers of America for their distinguished services rendered to the government during that great trial. The bill declares that the American coal miners by unremitting toil and patriotic devotion rendered a fundamental service to the country, but the committee to which it was referred did not consider it as it was thought inadvisable to applaud the workers for any great service rendered in the war.

Miners, West Virginia—(1920, p. 327) In the coal regions of West Virginia there are 40,000 mine workers who are yet arbitrarily denied the opportunity of becoming members of a labor organization and are also prohibited from enjoying many of the privileges and prerogatives which accrue to citizenship. The methods employed by the coal interests of that state to intimidate and coerce these citizens, through the employment of hundreds of armed detectives and gunmen who inflict unspeakable outrages upon the mine workers, have become a matter of national shame. The officers of the United Mine Workers of America have from time to time appealed to the governor of West Virginia for a correction of these conditions, and have even upon occasion brought before him in person the bruised, maimed and bleeding victims of the gunmen employed by the coal operators, and have in every instance failed to secure redress or an enforcement of the laws of the state. There has recently been a most serious armed conflict between agents of the Baldwin-Felts Detective Agency and the municipal officers of the town of Matewan, resulting in the loss of many lives. At the present time great numbers of these armed agents, acting without authority of law, are being mobilized in the counties of Mingo and McDowell, thereby threatening the further peace and security of the citizens of the state. Therefore the A. F. of L. favors a senatorial or congressional investigation into conditions obtaining in West Virginia.

(1921, p. 195) The A. F. of L. declares its sympathy with the striking mine workers of West Virginia in their struggle to maintain the right to belong to their organization and to improve their material well being, and urges the passage immediately of the U. S. senate resolution calling for a senatorial investigation.

Minimum Wage—(1919, pp. 114-327) A minimum wage law to fix reasonable wages for women and minor workers in the District of Columbia was enacted September 19, 1918. The act provides for an unpaid minimum wage board composed of three members to be chosen, so far as practicable, one as a representative of employes, one as a representative of employers, and one to represent the public. The board is given ample power to secure the attendance and testimony of witnesses, the production of books, papers and other evidence relative to matters under investigation, and to make rules and regulations to carry the act into effect. If, after an investigation concerning the wages of women and minors in any occupation, the board is of the opinion that any substantial number of them are receiving wages inadequate to meet with the necessary cost of living, maintain them in health and protect their morals, the board shall call and convene a conference, composed of not more than three representative employers and an equal number of representative employes in such occupation, and three disinterested persons representing the public; which conference, after considering all the information and evidence in its possession and in the possession of the board, shall make a report containing its findings and recommendations, including recommendations for minimum wages in the occupation under inquiry. If the board approves the recommendations, it shall hold a public hearing, at which all persons in favor of or opposed to such recommendations may be heard. After the public hearing, the board may make an order adopting the recommendations and carrying them into effect, requiring all employers in that occupation within the District to observe and comply with the minimum wages set forth in the order. The order becomes effective 60 days after it is made, and whoever violates the act, whether employer, agent, director, or officer or any agent of any corporation, shall be deemed guilty of a misdemeanor, and punished by a fine of not less than $25 nor more than $100, or by imprisonment of not less than 10 days nor more than three months, or by both such fine and imprisonment. Any employer who discharges an employe or in any other manner discriminates against one because such employe has served on any conference or has testified before such conference, is subject to similar punishment. The law requires the board to fix the minimum wage for one industry at a time, and the printing and publishing industry was selected as the first to be dealt with. This industry employs something more than 700 women in the District, about

76 per cent of whom receive less than $15, and about 47 per cent of whom receive less than $11 per week. The board found that $16 per week was the minimum cost of living for a woman in the District of Columbia. The final conclusion of the conference was that $15.50 per week was the lowest wage that should be paid to women employed in the printing industry in the District of Columbia. Before the adoption of this legal wage women were working for as low as $8 per week in this industry. (P. 288) The A .F. of L. refuses to approve of a plan to fix a standard minimum wage for workers not only by action of unions affiliated, but also by action through the legislatures of the various states of the nation.

(1923, p. 73) The minimum wage law of the District of Columbia was passed by congress and became a law on September 19, 1918. Shortly thereafter the constitutionality of the law was questioned by bills to enjoin the enforcement of orders of the minimum wage board. The Children's Hospital of the District of Columbia and an elevator operator employed by the Congress Hall Hotel Company were the parties contesting the constitutionality of the law. The hospital employed a large number of women with whom it had agreed upon wages, in some cases less than that fixed by the minimum wage board. The elevator operator was employed by the Congress Hall Hotel Company at a salary of $35 per month and two meals a day. These bills were dismissed by the trial court and on appeal to the court of appeals of the District of Columbia, the cases were decided June 6, 1921, by affirming the constitutionality of the law and on June 22, 1921, motions for rehearing were denied. The majority opinion held the act unconstitutional, and the case was thereupon appealed to the supreme court of the United States which sustained the lower court. The act was held invalid because in the eyes of the United States supreme court it authorized an unconstitutional interference with the freedom of contract included within the guarantees of the due process clause of the fifth amendment. Holding that there is, no such thing as absolute freedom of contract the court set out four grounds upon which interference has been upheld. These are (1) statutes fixing rates and charges to be exacted by business impressed with a public interest; (2) statutes relating to contracts for the performance of public work; (3) statutes prescribing the character, methods and time for payment of wages; and (4) statutes fixing hours of labor. The case of Muller vs. Oregon, in which the right to limit hours of labor for women is upheld, is dismissed with the thought that the nineteenth anmendment and other changes in the contractural, political and civil status of women have cured the ancient inequalities of the sexes, other than physical. The court then goes on to point out that this case differs from the four exceptions named above in every material respect. The court says: "It is not a law dealing with any business charged with a public interest or with public work, or to meet and tide over a temporary emergency. It has nothing to do with the character, methods or periods of wage payments. It does not prescribe hours of labor or conditions under which labor is to be done. It is not for the protection of persons under legal disability or for the prevention of fraud. It is simply and exclusively a price-fixing law, confined to adult women (for we are not now considering the provisions relating to minors) who are legally as capable of contracting for themselves as men." The following is worthy of attention: "It can not be shown that well paid women safeguarded their morals more carefully than those who are poorly paid. Morality rests upon other considerations than wages; and there is, certainly, no such prevalent connection between the two as to justify a broad attempt to adjust the latter with reference to the former." The law is also criticized because it compels the employer to pay at least the sum fixed, but required no service of equivalent value from the employe. The court evidently overlooked the fact that the employer can always exercise his right of terminating the emplloyment, and securing employes who will render a ;ervice of equivalent value. The court holds that while any attempt to fix a rigid boundary to the police power would be unwise and futile, that this legislation has passed the limits, and is therefore unconstitutional." In opposition to this, Mr. Chief Justice Taft in his dissenting opinion holds that minimum wage laws are passed oh the presumption that the "employes in the class receiving least pay, are not upon a full level of equality of choice with their employer and in their necessituous circumstances are prone to accept pretty much anything· that is offered." He also declares that the function of the court is not to declare acts invalid simply because they are to remedy economic conditions, which the court believes to be unwise or unsound. He is of the opinion that legislatures have the authority to limit the hours of employment on the score of the health of the employes, and that there is authority for the finding that low wages are equally harmful. Since congress took this view, the court can not say that it was not warranted in so doing. Mr. Taft holds that if the legislature finds as much support in experience for the view that a sweating wage has as great and as direct a tendency to bring about an injury to the health and morals of workers, as for the view that long hours injure their health, that the case of Muller *vs.* Oregon controls. This case limited the hours of women in industries in Oregon and has been upheld by the United States supreme court. According to him, the boundary of the police power should not be drawn to include maximum hours and exclude a minimum wage. Mr. Justice Holmes, who also dissented, had the following to say: "I confess that I do not understand the principle on which the power to fix a minimum for the wages of women can be denied by those who admit the power to fix a maximum for their hours of work. I fully assent to the proposition that here as elsewhere the distinctions of the law are distinctions of degree, but I perceive no difference in the kind or degree of interference with liberty, the only matter with which we have any concern, between the one case and the other. The bargain is equally affected whichever half you regulate. . . . The criterion of constitutionality is not whether we believe the law to be for the publîc good." In Knox *vs.* Lee, 12 Wall, 457, in discussing the power of the supreme court to declare laws unconstitutional, it is said: "The declaration (that an act of congress is void) should never be made except in a clear case. Every *possible* presumption is in favor of the validity of a statute and this continues until the contrary is shown beyond a rational doubt." The doctrine thus pronounced has been declared time and time again, and is asserted with favor in the majority opinion of the case now under discussion, but it is a question whether or not it has been always followed. This rule of construction has a special applica-

tion to all acts of congress, which for reasons not necessary to mention here does not always apply to the constitutionality of a state law. In spite of the language above quoted, which is the language of the supreme court itself, this tribunal insists and persists in declaring laws unconstitutional by a bare majority of one. Surely, one can be excused for refusing to believe that in such cases every rational doubt has been swept away. The minimum wage question received the attention of over 500 legislators, comprising the house and senate and was then signed by the president. Among these legislators was a considerable number of lawyers, skilled in the law and possessing a deep knowledge of things constitutional. Does the fact that five members of the supreme court thought differently not only from their other colleagues, but from the legislators, together with the executive, wipe away every rational doubt? Does this fact make the unconstitutionality of the minimum wage act a clear case? Our last three presidents, Roosevelt, Taft, and Wilson, thought that such an act would be constitutional as is evidenced by their language. President Roosevelt in his first inaugural held that measures to safeguard women and children in industry were among the primary functions of government. Chief Justice Taft in his dissenting opinion clearly is of the opinion that the law was sound. President Wilson in his first inaugural said: "There can be no equality of opportunity, the first essential of justice in the body politic, if men and women and children be not shielded in their lives, their very vitality, from the consequences of great industrial and social processes which they can not alter, control or singly cope with. Society must see to it that it does not crush or weaken or damage its own constituent parts. The first duty of law is to keep sound the society it serves. Sanitary laws, pure food laws, and law determining conditions of labor which individuals are powerless to determine for themselves, are intimate parts of the very business of justice and legal efficiency." (P. 226) The minimum wage law decision clearly emphasizes the uncertainties and dangers involved in attempting to correct evils arising out of industrial relations through the political power of the state rather than by the collective economic power of the wage earners. We are likewise deeply impressed with the great difficulties that make almost impossible, if not hopeless, the continued effort to prevent the exploitation of the women wage earners of our land by a maddened industrial and commercial world that only worships mammon and disregards the appeal of humanity. We are concerned with the serious and grievous problems that have developed as a consequence of this decision of the United States supreme court. That which is required is the organizing of all women wage earners in their respective trade unions and by industrial action enforce standards of work and of compensation and rewards for services given that shall be beyond and out of reach of those who would misuse the powers of state for the enrichment of a few and the impoverishment of the many. The president of the A. F. of L., with the approval and guidance of the Executive Council, is hereby empowered to call a conference of all international and national trade unions in whose trade or calling women wage earners are employed so that a more perfect plan of organizing the women workers may be devised and that all organized labor be called on to renewed efforts and activities to deal promptly and efficiently with the problems at present confronting the women toilers of America and in the manner herein outlined.

Minimum Wage, Nolan—(1919, pp. 115-327-354) The Nolan minimum wage bill was lost because no direct action could be secured in the senate. It could not be dragged out of a committee to which it had been committed consideration, and with the close of the session it died in the hands of that committee.

(1920, p. 110) H. R. 5726, known as the Nolan minimum wage bill for government employes, was introduced June 13, 1919, and passed the house July 22, 1919. This bill had been before the house for seven years. It sought to change the wages of the employes of the government that had been fixed by law as long ago as 1854. A most persistent but unsuccessful effort was made to destroy the benefits of the bill by an attempt to strike out the $240 bonus for government employes. (P. 359) Urged passage by the senate of the Nolan minimum wage bill.

(1921, p. 113) The Nolan minimum wage bill, which had passed the house again, died in the senate. Representative Nolan is to be highly commended for the persistency with which he has urged the passage of his bill. No member of congress has worked so earnestly for any measure than he for the $3 a day minimum wage bill. The bill was reintroduced in the 67th congress. (P. 372) About 80,000 employes of the United States are paid less than $3 a day, which is manifestly less than an adequate wage. Indorsement of the Nolan minimum wage bill reaffirmed.

(1922, pp. 114-328) Notwithstanding the defeat of previous efforts, Representative John I. Nolan, of California, is just as vigorously urging the passage of H. R. No. 2429, which provides that "no person employed by the District of Columbia shall receive less than $3 per day." When it is known that there are 80,000 employes of the government receiving less than $3 per day it is surprising that anyone in congress would try to prevent the passage of such a meritorious measure. The wages for which these government employes work were fixed by law in 1854 and in spite of every effort made to change it the law remains as originally passed. This should be a warning to all of those who advocate the fixing of wages and hours of employment or working conditions by law.

Mob Action and Lynchings—(1919, p. 321) President Woodrow Wilson issued from the capital city of our nation on July 26, 1918, a personal statement addressed to his fellow countrymen, defining mob-spirit action, called upon the nation to show the world that while it fights for democracy on foreign fields, it is not destroying democracy at home. While the president referred not alone to mob action against those suspected of being enemy aliens or enemy sympathizers, he denounced most emphatically mob action of all sorts, especially lynchings. In all wars, where our country and its interests were at stake, the colored race, with their white brothers, fought, shed their blood and died in defense of Old Glory and over there gave their all that others may live in peace and happiness ever after. Lynchings cowardly and unjust, is a blow at the heart of ordered law and human justice. The colored people, their workers, their bread winners, throughout the nation look with hope and anxiety in their hearts to those in the struggle for better conditions, for better homes and for the good things of life, as well as protection from mob rule and for a surging popular opinion behind them that will not tolerate a laxity in upholding the laws of our land. The hope of civilization is in democracy; the hope

of democracy is in justice; the only hope of justice is in the tribunals through which justice can be secured, and the only hope of the functioning of these tribunals is in the sentiment which demands that they, within their departments, shall be supreme and that any effort to incite mob violence shall be regarded as an attack upon the very foundatiions of society itself. The American labor movement knows no race, color or creed in its stand for the toiling masses to get justice. Therefore, the A. F. of L. declares against mob rule and lynchings and for the proper enforcement of the laws of our land.

Money, Soiled Paper—(1919, p. 318) Refused to ask congress to provide for the transportation to the treasury or sub-treasuries of soiled, dirty and worn paper money without any cost to the banks whatever.

Mooney Case—(1919, pp. 161-267-335) Previous conventions have taken a deep interest in the incidents connected with the trial and sentence of Thomas J. Mooney. Insistent demands have been made by these conventions that the accused be given a new trial. Despite our efforts the accused has been denied another opportunity of facing his accusers, or of presenting in open court the large volume of evidence and testimony secured since his trial, which has been the basis of a widespread belief that perjury and subornation of perjury was the basis upon which his conviction was secured. As a result of the activities and representations made by the officers of the A. F. of L., acting under the instructions of previous conventions, the president of the U. S. gave public expression of his belief that the accused should be given another trial. The St. Paul convention of 1918, realizing that the accused was in immediate jeopardy of his life, again instructed the president of the A. F. of L. to immediately appeal to the governor of California and again present the urgency of the case to the president of the United States. These instructions were carried out, but instead of a new trial, the death sentence was commuted to life imprisonment. This action, while saving the life of the accused, is intolerable under the circumstances. If the accused had been found guilty of the heinous crime charged as the result of unquestioned evidence which had been introduced against him, the commutation of his sentence was an outrage upon the community. If the evidence was of such a character as to cast a grave question of doubt over the acts of the prosecution itself, then the commutation was a outrage against the accused. We are firmly of the opinion that a new trial of the accused has become an imperative necessity in order that the evidence presented by the prosecutors' office may be reviewed by another court and jury; and, furthermore, that there may also be presented in court the tesimony and evidence, which have been circulated in this and other countries, which has aroused a widespread impression that motives and methods of a most sinister character, and evidence of a perjured nature, were responsible for T. J. Mooney's conviction. The Executive Council is therefore instructed to give early attention to the devising of such practical ways and means as will aid in securing a new trial to Thomas J. Mooney, and also the presentation before the court of the tesimony and evidence presented since the trial, the character of which has created the belief that a most grave miscarriage of justice and perjured testimony were responsible for the conviction and sentence.

General Strike—(P. 336) In connection with the case of Thomas J. Mooney Resolution No. 188 has been introduced calling upon the convention to take steps, through the officials of affiliated organizations, for the taking of a referendum vote of the membership they represent, upon the question of a general strike on Labor Day, 1919, should a new trial be refused him before that date. In connection with this proposition the A. F. of L. is forced to give consideration to the effort which was been made by the international workers' defense league to take a referendum vote of the membership of the American trade union movement upon the question of a general strike on July 4 of this year. With reference to the provisions of the resolution, it is essential first of all to indicate that the national and international unions comprising the A. F. of L. were guaranteed full autonomy when they affiliated with this organization. That is to say, they were assured of their unquestioned authority to make such laws for their self-government as their desires, wisdom and experience indicated. Upon the specific question of strikes, and the rules and regulations governing the taking of referendum votes upon any question, each affiliated organization is governed by the laws which its membership have enacted for their self-government. Neither the A. F. of L. nor any of its affiliated organizations have the right to interfere with the operation and application of the laws of any of the national or international unions. Such interference would usurp their right of self-government and would immediately destroy the voluntary character of membership in the A. F. of L. The membership of affiliated organizations have been informed of the action of the convention called by the international workers' defense league, which proposed a general strike on July 4, 1919, if Thomas J. Mooney was not given a new trial before that date. This membership, through the laws which they have created for their self-government in their respective organizations, have had at their disposal the methods by which they could express themselves upon the question. This convention has no power nor authority, neither can it assume the authority, to direct the taking of a referendum vote of the membership of affiliated organizations upon any question; it may recommend but it can not instruct. Upon the subject of the attempt which has been made to take a referendum vote upon the question of a general strike on July 4, 1919, we gather from the official published statements of those responsible for the attempt, that they were impelled to assume authority to issue a call for a referendum vote of the trade union membership of the U. S. and Canada, because they had taken exception to the attitude of the accredited trade union executive officers of affiliated organizations. The executive officers of affiliated organizations are not answerable to the A. F. of L. for whatever attitude they may have assumed upon the subject under consideration; they are not answerable to any of the affiliated organizations; they are not answerable to any other bodies or organizations unaffiliated with the A. F. of L.; they are answerable to the membership of their respective organizations only. The incident of an outside body irresponsible to the trade union movement assuming to usurp the functions of the executive officials of affiliated organizations is one which can not be ignored in connection with the subject under consideration. In this instance the general strike was advocated not to save a human life but for

the stated purpose of securing a new trial for Thomas J. Mooney before July 4, 1919. General strikes for other purposes have been advocated during the year by individuals and bodies outside of the trade union movement, equally irresponsible to the A. F. of L. If bodies unauthorized by the A. F. of L. are to assume the functions of polling the membership of the American trade union movement upon any question of their choosing, the machinery through which the trade union movement functions would be seriously injured, if not destroyed. If outsiders can force a vote of the membership and assume authority superior to that created by the organizations themselves for their administration, practical methods must cease to function. Irresponsible groups of men or individuals who were not even trade unionists would have it within their power to destroy the effectiveness of trade union discipline, tear down the structure which trade unionists have built up and create a condition of chaos. The orderly, systematic methods which the workers of America have adopted to protect their welfare and advance their interests as wage earners would be set aside, our organizations would become a rich field for exploitation by all those who believed it to be to their personal advantage. Those who are opposed to trade unionism and who attack its policies and methods would take full advantage of this opportunity of utilizing this method as propaganda for their own programs, policies and sentiments. Unquestionably, adventurers would promptly seek the opportunity offered. The machinery of the trade union movement must remain in the full and unquestioned control of the membership which comprises it. Our movement can not afford to tolerate the attempt of any outside individual or group to use its machinery for the purpose of securing or endeavoring to secure the sentiments or opinion of its membership upon any question. This convention, therefore, expresses its emphatic disapproval of the efforts which have been made by a body irresponsible to the A. F. of L. to poll the vote of the membership of affiliated organizations. An attempted general strike would seriously injure the effort to secure a new trial for Thomas J. Mooney and accomplish much harm to his interests. Representatives of the international workers' defense league who are its agents soliciting funds for T. J. Mooney's defense are doing him an incalculable injury and also creating internal disturbances within the trade union movement through their continuous attacks, unjust criticisms and misrepresentations of the A. F. of L., its officials and the officials of affiliated organizations.

1920, (P. 213) Our attorneys were of the opinion after studying the case that nothing of a legal nature could be accomplished through judicial proceedings in the courts and that the only hope was through a pardon by the governor of California, even though it might mean a trial upon one of the indictments still pending against Mooney and Billings. Therefore, upon our authorization a committee of five was appointed to wait upon the governor of California and urge that a pardon be granted to Thomas J. Mooney and Warren K. Billings. The committee entered into correspondence with the governor for the purpose of securing a pardon for Mooney and Billings. The governor emphatically refused the application. From information received there are indications that the probability exists for a better outlook in this case in the near future. (P. 367) Executive Council directed to continue its efforts to prevail upon the governor of California to grant a pardon.

(1921, pp. 293-395) The Executive Council is hereby directed to do all that lies within its power to secure a retrial or a pardon for Tom Mooney and Warren K. Billings, and that all affiliated national and international organizations be communicated with for the purpose of enlisting their influence with the authorities so that justice may bé done and the facts relative to the perjury and subornation of perjury in connection with the miscarriage of justice in this case may be given the widest possible publicity.

(1922, p. 352) The A. F. of L. respectfully and unanimously requests Governor Stephens to immediately issue a pardon to Thomas J. Mooney and Warren K. Billings and right the great wrong which has been done to these two men. Each affiliated national and international union, all state federations of labor, central labor bodies and federal and directly affiliated local labor unions are requested to make the same request to Governor Stephens and to urge the local unions to do the same.

(1923, p. 294) Again urged governor to pardon Mooney and Billings.

Motion Picture Censorship—(1916, pp. 114-278) In the recent past efforts have been made to secure both state and federal legislation providing for government censorship of moving pictures. These proposals have had the support of a number of well-meaning persons who really desire to protect the children of the country and to promote a sense of high morality. However, there is involved in the proposal something more than is generally appreciated. The number, the variety and the uses of motion pictures have been so greatly increased that they now constitute an important means of expression. Motion pictures are something more than an instrumentality for recreation. They are an agency for education, for dissemination of current information, comparable in many respects to the daily press and the public forum. They have a determining influence in directing and educating public thought and opinion. Motion pictures supplement the spoken and written word by a powerful appeal to the mind through the eye. The event or the thought to be conveyed is visualized. Since motion pictures are a means of expression and have become established as an agency supplementing our older methods, they must be protected by the same guarantees of freedom that have been bestowed upon oral utterance and upon the press. It is fundamental for the protection of free institutions that freedom of speech and discussion should be assured. Only when there exists most complete freedom to express thought or to criticize is there established a guarantee tht political and other representative agents shall not violate the rights of others and shall not arrogate to themselves power and authority that they do not rightfully possess. Freedom of speech is inseparable from free institutions and the genius of a free people. This freedom must be protected against abuse by holding the individual responsible for his utterances. Legal restriction in advance of presentation limits research, investigation and inquiry for broader and deeper truths. It has ever been the theory of the few that people can be "made to be good by law." This same theory underlies the efforts of those who propose governments censorship. By establishing either state or federal boards to review motion pictures, it is proposed to present to the public only such things as they may be permitted legally to see. This is putting very dangerous authority in the hands of a few for it enables the board of review to restrict and determine the very fountainheads of information. There has been worked out a voluntary system by which objectionable and vicious information can be eliminated from motion pictures. Since this is based upon no legislative enactment and exercises no governmental prerogative their decisions amount only to an expression of opinion, which carries weight in accord with the honesty, the discretion, and the wisdom of the members of the board. This matter is brought to the attention of the delegates to this convention with the recommendation that the convention take official action in opposition to government censorship of expression of opinion in any form, and that we endorse again the declaration that freedom of expression of opinion, freedom of speech, freedom of the press are the palladium of free institutions.

(1919, p. 134) The 1916 convention took decisive action against legalized censorship of moving pictures. The subject came up during this past year, as bills for such censorship were introduced into the legislatures of Nebraska, North Carolina and Michigan. The federations of labor in these states were advised of the action of the Baltimore convention and our understanding is that these bills were defeated. There was some agitation to prevent the exhibition of pictures portraying scenes of labor unrest and some further discussion of a federal censorship. A bill appeared in the house providing for censorship of motion picture films. It was referred to the judiciary committee, from which it never reappeared. We feel sure that a proper and judicious use of the moving picture would be of value in promoting better conditions of labor. It is impossible to be too vigilant in guarding the freedom of all the various modes of public expression. A difficult phase of the moving picture question was presented when we were asked to interfere in Tennessee and Indiana in relation to bills in the legislatures of those states allowing moving picture shows on Sundays. Our only proper course, as the A. F. of L. had taken no action on this proposition, was to refer the question to the decision of the local organizations.

(1920, p. 466) The moving picture screen, with such wonderful possibilities, truthful and artistic, is every day being put to more and more vicious service as an instrument of misrepresentation in the American-wide campaign against labor and labor organizations, all of which is evident in both news and feature pictures. Large open meetings of union men or strikers are shown as "mobs," their parades are termed "riots," and their cause is both ridiculed and falsified, to all of which labor is without proper answering. Therefore, the Executive Council should take cognizance of the situation and file protests with the leading producing, distributing and exhibiting picture concerns and demand in behalf of organized labor the truth and a fair deal for all. Labor should also interest itself in the use of the film to exploit its own educational work.

(1921, p. 334) The Executive Council was requested to investigate the advisability of the affiliated internationals and their local unions in establishing a chain of moving picture houses to show films portraying the true principles of labor.

(1922, pp. 109-138-360) By action of the Denver convention of the A. F. of L., the Executive Council was directed to investigate the feasibility and advisability of having the A. F. of L. institute and maintain a studio for the production and manufacture of moving pictures, to portray on the screen the true principles, objects and activities of organized labor and to investigate the advisability of affiliated international and local unions establishing a chain of moving picture theaters for the exhibition of films of pictures portraying the labor movement and the labor cause. Complying with these instructions, the Executive Council caused an investigation to be made of this entire subject. It is found that there are three methods of producing motion pictures for entertainment and instruction purposes. One is to build your own studio and laboratory, as has been contemplated in the instructions given to the Executive Council. Another is to lease or rent everything, and the third method is to contract with a competent film producing concern for the production of the pictures desired. It should be understood that the cost of building and equipping a motion picture studio depends entirely upon the size, location and scale or magnitude of pictures contemplated. In undertaking to provide one's own studio and laboratory suitable for general productive purposes, it is estimated that the building of a studio, with proper lighting, camera, laboratory and other essential equipment, exclusive of all labor cost, would approximate $225,000. To this must be added the permanent salaries for superintendence, watchmen, artisans and laborers, laboratory workmen and others at an estimated figure of $525 per week or approximately $27,000 a year. Thus it is estimated the building and equipment of a studio would approximate $225,000 with a maintenance charge of approximately $27,000 a year. The investigation made has clearly demonstrated that to build and maintain a moving picture studio would be an unprofitable venture unless it be in continuous and profitable use. This could only be accomplished if the A. F. of L. were to enter the motion picture field as a business venture, unlimited and unrestricted in the character of the pictures it was to produce. Another very important item entering into production of motion pictures is the talent and settings to be employed in the making of any given picture. It is impossible to estimate this item of expense as each picture varies in the cost of production dependent upon the number and character of actors employed as well as the dramatic and spectacular features involved. It is, therefore, evident that it is neither practical nor desirable that the A. F. of L. should undertake to own and maintain a motion picture studio. In looking into the practicability and advisability of a leasing plan, we find that the estimated cost of leasing a studio, laboratory charges involving 50 reels a week or 50,000 feet, and charge of superintendency, watchmen and other labor costs would approximate $160,000 a year. This estimate does not include the salaries of actors and other expenses in the taking of a picture. We are informed that the Labor Film Service Company spent $36,000 in the making of "The Contrast" film, outside of the cost of promotion and releasing. This picture is a six-reel film. It was produced in a studio that was rented only for the time required for its completion, and while the picture contains more characters than usually appear in the average production, it does not contain any stars. In these days of stupendous motion picture productions, none of the large producers attempt to make a production under $60,000, and modern feature pictures range in cost from $35,000 to $500,000 and more. It is esti-

mated that regardless of whether a picture is produced on the purchase or leasing plan, the average cost per picture, which could compete with the pictures now in the market, would range between $60,000 to $75,000. It is, therefore, evident that the leasing plan is likewise an undesirable venture for the A. F. of L. The third plan is to contract with a competent motion picture concern for the production of whatever pictures and films are desired. It is impossible to secure an estimate on the probable cost involved in this method, as the cost depends largely on the scale and magnitude embraced in the scenario. It is said that pictures that are not featured consisting of two to five reels range in cost from $5,000 to $10,000, but what may be termed as feature pictures range from $10,000 to $1,000,000. Therefore, the cost of contracting for the production of motion picture films depends largely upon how elaborate are to be the settings and the class of talent that is to be employed. We venture to suggest that this is not a field of activity into which the A. F. of L. can enter profitably either from a financial or practical viewpoint and, therefore, adversely to the proposal of having the A. F. of L. enter into the field of producing motion picture films. Our investigation into the proposal of having affiliated international and local unions establish a chain of motion picture theaters, while not as comprehensive as that of producing motion pictures, nevertheless indicated clearly the almost insurmountable difficulties that present themselves in such a large business enterprise and we do not hesitate to report adversely upon this proposal. The resolutions upon which this report is based are predicated upon the declaration that the motion picture industry is one of the greatest forces in molding public opinion and in the dissemination of knowledge, that it is a censor of activities and principles and that this influence is being used to arouse public opinion and prejudice against the trade union movement. Appreciative of the great influence of the motion picture productions upon the public mind and keenly alert to the dangers involved in presenting prejudiced and unfair picture productions of organized labor in its constant struggle with organized capital, the subject of presenting fairly and without bias the hopes and aspirations of the working people of our country by motion pictures, has been taken up with the motion picture producers. We are assured through William H. Hays, president of the Motion Picture Producers and Distributors of America, Incorporated, that it is the intent, desire and purpose of the motion picture producers of America to cooperate with the trade union movement to present fairly and accurately the activities and attitude of the wage earner, without prejudice and in the light of helping to uplift the great family of human toil. It is said that the motion picture producers have come to realize that if the screen is to serve humankind, it must not only be true to a correct presentation of conditions of life as it finds them, but that motion pictures must likewise encourage all movements and tendencies that tend to uplift mankind. In connection with this it is incumbent upon the workers to cooperate with the trade union movement in seeing that those promises of motion picture producers are shaped into realities and wherever and whenever motion pictures are shown which are prejudicial and unfair to labor that the attention of the A. F. of L. be directed to such productions so that steps may be taken to discourage such exhibitions and make them unprofitable. It is also essential, whenever and wherever there are produced and exhibited, pictures which are helpful to the realization of labor's hopes and aspirations and which fairly represent the activities of the trade union movement and its achievements, that support and encouragement be given to such producers and exhibitors and thus, by labor's patronage, reward those who would devote their time and effort in the workers' cause and for human uplift. Our investigation has led us to note a tendency of extreme danger to the general welfare in the subtle propaganda that is being promoted for the establishing of a political form of censorship of the motion picture method of communicating thought and action of the human race. It has been found that under the guise of protecting the morals and safeguarding the peace of a community, motion pictures depicting the brutal and unwarranted conduct of employers' hirelings and officers of the law against the working people engaged in an industrial struggle have been censored by these state censorship commissions. By that method the public has been denied the opportunity of becoming familiar with the vicious tactics used by employers in their mad attempt to suppress and depress the wage earners in their struggles for a better day and a brighter life. While appreciative of the need and desirability of exhibiting only clean and wholesome motion pictures and while unsympathetic with any means of communicating thought that tends to weaken the bonds so essential to an improved civilization, time and experience have demonstrated that the principles underlying governmental censorship are such as to threaten to convert the liberties of our people into license and subjugate the rights of free men to the whims and fancies of governmental censorship commissions. Because of the dangers inherent in these censorship commmissions to the rights and liberties of our people, the Executive Council is impelled to reiterate the approved declaration of a year ago in protest to the existing censorship laws as well as against the proposal to extend this fraternal form of government. The prediction made a year ago that the political censorship over motion pictures would ultimately extend over the stage as well as over printing and publishing has already developed to a considerable degree. Plans have been made by some of our so-called reform organizations to undertake the furtherance of legislation intended to establish a censorship over the stage, printing and publishing. Those engaged in the theatrical profession, alert to the dangers confronting the stage, have undertaken to provide a voluntary method of reviewing such plays and performances against which complaint is lodged. It is proposed by those directly engaged in these professions and allied crafts to exercise their economic power so as to attract public favor, raise the standards of theatrical productions and deny to those who commercialize public sentiment, the opportunity of attempting to foist on the American people a further extension of regulative rules of conduct which do not find their enforcement in an enlightened conscience but by the rigors of stautory law and the vesting of vast discretionary powers into the hands of censorship commissions. The plans under way likewise embrace the ultimate attempt of censorship of the press. Indeed, it is difficult to understand how the work of an author or writer, artist or painter can well be permitted the freedom of the press, when these self-same expressions if exhibited on the stage or on the screen may be censored or be denied freedom of expression. Thus, there is involved in this whole realm of censorship a danger boundless in extent and permeated with a purpose to stifle and suppress the venturous spirit of a free people and to enforce by law a predetermined moral, social, political and economic code and a bureaucratic form of government rather than to permit free expression, conflict of viewpoints and development of intellect and of a higher consciousness to determine the future moral, social, political and industrial relations of humankind. Sensitive to the grave dangers involved in this wave for state regulation over all methods of communicating and distributing thoughts and human expression, the Author's League of America, the Actors' Equity, the American Dramatists, the Screen Writers' Guild, the Stage Mechanics and Motion Pictures Union, the Cinema Camera Club, the Motion Picture Directors' Association, the American Federation of Musicians and the International Printing Trades Unions, have undertaken to provide a program which will embrace the advancement of all that is good, in motion pictures and on the stage, to inculcate into all those persons engaged in the production and promotion of motion pictures and plays and writings a higher ethical standard; to bring into a closer and more harmonious relationship all branches of the professions and trades having to do with the expressions and communicating of the thoughts and activities and relations of man, and to oppose all forms of political and bureaucratic censorship boards and commissions as an unwarranted and extremely dangerous infringement upon the freedom of expression and freedom of the press. We commend this voluntary and constructive program worthy of our approval and support and we reaffirm the declaration approved a year ago that we oppose all forms of political censorship over the freedom of expression and that if existing laws are insufficient to protect fully the morals of our people and the perpetuity of the democratic principles upon which our nation is founded, in that event additional and adequate laws be enacted but that freedom of expression, freedom of the press and freedom of assembly shall not be abridged or denied and that producers, exhibitors and publishers shall be held responsible for any transgression of the laws of our country or of the states.

Motor Boat Law—(1922, p. 484) Favored amendment of the 65-foot motor boat law "to fully protect all power boats engaged in any commercial industry."

Muscle Shoals—(1922, p. 350) Directed the Executive Council to secure favorable action on the final offer of Mr. Ford to lease Muscle Shoals as soon as possible to prevent deterioration of the property.

(1923, pp. 98-281) Executive Council authorized to deal with this subject as subsequent developments may warrant.

Naturalization and Americanization—(1919, p. 320) In response to public demand, and by direction of an act of congress of May 9, 1918, the bureau of naturalization of the U. S. department of labor has issued the federal text-book on citizenship to be distributed through the public schools of the states and cities of the union, for the purpose of fitting candidates for citizenship for their duties as Americans. The A. F. of L. recommends to all affiliated organizations, cooperation with the bureau of naturalization to the end that they shall assist the foreign-born to become citizens, to direct them into the citizenship classes established for their bene-

fit, and to aid them to an understanding of our customs and our institutions.
(1923, pp. 84-357) Companion bills, introduced by Senator Shortridge of California and Representative Johnson of Washington contain most dangerous provisions. They provide that all aliens shall register on coming to the United States and each year thereafter. Should such a law be enacted governing aliens it could be extended to citizens, which would Russianize and Germanize our republic. If the bills referred to become a law, and they are expected to be pushed in the next congress, it will give federal judges the power to cancel the citizenship of naturalized aliens who might be engaged in strikes. A year ago a judge in Pittsburgh refused to naturalize a number of miners because he said they were on strike. There was no law giving the judge power to deny citizenship on that score. Such a law as that proposed in the bills mentioned would make lawful the deportation of any alien engaging in a strike or any naturalized citizen who might also offend in the same manner. In 1892 a law was enacted providing that all Chinese in the United States should register with the internal revenue collector in their respective districts. This law was amended in 1893 to more thoroughly enforce the registration provisions and when carried to the supreme court it was declared constitutional. The object of the law compelling Chinese to register was to make it easier for the government to know that unless a Chinaman could show a registration certificate he was not entitled to remain in this country. While the Chinese registered in 1893 and 1894 the law apparently was never enforced afterwards. If aliens from western Europe were compelled to register it would not be long before that requirement would become a political issue and would divide our people by nationalities. It is a bad principle and should be opposed with all the influence of labor.

Natural Resources—(1921, p. 415) The natural resources of the country—coal, iron and copper ores, phosphates, nitrates, sodium, gas, water power, timber land, etc.—are still in public ownership and worth scores of billions of dollars. Private development of these natural resources which have been alienated by patent or lease, is extremely wasteful, and the owners thereof are making huge profits, and the system of distributing the products thereof affords equally large and unearned profits to the middlemen and consignors and reconsignors thereof. Therefore, the A. F. of L. opposes the alienation of any more of these natural resources still in public ownership and demands the prompt enactment by congress of legislation for strict federal control of the production and distribution of natural resources now privately held and privately developed.

Navy Yard Employes, Protection for—(1922, p. 109) Without a moment's warning, without even a hint that such action was contemplated, 18,000 employes of the navy yards of the country were laid off indefinitely. While the order read "furloughed," those who marched out of the navy yards knew that it was their last day. They also knew that their benefits under the retirement act had been taken away and that they were to become a part of the flotsam and jetsam of the unemployed. Representative Fairfield introduced a bill providing that all discharged employes of the government over 50 years of age who had worked 15 years would be given a retirement certificate. When they reached the age of 60, no matter whether they have been working for the government or not, they would be placed on the retirement roll. (P. 476) When the Washington conference on limitation of armament was convened the organized labor movement, in conformity with its traditional position, lent its whole-hearted support and sympathy to the administration in its efforts to prevail upon all the nations assembled to agree upon a substantial reduction in armaments. Organized labor expected, in view of this attitude, that when the final program adopted by the conference became effective in the United States, the interest of the workers at the government navy yards and arsenals affected thereby would be adequately safeguarded. Much to its disappointment, however, no steps were taken by the present administration in this direction or apparently even considered. With hardly an hour's warning, thousands of the faithful workers in the navy yards and arsenals were furloughed and discharged. There is invested in these navy yards and arsenal many millions of the people's money in the form of government securities and taxes; since the plants are among the most superior of their kind in the country, are absolutely indispensable to the naval and military establishments such as remains necessary under the limitation of armaments agreements. In order that this may be accomplished, that employment in these plants may be stabilized, that the temptation to profiteer at the expense of the government on the strength of war and war scares may be eliminated, that the people may be saved many millions of dollars each year through the intensive utilization of these plants for the manufacture of all governmental supplies, it is imperative that congress pass immediate legislation.

Near East Relief—(1921, p. 442) We recognize and approve the work of the Near East relief and continuation of its program, especially in the feeding of orphans and their training for self-support, which deserves the cooperation of our affiliated membership to the best of its ability, and recommend to the national unions, state and local organizations that they cooperate in the education of their members as to this great need and collect and forward through their national headquarters to the Near East relief such funds as may be contributed for this purpose.

Negroes—(1919, p. 304) Refused to grant an international charter to exclusively negro workers, as the term colored laborers, skilled and unskilled, is so broad it is a trespass upon the jurisdictional rights and claims of several organizations affiliated to the A. F. of L. (P. 305) Executive Council is directed to give particular attention to the organizing of colored workers everywhere and to assign organizers for that purpose wherever possible. (P. 305) Where international unions refuse to admit colored workers to membership, the A. F. of L. is authorized to organize them under charters from the A. F. of L.
(1920, p. 311) Reaffirmed. Negro organizers should be appointed where necessary to organize negro workers under the banner of the A. F. of L. (P. 375) The A. F. of L. has never countenanced the drawing of a color line or discrimination against individuals because of race, creed or color. It recognizes that human freedom is a gift from the Creator to all mankind and is not to be denied to any because of social position or the limitations of caste or class, and that any cause which depends for its success on the denial of

this fundamental principle of liberty can not stand. (1922, p. 265) Reaffirmed.

Newspapers, Labor Control of—(1920, p. 466) Executive Council directed to investigate the advisability of securing the control of a number of daily papers located in various sections of the country, such papers to be conducted as independent news arteries whose main purpose will be the fair presentation of matters in which labor is interested.

Newspaper Misrepresentation—(1921, pp. 317-336) The daily press has in many instances, especially during the past few years, when grave and far-reaching industrial issues confronted the organized workers, such as the steel strike, the miners' strike and the railroad controversy, printed matter at variance with the true facts involved in these issues. The president and Executive Council are therefore directed to make an investigation and report to the next convention the advisability of acquiring a chain of daily newspapers. Central bodies are urged to consider the advisability of establshing local labor papers.

News Print, Shortage of—(1920, p. 120) The shortage of news print caused the introduction in congress of a number of bills to govern the size of newspapers and to prevent the exportation of print paper from the United States. These bills were considered in extensive hearings before committees. The newspaper publishers agreed to take the matter in their own hands and conserve news print paper. This was done by reducing the size of the newspapers and periodicals by agreement. The plan, however, did not relieve the shortage and congress passed a bill providing that news print paper under 8 cents a pound would be admitted free of duty for two years. This was signed by the president April 24. The only feasible plan to relieve the shortage is for Canada to permit the importation of pulp wood.

Newswriters—(1923, p. 328) The president and Executive Council are hereby directed to issue local union charters to those employed as editorial writers, desk editors, feature writers, reporters and newsgatherers employed in the news departments or contributing to the news columns of daily and weekly newspapers.

Night Work in Postal Service—(1919, p. 351) The affiliated postal employes are endeavoring to eliminate unnecessary night work in the service by securing a reduction in the daily working schedule of 15 minutes in every hour worked after 6 p. m. and prior to 6 a. m., a legislative reform beneficial to the men and the service. The A. F. of L. endorses this effort to minimize night work and directs the Executive Council to cooperate in securing the necessary legislation. (1921, p. 320) Reaffirmed. (1922, pp. 360-473) Reaffirmed. (1923, pp. 87-358) The promised relief from excessive night work through postal administration has not been granted the postal workers. The fight for the desired remedial legislation will be carried to the next congress.

North Dakota Bonds—(1921, p. 379) Resolutions favoring the purchase of bonds of the state of North Dakota were directed to be sent to all affiliated organizations for their favorable consideration.

Occupational Diseases—(1923, p. 90) Government employes were much exercised in February last when the comptroller general of the treasury made a decision that under the workmen's compensation act those who suffered from occupational diseases were not

entitled to benefits. The workmen's compensation commission had since the passage of the law granted compensation to all those suffering from diseases contracted as a result of their employment. The decision reversing the original rule was so contrary to the intent of the law that members of congress immediately took up the matter and a bill was introduced to counteract the effect of the comptroller general's decision. The bill provided for the payment of compensation in cases of occupational diseases to those who already had been receiving it or any who might be eligible for such compensation in the future. Congress, however, refused to pass the bill in its entirety. The law as enacted, known as Public No. 537, provides that only those persons who had been receiving compensation for occupational diseases upon an award made by the compensation commission should until March 1, 1924, be entitled to receive the amount specified unless set aside by the commission. Every effort will be made in the next congress to have a satisfactory law enacted. (P. 281) It is a sad and deplorable commentary upon the congress of the U. S. that legislative proposals of such great human concern that would provide at least a meager measure of relief to those unable to toil for their living because of physical impairments, occasioned by the very nature of their employment, should have found so little sympathy and response by our national legislators.

One Big Union—(1919, pp. 183-278) A meeting held January 13-15, 1919, at Calgary, Alta., under the title of the western provincial labor conference, adopted this resolution: "That the aims of labor as represented by this convention are the abolition of the present system of production for profit, and the substitution therefor of production for use, and that a system of propaganda to this end be carried out." The resolution committee recommended the adoption of the undermentioned resolution as a substitute for the many resolutions presented on industrial unionism:

"*Resolved*, That this convention recommend to organized labor in this dominion the severance of the present affiliation with the international organizations, and that steps be taken to form an industrial organization of all workers, and that a circular letter outlining the proposed plan of organization be sent out to the various organizations, and that a referendum on the question be taken at the same time, the votes east of Port Arthur to be compiled separately from those of the west." The policy committee made a report embodying the wishes of the conference, viz: "1. We recommend the name of the proposed organization to be 'The One Big Union.' 2. We recommend the conference elect a committee of five irrespective of geographical location for the purpose of carrying out the necessary propaganda to make the referendum a success. 3. We further recommend that delegates from each province meet and elect a committee of five to work in conjunction with the central committee in carrying on the necessary propaganda to accomplish the wishes of the convention. 4. We recommend the drafting and issuing of the referendum be left to the 'central committee' also receiving and publishing returns of the vote. 5. In the opinion of the committee it will be necessary in establishing an industrial form of organization to work through the existing trades council and district boards and no definite plan of organization be submitted until after the referendum has been taken. The committee further recommends that after the return of the vote is received the 'central committee' call a conference of representatives of trades councils and district boards to perfect the plans of organization basis of referendum of affiliated membership of 5,000 or less to be one delegate, over 5,000, 2 delegates, over 10,000, 3 delegates. 7. We recommend that an appeal be made to the trades councils and district boards for the payment of two cents per member affiliated to finance the educational campaign for the inauguration of 'The One Big Union.'" After considerable discussion the report was declared adopted.

The Executive Council of the Trades and Labor Congress of Canada, in Bulletin No. 3, dated April 19, last said: "During the past month an attempt at disruption of our movement has taken place by the launching of a campaign for the secession from international trade unions and the formation of 'one big union.' This can not in any measure be considered as reform or progress, but purely a secession movement which will result, if given support, in division of our ranks. The international trade union movement has been making rapid strides during the past year, over three hundred new local unions and several thousand members being added in Canada in that priod. The present is the time when the full force of the organized labor movement should be exercised, and any action which will weaken our forces and delay our opportunities to achieve results should be discountenanced. We do not intend to allow either outside or inside influences to work unopposed for the destruction of the organizations we represent and federal labor unions chartered by the congress, trades councils, and provincial federations of labor are advised and warned to take no action in support of this 'one big union' propaganda which would in any way conflict with the obligations they have taken, and the constitution of the Trades and Labor Congress of Canada. This matter will be dealt with more fully in a further statement. In conclusion we would advise that organization work be vigorously proceeded with. Where workers are eligible for membership in an international trade union of their craft or calling, direct application should be made that body. Where workers are not so eligible federal labor union charters should be applied for to the A. F. of L. When workers are not eligible to established international trade unions, but are employed by civic, provincial or federal governments, where their working conditions are controlled by legislative bodies, the congress will be pleased to issue federal union charters to them." (P. 323) The following was approved: The Wilmington Central Labor Union believes that the growth of the trades union movement can be attributed to the policy of progress that has been inaugurated and carried out by the A. F. of L., President Samuel Gompers and the Executive Council of the A. F. of L. We realize that this progress has been steady and resultful in bringing about desired improvements in working conditions, the increasing of wages and the shortening of hours. We do not believe in the untried and unsound doctrines that are being preached in propaganda tracts and on soap boxes against Mr. Samuel Gompers, president of the A. F. of L., and the A. F. of L., under his leadership. The Wilmington Central Labor Union does not believe that "one big union" principles

should be adopted by the A. F. of L. We realize that the remarkable progress made by the American labor movement was made through constant education of the membership of the trade unions and progression gradually with each further step in the education of the rank and file of the members of the craft unions.

(1920, p. 206) It is gratifying that in the convention of the Canadian Trades and Labor Congress, held in Hamilton, Ont., September, 1919, 950 delegates disavowed and repudiated the so-called "one big union" movement, while only one delegate recorded his vote in support of that movement. The vote came after a debate lasting two hours and after the Canadian trade unionists had had ample opportunity to consider the question from a practical as well as from a theoretical viewpoint. The repudiation of the "one big union" fallacy in Canada was a magnificent triumph for trade unionism, and a vindication of the purposes, policies and achievements of the A. F. of L.

(1921, pp. 150-374) As a factor in the industrial life of both Canada and the U. S. the so-called "One Big Union" has practically ceased to exist. This movement, which has been on the decline since the Winnipeg strike, is no longer considered as an active movement of any consequence. When the Executive Council met in Washington in March, the president of the Canadian Trades and Labor Congress appeared before the council to discuss affairs relating to our movement in Canada. Following this conference the council directed that a questionnaire be sent to all international unions having membership in Canada, in order that full and accurate information might be had as to the secession movement and as to the relation between the international and the Canadian Trades and Labor Congress. The replies to this questionnaire show that so far as the "One Big Union" is concerned, those international originally affected have in nearly all cases recovered and that but little evidence remains of the work of misguided persons who engineered the rise of the O. B. U. The replies from international officers show clearly that in every case where active organization work is carried on by the bona fide trade union movement, and where there is energetic and persistent educational work carried on, the "One Big Union" is able to make no headway. With the exception of an inconsequential scattering of membership, all that remains of that concern is the lesson of fruitless experience culminating in the disastrous Winnipeg strike. Another question brought before the council was the need for affiliation to the Canadian Trades and Labor Congress by those international unions which have not yet affiliated. While the Canadian Trades and Labor Congress has with success and with credit to itself succeeded in defeating the "One Big Union" movement, it still has serious problems and difficulties to solve and to overcome. It needs the full strength of the bona fide trade union movement in its struggles and is, we feel, entitled to the affiliation and support of all internationals having membership in Canada. We urge and recommend that such internationals, where they have not already done so, seek immediate affiliation of their Canadian locals with the Canadian Trades and Labor Congress and that every effort be made to co-operate in strengthening the movement for the support and advancement of the interests of the working people of Canada.

(1920, p. 348) In reply to addresses of welcome President Gompers said in part: We had the experience, in part, of what has come to be known as the one big union. To us, to the men and the women of labor who have studied the history of the struggles of the workers throughout the whole world, and in each country and from all time, we know that there is a camaraderie among the men of labor of each particular craft, or trade, or industry—that is also true of all professions—and though they feel a wonderful regard for all others, that spirit of camaraderie evolves and maintains a position of unity and cooperation much closer than to all the world. We love our neighbors as ourselves, or at least we are commanded to do so, but it is doubtful that there is generally the concept that we love our neighbors quite' as well as we do ourselves. And so with the organizations of the workers. Indeed these facts are typical of every living creature, of every living thing. Whether it be the beasts of the forests, whether it be the birds of the air or the fish in the seas, there is a natural attrition of life with life and no amount of sophistry or pretention can wipe out that natural condition. The One Big Union! It reminds me of an attempt at breaking eggs for the purpose of making an omelet, and then the cook, finding that the omelet has not turned out as he would like it, undertaking to bring about the restoration of the omelet into the egg shells. In the A. F. of L. movement as represented by our two countries, and in the industrial affairs and the labor movement of Great Britain, we find that the unions of labor are constantly extending their powers, or their claims to power, in gathering in the unorganized workers. We say that our movement is not a close corporation, it is not a hidebound institution, but to open the doors of our movement wide and not only ask and urge, but send out our missionaries to the men and women of toil, asking them to come in and join with us, both in the advantages secured and to be secured, and to meet the obligations and duties devolving upon enlightened men and women. And in the American labor movement on both sides of the line we have established, in addition to our local unions, our city central bodies, our national or dominion congresses or conventions, departments of the organized workers of the various unions of an industry, or of kindred industries, working out the highest ideal of cooperative effort and yet maintaining the autonomy and integrity of every trade and calling. At the time when I attended the British Trades Union Congress at Derby two years ago I heard a remark made which seemed to me to be quite important then, as it does seem to me now, that a committee might be appointed, and which was subsequently appointed, for the purpose of working out a solution of the jurisdiction problems, "the overlapping," as it is more frequently called in England, and the expression was that the committee having the subject matter in charge would by its report to the next Trades Union Congress finally and forever settle these jurisdiction disputes. I remember very definitely that when I had the honor of addressing the congress I wished the committee luck in their project, and said if there was anything in the history of the American trade union movement that could contribute to the final solution of jurisdiction disputes and claims it was at the disposition of the committee. In reading the report of the proceedings of the last British Trades Union

Congress held at Glasgow, I find that the problem has not been solved once and forever, and I doubt that it will ever be solved so long as labor is essential to human civilization and so long as the human mind continues to work out new inventions, new tools, new machinery, new devices, and so long as the human mind shall offer substitutes for materials already in existence. As a matter of fact, though the jurisdiction problems rise up and create discord, disputes and sometimes conflicts, yet, uncomfortable as it sometimes makes me, I know it is the constant endeavor of the human race in industry to find a way out that shall establish the best possible relations and conditions. It is the struggle of the human family, it is part of the struggle in this great industrial problem. We all claim to be willing to aid in progress; we all look forward to the time when tomorrow shall find a better expression of human needs than today. Many of us fail to understand that for every gain in the progress of the human race there is some form of compensation that we pay for it, that the law of compensation obtains and that some of us are afraid of the pain and the trouble which encompasses and accompanies the human struggle for freedom and progress. The American labor movement, as I try to interpret it, is our willingness to bear whatever pain and trouble and sacrifice may be necessary in order that progress shall be made and civilization established. We realize the fact that there is no royal road nor any short cut to human disenthrallment, no more than the life and the renewed life of the human race can be accomplished without pain and travail, no more than we can expect the infants just learning to walk, with the falls and mishaps to which it is heir, can be entered in a marathon race and be expected to compete with the best athletes. It is the human struggle and human progress through struggle. I shall not attempt, particularly at this time, to speak of labor parties and political action. More than likely this will come before the convention in a concrete form. In any event, our policy has been outlined and declared. Forty years of experience, forty years of success and triumph, forty years of setbacks, but forty years of overcoming difficulties and problems and finally attaining the purpose for which we were organized. In human progress there is action and reaction. The pendulum of movements and of progress swings one way and then another. In the labor movement, for the interests, for the rights, for the advancement of the workers and for the advancement of the whole people, for centuries the pendulum stood still, not at the center of gravity, but always down, down, hard upon the workers of the world. The pendulum has swung partly toward the other side, and we breathe more freely, meet more openly, declare our position more manfully, and more intelligently. The demands which labor movements make, not only upon employers, but upon society, the demands made upon government and upon employers, upon society for the service labor performs and gives to society, and without which service progress would be impossible and civilization would come to a standstill. Labor makes the demand for a better and a higher life, to be regarded, not as men typified by the "Man with the Hoe," with bent back and receding forehead, not with a suppliant's knee, but as men demanding their just recognition and the reward to which they are so justly entitled. And we are going to press forward and onward and upward, never lagging in our effort and our course. There may be here and there some who will not subordinate their individual preferment to the general good. The labor movement, while it does not attempt to express the unanimous views of all those in whose name it speaks, does expect that the moral obligation devolves upon all of us to see to it that the standards and the banner under which we struggle and the demands which labor makes shall receive the moral support of all our people. We do not set ourselves up as part of or superior to the governments in whose countries we live; we do not claim anything of this character, but the men and the women in the labor movement are the militant forces which appeal to the conscience of all our people. Even Canada, with her wonderful activities and all the sacrifices of her people in this great and awful struggle which has come to a close, did not send her entire manhood to France and to Flanders. Canada sent her available fighting men. The manhood and womanhood of Canada were no less interested and vitally affected by the war than were those who went to the front. It is the comparative few in a nation who are the militant defendants and advocates of the rights and hopes and the interests of the people at home. And so with the labor movement industrially. All the workers are not organized men. Regrettable as that may .be, it is true. But those who are organized, even though we use the term militantly, those who are by peaceful and lawful means exercising their industrial rights, are the vanguard and form the great army of labor in defense of and for the protection and promotion of the rights and interests of all the people. Honored Sir, may I say that I am profoundly impressed and appreciative of what you have said in regard to our movement in our common countries, and the very high compliment you have seen fit to pay me. With you, we are one in believing that it is pitiable that the U. S. has not ratified the covenant of the league of nations, not only for the great ideal of making a sincere effort to maintain the peace of the world, and that such a catastrophe as that which came over the world six years ago shall never again be possible; at least, the effort might be made that such a war should never again occur. In addition to this labor draft convention by which all should help, all the peoples and all the governments should help, in raising the standards of the working people of this work-a-day world, and particularly to help the workers in the most backward countries. They can do little or nothing for the working people of the U. S. or of Canada. As a matter of fact, we want little of their help, but we can help others, and I hold it to be the duty of far-seeing, thinking, humane men and women to give a helping hand to lift those who are so far down to take their places among the civilized manhood and womanhood of the world. I believe if the question itself were submitted to the people of the U. S. to ratify or defeat the covenant of the league of nations, without any other entangling question, the people of our country would by an overwhelming vote show that they desire a league of nations. If a question of this character is brought into a campaign and is part of declarations of all the political parties, enveloped and covered and perhaps overwhelmed by other problems of an internal character, with the

person of one candidate to represent all these ideas, the whole question of a league of nations may be lost. It is regrettable that the question in itself might not have had the opportunity for the consideration and the determination of the people of our country. In any event, we are as we are; we are making the best progress that it is possible and giving our aid to any movement that shall help to bring about that day for which the poets have sung and of which the philosophers dreamed and for which the masses of the people have always found it necessary to struggle, the day when universal peace and brotherhood and good will shall obtain now and forever.

"One Big Union" in Canada—(1920, p. 231) The "one big union" has continued its campaign of vilification against the officers of international trade unions, the A. F. of L. and the Trades and Labor Congress of Canada and have succeeded in temporarily alienating many members of the international labor movement by these methods. Their policy of general strike, though ending in failure whenever put into operation, nevertheless still finds some favor with workers who have little experience of organized effort. While claiming a membership of 41,000 the figures submitted for the amount of per capita tax paid up to the time of their convention in Winnipeg in January this year their balance sheet shows a per capita tax collected of $5,200 which can not mean more than 5,000 dues paying members. Increased activity is also being shown by the national catholic unions who are waging an aggressive warfare in the province of Quebec against international trade unionism. They submit a claim to the dominion government directory of labor of a membership of 35,000, but for the purpose of showing this membership have changed their name from National Catholic Federation of Labor Unions to the National Catholic Union and have included in their aggregate membership many forms of organization which can not by any stretch of the imagination be classed as labor organizations.

"Open Shop"—(1921, p. 422) Following is from a bulletin sent out by employers in the printing industry to members of their association in advocacy of the non-union shop: "Don't give the unions a toe-hold in your plant or they will soon have you in a headlock. Whenever you put a union member on your pay roll you are simply contributing your good money to funds that will be used to fight you. Let the men come back only when they decide to tear up their union cards and sign individual contracts." There is the entire open shop question and is a statement from employers themselves that the open shop means that no member of a labor organization can get employment in such an institution.

(1922, pp. 72-263) During the year the efforts of employers to disrupt the trade union movement by means of a campaign for the so-called "open shop" have continued with great vigor but with little result. The instinctive resistance of the workers to the deception offered by employers has been sufficient to prevent any noteworthy progress in the establishment of the so-called "open shop" in any of its forms. One of the variations of the non-union shop idea fostered by employers is the so-called "American plan." There is nothing American about this plan, since it contains none of the elements of true democracy but contains all of the elements of autocracy. This has been obvious to the workers everywhere and they have generally declined to be deceived. We are unable to say that the danger of the anti-union shop movement has passed because that danger will persist as long as there are employers who are short-sighted enough not to see the tremendous advantages to be derived from the establishment of better relations with organized workers. We are able to say, however, and we say with much pride and satisfaction, that the labor movement has held its lines everywhere, and this despite most unfavorable conditions caused by the widespread industrial depression. It would have been an achievement under any circumstances to have resisted the tremendous campaign of employers to establish what they are pleased to call the "open shop." It is an immeasurably greater achievement and an immeasurably higher testimonial to the intelligence and solidarity of the workers to say that they have so successfully resisted during a period of unexampled unemployment and suffering. There is scarcely a trade in which there has not been conducted an organized campaign for the establishment of the so-called "open shop." Not only employers but big business and high finance throughout the country have contributed financially to this campaign and an enormous fund has been used in propaganda work. Indeed, it is an undisputed fact that to a large extent the campaign was the result of the work of professional propagandists who make it their business to sell their services to the highest bidder without regard to the character of the work to be done. They are exactly comparable to that with which European labor for decades has had to contend, the despicable *agents provocateurs*. Chambers of commerce throughout the country, with certain notable exceptions, have lent themselves to this disruptive propaganda. The U. S. chamber of commerce, which seeks to be the guiding spirit of all local chambers of commerce, has supported the movement, although we are informed there is much sentiment within the U. S. chamber of commerce to the effect that a grave error has been committed and that the organization should not have given its sanction to the campaign. However, having committed itself, it apparently feels under the necessity of making as brave a showing as possible in the direction of consistency. The organization is about to begin the construction of a three-million dollar headquarters building in the city of Washington and has announced its purpose of constructing this building on the "open shop" basis. The experiment to be tried in the capital of the nation on so pretentious a scale will undoubtedly be watched with great interest by workers and employers alike. There is but one answer to the entire campaign of employers for the disruption and destruction of the labor movement and that is continued organization, eternal vigilance and the highest degree of solidarity. There is no complicated device by which the campaign of employers may be met; the answer is simplicity itself. It is merely that the workers must organize and must stay organized. They must use every effort to gain an intelligent understanding of all industrial problems and they must bring to their organized efforts the highest quality of industrial statesmanship. The struggle is one between organization and disorganization. Nothing else is involved and organization is the complete answer. There can be no "open shop" where the workers are 100 per cent organized.

(1923, pp 58-208) "It is an ill wind that bloweth no man good." There is no better exemplification of that axiom than the defeat of that most disgraceful campaign to introduce autocracy in industry through the subterfuge of the so-called "open shop." That un-American scheme was the means of uniting the organized wage earners more solidly. The hypocrisy of the movement was so apparent that the great public had no sympathy with it or its purpose. The Executive Council believes that the unfair employers overstepped themselves and instead of securing benefits to gratify their power and satisfy their greed they have caused labor to place itself in a better position than ever before. Before the war ended and while our boys were offering the supreme sacrifice certain unfair employers who were profiting by the conflict arranged for an insidious propaganda campaign to break down American standards by introducing the so-called "open shop" in industry. They folded about themselves the cloak of patriotism and called their un-American plan the "American" plan. Lawyers who had gained notoriety through prosecution of wage earners engaged in normal trade union activities organized groups of employers who were willing to degrade the wage workers for their personal gain. The Associated Employers' Association, Inc., of Indianapolis, launched a campaign for the "open shop." It sent letters to as many employers whose names they could learn in nearly every city in the country. It was urged that these employers get together and form an "open shop" association. The newspapers were full of the bitter warfare on labor and how labor was to be driven to the wall by the "open shop" movement. The real object behind the "open shop" movement was to reduce wages. It was thought that by breaking up or disorganizing the unions it would be an easy matter to cut wages to the bone and thus break down American standards. During this time the big interests through the federal reserve board and in other ways began a campaign of deflation of labor and of the farmers. Unemployment grew at an alarming rate until according to the secretary of labor more than 5,000,000 workers were walking the streets in 1921. Then the unfair employers took advantage of the situation to carry out their scheme of establishing autocracy in industry. First the printing trades were attacked. The employers had made an agreement that on May 1, 1921, they would grant the 44-hour week in the book and job offices of the country, but before May 1 by a series of lockouts, demands for reductions in wages and other acts to cause dissension, they endeavored to force the printing trades to take the offensive and save the employers from the obloquy of their acts. However, the printers remained at work until May 1 and then were forced to quit because the employers violated their contract. The coal operators refused to meet representatives of the miners to make a contract for the year beginning April 1, 1922, and demanded a reduction in wages. The miners could not work after April 1 without a contract and they ceased work. The textile workers after repeated reductions in wages protested in the only way they could protest and that was by ceasing work. So did the railroad shopmen and granite cutters. But those who would reduce wages and establish autocracy in industry failed. After five months' cessation of work an agreement was reached by the miners and they returned to work at the same wages they had received the previous year. The textile workers were largely successful, the printers as well as the granite cutters and the railway shopmen. The railway shopmen not only stopped reduction in wages by the labor board, but they have restored negotiations so that now the greater number of individual roads treat with them instead of the nation-wide association controlled by the Pennsylvania Railroad. The A. F. of L. is of the firm opinion that the successful strikes of the nearly 2,000,000 wage earners in the U. S. are responsible for the prosperity the country is enjoying since these strikes were adjusted by collective bargaining. It must also not be forgotten that where organized labor maintained its wage scales and secured increases the unorganized benefited thereby so that the great struggle of organized labor to defeat the purposes of a small band of unfair employers not only brought prosperity to themselves but to the unorganized as well as to all our people. So much has been printed about the membership of the Associated Employers' Association and its alleged success in making Indianapolis an "open shop" city than an investigation was made that showed that organization was mostly on paper. In March of this year it was found that the association had only 50 members in that city and only about 1,000 in the entire U. S. and Canada. March 21, 1923, the Association had a meeting to which all the enemies of union labor that would attend were invited. It was addressed, however, by the president of the Illinois Brick Company which for many years has made agreements with the brick and clay workers' union and with other unions of wage earners. Instead of being an "open shop" city Indianapolis in a number of trades is one of the best organized cities of its size in the United States. Even the president of the Associated Employers' Association, Inc., had to employ union men exclusively on a residence he had erected for himself. There were few strikes in Indianapolis because the employers believe in collective bargaining and this association is securing publicity under false pretenses. The building trades are nearly 100 per cent organized. The machinists noted no effect of the campaign carried on by the association. In fact, the conditions of the machinists in Indianapolis compare favorably with any other city of the same size. What will surprise people outside of Indianapolis is the fact that the machinists scarcely know there is such an association as the Associated Employers' Association, Inc., in existence. Another important fact should not be overlooked. Approximately 95 per cent of the newspapers of the country conduct union shops. Still the great majority of them give publicity to the propaganda of the "open shoppers." This is not because they believe in the "open shop," for they prefer the "closed shop," but that those who are establishing autocracy in industry are the advertisers upon whom they must rely to pay the expenses of publishing the newspapers and give them profits. The A. F. of L. is therefore decisively of the opinion that the "open shop" campaign received publicity that was not only unwarranted, but most deceptive and undoubtedly many people believed it had made great headway in establishing autocracy in industry. But this is not the case. However, the president of the A. F. of L. should continue to acquaint labor organizations of the true status of the fight of unfair employers for the "open shop" and their humiliating defeat.

"Open Shop" in Canada—(1921, p. 172). The campaign for the open shop which is being

so vigorously carried on in the U. S. is also vigorously propounded in Canada, and is designated under the title of "optional plan of employment and the open shop." Wage reductions have also been forced wherever the workers have been too weakly organized to resist them and in general the organized workers of Canada are being faced with much the same industrial problems as those existing in the U. S. With the continued solidarity of the workers of the North American continent, as represented in the international trade union movement, the A. F. of L. and the Trades and Labor Congress of Canada, the future can be confidently looked forward to and though unemployment is still ripe and has been very serious all through the past winter we have every reason for optimism for the future.

"Open Shop," Religious Declarations Against—(1921, p. 385) Declarations by the National Catholic Welfare Council, Federal Council of the Churches of Christ in America and the Central Conference of American Rabbis against the "open shop" are hereby recognized as intelligent and most humane documents of inestimable value to the organized workers and the public in general.

"Open Shop" Scheme—(1921, p. 384) Denounced the action of a firm in Springfield, Mass., that had endeavored to fasten on the working people the sinister liberty destroying employment of individual contract to aid the "open shop" campaign of various employers' associations.

Organizers—(1919, p. 163) During the year jut closed the 2,091 organizers of the A. F. of L. have rendered a service to the cause that is beyond estimate. The great growth of the Federation is in great part due to the loyal and unremitting efforts of these men and women, many of whom give their time after their day's work is done, with no remuneration beyond that which come as of sense of service given to a great cause. The great work done by the organizers, as chronicled monthly in the *American Federationist*, has been we feel sure, a source of gratification and inspiration to the entire labor movement. We desire to express our deep appreciation of this splendid service and of the devotion which prompted it.

(1920, p. 208) During the year just closed, organizers for the A. F. of L. have done exceptionally valuable work, for which they are deservedly commended by the federation. Not only have the organizers regularly paid by the federation done work of great value, but the hundreds of volunteer organizers have been unusually active and unusually effective. The great growth of the federation during the year is the best testimony to the character of the work which has been done. Organizers, both salaried and volunteer, have during the year worked at time under most trying circumstances and, in some cases, in positions of actual danger to their own safety. This has been the case particularly in the organization work done in the steel industry. We commend most sincerely the splendid work done during the year just closed. While the results that have been achieved have been of the most satisfactory nature there is still much to be done. Many workers remain unorganized and are consequently voiceless. Great have been the efforts made in the past. The future must, we feel, bring forth still greater efforts in the work of organization. It is imperative that organization work proceed intelligently, both for the sake of those who remain unorganized and for the sake of those who are organized. There is in America no more potent factor for progress than the bona fide labor movement. The more effective the organization of the workers, the greater will be the beneficent results schieved. Every possible effort must be made during the coming year to strengthen the organized labor movement, and to this end we call upon national and international trade unions, state federations, central bodies, and local unions as well as organizers generally in America, to put forth their best efforts and to surpass in effectiveness the magnificent achievements already acccomplished.

(1921, p. 146) During the year A. F. of L. organizers have faced a task made more difficult by the campaign conducted by employers to break down the labor movement. Despite economies that have been necessary in the organizing staff, both the salaried and volunteer organizers have rendered exceptional service under trying circumstances. We wish heartily to commend the work of our organizers and to encourage them in their most valuable and necessary work. The work of organizing is of first importance. It is to a large degree through the efforts of these paid and unpaid men and women that the message of the trade union movement is brought to the unorganized to light their lives and their work. We wish to express our appreciation of this loyal and faithful work and to bespeak for our organizers the hearty and cordial support and assistance of the movement throughout our country.

(1922, pp. 145-262) More than ever the work of our volunteer organizers has been of importance during the last year. The fact that our movement has been able to withstand attack so successfully is in part due to the splendid efforts of voluntary organizers who have been unremitting in their vigilance and untiring in their work. We bespeak for them the gratitude of the movement and we feel confident that their efforts in the future will be as energetic and successful as in the year that has passed. In connection with the work of the salaried organizers of the A. F. of L. there should be borne in mind the fact these organizers whenever they are called upon or whenever the occasion requires give every possible assistance to the national and international unions, not only in organization work but in helping to avert trade disturbances and in adjusting trade disputes. Through this assistance and cooperation a number of strikes have been averted that would have cost the A. F. of L. as well as affiliated unions large sums of money. Our organizers have proven helpful likewise in adjusting differences with employers and in securing to the unions concerned the conditions of employment desired. In addition, they have been frequently called upon to give their helpful service to the state labor movements in legislation advocated by the state movements and endorsed by the A. F. of L.

(1923, pp. 34-209) The work of the volunteer and salaried organizers has been of unusual importance during the year just closed. We wish particularly to record our appreciation of the work of the great number of volunteer organizers whose services have been given cheerfully and unselfishly for the advancement of labor's cause. It would be difficult if not impossible to conduct the organization work of the A. F. of L. without the assistance of the constantly growing number of volunteer organizers. Our salaried organizers have continued to render valuable services not only in the organization of the unorganized but in the adjustment of grievances and disputes which otherwise might have resulted in strikes costly to affiliated national and international unions, the A. F. of L. and the individual workers directly involved. In addition to this our organizers have been of material assistance to state federations of labor in various legislative campaigns. We commend the work of the organizers and urge upon them renewed efforts in behalf of the organized and in the organization of the unorganized.

Overtime—(1919, p. 450) It is necessary to provide for price and one-half or double price for time worked over a specified number of hours and time worked on Sunday and holidays in order so far as possible to prevent the working of members of labor organizations beyond what are recognized to be reasonable hours and those named in contracts and wage scales. The employers of labor frequently ridicule the penalizing of overtime with the statement that it is inconsistent for labor organizations to demand a shorter work day and then provide for a different price for time worked beyond the hours named. This is a specious argument and put forth only for the purpose of confusing and clouding the issue. The increased price for overtime, Sundays and holidays is made for the purpose of, so far as possible, preventing the working of people during these times and hours. Practically all, if not all of the international unions have been able to secure the adoption of overtime rates in contracts with private employers. We can see no possible reason why the government under which we live should not give to its employes at least as good conditions, as good wages and as short hours as is given in any of the industries conducted by citizen employers of labor. (P. 454) We believe that no matter what workday may be established, sufficient remuneration should be received by the workers to make it possible to live comfortably without working overtime or on Sundays or holidays. It may be true that in certain industries "extraordinary emergencies" arise that at times make it necessary for a certain amount of overtime or Sunday work to be done. In order to as much as possible prevent these "extraordinary emergencies" arising it is necessary to provide a special rate of pay for this overtime work. It has been found necessary in most of the industries to provide for time and one-half or double time for this class of work, and in some of these crafts it would be disastrous to eliminate such provisions. All national and international unions should impress upon their subordinate unions as strongly as possible the necessity for preventing overtime work.

Panama Canal Zone—(1919, p. 380) Executive Committee directed to investigate charges that rules under which employes on the Canal Zone work are made by presidential executive orders, official circulars and by the administration of the Panama Canal and Panama Railroad without consultation with or advice of the workers. (P. 460) Executive Council was also directed to investigate protest of the Panama Canal Central Labor Union against the organization of aliens.

(1920, p. 375) Executive Council directed to take up with the proper authorities the amendment of the manual of information in order to eliminate the employment of alien labor in the operating and mechanical departments and also to urge the Panama

Canal Commission to employ American citizens only in those departments.

(1921, pp. 150-329) The matter of amending the manual of information of the Canal Zone with a view of eliminating the emergency clauses that permit the employment of alien labor in the operating and mechanical departments was taken up with the secretary of war, who, in reply, contended that "we ought all to recognize the desirability of a change when it can be made which will reduce the number of people from the states who are required in the operation and maintenance of the canal." The secretary also contended that it had been definitely shown that life in the tropics was injurious to the health of the people from the states. For that reason he said the U. S. should as far as possible refrain from sending its own citizens to the zone and that all work there which could be done by workers who are acclimated ought to be done by them. During the war the secretary was requested by the building trades department of the A. F. of L. to eliminate the emergency clauses, but it was mutually agreed to defer action until hostilities had ceased. Since the war, however, American citizens are being separated from the service in the Canal Zone and their places are being filled by aliens. The request for affiliation with the A. F. of L. of the Union Obrera de Panamenos of Balboa Heights, Canal Zone, was referred to the various international unions interested. They declared: "It is our belief and understanding that the applicants or a major portion of them are not citizens of Panama nor have they any intention of ever becoming citizens of Panama or of the U. S. That to issue the latter (aliens) a charter would overwhelm our central bodies with aliens whose apparent intention is to invade the jurisdiction of the established organizations at a rate of pay fixed by the Panama Canal authorities and known as the silver roll, far and away below the rate of American standard. We firmly believe that in all such important projects as the Panama Canal, American citizens only should be employed at least in the operating and mechanical departments as a measure of safety to American interests." In view of the action of the conference the application for the charter of the Union Obrera de Panamenos (composed of workers alien to Panama and the United States) was denied.

(1922, pp. 105-485) While looking over government departments to determine where further reductions in wages could be made the secretary of war found the Canal Zone. He sent a commission to Panama to make an investigation. It recommended that conditions granted to employes because of the sacrifices they had to make in going there to work should be taken away from them. These included house rent, light, heat and transportation to and from work. The secretary of war approved of the report. He also ordered that, thereafter, all dealings should be through "committees or representatives composed of employes whether representatives of labor organizations or not." It was ordered that it would not be necessary to pay the union rates in force in the U. S. but those actually paid for similar services whether it be union or non-union rates. All agreements limiting the use of alien laborers were abrogated, and their wider use recommended with the modification that aliens could not work in the responsible positions.

Pan-American Federation of Labor— (1919, p. 87) The first international labor conference of the Pan-American countries was held in Laredo, Texas, on November 13, 14, 15 and 16, 1918. The labor movements of the U. S. of America, of Mexico and the Central and the South American States of Guatemala, Costa Rica, Salvador and Colombia were represented by a total of seventy-two delegates. Antonio Correa of Cuba and Cardenio Gonzalez S. of Chile, both accredited members of the Pan-American Federation of Labor Conference Committee, were unable to be present. Honorable W. B. Wilson, secretary of labor, attended the conference as the representative of President Wilson. General Pablo de la Garza, the personal representative of President Carranza, in like manner conveyed the greetings of the president of Mexico to the conference. Honorable George W. P. Hunt, governor of Arizona, addressed the conference, declaring that the meeting laid the basis for fraternal cooperation between the workers of North and South America. The welcome by unions of carpenters, painters, blacksmiths, retail clerks, and other trade unions whose members spoke Spanish, the enthusiastic reception given to this international meeting, can best be appreciated by those who know the long history of strife upon the border caused by the lack of direct understandings and conferences between the workers of the two countries. Secret diplomacy has been the rule upon the border causing in great part the strife engendered in the last fifty years. The international labor conference established the precedent of open diplomacy conducted directly between peoples of the two countries involved. It followed, therefore, that the residents all along the border, especially those of Mexican blood, welcomed the conference with an enthusiasm never given before to any public assemblage on the boundary line. The conference unanimously voted to form the Pan-American Federation of Labor to be composed of the organized labor movements of the U. S. of America, the United States of Mexico, and the labor organizations of the Republics of Central and South America. The objects of the Pan-American Federation of Labor were declared to be: "1. The establishment of better conditions for the working people who emigrate from one country to another. 2. The establishment of a better understanding and relationship between the peoples of the Pan-American Republics. 3. To utilize every lawful and honorable means for the protection and promotion of the rights, the interests and the welfare of the peoples of the Pan-American Republics. 4. To utilize every lawful and honorable means for the purpose of cultivating the most favorable and friendly relations between the labor movements and peoples of the Pan-American Republics." From the beneficial results already achieved in creating mutual respect, good will and confidence among the workers and the peoples of Mexico and of the U. S. and further with the representatives of labor and peoples of several of the Latin and Central American countries, we regard the establishment of the Pan-American Federation of Labor as an augury that still greater mutual respect, good will and confidence will ensue between the peoples and the governments of the Pan-American countries. (P. 417) The A. F. of L. determined several years ago to inaugurate trade union movements in our southern sister republics. Efforts were first made in Mexico, where a formidable labor movement had been organized. The labor movement in Mexico, crude and imperfect though it was at that time, was an effective means for bringing about a better understanding between the workers of our own country and those in Mexico, and of doing more than any other agency in preventing a war between the U. S. and that country in the year of 1912 and since. This was accomplished through the president of the A. F. of L. bringing into correspondence and personal conferences the representatives of both countries. The leaders of our trade union movement foresaw the absolute necessity of organizing the workers of South America along trade union lines for the purpose of protecting their interests and advancing their economic conditions. In all parts of Central and South America the attention of the workers was purposely misguided and kept at fever heat over politics by the privileged few, the exploiters of labor, the predatory rich. Just so long as they were kept in this frame of mind they paid no attention to the only real movement—a trade union movement, that would have protected their working and living conditions. They kept on shouting politics but worked for 70 cents a day. After all the question is predominatingly economic. Back of the cause of unrest is the economic condition of the masses. There is just as much unrest and discontent in the republics in Europe as there is under constitutional monarchies. The degree of virility and constructive work and results in the improvement in the life of the masses is measured absolutely and exclusively by the power, strength and effectiveness of the trade union movement. South and Central America is composed exclusively of republics. There is plenty of political activity but a dearth of trade union energy. It is a subject of general comment that the frequency of political revolutions in many of the South American republics accomplish nothing insofar as the economic well-being of the industrial workers is concerned. The thing that will bring practicable results there, here, or elsewhere, is fair wages, shorter hours and reasonable working conditions. This can be accomplished through and only through the trade unions. The formation of trade unions in Mexico and the substantial advances and achievements that followed roused attention and the desire to form trade unions in the republics of Central and South America. This movement met with a fair degree of success. There followed in South and Central American countries the formation of federations of labor. The connecting link between the labor movements of North and South America was the formation of the Pan-American Federation of Labor.

(1920, p. 121) The second Pan-American Federation of Labor convention was held in New York City beginning July 7. 1919. The labor movements of the U. S., Mexico, Honduras, Nicaraugua, El Salvadore, Dominican Republic, Ecuador and Peru were represented. Resolutions were adopted urging upon the U. S. secretary of the treasury that no financial, industrial or commercial plans can be wisely determined without due consideration to the interest of human agents necessary to carry out all projects, and that in order for the Pan-American financial conference to develop most effective plans there must be provided in that conference representation for the wage earners of those countries concerned, as well as for the managements of industry and commerce. Also, hailing with satisfaction the ending of the unfortunate war and heartily approving and endorsing the covenant of the league of nations as part of the peace treaty as an earnest effort to maintain the peace of the world; to do justice to every nation large and small and thus safeguard the peoples and nations from a recurrence of such a slaughter and destruction as the world has witnessed in the war just closed, and also the labor draft convention and the labor charter in the covenant of the league of nations of the peace treaty and earnestly express the hope that the time may soon be reached when under the covenant of the league of nations and the labor draft convention, all the workers and representatives of the countries of the world may be leagued in a common heritage of internationality, fraternity, justice, freedom, and democracy," that all nations, including all of the American countries, shall be eligible to membership in the league of nations. Other resolutions were adopted recommending the issuance by the officers of the Pan-American Federation of Labor of a manifesto setting forth the objects and principles of the organization; declaring for the autonomy of all the affiliated labor movements within their own country; recommending a closer touch with the European labor movements; calling upon the workers of all the American countries to organize in trade unions, these to create a central or national labor federation; declaring for the establishment of the eight-hour working day where not yet established; for the cultivation of uncultivated lands as a means of increasing production and reducing the high cost of living; favoring a larger distribution of free scholarships in colleges and universities for the sons and daughters of workingmen, and the building of hygienic homes for the workers by government enterprise on easy payments and low rates of interests; approval of the proposition to organize an International Federation of Trade Unions, representative of the workers all over the world; favoring the establishment of cooperative socieites and stores; holding inviolate the right of the workers to use the strike as the last resort in their efforts to improve their conditions; recommending the passage of workmen's compensation laws, and an increase in educational institutions for workers and their children. The New York Pan-American Congress also declared in favor of a peaceful solution of the territorial dispute of long standing between the South American Republics of Chile and Peru which has assumed alarming proportions during the last two years and recommended to the workers of both countries that they put forth their best efforts to prevent any serious friction and to maintain the best friendly relations between their peoples as a means of helping to a peaceful solution of their problem. Other resolutions asked for an investigation of the abnormal situation in the Central American Republic of Nicaragua where it is claimed the U. S. has exercised a certain form of control in its domestic affairs during the last eight or ten years, declared its determination to maintain and improve the relations between Mexico and the U. S., and denounced the selfish interests which are seeking to have the U. S. intervene by armed force or otherwise, in the affairs of our sister republic. (P. 124) Executive Council reported: "Relations with the Latin-Americans, Mexico in particular, have been constantly made more difficult and complicated by reason of the propaganda emanating from those who have selfish interests to serve and by reason of the utterances of those whose thought is chiefly or entirely of the employers and exploiters. It is an established fact that American interests with large holdings in Mexico maintain an organized propaganda, the object of which is to discredit the people and the government of that country. We condemn this propaganda as vicious and as a danger to our national welfare. By this propaganda our national good will is brought into question in all Latin-American countries and suspicion is fastened upon our people, unjustly but not without reason. In addition to the organized, purposeful propaganda, there has been in recent months a subcommittee of the foreign relations committee of the U. S. senate, under the chairmanship of Senator Albert B. Fall, of New Mexico, engaged in the work of gathering testimony relative to conditions in Mexico. Senator Fall's committee has done much to destroy Latin-American faith in the American government. Its work has been colored by an evident prejudice and its report is discredited in advance with all thinking people. From the authentic information we have upon which we base our report we are firmly persuaded that it is the duty of this convention to condemn such biased and partisan operations, the more so when they are cloaked with senatorial authority and we call upon the senate to repudiate the report of Senator Fall's committee as unworthy of America, for whatever the report may recommend is made valueless by the prejudiced methods followed by the committee in conducting its hearings." (P. 474) Relations between the U. S. and the other nations on the American continent are constantly becoming more intimate in every direction; and it is essential for our common welfare that the relations of the labor movements of these countries be developed to keep pace with the development of the relations of other interests. We heartily commend the work of the Pan-American Federation of Labor in general and recommend that every possible effort be made to strengthen the organization, so that it may fully and efficiently meet the needs of the working people of all American nations and fully conserve their rights, interests and welfare.

(1921, p. 82) The third convention of the Pan-American Federation of Labor was held in Mexico City January 10-16, 1921. (P. 85) The character of the labor movements of most of the Latin-American nations differs considerably from that of our own. This is but natural, considering their industrial and political struggles and the influence of radical European literature, the readiest at hand and redolent of socialism, syndicalism and their various allies. Also they are almost exclusively agricultural countries. Of more than ordinary gratification, therefore, was the adoption by an enthusiastic unanimous vote of a resolution introduced by the American delegation based upon constructive trade unionism and a complete and absolute repudiation of all doctrines subversive of evolutionary progress and democracy. The adoption by the Pan-American Federation of Labor of this platform is regarded as one of the great labor events of the year. This program or declaration of principles, which was ordered printed in Spanish and English for distribution in all Pan-American countries is as follows: "Political freedom, the right of the workers to have a voice and vote equal to that of every other citizen is the first practical step toward those individual rights which are essential to liberty. But political liberty, working through the legislative, executive and judicial departments of the organized government of a free people does not, and should not be permitted to enter into that personal (non-governmental) relationship between wage earner and employer through which the terms of employment are determined by the recognition of equality of rights and the joint agreement of both parties. The trade union movement holds that the principle of self-government by free peoples and the principle that in industry and commerce the wage earners through their organization should freely and fully participate in determining the terms of employment, are identical. The principle that governments should only exist with the consent of the governed is identical with the principle that the terms of employment, conditions of labor and the rules and regulations of employment should only exist with the consent of the employed. We regard it as essential to the success of our movement that there be a clear and definite statement as to the attitude of this federation toward questions subject to controversy and honest difference, not only because of our desire to promote understanding among those now affiliated to the federation, but so that those not yet affiliated may the more readily understand the character of our federation and the more quickly assume their proper responsibilities by seeking affiliation. We, the delegates assembled in this congress, regard it as essential that it be established as a foundation principle that progress can be achieved only through agreement. The aim of our federation must be to find those programs, principles and tactics upon which agreement can be had. This federation has a right to life only because it is of service to the workers and there is no service in disunity and disharmony. Those matters regarded as essential by some, but not by all, should be held in abeyance until the processes of education, understanding and experience develop agreement among all. Any effort to force upon minorities principles or tactics to which they can not give consent, must, in an international federation such as this, lead to destruction. In like manner any effort of minorities, through strategy or otherwise, to thrust their decisions upon majorities must be equally fatal. We call the attention of all workers to the vital need of education as a prime requisite of intelligent progress. We set it down as a fundamental fact that a high state of democratic civilization and enlightenment can not be founded upon ignorance. The more highly our civilization is developed, the more complete must be the degree of education, enlightenment and understanding of the workers if democracy is to be preserved and its opportunities kept open to those who do the useful work of all nations. We urge upon all affiliated organizations, and upon labor movements everywhere, the prime necessity of encouraging education, of insisting upon education and of securing the just right to participation in the development and administration of education. Our movement is a movement of protest against wrong and injustice and a movement of constructive progress. We can not develop beyond the understanding of the working people everywhere. Without an intelligent and understanding labor movement, capable of receiving and transmitting thought and capable of a proper appraisal of facts, conditions and theories, there can be only chaos or tyranny. Proper education is a first requisite of democratic constructive progress. One of the primary conditions essential to the success of our movement in our respective countries as well as that of the Pan-American Federation of Labor is the organization of the yet unorganized wage workers, whether skilled or unskilled, into unions of their trades, callings or industries and the unity of these organizations for the cultivation of the spirit and action of fraternity and solidarity. We regard as essential the extension of democracy in industry and we declare our unalterable opposition to interference in the processes of industry by forces outside of the industrial field and therefore incompetent to deal with its problems. We urge upon the labor movement everywhere the extension of the practice of negotiation between the employers and the workers and the making of trade agreements. We hold this to be the first great step in the development of democracy in industry and we hold that in no other way can such democracy be developed. There is no democracy while the workers are inarticulate and the workers can have no effective voice except through organization on the industrial field." (P. 444) The A. F. of L. has been from the first the ardent champion of freedom for the Mexican people, and it is to us a source of the deepest gratification to know that our hopes are finding fruition. Mexico has been and is beset with problems of the most difficult nature. Her working people struggle and labor under grave and complex burdens. We can only offer our help and encouragement. The fundamentals of solution must be the fruit of the thought of the Mexican workers and of their experience. We are mindful of the greed which still seeks satisfaction in the rich resources of Mexico and in so far as that greed emanates from our country we must feel bound to place ourselves in opposition to it. It is not going beyond the bounds of good citizenship to express here the hope that relations between our govenment and the Mexican government soon may be re-established on a basis of honor and respect, in order that our people may have that official contact and communication which is essential in modern society. We believe that an early adoption of such a course, re-establishing the relations of the two nations on a sound and friendly basis, will do much to bring speedy solution to other problems of importance, which, in the absence of official friendly relations, are less likely of speedy and amicable settlement. In addition, we believe there should be the closest contact between the movements of the workers in both countries. The Mexican workers have a bona fide trade union movement. To the end that there may be a better understanding and a more harmonious relationship where it is so essential, the Executive Council of the A. F. of L. is directed to keep in the closest possible relations through correspondence with the Mexican Federation of Labor.

(1922, p. 145) No convention of the Pan-American Federation of Labor has been held since the last A. F. of L. convention. We are informed that it is not the intention of the Pan-American Federation of Labor to hold a convention this year; meanwhile the relations of the A. F. cf L. with the labor movements of the various Pan-American countries have continued to be of the most friendly and helpful character. The officers of the A. F. of L. have been of assistance wherever possible to representatives of the labor movements of other countries, particularly of Mexico and Santo Domingo. We have repeatedly expressed our conviction that there should be a readjustment of American relations with the Dominican Republic and that the government of the United States should extend recognition to the Republic of Mexico. We desire to call attention here to the unique service which the labor movement can render to the peoples of the American continents. In practically all governmental international relations it is the almost unvarying practice to ignore the Latin-American republics. Therefore, the Latin-American republics are prevented from making their proper contribution to the welfare and progress of the world. The nations to the south of us have no great menacing naval or military strength and perhaps for that reason they are not invited to participate in the international councils of governments. They have, however, a considerable wealth of thought, knowledge, and idealism which they should be encouraged to contribute to the councils of the world. We believe that it should be a matter of some pride to the A. F. of L. that it assisted so materially in bringing into being the first international organization through which the Latin-American countries might offer to the world their progressive and constructive thought and through which they might come to have a better understanding of each other. It is our conviction that the Pan-American Federation of Labor is but at the beginning of the period of its greatest usefulness and opportunity for service. Relations with Latin-American countries are of constantly growing importance. The opportunity of the A. F. of L. through its participation in the Pan-American labor movement is therefore one of great promise and one which we feel should be developed to the utmost. Understanding between peoples is of infinitely greater moment than understanding between the officers of governments. The labor movement can best foster and develop this understanding between peoples. (P. 490) The A. F. of L. believes it is the duty of the American labor movement to inspire the workers of all America to organize along economic lines and affiliate with the Pan-American Federation of Labor. (P. 492) The A. F. of L. urgently calls the attention of the labor movements of all the Latin-American republics to the necessity of using their influence to prevail upon their respective governments, when negotiating with foreign banking institutions, that the future welfare of their peoples, as it may be affected by such negotiations, be the first consideration before agreeing to terms and conditions imposed upon them by the bankers.

(1923, p. 112) Our relations with the Latin-American nations through the Pan-American Federation of Labor have continued mutually satisfactory. We have been able to be helpful in a number of situations, more than justifying our participation in the Pan-American Federation of Labor and offering conclusive reasons for its continuance and enlargement. It has not been possible to hold a convention of the Pan-American Federation of Labor during the year, but the hope is entertained that such a convention may be held during the coming year. Through the Pan-American Federation of Labor we have consistently sought to develop understanding between the masses of the people of our own country and the countries to the south. We are convinced that our efforts have been fruitful. Specifically in the case of Mexico much has been done in an effort to end the long period of official estrangement and the conference between representatives of the Mexican and American governments was regarded as a hopeful and constructive development. W presented to the official commissioners the viewpoint of the workers of the United States and of Mexico and we are persuaded that this expression was of some value to the commissioners in approaching their task. An expression of labor's point of view and labor's hope for an amicable adjustment was likewise presented to the commissioners who met in Washington in an effort to adjust the long-standing Tacna-Arica dispute. We express our gratification over the opportunities for service that have presented themselves through our affiliation with the Pan-American Federation of Labor and we express our confidence in the continued effectiveness and strength of that organization. (P. 363) We take satisfaction over the demonstrated fact that our federation was of material assistance in forming the Pan-American Federation of Labor and of its helpfulness in directing its activities along constructive trade union lines. For the first time in the history of a president of a sister republic, together with other responsible officials, they have given expression to their high appreciation of and acknowledgment for the sustaining action of the president and Executive Council of the A. F. of L. and of their helpfulness in expediting the official recognition by our government of our sister republic of Mexico and of the treaty that finally brought about political and commercial relations between the two great countries.

Pan-American Financial Congress— (1920, pp. 128-389) Upon the convening of the first Pan-American Financial Congress in 1915, protest was filed with the Hon. Wm. G. McAdoo, then secretary of the treasury, because of failure to appoint among the delegates representing the U. S. any representative standing conspicuously for human rights and human welfare. In this protest by the president of the A. F. of L. it was set forth that the men appointed represented "great business and financial interests of our country. They are interested primarily in the material affairs of business, industry and commerce— the natural resources of countries." The letter of protest continues: "As a representative of the organization which stands primarily for human rights and human welfare, I desire to bring to your consideration the advisability of appointing on some of these commissions that have to do with things that will so affect the future development of America, men who represent directly the great masses of the citizens of our nation—the wage earners." In its report to the San Francisco convention in that year, the Executive Council discussed the matter at length. The following paragraph conveys the viewpoint which the Executive Council had at that time:

"It requires no great imagination or discernment to understand that these able representatives of the interests would so plan and manipulate conditions and events, that the great corporate interest of the various countries would be in a position to control, not only the industries and commerce within their own countries, but international regulations for commerce and industry. In other words, this conference plainly would enable the corporate interests to entrench themselves in a powerful position that would require years of struggle to enable the people of the nations, the masses of the wage earners, to secure for themselves protection and a right to opportunities in accord with their importance. This conference would determine the tone of international relations, the standards and ideals that would dictate policies and would

thus establish a whole line of intangible powerful influence that would make doubly difficult the age-long struggle for freedom that the workers everywhere have waged."

Because of the failure to name a representative of the wage earners to attend the Pan-American Congress, the Executive Council recommended that the convention authorize the council "to consider this matter during the coming year and to enter into correspondence with representatives of organized labor movements of those various countries, for the purpose of promoting a better understanding and closer relationship to the end that all workers of the various countries may be prepared to act concertedly for mutual advancement and protection." This protest of 1915 gave impetus to the movement to establish the Pan-American Federation of Labor and had its effect when the second Pan-American Financial Conference was organized in January of this year. By appointment from Hon. Carter Glass, secretary of the treasury, the president of the A. F. of L. was made a member of one of the group committee of the Second Pan-American Financial Congress, held in Washington, January 19-24, 1920. The congress was held under authority conferred upon the president in Public Act 379, of the 64th congress, and was composed of ministers of finance representing the Pan-American nations, together with representative financiers, trade experts and exporters. In the sessions of the group to which he was assigned the president of the A. F. of L. suggested the advisability of consideration by future conferences of the questions having to do with the material standards of life and labor of the masses of the people. The matter was not placed before the group in the form of a motion or resolution, but was laid before them as a suggestion. The Gautemalan delegates stated that their instructions limited their freedom of action, and they expressed a disinclination to exceed their instructions

Paper, Union Water-Marked—(1921, p. 287) The president and secretary of the A. F. of L. are directed to urge by correspondence with the officers of the various international unions, either individually or collectively, the consistent 100 per cent use of union watermarked paper; and all trade unionists and friends of labor having printing or bookbinding done be urged to use only union watermarked paper. (1922, p. 281) Reaffirmed.

Parcel Post—(1922, p. 361) Directed the Executive Council to endeavor to secure a congressional investigation of parcel post rates for the purpose of determining a fair and reasonable rate of postage, commensurate with the cost of service.

Patents—(1922, p. 475) Executive Council directed to investigate patent laws and practices under which laws of other nations operate and to take such further action as will stimulate American production under all patent laws and under such conditions as will bestow the full benefits of all patents rendered upon the American people as a whole.

(1923, pp. 57-244) The Cincinnati convention referred resolution No. 102 to the Executive Council for the purpose of investigating patent laws and practices and to take such action as would stimulate American protection under all patent laws and under conditions which would bestow upon the American people as a whole the benefits of all patents granted. This investigation was made. The information obtained has but indicated the many complexities and perplexities involved in this subject. Ten years ago the Oldfield bill, which called for compulsory licensing of patents with the object of having them worked within a certain length of time, received a favorable report from the house committee on patents. So overwhelming, however, was the opposition to the Oldfield bill by inventors, manufacturers, publicists, patent lawyers, scientific socieites and business men's associations that the bill was never brought to vote in either branch of congress. On April 5, 1922, Senator Stanley presented a bill compelling the patentee to start production of the article patented inside of two years. It was proposed that if this was not done the government would reserve the right to license anyone desiring to use and manufacture the product of that patent. This bill was opposed by every organization and association having to do with patent law legislation and administration. Briefly their opposition was this: A patentee creates something that has never existed before, something new, something which no one else has ever made. Before a patentee can manufacture this new article a large expenditure of moneys is often involved. Moreover, inventors are sometimes so far ahead of the times that they can not obtain means for such articles. For example, the first patent on the pneumatic tire expired many years before any pneumatic tires had ever been used. Under the present law a patent is granted for seventeen years. It has been pointed out that no patent of merit has ever been brought to a marketable condition in less than an average of ten years so that the effective life of the patent is about seven years. No patent that has ever come out of the patent office with merit has been effective immediately. "As a rule," the chairman of the Inventors' Guild said, "it takes seven and eight and sometimes ten, twelve and even fifteen years to develop an absolutely new invention." Commissioner of Patents Robertson has informed us that that part of the resolution which says that "holders of American patents are working or operating their patents in foreign lands while not doing so in this country" is only true in a comparatively few patents and is certainly not true with respect to inventions which have been made by American inventors. If the purpose of the proposed resolution is to compel foreigners to manufacture in this country, it would seem to be against our treaty, since the convention to which the United States is a party provides that "subjects or citizens of each of the contracting countries shall enjoy in all the other countries of the union the advantages which the respective laws now grant or may hereafter grant the citizens of that country." This treaty, it would seem, would prevent us from compelling foreigners to work their inventions in this country unless we also compelled our own citizens to manufacture the products of their patents in the countries abroad and in which they have taken out patent rights. England, Germany, Switzerland, Belgium and France have compulsory working laws, but it has been pointed out that none of these countries, with the exception of Germany, can approach us in producing worth while new patents. In Germany, as a matter of fact, there is a working provision affecting all nations except the U. S. The U. S. has a treaty with Germany which provides that working in the home country is the equivalent of working in Germany. In view of these difficulties the A. F. of L.

does not deem it wise to act upon the suggested procedure contained in the resolution. Instead, further inquiry should be made into this subject and if it be found that the desired relief set forth in the resolution is at all feasible or possible that action be taken accordingly or such other action as a further consideration of the subject may warrant or justify.

Peace, Call to—(1919, p. 444) Referred to the Executive Council the matter of taking part in the "Call to Peace" parade and pageant to be held in Washington, D. C., July 4, 1919.

Peace Conference—(1919, p. 13) REPORT OF THE A. F. OF L. DELEGATION TO THE PEACE CONFERENCE: "Realizing the difficult problems of peace and reconstruction your conventions of 1914, 1915, 1916, 1917 and 1918, after declaring that a labor conference should be held at the same time and place as the official peace conference, adopted resolutions providing that an A. F. of L. delegation not to exceed five in number, one of whom should be the president, should attend, to promote and protect the rights and welfare of the work people. Accordingly, shortly after the signing of the armistice, at a meeting of the Executive Council at Laredo, Texas, November 12, 1918, the delegation was appointed. On the steamer en route to Liverpool meetings of the delegation were held daily, and the records, declarations and war aims of the A. F. of L. and the European labor organizations were read and discussed. The delegation arrived in Liverpool January 17, proceeding directly to London, where the following day a conference was held with Hon. John W. Davis, United States Ambassador to Great Britain. On Monday, January 20, a conference was held with the parliamentary committee of the British Trades Union Congress, at which there were also present representatives of the Metal Workers' Federation of Great Britain and the Trades and Labor Congress of Canada. A letter was read from the secretary of the Confederation Generale du Travail explaining that it had been decided not to attend this meeting for the reason that the matters could be discussed when our delegation arrived in Paris. Two matters were considered: The proposed international conferences at Berne, Switzerland. The formation of an international trade union organization. As to the proposed Berne conference, it appears that the British parties had given Mr. Arthur Henderson complete liberty of action in regard to the bringing about of the conference. He proposed that the call should be issued by Vandervelde of Belgium, Thomas of France, Henderson of England and Gompers of the U. S., a committee without jurisdiction or authority to convoke any conference. President Gompers refused to allow his name to be used, but a call for a conference at Lausanne was sent out for January 13. Chairman Bunning, of the parliamentary committee, explained that the conference was called for Lausanne, Switzerland, because the French government found itself at this early period unable to guarantee the personal liberty of German and Austrian delegates at Paris. Therefore, that part of the mandate directing that the conference should be held "at the same place" as the official peace conference was ignored by those convoking the conference and all its opportunities and advantages sacrificed in order to meet with representatives of the enemy countries. It then developed that the feeling of the French-Swiss population at Lausanne was so manifestly hostile to the Germans and Austrians that the government forbade the holding of the conference at that place, whereupon those who convoked the conference decided to call it at Berne, Switzerland, the people of which city were known to be more in sympathy with German thought and feeling. On the part of the British delegates there seemed to be some doubt and confliction of opinion with regard to the Berne conference, yet the general view was that they were committed by instructions of their congresses to send their committee of five to said conference, regardless of its makeup, place of meeting, or the legality of its convocation. This position was adhered to, although three of the original delegation of five resigned because there were not in sympathy with the conference. Our position was made perfectly clear and plain, namely, that the American delegates were ready and willing to meet the representatives of labor of the allied countries in a purely trade union conference, but that we were disinclined to sit in conference with representatives of enemy countries for the present at least, or in a conference in which the aims and purposes of organized labor would be subordinated to those of any partisan political movement. It was also made plain that in all the the official declarations of the A. F. of L. in conventions it was clearly set forth that a labor conference should be held at the same time and *place* as the official peace conference, and that we believed no good purpose could be served by a premature conference with representatives of the central powers in a neutral country, which would destroy interallied labor's opportunity of presenting through personal contact demands untainted by enemy influence or propaganda. As to the formation of an international trade union movement, following our appeal for action relative thereto, the following resolution was unanimously adopted by the parliamentary committee:

" 'That this parliamentary committee welcomes the invitation of the A. F. of L. to take part in the formation of an international trade union movement, and hereby pledge our support to the formation of such movement, and will appoint representatives to attend the first meeting, to be held at a time and place to be mutually agreed upon.'

With this accomplished we proceeded to Paris, arriving there late in the evening of January 22, 1919, having arranged for a conference with the executive of the Confederation Generale du Travail the following morning. Secretary Jouhaux, after welcoming our delegation, confirmed that the labor conference was not to be held "at the same place" as the official peace conference because the French government could not guarantee the personal liberty of the Austrian and German delegates at Paris. At this conference we stressed the extreme importance of holding an inter-allied conference immediately at Paris, as directed by our conventions and the inter-allied conference at London in September, 1918, not only for the purpose of personally presenting to the inter-allied commissioners then in session in Paris the demands of inter-allied labor, but to remove the international trade union secretariat from Berlin. The Executive of the Confederation Generale du Travail was entirely agreeable that an inter-allied conference should be held as soon as possible, but at the same time expressed the belief that those things which labor intended to present to the Peace Conference should be pre-

sented as the expression of the labor representatives of all countries in conference at Berne. The tenor of the discussion throughout was that the French delegates were willing to attend a conference of the British, French, Canadian, Belgian and American representatives, but that it must be purely informal in the way of a "conversation" and that the proposed conference at Berne was the one they looked to for an official expression of labor's demand to be presented to the Peace Conference. It was finally agreed that such informal meeting should be called within a week to convene at paris and that the representatives of the British, French, Belgian, Canadian and the United States trade union movements be invited to attend. This second conference was held on January 31 at the headquarters of the Confederation Generale du Travail, with representatives of the French, Belgian, Canadian and American trade union movements present. The British Trade Union Congress sent a letter stating that the invitation arrived too late to permit of their being present. Here again the French delegation made it clear that the only conference they would officially recognize was the Berne conference, in spite of our determined stand that this proposed conference was premature and that our mandate to meet at "the same place" as the official peace conference would be violated if we were to meet an unrepentent enemy representing a city dominated by German and Austrian thought and sentiment. President Gompers also explained that he had refused to allow his name to be used in connection with the call, and that the other two men suggested by Mr. Arthur Henderson—Thomas of France and Vandervelde of Belgium—denied giving authority to use their names, although Vandervelde had explained to our delegation that he had given authority to use his name to call an *inter-allied* meeting to consider the question of an *international* conference, as directed by the labor organizations of Belgium. The Belgian delegation expressed a willingness to attend an inter-allied conference, but opposed the Berne conference because it was premature and included representatives of the enemy countries. They also spoke in favor of the removal of the Trade Union Secretariat from Germany. A third conference was held Saturday, February 1, at which our delegation made a final statement confirming its determination not to participate in the Berne conference and at the same time renewing its declarations in favor of the holding of an inter-allied conference in Paris. We made the further statement that when the terms of peace had been finally signed and the representatives of the inter-allied countries had formulated and presented labor's demands for incorporation in the peace treaty, we would then be willing to sit in a general conference with the workers of all nations for the purpose of forming a convention that would be a true federation of the organized workers of the world. The Belgian delegation also declared they would not attend the Berne conference, but the French held firmly to their pledge to send representatives to Berne. We were asked by the representatives of the Confederation Generale du Travail not to make public the reasons for our refusal to participate in the Berne conference, but much to our surprise there appeared the following day in "La Bataille," the official journal of the Confederation Generale du Travail, an article giving their reasons for sending delegates to Berne. We then found it necessary to prepare and make public the following statement of our reasons for not attending the Berne conference:

Position of American Labor.—Owing to the distance between America and Europe, and there not having been a united program between representatives of organized labor in continental Europe and Great Britain, detailed correspondence with reference to united procedure of all parties concerned at the present time was next to impossible. For these reasons the delegation representing organized labor in America went to London and to Paris to enter into preliminary conferences with other groups of labor representatives to bring about an allied convention at Paris. At a labor meeting held in London in September, 1918, an agreement was reached that as soon as possible after peace was declared in Europe there should be a conference called of the labor representatives of the inter-allied countries and America, to be convened at the same time and place as the official peace conference. A group of men principally interested in their several political parties arranged for a conference at Berne, Switzerland, and at the same time assumed to call, without authority, a labor convention to be held at Berne concurrently with the political convention. This situation becoming known to the American labor delegation, the members of it sought a conference with the representatives of organized labor in Great Britain in London and invited the French labor representatives to attend. In this way the American delegates expected to bring about a convention at Paris, where the official peace conference is now in session, which action would not only be in accord with the decision reached at London last September, but in full accord with the action of the A. F. of L. at several conventions in which it was decided to send representatives at the same time and place as the official peace commissioners would be in session. This action as well as the decision of the London convention last September, was primarily and chiefly prearranged in order to bring all possible influence upon the peace commissioners and, in a general way, to incorporate in their conclusions conditions representative of organized labor, which it was expected would be of benefit, not only to the workers in the allied countries and in America, but also similarly to all workers throughout Europe, and in a very great measure thereby influencing progressive and just policies to all the workers of the world. A conference was held in London between the American delegates and the parliamentary committee of the British Trades Union Congress at which information was given that the French labor representatives above referred to deemed it not necessary for them to visit the London conference, because the American and British labor representatives, would be immediately in France and at Paris, at which time the conference which had been suggested to be held in London could be convened, perhaps informally, but with the hope of arriving at a course of procedure which would be mutually satisfactory to organized labor as represented by the three groups of delegates. Several conferences were held at Paris, but owing to some misunderstanding about when the Paris conferences would be held the British representatives did not attend. Instead they sent a letter indicating their friendliness to the purposes of the meeting. At the London and Paris conferences it was evident that the British and French representatives had already concluded

to attend the Berne conference above referred to, although admitting the irregular course pursued in calling it. The American delegation thus ascertained that the purpose of meeting at Berne was because delegates from the countries of the central powers had been invited and would also be present, and that the main reason for meeting at Berne was for the purpose of arranging socialist procedure of an international character. Berne had been selected as the place of meeting owing to peace terms not yet being prepared and signed, and it would not therefore have been diplomatically proper nor advisable to have had German Austrian, and Bulgarian delegates at a meeting held in Paris. In addition to this the American delegation considered that if such a convention hoped to have influence with the official peace commissioners now in session at Paris that purpose would not be enhanced; in fact, might largely be hampered if labor conditions and provisions were submitted to them in which labor delegates representing the countries which had composed the central powers in the war participated, for it would have been obvious that the proposals submitted were largely "German made." The Berne conferences were originally proposed as conferences of citizens of the allied countries. By a device that we can not approve this purpose was covertly altered so as to include delegates of the nations with which our countries were and technically are still at war. While, therefore, the official peace conference is in session and before it has admitted to participation therein representatives of the Teutonic powers, it was proposed that we should sit side by side and face to face with such representatives, call them comrades and in this public way condone the hideous and unforgettable crimes against humanity and democracy committed by their nations. This, for the present, we declined to do. The peace deliberations are based upon the program of meeting delegates from the central powers only after the allies and the United States have agreed among themselves and are in accord as to the terms to be insisted upon at the peace table. The commissions representing the allies and the U. S. and the other countries interested are now in session in Paris, and it would seem to be the logical course, and we are so instructed by several conventions of the A. F. of L. to prevent labor's demands at this time and place. Labor of the central empires has the same equal right to present their demands to the commission which will represent them at the peace table. Had we overlooked the irregular manner of calling the Berne conference and the fact that it is called to be held in a neutral, instead of an allied country, and decided to go to Berne, where would the commissions of the allies and the U. S. get a truly bona fide statement of the allied and American labor demands? We declare the Berne conference to be irregular in conception and we can conceive of no good which will result from our attendance. For these reasons the American labor delegation concluded not to participate in the Berne conventions. The Belgian labor delegation also concluded not to attend. In order, however, to be as useful and as constructive as possible, the American delegation proposed that a convention be yet held in Paris at the earliest possible date of the labor delegation from America and representatives of organized labor of the allied countries. This was approved by the Belgian delegates and may yet be held, for there is nothing the representatives of organized labor of America and of the allies need to go to a neutral country to discuss. Besides, such action would be, as already stated, in accordance with the original course mapped out. This would also afford opportunity from time to time to take action while such a convention was in session in Paris to present to the official peace commissioners at close range the deliberations of the inter-allied delegates thus in session at Paris. The delegation from America is not entirely opposed to going into conference with delegates from the countries of the central powers, but they believe the present is not an appropriate time to do so, and that when the peace commissioners have so far proceeded with their deliberations that they can invite the representatives of the central powers to sit with them and to sign the terms, would, instead, be the opportune time, or as soon thereafter as possible, to hold a great general labor convention for the purpose of a better understanding and for arranging methods of procedure which would be of benefit, not only throughout America and Europe, but to the whole world. For the present the American delegates prefer to officially meet and transact business with representatives of labor from the countries which had to defend themselves against the ruthlessness of imperial Germany, and in which inhuman precedure there is ample evidence of the socialist and labor representatives, particularly of Germany, having almost unitedly supported the German war activities and atrocities. The American proposition to hold an inter-allied conference of the representatives of organized labor is now before groups of union representatives of the allied countries and it is hoped and expected that as soon as a full interchange of views has taken place among the representatives of these countries, the proposition of the American delegation will be accepted. In the meantime, in accordance with the action of the A. F. of L., its delegates now in Paris will hold conferences from time to time with the official peace commissioners of America for the purpose of general understanding and so that, through these commissioners the essential and progressive principles of organized labor will be fully submitted to the official peace conference. After several conferences with representatives of the Belgian Federation of Labor in Paris, upon their invitation we went by automobile to Brussels, Belgium, which afforded the opportunity enroute to view the wanton destruction and devastation wrought in Northern France and Belgium by the invading German army. A conference was held with the president and secretary of the Belgian Federation of Labor at the Palace Hotel, Brussels, February 15. After welcoming us and expressing their pleasure at our visit the Berne conference was discussed at some length, particularly the action providing for the convocation of an international trade union conference some time in May. The Belgians reiterated that they were ready at any time to meet in an inter-allied conference at Paris, but that they did not favor an international conference until after an inter-allied conference had first been held. It was agreed that upon the return of the A. F. of L. delegation to Paris, an effort should be made, in conjunction with the Confederation Generale du Travail, to call a conference of the labor representatives of all the allied nations, the Belgians giving assurance that if such a conference could be arranged they would be present. Upon our return to Paris the question of holding a

conference of the labor representatives o f the allied countries in Paris at an early date was again discussed and a committee of two from our delegation, consisting of Vice-Presidents Duncan and Alpine, was authorized and directed to confer with the Executive of the Confederation Generale du Travail with the end in view of having such a conference called. An agreement was reached and the call was issued for March 8 to labor representatives of England, France, Belgium, Italy and the United States. At the time set for the meeting, however, only the French and American delegations were present. A communication was read from the parliamentary committee of the British Trade Union Congress, explaining that they had not received the invitation in sufficient time to arrange passport difficulties; also, a letter from the General Federation of Trade Unions of England, explaining why they could not be represented. Secretary Jouhaux explained that the Italian delegation had been delayed and could not arrive on time. We later learned that the Belgian delegation was unavoidably delayed on account of transportatiion difficulties, but upon their arrival the following Monday morning they approved of what had been done. Secretary Jouhaux explained that he and Oudegeest of Holland had been authorized by the Berne conference to arrange for the calling of an international trade union conference at an early date, preferably in May, at Amsterdam, Holland. We explained that it was absolutely essential that our delegation return to America as soon as possible, and that upon our return our duties would require our attention for some time, not only in connection with our own organizations, but in connection with the convention of the A. F. of L. in June. It would therefore be impossible to attend a conference in April, May or June, or to return to the United States and have another delegation come to Europe during those months. We therefore suggested two possibilities: August or September, when the A. F. of L. fraternal delegates to the British Trade Union Congress could attend a conference in Europe or October, in Washington, D. C., at which time and place the first meeting of the conference created by the commission on international labor legislation would be held. Mr. Jouhaux gave as the principal reason for desiring to hold the conference promptly the necessity of labor giving expression to its views on the propositions affecting labor decided by the peace conference. He stated, however, that in about 10 days he would meet with Mr. Oudegeest for the purpose of discussing preliminary arrangements for the conference and that he would make known our views, and even if it was decided to hold a conference in May, another international conference might be held in October. In the meantime, while the Berne conference was refusing to condemn the bolsheviki, failing to fix the war responsibility upon the Germans or to remove the International Secretariat from Berlin, and declaring for an impossible international super-parliament, the A. F. of L. delegation remained at Paris in close touch with the peace commissioners. Conferences were held with President Wilson and the American commission to negotiate peace and the just hopes and aspirations of the working people were presented and explained. We also made known our reasons for refusing to attend the Berne conference and our position in the matter was approved by the President and the American commissioners. A draft covenant of the league of nations was the first document presented to the public by the peace conference. In this draft of the covenant the labor question was dealt with in Article X X, as follows:

"The high contracting parties will endeavor to secure and maintain fair and humane conditions of labor for men, women and children, both in their own countries and in all countries to which their industrial and commercial relations extend; and to that end agree to establish as part of the organization of the league of nations a permanent bureau of labor."

In reporting the draft covenant to the peace conference, President Wilson said:

"It is not in contemplation that this should be merely a league to secure the peace of the world. It is a league which can be used for cooperation in any international matter. This is the significance of the provision introduced concerning labor. There are many ameliorations of labor conditions which can be effected by conference and discussion."

Lord Robert Cecil, after stating that the problem before the conference was to devise some really effective means of preserving the peace of the world consistent with the least possible interference with national sovereighty, said: "I do not regard the clause which deals with labor as any such interference, for it is quite certain that no real progress in ameliorating the condition of labor can be hoped for except by international agreement. Therefore, although the conditions of labor in a country are a matter of internal concern, yet under the conditions under which we now live, that is not so in truth, and bad conditions of labor in one country operate with fatal effect in depressing conditions of labor in another.

Mr. George N. Barnes, labor representative on the British Peace Commission, expressed himself as follows:

"Hitherto, nations have endeavored to protect themselves against low-paid labor by the imposition of tariff barriers. I hope we shall, in the future, under the authority of the league of nations seek and find a better way of abolishing low-paid labor altogether. We hope to raise life and labor from the mere struggle for bread on to higher levels of justice and humanity."

To give effect to Article X X, on January 25, 1919, the supreme allied council at Paris created the commission on international labor legislation to deal with the all-important economic, sociological and human problems of peace and reconstruction, and President Gompers was appointed one of the delegates to represent the United States. At the first session of this international commission a great honor was bestowed upon President Gompers and the American labor movement as represented by the A. F. of L. by unanimously electing him President of the commission. The only representative labor man on the commission, a great majority of the time Mr. Gompers found himself in the minority, insisting upon and fighting for the rights and interests of the toiling masses. However, after thirty-five strenuous sessions and numerous advisory consultations with the A. F. of L. delegation, results were achieved which were acknowledged to be of a practical and constructive character, and a glorious advance in labor's triumphant struggle for the new concept and a better understanding between man and man and nation and nation. The commission drew up its conclusions in two parts: First:—A draft convention creating a permanent organization for international labor legislation. Second: What is known as the "labor clauses" or "labor's bill of rights,"

consisting of nine essentially fundamental principles proposed for insertion in the treaty of peace. The draft convention, slightly amended, and the report of the commission, as unanimously adopted by the plenary session of the Peace Conference, April 11, 1919, are printed below in full:

Report of the Commission on International Labor Legislation: "The commission on international labor legislation was appointed by the supreme allied council on the 31st of January, 1919, consisting of two representatives of each of the great powers and five representatives of each of the other powers. The terms of reference were as follows: 'That a commission, composed of two representatives apiece from the five great powers, and five representatives to be elected by the other powers represented at the peace conference, be appointed to inquire into the conditions of employment from the international aspect, and to consider the international means necessary to secure common action on matters affecting conditions of employment, and to recommend the form of a permanent agency to continue such inquiry and consideration in cooperation with and under the direction of the league of nations.'

The commission has held thirty-five meetings, and has drawn up its conclusions in two parts. The first is a draft convention containing provisions for the establishment of a permanent organization for international labor legislation, since such an organization seemed essential for its promotion. This convention, which was based on a draft presented by the British delegation, has been the subject of the most careful examination and discussion. The first part of this report may conveniently take the form of a commentary thereon. The second part of the commission's conclusions is in the form of clauses containing declarations of principle in regard to a number of matters which are of vital importance to the labor world. At the opening sittings, the various delegations agreed on the need for such declarations, which the commission suggests should be included in the treaty of peace, in order that it may mark not only the close of the period which culminated in the world war, but also the beginning of a better social order and the birth of a new civilization."

Part I. Permanent Organization Preamble: "The main idea underlying the scheme embodied in the convention is that the constitution of the league of nations will not provide a real solution of the troubles which have beset the world in the past, and will not even be able to eliminate the seeds of international strife, unless it provides a remedy for the industrial evils and injustices which mar the present state of society. In proposing, therefore, to establish a permanent organization in order to adjust labor conditions by international action, the commission felt that it was taking an indispensable step towards the achievement of the objects of the league of nations and has given expression to this idea in the preamble, which defines the objects and scope of the proposed organization."

Chapter I. "Chapter I provides the machinery of the permanent organization proposed. In the first place, it is stipulated (Article 1) that participation in this organization shall be a condition of membership of the league of nations, since every state member of the league is morally bound to accept the principles set forth in the preamble, if it has really at heart the promotion of the cause of justice and humanity. The organization itself is divided into two parts:

(1) The International Labor Conference: (2) The International Labor Office controlled by a government body. (Article 2.)"

1. *International Labor Conference*: "This conference will meet at least annually and will consist of delegates nominated by each of the high contracting parties, two of whom will be directly appointed by the government, and the other two will be chosen in agreement with the industrial organizations representative of their employers and work-people respectively (article 3). Each delegate will vote individually (article 4). It was strongly felt by the commission that if the conference was really to be representative of all those concerned with industry and to command their confidence, the employers and work people must be allowed to express their views with complete frankness and freedom, and that a departure from the traditional procedure of voting by national units was therefore necessary. It was accordingly thought that the employers' and work people's delegates should be entitled to speak and vote independently of their governments. Some difference of opinion made itself felt on the commission as to the relative numbers of the delegates representing the governments, the employers and the work people respectively. The French, American, Italian and Cuban delegations contended that each of these three parties should have equal voting power. They maintained that the working classes would never be satisfied with a representation which left the government and the employers combined in a majority of three to their one. In other words, the proposal amounted to giving the states a veto on the proceedings of the conference which would create so much distrust of it among the workers, that its influence would be seriously prejudiced from the start. This view was contested by the British, Belgian, and other delegations, who pointed out that as the conference was not simply an assembly for the purpose of passing resolutions, but would draw up draft conventions which the states would have to present to their legislative authorities, it was essential that the governments should have at least an equal voice. Otherwise, it might often happen that conventions adopted by a two-thirds majority of the conference would be rejected by the legislatures of the various states, which would have the effect of rendering the proceedings of the conference nugatory and would quickly destroy its influence and prestige. The adoption of a proposal to which the majority of the governments were opposed would not lead to any practical result, as the legislative authorities of the government whose delegates were in the minority would in all probability refuse to accept it. Moreover, it was likely, especially in the future, that the government delegates would vote more often with the workers than against them. If this were so, it was obviously to the advantage of the latter that the governments should have two votes instead of one, as it would render it easier for them to obtain a two-third majority, which under the Franco-American proposal would be practically impossible if the employers voted in a body against them. The commission finally decided by a narrow majority to maintain the proposal that each government should have two delegates. The Italian delegation, which united with the French delegation in urging the importance of securing representation for agricultural interests, were to some extent reconciled to the above decision by the consideration that, as the government would have two delegates, it would be easier to secure such representation. It should also be observed that, as different technical advisers may be appointed for each subject of discussion, agricultural advisers may be selected when necessary."

2. *International Labor Office*. (*Articles 6 to 13*.) "This office will be established at the seat of the league of nations, as part of its administrative organization. It will be controlled by a governing body of 24 members, the composition of which is provided for in the protocol to article 7. Like the conference, the governing body will consist of representatives of the governments, employers and work people. It will include 12 representatives of the governments, 8 of whom will be nominated by the states of chief industrial importance, and the remaining 12 will consist of six members nominated by the employers' delegates to the conference and 6 nominated by the workers' delegates. The objects and functions of the office are sufficiently explained in the articles referred to."

Chapter II.—1. *Procedure* (*Articles 14 to 21*). "This portion of the convention contains one article of vital importance, namely, article 19, which treats of the obligations of the states concerned in regard to the adoption and ratification of draft conventions agreed upon by the international conference. The original draft proposed that any draft convention adopted by the conference by a two-thirds majority must be ratified by every state participating, unless within one year the national legislature should have expressed its disapproval of the draft convention. This implied an obligation on every state to submit any draft convention approved by the conference to its national legislature within one year, whether its own government representatives had voted in favor of its adoption or not. This provision was inspired by the belief that although the time had not yet come when anything in the nature of an international legislature, whose decisions should be binding on the different states was possible, yet it was essential for the progress of international labor legislation to require the governments to give their national legislatures the opportunity of expressing their opinion on the measures favored by a two-third majority of the labor conference. The French and Italian delegations, on the other hand, desired that states should be under an obligation to ratify conventions so adopted whether their legislative authorities approved them or not, subject to a right of appeal to the executive council of the league of nations. The council might invite the conference to reconsider its decisions and in the event of its being reaffirmed there would be no further right of appeal. Other delegations, though not unsympathetic to the hope expressed in the first resolution (printed at the end of the draft convention), that in course of time the labor conference might, through the growth of the spirit of internationality acquire the powers of a truly legislative international assembly, felt that the time for such development was not yet ripe. If an attempt were made at this stage to deprive states of a large measure of their sovereignty in regard to labor legislation, the result would be that a considerable number of states would either refuse to accept the present convention altogether, or if they accepted it, would subsequently denounce it, and might even prefer to resign their membership of the league of nations rather than jeopardize their national economic position by being obliged to carry out the decisions of the international labor conference. The majority of the commission therefore decided in favor of making ratification of a convention subject to the approval of the national legislatures or other competent authorities. The American delegation, however, found themselves unable to accept the obligations implied in the British draft on account of the limitations imposed on the central executive and legislative powers by the constitution of certain federal states and notably of the U. S. themselves. They pointed out that the federal government could not accept the obligation to ratify conventions dealing with matters within the competence of the 48 states of the union with which the power of labor legislation for the most part rested. Further, the federal government could not guarantee that the constituent states, even if they passed the necessary legislation to give effect to a convention, would put it into effective operation nor could it provide against the possibility of such legislation being declared unconstitutional by the supreme judicial authorities. The government could not therefore engage to do something which was not within their power to perform, and the non-performance of which would render them liable to complaint. The commission felt that they were here faced by a serious dilemma, which threatened to make the establishment of any real system of international labor legislation impossible. On the one hand, its range and effectiveness would be almost fatally limited if a country of such industrial importance as the U. S. did not participate. On the other hand, if the scheme were so weakened as to impose no obligation on states to give effect to, or even to bring before their legislative authorities, the decisions of the labor conference, it was clear that its work would tend to be confined to the mere passage of resolutions instead of resulting in the promotion of social reforms with the sanction of law behind them. The commission spent a considerable amount of time in attempting to devise a way out of this dilemma and is glad to be able to record that it ultimately succeeded in doing so. Article 19 as now drafted represents a solution found by a subcommission consisting of representatives of the American, British and Belgian delegations specially appointed to consider the question. It provides that the decisions of the labor conference may take the form either of recommendations or of draft conventions. Either must be deposited with the secretary-general of the league of nations and each state undertakes to bring it within one year before its competent authorities for the enactment of legislation or other action. If no legislation or other action to make a recommendation effective follows, or if a draft convention fails to obtain the consent of the competent authorities concerned, no further obligation will rest on the state in question. In the case of a federal state, however, whose power to enter into conventions on labor matters is subject to limitations, its government may treat a draft convention to which such limitations apply as a recommendation only. The commission felt that there might in any event be instances in which the form of a recommendation affirming a principle would be more suitable than that of a draft convention, which must necessarily provide for the detailed application of principles in a form which would be generally applicable by every state concerned.

Subjects will probably come before the conference, which owing to their complexity and the wide differences in the circumstances of different countries will be incapable of being reduced to any universal and uniform mode of application. In such cases a convention might prove impossible, but a recommendation of principles in more or less detail which left the individual states freedom to apply it in the manner best suited to their conditions would undoubtedly have considerable value. The exception in the case of federal states is of greater importance. It places the United States and other states which are in a similar position under a less degree of obligation than other states in regard to draft conventions. But it will be observed that the exception extends only to those federal states which are subject to limitations in respect of their treaty-making powers on labor matters, and further that it only extends in so far as those limitations apply in any particular case. It will not apply in the case of a convention to which the limitations do not apply or after any such limitations as may at present exist have been removed. Though reluctant to contemplate an arrangement under which all states would not be under identical obligations, the commission felt that it was impossible not to recognize the constitutional difficulties which undoubtedly existed in the case of certain federal states, and therefore proposed the above solution as the best possible in the circumstances. Attention should be drawn to the protocol to article 19. The fear was expressed that the article might be interpreted as implying that a state would be required to diminish the protection already afforded to the workers by its legislation as a result of the adoption of a recommendation or draft convention by the conference: and in consequence, the protocol was added in order to make it quite clear that such an interpretation was inadmissible. It should be added that the Japanese delegation abstained from voting on article 19, as they had not yet received instructions from their government in the matter. The Italian delegation also abstained on the ground of the inadequacy of the powers given to the conference.

2. *Enforcement.* (*Articles 22 to 34.*) These articles provide machinery whereby a state which fails to carry out its obligations arising under article 19, or which fails to enforce a convention which it has ratified, may be made subject to economic measures. This machinery is briefly as follows: An industrial association of employers and work people may make representations to the international labor office which the governing body may at its discretion communicate to the state complained of for its observations (article 23). If no satisfactory reply is received, the governing body may publish the correspondence (article 24), which in most cases will probably create sufficient pressure by public opinion to cause the condition to be remedied. The governing body also has the power either on its own motion or on receipt of a complaint from a government or from a delegate to the conference to apply to the secretary general of the league of nations to nominate a commission of inquiry. For the purpose of such inquiries, each high contracting party undertakes to nominate one employer, one workman and one person of independent standing and each commission shall consist of one person drawn from each of these three categories (articles 25 and 26). The commission will report on the facts, recommend the steps which should be taken to meet the complaint, and indicate

the economic measures, if any, which it considers would be appropriate in the event of the condition complained of not being remedied (article 28). Appeal may be made to the permanent court of international justice of the league of nations, which shall have power to review the findings of the commission (articles 29 and 32). If the defaulting state fails to carry out the recommendations of the commission or the permanent court, as the case may be, within the specified time, it will then be open to the other states to take the economic measures indicated against it (article 33). It will be seen that the above procedure has been carefully devised in order to avoid the imposition of penalties, except in the last resort, when a state has flagrantly and persistently refused to carry out its obligations under a convention. It can hardly be doubted that it will seldom, if ever, be necessary to bring these powers into operation, but the commission considers that the fact of their existence is nevertheless a matter of almost vital importance to the success of the scheme. The representatives of the working classes in some countries have pressed their delegates to urge more drastic provisions in regard to penalties. The commission while taking the view that it will in the long run be preferable as well as more effective to resort to the pressure of international public opinion rather than economic measures, nevertheless considers it necessary to retain the possibility of the latter in the background. If all forms of sanctions were removed, the effectiveness of the scheme, and, what is almost equally important, the belief in its effectiveness, would be in a great measure destroyed.

Chapter III.—General: This chapter does not call for much comment, but attention should perhaps be drawn to the provisions of article 35 which provide that the British Dominion and India, and any colonies or possessions of any state which may hereafter be recognized as fully self-governing by the executive council of the league of nations, shall have the same rights and obligations under the convention as if they were separate high contracting parties. It seemed evident to the commission that colonies which were fully self-governing, not only as regards labor legislation, but generally, must be regarded as separate entities for the purposes of the labor conference, but it was decided that a state and its self-governing colonies should not have more than one seat in the governing body. In the case of colonies which are not fully self-governing, the mother country undertakes the obligation to apply labor conventions to them unless local conditions render it impossible to apply them either wholly or in part.

Chapter IV.—Transitory Provisions: This chapter provides *inter alia* for the holding of the first conference in October, 1919. The commission felt it was essential that the conference should meet at the earliest possible moment, but that if it was to do its work effectively some time must be allowed for the collection of information and for the different countries to prepare their views on the various subjects for discussion. The conference could, therefore, hardly meet earlier than October. In the schedule to article 39, it is proposed that the arrangement for this conference should be made by an international committee—consisting of representatives of the states named, with power to invite other states to send representatives if necessary. It is suggested that the U. S. government might be willing to convene the conference at Washington, and the commission much hopes that they will be willing to undertake this task. It is also suggested that the peace conference should approve the agenda set out in the same schedule. The Italian delegation proposed that all nations should be admitted to the conference immediately after the signature of the peace treaty, but the commission confined itself to passing the second resolution attached to the draft convention. In conclusion, it should be remarked that after a long discussion on the question of adopting certain measures in the interest of seamen, the commission thought that the very special questions concerning the minimum conditions to be accorded to seamen might be dealt with at a special meeting of the international labor conference devorted exclusively to the affairs of seamen, and at which the delegates and technical advisers could accordingly be chosen from the shipping community. (See resolution attached to the convention.)

Part II.—Labor Clauses: The commission were unanimous in thinking that their work would not be complete if it were simply confined to setting up a permanent machinery for international labor legislation. It was not within their competence or within the terms of reference to deal with specific questions relating to industrial conditions and to work them out with the detail necessary for the framing of proposals which could be accepted in a binding form. So impressed were they, however, with the urgent need for recognizing explicitly certain fundamental principles as necessary to social progress, that they decided to submit a series of declarations for insertion in the peace treaty. They did not feel called upon, however, to draw up a charter containing all the reform which may be hoped for in a more or less distant future but confined themselves to principles, the realization of which may be contemplated in the near future. It will be seen that the high contracting parties are not asked to give immediate effect to them, but only to endorse them generally. It will be the duty of the international labor conference to examine them thoroughly and to put them in the form of recommendations or draft conventions elaborated with the detail necessary for their practical application. Proposals were placed before the commission by the Italian, French, American, Belgian and British delegations as to the declarations which should be made. The commission decided that no declaration should be submitted to the peace conference, unless it were adopted by a two-thirds majority, and it now has the honor of submitting nine declarations, all of which obtained such a majority and some of which were adopted unanimously. It should be added in conclusion, that a majority, but not a two-thirds majority, was obtained for a proposal couched in very general terms which suggested the application to agriculture of the general principles of labor legislation, and which arose out of an Italian proposal in regard to the limitation of the hours of work in agriculture. The delegates who voted against this proposal were, as they explained, by no means hostile to its general idea, but they thought that a proposal in such wide terms was not suitable for inclusion among the declarations to be put forward."

Commission on International Labor Legislation—A Draft Convention Creating a Permanent Organization for the Promotion of the International Regulation of Labor Conditions, Preamble "Whereas the league of nations has for its object the establishment of universal peace, and such a peace can be established only if it is based upon social justice and whereas, conditions of labor exist involving such injustice, hardship and privation to large numbers of people as to produce unrest so great that the peace and harmony of the world are imperiled; and an improvement of those conditions is urgently required: as, for example, by the regulation of the hours of work, including the establishment of a maximum working day and week, the regulation of the labor supply, the prevention of unemployment, the provision of an adequate living wage, the protection of the worker against sickness, disease and injury arising out of his employment, the protection of children, young persons and women, provision for old age and injury, protection of the interests of workers when employed in countries other than their own, recognition of the principle of freedom of association, the organization of technical and vocational education and other measures. Whereas also the failure of any nation to adopt humane conditions of labor is an obstacle in the way of other nations which desire to improve the conditions in their own countries. The high contracting parties, moved by sentiment of justice and humanity, as well as by the desire to secure the permanent peace of the world, agree to the following convention:

Chapter I.—Organization.—Article 1: The high contracting parties, being the states members of the league of nations, hereby decide to establish a permanent organization for the promotion of the objects set forth in the preamble, and for this purpose hereby accept the provisions contained in the following articles. *Article 2:* The permanent organization shall consist of (i) a general conference of representatives of the high contracting parties and (ii) an international labor office controlled by the governing body described in article 7. *Article 3:* The meetings of the general conference of representatives of the high contracting parties shall be held from time to time as occasion may require, and at least once in every year. It shall be composed of four representatives of each of the high contracting parties, of whom two shall be government delegates and the two others shall be delegates representing respectively the employers and the work people of each of the high contracting parties. Each delegate may be accompanied by advisers, who shall not exceed two in number for each item on the agenda of the meeting. When questions especially affecting women are to be considered by the conference, one at least of the advisers should be a woman. The high contracting parties undertake to nominate non-government delegates and advisers chosen in agreement with the industrial organizations, if such organizations exist, which are most representative of employers or work people, as the case may be, in their respective countries. Each delegate may be accompanied at each sitting of the conference by not more than two advisers. The advisers shall not speak except on a request made by the delegates whom they accompany and by the special authorization of the president of the conference, and may not vote. A delegate may in writing addressed to the president appoint one of his advisers to act as his deputy, and the adviser, while so acting, shall be allowed to speak and vote. The names of the delegates and their advisers will be communicated to the international labor office by the government of each of the high con-

tracting parties. The credentials of delegates and their advisers shall be subject to scrutiny by the conference, which may, by two-thirds of the votes cast by the delegate present, refuse to admit any delegate or adviser whom it deems not to have been nominated in accordance with the undertaking contained in this article. *Article 4:* Every delegate shall be entitled to vote individually on all matters which are taken into consideration by the conference. If one of the high contracting parties fails to nominate one of the non-government delegates whom it is entitled to nominate, the other non-government delegate shall be allowed to sit and speak at the conference but not to vote. If in accordance with article 3 the conference refuses admission to a delegate of one of the high contracting parties, the provisions of the present article shall apply as if that delegate had not been nominated. *Article 5:* The meetings of the conference shall be held at the seat of the league of nations, or at such other place as may be decided by the conference at a previous meeting by two-thirds of the votes cast by the delegates present. *Article 6:* The international labor office shall be established at the seat of the league of nations as part of the organization of the league. *Article 7:* The international labor office shall be under the control of a governing body consisting of 24 members, appointed in accordance with the provisions of the protocol hereto. The governing body shall, from time to time, elect one of its members to act as its chairman, shall regulate its own procedure and shall fix its own times of meeting. A special meeting shall be held if a written request to that effect is made by at least 10 members. *Article 8:* There shall be a director of the international labor office, apponted by the governing body, who shall, subject to the instructions of the governing body, be responsible for the efficient conduct of the international labor office and for such other duties as may be assigned to him. The director or his deputy shall attend all meetings of the governing body. *Article 9:* The staff of the international labor office shall be appointed by the director, who shall, so far as is possible with due regard to the efficiency of the work of the office, select persons of different nationalities. A certain number of these persons should be women. *Article 10:* The functions of the international labor office shall include the collection and distribution of information on all subjects relating to the international adjustment of conditions of industrial life and labor, and particularly the examination of subjects which it is proposed to bring before the conference with a view to the conclusion of international conventions, and the conduct of such special investigations as may be ordered by the conference. It will prepare the agenda for the meetings of the conference. It will carry out the duties required of it by the provisions of this convention in connection with international disputes. It will edit and publish a periodical paper in the French and English languages, and in such other languages as the governing body may think desirable, dealing with problems of industry and employment of international interest. Generally, in addition to the functions set out in this article, it shall have such other functions, powers and duties as may be assigned to it by the conference. *Article 11:* The government department of any of the high contracting parties which deal with questions of industry and employment may communicate pirectly with the director through the representative of their state on the governing body of the international labor office, or failing any such representative, through such other qualified official as the government may nominate for the purpose. *Article 12:* The international labor office shall be entitled to the assistance of the secretary general of the league of nations in any matter in which it can be given. *Article 13:* Each of the high contracting parties will pay the traveling and subsistence expenses of its delegates and their advisers and of its representatives attending the meetings of the conference or governing body, as the case may be. All the other expenses of the international labor office and of the meetings of the conference or governing body shall be paid to the director by the secretary general of the league of nations out of the general fund of the league. The director shall be responsible to the seretary general of the league for the proper expenditure of all moneys paid to him in pursuance of this article.

Chapter II.—Procedure.—Article 14: The agenda for all meetings of the conference will be settled by the governing body, who shall consider any suggestion as to the agenda that may be made by the government of any of the high contracting parties or by any representative organization recognized for the purpose of article 3. *Article 15:* The director shall act as the secretary of the conference, and shall circulate the agenda to reach the high contracting parties, and through them the non-government delegates when appointed, four months before the meeting of the conference. *Article 16:* Any of the governments of the high contracting parties may formally object to the inclusion of any item or items in the agenda. The grounds for such objection shall be set forth in a reasoned statement addressed to the director, who shall circulate it to all the high contracting parties. Items to which such objection has been made shall not, however, be excluded from the agenda, if at the conference a majority of two-thirds of the votes cast by the delegates present is in favor of considering them. If the conference decides (otherwise than under the preceding paragraph) by two-thirds of the votes cast by the delegates present that any subject shall be considered by the conference, that subject shall be included in the agenda for the following meeting. *Article 17:* The conference shall regulate its own procedure, shall elect its own president, and may appoint committees to consider and report on any matter. Except as otherwise expressly provided in this convention, all matters shall be decided by a simple majority of the votes cast by the delegates present. A vote shall be void unless the total number of votes cast is equal to half the number of the delegates attending the conference. *Article 18:* The conference may add to any committees which it appoints technical experts, who shall be assessors without power to vote. *Article 19:* When the conference has decided on the adoption of proposals with regard to an item in the agenda, it will rest with the conference to determine whether these proposals should take the form (a) of a recommendation to be submitted to the high contracting parties for consideration with a view to its being given effect by national legislation or otherwise, or (b) of a draft international convention for ratification by the high contracting parties. In either case a majority of two-thirds of the votes cast by the delegates present shall be necessary on the

final vote for the adoption of the recommendation or draft convention, as the case may be, by the conference. A copy of the recommendation or draft convention shall be authenticated by the signature of the president of the conference and of the director and shall be deposited with the secretary general of the league of nations.' The secretary general will communicate a certified copy of the recommendation or draft convention to each of the high contracting parties. Each of the high contracting parties undertakes that it will, within the period of one year at most from the end of the meeting of the conference (or if it is impossible, owing to exceptional circumstances, to do so within the period of one year, then at the earliest possible date and in no case later than 18 months from the end of the meeting of the conference), bring the recommendation or draft convention before the authority or authorities within whose competence the matter lies for the enactment of legislation or other action. In the case of a rcommendation, the high contracting party will inform the secretary general of the action taken. In the case of a draft convention, the high contracting party will, if it obtains the consent of the authority or authorities within whose competence the matter lies, communicate the formal ratification of the convention to the secretary general and will take such action as may be necessary to make effective the provisions of such convention. If on a recommendation no legislative or other action to make such recommendation effective is taken, or if the draft convention fails to obtain the consent of the authority or authorities within whose competence the matter lies, no further obligation, shall rest upon the high contracting party. In the case of a federal state, the power of which to enter into conventions on labor matters is subject to limitations, it shall be in the discretion of the government of such state to treat a draft convention to which such limitations apply as a recommendation only, and the provisions of this article with respect to recommendations, shall apply in such case." (In regard to the interpretation of this article reference should be made to the Protocol.) *Article 20:* "Any convention so ratified shall be registered by the secretary general of the league of nations, but shall only be binding upon the states which ratify it, subject to any conditions which may be contained in the convention itself." *Article 21:* "If any convention laid before the conference for final consideration fails to secure the support of two-thirds of the votes cast by the delegates present, it shall nevertheless be within the right of any of the high contracting parties to agree to such convention among themselves. Any convention so agreed to shall be communicated by the governments or the states concerned to the secretary general of the league of nations, who shall register it." *Article 22:* "Each of the high contracting parties agrees to make an annual report to the international labor office on the measures which it has taken to give effect to the provisions of conventions to which it is a party. These reports shall be made in such form and shall contain such particulars as the governing body may request. The director shall lay a summary of these reports before the next meeting of the conference." *Article 23:* "In the event of any representation being made to the international labor office by an industrial association of employers or of work people that any of the high contracting parties has failed to secure in any respect the effective observance within its jurisdiction of any convention to which it is a party, the governing body may communicate this representation to the state against which it is made and may invite that state to make such statement on the subject as it may think fit." *Article 24:* "If no statement is received within a reasonable time from the state against which the representation is made, or if the statement when received is not deemed to be satisfactory by the governing body, the latter shall have the right to publish the representation and the statement, if any, made in reply to it." *Article 25:* "Any of the high contracting parties shall have the right to file a complaint with the international labor office if it is not satisfied that any other of the high contracting parties is securing the effective observance of any convention which both have ratified in accordance with the foregoing articles. The governing body may, if it thinks fit, before referring such a complaint to a commission of enquiry, as hereinafter provided for, communicate with the state against which the complaint is made in the manner described in Article 23. If the governing body do not think it necessary to communicate the complaint to the state against which it is made, or if, when they have made such communication, no statement in reply has been received within a reasonable time which the governing body considers to be satisfactory, the governing body may apply for the appointment of a commission of enquiry to consider the complaint and to report thereon. The governing body may adopt the same procedure either of its own motion or on receipt of a complaint from a delegate to the conference. When any matter arising out of articles 24 or 25 is being considered by the governing body, the state against which the representation or complaint is made shall, if not already represented thereon, be entitled to send a representative to take part in the proceedings of the governing body while the matter is under consideration. Adequate notice of the date on which the matter will be considered shall be given to the state against which the representation or complaint is made." *Article 26:* "The commission of enquiry shall be constituted in accordance with the following provisions— Each of the high contracting parties agrees to nominate within six months of the date on which this convention comes into force, three persons of industrial experience, of whom one shall be a representative of employers, one a representative of work people, and one a person of independent standing, who shall together form a panel from which the members of the commission of enquiry shall be drawn. The qualifications of the persons so nominated shall be subject to scrutiny by the governing body, which may by two-thirds of the votes cast by the members present refuse to accept the nomination of any person whose qualifications do not in its opinion comply with the requirements of the present article. Upon the application of the governing body, the secretary general of the league of nations shall nominate three persons, one from each section of this panel, to constitute the commission of enquiry, and shall designate one of them as the president of the commission. None of these three persons shall be a person nominated to the panel by any state directly concerned in the complaint." *Article 27:* "The high contracting parties agree that in the event of the reference of a complaint to a commission of

enquiry under article 25, they will each, whether directly concerned in the complaint or not, place at the disposal of the commission all the information in their possession which bears upon the subject-matter of the complaint." *Article 28:* "When the commission of inquiry has fully considered the complaint, it shall prepare a report embodying its findings on all questions of fact relevant to determining the issue between the parties and containing such recommendations as it may think proper as to the steps which should be taken to meet the complaint and the time within which they should be taken. It shall also indicate in this report the measures, if any, of an economic character against a defaulting state which it considers to be appropriate, and which it considers other states would be justified in adopting." *Article 29:* "The secretary general of the league of nations shall communicate the report of the commission of enquiry to each of the states concerned in the complaint, and shall cause it to be published. Each of these states shall within one month inform the secretary general of the league of nations whether or not it accepts the recommendations contained in the report of the commission; and if not, whether it proposes to refer the complaint to the permanent court of international justice of the league of nations." *Article 30:* "In the event of any of the high contracting parties failing to take within the specified period the action required by article 19, any other of the high contracting parties shall be entitled to refer the matter to the permanent court of international justice." *Article 31:* "The decision of the permanent court of international justice to which a complaint has been referred shall be final." *Article 32:* "The permanent court of international justice may affirm, vary or reverse any of the findings or recommendations of the commission of enquiry, if any, and shall in its decision indicate the measures, if any, of an economic character against a defaulting state which it considers to be appropriate and which other states would be justified in adopting." *Article 33:* "In the event of any state failing to carry out within the time specified the recommendations, if any, contained in the report of the commission of enquiry, or in the decision of the permanent court of international justice, as the case may be, any other state may take against that state the measures of an economic character indicated in the report of the commission or in the decision of the court as appropriate to the case." *Article 34:* "The defaulting state may at any time inform the governing body that it has taken the steps necessary to comply with the recommendations of the commission of enquiry or in the decision of the permanent court of international justice, as the case may be, and may request it to apply to the secretary general of the league of nations to constitute a commission of enquiry to verify its contention. In this case the provisions of articles 26, 27, 28, 29, 31 and 32 shall apply and if the report of the commission of enquiry or decision of the permanent court of international justice is in favor of the defaulting state, the other states shall forthwith discontinue the measures of an economic character that they have taken against the defaulting state."

Chapter III—General, Article 35: "The British Dominions and India shall have the same rights and obligations under this convention as if they were separate high contracting parties. The same shall apply to any colony or possession of any of the high contracting parties which on the application of such high contracting party is recognized as fully self-governing by the executive council of the league of nations. The high contracting parties engage to apply conventions which they have ratified in accordance with the provisions of the present convention to their colonies, protectorates and possessions, which are not fully self-governing. 1. Except where owing to the local conditions the convention is inapplicable, or 2. Subject to such modifications as may be necessary to adapt the convention to local conditions. And each of the high contracting parties shall notify to the international labor office the action taken in respect of each of its colonies, protectorates and possessions which are not fully self-governing." *Article 36:* "Any state not a party to this convention which may hereafter become a member of the league of nations, shall be deemed *ipso facto* to have adhered to this convention." *Article 37:* "Amendments to this convention which are adopted by the conference by a majority of two-thirds of the votes cast by the delegates present shall take effect when ratified by the states whose representatives compose the executive council of the league of Nations and by three-fourths of the states whose representatives compose the body of delegates of the league." *Article 38:* "Any question or dispute relating to the interpretation of this convention or of any subsequent convention concluded by the high contracting parties in pursuance of the provisions of this convention shall be referred for decision to the permanent court of international justice."

Chapter IV—Transitory Provisions. Article 39: "The first meeting of the conference shall take place in October, 1919. The place and agenda for this meeting shall be as specified in the schedule annexed hereto. Arrangements for the convening and the organization of the first meeting of the conference will be made by the government designated for the purpose in the said schedule. That government shall be assisted in the preparation of the documents for submission to the conference by an international committee constituted as provided in the said schedule." The expenses of the first meeting and of all subsequent meetings held before the league of nations has been able to establish a general fund, other than the expenses of delegates and their advisers, will be borne by the high contracting parties in accordance with the apportionment of the expenses of the international bureau of the universal postal union." *Article 40:* "Until the league of nations has been constituted all communications which under the provisions of the foregoing articles should be addressed to the secretary general of the league will be preserved by the director of the international labor office, who will transmit them to the secretary general of the league when appointed." *Article 41:* "Pending the creation of a permanent court of international justice, disputes which in accordance with this convention would be submitted to it for decision will be referred to a tribunal of three persons appointed by the executive council of the league of nations." *Protocol to Article 7:* "The governing body of the international labor office shall be constituted as follows: Twelve representatives of the governments. Six members elected by the delegates to the conference representing the employers. Six members elected by the delegates to the conference representing the work people. Of the 12 members repre-

senting the governments, eight shall be nominated by the high contracting parties which are of the chief industrial importance, and four shall be nominated by the high contracting parties selected for the purpose by the government delegates to the conference, excluding the delegates of the eight states mentioned above. No high contracting party, together with its dominions and colonies, whether self-governing or not, shall be entitled to nominate more than one member. Any question as to which are the high contracting parties of the chief industrial importance shall be decided by the executive council of the league of nations. The period of office of members of the governing body will be three years. The method of filling vacancies and other similar questions may be determined by the governing body subject to the approval of the conference." *Protocol to Article 19* "In no case shall any of the high contracting parties be asked or required, as a result of the adoption of any recommendation or draft convention by the conference, to diminish the protection afforded by its existing legislation to the workers concerned. In framing any recommendation or draft convention of general application the conference shall have due regard to those countries in which climatic conditions, the imperfect development of industrial organization or other special circumstances make the industrial conditions substantially different, and shall suggest the modifications, if any, which it considers may be required to meet the case of such countries."

Borden Amendment Adopted. "The conference authorizes the drafting committee to make such amendments as may be necessary to have the convention conform to the covenant of the league of nations in the character of its membership and in the method of adherence."

Schedule referred to in Article 39—First Meeting of Annual Labor Conference, 1919: "The place of meeting will be Washington. The government of the U. S. of America is requested to convene the conference. The international organizing committee will consist of seven members, appointed by the U. S. of America, France, Great Britain, Italy, Japan, Belgium and Switzerland. The committee may, if it thinks necessary, invite other states to appoint representatives: Agenda, 1. Application of principles of 8 hours day or of 48 hours week: 2. Question of preventing or providing against unemployment: 3. Women's employment: (*a*) Before and after childbirth, including the question of maternity benefit. (*b*) During the night. (*c*) In unhealthy process. 4. Employment of children: (*a*) Minimum age of employment. (*b*) During the night. (*c*) In unhealthy processes. 5. Extension and application of the international conventions adopted at Berne in 1906 on the prohibition of night work for women employed in industry and the prohibition of the use of white phosphorus in manufacture of matches."

I.—Resolutions Proposed by the Belgian, Resolutions Adopted by the Commission, French and Italian Delegations: "The commission expresses the hope that as soon as it may be possible an agreement will be arrived at between the high contracting parties with a view to endowing the international labor conference under the auspices of the league of nations with power to take, under conditions to be determined, resolutions possessing the force of international law."

II.—Resolution Proposed by the Belgian,

French and Italian Delegations: "The commi sion being of opinion that an international code of labor legislation which will be really effective can not be secured without the cooperation of all industrial countries, expresses the wish that pending the signature of the treaty of peace, which will permit all such countries to be approached, the peace conference will communicate the present draft convention to the neutral powers for their information before finally adopting it."

III.—Resolution Proposed by the French Delegation: "The commission considers that the very special questions concerning the minimum conditions to be accorded to seamen might be dealt with at a special meeting of the international labor conference devoted exclusively to the affairs of seamen. The "Bill of Rights" as proposed by the commission on international labor legislation for insertion in the treaty of peace was adopted by that commission after carefully considering and debtaing the proposals submitted by the delegations of the various nations represented. The proposals of the American delegation appear below, from which it will be seen to what extent the basic principles underlying the American trade union movement as represented by the A. F. of L. were adopted by the commission and actually written into the treaty of peace. The hieh contracting parties declare that in all states the following principles should be recognized, established and maintained: 1. That in law and in practice it should be held that the labor of the human being is not a commodity or an article of commerce. 2. That involuntary servitude should not exist except as a punishment for crime whereof the party shall have been duly convicted. 3. The right of free association, free assembly, free speech and free press should not be denied or abridged. 4. That the seamen of the merchant marine shall be guaranteed the right of leaving their vessels when the same are in safe harbor. 5. That no article or commodity should be shipped or delivered in international commerce in the production of which children under the age of sixteen years have been employed or permitted to work. 6. That no article or commodity should be shipped or delivered in international commerce in the production of which convict labor has been employed or permitted. 7. It should be declared that the workday in industry and commerce should not exceed eight hours a day, except in case of extraordinary emergency, such as danger to life or to property. 8. It should be declared that an adquate wage should be paid for labor performed—a wage based upon and commensurate with a standard of life conforming to the civilization of the time. 9. That equal wages should be paid to women for equal work performed. 10. That the sale or u e for commercial purposes of articles made or manufactured in private homes should be prohibited."

As adopted by the commission on international labor legislation, "labor's bill of rights" was proposed for insertion in the treaty of peace as follows: "The high contracting parties declare their acceptance of the following principles and engage to take all necessary steps to secure their realization in accordance with the recommendation to be made by the international labor conference as to their practical application: 1. In right and in fact that labor of a human being should not be treated as merchandise or an article of commerece. 2. Employers and workers should be allowed the right of association for all lawful purposes. 3. No child should be permitted to be employed in industry or commerce before the age of fourteen years, in order that every child may be ensured reasonable opportunities for mental and physical education. Between the years of fourteen and eighteen young persons of either sex may only be employed on work which is not harmful to their physical development and on condition that the continuation of their technical or general education is ensured. 4. Every worker has a right to a wage adequate to maintain a reasonable standard of life having regard to the civilization of his time and country. 5. Equal pay should be given to women and to men for work of equal value in quantity and quality. 6. A weekly rest, including Sunday, or its equivalent for all workers. 7. Limitation of the hours of work in industry on the basis of eight hours a day or forty-eight hours a week, subject to an exception for countries in which climatic conditions, the imperfect development of industrial development or industrial organization or other special circumstances render the industrial efficiency of the workers substantially different. The international labor conference will recommend a basis approximately equivalent to the above for adoption in such countries. 8. In all matters concerning their status as workers and social insurance foreign workmen lawfully admitted to any country and their families should be ensured the same treatment as the nationals of that country. 9. All states should institute a system of inspection in which women should take part, in order to ensure the enforcement of the laws and regulations for the protection of the workers."

The adoption of the "bill of rights" as adopted by the commission on international labor legislation was moved at the plenary session of the peace conference, April 28, 1919, whereupon the following redraft was moved as an amendment, adopted and inserted in the treaty of peace:

"The high contracting parties, recognizing that the well-being, physical, moral and intellectual, of industrial wage earners is of supreme international importance have framed a permanent machinery associated with that of the league of nations to further this great end. They recognize that differences of climate, habits and customs of economic opportunity and industrial tradition makes strict uniformity in the conditions of labor difficult of immediate attainment. But, holding as they do, that labor should not be regarded merely as an article of commerce, they think that there are methods and principles for regulating labor conditions which all industrial communities should endeavor to apply so far as their special circumstances will permit. Among these methods and principles, the following seem to the high contracting parties to be of special and urgent importance: First. The guiding principle above enunciated that labor should not be regarded merely as a commodity or article of commerce. Second. That right of association for all lawful purposes by the employed as well as by the employers. Third. The payment to the employed of a wage adequate to maintain a reasonable standard of life as this is understood in their time and country. Fourth. The adoption of an eight-hours day or a forty-eight hours week as the standard to be aimed at where it has not already been obtained. Fifth. The adoption of a weekly rest of at least twenty-four hours which should include Sunday whenever practicable. Sixth. The abolition of child labor and the imposition of such limitations on the labor of young persons as shall permit the continuation of their education and assure their proper physical development. Seventh. The principle that men and women should receive requal renumeration for work of equal value. Eight. The standard set by law in each country with respect to the conditions of labor should have due regard to the equitable economic treatment of all workers lawfully resident therein. Ninth. Each state should make provision for a system of inspection in which women should take part in order to insure the enforcement of the laws and regulations for the protection of the employed. Without claiming that these methods and principles are either complete or final, the high contracting parties are of opinion that they are well fitted to guide the policy of the league of nations and that if adopted by the industrial communities who are members of league and safeguarded in practice by an adequate system of such inspection, they will confer lasting benefits upon the wage earner of the world."

Among the many congratulatory messages and expressions of praise, the following cablegram from President Wilson best explains how the work of the commission on international labor legislation is regarded by those familiar with the difficulties overcome and the results achieved:

"The labor programme which the conference of peace has adopted as part of the treaty of peace constitutes one of the most important achievements of the new day in which the interests of labor are to be systematically and intelligently safeguarded and promoted. Amidst the multitude of other interests this great step forward is apt to be overlooked, and yet no other single thing that has been done will help more to stabilize conditions of labor throughout the world and ultimately relieve the unhappy conditions which in too many places have prevailed. Personally I regard this as one of the most gratifying achievements of the conference. In addition to the work and conferences herein outlined, members of our delegation went to various industrial centers in the different countries visited, meeting, discussing and holding conferences with trade union representatives in a helpful interchange of opinions and information as to labor conditions and policies. A rendezvous was effected in London, March 27, 1919, for which date a conference had been arranged with a special committee of the Parliamentary committee of the British trades union congress to discuss matters relative to the proposed international trade union conference and if possible agree to some mutually satisfactory time and place for holding such conference. Our delegation went into the matter in detail with the result that the special committee agreed to favorably recommend to the parliamentary committee our desire that the proposed international trade union conference suggested for May be postponed until a later date, preferably October, in Washington, D. C. It is the unanimous feeling of the delegation that its objects in going abroad were fulfilled and that its efforts were successful. We feel that we accomplished everything that was possible under the circumstances and that the mark of American labor's constructive purpose was left indelibly written into the structure of the future peace. If it was not possible during our stay in Europe to hold an international trade union conference, no effort was spared in that direction and there is every reason to expect that a meeting of this kind will materialize as the result of our efforts. We feel that our work in connection with the peace conference amply justified the effort expended and it is with some pride that we point out to the workers of America the fact that the deliberations held in connection with the peace conference clearly demonstrated the position of leadership held by the American labor movement, a leadership that rests upon the solid achievements gained for the workers of America by the trade union movement of our country. We did not accomplish everything that we had hoped to accomplish. We did, however, gain as much as it was possible to gain. If there remains much unfinished work it is simply an indication that the world has not yet reached a stage where the right can be won for labor without continuing to struggle. We are more firmly convinced than ever of the practical success of the policy of the A. F. of L. and of its constructive effect in realizing the ideals and aspirations of the working people for a greater and ever greater measure of freedom and justice and democracy. Our experience has taught us afresh that the sure way to progress is the way that lies through a constant contact with the facts and conditions of life which has always been the purpose of the A. F. of L. We feel that we have a right to say that the world will better understand the needs of labor in the future as the result of our work abroad and that the world will more readily find a way to satisfy those needs.

Peace Treaty and League of Nations— (1919, p. 86) The treaty of peace formulated in Paris acknowledges the complete justice of the five points set forth by the Buffalo convention and reaffirmed at St. Paul (pages 53-54, 334-335, St. Paul Proceedings), which are based upon declarations of the president of the U. S. and contains two of the four propositions added at St. Paul. Thus is justified the high confidence felt by the American labor movement and expressed in these declarations that the result of the world war would be to place the conduct and morals of the governments of the world upon a higher plane and the establishment and maintenance of international relations which shall safeguard the peoples of the world in the enjoyment of a permanent peace. The treaty of peace as drafted by the allied and associated governments sets a new standard in the relation of nation to nation and gives to government a purpose that has been lacking where the monarchical and bureaucratic concept obtained. The Prussian idea, defeated on the field of battle, is now forever made impossible of revival by the treaty of peace submitted to the German envoys. The five guiding principles laid down at the Buffalo convention of the A. F. of L. as basic principles of a lasting peace are firmly imbedded in the draft and we feel that with a peace so built the world has in truth been made safe for democracy. Under the guiding principles now laid down as the standard of conduct for all nations the peoples of the world may go forward in security and freedom to work out their own concepts of democracy and their own ideals of freedom. The covenant of the league of nations, written into the treaty of peace, must meet with the unqualified approval and support of the American working people. It is not a perfect document and perfection is not claimed for it. It does, however, mark the nearest approach to perfection that ever has been reached in the international affairs of mankind. It provides the best machinery yet devised for the prevention of war. It places human relations upon a new basis and endeavors to enthrone right and justice instead of strength and might as the arbiter of international destinies. It is, we feel, well to recall the adoption of the constitution by our own federal government in the early days of its life. Perhaps no document in the history of the world was more attacked, criticised, and opposed than was the constitution of the U. S. when it was first formulated and adopted by the congress. On several occasions that constitution has been amended, yet no one would presume to say, because of these amendments, that the constitution was not good when it was adopted, or is not good today. Opportunity is afforded for amendments to the covenant of the league of nations in order that the human family may from time to time make such improvements as may be needed and may so readjust its guiding rules of conduct as to make for the highest good of all the world. We declare our endorsement of the triumph of freedom and justice and democracy as exemplified in the covenant of the league of nations. The introduction of the nine specific labor clauses in the peace treaty declares that "the well-being, physical and moral, of the industrial wage earners is of supreme international importance." No such declaration has ever been written into international law through any previous treaty of peace and it is due to the efforts of the American labor movement more than to any other single factor that it appears in this emphatic form in the present treaty. The labor section of the treaty as it apears in its final form is, of course, a compromise. It must, however, be a source of deepest satisfaction to the American working people to know that the American position and American declarations as presented for insertion in the treaty ranked above all others in point of progress measured and in point of actual and practical application in the lives of working people. Whatever of compromise appears, was made because of the claim that other nations of the world could not pledge themselves to an immediate and definite acceptance of the standards maintained by the American labor movement as the established practices of our day. (P. 399) Attention is called to the preamble of the draft convention adopted by the Commission on International Labor Legislation and approved by the plenary peace commission and incorporated as part of the peace treaty. The preamble is as follows: "Whereas the league of nations has for its objects the establishment of universal peace, and such a peace can be established only if it is based upon social justice; and whereas conditions of labor exist involving such injustice, hardship and privation to large numbers of people as to produce unrest so great that the peace and harmony of the world are imperiled; and an improvement of those conditions is urgently required; as, for example, by the regulation of the hours of work, including the establishment of a maximum working day and week, the regulation of the labor supply, the prevention of unemployment, the provision of an adequate living wage, the protection of the worker against sickness, disease and injury arising

out of his employment, the protection of children, young persons and women, provision for old age and injury, protection of the intrests of workers when employed in countries other than their own, recognition of the principle of freedom of association, the organization of technical and vocational education and other measures; whereas, also, the failure of any nation to adopt humane conditions of labor is an obstacle in the way of other nations which desire to improve the conditions in their own countries.'

The high contracting parties, moved by sentiment of justice and humanity, as well as by the desire to secure the permanent peace of the world, agree to the following convention: In connection with the term "convention" as used in the title of the labor draft convention as adopted by the commission on international labor legislation, the term "convention" is understood to mean a covenant or agreement. Special attention is directed to the protocol of article 19, which reads as follows: "In no case shall any of the high contracting parties be asked or required as a result of the adoption of any recommendation or draft convention by the conference to diminish the protection afforded by its existing legislation to the workers concerned." The treaty embodying the covenant of the league of nations provides that international disputes between nations shall be settled in the calm light of reason and justice, rather than by the arbitrment of war, with its consequent slaughter of priceless human lives and destruction of untold wealth. No human being in possession of his moral senses can deny the adoption of a measure that will tend to prevent the indescribable horrors of another world war. Civilization must turn to a point where international disputes will be settled in the calm light of reason rather than by the repetition of the horrors we have just witnessed. While the covenant of the league of nations with its labor provisions is not perfect, is not all that we desire, it is in the right direction for the reason stated and a multiplicity of others and (p. 413) is adopted in principle. (P. 404) Nothing in the league of nations as endorsed by this convention can be construed as denying the right of self-determination and freedom to Ireland as recognized by the vote of this convention on Tuesday, June 17, 1919. (P. 438) Cable of President Wilson to President Gompers, dated June 21, 1919: "Comparison between your draft labor convention as reported to the plenary conference and the labor provisions as they now appear in the treaty of peace shows the following categories of changes: First, redraft of what is called in commission's report 'clauses for insertion in treaty of peace.' In actual treaty they appear under the title 'General principles' and read as follows: 'The high contracting parties recognizing that the well-being physical, moral and intellectual of industrial wage earners is of supreme international importance have framed order to further this great and the permanent machinery provided for in section 1 and associated with that of the league of nations they recognize that difference of climate, habits and customs of economic opportunity and industrial tradition make strict uniformity in the conditions of labor difficult of immediate attainment, but holding as they do that labor should not be regarded merely as an article of commerce they think there are methods and principles for regarding labor conditions which all industrial communities should endeavor to apply so far as their special circumstances will permit. Among these methods and principles the following seem to the high contracting parties to be of a special and urgent importance; first, the guiding principle above enunciated that labor should not be regarded merely as a commodity or article of commerce; second, the right of association for all lawful purposes by the employed as well as by the employers; third, the payment to the employed of a wage adequate to maintain a reasonable standard of life as this is understood in their time and country; fourth, the adoption of an eight-hour day or a forty-eight hour week as the standard to be aimed at where it has not already been attained; fifth, the adoption of a weekly rest of at least twenty-four hours, which should include Sunday wherever practicable; sixth, the abolition of child labor and the imposition of such 'limitations of the labor of young persons as shall permit the continuation of their education and assure their proper physical development; seventh, the principle that men and women should receive equal remuneration for work of equal value; eighth, the standard set by law in each country with respect to the conditions of labor should have due regard to the equitable economic treatment of all workers lawfully resident therein; ninth, each state should make provision for a system of inspection in which women should take part in order to ensure the enforcement of the laws and regulations for the protection of the employed. Without claiming that these methods and principles are either complete or final, the high contracting parties are of opinion that they are well fitted to guide the policy of the league of nations and that if adopted by the industrial communities who are members of the league and safeguarded in practice by an adequate system of such inspection, they will confer lasting benefits upon the wage earners of the world. The second part of your cable seven has been transferred into body of the convention and now appears under article 405 of the Treaty of Peace under clause 19 of your report. I am convinced that except for changes in wording which do not affect the substance and spirit of these clauses they remain the same; second, likewise your protocol to article 19 has been transferred to body of treaty under article 405. The 'resolutions' adopted by the commission do not appear in the treaty inasmuch as they were merely proposals of separate delegations and no part of the report as unanimously adopted for incorporation in the treaty. Third, a number of changes of form have been through the draft convention to make it conform in phraseology with the covenant of the league of nations as redrafted by the league of nations commisssion. For example, the words 'The high contracting parties' now reads 'members' and other similar unimportant changes. Fourth, on April 11 at the plenary conference which adopted the report of labor commission, Sir Robert Borden made the following remarks: 'This convention is linked in many ways by its terms to the covenant of the league of nations and I think it desirable to make it perfectly plain that the character of its membership and the method of adherence should be the same in the one case as in the other.' He then offered the following resolution, which was unanimously adopted by the conference: 'The conference authorizes the

drafting committee to make such amendments as may be necessary to have the convention conform to the covenant of the league of nations in the character of its membership and in the method of adherence.' In pursuance of this resolution the following changes were made: article 1 your commission reports together with the first two clauses of your article 35 together with article 36 have been combined as article 387 of the treaty to read: 'A permanent organization is hereby established for the promotion of the objects set forth in the preamble; the original members of the league of nations shall be the original members of this organization and hereafter membership of the league of nations shall carry with it membership of the said organization, as you doubtless have in mind the changes have the effect of giving the British dominions and colonies separate representation on the general conference. When you give your final judgment upon the importance of these changes I earnestly urge you to entertain the following consideration; One, that Borden could not go back to the Canadian people who occupy a position of considerable importance in the industrial world and tell them that they were not entitled to representation on the general labor conference at Versailles; two, that the changes did in fact bring the labor convention into harmony with the league of nations covenant; three, that the changes are not substantially important inasmuch as every labor convention adopted by the conference must be submitted to our government for ratification; thus the choice of acceptance or rejection lies in our own hands irrespective of the constitution of the general conference; four, that the problems of the chief British colonies and dominions are much more our own than like Great Britain's, so that their representation will be a source of strength to our point rather than an embarrassment; five, that in my opinion the changes do not introduce any weakness or threat of particular weakness into the labor provisions. They still stand, thanks to your efforts and guidance as one of the great progressive achievements of the peace conference, something from which peoples the world over may take courage and hope and confidence in a better future. I am sure that you will agree that nothing could be more fatal to these first aspirations than any failure to endorse these provisions. I count upon your support and sponsorship." (P. 399) Executive Council directed to aid in every way the holding of the inernational labor conference, which, under the treaty of peace, will convene in Washington, D. C., in October, 1919.

(1920, pp. 169-477) By a vote of 29,909 to 420 the 1919 convention declared its approval of the covenant of the league of nations and the labor draft convention and strongly urged ratification by the U. S. senate of the treaty of peace. Since our last convention the treaty of peace has twice been before the senate of the U. S. for ratification and has failed of ratification on both occasions. We can not escape the conviction that the failure to secure ratification of the treaty was due to causes having but little relation to the merits of the treaty. It must be clear to everyone that partisan political consideration and selfish interests were the dominating factors throughout the discussion in the senate. We are convinced that the decision reched by the Executive Council a year ago and confirmed by the convention needs no revision in the light of what has happened since. The principles for which we took our stand a year ago are principles which are as deserving of support today as then. Careful study of the senatorial debate and of the reservations offered in the senate, compel us to conclude that the covenant of the league of nations ought, at the earliest possible moment, to receive the support of the U. S. through ratification of the treaty by the senate. Reservations, whether offered for partisan political purposes or otherwise, ought not be used as instruments for further delay in ratification of the treaty. It has been pointed out in the senate and elsewhere that certain of the provisions in the treaty, outside of the covenant of the league of nations, are impossible of fulfillment and without justification from the American point of view. We recognize now, as we have always recognized, that the treaty is not a perfect document and that the imperfections extend both to the covenant of the league of nations and to the treaty provisions proper. In regard to these imperfections we call attention to our report of 1919, where it was set forth that the treaty itself provided machinery for the correction of mistakes and for the remedying of imperfections. Those who have followed European developments in connection with the treaty of peace will have noticed that in several instances treaty provisions already have been modified, because it was found that they were impracticable. While it is true, as American labor recognized from the outset, that there were faults in the treaty, the actual developments in relation to the correction of faults already discovered, and the machinery set up by the treaty itself to facilitate corrections and readjustments, should be sufficient to remove objection on grounds of that character. The people of the U. S. have suffered materially through failure of the senate to ratify the treaty. The interests of the working people of the country are seriously affected by this failure. In our internaional relations, which are as important to working people as to any other, the country has been placed at a serious disadvantage. It is of the utmost importance that the senate alter its position and ratify the treaty at the earliest possible moment in order that the U. S. may play its full part in world affairs and may exercise its democratic influence most effectively in a world which continues to need all the democratic influence that can be brought to bear. Labor, we believe, views the manner in which the treaty has been dealt, with the most profound regret, and it condemns without reservation the action of those who have deliberately produced the resulting state of confusion out of a desire to secure partisan political advantage. In addition to labor's broad interest in the treaty from the viewpoint of American citizenship, it has a specific and definite interest in the labor section of the treaty. American labor was unable to have representation, except through courtesy and without vote, in the first international labor conference under the terms of the treaty of peace, and it is unable to have representation in the international labor bureau until such time as the treaty is ratified. This is of the utmost importance, since work is continually in progress in which American labor has a vital interest and since decisions are being reached constantly in which American labor has an interest but no voice. We feel that as citizens and as workers, we can only renew our demand for speedy ratification of the treaty of peace, and this we believe should be done in the most emphatic manner possible.

We therefore urge the convention to make most earnest protest against the tactics which have resulted in postponing the ratification of the treaty and to urge upon the senate of the U. S. the necessity of ratification without any reservations which would tend to injure the effectiveness of the covenant of the league of nations.

Pennsylvania Legislature. Appeal to— (1919, p. 440) The A. F. of L. urgently appeals to the members of the Pennsylvania legislature to protect the rights of the workers and the masses of the people of that great state from further infraction and invasion, and to vote against any bill or measure which is, or may be brought before that legislature having for its purpose the causes against which this resolution protests.

Pennsylvania Railroad Company— (1923, p. 303) It should be distinctly understood that the Pennsylvania Railroad Company and its management is regarded the most autocratic organization and most hostile opponent to the cause of trade unionism in general and the railway shopmen's unions in particular.

Pensions, Old Age—(1920, p. 424) Refused to authorize the Executive Council to make such provisions as shall be necessary to establish a system whereby employes in private employment may have assistance in making provision for old age and such disabilities as may prevent them from working.

(1921, p. 330) The advisability of urging congress to enact an old age pension law was referred to the Executive Council for such investigation and action as may seem proper or necessary.

(1922, p. 141) The problem of providing old age pensions to all the citizens of the U. S. presents a number of constitutional difficulties in that our form of government is one of constitutional limitations designed to safeguard the sovereignty and the individual rights of the citizens, and is founded on the conception that our federal government shall be vested only with such powers and authority as may be delegated to it by the several states. In determining and defining the powers of our national government, we find its constitutional grants of authority extremely limited, and its sovereignty over the citizens of the several states provided only by the general declaration in the preamble of the constitution. While the expressed intents and purposes of our national government embrace the establishment of justice and the promotion of the general welfare, the attainment of these objectives has been confined by judicial interpretation to include only such practical methods as are more particularly defined in the constitution itself and in the amendments enacted thereafter. To accept this judicial interpretation of the powers of our national government as final is to deny the flexibility of our judicial mind; the historical development of our supreme judicial institution indicates otherwise. Were we to accept as final the present judicial point of view of the powers of our national government it would be impossible to provide old age pensions to all citizens of the U. S. without securing additional authority to our national government by constitutional amendment. This procedure would involve a gigantic undertaking and would immediately arouse the whole question of state rights, which, considered with the opposition such a proposal would inevitably awaken among the selfish possessors of wealth, would render this task an almost hopeless one. Then, too, proceeding in the form of a constitutional amendment would preclude any other possible procedure in that such an attitude would be expressive of the weakness of our national government in undertaking to provide old age pensions under existing delegated authority. It is conceivable that with a proper public conscience aroused, the constitutional declarations to establish justice and promote the general welfare might be broadened by subsequent judicial interpretation to include provision for an old age pension to all citizens, especially if predicated on the existing recognition of the duty and need of society to care for the aged as is evidenced at the present time in the form of poorhouses, hospitals, etc. The recognition of this social duty is demonstrative of the need of an enlargement in providing justice and promoting the general welfare of the citizens of the U. S. Society should undertake the performance of this duty, not as a matter of charity but as a matter of right and of justice. Supplemental to this general constitutional declaration of intents and purposes is the specific authority delegated to the national government to regulate commerce between the several states. It is under this constitutional provision that the existing national compensation law is predicated. Unfortunately, however, we find that in the enforcement of this act the workers are involved in many subtle questions of conflict arising between interstate and intrastate employment. Altogether too often the wage earners are without relief or redress in what is clearly recognized in law as a compensatory injury. Thus, a railway worker may be engaged within a state in switching or hauling a car of freight destined for another state and yet if he does not pass the state line in the performance of his service, he is said not to have been engaged in interstate commerce. Then, too, there is the further possibility of our courts ruling against the constitutionality of an old age pension predicated upon the power of congress to regulate interstate commerce in that immediately upon resigning from his employment a man would no longer be in the employment of interstate commerce and therefore not subject to the authority of the U. S. government. Evidently, this method of providing for old age pensions presents too many present day difficulties to be given serious consideration. Another method of providing old age pensions would be through the exercise of the contracting power of our national government. It was during the period of war when the contracting power of our national government became the real dominating power and influence in our industrial life that through this power our national government was enabled to regulate private industrial activities and relations to meet the requirements of our national emergency and without involving many of the constitutional questions which would have arisen had any other method of procedure been followed. To exercise this power so as to require those who furnish materials, supplies or fulfill the needs of our national government in providing old age pensions, and to consider this additional authority in connection with the power the government now possesses and exercises in granting pensions to its own employes, a much larger scope and percentage of wage earners would be required to be included in a na-

tional plan for old age pensions. However, this method would involve so many intricacies and complexities and be subject to so many uncertainties that the value of such a plan, to say the least, is extremely doubtful. It may be suggested that if it is impractical to secure the enactment of an old age pension system through federal legislation that the same ends might be attained through state legislation. Practically the same legal difficulties may be urged against this procedure. While we believe that the several states have the authority to enact old age pension laws this procedure and method would not embrace all citizens of the United States. Then, too, the difficulty in securing favorable legislation in the forty-eight separate states, the District of Columbia and in all of the possessions of the United States is so apparent that it needs only to be mentioned to be fully understood. Another thought that has been advanced is to have the national government encourage state legislatures in providing old age pensions by contributing a proportional sum of money equal to that expended by each state for this particular purpose. That this method is perfectly constitutional is well demonstrated in the making of similar financial contributions by congress in providing for the educational facilities of our people, in promoting good roads, building plans, and in providing maternity benefits. However, this procedure is subject to the same difficulties embraced in the proposal to have the several states provide old age pensions. It is evident that it is extremely difficult to devise a direct method for the payment of old age pensions by the national government unless recourse is had to the creating of an additional relationship of the individual citizen to the national government and upon which payment of services during old age might be predicated. There is contained in the constitution of the U. S. the provision that congress shall have the power "to raise and support armies." From the inception of the national government and without question congress has exercised that power and under this constitutional provision congress may fully regulate the age and qualifications of enlistment, terms of service and rates of compensation. It is upon that principle of constitutional law that the convention of the A. F. of L. held in Toronto in 1909, declared for a national old age pension system and caused a bill to be introduced into the national congress as follows:

"An act to organize an army corps, prescribe qualifications for enlistment therein, define the duties and fix the compensation and term of enlistment of privates and for other purposes. Be it enacted, etc. That immediately after the passage of this act, an army corps shall be organized in the department of war, under the direction of the President, to be known as the old age home guard of the U. S. army. Sec. 2. The old age home guard of the U. S. army shall be composed of persons not less than 65 years of age. Sec. 3. Any person who is 65 years of age, or upwards, and who has been a resident of the U. S. twenty-five consecutive years, and a citizen of the U. S. fifteen consecutive years next preceding the date of application, and who is not possessed of property amounting to more than $1,500 in value, free of all incumbrances, or an income of more than $240 per annum, and who has not sequestered, or otherwise disposed of property or income for the purpose of qualifying for enlistment as hereinafter provided, may make application, in writing, to the secretary of war, for enlistment in the old age home guard of the U. S. army, and it shall be the duty of the secretary of war to enlist and enroll such applicant, for the term of his or her life, as a private in the old age home guard of the U. S. army, without regard to the physical condition of the applicant, provided that persons related as husband and wife shall not both be eligible for enlistment, enrollment and service therein at the same time, and in case of dispute as to whether husband or wife shall be enlisted and enrolled, as herein provided, the question shall be decided by the secretary of war, by and with the approval of the president. Sec. 4. The pay of a private in the old age home guard of the U. S. army shall be $120 per annum, to be paid in quarterly installments, as pensions are now by law paid, provided, that $10 per annum shall be deducted from the pay of each private, and retained in the treasury of the U. S. for every $100 worth of property in excess of $300, and for every $10 per annum income in excess of $120 possessed by such private. Sec. 5. Arms and ammunition shall be furnished to privates in the old age home guard of the U. S. army at the discretion of the secretary of war, but no sustenance shall be furnished to them except the pay herein provided. Sec. 6. No private, or applicant for enlistment as private, shall be required to leave his or her home for the purpose of enlistment, enrollment or service in the old age home guard of the U. S. army, nor shall they be required to assemble, drill or perform any of the other manoeuvres, nor be subject to any of the regulations of the U. S. army, except as herein provided. Sec. 7. Privates in the old age home guard of the U. S. army shall be required to report annually, in writing, to the secretary of war, on blanks furnished by him for the purpose, the conditions of military and patriotic sentiment in the community where such private lives, but no private shall be discharged, disciplined, or otherwise punished for failure to make such report. Sec. 8. The number of persons enlisted in the old age home guard of the U. S. army shall be in addition to the number of officers and privates now required by law in the U. S. army. Sec. 9. All acts and parts of acts inconsistent with the provisions of this act are hereby repealed."

Unquestionably, the principle upon which this bill is predicated is well founded though the particular provisions relating to eligibility, conditions of service, terms of compensation, are subject to varying opinions and conclusions. This plan, however, seems to be the most feasible one yet presented or devised in that it provides the opportunity of old age pensions for all citizens who have reached a certain age, places the pensioner in the direct employment of the government and lists him in the army of the U. S. under the direction of the president who is the commander-in-chief of the army and navy, enumerates the duties to be performed, limits the punishment for failure to perform them and stipulates the compensation to be received for the service required. It will be noted that this method of providing old age pensions is devoid of the element of poverty or charity, and that it is not conceived as the payment of deferred wages. It is founded entirely upon a relationship of service and for which compensation is provided. It is a method of providing old

age employment compensation and therefore, it applies to all wage earners regardless of the regularity or irregularity of employment. It reaches all classes of persons. It will not lessen the quality of self-help and self-reliance on the part of the individual. It will secure its contributions through means of taxation. It avoids the character of compulsory insurance in that it is not an insurance but it is in the nature of payment for services rendered. It does not infringe upon the inherent and natural right of individuals guaranteed freedom for life, liberty and the pursuit of happiness, nor does it deprive any person of property without due process of law. It seems more clearly to avoid all of the constitutional limitations which may be urged against all other plans and proposals. The principle of the legislation herein reported is again reaffirmed, and the E. C. is authorized to cause this bill to be introduced in the national congress modified in so far as the compensation features are concerned more nearly to meet the requirements of the living conditions of today. (P. 360-472) The A. F. of L. declares in favor of the revival of the old age pension system advocated by the Toronto convention (the old age home guard measure). Since the whole question of constitutional checks on progressive legislation is one of the main issues to which the labor movement must devote itself, it may be deemed advisable to concentrate on the removal of such checks. (1923, p. 293) The A. F. of L. indorses the principle of old age pensions for those who have given the best period of their lives to industry in order that they may have sustenance without charity when they are no longer able to work. The officers and Executive Council of the A. F. of L. are requested to investigate or cause to be investigated the several state constitutions with particular reference to the enactment of appropriate legislation herein contemplated and that consideration be given by the Executive Council to the preparing and drafting of constitutional amendments or legislative proposals embracing the principle and purposes herein declared for. All national and international unions are requested to assist the wage earners of Ohio to secure adoption of old age pensions referendum at the November election.

Personnel Research Foundation—(1921, pp. 145-374). As the result of a preliminary conference held November 12, 1920, in Washington under the auspices of the National Research Council, the Personnel Research Foundation was organized and the A. F. of L. was invited to participate as an affiliated member organization. The Executive Council considered the invitation and voted to accept membership. Final organization plans and the outline of work were agreed upon at a meeting held in Washington, March 15, 1921. The plan of the Personnel Research Foundation contemplates for the present, at least, no original research. It is the purpose of the foundation to serve as a clearing house to gather and to make readily available all existing information, to coordinate work under way, to indicate what additional investigation is desirable or necessary to stimulate activity and help in molding the purpose of research. The earlier errors of those who sought under the leadership of Taylor to adjust employment regulations by mathematical rules and to increase production by stop-watch methods, have been discarded by all except a few of the less intelligent engineers and employers. Management, having discovered the importance of the human element in production, and having discarded the time study and stop-watch in its efforts to find out how best without regard to human consequences to drive that force, has turned in a direction that makes the cooperation of the trade union movement not only advisable, but inevitable. It was largely because of the efforts of the trade union movement that the old methods were broken down and discarded and it is but fitting that it should join in the development of proper methods for the stimulation of proper relations. There is in process of development a sense of management and this involves the finding of principles for associated effort in production. Wherever management has begun to have a scientific regard for its work, it finds as one of its first obligations the necessity and the desirability of earning the good will of the workers. The Personnel Research Foundation will have to do with the correlation of research and the dissemination of information concerning management methods of earning the good will of workers—it will have to do with employment, absenteeism, placement and replacement, quits and discharges and methods of finding and recording the causes thereof. It will have to do with research into the various causes of economic waste which add to production costs and which make for remedial lack of production. It becomes more and more clear that many of the ills of industry which old-time employers were in the habit of attributing to labor, are in reality the fault of management. One of the greatest of these is labor turnover. The gathering and dissemination of information concerning these evils and the manner in which they are being overcome is a matter of keen interest to the workers. It also is necessary that there be continued vigilance in guarding against unscientific methods and methods which operate to place unwarranted blame for faults upon the workers and which seek to place upon them all of the burden for improvement. We are convinced that the efforts of the Personnel Research Foundation, with which the A. F. of L. has joined, will be helpful to that end.

(1922, pp. 68-339). The Personnel Research Foundation, of which the A. F. of L. is a part, is now upon a permanent working basis. Its membership totals twenty-five research organizations of national repute classified on a basis of contributions as follows: Voting members, 10; cooperating members, 14; sustaining members, 1. The purposes of the Personnel Research Foundation are: 1. To learn in a general way what organizations are studying one or more problems relating to personnel in the industries, and the scope of their endeavors. 2. To determine whether these endeavors can be harmonized, duplication minimized, neglected phases of the problems considered and advanced work undertaken. 3. To create a clearing-house for dependable, unprejudiced information about personnel in industry. 4. To formulate a comprehensive general plan into which all useful efforts may be fitted and in accordance with which future work may be directed. 5. To plan for the inauguration and support of coordinated studies in the several fields of industrial employment, by scientific methods, under unprejudiced direction, for the benefit of all concerned. 6. To devise ways and means of supporting the project. At the annual meeting in November, 1921, research

proposed or under way was reported upon the following subjects: "Job analyses of managers; interest analyses, will temperament traits and vocational aptitudes; selection, training, and supervision of salesmen; prediction of success for comptometer operators; causes of leaving; organization of work in the bituminous mines with special reference to personnel problems; occupational description of faculty position in a large university; methods of organizing personnel work for a university; women in trade unions in Philadelphia; methods of industrial training; women in chemistry; studies in hygiene and safety in a variety of industries." This foundation effected arrangments for the publication of an official journal, the *Journal of Personal Research*, the first number of which was issued for April, 1922. Complete editorial control is in the hands of the Personnel Pesearch Foundation. The A. F. of L. is represented on the board of editors by Matthew Woll. We believe it is fitting and expedient for the A. F. of L. to continue such active participation in this work so as to insure most helpful progress in developing information on the problems of human relations in industry. We feel confident that the future work of this movement will be extremely helpful in aiding in the solving of the many complex problems that our ever growing and varying industrial life constantly presents.

(1923, pp. 124-277) The significant undertaking of the Personnel Research Foundation has been that of exploring the general field of personnel research. In so far as opportunities and resources have been available, the Personnel Research Foundation has been seeking to discover and become acquainted with individuals and organizations that are trained and competent in the execution of research progress. Through its periodical publication, "The Journal of Personnel Research," some fifty courses in personnel and allied subjects have been given up to the present time. It is hoped that this particular function may serve not only as a source of information to the constituent and associate members of this organization, but also as a medium through which the results of the work done may be published as an incentive to others to interest themselves in similar undertakings. The personnel research foundation has found need for an additional outlet for monograms and studies and has consequently arranged for a series of books, the first of the series having appeared to date and additional volumes being under way, ranging all the way from studies of the labor problems in the printing industry to such material as that for use in vocational guidance. Unquestionably this organization has served as an effective and helpful clearing house and has on some occasions been of great assistance. Pursuant to the action of our Cincinnati convention, the A. F. of L. has continued its participation in the work of this organization. The total voting membership is ten. The cooperating membership is forty-two, and the sustaining membership is two. Because of the growing importance of research work and the great possibilities of the Personnel Research Foundation the A. F. of L. will remain in active affiliation.

Peru, Tribute from Workers of—
(1919, p. 191) Through the Peruvian ambassador the following was received

by the president of the Pan-American Federation of Labor and of the A. F. of L. from the labor movement of Peru: "I respectfully salute you and at the same time wish to inform you that in sending you this pamphlet through our ambassador Dr. Francisco Tudela y Varela, I was prompted to do so because I am convinced of the sincere affection you feel for Peru. I take this opportunity to state that our honorable ambassador is a convinced patriot dearly loved by the workers. To extend to him all the courtesies and to esteem him is to be attentive to Peru. Accept my esteem and the assurance of the sincere friendship of the Peruvian workers." The pamphlet was engrossed in colors and contained this testimonial: "The president of the American Federation of Labor, Mr. Samuel Gompers, homage of the workers of Peru in remembrance of the feast offered in honor of the workmen of the nations of the allies. Lima, 5th of December, 1918."

Philippine's Competition—(1923, p. 327) The introduction of many of the products of the Philippine Islands into the states duty free comes in direct competition with the higher paid working men and women of the mainland thus making it practically impossible for employes and independent manufacturers to meet competition. The Executive Council of the A. F. of L. is hereby authorized and instructed to appoint a special committee for the purpose of a general survey of working and living conditions of the workers of the Philippine Islands, and report its findings to the Executive Council of the A. F. of L.

Picketing—(1922, pp. 112-339) Executive Council commended for defeating an anti-picketing bill submitted to congress.

Piece Work in Navy Yards—(1919,p. 451) We believe the system of putting artisans upon a piece basis is most objectionable in private industry, and when put into effect in governmental departments is wholly unsuccessful and without justification. There can be no question that the proper method to be employed in government departments is upon a fixed price for certain hours of work.

Policemen—(1919, p. 302) The A. F. of L. favors the organization of policemen and the officers are directed to issue charters for such unions when application is made.

(1920, p. 304) The issuance of a charter to an international union of policemen was directed when the local unions had a combined membership of 6,000 and application was made.

(1921, p. 120) In 1919, the policemen and firemen of the District of Columbia were affiliated to the A. F. of L. A bitter campaign to force them so withdraw was begun in the house and the senate. At that time there were receiving niggardly wages, were working under unbearable conditions and controlled by rules more arbitrary than those of any police force in the U. S. They had appealed to congress for several years for a sufficient wage to support themselves and dependents, but no attention was paid to them. After they had affiliated to the A. F. of L. members of congress became zealous in their behalf. However, it was made a condition for granting an increase in wages and better working conditions that the policemen and firemen should withdraw from the labor movement. This was done and their wages were increased and a bonus of $240 a year granted. A year later the bonus was reduced to $120. After the next twelve months had passed the $120 bonus was taken away because the policemen and firemen could make no protest. They were unorganized and therefore helpless. However, representatives of the A. F. of L. persisted in the effort to have the bonus restored and this was accomplished.

Political Labor Party—(1923, p. 284) The development and history of the A. F. of L. disproves all the false imputations, allegations and charges hurled against the American trade union movement by those who would pervert economic and industrial problems into political discussions and who would confuse the minds and dissipate the power of the wage earners in the economic and industrial field for the temporarily radiant but ever elusive rainbow of political action that follows the stress of storm but is dissipated in the dawning of the bright rays of the sunshine of tranquility and prosperity. The records of the A. F. of L. clearly evidence that the American trade union movement considers of first and foremost importance the organizing of the wage earners into their respective trade unions, and, through their constant economic and industrial power and influence, redress wrongs inflicted, secure rights infringed upon, and protect and promote their conditions of employment and enlarge their rewards for services given, The records further demonstrate that the A. F. of L. is not unmindful of the necessity, advisability or desirability of massing and guiding the potential political power of the wage earners and of all groups sympathetic to the cause of organized labor; first, to prevent infringement upon the civil, economic and industrial rights of the wage earners, whether exercised individually or collectively; secondly, to safeguard and promote the welfare and well-being of the wage earners and of all citizens, and to prevent the powers of government being used by any one group for the exploitation of another. In undertaking to mass and direct this potential political power, the American trade union movement deems it of primary importance that the economic organizations and power of labor shall in no way be impaired. Then, too, in our peculiar form of duality of government and tripartite, divisions of the powers of government, experience has demonstrated that any attempt to mass and direct the potential and actual power of the wage earners through any form of fixed party scheme is to destroy that efficiency that comes from flexible mobility of power to meet whatever emergency may arise and from whatever source it may emanate. The policy and practice of the A. F. of L. to be partisan to principles and not to be partisan to political parties has been fully justified by experience. That weaknesses have developed in the application of this political policy is unquestioned. These weaknesses, instead of disproving the validity of this policy emphasize its effectiveness and indicate a proficient method of improvement by extending this policy into all primary elections within political parties and by the enactment of open, liberal and democratic primary election laws.

Political Policy, Labor's—(1919, p. 102) With independent political labor activity engaging attention in a number of localities during the year, the views of President Gompers were sought by a great many members of the labor movement. In December, 1918, President Gompers took advantage of a gathering of the committees on health insurance and reconstruction to express his views on the question of political policy. A number of representative men and women of labor were invited to meet with the members of these two committees in New York City on December 9, 1918. The address was later considered by the Executive Council and endorsed by the council as expressing the views of the council. The address is therefore presented here in full as follows:

"And, now, a consideration of the subject I have in mind and for which I have asked the gentlemen of the committees and the ladies and gentlemen of labor to participate in this conference. In the last few weeks there have been published certain situations which exist and certain movements which were about to be inaugurated. In a few of the cities that situation and that movement have become accentuated. In Chicago, New York City, and two or three other places the labor movement has expressed itself through the central bodies in favor of the formation of a political labor party. No man has the right to look upon such a move lightly or without deep consideration or deep concern. Either the proposed movement about to be inaugurated for the establishment of a political labor party is good, or it is bad. Either it is advantageous or it is injurious, and the purpose of my asking that we meet this afternoon is to present to you some facts upon that subject. You who were in the movement of long ago will remember that to which I refer. We had in the U. S. a fairly growing labor movement of some trade unionists in some form of a federation called the National Labor Union. That organization went along, inspired good spirit and activity among the workers, and then called a national convention for the purpose of nominating a president of the U. S. That convention met and nominated Justice David Davis, a judge of the supreme court of the United States, as its candidate for president and after nominating Mr. Davis adjourned and never met again. The trade unions then in existence fell off in membership until the organizations became very weak and ineffective. Some organizations fell by the wayside. Labor was in a most deplorable condition, without opportunity for defense and robbed entirely of any power to press forward its rightful claims. In 1885-1886, after a few years of precarious early existence, the A. F. of L. tried to build up and extend its influence and organize the workers into their unions. In 1884 the A. F. of L. declared for the introduction of the eight-hour workday, May 1, 1886. It proposed negotiations with the employers to the accomplishment of that high purpose. The movement gained great impetus and large advantages followed, but on May 2 or 3, 1886, a bomb was thrown at a meeting which was being held at Haymarket Square, Chicago which killed and maimed more than twenty policemen. The meeting was supposed to have been held in the interest of the eight-hour movement. The wrath of the people which was aroused against those in charge of the Haymarket meeting gave the eight-hour day a severe blow and set-back. However, the eight-hour day was secured for the workers in several industries and a reduction in the hours of labor from 16 to 12, or from 12 to 10 became almost universal in the United States. But the eight-hour movement as such was destroyed for the time being. Due in part to that incident and to the resentment of the workers because they had lost so much that they could have obtained and due to certain local conditions, political rather than economic, in various cities the local movement undertook political campaigns and organized a political party in Chicago, Milwaukee, St. Louis, Boston and New York. This resulted in the organized labor movement of New York city launching into a campaign which nominated Henry George as mayor of the city. It was my privilege to enter into that campaign with the men (there are a few of them in this room now) who were active at the time. I-aided to the very best of my ability. Henry George received 68,000 votes and came very near election. Some claim that he was really elected, but that in the last hours many of the supporters of Theodore Roosevelt who was the mayoralty candiate of the republican party abandoned him and cast their votes for Abraham S. Hewitt who was the democratic candidate for mayor. After the campaign closed and the election was held, the movement took on another phase. It was called the progressive labor party. They admitted to membership not only the men of organized labor but what had popularly been called by a great many the "brain with brawn" or "brain with labor." The campaign was carried on with such scandalous results, that nearly all the men of labor who had some self-respect had to hold themselves in the background for fear that they might be besmirched with the incidents which occurred in the campaign. A man, an extremely rich man, in business in the city of New York at the time, was induced to become the candidate for mayor as the representative of labor. I think it was Mr. Coogan, a man engaged in the furniture business. Mr. Coogan, had, I was informed, wonderful experience in financials transactions of which he was not entirely and fully aware until it was all over. By the way, there was a popular phrase which came into effect right at that time, 'Wass ist loos mit Coogan.' (What is the matter with Coogan.) I mention these things of our own country, and now I want to mention a few things of other countries of which I have been a personal, intimate, and close observer. In Germany, the trade union movement having been dissolved by Bismark and the organizations of labor not having the right to exist, went to its death for the time. Then when there was a slight moderation of that order, the trade union movement of that country was organized from the top down. There were executive officers who imposed their will upon the rank and file. There was no democracy of administration, of construction, or of the right of the membership to determine policies. Benefits were paid by the officers of the general organization. These officers had the power to determine whether the workers were entitled to the insurance and other benefits. It was a matter of power vested in the executives. You can imagine how necessary it was for the rank and file to endeavor to curry favor with the executives in order that they might not be discriminated against unfairly. In 1905 I was in Hamburg and Bremen, in consultation with the officers of the general labor movement of Germany, among whom were Legien and Von Elm. They were not permitted to hold public meetings dealing with any subject affecting labor or the government. Before I reached there Mr. Von Elm, with whom I had been in correspondence because he belonged to the Cigarmakers' International Union here, of which I am a member, invited me to deliver an address in German in a public meeting before five or ten thousand persons, but it was necessary for me to address them in German because an address in any other language but German would not be permitted. I could speak and read German but I did not feel competent to deliver an address in the German language before a gathering of five or ten thousand people. I was afraid of my own weakness and that possibly by reason of grammatical errors some might say: 'Well, if he can not speak he ought not try to speak to us,' and thereby discount anything I might say. Therefore, I declined it. They agreed however, to call a social gathering. Invitations were sent out to 132 people to attend. The full number responded. I spoke to them in the German language, but the meeting was secret. The unions were struggling for the right to meet as unions and to have the guarantee of the law for their legal right to maintain their organizations and to hold such meetings; in other words, the right of free association. I had the assurance of Von Elm, Legien and others that the socialist political party of Germany denied the demand made by the trade unions to work to secure from the government a law guaranteeing the workers the right to organize as a free association of workers. The socialist political party of Germany, which is the only political party claiming to be the workmen's party, denied the nuion labor movement of Germany the right to take political action in order to secure the lawful right for its existence. The French organized labor movement is not extensive. Some of the most completely organized unions are wholly out of touch with the Confederation Generale du Travail, that is, the French Federation of Labor, because they want to exercise their individual right of trade unionism and trade union action. To the inter-allied labor conference in London in September, there came a delegation from France of three or four men representing the French Federation of Labor and then a delegation of about seven, eight or ten representing the majority socialist party of France and about that same number representing the minority socialist party. The vote of the delegation was divided between the majority and minority Socialist party and the French Federation of Labor. The political party dominates the trade union movement of France.

In England there is the British Trade Union Congress, the British Federation of Trade Unions, and the labor party. For the discussion of business when the conventions of either party are not in session, they meet jointly in conference through the parliamentary committee of the British Trade Union Congress and the executive committee of the labor party. Quite a number of the members of the parliamentary committee of the British Trade Union Congress are members of the labor party, and quite a number of them who hold their seats in parliament are members of the labor party. As a matter of fact, the executive committee of the labor party dominates the entire movement of England. At a conference held at Derby, England, in September, 1918, the executive officers of the labor party presided and dominated the proceedings. And all the time that I was in England I never heard of a phrase like this: 'The British trade union movement and the labor party.' I never heard it said: 'The parliamentary committee of the British Trade Union Congress and the executive committee of the labor party.' It was always the labor, party and the Trade Union Congress. The labor party of England dominates the labor movement of England. When the inter-allied labor conference opened in London, September 17, early in the morning there were sent over to my room at the hotel, cards which were intended to be the credential cards for our delegation to sign and hand in as our credentials. The card read something like this: 'The undersigned is a duly accredited-delegate to the Inter-Allied Socialist Conference to be held at London,' etc., and giving the dates. I refused to sign my name, or permit my name to be put upon any card of that character. My associates were as indignant as I was and refused to sign any such credential. We went to the hall where the conference was to be held. There was a young lady at the door. When we made an effort to enter she asked for our cards. We said we had no cards to present. 'Well,' the answer came, 'you can not be admitted.' We replied: 'That may be true, we can not be admitted, but we will not sign any such card. We have our credentials written out signed, and sealed, and will present them to any committee of the conference for scrutiny and recommendation, but we are not going to sign such a card.' Mr. Charles Bowerman, Secretary of the parliamentary committee of the British Trade Union Congress, at that moment emerged from the door. He asked why we had not entered. I told him the situation and he persuaded the young lady to permit us to pass in. We entered the hall and presented our credentials. Mr. James Sexton, officer and representative of the Dockers' Union of Liverpool. arose and called the attention of the conference to this situation, and declared that the A. F. of L. delegates refused to sign any such document. He said that it was not an Inter-Allied Socialist Conference but an Inter-Allied Socialist and Labor Conference. Mr. Arthur Henderson, of the labor party, made an explanation, something to this effect, if my memory serves me: 'It is really regrettable that such an error should have been made, but it has been made. It was due to the fact that the old card of credentials which had been used in former conferences was sent to the printer, no one paying any attention to it, and thinking it was all right.' I want to call your attention to the significance of that explanation. That is, that the trade union movement of Great Britain was represented at these former conferences, but at this conference the importance of labor was regarded as so insignificant that everybody took it for granted that it was perfectly all right to have the credential card read, 'Inter-Allied Socialist Conference,' and with the omission of this more important term 'Labor.' The fact is that an independent political labor party becomes either radical, so-called, or else reactionary, but it is primarily devoted to one thing and that is vote-getting. Every sail is trimmed to the getting of votes. The question of the conditions of labor, the question of the standards of labor, the question of the struggles and the sacrifices of labor to bring light into the lives and the work of the toilers—all that is subordinated to the one consideration of votes for the party. I have read the fourteen points which have been formulated for the proposed labor party here. Is there one of them of an essential character to the interests and welfare of the working people of the U. S. which is not contained in the curriculum, the work and the principles of the bona fide labor movement of our country? Which movement, economic or political, in any country on the face of the globe has brought more hope and encouragement, more real advantage, to the working people than the trade union movement of America has brought to the wage-earning masses of our country? The organization of a political labor party would simply mean the dividing of the activities and allegiance of the men and women of labor between two bodies, such as would often come in conflict. In the British Trade Union Congress at Derby there were divergent views. There were four different points of view upon one subject before the congress. In order to try to unite the thought a committee of four was appointed for the purpose of trying to bring in some agreed proposition and recommendation for adoption by the congress. In the course of a few days the committee reported a resolution. For the purpose of conserving time the four members of the committee representing the divergent views were called upon in turn to express their views. Each in turn expressed his own view and placed his own construction upon the resolution recommended. Then each declared that he was going out to fight for his own view. In our movement we have done some things. We have brought together more than three million workers, organized into our trade unions and belonging to the A. F. of L. In addition there are between four and five hundred thousand workmen in the railroad brotherhoods not affiliated with us, but yet in accord with our work and our policies. In other words, there are nearly four million of organized trade unionists in the U. S. There is not always harmony; there is disagreement; there is opposition, all of it important, all of it tending to crystallize the sentiment of unity and devotion to the cause of labor. The American labor movement occupies the field of activity without yielding one inch to any other body. Mr. Longuet, representing the majority socialists of France, at the Inter-Allied Labor Conference in London, expressed his regret that what he called the American socialist party was not represented in the conference. He proposed that the votes of the A. F. of L. delegates should be reduced because the American socialist party was not represented. Who are we going to have as the leaders of this new political labor party here? I understand that there is impatience among our fellows. It is creditable to them that they are impatient. There is not any man in America, or in all the world, more impatient than I with the progress that has been made, with the position we occupy. I want more, more, more for labor. I think I have tried and am trying to do my share. My associates of the Executive Council have tried to do their share, but there is such a thing as attempting to overrun, and by overrunning to defeat the object we would gain for the wage earners and to throw them into the hands of those who do not know the honest aspirations of labor or who would direct them for personal aggrandizement. I have been the president of the A. F. of L. for many, many years. I regard that position as the most exalted that I could occupy. I have no aspiration to hold this or that position. It is not that I ask you to follow me. I ask that the trade union movement be given its fullest opportunity for growth and development so that it may be the instrumentality to secure better and better and better and constantly better conditions for the workers of our country. Here we are in this transition period from war into peace, with all that it may mean. A week ago last evening; that is, on Sunday evening, December 1, at the Century Theater, I delivered an address. I am proud of the address I delivered there on that night. I do not think that anyone realizes all the dangers which I felt and tried to express as to the situation now and which may arise in the near future. I ask you whether the creation of a political labor party, and particularly at this time, would help to solve these problems and meet these dangerous conditions? If ever unity was needed for the toilers, it is now. It is not true as some carping critics allege, that the A. F. of L. is a non-political organization. As a matter of fact, the workers of the U. S. and the organized labor movement act voluntarily in the exercise of their political right and power. We have changed the control of our government from the old-time interests of corporate power and judicial usurpation. We have secured from the government of the U. S. the labor provision of the Clayton Anti-trust law, the declaration in the law that the labor of a human being is not a commodity or article of commerce. In that law we have secured the right of our men to exercise functions for which, under the old regime our men were brought before the bar of justice and fined or imprisoned. We have secured the eighthour workday not only as a basic principle, but as a fact. We have secured the seamen's law, giving to the seamen the freedom to leave their vessels when in safe harbor. The seamen of America are now free men and own themselves. We have secured a child labor law, and although it has been declared unconstitutional, we are again at work to secure a law for the protection of our children. Better than all, we have established the concept in law and in administration that the interest and welfare of the workers are paramount, and this not only in the laws of our republic, but in the laws of our states and municipalities. There are other laws in the interest of labor which we have secured, more than I can mention off-hand, but far above all these are the improvements brought into the lives and work of the toilers by their own actions as organized workers. We have established unity of spirit; we have brought about the extension of organization among the formerly unorganized, and our organized free existence to function and to express ourselves is now practically unquestioned. Suppose in 1912 we had had a labor party in existence; do you think for a moment that we could have gone as the American labor movement to the other political parties and said: 'We want you to inaugurate in your platform this and this declaration.' If one of the parties had refused and the other party consented and took its chance, would the A. F. of L. have been permitted to exercise that independent political and economic course if the labor party had been in existence? How long would we have had to wait for the passage of a law by Congress declaring in law, in practice and in principle that the labor of a human being is not a commodity or an article of commerce—the most far-reaching declaration ever made by any government in the history of the world. I say this to you. I am 68 years of age. I have been tried and seared as few men have. I have almost had my very soul burned in the trials of life. With my two associates, Mr. Mitchell and Mr. Morrison. I have suffered the indignity of being brought before the courts of our country and adjudged guilty and sentenced to imprisonment. Our eyes were wide open. I do not think that it is improper for me to say that I led in the thought and activity of that work, of that willingness to suffer, but it was not a very nice thing to have the endeavor made to besmirch our honor by a sentence of imprisonment—Mr. Morrison six months, Mr. Mitchell nine months, and I 12 months. We fought that sentence, fought it and fought it, supported by the activity of the organized labor movement in all the states and towns of our country, until the principle for which we were contending through that action brought about the incorporation of those provisions in the Clayton Anti-trust law which confirmed and legalized the very things for which we were sentenced to imprisonment. They were legalized, not for us alone, but for labor. I repeat, we have secured the enactment of the seamen's law, the right of a seamen to quit his vessel whenever his vessel is in safe harbor in any part of the world, a law which does not exist in any other country—secured it by our political activity and by our economic powers. Has anything like that been accomplished in any country of the world? Our delegates proposed it at the Inter-Allied Labor Conference in September, and there was not a hearty agreement to stand for it as an international demand. I think you know that I have been most cruelly hurt in the recent past. Some how or other I believe that there are yet considerable years of fight in me for labor. I have said that I hold the position of president of the A. F. of L. in the most exalted estimation, but it is not that for which I am contending; it is not that which I would want to keep one moment beyond the time when I can no longer be of service to my fellows. The only thing that I can leave to my fellow men is that I have helped in trying to bring about a labor movement in our country that is better, more comprehensive and more united than in any other country on the face of the globe. I wanted to present these thoughts to you. I did not have in mind any particular theme or course to present to you. I know I feel and understand and apprehend the danger which is involved in the project which is now being so very actively agitated in some quarters of the labor movement of our country. I fear no danger, I am just as good a follower, perhaps a better follower, than I am a leader, and I am perfectly willing to occupy either position. I would be recreant to the great labor movement and all it portends now and for the future if I did not take you into my confidence, men and women of labor. and tell you what I have told you. I am apprehensive, justly so, justified by every event in the whole history of labor, that a great mistake may be made, a great injury inflicted upon our fellows, not for a day, not for a year, not for a decade, but perhaps for many, many, many years to come. I want to present that view to you so that you may understand the situation clearly. I have spoken calmly and without ceremony or attempt to touch your feelings, but simply to touch the innermost recesses of your minds and to lay before you the responsibility which rests upon you."

The Executive Council meeting which considered the address and the whole question of political policy was held in New York City on December 28. It expressed its approval of the address and its position in the matter as follows: "The address expresses the judgment of the Executive Council to protect and to promote the best interests of the workers and of the labor movement of America. It conforms to the letter and spirit of the provisions of the constitution of the A. F. of L., Article III, Section 8: 'Party politics, whether they be democratic, republican, socialistic, populistic, prohibition, or any other, shall have no place in the conventions of the A. F. of L.' While local and central bodies and state federations may enter into the political field, either independently or otherwise, it is not within their province to form or become part of a national political party."

Political Prisoners—(1919, p. 392) No recommendation is presented for a general pardon of all those who have been sentenced under the espionage act or in connection with industrial crimes. There are instances where commutations of sentences or pardons are warranted; there are undoubtedly many instances where the sentences imposed were fully justified.

(1920, pp. 212-364) The experience of being compelled to detain large numbers of people for what in European countries have long been known as political offenses is an experience practically new to the United States and hitherto unexperienced by the present generation. The necessities of war, however, made it a question of national safety to imprison those who violated the emergency statutes of wartime. The congress enacted an espionage law for the protection of the republic from enemies within its gates and under this act numbers of people were detained as a war precaution. In the tense hour of warfare sentences were imposed which were easily justified under the unusual circumstances of national peril, but which, as was to have been expected, have lost their meaning with the return of peace. Sentences were imposed during the tense months of war which were thoroughly justified under war conditions. The life of the nation was at stake. We do not condone the conduct of those who sought by any means to make more difficult the progress of our government toward victory. We condemn those activities as severely now as during the war. But we believe that many still detained in prison have satisfied justice and should be released. We believe this is in harmony with the thought of our people. We see no cause to be served by detaining further those whose violation of the espionage law was by speech or writing in the expression of views. The principle nations of Europe have already pursued the course here indicated. America is unaccustomed to such problems and it is undoubtedly for that reason that our authorities have hesitated to take a step which is regarded as but natural in those countries where the problem is an old and common one. It is not democratic to inflict continued punishment for the mere sake of punishing. Despicable as was the conduct of many of those still imprisoned we shall not build well for our republic if we allow ourselves to build upon resentment. We believe the welfare of our country and the nobility of our institutions call upon us to urge the release of those political prisoners held for the expression of views and whose detention has already satisfied the ends of justice and the safety of our republic. (P. 364) It is the sense of the A. F. of L. that the further prosecution and imprisonment in the U. S. of political offenders is contrary to the democratic idealism and the traditions of freedom to which our country is committed.

(1921, p. 118) In pursuance of the action of the Montreal convention many conferences were held with government officials and members of congress to urge the release of political prisoners. After the exchange of a number of letters and telegrams a conference was held with the attorney general of the U. S. September 14, 1920. The president of the A. F. of L. pointed out that the issuance of an amnesty proclamation by the president would have a most beneficial effect upon the larger portion of our people, would help to allay feelings that had been aroused, and in fact would have a general tranquilizing influence. The attorney general replied that the president could not under the law issue a general proclamation, that each case would have to be handled separately and upon its individual merit. He further stated that he would be glad to call the attention of the president to the suggestions made, The president of the A. F. of L., on December 21, 1920, appeared before the subcommittee of the committee on judiciary of the senate on S. J. Res. 171, providing for the recommendation of amnesty and pardon for political prisoners. He advocated passage of the resolution. Efforts were continued in the interest of political prisoners up to and after the inauguration of President Harding. On February 25, 1921, a request was made by the president of the A. F. of L. for a conference with President Harding. In company with representatives of national and international unions and departments of the A. F. of L. a conference was held with the president on April 4, during which the desires of the American labor movement were set forth. President Harding stated he had the question of amnesty under consideration, but that under the law each case would have to be treated individually.

(1922, pp. 137-340) The work of the A. F. of L. in behalf of political prisoners was carried on largely in cooperation with the central labor bodies conference for the release of political prisoners. During the war there were approximately 15,000 military offenders and about 600 conscientious objectors placed in confinement. All of the conscientious objectors have been released and about 14,000 military offenders have been freed. About 1,484 convictions under the espionage law were secured by the U. S. department of justice. On December 25, 1921, President Harding liberated a group of political prisoners, leaving only about 45 still in confinement. It was understood at the time that these remaining prisoners were shortly to be released, providing demonstrations were not made in their behalf. Following this the work of the central labor bodies conference was concluded and we are of the opinion that a discontinuance of the work was proper and justified inasmuch as a full measure of success had been achieved. The war-time laws were repealed by congress and nearly all of the political prisoners have been released. There is no doubt that the few remaining in prison would have been released had not their false friends made earlier action by the government difficult. As a matter of fact, throughout the whole campaign for the release of political prisoners, it was necessary not only to convince government officials of the wisdom and justice of our proposals, but it was necessary to contend against the propaganda activities of those who sought to exploit the prisoners for either personal or political purposes. Once again we wish to make clear what has been frequently stated, that our efforts have been solely in behalf of those who were imprisoned for the written or spoken expression of thought or opinion during the war, on the ground that the war having been ended, no further reason for the imprisonment of these purely political offenders remained. (P. 340) The A. F. of L. favors a new trial for Vanzetti and Sacco.

Political Rights of Railroad Workers— (1919, p. 443) The director general of railroads issued an order forbidding railroad employes from engaging in politics and warning them on pain of immediate dismissal scrupulously to abstain therefrom. This order has a tendency to infringe upon and to a certain extent abridge the constitutional rights of millions of American citizens because it is an extension on a vast and far-reaching scale of an old policy which has hitherto attracted but little attention because it affected but a comparatively small number of men but which in its effects has sufficiently revealed the danger and unwisdom of its further enlargement. We believe it is unjust and unnecessary to deprive any class of American citizens of any of the rights of citizenship or to set them aside as a body of partially disfranchised citizens. Therefore the Executive Council is not only directed to secure the rescinding of this particular order but also strive to have their political rights restored to those federal employes now affected injuriously by similar but older orders.

Political Rights—(1919, p. 430) As the constitution of the U. S. was intended to guarantee full political rights to all citizens and this right has in the case of government employes been to a large extent abrogated by executive order, therefore this convention of the A. F. of L. goes on record as opposed to the policy of denying government employes the privilege of participating in political activities. The Executive Council is directed to respectfully represent to the president of the U. S. that these executive orders be withdrawn.

Politics, A. F. of L. Non-Partisan— (1919, p. 374) No one will gainsay or deny the importance of political action on the part of wage earners in their constant struggle to right the wrongs and to secure to the workers a full and equal opportunity to life and liberty and the pursuit of happiness. Differences arise not on the principle of political action, but to the extent to which economic trade union determinism should be supplemented by political parliamentarism and the methods and procedure by which the political power and influence of the wage earners should be manifested. The A. F. of L. has not attempted to interfere with the attitude or inclination of any of its affiliated international unions, either to encourage, limit, restrict or prohibit their membership in this field of endeavor though it has counselled and advised that procedure which would permit of full development and uninterrupted advantages of economic trade union determinism. In that counsel and advice it has been followed by nearly all, if not all, of the international trade unions. Nearly all, if not all, have predicated membership in their organization on the guarantee of the right to political freedom. Recognizing the necessity for legislative redress in more general affairs they have designed their rules and regulations to encourage the workers in the exercise of their political suffrage so as to favor helpful legislation and promote to public office and authority aspirants who are known to be friendly and helpful to labor regardless of their political affiliations. The wisdom of this attitude and procedure is well demonstrated by the many efficient and proficient economic trade union organizations which now dominate in our industrial life. In so far as central labor unions are concerned, equal freedom is allowed and the same counsel and advice are extended, though the activities of these federated bodies are further restricted in that they are prevented from invading the rights and prerogatives and from disregarding the guarantees to the complete autonomy accorded to all affiliated international unions. Considered from this point of view, the relations, attitudes and activities of the many organizations comprising the A. F. of L. can not be interfered with without subjecting ourselves to the dangerous and harmful consequences which necessarily and logically follow the sweeping aside of the rights privileges and guarantees of our associated organizations. That there is room for improvement in the efficient exercise of the political power of the wage earners is freely admitted. The dangers of exercising this power from a purely partisan political standpoint is convincingly portrayed in the report of the Executive Council. With the increasing tendency to place employes in public and semi-public utilities under public and governmental control there is an increasing need of more closely solidifying the forces of labor in all their varied manifestations and in such a manner as not to interfere with the workers' freedom or choice and freedom of action. To render ineffective or to hamper in any degree or to lessen the importance and value of trade union economic determinism merely to attain possession of political authority to place into dominance political parliamentarism will not have been a gain but a loss to the advancement of the workers to a fuller, a freer, a better and a nobler life For these reasons the A. F. of L. directs the continuance of the policies which have heretofore governed the political activities of labor.

(1920, pp. 74-383) The following report of the Executive Council was unanimously adopted: "In accordance with the instruction of the Atlantic City convention, unanimously adopted, recommending "the continuance of the policies which have heretofore governed the political activities of the American Federation of Labor," the Executive Council at its meeting in Washington

December 11-18, 1919, adopted a resolution declaring: "This is a crucial time in the struggle of the workers for the advancement of their industrial and social welfare and never before has it been so necessary for them to demonstrate their convictions at the ballot box and their earnestness in the matter of holding to account legislators who have no regard or are unmindful of the great fundamental principles for the recognition of which the organized labor movement is struggling." This action was taken by the Executive Council in view of the established policy of the American labor movement, and in view of the extremely grave issues which confronted the American workers as citizens and as trade unionists. At this meeting the Executive Council, pursuant to the declared policy of the federation and the previous action of the council, instructed the president of the A. F. of L. to appoint a committee consisting of the heads of the departments affiliated to the A. F. of L. and the Executive Council of the A. F. of L. to carry into effect the non-partisan political policies of the A. F. of L., and to conduct a campaign as declared in the report of the conference of officials of national and international unions held in Washington, December 13, 1919. The committee on declarations, after a thorough consideration of the situation that confronted the nation, and having in view the declared policies and principles of the A. F. of L., presented a draft of a declaration to all organized labor, which was adopted and which was issued to the entire labor movement under date of February 12. This declaration follows:

"'Washington, D. C., February 12, 1920. To All Organized Labor: Dear Sirs and Brothers: In compliance with the directions of the last convention of the A. F. of L. and of the December 13, 1919, conference of representatives of Labor and the farmers' organizations a three days' conference was held at the federation headquarters in this city to consider the part which labor should take in the coming campaign, primaries and election. The following declaration was unanimously adopted: The inherent rights and principles of our people are threatened. The free institutions of our country are menaced. The ideals of democracy are in danger. The congress of the U. S. has failed to do its duty. It has failed to meet the emergency. It has given encouragement and support to autocratic and reactionary policies. Its dominating thought has been the repression of labor. Every effort to secure remedial and constructive legislation has been strangled. Every appeal for redress has met with subtle and open hostility. The halls of congress have been used by labor's enemies to foster and spread a vicious propaganda against the efforts of the toilers to exercise their normal and lawful activities for the protection and promotion of their interests and welfare. Labor has appealed for relief in vain. The hour has arrived when those who believe in the maintenance of democratic institutions must marshal their forces in defense of their rights and ideals. It is intolerable that a people who spared no cost to make the world safe for democracy should be forced to submit to any restriction of the glorious liberties inherited from the founders of our nation. The perpetuation of our fundamental rights and the enactment of essential constructive legislation demand the election of men, regardless of their political affiliations, who are truly representative of American ideals of liberty. Conscious of its responsibilities, impressed by the grave problems resulting from the great war, the A. F. of L. at its annual convention in June, 1919, adopted a reconstruction program. This program defined the essential industrial policies and legislative enactments required to establish a full measure of justice and opportunity for Labor. Because of grave emergencies which have arisen since that convention, it became imperative that the representatives of organized labor and of farmers should assemble and confer to devise ways and means for safeguarding their rights and liberties as freemen and citizens. On December 13, 1919, a conference of representatives of labor and of farmers met in Washington, D. C. This conference expressed "Labor's Grievances, Protests and Demands." No favorable legislative action upon the recommendations contained in the A. F. of L. reconstruction program, or those expressed at the December conference, has been taken by congress. Instead many congressmen have endeavored to enact legislation providing for compulsory labor. Despite the patriotism and sacrifice of the masses of labor of America during the world war, under the guise of anti-sedition laws the effort has been made to repress free association, free speech and free press. Scorned by congress, ridiculed and misrepresented by many members of both houses, the American labor movement finds it necessary to apply vigorously its long and well-established non-partisan political policy. Confronted by a succession of hostile congresses, the A. F. of L., in 1906, announced its historic "Bill of Grievances." This was followed by a vigorous and successful non-partisan political campaign. In 1908, 1910, and 1912, the same program was energetically applied. As a result, many of Labor's enemies in congress were defeated and all of the essential legislation in "Labor's Bill of Grievances" of 1906 was enacted. Constructive legislation has never been so necessary as at present. Never has it been so essential to secure the defeat of labor's enemies and the election of its friends and supporters. Sinister forces are already actively engaged in efforts to confuse and nullify labor's political power. Their object is to divide the labor vote so that the election of reactionaries and enemies of labor will be assured. Unless labor holds steadfastly to its non-partisan political policy, the enemies of labor will be successful in their efforts. Labor can not, labor must not, permit its political strength to be divided in the present crisis. Organized labor owes allegiance to no political party. It is not partisan to any political party. It is partisan to principles—the principles of freedom, of justice and of democracy. It is the duty of trade unionists, their friends and sympathizers, and all lovers of freedom, justice and democratic ideals and institutions, to unite in defeating those seeking public office who are indifferent or hostile to the people's interests and the rights of labor. Wherever candidates for re-election have been friendly to labor's interests they should be loyally supported. Wherever candidates are hostile or indifferent to labor's interests, they should be defeated and the nomination and election of true and tried trades unionists or of assured friends should be secured. Complying with the instructions of the last convention and the labor and farmer conference of December, 13, 1919, the A. F. of L. announces its determination to apply every legitimate means and all of the power at its command to accomplish the defeat of labor's enemies who aspire for public office, whether they be candidates for president

for congress, for state legislatures, or for any other office. The A. F. of L. calls upon all affiliated and recognized national, international and brotherhood organizations, state federations of labor, central labor bodies, local unions and labor's friends and sympathizers to unite and give loyal support to the non-partisan political campaign now set in motion. This political campaign must begin in the primaries. The record of every aspirant for public office must be thoroughly analyzed, stated in unmistakable language and given the widest possible publicity. Labor's enemies and friends must be definitely known. To this end the A. F. of L. has created the National Non-Partisan Political Campaign Committee and it now calls upon all affiliated and recognized labor organizations to create district and local committees to cooperate with the national committee and coordinate their efforts. The future welfare, the very ability of the trade union movement to carry on its work for humanity depends upon the success of the campaign herewith inaugurated. There can be no hesitancy. There must be no turning aside. The time for vigorous and determined action is here!"

It is with a sense of satisfaction and gratification that the Executive Council views the splendid enthusiasm with which the labor movement has responded to the call to action. Throughout the nation there has been a spontaneous rallying of the movement, which indicates the intense earnestness with which the working people of the country look upon the present political struggle and their profound determination to carry into effect at the polls the slogan of the A. F. of L., "stand faithfully by our friends and elect them; oppose our enemies and defeat them, whether they be candidates for president, for congress or other offices, whether executive, legislative or judicial." The only note of dissension which has made itself manifest has come from those who have endeavored to thrust into the campaign situation an independent national political labor party. In every case where our attention has been brought to efforts to form a national political party in violation of the policy laid down by the A. F. of L., we have remonstrated and made every effort to make clear the position of the Federation and to explain at length the historical reasons which form the background and the substance of the policy as laid down by the Federation in conventions. No effort has been made nor has any desire been expressed to interfere with the freedom of action guaranteed to central bodies, nor with the autonomy guaranteed to international unions in respect to political action. Numerous pamphlets and circulars have been issued by the executive committee of the national non-partisan political campaign committee and all possible energy has been directed toward the organization of labor's forces in such a manner as to result in the greatest possible success at the polls. It is with extreme satisfaction that we report a growing solidarity in support of the national non-partisan political policy and a constantly diminishing desire to experiment with political theories not in accord with that policy. There has never been a greater spirit of unity nor has there ever been a higher enthusiasm nor a greater determination to achieve results. The intolerable spirit of repression which has made itself manifest in legislation adopted in the state legislatures as well as in the national congress and in legislation proposed in these same bodies, has aroused in the working people everywhere a feeling of deep resentment and has thoroughly awakened them to the necessity of defeating those elected officials who have proven themselves either unable or unwilling to follow in legislative matters the desires of the people and to take into consideration their needs and their welfare in the enactment of laws. We stand at the parting of the ways. Only the determination of the working people of the U. S., supporting the non-partisan political policy of the A. F. of L., can save the nation from pursuing the road toward reaction. Let there be unity. Let there be solidarity. Let the great voice of the working people of America in their organized capacity be heard for the progress, for the welfare, for the liberty of our country"

(1921, p. 148) Report of Executive Council: Under instruction of the 1919 convention, adopted by unanimous vote, your Executive Council continued the policy which has heretofore governed the political activities of the A. F. of L. We were able to report to the 1920 convention a large part of the work done in the national campaign and we here continue to report on our activities subsequent to that convention. The proposals of labor which were laid before the republican convention and which were reported to and adopted by our 1920 convention, were placed in identical form before the democratic national convention and the report submitted and published in the *American Federationist* for July, 1920. In pursuance of the established policy, the Executive Council appointed the national non-partisan political campaign committee, to which was delegated the work of actively directing the campaign. Following our 1920 convention this committee continued the work of apprising the working people and people generally through the organizations of labor in the congressional and senatorial districts of the records of representatives and senators in congress and of the platform declarations of political parties. The work of the campaign committee and of the bodies created in cooperation with it, was limited to the supplying of information, the stimulation of effective organization and the allocation of speakers. As the campaign progressed, practically all domestic questions were overshadowed by questions of an international character. Issues pertaining to relationships at home were subordinated to the relationship of our nation with all other countries abroad. Indeed, this entire campaign was unprecedented in American politics and the conclusions reached leave in doubt the political expression of the electorate upon the internal problems which require consideration and solution at the hands of congress. It is likewise difficult to appraise accurately the temperament and attitude of many of the men elected to both the house of representatives and to the senate. Sixteen of the men in the house of representatives are members of organized labor, the same number that were in affiliation with organized labor in the last congress. In view of these uncertainties, it is urged that labor should continue to impress its views, hopes, desires and aspirations upon congress and those charged with administrative authority and press forward more vigorously than ever its campaign for helpful and constructive legislation which will safeguard and promote labor's interest, organized and unorganized, and that of all our people. We should likewise be prepared and be in readiness to continue labor's non-partisan political

activities to the end that the rights and privileges of the workers and of the people shall not be invaded but shall be freed from transgression and be made secure for all time. (P. 309) The Executive Council is directed and empowered to provide for the setting up of the proper agency for the distribution of digested information with regard to the doings of congress and the record of the members of congress. Through this means will be provided the essential organization on which the success of the non-partisan campaign must rest, and through such systematization and co-ordination of effort the endeavors of organized labor to exercise properly its power at the ballot box may be made more effective. (P. 310) President Gompers: "May I make a brief explanation of a matter upon which some criticism was indulged, the criticism being that the committee which appeared before the convention of the democratic party at San Francisco did not present to the committee on resolutions of that convention the declaration of the Montreal convention upon the subject of government ownership and democratic control of the railroads. You will recall that the committee left Montreal and attended the national convention of the republican party at Chicago and returned within a day and a half. At the time when the committee appeared before the platform committee of the republican party convention, the Montreal convention itself had not then declared for government ownership of railroads. Hence, when the committee appeared before the democratic national party convention at San Francisco, it could not change the demands made upon the republican party convention. It was necessary to present the identical demands to both parties, so that it was not within the power or the province of the committee to present different demands to one political party than it had already presented to the other."

(1922, p. 79) The deplorable economic conditions which the people of our country have suffered in the past two years and from which they are still suffering have awakened them to the necessity of removing from power those responsible for such conditions. This has been most effectually and emphatically shown by the activities of the 40,000 local unions in preparing for the primaries and elections that will take place this year. Many communications have been received by the officers of the A. F. of L. in which emphatic complaints are made because of conditions arising from the failure of congress to enact legislation for the relief of the people from the conditions resulting from the aftermath of war. Millions of idle men have been earnestly and persistently seeking employment. Their appeals are unheeded; the destitution caused by unemployment is not relieved. Congress is unresponsive. Pre-election promises seem to be forgotten. Conforming to the directions of the Denver convention and desirous of speedily arousing the men of labor to the urgent need for action at the polls, the president of the A. F. of L. with our approval from month to month sent to national and international unions, state federations and city central bodies, building trade councils and the labor press, a summary of the report of the legislative committee so that these officials might keep fully in touch with congressional activities. An extensive campaign was also conducted through the publicity service of the A. F. of L. On March 8, 1922, the A. F. of L. Non-Partisan

Political Campaign Committee issued the following:

"To All State Federations of Labor and City Central Bodies: The time is here when the thousands of non-partisan political campaign committees appointed by unions affiliated to the A. F. of L. should become more active than ever before. The reactionary members of congress and of the state legislatures, aided and abetted by the unfair employers of our country, have taken the reins in their hands and are riding rough shod over the hopes and aspirations of labor and the people. They have shown no mercy, and by their actions declare they will show no mercy to those who seek to better their economic condition through the normal activities of the trade union movement. Members of legislatures in various states have presented bills that would, if enacted, take America back to the sixteenth century. While the unfair organizations of employers are demanding of congress repressive legislation against labor they are at the same time demanding that no employers shall make agreements with employes. The un-American campaign of the profiteering interests to establish autocracy in industry has failed in its purpose and they are now endeavoring to obtain the same wished-for results through congress and the state legislatures. Although the constitution of the U. S. forbids compulsory labor except for crime, here and there bills have been presented in congress and various legislatures having for their purpose the compelling of wage earners to work against their will. Economy is the watchword of most new administrations. It is useless as a watchword when ignored in practice, or when the practice results in removing the burdens from the rich and predatory and placing them on the shoulders of the wage earners. We are in the midst of an amazing kind of muddling with tax and tariff questions where a little regard is had for the interests of the great masses of our people. Not a genuine constructive measure has been enacted by congress since March 4, 1919. Every means used to secure legislation that will aid in relieving unemployment has been met with rebuff. The present deplorable condition of our country, artificially made, and in which labor and the farmers have been deflated until it hurts, has been ignored by congress. Only appeals for subsidies for shipowners, railroads and other interests find listeners. To all legislation in the interest of the people congress is deaf. In a circular sent to all organized labor December 1, 1921, the president of the A. F. of L. said: "In the A. F. of L. headquarters we are keeping accurate record of the members of both houses of congress. Records of every member of a local legislative body should be kept by the respective legislative committees. During political campaigns the legislative committees of each organization may automatically become non-partisan political campaign committees. They will make public at the proper time the labor records of all legislators who have been false to the people as well as of those who have been true to the people." The coming political campaign demands the utmost vigor from every state federation, city central body and all local unions in the U. S. in order that success may be assured. The Executive Council of the A. F. of L., at its meeting held February 21, 1922, directed that a vigorous campaign in the interest of labor and the people generally shall be planned and conducted. Members of unions,

their friends and sympathizers, are urged to go to the polls primary day and vote only for those candidates for the senate and the house the state legislatures or any other public office who have shown a fairness to labor and the people in order to defeat those who openly or covertly aim to throttle the normal activities of the toilers. Wherever necessary labor should place candidates in the field. This should be done where the candidates on both dominant party tickets are unfriendly to our cause. The records of the members of congress will be furnished to the non-partisan political campaign committees and all interested friends for the purpose of obtaining as great publicity as possible. To be effective in the primaries we suggest that meetings be called as soon as possible by all non-partisan political campaign committees in the U. S. at which plans should be made and measures taken for a most intensive campaign of education of not only members of trade unions, but of the great masses of the people. Where non-partisan political campaign committees have not remained in existence since the last election it is urgently requested that they be immediately selected and begin active preparations for the primaries. Every state federation of labor, every city central body should create non-partisan political campaign committees. Every local union should appoint committees to cooperate with the state and central bodies. Mass meetings should be held. The real conditions facing the workers in industry and agriculture should be clearly set forth in order that those who have been misinformed and misled by the publicity agents of the reactionaries will know how to vote. Agitate! Agitate! Agitate! The campaign should not be among the organized workers alone but should be extended so that the truth will be known to all just minded citizens of our beloved country. Since the armistice the most flagrant and malignant denunciation of the hopes and aspirations of the masses of our people has been made. The present campaign in the primaries and in the fall elections offers opportunities which may not come again in a decade to redress wrongs and attain justice. It is, therefore, important and necessary that not a moment should be lost in launching a most active campaign that will bring about the election of men and women who will restore to our people the rights taken from them since fighting ceased in the great war. Therefore, all are urged to be up and doing. Please report fully and frequently to the A. F. of L. Non-Partisan Political Campaign Committee, A. F. of L. Building, Washington, D. C." In the meantime many communications pertaining to the non-partisan campaign were received and answered. Others were sent to officers of organizations requesting and giving information as to the necessity for making an intensive effort to arouse the wage earners and the people to existing conditions and the need for action. Much correspondence was had with the farmers' organizations, looking to an amalgamation of efforts to defeat enemies and elect friends of the people. This bore fruit in a number of states where labor and the farmers have united on a non-partisan political basis. In order to carry on an aggressive campaign and one that would bring success to our cause requests were sent to all labor organizations for contributions necessary to carry on the work of the national non-partisan political campaign committee. In order to bring about greater cooperation of the wage earners, the executive committee of the non-partisan political campaign committee directed that another circular be sent out by the president of the A. F. of L. The following was addressed to all national and international unions, city and state central bodies and 40,000 local and federal labor unions:

"To All Organized Labor: The reactionary elements in the legislative bodies of our country, both federal and state, endanger American standards and threaten to graft laws on our people that will interfere with their evolutionary progress toward a higher and a better life. No thought is given to the needs of the people. No constructive legislation that will remove the artificially made business depression has been seriously considered by the reactionaries who control legislation. No thought is given to the millions of unemployed. In fact, every effort has been and is being made to lull the people into a feeling of false security in order to permit the privileged few to conceive and enact legislation of benefit only to themselves. There has been no time in the history of our country when the predatory interests have so unblushingly sought legislation for their especial benefits. It is most imperative that all union men and all local unions in the U. S. should take to themselves the duty of protesting against such a reactionary course. The A. F. of L., realizing that there is an urgent necessity for united and intensive action, adopted a plan providing that every local union throughout the country should appoint a permanent legislative committee to further beneficial legislation and oppose legislation inimical to the rights and interests of labor. If your local union has not a legislative committee you are, therefore, most earnestly urged that one be immediately selected and that this office be advised of compliance with this request, together with the names and addresses of your permanent legislative committee. The A. F. of L. keeps a record of the votes of every U. S. senator and member of the house of representatives on matters of interest to labor and the people. There will be an election in November for senators in some 34 states and an election for members of the house of representatives in every congressional district in the U. S. It is the desire of the A. F. of L. that your legislative committees should send here for the records of congressmen in your respective districts through the central bodies or direct. I would also urge that your legislative committee keep in touch with the A. F. of L. so that your committee may be supplied with all information desired to carry out the legislative policy of the non-partisan political program, local, state and national. Through the formation of these permanent legislative committees by the various local unions it will be possible to keep all members continually informed of the work of congress. The state federations can keep these committees informed of all matters pertaining to state legislation. In outlining this plan of organization of the organized forces of labor, the Denver, 1921, convention unanimously declared: "Through this plan means will be provided for the essential organization, on which the success of the non-partisan political campaign must rest, and through such systematization and co-ordination of effort the endeavors of organized labor to exercise properly its power at the ballot box may be made more effective." Permit me to impress upon all local unions the deep significance of the action of the A. F. of L. as its intent is to unite in a solid phalanx the organizations and the rank and file of the trade union movement and its sympathizers. It is my desire and hope that these committees will not hesitate to write me for any information that will be helpful in carrying out the policies enunciated by the A. F. of L. in bringing the greatest possible success to the cause so dear to the hearts of the men in the organized labor movement of our country."

The responses from this circular were so general and the interest so intense that it can be stated that labor will be more active than ever, not only in the primaries but also in the elections. It is in the primaries that initial effective work can be done. The confident belief is expressed by those who have written of conditions in the various localities that satisfactory results will be accomplished. The workers have never been more united to translate into action the discontent with existing political and economic conditions. There is now no independent political labor movement in the field to interfere with or minimize the efforts of our people to gain victories. Organizations that have heretofore stood for partisan politics have discovered the futility of such a course and are heartily supporting the non-partisan political policy of the A. F. of L. This is most gratifying. It demonstrates that the repeated declarations of the A. F. of L. against partisan politics, gained from 41 years of experience, are for the best interests of labor and the people. It is the only policy through which success can be gained. Labor in Illinois is united on a non-partisan basis. The workers in Indiana have a state-wide organization and many local organizations that will demonstrate their value in the November elections. In Kansas the organizations have centered their efforts upon electing members of the state legislature who will vote for a repeal of the court of industrial relations act. In Minnesota, Nebraska, North Carolina, North Dakota, Ohio, Oklahoma, Pennsylvania, South Dakota, Tennessee, Texas, and Iowa most effective non-partisan campaign organizations have been formed. In some of these states labor and the farmers have joined together to elect friends and defeat foes of the people. Although the primaries in a great many of the states will not be held until after the adjournment of this convention, it is definitely known that there never has been in an off year such intense interest in political campaigns. In Pennsylvania it is a struggle for liberty. It is a struggle to maintain rights guaranteed by the constitution of the U. S. In no other state except West Virginia have the authorities exercised more assumed power to prohibit free speech, free press and free assembly. The tentacles of the monstrous steel trust, united with anti-union coal operators and other great interests antagonistic to the wage earners have strangled liberty in both states for many years. Another blow aimed at the interests that have preyed upon Pennsylvania for so many years is the candidacy for governor of a man who is the representative of the farmers and who is most earnestly supported by labor of that state. In all communications sent from headquarters to local non-partisan political campaign committees, labor is urged to spread broadcast the following principles: "No freedom-loving citizen should vote for any candidate who will not pledge himself to oppose any form of compulsory labor law. No justice-loving citizen should vote for a candidate for any office who will not pledge himself to oppose injunctions and contempt proceedings as a substitute for trial by jury." The Executive Council desires to express its satisfaction over the wonderful enthusiasm exhibited by the state bodies, the city central bodies and the local unions. Not only the wage earners but the great mass of our citizenship are crying aloud for relief. Congress has failed to meet the responsibility placed upon it by a great war. It has proved its inefficiency in a great crisis. It has proved that only those who are well-to-do or control great interests can induce congress to listen. Those who favor subsidies for railroads and shipowners; those who believe in paying back to the profiteers in food the fines assessed against them; those who believe in relieving the business of the well-to-do from taxation by substituting the sales tax, and those who believe in compulsory labor find ready listeners to their demands for legislation. When a sufficient number of members of the senate banded together in an effort to obtain at least some relief for the farmers the privileged few immediately began to denounce them. Nothing can be expected from the present congress except legislation giving fortunes to those who already possess them and adding to the burdens of the people by higher and higher taxation. These facts are slowly penetrating the minds of the people. They are beginning to realize that the change they thought they wanted and for which they voted has been an injury instead of a benefit. Therefore, it is expected that many changes will be made in the personnel of the senate and the house. And unless there is a change in such personnel the people can prepare themselves for still greater and greater suffering and injustice. (P. 476) The A. F. of L. in the forty-second convention assembled demands of the union men and women of the United States that for their own good and their own liberation and freedom from political enslavement, that they do take a more active interest in the precinct, county, state and national conventions and assemblies of the two old parties, thereby getting control of the two old parties' machinery by electing only men who are fair and honest with labor in the precinct, county, state and national assemblies. Both the old parties are ultimately controlling the machinery of our national government.

(1923, p. 46) The belief expressed by the Executive Council in its report to the Cincinnati convention that the national nonpartisan political campaign of the A. F. of L. would be a success in 1922 became a fact. It was a most remarkable campaign, as it was the first time in many years that alleged political labor parties failed to make much of an impression on the result. This was most convincing evidence that where labor will unite on a non-partisan political program there is no doubt of the certainty of success. As reported at the last convention the non-partisan campaign began in the fall of 1921. Circulars were sent to all national, international local unions, and state and city central bodies outlining plans to re-elect public officials who had been true to labor and the people and to defeat those who had proved untrue to them. Due to the favorable results of the campaign the Executive Council believes that it should report some of the correspondence that did so much to bring about the desired result. On May 1, 1922, too late to be incorporated in the report to the Cincinnati convention, a circular was sent to all organizations of labor affiliated directly or indirectly to the A. F. of L. as follows:

"To All Organized Labor—Greetings: The primaries this year will largely determine whether misrule shall hold sway for another two years or more in congress and state legislatures or whether the people will be represented by those who believe in progress and even-handed justice. All hope of remedial legislation of a really constructive nature by the present congress was lost months ago. Subsidies for railroads and shipowners, relieving the well-to-do from taxation by placing the burden through a sales tax on those least able to bear it, rémission of fines for food profiteers, adding to the number of judges in order to make the jobs more worth while and the issuance of injunctions in labor disputes more easy, have constituted the ruling passion of the reactionaries in congress. At the same time reactionaries just as active have held the reins in state legislatures, some of which have attempted to pass legislation as vicious as that in which congress has been interested. It is therefore most imperative that the wage earners of our country awaken to the serious dangers ahead. It will require the greatest unity of action and determination to defeat those who, because of their lack of regard for the interests of the people, will have all the antagonistic reactionary forces united in their support. Upon the shoulders of those who control legislation must rest responsibility for the present unemployment. Through no fault of their own more than 5,000,000 wage earners are idle. They are all willing and anxious to work but they can not find work. The same influences that are striving to break down the standards of labor have also chosen as victims the farmers of our country. Not only are the wage earners crying for relief but the farmers have their backs to the wall and are just as earnestly and insistently demanding of congress to do something to save them from bankruptcy. The A. F. of L. Non-Partisan Political Campaign Committee therefore appeals to all organized labor and to all justice-loving citizens without regard to political party affiliations to unite to defeat those who have proved false to the people, and to support those who have proved by their public acts that they will work and vote for no legislation that will injure the many in order to benefit the privileged few. The injunction abuse with its attending contempt proceedings has become so flagrant that even a judge here and there has called attention to attending dangers. Members of the U. S. senate have declared in open session that federal courts (except the U. S. Supreme Court) should be abolished as they are not only duplicating the work of the state courts but are definitely recognized as "rich men's courts." Hon. William H. Taft, now chief justice of the U. S. Supreme Court, has declared there is "no more important question than the improvement of the administration of justice," and to accomplish that end he advised: "We must make it so the poor man will have as nearly as possible an equal opportunity in litigating as the rich man, and under the present conditions, ashamed as we may be of it, this is not a fact." The president of the Carnegie foundation in the introduction to a report on "Justice and the Poor," said: "The very existence of free government depends upon making the machinery of justice so effective that the citizens of a democracy shall believe in its impartiality and fairness." The chief justice of the municipal courts of Chicago also adds this warning: "When litigation is too costly the result for most persons is a denial of justice. Such denial or partial denial of justice engenders social and commercial friction. The sense of helplessness this causes incites citizens to take the law into their own hands. It causes crimes of violence. It saps patriotism and destroys civic pride. It arouses jealousy and breeds contempt for law and government." These warnings, however, failed to appeal to a West Virginia federal judge. He granted an injunction which forbade not only the lawful right of the workers to organize but evicted several thousand boycotted and nearly destitute men, women and children from their homes. Judges in the fifteenth century did not assume more arbitrary power. Then there is the persistent demand of unfair employers that involuntary servitude should be once more established in the U. S. This is to be brought about by compulsory labor laws, which would compel men and women in industry to work for whatever their employers are willing they shall have or be imprisoned. Every effort has been made to prohibit the normal activities of labor. Such laws would make wage earners the wards of their employers and they would no longer be free men and free women. The people are permitted no voice on the most important issues that come before congress and the state legislatures. This was most flagrantly demonstrated in the passage of the Volstead prohibition enforcement act. Believing that this should be called to the attention of the people the Executive Council issued a statement on February 25, 1922, as follows: "To the American people: The A. F. of L., as the spokesman of the unorganized as well as the organized toilers, having in mind the interest and the welfare of our people, decided by unanimous vote in its convention held in Denver, in June, 1921, that the Volstead enforcement act must be modified so as to promote the manufacture and sale of beer and light wines. Before this decision was reached the Executive Council of the A. F. of L. had caused to be made an exhaustive investigation of the effects of the Volstead act. It was shown by this investigation that there had been: 1. A general disregard of the law among all classes of people including those who made the law. 2. Creation of thousands of moonshiners among both country and city dwellers. 3. The creation of an army of bootleggers. 4. An amazing increase in the traffic in poisons and deadly concoctions and drugs. 5. An increased rate of insanity, blindness and crime among the users of these concoctions and drugs. 6. Increase in unemployment due to loss of employment by workers in 45 industries directly or indirectly connected with the manufacture of liquors. 7. Increase in taxes to city, state and national governments amounting to approximately one thousand million dollars per year. Having in mind these results of the extreme interpretation of the prohibition amendment contained in the Volstead act, as well as the enormous expense of the attempt to enforce that unenforceable legislation, it is our conclusion that the act is an improper interpretation of the prohibition amendment, that it is a social and a moral failure, and that it is a dangerous breeder of discontent and of contempt for all law. Something of the economic effect of the Volstead law may be seen by considering the fact that in 1918, according to government statistics, $110,-000,000 worth of farm products were consumed by breweries, and that the transportation of

these products to the manufacturer and thence to the consumer necessitated the use of 133,666 railroad cars. In addition to this, breweries in operation in 1918 consumed 50,000 carloads of coal. It must be obvious that the total economic effect of the destruction of this industry is tremendous. The A. F. of L. always has been the advocate of law and order and always has endeavored to create conditions which would make possible the highest type of citizenship. We do not protest against the eighteenth amendment to the constitution which is now a part of the fundamental law of the land. We do not protest against the principle established by the eighteenth amendment. It is our contention that the eighteenth amendment under a reasonable and proper legislative interpretation would be beneficial to our country and would have the support of the great majority of our people. The eighteenth amendment, however, under the present drastic and unreasonable legislative interpretation has a destructive and deteriorating effect and influence in every direction. We seek no violation of the eighteenth amendment but on the contrary, we declare for a reasonable interpretation of that amendment in order that the law may be enforceable and enforced, and in order that the people of our country may not suffer from an unjust and fanatical interpretation of the constitution. We urge, therefore, that all citizens in every walk of life demand from their representatives and senators in Washington immediate relief from the unwarranted restriction contained in the Volstead act; and we likewise suggest to the citizenship of our country the wisdom and advisability of bearing in mind the attitude toward this issue of office-holders and aspirants to office in coming elections in order that there may be restored to the people the lawful use of wholesome beer and light wines, which, under the provisions of the eighteenth amendment, can and should be rightfully declared as nonintoxicating beverages. It is to the issues hereinabove presented that the people of our country must direct their activities. If they do not replace the present members of congress and the state legislatures who have brought on these conditions they will have another two years of struggle and sacrifice. Therefore, the A. F. of L. Non-Partisan Political Campaign Committee directs the attention of the wage earners and their sympathizers to two principles that should be followed in the campaign. These are: No freedom-loving citizen should vote for a candidate who will not pledge himself to oppose any form of compulsory labor law. No justice-loving citizen should vote for a candidate for any office who will not pledge himself to oppose injunctions and contempt proceedings as a substitute for trial by jury. Let your slogans be: No judge-made laws. Abolish the injunction abuse. Make justice blind in fact as well as in theory. Amendments to the constitution of the U. S. should guarantee rights, not take them away. No compulsory labor laws. No sales tax. No wage earners or farmers to be enslaved. No subsidies for the privileged few. No remission of fines to food profiteers. These issues, upon all of which depend the future of our republic should be discussed with the organizations of farmers. Whatever injures labor injures the farmer. Whatever benefits labor benefits the farmer. Whatever is for the interest of labor and the farmer is for the best interest of all the people except the privileged few.

We urge you to be up and doing. The democracy of our republic must be maintained by labor and the farmers and all others who believe in good government. By authority and direction of the Executive Council of the A. F. of L.

August 14, 1922, a circular was sent to all organizers of the A. F. of L. to energize their activity. It was in part as follows: "We have much to fight against. We have much to fight for. The success of our efforts will depend as much upon the organizers of the A. F. of L. as upon any other representatives of the trade union movement. We want you to keep us informed of the political conditions in your locality. Send in frequent reports. Do not hesitate to give all the facts in your possession. What has been done in Indiana, in North Dakota, in Iowa, and other states can be done in your respective states if you will give your whole heart and soul to the work. You are fighting for the cause of humanity. You are fighting for progress and against reaction. Be alert. Be aggressive. Be faithful to labor and the people. Let it be said after the elections in November that there is not an organizer in the U. S. who did not show results. Whatever success you may have will not be for yourself alone. It will bring happiness and hope to all those benefited by your activities." In October just before the election circular letters were sent to all labor organizations in the U. S. Special circulars also were were prepared for each state giving the records of senators. Where congressmen at large were to be elected they were also included. To each congressional district the records of the respective congressmen were also sent. The circulars pointed out the necessity for united action and contained the following: "This is a most crucial time in the history of our country and it is most necessary that the wage earners and all liberty-loving citizens awaken to the dangers ahead if the elections in November are in favor of reaction. The reactionaries are running mad in demanding legislation most abhorrent to the people of a free country. Included in the proposed legislation are: Compulsory labor, which means that the wage earners must work for wages, hours and under any conditions that may be determined by governmental court or board. In fact, they propose involuntary servitude in this land of the free. Giving jurisdiction to federal courts over matters strictly within the jurisdiction of the state courts. The enactment of legislation in support of the nation-wide injunction issued despite the constitution and laws of the land by a newly appointed federal judge in Chicago on the application of the attorney general of the U. S. who was instrumental in his selection. Establishment of a sales tax, which would relieve the well-to-do from taxation and place the burden upon those least able to bear it. Granting millions of dollars in ship subsidies to political friends while at the same time refusing to recompense soldiers and sailors who offered the supreme sacrifice. The destruction of the direct primary system so that candidates for public office will be selected by boss-ruled conventions." Through the activities of the A. F. of L. National Non-Partisan Political Campaign Committee, as directed by the Executive Council 23 candidates for U. S. senators who had been loyal to labor and the people were elected and 11 reactionary senators defeated. Of the friendly senators elected, 18 were democrats and five republicans. Of the candidates for representatives 170 were elected either because directly supported by the A. F. of L. national non-partisan political campaign committees or by reason of the opposition to their opponents. Of these 105 were democrats, 63 republicans, one farmer-labor and one independent. The slogan that led to victory was: "Stand faithfully by our friends and elect them. Oppose our enemies and defeat them; whether they be candidates for congress or other offices; whether executive, legislative, or judicial." After the result of the election was known the national non-partisan political campaign committee sent out the following circular November 22: "During the year 1921, the A. F. of L. National Non-Partisan Political Campaign Committee, by direction of the Executive Council, began to plan for the elections in 1922. It was believed that frequent communications with all labor organizations would be the means of stirring the membership to the necessary enthusiasm to bring about results when the time came for them to select candidates either in the primaries or elections. In December, 1921, by authority and direction of the Executive Council, circular letters were sent all state federations and city central bodies warning the wage earners of the country of the reactionary forces that were guiding legislation. All organizations in their respective localities were urged to appoint legislative committees to keep a record of the votes on measures of interest to labor by members of their respective state legislatures. These committees were advised that during the then forthcoming political campaign they could become non-partisan political campaign committees to further the interests of labor and the people. They were also informed that the records of all members of congress in their respective states or districts would be sent them when the campaign opened. Printed reports on legislation before congress under the heading, "What Congress is Doing or Not Doing," were sent to all colleges, state federations, city central bodies, all councils of our departments and to the labor press. March 8, 1922, circular letters were sent to all state federations of labor and city central bodies in which it was urged that all municipal and state non-partisan political campaign committees should become more active than ever. They were advised to hold mass meetings and to confer with farmer and other organizations of liberty-loving people for the purpose of acting in harmony in the primaries and on election day. April 4, 1922, another circular was addressed to all organizations of labor informing them that it was vital to the protection of labor's interest and welfare that a vigorous campaign be conducted to place in the national congress and the state legislatures men who, without regard to party affiliation, would serve the dictates of justice and not the autocratic domination of the exploiting interests. This was followed by a circular being sent to all organizations of labor on May 1, 1922, calling attention to the fact that every energy should be used in the primaries to nominate members of congress and the state legislatures who believed in progress and even-handed justice. Encouraging reports were received from many of these committees. On July 29, 1922, a special circular was sent to nearly 40,000 non-partisan political campaign committees outlining what should be done to make the campaign a success and in which they were urged to give as wide publicity as possible to the following principles: "No freedom-loving citizen should vote for any candidate who will not pledge himself to oppose any form of compulsory labor law. No justice-loving citizen should vote for any candidate for any office who will not pledge himself to oppose injunctions and contempt proceedings as a substitute for trial by jury. No freedom-loving citizen should vote for any candidate who will not pledge himself to vote for legislation abolishing child labor." Early in the year conferences were held with the representatives in Washington of the various farmers' organizations. These were very helpful in reaching an understanding as to many of the candidates. During the campaign the committee was repeatedly asked by the farmers if certain candidates for congress were acceptable to labor as they did not wish to endorse anyone unfriendly to labor or oppose those friendly to labor. A remarkable feature of this questioning, as to legislative records, showed that in every instance the farmers were supporting or were willing to support the same candidates as labor. The committee feels that this cooperation will continue to a greater extent in the future. A situation arose in Iowa which required your committee to take some action to endeavor to secure the nomination of some outstanding man in the primaries for the U. S. senator from that state. Representative Sweet, of Iowa, announced his candidacy. Mr. Smith W. Brookhart, a man of sterling qualities, sympathetic to the cause of labor and justice, announced his candidacy. It was exceedingly difficult, by reason of the fact of the excellent record of both Mr. Sweet and Mr. Brookhart and in addition because Mr. Brookhart had made such a wonderful showing in his candidacy against Senator Cummins in 1920, to choose between them. It was understood before the election that whichever one received the nomination he would in turn receive the hearty support of the other. Many of the conferences with members of congress or candidates were held by the committee or the chairman concerning the attitude of labor toward certain candidates. In the meantime hundreds of letters from individuals were answered on all phases of the political campaign. Officials of labor in Kansas were urged to begin a campaign to defeat supporters of the Kansas Court of industrial relations act. Arizona was voting on amendments to the constitution that should be defeated. Nebraska had a referendum vote on an amendment to the constitution permitting the legislature to pass compulsory labor laws. Missouri, Rhode Island, Massachusetts and other states were also taking referendum votes on questions pertaining to labor. Illinois was preparing for a vote December 12 on a new constitution which disfranchised thousands of voters in Cook county by limiting their representation in the legislature. This necessitated much correspondence. Circulars have been sent to all state federations of labor asking for the result of the referendum votes. While this agitation began to show results, up to August 14 eighteen states had held their primaries and the outcome was most encouraging. August 14 and 24 additional circulars were sent to 2,400 organizers of the A. F. of L. and of its various departments. These directed the organizers to visit the various central bodies and local unions, inform them of the dangers ahead if the wage earners and all other liberty-loving people were not awakened to the situation. During September, 1922, the individual records of every member of the U. S. senate and house of representatives were brought down to date and sent to all central bodies and nearly 40,000 local unions in the respective states and districts. Special circulars were also prepared for each state, which were sent to all central bodies and local unions. These circulars pointed out the legislation which reaction had prepared for passage in the forthcoming session of congress. They also called special attention to the attitude toward labor of members of the senate. During the primary and election campaigns, organizers were active in North Dakota, Minnesota, Wisconsin, Iowa, Kansas, Colorado, New York, New Jersey, Indiana, California, Idaho, Washington, and Pennsylvania. Special circulars were sent into Nevada in the interest of Senator Pittman, to Wyoming in the interest of Senator Kendrick, to Minnesota in opposition to Senator Kellogg, to Wisconsin in favor of Senator La Follette, to New York state for the purpose of organizing non-partisan political campaign committees to oppose Governor Miller, Senator Calder and other antagonists of labor. The publicity department of the A. F. of L. was very helpful in spreading broadcast the principles of labor and in acquainting the voters with the issues at stake. Never in the history of the non-partisan movement has there been such activities among central bodies, local unions and individual members. Applications by unions and individuals for legislative records of members of congress on measures of interest to labor were received in great number and promptly complied with. The members of the committee took an active part in public addresses and in conferences during the campaign. President Gompers attended the American Legion convention in New Orleans, and spoke in New Jersey and Connecticut. At the same time he held numerous conferences in the cities he visited during the primary and election campaigns and consulted and advised with the officials of labor as to candidates. He wrote many articles for the *American Federationist* bearing upon the political situation and the necessity of the people to safeguard their interest by being sure to vote only for those who by their past records demonstrated that they would faithfully carry out the wishes of the people. Statements for the press on political and labor questions were frequently written by him and received wide publicity. Just before election an article entitled "The Bugle Call," was issued by the committee. It was printed in a great majority of the daily papes, in the entire labor press and the- *American Federationist*. The committee is confident in asserting that many of the tremendous victories secured in the recent elections are due to the non-partisan political campaign carried into effect by us and by the rank and file of the labor movement. In Minnesota, labor supported Mr. Shipstead, independent candidate for senator. Although the democrats had a candidate, Mr. Shipstead was successful over Senator Kellogg. We held a number of conferences and wrote many letters to Minnesota labor officials in an endeavor to have the situation cleared in that state by the withdrawal of the democratic candidate. In Washington, Mr. James A. Duncan was nominated for the U. S. senate. President Gompers in a letter to Mr. Duncan, the labor candidate, informed him that his candidacy was apt to draw enough votes away from Mr. Dill, the democratic candidate, to permit the election of Mr. Poindexter and suggested that Mr. Duncan withdraw. He refused to do so. This correspondence will be printed in the *American Federationist* for December. The vote given Mr. Duncan, however, was not large enough to re-elect Senator Poindexter. Your committee believes that no individual member of the labor movement should allow himself to be forced into a political contest which would result in the election of a bitter and relentless antagonist to labor. The result in Kansas was a victory for labor. A conference of representatives of all labor organizations in Kansas was called by the committee to meet in Emporia, September 18, 1922, to arrange for a campaign that would defeat all candidates in favor of the Kansas court of industrial relations act. As a result of that confidence, Governor Allen's candidate for governor was defeated by an avowed opponent of the act. The election of Mr. G. W. P. Hunt as governor of Arizona was also a victory for labor. By letters and telegrams from us we were very helpful in the election of Mr. Hunt. The election of Mr. Smith as governor of New York was heartily supported by the national non-partisan political campaign committee. The elections of Mr. J. J. Blaine for governor of Wisconsin, Mr. A. Victor Donahey for governor of Ohio, Mr. Fred H. Brown for governor of New Hampshire, Mr. Wm. H. Flynn for governor of Rhode Island, Mr. William E. Sweet for governor of Colorado, and Mr. J. J. Scrugham for governor of Nevada, were also the result of labor's activities. Early in the campaign the committee sent circular letters to all national and international unions requesting that they urge the local unions in each state to give all the assistance within their power to the non-partisan campaign. Much correspondence followed and labor in the various states was organized effectively to enter the primary and election campaign. At a meeting of the New York State Federation of Labor the president of the A. F. of L. mentioned former Governor Smith as the next governor of New York. The sentiment expressed in that convention set the state aflame for Smith. The enormous majority he received demonstrates conclusively that he had the solid support of labor and the forward-looking citizenship. The election of Mr. J. C. Walton as governor of Oklahoma was another victory for the wage earners. They had joined with the farmers and made an excellent campaign for the progressive candidate for governor. The re-election of Governor Blaine in Wisconsin was the result of his progressive adminisration. He was heartily supported by labor. One of the pleasant surprises of the campaign was the many requests made before and after the primary election of members of the U. S. senate and house of representatives for their legislative records on measures of interest to labor. The committee was very active in the primary campaign which resulted in the defeat of a number of anti-labor members of Congress. Among them were senators New and McCumber and representatives Campbell and Coply. It was believed that the greater agitation for acceptable candidates in the primaries the more interest would there be in the elections. While the newspapers were daily printing statements that there seemed to be no interest being taken in the campaign in the various states the correspondence received by the committee proved otherwise. Much attention was given to the determination of the politicians to destroy the direct primary system in some of the states. Organizers were active in Idaho to help defeating a plan to destroy the direct primary. This question was called to the attention of the labor organizations in all states. President Gompers also wrote a letter to Senator Borah which

was used in the campaign. It is now said tha˄ the abolishment of the direct primaries for state officials helped to defeat both Governor Miller and Senator Calder and resulted in the election of Governor Smith and Dr. Copeland. The people are aroused in the primaries and have more interest in the election. Early in the year the publicity bureau of the national republican party began criticizing the A. F. of L. and labor generally. Undoubtedly it was believed that the propaganda spread against labor since the armistice had been so effective that any attack on labor would discredit those whom labor supported. Instead, the propaganda aroused the wage earners to the dangers of re-electing the present members of congress. Some confusion was caused by the distribution of legislative records of members of congress that appeared to be sent out in the interest of organized labor. However, these records were not intended to apply to strictly labor questions but to issues which were said to affect the whole people. The influence of the American labor movement was so effective that misunderstandings were soon eliminated. While a report was made to the Executive Council and to the A. F. of L. convention held in Cincinnati on the activities of the national non-partisan political campaign committee up to that time it was deemed best to include that portion in the full report of what was done during the entire primary and election campaigns. The result has been gratifying. The lack of funds proved a hindrance in sending out as many speakers as it was hoped to the various states. Too much credit can not be given to the rank and file of the labor movement and to the volunteer organizers, all of whom contributed much to the successes above recorded. Most of the meager funds at our disposal were utilized in the printed word. The A. F. of L. is most fortunately situated to be of service not only to labor, but to the high aspirations of the masses of our people. Our international unions, state federations, city central bodies, their non-partisan legislative committees and our organizers are permanent bodies through whom may be conveyed the necessary activities in order that the rights and welfare of the masses of our country may be protected and promoted not only upon the economic but also political field. We can not too highly commend the spirit of solidarity and activity so excellently displayed. For our part, we may also add that we gave every effort within our power to contribute to the accomplishment of the results both in the primaries and the recent elections. Your committee recommends that it be authorized in the name of the Executive Council to endeavor to bring about cooperation of all labor and progressive organizations and groups so that there may be unity of action to protect and promote the rights and interests of the working people and the people generally."

It has been suggested, and wisely, that state federations of labor would have more influence on federal legislation if they took a more active interest in congressional elections. In the past most of the state federations have confined their efforts almost exclusively to the election of members of their respective legislatures. The Executive Council believes that if the state federations would take a more active interest in flooding the various congressional districts of the state with literature furnished by the A. F. of L. National Non-Partisan Political Campaign Committee it would increase their influence when supporting legislation under consideration by congress. While the non-partisan campaign brought many victories to labor and the people the A. F. of L. National Non-Partisan Political Campaign Committee was hampered by the lack of necessary funds. In many districts more effective work could have been done were sufficient funds available. The convention should consider this phase of the nonpartisan campaign and devise some method by which during the elections of 1924 a most thorough campaign can be inaugurated and carried to a successful conclusion. It would be dangerous not to give this subject the most careful consideration, as failure to finance the next campaign will make it possible for the reactionaries to gain their ends through insidious propaganda that could not be counteracted.

(P. 155) An appeal was issued April 4, 1922, by the national non-partisan political campaign committee of the A. F. of L. for contributions to assist in carrying out the instructions of the A. F. of L. convention, to defeat candidates for office hostile to the trade union movement, and elect candidates who may be relied upon to support measure favorable to labor. The amount received in response to the appeal to carry on the 1922 congressional campaign from April 12, 1922, to and including October 25, 1922, was $4,928.33. (P. 312) The circulars sent out by the national non-partisan political campaign committee with the suggestions made and the principles enumerated afford most excellent illustrations of the very practical and effective methods adopted by the A. F. of L. in pursuance of its policy dealing with political questions from a non-partisan standpoint. Some of the results that were attained are recorded in the report, one of the outstanding achievements being the election of 23 candidates for the U. S. senate who had been loyal to labor and to the people, and the defeat of 11 candidates whose record was that deserving the classification of reactionary. In the house of representatives, 170 candidates owe their election to the activities of the A. F. of L. National Non-Partisan Political Campaign Committee. This result should encourage the workers to continue their confidence in the policies of the A. F. of L., which have been productive of beneficial results. The concluding paragraphs of the report are especially recommended, particularly the last sentence, which reads: "It would be dangerous not to give this subject the most careful consideration, as failure to finance the necessary campaign will make it possible for the reactionaries to gain their ends through insidious propaganda that could not be counteracted." We realized the many difficulties that surrounded this phase of the question, because of the restrictions placed on the various national and international unions affiliated to the A. F. of L. by their own laws, which prevent any part of their funds being devoted to this purpose. We suggest that each national and international and directly affiliated organization impress upon its individual membership the vital necessity of providing ample and sufficient means for carrying on the work of the A. F. of L. national nonpartisan political campaign, and that to this end each urge upon its members the desirability of individually contributing money to this fund. (P. 368) In order to most effectively further the political and economic interests of the wage earners as expressed by the A. F. of L., the Executive Council of the A. F. of L. and the executive councils and officers of state federations of labor are urged to avail themselves of every opportunity to present labor's position and to press for the fulfillment of its just demands, in the formulation of political platforms, national and state, and through any other channel that may be afforded.

Porto Rico and San Domingo—(1919, p. 127) Persistent requests of Porto Ricans for statehood or independence for the people of that island at last gained enough attention from congress to secure the introduction and committee consideration of a joint resolution authorizing the president to appoint a commission of three members to study and report upon the industrial and economic conditions of the island. The committee on Pacific islands and Porto Rico reported favorably on the resolution, but no further action was ever taken upon it. A party of 20 members of the house, however, went to Porto Rico early in April, for investigation and information, with a view to future legislation. A representative of the A. F. of L. also went to Porto Rico at about the same time in connection with the extensive strike of tobacco workers and cigarmakers then prevailing on the island. (Pp. 174-377) Conditions to which the Porto Ricans have been constantly subjected should be condemned and every possible effort should be made to right the wrongs which are being perpetrated on the wage earners of this possession of our nation. Unfortunately, the bureau of insular affairs of the war department has failed to exercise that power it possesses over Porto Rico to the advantage of the people of this island, and it is our belief that the control over this possession of our nation should be transferred to the department of interior. The Executive Council should give every possible assistance in furthering the legislative program proposed by the Porto Rican trade unions affiliated with the A. F. of L. We are in full accord with the complaint of these workers regarding the evils and oppression of the monopolies whose profits are taken from the industrial masses by compelling the wage earners to labor under the lowest and most miserable conditions of work. All necessary and adequate steps should be taken to relieve this situation and to subject the non-resident owners to the same restrictions and conditions which apply in the U. S. The charges against Arthur Yager, governor of Porto Rico, should be again presented to President Wilson and that organized labor's protest should be continued until he has been removed from this position of power and influence. If we are to aid the trade union movement of Porto Rico, it is essential that we exercise that support and influence during this period of reconstruction so as to increase the number of organizations and membership which now approximate 143 organizations, with 18,000 members, affiliated with the A. F. of L. It is reported that the Porto Rican American Tobacco Company since December 31, 1918, has locked out all of its employes, involving approximately 15,000 men and women. This industrial conflict covers 17 cities and towns and involves almost the entire tobacco industry. We here in America can and should assist these workers by refusing to purchase goods manufactured by this or other oppressive corporate combinations. We are of the firm conviction that proper labor conditions are of more importance to Porto Rico than any other proposal that can be suggested; and to attain improvements in these conditions the president of the A. F. of L is authorized and directed to appoint a committee of three to visit the island for the purpose of investigating labor conditions, to submit their report to the Executive Council, and that thereafter the Executive Council take such steps to give the widest possible publicity to the information obtained of existing conditions to the end that the recall of Governor Yager may be hastened, that necessary legislation may be enacted to give to the people of Porto Rico a civil form of government and that the affairs of this island may be taken out of the hands of the bureau of insular affairs of the war department in order to bring into the lives and homes of these people the hope for a better and a freer life and greater opportunities for the enjoyment thereof.

(1920, pp. 126-232) The 1919 convention directed the president of the A. F. of L. to appoint a committee of three to visit the island of Porto Rico for the purpose of investigating labor conditions. This action was the result of frequent complaints against labor conditions existing in Porto Rico which had culminated in the filing of charges against Arthur Yager, governor of the island. The Pan-American Federation of Labor meeting in New York City in July, 1919, adopted a resolution requesting the A. F. of L. to investigate complaints and grievances in relation to the condition of the workers of Santo Domingo, and urged the federation to do whatever might be possible "to secure to the workers of San Domingo the full opportunity of freedom of expression, freedom of action, the right of voluntary association and the right of collective bargaining to the same degree that those rights are recognized to the wage earners of the U. S. and all other governments of free peoples." Having before it both the instructions of the 1919 convention of the A. F. of L. and the request of the Pan-American Federation of Labor, the council deemed it advisable that a committee be authorized to investigate conditions in both places. Prior to authorizing the commission to visit Porto Rico and San Domingo the Executive Council had exhausted every means of securing relief from oppressive conditions. In a letter to President Wilson, dated November 29, the president of the A. F. of L. called attention in detail to the grievances of the San Domingo working people and summarizing the three principal grievances as follows: "First. Non-enforcement of the immigration laws of the republic. Second. Too severe censorship established. Third. The manifest unfairness of the provost marshals in the administration of justice." (P. 243) The A. F. of L. commission made the following recommendations for the relief of the people of Porto Rico: "1. The transfer of the administration of Porto Rico from the bureau of insular affairs of the war department to the department of the interior. 2. Congressional investigation of the administration of Porto Rico by the bureau of insular affairs of the war department. 3. Demand for the general introduction of a maximum 8-hour day for men, women and children as a means of providing employment and relieving the enormous over-supply of labor. 4. The establishment of a minimum wage for all women and children. 5. That all child labor under 16 be prohibited, and also the employment of children up to 18 years unless they have been graduated from an elementary school; the establishment of compulsory continuation schools for all children up to 18 years; that the American language only be used by all public officers and taught as the principal language in all grades of the schools. 6. The

establishment of sufficient schools with every necessary facility and equipment to provide accommodations for every child; erection of additional high schools and schools for industrial and vocational training for boys and girls up to 18 years of age; increased pay for teachers, scholarships for school children who are graduates of elementary and high schools to come to the U. S. for additional education; lunches to be provided in the schools for the purpose of giving the children nourishing food and demonstrating food values. 7. Establishment of children's courts to care for and handle all kinds of juvenile delinquency; adoption of a system of physical training in health and careful living for all boys up to 21, and girls up to 18 years of age. 8. An amendment to the Porto Rico laws to declare that the labor of a human being is not a commodity or article of commerce, and a law limiting the use of injunctions in strikes and other industrial disputes and prohibiting women from being employed at night and in occupations which may be injurious to their health; elimination of the present sweatshop and insanitary methods of home-work, on lace, embroidery, drawn work, sewing, and hats which should be done in well-ventilated and sanitary factories. The adoption of a law which will keep women out of the fields and the factories who have other means of support and who would not become a public charge, if denied employment, so that mothers could stay home to look after the children. 9. Enforcement of the law and prosecution of individuals, companies, and corporations for violating the law against the importation of strike-breakers. Appointment of inspectors, experts, and office employes in sufficient numbers to efficiently enforce all the laws for the protection of working men, women and children. Extension of the workmen's compensation and relief law to occupational diseases and establishment of training schools for those crippled in and out of industry. 10. Establishment of a pension for maintenance of widows, children, cripples, and old people having no other means of support. 11. Prisoners and inmates of other state institutions to be used on government farms and in industries for the purpose of training them in agricultural and industrial vocations and for the raising of foodstuffs and the manufacture of equipment and supplies for the maintenance of themselves and the inmates of other eleemosynary institutions; people so employed to be paid for services rendered. 12. Immediate enforcement and application of the homestead law which will give the people a chance to own their own homes and some land on a self-supporting basis, and enforcement of the law which prohibits individuals, companies, and corporations from owning and controlling more than 500 acres of land; prosecution of all those who have violated its provisions with confiscation to the state of all land they have bought or over which they have secured control since the law was adopted. State-owned lands to be drained, cleared off, and prepared for cultivation under the direction of the Mayaguez agricultural experimental station as a demonstration of the foodstuffs and other products which can be successfully grown and marketed in Porto Rico and for export; this demonstration to be used in such a way as to point out the success and efficiency and community benefits of the small farm and home. 13. Establishment of municipal markets in city, town, and village as a means toward reducing the high cost of living. 14. Enactment of laws which will give the policemen of Porto Rico a living wage, and provide them with uniforms and equipment. The erection of barracks and the necessary jails so that the enforcement of law will be fair and impartial, and they no longer will be obliged to sleep and eat on corporation premises or depend upon employers for the use of horses and automobiles when strikes exist. 15. Amendment to the federal law which will give Porto Rico the benefits of rural credits and vocational and industrial education aid. Amendments to income tax laws by increasing the rates on excess profits, large incomes, and inheritances in such a way as to put the expense of maintaining the island upon those best able to bear it, and especially those companies, corporations, and individuals outside the island of Porto Rico. 16. A complete survey of the agricultural and industrial resources and possibilities, the health and education, and living and working conditions of Porto Rico and its people, to the end that a plan may be adopted to provide continuous employment and give to every person a chance to live in decency and comfort. 17. That a special session of the Porto Rico legislature be urged to immediately convene and give favorable action to this program for securing relief for the starving and neglected Porto Rican people. If these recommendations do not receive immediate attention and favorable consideration by the Porto Rico legislature that the United States suspend the organic act of 1915, and establish a receivership for Porto Rico. 18. That all international unions, the jurisdiction of which would extend to industries and occupations in Porto Rico, be urged to join with the A. F. of L. and Free Federation of Labor in Porto Rico to assign organizers and representatives for a labor forward movement to thoroughly organize the working people of Porto Rico so that they may be able to protect themselves from the inhuman treatment they now receive at the hands of unfair employers, and biased and prejudiced public officials. Your commission made a searching inquiry into the working and living conditions of the people of Porto Rico and their just complaints against the police, judges, district attorneys, and other public officials, and we have secured a great amount of evidence, both oral and documentary, which can be submitted in support of our findings and recommendations.'' (P. 386) The island of Porto Rico is a part of the U. S., and it is a matter of deep reproach to the government of the U. S. that in the years since these islanders came to be an integral part of that great nation, so little has been done to improve conditions or produce a better way of living for the people who had been so long repressed by the monarchy under which we found them. It is to our shame that it may be truthfully said that these unfortunate human beings were merely transferred from Spanish to American exploitation. The Executive Council is directed to take whatever action is necessary to carry out the plans for improvement in the social and industrial conditions in Porto Rico.

(1921, p. 172) The sugar corporations and others have reduced the poor wages of the agricultural workers in many sections of the island. Many thousands of the workers have resisted such great reductions and in many sections they have prevented at least the employers going farther in their designs. Bulldozing and brutalities and illegal interference of the local police have been again repeated against the workers. The railroad companies at the expiration of the agreement had the purpose of reducing the wages of the members of the machinists' lodges all over the island, but thanks to the determination of the workers, the company renewed their agreement with slight concessions over the last schedule of wages for another year. The forces of reaction and greed have shown great aggressiveness during the last year. All that could be done to destroy existing labor organizations and to prevent the organization of new ones in the island has been done. The efforts of the A. F. of L. are being antagonized by those who have interests in keeping this island as a large factory worked by slaves. In spite of that, during the past year the toilers have advanced along the road of progress toward the achievement of a better social, economical and political independence by means of a methodical and persistent labor fight, both collectively and individually.

(1922, pp. 111-326) Several bills were introduced in congress to define the status of Porto Rico owing to a decision of the supreme court that it is not an incorporated territory. Therefore the constitution of the U. S. is not applicable in many respects to American citizens in that island. Representative John I. Nolan, of California, introduced H. R. 9934, ''to make Porto Rico an incorporated territory of the United States.'' The bill would also give the internal revenues and customs duties collected in the island for the purpose of education, sanitation and permanent public works. The A. F. of L. has approved the bill and is urging its passage. (P. 156) The solution of the economic and social problems of Porto Rico has been delayed for years because of the fact that the president of the U. S., the secretary of war, who has jurisdiction over insular affairs, and the congress of the U. S. have not been sufficiently informed as to these problems. As a matter of fact, Porto Rico has not the proper standing in the national life. Very few officials of the federal government have had a thorough knowledge regarding the living conditions of the people of that island and especially of the economic and financial organization imposed upon them through a colonial system of unlawful monopoly of the lands and business controlled by non-resident enterprises. Consequently, two-thirds of the annual profits yielded by the agricultural and industrial producing masses of Porto Rico leave the country in the shape of rents, commissions and dividends estimated at 60 per cent, to be distributed and invested in other communities outside of the island. It is not strange then that more than half of a million of workers, men, women and children, engaged in farm and industrial work are continually in a depressing condition. The exportation of the profits in such amount has prevented the reinvestment of same in new enterprises and industries within the island for the last 20 years. Many million of dollars have already been lost to the progress and welfare of the people of Porto Rico. It has been proved by a legal document transmitted to the senate by the president of the U. S. on January 18, 1919, that a number of American, Spanish, and French corporations and individuals of other nationalities, non-residents, own and monopolize over 1,000,000 of acres of land and franchises of all classes, including hills, rivers and falls, valued at over $100,000,000, and in violation of the organic law of Porto Rico, which does not allow any corporation to hold or possess in Porto Rico over 500 acres of land. General McIntyre, in regard to the land question, has made the following comment: "The difficulty, then, with large holders of agricultural lands arises not from the size of the holdings, but from the disposition of corporations and large absentee owners holding lands in the tropics to loot the property annually; that is, instead of studying the situation with a view of developing a property for all the time, with tenants and laborers living under real living conditions and with a fair share of contentment, the disposition is to secure for each year the maximum return on the money invested. It is for this reason that suitable land for food crops will not be available for that purpose normally and it is also for this reason that the labor troubles are almost continuous where this condition prevails." The commissioner of agriculture and labor of Porto Rico on January 9, 1922, in a meeting held at the agricultural experimental station of Porto Rico, has stated that out of the 200 million of acres of cultivable land in Porto Rico, only about 500,000 are cultivated, or used for agricultural purposes. He also stated that in 1910 Porto Rico had 59,000 of small farm owners, while in the last 10 years that number has been reduced by 17,000, leaving 41,000 farm owners at present according to census of 1920.

Organization and Strikes.—On account of the conditions above referred to, our unions have had to confront a most unusual situation in an effort to preserve the wages and living conditions which were the product of years and years of struggle and hard work throughout the island. With the people confronting almost starvation conditions a cut in wages followed hand in hand with changed working conditions by which almost all the achievements secured by labor in years past were done away with, leaving the workers deprived of all means of defense in the shops, factories and agricultural fields and with no voice in determining the conditions under which they shall work. The workers could not yield willingly and voluntarily to the establishment of such conditions and the employers determined as they were to break down the organization, to do away with the unions and of industrial bargaining collectively established, brought about conditions that were unbearable for the workers, thus causing unrest and trouble. Many protests were recorded on account of the attitude of the employers. Minor cases were registered in which the bakers and some of the building trades had to fight to preserve their conditions. The railroad men affiliated with the International Association of Machinists, the cigarmakers affiliated with the Cigarmakers' International Union of America and the agricultural workers in agricultural unions directly affiliated with the A. F. of L., had to fight the hardest and more important battles on account of their number and the grade of their organization. (P. 159) As it is very well known the administration of Governor Arthur Yager in Porto Rico was a disgrace for the laborers of the island, and for the good name of the American institutions as represented by him. He not only absolutely ignored labor in the administration of the island and even in all those matters connected with their living conditions, but also permitted these to be killed by dozens when trying to improve their working and living conditions by means of the strike after having exhausted all means of conciliation, mediation and arbitration, and jailed and beaten by hundreds, while those responsible for such conditions were left unpunished and unmolested. To his attitude is due the encouragement taken by the advocates of secession of the island from the U. S. and all the economic, social and political evils that have lately brought this island to a state of unrest and general uneasiness. The inauguration of the new governor of Porto Rico, E. Montgomery Reily, took place in San Juan on the 30th of July, 1921. Governor Reily made clear his intention to deal fairly with labor and by his actions subsequently demonstrated his sincerity in that expression. In his opposition to the secession movement in the island he took a position which had been sustained for more than 20 years by Porto Rican labor. One of the first requests to him was for the prompt appointment of a mediation and conciliation commission, as provided for in the insular laws. The former governor had constituted a commission without regard to representation for bona fide organizations of labor. Governor Reily granted the request in this connection. Another act of justice to the labor movement was the granting of a pardon upon request for a number of strike leaders who were imprisoned under Governor Yager's administration. He also assisted in conferences in Washington in the efforts to settle strikes of cigarmakers, railroad workers and longshoremen. He further demanded the resignations in Porto Rico of certain judges and police officers whose conduct had been improperly hostile to labor. A new chief of the insular bureau of labor was appointed from the ranks of organized labor by Governor Reily. So far as we have been able to observe his official acts in Porto Rico, we believe they have been inspired by the best of motives and that it has been his aim to promote justice and fair dealing for everyone. These being the feelings and sentiments of Governor Reily as expressed by himself labor could not help giving him its sympathies and the respect for his position that was thought to be fair and for his high regard for the A. F. of L. We had the right to think such expression to be honest and sincere and we still think the same way. Being in sympathy with the new executive for his declaration with reference to labor and having also concurred with his views of Americanism in the island as against secessionism, an issue advocated by us for more than 20 consecutive years against all tendencies to the contrary, it is needless to say that the best relations were established in an effort to help and cooperate to the success of the new administration. (P. 162) A federal high industrial commission should be appointed by the president with broad powers to investigate the unbearable economic and industrial situation of the people of Porto Rico making recommendations on the basis of their findings that would build another form of economic standing for the country, bettering the living conditions of the workers of the island and helping the prosperity of the people generally. Besides this, federal high commission should report to the president the means of establishing and developing industries essential to the welfare of the people, its sanitation and education.

(1923, p. 361) The A. F. of L. has repeatedly expressed its deep sympathy with the aspirations of the workers of Porto Rico and we have time and again aided them in their righteous struggle for larger measure of freedom and a fuller life. It is vitally necessary, in order to make the relation between continental and insular Americans harmonious and cordial as well as permanent and indestructible that a full measure of self-government, compatible with American sovereignty, shall be granted to the island.

Postal Employes, Wages of—(1919, pp. 34-329) Supported by the legislative influence of the A. F. of L., the organized postal employes made a determined fight for higher permanent salary classifications. They were in part successful. The congress adopted the wage standards urged by the organized employes, but limited the application of these standards to the next fiscal year. An investigation into the subject-matter of postal wages is now being made by a congressional commission with a view of recommending appropriate wage legislation to the next congress. The organized employes are hopeful of securing some constructive remedial legislation based on the commission's report.

(1920, p. 111) A joint commission on postal salaries was appointed by the 65th congress to investigate the subject of postal wages. This commission has made an exhaustive investigation of the subject, holding hearings in 11 representative cities throughout the country. Hundreds of witnesses from all groups of postal employes were heard. The fact that postal wage standards and working conditions in general are too unattractive to enable the government to properly man the postal service was brought home to the commission by the testimony of the workers and their representatives. A substantial betterment in postal employment it was pointed out to the commission, is imperative if the service is to be saved fom a complete demoralization. (P. 360) The Executive Council is directed to cooperate with the representatives and officers of the affiliated organizations of postal employes in securing a higher wage standard than that now existing in the postal service, and in perfecting the legislation to secure better working conditions and classification. Also to assist the affiliated postal organizations to maintain the right to participate in determining the proper allowances and apportionment of the eight hours for the various duties required of them.

(1921, p. 114) June 5, 1920, congress enacted a postal wage reclassification law that benefited all groups of postal employes. While there was some disappointment among the members of the affiliated postal organizations because the wage reclassification was not more liberal, it now is realized that postal wage standards are more satisfactory than heretofore. There are a number of minor inequalities in the reclassification act that must be adjusted and every assistance has been given the affiliated postal bodies in securing the desired legislation from congress. The 66th congress did not enact the legislation for shorter working hours for night workers, punitive pay for overtime, a court of appeals and other remedial measures for which the affiliated postal organizations have been agitating.

(1922, pp. 114-327) The senate committee on post offices and post roads is conducting an investigation at the request of the affiliated postal workers of the question of night work in the postal service. Strong efforts are being made to secure at this session of congress the long-deferred action on remedial legislation granting a time differential for night employment in the service. This reform has been repeatedly urged by the labor movement.

(1923, p. 359) The A. F. of L. directs 'the Executive Council to cooperate in every possible way with the affiliated postal organizations in urging upon the 68th congress the need for a substantial increase in postal pay rates.

Postal . Rates, Second Class—(1919, p. 129) In compliance with the instructions of the St. Paul convention, as embodied in resolution No. 123, copies of that resolution were sent to President Wilson, Postmaster General Burleson, and to all members of congress, together with a protest signed by the president of the A. F. of L., against the taking effect on July 1, 1918, of the increased rates and the postal zone system for second-class publications. In spite of this protest the increased rates took effect on July 1, as provided by section 1101 of the revenue act of 1917. An effort was made to secure a repeal of the increased rates and the postal zone system in the new revenue bill approved February 24, 1919, and an amendment to the revenue bill to repeal the zone system in relation to second-class postage was adopted in the senate December 23, 1918, but the repeal was not contained in the revenue bill when finally passed. So this effort also failed, but the increased rate of one cent on all mail matter of the first class was repealed, to take effect on July 1, 1919.

(1923, p. 296) The A. F. of L. directs the Executive Council to cooperate with the affiliated postal and other organizations in obtaining from congress appropriate action, based upon the findings of the present investigation, to revise postal rates in order that the revenues may approximate operating costs.

Post Office Not for Profit—(1921, p. 335) A number of recent conventions of the A. F. of L. have very properly critized the labor policies of the post office department and have indicated the necessary reforms that should be established for the protection of the rights of the postal workers and the improvement of service efficiency. In thus endeavoring to call public attention to industrial deficiencies in the largest governmental agency, one that comes into more intimate contact with the people than any other public utility, the A. F. of L. has realized that an enlightened postal labor policy is certain to have a profound influence on both public and private employment. The postmaster general has made made known his administrative policy, the main essentials of which are: The post office is an institution for service and not for profit or politics; labor is not a commodity; the service shall be humanized; employes shall have the right to be heard through chosen representatives without discrimination because of membership in any organization. The A. F. of L. commends this action of the postmaster general and believes that a strict adherence to his policies will insure complete restoration and maintenance of service efficiency.

Power, Super or Giant—(1923, p. 229) The A. F. of L. is unanimously opposed to the subsidizing or granting of government financial aid to any private corporation or corporations for the purpose of establishing a privately owned and operated power system, or to any encouragement whatever to a privately owned and operated super-power system. We individually and collectively urge upon our respective state legislatures and upon the federal government, and cause to be given the utmost publicity, the necessity for a co-ordinated public development and control of said water resources for the service of the people at cost, giving due regard to the four-fold duty of water for domestic supply, for irrigation, power production, and navigation, and to the necessity for flood-water storage and control and to the rights of political sub-divisions to the measure of local control in these matters; and that we favor and urge the withdrawal and curtailment of special privileges to private interests controlling this natural resource for incomplete and costly development for private profit. (P. 229) The president of the A. F. of L. reported: "It came to my knowledge that in connection with some exposition about to be held in England in 1924 a congress has been called of representatives of all countries where power has been generated. I learned that an American organization had been formed for the purpose of cooperating with the interests there when the movement begins in England. It is for the co-ordination of all the power and super-power in the world. It made such a great impression upon my mind that I consulted with several of my associates in the office of the A. F. of L. and concluded to communicate with the executive secretary of the American section, so that the whole procedure, so far as our country is concerned, should not be left in the hands of private corporations or business interests, and that there should be representation from our government and representation from the men engaged in the production and use of power. The executive secretary of that American organization came to my office and we had a most interesting discussion upon the subject. He said he would take it up with his associates and decide as to the representation of the men of labor in the various trades, occupations and professions. In addition I might say that then, not knowing that there had been a change in the secretaryship of the British Trades Union Congress General Council, I addressed a letter to Mr. Charles Bowerman, the secretary for many years informing him of this situation and calling upon him in turn to bring the subject matter before the general council of the British Trades Union Congress so that there might be not only cooperation between us, but representation of the men of labor, who know about as much, if not more, than all other agencies as to power and super-power. It seemed to me that I should communicate this information to the delegates to this convention."

Prayer at Cincinnati Convention Opening by Rev. Peter E. Dietz—(1921, p. 1) "You have come together in this city, trade union representatives from all over the land, to exercise the rights and to share the responsibilities of the great American Union Parliament. You stand ready, in the name of God, to begin. For you and for your constituents I appeal to the God who rules the universe to witness the justice of your cause and the rectitude of your intentions. I appeal to Him to preside in your councils, to supply your defects, to bless all your efforts for the preservation and extension of the liberties and prosperities of the American people. Great deeds do not come from indecision and inaction. Your purpose is to decide and to act. Power without truth and wisdom leads but to anarchy. God give to you His inspiration, His truth and His guiding power! The freedom to fulfill your human destinies, the liberty to serve mankind can not be achieved and preserved without vigilance. May God keep you, as

you have been, the minute men of Americad liberties! The noblest purposes are wrecken through imprudence; prudent men abide both the time and the circumstance. God grant that more and more there shall rise from your ranks the noblest statesmen of the future! Justice is the foundation of empire, without it no law will stand and no government is secure. This justice we implore at Thy hands, Supreme Judge of the world! Fortitude is the finest test of manhood; to suffer and to wait while the ends of justice are in the balance, to be strong in adversity, this fortitude, oh God do Thou bestow upon Thy servants here assembled that they may go forth once more, bearing aloft the burdens of men with spirit unbroken! Men have been strong in defeat and weak in victory. To be temperate, to be magnanimous when victory comes, when you shall wipe away the tears of the fatherless and the widows, when the weak and needy shall be lifted up from their lowliness—the fruits of victory long delayed—unto that day, oh Loving Father, prepare in our hearts the virtue of victory! We pray Thee, Father, through Christ Our Lord, to stir up in this assembly the spirit of wisdom and of understanding, the spirit of counsel and fortitude the spirit of knowledge and of godliness, the spirit of the fear of the Lord! Come, Thou Holy Spirit and fill our hearts that we may be created anew to renovate the face of the earth. Give us peace in this Thy day, remove from us the rumors, the tumults, the agonies of civil and industrial strife, and make Thou, O God, secure the borders of the nations. Go now to your tasks, ye men of labor, with the hope of all these things in your hearts. God and all good men are with you. The blessing of The Almighty, The Father, The Son and The Holy Spirit descend upon you and abide with you forever, Amen."

President A. F. of L., Address of—(1923, p. 4) "In so far as I have the authority to speak—and I believe that I bespeak the sentiments of the delegates to this convention of the A. F. of L., as well as I express my own innermost feelings—I thank you in their name and in my own for the welcome you have extended to the officers and delegates of this 43rd convention of the A. F. of L., not only for the earnest and cordial welcome which you have extended to us, but for the sentiments in which you have couched that welcome, as well as the historical events which you have pointed out to us, and for the friendly solicitude you have expressed for our welfare and success. It has been now nearly 38 years ago since I first visited Portland and other cities of your great state. I think you men of Oregon will agree that in that time it was part of the great woolly west. Today it is not only large and great and wonderful in its resources, but in its development of man. The resources of Oregon are great, and several of them have been pointed out to us, but the resources of Oregon are not comparable with the resources of the men and the women and the children of Oregon, as the resources of our great America, wonderful and boundless and fruitful as they are, are no comparison to the one hundred and ten millions of Americans within our borders. And it is for the protection and the promotion of the rights, the welfare and the interests of these 110,000,000 of America's citizenship that the A. F. of L. functions. Having the human equation in the development of America, we can not leave out of consideration one of the vital questions with which the American people are confronted. Modern history, modern industrial development, has brought in its wake not only great civilizing influences, but it has brought evils of great moment and menace. There can be no greater menace to the progress and civilization of our time than the sacrifice of young and innocent children upon the altar of mammon. The conscience of the American people has been awakened, and a cry has gone forth from one end of America to the other that the child life of our country must be conserved at all hazards. To say 'to this universal demand of our people that the constitution of the United States is impotent for the people to protect the children of our time is begging the question. The courts have decided that two laws which the congress of the U. S. enacted, upon the demand of the people of our country to protect children and minors from undue exploitation, are null and void, are unconstitutional. That the people, through their chosen represehtatives, can not pass a law to protect the child life of America, the children of today upon whom the perpetuity of our republic and our civilization depend—that is to lay the greatest indictment against our competency. When the report of the Executive Council of the A. F. of L. shall, during the course of the day, be presented to you, you will observe a report and recommendation to this convention upon this subject which we regard—and I desire to emphasize this—as the vital question of the hour. This movement of ours, commonly known as the labor movement, and, as we term it, the trade union movement, and this, its federation, is not born necessarily out of an idea; it is born of necessity, it is the result of conditions; it is born in the beginning by hunger—hunger for food, hunger for shelter, hunger for better food, hunger for better shelter, and as time in its course developed new conditions, hunger for still better food, hunger for still better shelter, better homes, hunger for rest, hunger for recreation, hunger for music, for the arts, for literature, for all that goes to make up a fuller, a broader and a higher life—hunger to make this life and world better for our being in it and contributing our share of our work and our service in the solution of the great problems yet before us. Reference has been made here this morning to reds and radicals. With the reference to those who come under the general terminology of 'reds,' I fully agree, and those who know me or know anything of me and the work that I have tried to perform and the service I have endeavored to give know that I am not even pink. But I think that there is some general misconception of the term 'radical.' There are so many varieties of them. I believe in the expression of conservative demands, radical in the effort to get them. The devil of the thing is that those who would label themselves as 'radicals,' as a rule, know nothing of the great, fundamental principles of the labor movement or of the ideals toward which it is striving. It takes all sorts of people to make up a nation, and it takes all sorts of people to make up a labor movement. All we ask is that this labor movement of America and all America shall be and continue to be a movement of wage earners, for wage earners, and by wage earners. We are not always able to determine who these shall be. The trade union movement has not the choice of the material with which it must work. Big business, large employers of labor, have kept a wide open channel for years for the purpose of bringing

peoples to our country so far below the standards of life and work which prevail in America that it has been a matter of little choice with us. We have held and hold that if the hordes of men from these backward couunt ries of Europe are brought into the U. S. with all of the omissions and commissions upon their heads, if they are good enough to be brought to our America for profit, they are good enough for us to try to organize them and make better Americans out of them. And if, here and there, there is a red or a radical, it is not our fault, but the sin must be upon the heads of those who brought them to America. We realize that so long as they are wage earners and organizable we will organize them, not as reds and radicals, but to try to make better men and better citizens of them. And not only do they regard us an opponent worthy of their steel, but they have felt its point of contact. While sitting upon this platform this morning we heard a beautiful orchestra rendering sweet artistic music. It brought a thought to my mind quite apropos of this matter which I have just for a few moments been presenting to you, and it occurred to me—what, after. all, is music but a succession of harmonious sounds? Now, one member of that splendid orchestra might entertain us with his renditions, but there were about a hundred of them. Suppose they had, by a majority of 98 to 2, decided they would work in harmony and then render their pieces of music in harmony with each other to attain one common purpose—this succession of harmonious sounds; and suppose, for instance, the piccolo player and the drummer, being the two in the minority, would say, 'No, we will not be bound by you 98, you reactionaries.' One of them will say, 'I am going to blow my piccolo just when I feel like it,' and the other one will say, 'I'll beat the drum to beat the band.' I wonder if any such a performance had been given this morning you would have risen and given the cheers of approval to this wonderful orchestra, each man knowing the part that he has to play in the accomplishment of the given whole harmonious sound. The application is exactly the same with our trade union movement. Your governor, both your governor and our friend, and his honor the mayor, have spoken well and truthfully upon the condition of the farmers of our country. I wonder when the time shall come—and let us pray that it may be soon—when the men on the farm and the men in the factory and workshop and mine shall come together for the purpose of protecting each other and all against their common enemy, their common exploiter. When I had the honor and the privilege of addressing the wheat conference at Chicago a few months ago, upon the invitation of the committee having the conference in charge, I called attention to this specific thing; that the difficulty with the farmers, the trouble with the farmers was that they were led by gentlemen farmers, by political farmers, by trust farmers, by manure trust farmers, and magazine owner farmers, and that what they wanted and the goal to which I believed they should strive was, as the American trade union movement is made up of wage earners, for wage earners and by wage earners, they wanted a movement of dirt farmers, real farmers who are working upon the soil. The antagonists, natural or ignorant, have at all times and up to the present time fairly successfully kept- the agricultural and industrial workers from each other. They have con-

sistently interjected something as a schism
between the two. Some of the ststisticians
employed by that particular interest to which
I have referred have pointed out a certain
class of workers and a comparison of their
daily wage with the income of farmers upon
certain products. No reference was made to
the fabulous profits made by the stock jobber,
by the exchanges, by the money lenders and
the intermediary commissioners, and on both
sides. Who of the population of America are
the greatest users and consumers of the farmer's products, if not the great mass of the
wage earners? And who are those who use
and consume the products of man's industrial
labor if not the farmers? The profiteers on
both sides have taken more out of the product
of each than was given in the form of returns
to the farmers and wages to the workers.
There is an abiding faith I have that
in our America, slow moving as we often
are, the trend of events and the intelligence
and stamina of our people will bring the
farmer and the worker in industry together
in the solution of the great problems confronting both. Reference has been made
to the American labor movement in post-
war activities. And may I add a word, perhaps not informing to the seasoned delegates
to the A. F. of L., but to those who may be
uninformed, what the activities of the organized workers of America were before the
war and during the war, as well as after the
war; and there has been no group of citizens in all America or in all the world who
stood more firmly and sacrificingly behind
their government in determining to beat down
and overwhelm political and military autocracy
than the much misunderstood organized labor
movement of America. It was with bad grace
that men of big business and high finance, almost immediately after armistice day, organized
and undertook to drive the men of labor
down in their standards of life and work and
to destroy or weaken the only body which
stands and has stood as the defender, the protector and the advocate of the rights and
interests of American labor. To refer to the
falsely termed 'open shop' and the treasonable
appellation of that as the 'American plan.'
The American plan must consist of a virile
citizenship, and American workers can only
maintain that virility and vision and insistence upon progress when they are united
and federated. Well, the drive was on and
wage reductions were demanded. In some
instances we had to yield some things, yet
despite the calamitous howls of the interests
it was the most fortunate thing for our country and our people that in 1922 the organized
working men and women of America resisted
reductions. To paraphrase the old couplet
that 'it is better to have loved and lost than
not to have loved at all,' 'it is better to resist
and lose than not to resist at all.' The
results of that resistance in 1922 gave the
employing interests and big business to understand this, that even if they succeeded in
wage reductions it would cost them more in
the end than to pay the scale which prevails,
and as for the losses to the working people, we
have little to lose and can afford to lose it.
With the prevention of wage reductions,
to turn the tide of industry as we have, to
secure that which we have lost and to go
forward, we will soon make up the losses which
we sustained duing the contest. I don't want
any man to believe that I am an advocate
of strikes or strifes, but I do hold that when
the time shall come in the history of industry
when men can not maintain themselves and
those dependent upon them in a manner con-

forming to the standards of American life, if
they would not strike they would write
themselves down as cowards and poltroons.
I thought of this period often when there
were more than five millions of American
workers unemployed, walking the streets and
highways and byways of our country vainly
seeking for employment. To put into effect
at that time a drive for wage reductions—
was that the way out? To cut wages and
reduce the using, purchasing and consuming
power of the people, whose wages had been
reduced? When you reduce the purchasing,
using and consuming power you necessarily
throw others out of employment, and when
they are unemployed the same thing goes on
like an endless chain, until it reaches the
lowest rung in the industrial ladder; then
it begins over and over again, from the top
down, cutting more and more and more. If
there is anyone who can give me any good
cause for the transition from this terrible
situation of unemployment and the return
to what we are pleased to call industrial
activity and industrial prosperity, except the
movement of labor of America in resisting
these wage reductions (and in many instances succeeding in their resistance, which
brought about the return of men to their employments, and as workers when employed,
giving the opportunity for others to work
and use and consume), if there be any other
cause that anyone can ascribe than the one
which I have just inadequately mentioned, I
would like to know it. We are now in a most
fortunate position. Our movement is growing.
The spirit of our movement has caught the
idealists as well as the practical men and
women of America. They are beginning to
understand us better, that we have not a
purely selfish motive and purpose to serve.
Selfishness? In part, yes, but that higher and
nobler selfishness which recognizes that this
is a world of activity, that service and good
faith, honor, progress and civilization are the
ends to be served. We have many grievances of which we justly complain, and giving
credit to any and all countries which have
striven and are striving to reach the goal
of freedom and democracy, we still hold, yes,
and I, as an adopted citizen of the U. S. of
America, declare verily and on my honor as a
man that I believe the republic of the U. S.
of America is the best government on the face
of the globe. I said I was an adopted citizen.
Out of my 73 years of life I have been in
America 60 years, longer than most Americans
have lived here. I repeat that we have many
grievances against which we protest, and we
are going to make our protest effective.
Wonderful and splendid as is our American
republic it is not good enough for us or for
those who are yet to come, and we are going
to do our duty under the laws of our country;
and our labor movement, conforming to those
laws and to the ideals of our republic, will
help to contribute its share toward making
this not only the most wonderfully productive
country in the world, but the leader in the
onward march of progress and civilization."

Prices by Law, To Fix—(1919, p. 357)
Refused to instruct legislative committee of
the A. F. of L. to prepare a bill to introduce
in congress to govern all prices and profits
throughout the country as far as possible.

Professions Underpaid—(1920, pp. 181-
464) Large numbers of our people, either
poorly organized or not organized at all, have
felt the burden of the rising cost of living
most keenly during the year just closed.
Large classes of workers employed directly
or indirectly by the public, in public service,

have been driven to the point of desperation by economic conditions. Among these are the school teachers, nurses in hospitals, various kinds of clerical workers, and technical or semi-technical workers. It is clear that there must be an upward revision in the compensation which workers in these and similar classes are to receive. It should be considered the duty of all citizens to give expression to this thought upon every proper occasion. School efficiency is imperative in America. It can not be had unless proper salaries are paid to teachers. In many of the cities and towns in nearly all the states of the union, teachers have gone into other lines of endeavor, industrially or professionally, and there are compartively few young men or young women who now enter into the important work of teaching in the public schools. It is a dire need for the perpetuation of our republic that full opportunity shall beafforded to its children for adequate education. We urge all possible assistance to the teachers in their efforts to improve their standard of living and we call the attention of the teachers of America to the need for organization in order that their efforts may be effective. We commend to all teachers the good work of the American Federation of Teachers and we point to the necessity for making it the great medium of expression for the needs of teachers everywhere. Among nurses conditions are even more intolerable. We are informed that many hospitals have found it necessary to close their doors because of their inability to secure nurses. In others it has been necessary to discontinue classes for trained nurses because an insufficient number of students came forward, owing to the low wages involved and the hard conditions imposed. The conditions in the hospitals directly affect the nurses and those who find it necessary to go to hospitals as patients. In those hospitals maintained by charity it is often impossible to increase the benefactions sufficiently to allow proper conditions and wages for nurses. In too many publicly owned hospitals the exigencies of politics result in niggardly policies. Hospital service is a matter of public concern. Proper wages and humane conditions for those who render service in hospitals is likewise a matter of public concern. We believe this convention should give expression to constructive views in relation to this important subject. Organization of nurses will be of direct benefit, but there must be the additional remedy of proper control and financing of hospitals before the situation can be fully corrected. As to technical and semi-technical workers we are of the opinion that the valuable organization work already done should be extended with vigor. We believe the trade union movement is fully apprecoative of the service to society rendered by these workers and is likewise fully alive to their needs and ready to extend all possible assistance. Nothing can be done, however, unless there is among the oppressed themselves a desire for betterment, a spirit of organization. The attention of the officers of the organized labor movement throughout America is directed to the situation here set forth and they are urged to use every effort to assist in developing a remedy. Where political action or the action of political bodies is necessary to provide a remedy in whole or in part organizers and officers and the members of organized labor are asked to assist in securing such action. The health, comfort, welfare and standard of living of thousands of working men and women depend upon conditions in the occupations to which we have

here called attention. It is urgent that every possible effort to be of assistance be extended.

Profiteering—(1919, p. 381) Directed Executive Council to take such measures as would induce congress to enact legislation that would make speculating, gambling and profiteering in the necessaries of life equally as dangerous as perjury or extortion.

(1920, pp. 105-381-385) Notwithstanding the needs of the masses of our country congress failed to enact a single constructive measure that would aid in checking profiteering. Many investigations were started in the District of Columbia and other localities to find out why the cost of living was so high. Much information was gained to the detriment of the profiteers but no action followed that would bring practical results. One measure was enacted. It was an amendment to the Lever act, and was: "An act to provide further for the national security and defense by encouraging the production, conserving the supply, and controlling the distribution of food products and fuel." The reasons given for the enactment of the law were that a state of war still existed and it was necessary for the "national security and defense, for the successful prosecution of the war and for the support and maintenance of the army and navy, to assure an adequate supply and equitable distribution, and to facilitate the movement of foods, feeds, wearing apparel, containers, primarily designed or intended for containing foods, feeds, or fertilizers; fuel, including fuel oil and natural gas, and fertilizer and fertilizer ingredients, tools, utensils, implements, machinery, and equipment required for the actual production of foods, feeds, and fuel; to prevent, locally or generally, scarcity, monopolization, hoarding, injurious speculation, manipulation, and private controls affecting such supply, distribution, and movement; and to establish and maintain governmental control of such necessaries during the war." Practically the only persons proceeded against under the Lever act were the miners who were seeking relief from the high cost of living. Notwithstanding the amendment, hoarders of food continued their nefarious practices. Profiteers in food, wearing apparel, shoes, and other necessaries of life continued to add to the prices. In order to hide this profit making from the public attacks were made on labor. Nothing that would misrepresent the workers, in order that the general public might be prejudiced against them, was left unsaid. While the bill was in the senate a rider providing for a rent commission to control the renting of property in the District of Columbia was placed in the bill. This provides that tenants who object to the rent they are paying, either for apartments, hotels, dwellings or rooms, can protest to the rent commission. H. R. 217 directing the federal trade commission to inquire into the increased prices of shoes, and ascertain the cause and necessity for the increases, was reported favorably by the interstate and foreign commerce committee. The report of the committee contained this statement: "As there does not appear apparent reason or justification for the high prices that are now being charged the public for shoes, or for the general increase of such prices which has been and is currently reported in the press of the country, the committee believes that the federal trade commission should make a thorough and immediate investigation of the subject and report to congress. Interesting and valuable information would thereby be given to the congress and to the public and possibly there would thereby be afforded sufficient justification for remedial legislation." Notwithstanding this emphatic charge that there is no "justification for the high prices of shoes," the passage of the resolution was prevented. The same influence that has protected the profiteers in food appears to have been able to prevent action against profiteers in shoes. Profiteering in sugar was so open and discreditable during the fall and winter of 1919, that several bills were presented for the purpose of giving relief to the people. During the hearings by the committee on the prices of shoes, the manufacturers and dealers who testified admitted that they made from 30 to 50 per cent and more on their investment and from 10 to 15 per cent more on sales. Their defense for such exorbitant prices was that the Washington people demanded luxuries in shoes. It was brought out, however, that instead of luxuries the people had demanded leather instead of paper heels and soles and that the prices charged for paper shoes would be unreasonable even for leather shoes. April 6, 1920, the senate adopted a resolution providing that the committee on manufactures be directed to ascertain in every practical way the reasons for the increased prices of shoes in the United States. A sub-committee making the investigation reported a "federal shoe branding bill." It provided that shoes which go into interstate commerce and are shipped into the District of Columbia must be branded in plain and legible letters at least one-fourth inch in height showing the price at which the manufacturers sold the shoes. This is to acquaint the public with the manufacturer's price and that of the retailer in order that profiteering can be eliminated through public protest. Heavy penalties are provided for persons or corporations who violate the law. As the boot and shoe workers are employed by the piece the charge that the workers are limiting the output can not be sustained. It is only necessary to give one instance to show the great profiteering that is being carried on. Shoes that sold in 1913 for $4, are now sold pretty generally for $12. The increase in labor cost is only 40 cents. The investigation should have been made months ago, but the influence of the profiteers on congress prevented it.

(1923, p. 326) It is common knowledge that high living costs can be traced directly to profiteering. The profiteers in the necessities of life are moving along in the even tenor of their ways, continuing their nefarious practices without much opposition or hindrance from those in public life. The officers of the A. F. of L. are directed to use their best efforts to bring to the attention of the public the truthful causes of the high living costs. The president of the A. F. of L. is directed to bring the subject matter of this resolution to the attention of the president of the U. S. and request that he take such steps as he deems necessary to bring about reduction in living costs.

Profiteers, Rewarding the—(1922, pp. 105-327) Condemned bill introduced in congress providing for the refunding of all fines levied during and since the war on every person, partnership, association and incorporation convicted of violation of the food control act.

Profiteers Taxes on—(1919, p. 134) The 1918 convention of the A. F. of L. urged congress to levy taxes on "war profits, swollen incomes and on land values, to an extent that during the period of the war will provide by taxation at least 50 per cent of the expenditures of the government in each year." The revenue bill as finally passed bore heavily upon war profits and large incomes but land values were not taxed.

Propaganda, Extremist—(1920, pp. 210-364) During the year just passed the labor movement has stood its ground solidly and maintained the progressive, constructive policy which has marked it apart from most of the labor movements of the world throughout the whole period of the war. But the nation has witnessed sporadic outbreaks of extremist sentiment and has been compelled to deal with extremist propaganda in a number of cases since the war period came to an end. This tendency toward unreasoned conduct and unreasoned thought has been most unfortunate for the nation and still more unfortunate for those who have been the participants. Bolshevism has been a lure for some of our people and its doctrines have been propagated with great vigor. This hideous doctrine has found converts among two classes of people principally—those intellectuals, so-called, who have no occupation save that of following one fad after another, and those so beaten in the game of life that they find no appeal in anything except the most desperate and illogical schemes. The rank and file of the organized labor movement, as was to have been expected, has given no countenance to the propaganda of Bolshevism, but has, on the contrary, been its most effective opponent in America. The propaganda of revolutionary thought has not been limited to the propaganda of bolshevism. It has taken other forms. The "one big union" idea has had its adherents, despite the disastrous results of the experiment in Canada with its treacherous machinery during the year preceding our 1919 convention. It is gratifying to note that everywhere the ostensible strength of this propaganda has been lost and that its fallacies are daily becoming clearer to its former victims. Of more importance than the results of studied propagada of revolution and extremism is the feeling of unrest among our people which is due to abuses in our political and industrial life and which seeks relief and freedom and not revolution and castastrophe. So long as this unrest finds its expression in the orderly, constructive and democratic activities of the bona fide trade union movement it is of incalculable benefit to the nation. So long as it finds the trade union movement an effective weapon for the righting of industrial wrongs and for the enlargement of opportunity and the extension of liberty, it is an asset to the national character and stability. It is the expression of the masses of the people against injustice and reaction and an expression of their unalterable determination to persist in the constructive effort to press home to a successful conclusion the fight for rights too long denied and for the abolition of wrongs too long endured. The greatest disservice that the great interests of reaction and bourbonism can do for America is to repress and deny the legitimate aspirations of the workers and to seek by restrictive legislation to make ineffective their bona fide trade union organizations. Protest denied will still be protest. Upon the signing of the armistice it became clear some employers and some reactionary forces in our political life were bent upon a career of exploitation and suppression, regardless of the needs and just desires of the masses of our people. The nation has already witnessed effort after effort to enact legislation of a restrictive, coercive character, in defiance of the interests of the people and in defiance of American liberties guaranteed in the constitution of our republic. The Esch-Cummins railroad law and the Kansas court of industrial relations law are examples of bourbon success. The Graham-Sterling peace-time sedition bill, the Palmer anti-sedition bill and other proposed legislation was of a similar mould, but was defeated by reason of labor's energetic and angry protest. The injunction in the case of the coal miners was another example of the lengths to which employers and government officials were ready to go in suppressing the aspirations of the workers and in making ineffective their lawful and constructive trade union organizations as agencies of progress. There was immediate evidence of the same trend in the purely economic life of the land. The position assumed by the U. S. Steel corporation typified a spirit too prevalent—a spirit of bludgeoning wrath and enraged opposition to all progress for the working people, a spirit of intolerance of the rights of man and of arrogance in the face of a struggle for elemental justice. In a score of communities employers' associations have reopened the struggle of a decade ago for what they term the open shop—in reality the shop which is closed against union men and women. At a time when vision and statemanship should guide the employers and the political authorities of the country there has been a resurgence of the concept of brutality and oppression. During the whole period since the armistice, price inflation has continued. Profiteering, for which constructive remedies are recommended elsewhere in this report, has run wild. It has scourged the land like a plague. It has burned through our arteries of trade like a fever and ravaged our people like a pestilence. Profiteers have been insatiable "devourers of men, women and children," intent upon heaping up hoards of gold without precedent, at the expense of human life and happiness. Inflation in staple commodities has reached a point of all but unbelievable extremes. Efforts of the department of justice to restrict profiteering have merely constituted comic interludes in one of the great tragedies of the post-war period. The written and spoken propaganda of unreason and extremism can be met and defeated by truth. But legitimate unrest, growing out of conditions of injustice can be met and overcome only by intelligent dealing with conditions. Those who drink from a poisoned well will be poisoned until the well itself is cleansed. The A. F. of L. has given constant attention to the whole matter in contemplation here. It has caused constant attention to be given to the work of exposing the fallacies of false and misleading propaganda. But those who by means more effective than any propaganda have brought disturbance upon our country and suffering to our people must be dealt with directly by forces which they can understand and from which they can not escape. They are afflicted with a madness, and reason has ceased to affect them. The powerful economic organization of the American wage earners offers to the workers their most potent agency of relief, but not in every case can relief be had before desperation begins to make itself felt. The opposing forces are strongly intrenched and seem to know no sobering sense of responsibility or conscience. During the year the officers of the labor movement have issued repeated warnings to the people and have put forth definite suggestions for remedial action. Congress, which might have done much, has done nothing. Great industrial leaders have laughed at warning words and have gone back to their counting rooms. Keeping pace with the extremits propaganda and with the forces generative of unrest there has been what appears to have been a studied attempt to discredit the organized labor movement and to throw upon it the onus and burden of most of our national ills. Employers and their publications have sought steadily to spread the belief that the labor movement is responsible for high prices, responsible for unrest and an antagonist of the public welfare in every strike. Therefore this convention utters a solemn warning to the country, calling upon it to demand of congress measures of fundamental relief from oppressive legislation, measures of fundamental character looking toward reduction in cost of living and warning the nation that if the just and reasonable demands of the working people, presented for orderly negotiation through their properly accredited representatives, are not given consideration and made the subject of prompt action it is but logical that it should face the disordered protest of unorganized masses driven to desperation by the disdain and autocracy of those in control of industrial management and political parties. We call upon all loyal citizens of our republic to aid in the work of bringing relief to the wage earners and that it should make clear the abuses that afflict the country and the forces that are responsible. It should be made clear to all—as it should have been clear long since—that labor's right of protest has been held in restraint out of motives of the highest patriotism and that largely because of this high patriotism the profiteers of the country have been able to force a price piracy without parallel in history. It is a matter of vital necessity that the program of social reconstruction adopted by the 1919 convention and the declaration of labor's representatives adopted in Washington December 13, 1919, be pressed for adoption. The American nation has reached a grave crisis. It stands at the cross roads. Progress must come. Justice must be done. Bourbonism must be dethroned. Criminal profiteering and exploitation must cease. These things are so because the endurance of the people has been strained beyond their willingness to bear and because all of these things are possible of achievement. The illogical fantastic propaganda of revolution has been met and will continue to be met by the truth about democracy. The terrible pressure of injustice within democracy can be removed only by the functioning of democracy and if the forces of greed so obstruct and distort the processes of democracy that they no longer work in normal, healthful manner to satisfy the needs of the people, it is the first duty of the nation to free those processes and remove those obstructions. The unrest born of need can be met and allayed only through definite, constructive action. The program for this action has been offered by the labor movement and is before the country. The weight of this convention should be added to the force of the great movement for relief.

Public Building Work—(1919, p. 383) The A. F. of L. urges congress to pass as quickly as possible the public buildings bill that failed at the last congress, so that the U. S. government can go ahead with its building projects, that will give employment to many thousands of building mechanics and will tend to quickly stabilize the building industry of our country.

Publicity, Information and Lecture Bureau—(1920, p. 465) The value of a lecture bureau to assist in meeting campaigns of misrepresentation and in bringing home to the public the true meaning of the organized labor movement is not open to argument. We believe that an effective start toward the establishment of such a bureau can be made with little expense. If the Executive Council should secure the compilation of a list of competent speakers on labor subjects in the various sections of the country, giving such data concerning the speakers as is deemed advisable, and announced that this list was available to open forums, civic clubs, and any groups who desired it, the information would be welcomed and frequent and valuable use made of it; the expense of securing the speakers being borne by the groups themselves. From this as an immediately practicable step a lecture bureau on a larger scale and with more effective organization could later develop. The Executive Council is instructed to secure the compilation of a list of competent speakers on labor subjects, and to make this list available to open forums, civic clubs and such groups as may desire it.

(1921, p. 67) The Executive Council reported that by direction of the 1920 convention a conference was called to meet February 23 to consider the creation of a lecture bureau. It was the decision of the council that in view of the situation it was necessary and advisable systematically to organize the entire work of information dissemination in order that facts about the labor movement and the industrial struggle in general might be more readily obtainable by those who are and should become interested in our movement and its work. Accordingly, we laid before the conference our suggestions and the conference voted its enthusiastic approval. Under the plan thus approved it was directed that there should be a coordination of all agencies within the A. F. of L. having to do with the gathering and dissemination of information about our movement and that for this purpose there should be established in the headquarters a separate bureau under the direction of the president, secretary and Executive Council. Since such a work will entail an expenditure of a considerable amount of money the conference directed the president to appoint a committee to report upon ways and means of raising necessary funds. Upon recommendation of this committee the council decided to issue an appeal to the affiliated organizations for such contributions as the organizations might see fit to make. This appeal has been issued and some results have been obtained, but not sufficient at this time to indicate fully what the scope of the work will be. Under the instructions of the 1920 convention, the council undertook to organize a corps of competent speakers and a large list already has been compiled and is available at headquarters. This list will be placed in charge of the new bureau and every effort will be made to see that forums and all other organizations desiring trade union speakers are promptly and properly supplied. We believe that the work undertaken by the council in this connection is of the very greatest importance. (P. 314) The A. F. of L. has seldom taken an advance step of greater value than the establishment of a bureau for the gathering and dissemination of information concerning the labor movement. The enemies of organized labor and of all progressive movements have utilized to the full the tremendous power of organized and

misleading publicity. In no other way could reaction have gained such impetus. The indispensable remedy is to make available to the public in the most effective way the facts of the industrial and social situation today. This requires expert service and adequate finance. But the finance must be found, since this is a key activity which supplements and facilitates all other activities, and upon which in a very real sense all others depend. We earnestly urge all affiliated organizations to make substantial contributions to the fund for the maintenance of this most essential bureau. (P. 333) We authorize the Executive Council to issue an appeal for funds from the affiliated organizations in order: 1. That our recently established lecture bureau may function; and qualified speakers be enlisted who will enter into all portions of the nation in furtherance of the program of principles of the A. F. of L. 2. That our campaign of publicity may be enlarged, to the end that no misstatement or attack on our movement may go unanswered and the people of the nation may be made more familiar with our humanitarian purposes and patriotic impulses. 3. That our force of organizers may be increased by the appointment of additional qualified men and women who will cooperate with all agencies now in existence in an intensive campaign to organize the unorganized and educate those already organized in the philosophy of our movement.

(1922, p. 61) Following the Denver convention, and in pursuance to the action there taken, the Executive Council directed the president and secretary to organize an information and publicity service. The president and secretary accordingly established the A. F. of L. information and publicity service. It was the intention that there should be developed under this head the publicity work of the A. F. of L., a constantly growing volume of research work, and that in general it should be an information gathering and information disseminating agency of the labor movement. It should be borne in mind that in addition to the information and publicity service thus established, there are a number of other agencies within the headquarters of the A. F. of L. engaged in similar efforts, and it seems proper that there be set forth here a concise summary of all these efforts.

American Federationist—(1922, p. 61) The *American Federationist*, the official organ of the A. F. of L., is published monthly under the editorship of the president of the A. F. of L. It serves as a medium for conveying to organized labor and to the public the official expressions of the labor movement. There has been a rapidly growing tendency on the part of daily newspapers and periodical publications to quote from the pages of the *American Federationist* and to comment editorially upon its articles and editorials. While it would be difficult, if not impossible, to check accurately the amount of newspaper quotation and comment of this character, it has, beyond doubt, within the course of a year run into hundreds of columns. The editorial value of this constantly growing tendency toward general use of the *American Federationist* for republication purposes is an asset to the labor movement beyond estimate. It has been the good fortune of the *American Federationist* within the past year to be able to present to its readers a considerable number of contributions of great worth. Shortly after the 1921 convention, the services of the Hon.

John M. Baer, former member of congress and famous cartoonist, were engaged for the *American Federationist*. Mr. Baer's cartoons are among the most forceful in the country and would be considered an asset by publications of the first rank. They have materially added to the attractiveness and value of our official magazine. Through the information and publicity service these cartoons have been furnished each month to the labor press and they have been widely used, especially by the official journals of the various national and international unions, thus adding value to a large number of labor publications.

(1923, pp. 129-253) We wish to record our approval of the great benefits resulting from the publication of the *American Federationist* and to urge labor and other publications everywhere to take advantage of the opportunity offered by our official magazine to obtain authentic information regarding the various phases of labor's struggles.

Weekly News Letter—(1922, p. 62) The *Weekly News Letter* is one of the established branches of the A. F. of L. educational work and has continued as formerly, with the exception of a change in title authorized by the Executive Council. It now is known as the A. F. of L. *Weekly News Service*. This, as is generally known, is a service of labor news gathered primarily for the labor press. In this manner a printed sheet the size of a newspaper page is furnished to the labor press each week, going in addition to a considerable number of publications and to a large number of individuals interested for one reason or another in the labor movement and its welfare.

(1923, pp. 129-253) The A. F. of L. *Weekly News Service*, formerly known as the *Weekly News Letter*, one of the established branches of A. F. of L. editorial work, has continued as formerly. It has been and continues to be the purpose of the *Weekly News Service* to supply to the labor press of the country authentic news of the trade union movement. The *Weekly News Service* is furnished free also to a considerable number of non-labor publications and individuals who are interested in securing accurate information about labor events. The *Weekly News Service* is a valuable asset to labor's channels for the dissemination of labor information. In the course of the near future it is proposed to carry the instructions of the Cincinnati convention into effect; that is, for the more thorough coordination of the *Weekly News Service* with other branches of our federation's publicity and educational services.

Legislative Committee's Report—(1922, p. 62) There has been a standing practice of publishing each month in the *American Federationist* the report of the A. F. of L. legislative committee. During the year there was inaugurated an extension of this work. The monthly report of the legislative committee is now furnished to the labor press, to all of the colleges in the U. S. and to a number of other institutions and to persons.

Speakers' Bureau—(1922, p. 62) It has not been possible to organize a systematic effort in this direction. This has been solely because sufficient financial support was not available. The necessity for a well-organized speakers' bureau is of course apparent and no argument in that direction is necessary. It was not possible during the past year, however, to do more in the way of furnishing speakers. It is to be hoped that the coming year may offer a possibility of establishing a speakers' bureau, in order that there may be a consistent effort in the furnishing of speakers in response to a demand that is constantly growing. There are many platforms open to labor, but the advantages thus offered can not be utilized until there is a regularly established agency for the conducting of that work at A. F. of L. headquarters.

Newspapers—(1922, p. 62) We are of the opinion that a daily newspaper or a chain of daily newspapers for the labor movement must come as the result of evolutionary growth and that it is not a venture upon which to embark at this time. The argument against hasty entry into the field of daily newspaper publication is purely one of utility, expediency and business judgment. We believe it will not be necessary to present any lengthy argument to justify this point of view. We merely say that we are of the opinion first of all, that the financial undertaking involved in the conduct of a chain of daily newspapers at this time would be much greater than our movement is prepared to meet, and furthermore we are of the opinion that expansion of the work of our information and publicity service will result in a constantly improving standard of accuracy in daily newspapers even though not owned or controlled by labor. We have given consideration not only to the field of daily newspaper publication but to the field of weekly newspaper publication and to the field of publicity in general. It is our conclusion that while it is impossible to enter at this time upon the publication of a daily newspaper it may be entirely feasible within the coming year to begin the publication of a weekly newspaper to serve as a great spokesman and champion for our cause. We are impressed with the value of a properly conducted weekly publication, believing that it would serve as a constant source of inspiration to our membership in addition to being a constant source of information. More and more the question of making available accurate information about important events in the world of industry becomes one of first importance. Most of the established channels for the dissemination of news are either in the service of those opposed to the labor movement or they display a degree of unintelligence in connection with industrial affairs that is deeply disappointing and that makes for unenlightened information likely to reach unintelligent and unfounded conclusions.

Information and Publicity Service—Through this new agency the A. F. of L. has conducted during the past year a considerable work of disseminating information in relation to the labor movement. For many years prior to the establishment of this service a need was felt for some agency which would be at all times in readiness to respond to requests for information and which would at all times serve as a channel through which information and news concerning the labor movement might be available to the public through the daily press, through periodical publications and through direct contact with individuals seeking information. The effort made in this direction has been, we feel, amply justified and it demonstrates not merely the need which existed for the establishment of this service, but makes clear the pressing need for its extension. By authority of the convention there has been gathered a fund of approximately $5,000 by voluntary contribution for the purpose of financing the work. This was made necessary because no other finances were available. If this work is to be a success and if it is to be possible to continue it on a sound, stable basis that will not fluctuate from year to year, or perhaps from month to month, some other method of financing must be devised. It has been possible during the year, with the available finances, to develop the work to a degree, but falling far short of what could be otherwise accomplished. It has been necessary to practice the utmost economy, even in the ordinary routine work of information dissemination. Only a trifling amount of research work has been possible and when it is considered that the great volume of the most valuable kind of information and news material must be based upon painstaking research work the necessity for that work becomes apparent. Vast resources are continuously at the command of the enemies of labor for use in the dissemination of the propaganda of untruth. It will never be possible, and it will never be desirable, to match the efforts of our enemies in a financial way. We must, however, at the earliest moment make possible a thoroughly effective and adequate presentation of labor's story. More and more as time passes and as the world of industry becomes more complicated the work of properly gathering facts becomes more difficult and requires more painstaking effort. Superficial work can only be harmful. Statements presented to the public by labor must be impossible of successful contradiction and all compilations and research results must be able to withstand the most painstaking scrutiny. While what is popularly and properly known as propaganda is passing more and more into disrepute and is more and more resorted to only by those who have greedy and illegitimate ends to serve, there is a growing field and a growing need for legitimate, honorable publicity work. Every effort ought to be made to enlarge upon the excellent beginning that has been made by the A. F. of L. in this direction and that it should be made possible to feed and re-enforce this publicity work with proper and adequate research efforts.

American Federationist Index—The analytical index of the *American Federationist* which is now in the course of preparation will be a reference book of the history of the achievements of the labor movement in so far as they have been recorded in the official magazine. It is designed to be a guide to what labor has thought, written and accomplished in its practical everyday work of improving the conditions of the working people.

Material for Debates—During the past year a number of requests for material to be used in debates in colleges, universities, high schools and the various social organizations increased at an amazing rate. Great care has been exercised in filling them. No letters for literature have been left unanswered nor has anything been left undone to give the fullest information on all questions asked. This part of the work of the A. F. of L. has proved of great value not only to the trade union movement, but to people in all walks of life generally and has contributed to a better understanding of the fundamental principles and the general purposes of our movement. Among the subjects used most in debates are compulsory arbitration, Kansas court of industrial relations, immigration, union and non-union shops, collective bargaining, unemployment insurance and should trade unions incorporate. Each applicant for date on the various subjects is requested to inform the officials of the A. F. of L. as to the result of the debates. It is surprising the number reported to have resulted in favor of labor's attitude upon these subjects. A great majority of the letters from students express a high regard for the trade union movement and commend the A. F. of L. for the great results it as accomplished in bettering the standards and conditions of the wage earners. Upon request much material also has been supplied to many libraries.

Labor Press—The labor papers are sentinels on guard throughout the country for the cause of mankind. They are extremely valuable advocates and defenders of the cause of the wage earners. Their struggle for existence is frequently a difficult one. The labor movement owes to the labor papers a great debt of gratitude for giving voice to labor's cause when often other avenues of publicity are closed. Every possible support should be given to the bona fide labor press in order that it may be strengthened for still greater work that lies ahead.

(P. 354) The A. F. of L. directs the Executive Council to provide adequate funds for the maintenace an development of the information and publicity service by levying an assessment of one-half cent per capita, when in its judgment conditions make it feasible, and in the meantime through a vigorous campaign for voluntary contributions. Because of the danger of duplication and waste in a multiplicity of unco-ordinated efforts, all publicity activities are hereby unified in one department under the direction of the president of the A. F. of L. (P. 355) The Executive Council is hereby authorized to make such arrangement as it may find practical for the publication of a weekly newspaper at such time as its success will be reasonably assured.

(1923, p. 125) This deals with some of the more important work conducted through our information and publicity service since our last convention. We are by no means content with the work that has been accomplished, but limited finances made further expansion impossible. It is gratifying, however, that efforts in this direction have exceeded previous efforts and we look forward with assurance to more effective efforts as rapidly as more adequate financial support becomes possible.

Charting the Form and Scope of A. F. of L. Work—At the beginning of this calendar year the work of depicting the form and scope of the organization and work of the A. F. of L. by means of a series of graphic charts was undertaken. This series of charts is a demonstration of the work performed by the A. F. of L. and a revelation of the enormous field which it covers in carrying on its great number of diversified activities. Each chart is accompanied by an explanatory note or legend, but the aim throughout has been to make the charts so direct and simple as to tell their own story. No other organization of labor has ever undertaken to prepare such an exhaustive survey of its own activities. This work has been completed and will shortly be published in book form for distribution throughout the world. No American trade unionist can fail to be proud of a movement capable of making the magnificent showing revealed by this book of charts. There are more than 100 pages in the book and fully half of these are required for the charted illustrations. It is impossible at this time:

to determine upon a price for the book, but it will not be more than sufficient to cover the cost of publication. It is highly desirable that distribution be as wide as possible. A copy of the chart complete will be placed in the hands of the committee to which this subject will be referred.

Labor Information is a pamphlet publication having a minimum of four pages designed to carry information about the labor movement to persons who have no trade union affiliation but who occupy positions from which they exercise an influence in the forming of public opinion. It has long been felt that it was desirable to have a means of direct contact with men and women of this type. Publication of *Labor Information* was begun in March. It has been the aim to produce an issue of this new publication approximately once a month but no definite date of publication is fixed because the real object is to issue the publication whenever the opportunity seems to offer itself or whenever the need arises for stating either labor's point of view or important information regarding the trade union movement. The publication goes to a large list of persons in academic, professional and literary fields. When the first issue was produced every person to whom a copy was sent was requested to sign and return a card asking for future copies. The response, almost 90 per cent, was most unusual. In every case since that time the same method has been employed. Thus no person continues to receive *Labor Information* unless a specific request is entered. We feel that this new publication is serving a most useful purpose in taking the truth about the trade union movement to those whose information hitherto has been derived from sources not directly connected with the trade union movement. *Labor Information* is furnished without charge.

The News Budget is a small clipsheet of very brief items and quotations and is furnished to daily and weekly paper in the smaller cities. The importance of establishing contact with the multitude of newspapers in cities ranging in population from 15,000 to 50,000 is evident to all who understand the importance of these publications in American life.

International Labor News Service—Through the International Labor News Service the A. F. of L. Information and Publicity Service is rendering assistance to the labor press of the country and assisting it in the establishment of what it is hoped eventually will be a powerful self-supporting news-gathering agency, owned cooperatively by the trade union publications of the U. S. The International Labor Press of America, which is the organization of bona fide trade union publications in the U. S. and Canada, believed it necessary to establish a news service in which trade union publications could have faith and over which the labor press could exercise control. The cooperation of the officers of the A. F. of L. and of the Information and Publicity Service was requested. This cooperation was gladly extended. The International Labor News Service is edited in the offices of the A. F. of L., the cost of the editorial work and the cost of mailing being borne by the A. F. of L. The mechanical cost of producing the service is borne by the International Labor Press of America through a nominal charge collected from papers receiving the service.

Mats and Cartoons—A considerable demand has been made upon the A. F. of L. by trade union publications for cartoons and cuts or matrices for their reproduction. There have

been in operation at various times a number of so-called services furnishing cartoons for labor papers, but in many instances these have been as harmful as helpful to the trade union cause. The A. F. of L. desires only to be helpful to the labor press and it believes that the labor press should do for itself everything that can possibly be done in that manner. We would welcome the establishment of a service furnishing mats or cuts of cartoons or other illustrations if such a service could be established on a basis of thoroughgoing support of the trade union movement under complete trade union control.

Guide to Sources of Information—As the result of repeated inquiries as to sources from which certain types of statistical information might be had and from which reports of investigations and hearings might be had, the task of compiling the sources of authentic and available information was undertaken by our Information and Publicity Service. The object was to place at the command of the executives of international unions a reference book which would serve as a reliable guide to sources of information valuable to trade unions. *The Guide to Sources of Information* was issued primarily for the use of officers of international unions. Copies are available, however, to those who have particular need to be in touch with the more important sources from which information in statistical and other forms is regularly available.

Informing the Daily Press—The work of conveying information to the daily news papers and press associations of the country has expanded considerably during the year. We have regarded it as of the utmost importance that authentic information be made available to the daily newspapers and every effort has been made to see that all information that is legitimately of a public character is conveyed to the public through the newspapers at the earliest possible moment.

Periodical Publications—One of the reasons why labor appears frequently at a disadvantage in articles in the periodical press is because writers are poorly informed. Of course outright bias, either of author or publication, is not infrequent, but there are many cases in which lack of information is not willful and where the deficit may be supplied. During the past year much has been done in this direction. A great number of writers have sought authentic information and every effort is being made to encourage such requests. In addition to supplying information in this manner a large number of special articles for various periodical publications have been prepared in response to requests. Not less than a 100 such articles have been furnished by the president of the A. F. of L. alone.

Lecturers—It is recognized as highly desirable that capable lecturers should be available in all parts of the country for addresses before organizations of labor and organizations that are interested in the problems of wage earners. It is of great value that trade unionists should train themselves and be aided in developing themselves as public speakers with a clear understanding of the historic development of the trade union movement and its philosophy, particularly in America and we urge upon our organizations that they undertake the creation of a committee or bureau in which the art of public speaking be taught.

Information Gathering—Any consideration of publicity as contemplated in the establishment of the A. F. of L. Information and Publicity Service must take into account the complete operation, which consists of getting information, systematizing it and passing it on through one channel or another. The greatest efforts were made in connection with the International Conference for the Limitation of Armament, the defeat of the ship subsidy bill, the so-called open shop movement and the activities of revolutionary propagandists within the labor movement and in the U. S. in general.

Range of Subjects Dealt With—The range of subjects in connection with which information was required during the course of the year reaches into almost every phase of human activity. It is an indication of the all-embracing interests of the trade union movement and of the wide interest of others in the trade union movement. (P. 250) We desire to express our appreciation and our approval of the remarkable progress in publicity made during the year. We desire to proceed as rapidly as possible with the development of this work. We believe that the work of intelligently informing the public concerning the work and the aims and policies of the trade union movement is of the highest importance and that every facility for this work should be made available. We believe it of the utmost importance that our affiliated national and international unions should continue voluntary contributions, and we earnestly express the hope that they will see the wisdom of so doing. We are confident that the convention will join enthusiastically in expressing the gratitude of our movement to those organizations which by their generous contributions have made possible the development of the publicity service. They have assumed a burden which properly belongs upon the movement as a whole and in doing so have made possible a measure of helpfulness and progress of value, not only to our movement, but to all who have an interest in the cause of constructive and progressive development toward a higher and better order of things.

Pueblo Disaster—(1921, p. 15) We urge all members of organized labor to come to the assistance of the people of the city of Pueblo. Particularly we believe it fitting that the international unions should contribute their support, but in addition we call upon all bodies of organized labor and the individual membership in this grievous emergency.

Railroad Labor Board—(1923, pp. 72-88) The U. S. railroad labor board brought into existence under the provisions of the Esch-Cummins act, has by its record fully justified and warranted the condemnation expressed by vote of our last convention. It has proven its inability to function in accordance with the claims and promises made by its sponsors at the time of its enactment, and has proven itself much more an agency for the promotion of discord than for the inauguration of constructive effort. There could have been no other development, as has been repeatedly pointed out, because·of the fact that the railroad labor board in so far as it had any power or influence was a coercive institution, thrust into the situation by legislative enactment in defiance of the natural evolution of the relation between workers and employers in the railroad world. It is noteworthy that while the railroad labor board was given no power to enforce its finding it sought to exercise power in dealing with the workers but confessed its lack of power when dealing with railroads. The futility of the railroad labor board has, we are confident, become apparent to observing Americans as a result of its performance. Whether it will become apparent to legislators that such methods of dealing with industrial

problems can result only in harm to all concerned, is a question which can be answered only by the future conduct of legislators. The viewpoint expressed by labor at the time of the creation of the railroad labor board has been so fully borne out by events, that we point to the record not so much in satisfaction as in the earnestness of our desire to bring about the cessation of political tinkering with the machinery of industry in the vain effort to provide instantaneous remedies for problems that can not be thus successfully dealt with. The natural and rational processes of industrial evolution must and will develop remedies for every situation arising in relations between wage earners and employers whatever the industry may be. It is high time that industrial difficulties ceased to offer campaign material to those whose prime interests are all too frequently the harvesting of votes for reelection. At the risk of uttering what may sound like a platitude we reaffirm that industry is and must remain industrial and that it is not and should never be political. The railroad labor board is but one evidence of the mania for political intrusion into the industrial field. Its failure has been complete. The law under which it was created should be removed from the statute books by the forthcoming congress. The removal of this provision of the law from the statute books should mark the end of legislative efforts toward political invasion of the field of wage fixing and employment relations. (P. 274) Having demonstrated its impotency to deal properly, fairly and justly as a board of mediation and conciliation, the railroad labor board, like all similar institutions, attempted to assume dictatorial powers. The railway shopmen effectually challenged this assumption of power, and, having failed in its accomplishment, we now find the chairman of the railway labor board assiduously at work endeavoring by might and main to have himself and his associates in the railway labor board vested with power to decide the wages and conditions of employment under which millions of wage earners shall be forced to give service. In the palmiest days of tyrannical government no such colossal power has ever been vested in any king or monarch, or exercised by them. Even that most brutal proposal to conscript men during a "national emergency" palls into insignificance when compared to the proposal to conscript the railway workers and to place them under the complete domination, first, of the railway magnates, and, if their mastery fails, then under the lash of the railway labor board. The railway labor board is a constant menace to the freedom and well-being of the railway workers, and its early elimination would be but a belated act of justice.

Railroad Law, Esch-Cummins—(1920, p. 97) Enactment of a law to turn the railroads back to their owners caused a most bitter campaign to include provisions that would prohibit employes from striking. Furthermore, when the committee on interstate commerce reported a bill to the senate it was first intended that no hearings would be held upon it. It was to be presented in the morning, a week given for its consideration, and it was to be rushed through before the people really became aware of what it contained. This policy was prevented through a most aggressive protest from the A. F. of L. and the railroad brotherhoods. The house bill, however, was submitted at midnight on Saturday and no one knew what it contained until the following Monday. A week was given for its consideration and then it was jammed through in scheduled time. An aggressive campaign against this reactionary legislation was conducted. President Gompers appeared before the interstate commerce committee of the senate, and in an extended hearing declared that if such a aw was enacted it would mean a violation of the thirteenth amendment to the constitution of the U. S. which forbids involuntary servitude except for those who commit a crime. He declared: "When the government during the stress of war took over the railroads the employes were free men. Now you are preparing to turn them back to their owners with the employes handcuffed." Senator Cummins, the author of the bill, was so determined that the normal activities of labor should be prevented, not only in the railroad industry, but in many others, that he made this threat on the floor of the senate: "Not only has there been no hesitation, so far as I am concerned, with respect to these provisions of the railroad bill, but I intend when the measure comes before the senate to propose an extension of the principles of the bill, which are now applied only to transportation, to the basic industries of America, to the production of fuel, or iron and steel, to the production of the foodstuffs and of lumber and of building material and of clothing; for I can not conceive that the people of this country are to be continuously at the mercy of any class so far as these fundamentals in American life are concerned." A more successful fight was made in the house against reactionary labor legislation in the railroad bill. After several months of hearings the interstate and foreign commerce committee of the house presented the Esch bill. It contained the following drastic penalty for violation of the law: "Any union which authorizes any member to break any term or terms of any such contract of hire, or in case such contract is modified by any decision of the adjustment board or board of labor appeals, then of such contract as so modified, or which aids, abets, counsels, commands, induces, procures, or consents to, or conspires to effect any such breach by its members shall be liable for the full damages to the carrier arising from the breach." This would make the unions financially liable for damages to a carrier suffered during a strike. Efforts to rush this bill through with the pernicious labor provisions aroused the entire country. It united the labor group and the friends of labor in the house in a solid phalanx. Nevertheless, the enemies of labor, bolstered up by the denunciation hurled at labor, and believing that they were rising to great heights of notoriety, sought to amend the section by making it more objectionable. Representative Webster contended that the labor clauses were not drastic enough and submitted an amendment which he declared had "teeth" in it. This amendment was the most far-reaching of any suggested. It provided that individual members of unions as well as organizations themselves would be financially liable for damages. The amendment reads: "The action shall run against the union or organization jointly and severally against it and the members thereof, or against the employes individually as the carrier or carriers may elect; satisfaction of any judgment rendered shall be made from the property of the union or organization or any member or members of the offending union or from the property of any offending employe or group of employes sued by name." Representatives of the A. F. of L. and the brotherhoods called meetings of the labor group and friendly

congressmen and considered plans for effectually defeating such drastic legislation. The railroad brotherhoods recommended that an effort be made to substitute an amendment to both the Webster amendment and the clauses in the Esch bill. This amendment was submitted by Representative Anderson, of Minnesota, and was adopted after a most aggressive verbal battle. Then the senate and house bills went to conference. After eight weeks' consideration by the conference committee of the two bills, during which all efforts to appear before it to enter protest against the reactionary clauses pertaining to labor had failed, a completed bill was reported to both houses. The vigorous protests, coming from all parts of the U. S. against the labor clauses proposed in the bills caused a change in the policy of the conference committee. The labor clauses were submitted to Director General Walker D. Hines, of the railroad administration, with instructions to eliminate all of the features objectionable to labor in the Cummins and Esch bills. During a protest meeting held in the house office building, February 19, 1920, by representatives of labor and friendly congressmen, Representative Barkley, of the conference committee, who objected to the report, declared that the director general had admitted to him that his work in amending the bill was imperfect and that he was not at all satisfied with it. A telegram sent to a number of railroad officials by one of their confidential attorneys was read to the meeting. It said: "The only difference between the anti-strike clause in the Cummins bill and the one in the conference report is that in the former a penalty is affixed which has to be tried by a jury, while in the latter an injunction method will be followed and the penalty fixed and assessed by a court and not a jury in contempt proceedings. This is better for the railroads, as it is more effective, and because it would be harder to convict a union man before a jury.". The labor clause in the conference committee's report was condemned because of its concealed menace to the workers. It surreptitiously provided for compulsory arbitration. The workers could be proceeded against for damages in an equity court if they did not use reasonable efforts to avert trouble. A labor board with great powers could order raids on homes of individual workers for books and papers. One of the most objectionable features of the bill provided that any 100 unorganized employes could present grievances. This would permit enemies of the trade union movement to work secretly and menace the efforts of the organization for better working conditions. Any desire of the organized workers to build up their standard of living could be defeated by the railroad officials secretly inciting small groups to make demands that would discredit legitimate unions. Early in the agitation for a law providing for the turning over of the railroads to their owners it was decided that arguments for and against the success of government control were based on the experiences that did not give a fair test. These experiences were gained during a great war. It would be necessary therefore to extend such government control during a period in peace times so that a proper test could be made. The president of the A. F. of L. called a meeting of the railroad brotherhoods and shopmen and they agreed to confine their efforts to the defeat of all labor clauses in the railroad bill and to urge the retention of the railroads for two years for the purpose of giving a fair test to government control in peace times. The conference adopted the following: "That it is the sense of the conference that the control of the railroads should be exercised by the government of the U. S. for a period of not less than two years in order that a proper test may be made as to government control. That such test has not been given a fair opportunity during war times or since. This conference is opposed to legislation making strikes of workers unlawful. It is the sense of this conference that penalty clauses in pending legislation on. railroads against workers ceasing their employment should be eliminated. That the conference favors the enactment of beneficial features of the bills which tend to establish better relations between the employes and the carriers. That the beneficial clauses should be extended to the sleeping car and Pullman company employes." After the railroad bill passed both houses and was signed by the president, the representatives of the brotherhoods and shopmen agreed that the only method of procedure would be to accept the provisions of the bill and proceed as quickly as possible in negotiations for sufficient wages and better working conditions. By the terms of the bill any increases in wages must be approved by at least one representative of the public if it is necessary in paying them to increase rates. If the representatives of the workers and the three representatives of the railroads vote for increases in wages they are defeated unless one representative of the public votes in its favor. Although six of the nine members of the board may vote to approve the increase it is obligatory for one of the public representatives to vote for them, thus requiring seven out of the nine votes to approve. (P. 373) The convention unanimously declared unyielding opposition to any legislation which would establish a condition under which workmen may not quit their employment singly or collectively whenever their terms of employment or conditions of labor become unsatisfactory or intolerable.

(1921, p. 69) Report of the Executive Council: "Pursuant to resolution No. 66, of the 1920 convention, your council has earnestly sought to find means of giving effect to the terms of that declaration. Perhaps no part of our industrial machinery has been subjected to greater controversy or greater strain due to conflict of interest and conflict of opinion and judgment. The Executive Council directed the officers at headquarters to meet with the representatives of the 16 organizations having jurisdiction over railroad employes. Two conferences were called, the first on December 6, 1920, which was postponed in compliance with the expressed wish of a number of the organizations. The second conference was held April 12, 1921, when the question of railroad legislation was discussed in all its phases and there decided by unanimous vote that a policy committee be appointed whose duties would be to look after legislation affecting railroad employes. The Esch-Cummins law was enacted, under the terms of which the railroad labor board was created and a government guarantee of railroad dividends for a period of six months was established. By a subsequent amendment to the Esch-Cummins law the U. S. treasury was compelled to pay alleged losses incurred during the period of governmental operation of the roads. The conference of national and international trade union representatives held in Washington, February 23-24, 1921, protested against the enactment

of this amendment and requested its veto by the president. The amendment, however, was not vetoed and became law. In addition congress also provided that for two years after the probationary period the owners of the railroads should be aided in earning 5½ per cent annually on $19,000,000,000, largely watered, and an additional ½ per cent on the $19,000,000,000, to make provision for improvements and equipment which under the accounting system prescribed by the interstate commerce commission are charged to capital account. To make it possible to earn that profit the interstate commerce commission was authorized to increase freight and passenger rates no matter how burdensome the change would be to the people of the country. The A. F. of L. has from the outset understood the unsoundness of the Esch-Cummins legislation and has continually pointed out the mistake and failure. When the original Esch-Cummins measure was under consideration, protest was made and it was pointed out that in addition to the fact that the bill was wrong in principle, it would be a failure in practice unsatisfactory to all parties. The operation of the law has created a situation by virtue of which even its promoters and advocates now freely acknowledge that absolute failure and collapse was predicted by labor in the very beginning. Labor's protest also was directed against the government guarantee of interest and dividends, by which it placed a premium upon ineffective and uneconomical management. In addition to this, we wish to call attention to the practice adopted by the railroads since the termination of government control, by which a large part of railroad repair work is done in private repair shops not owned by the railroads themselves. The former custom of the roads was to do their repair work in their own shops. The result of this change in practice is that repair work is costing three and four times its former cost in railroad repair shops. It is further stated that various railway directors are part owners of these private repair shops in which work is now being done and consequently derive additional profit as a result of the new policy, while the burden of the increased cost is thrown on the railroads as an unjust and improper burden upon operating expenses. These are some of the developments in the railroad situation. They indicate the main centers of turmoil and they indicate also the impossibility, for the time being, of making appreciable progress toward the development of a sound railroad policy, or toward giving any particular impetus to such constructive proposals as labor might have to offer. The Esch-Cummins legislation, having been enacted it was necessary that a sufficient time elapse to prove to the country the folly and impracticability of that legislation. That folly and impracticability now stand proved, as labor declared it would be, to the satisfaction of practically everyone. A review of the decisions of the railroad labor board shows nothing of constructive statesmanship, nor could such a showing be expected. The outstanding decision of the board was that by which the national agreements were abrogated. This decision undid a notable achievement in the direction of justice, uniformity and economy. It constituted a deliberate backward step. Decisions in wage cases have betokened no progressive thought. At best the board has merely refused to sanction certain proposed wage reductions. But whatever may have been the character of the decisions, the central and all-important fact is that they have not brought satisfaction to either workers or management and have left the general railroad morale in a seriously impaired condition. This is so because court or tribunal decisions must of necessity deny all expression of mutuality and agreement and only through such expression can harmony, justice and cooperation be secured or developed. The railroad labor board has made voluntary agreement a relic of history. The maximum demands are presented in preliminary meetings, with the board as a court of appeal always in the background. Thus, questions of wages, working conditions, and hours become matters for litigation instead of negotiation. Neither party is satisfied, as is abundantly evident. Only a minor fraction of the cases presented has been decided. The breakdown is complete. Another feature to which it is necessary to call attention is the fact that under the law provision was made for representation on the labor board by three representatives of management, of the public and of labor, and that the three representatives of labor were divided as follows: One member representing the train service, one the railroad shop employes and one the miscellaneous trades and callings in the railroad service, and in the organization of the labor board these classifications of workers were each represented by one of their own choosing and in that manner the board was organized. The first vacancy occurred by the expiration of the term of the representative of the workers in the miscellaneous branches of the service. Upon his retirement a member was appointed by the president to fill that vacancy who was not of the miscellaneous trades and callings but is one who was engaged in the train service, thus leaving without direct representation the men engaged in the miscellaneous trades and callings who represented nearly 50 per cent of all the employes of the railroads. This statement is not made in adverse criticism of the personnel of this representative, but to remind all whom it concerns that unless the original thought and practice are put into operation we may find in the future that the three representatives of labor may belong to one classification in the railroad service, not familiar with the work of the others, and leave the two other branches of the men in the railway service without any direct representation at all. It is therefore necessary to look to the future for the development of a sound, constructive program under which the nation may be assured of competent, fair and economical operation and control of the railroads with labor's right to exercise its normal activities and freedom safeguarded. There is now before the country, proposed by the railroad security holders a plan for the unification of the railroads and the stabilizing of their securities by the incorporation by the interstate commerce commission of a national corporation to take over the roads. Their plan is neither for government ownership nor for government operation, but for a joint control by stockholders, classified labor and the public. Without expressing preference for any specific basis of representation the railroad security holders declare they are willing to accept any basis by which these three interests are represented. Organized labor is open to the consideration of all serious proposals. The first basis of representation recommended by the railroad security holders is a board of 15 directors, as follows: Five of these directors might be elected by the stockholders for say, five-year terms; five by classified labor, and five appointed by the president representing purely public interests.

Organized labor is not prepared at present to give its conclusions upon the security holders' proposals, but it believes that the above basis of representation is fully justified for a national commission to investigate the present crisis and to make recommendations to congress for action. The commission should have seven representatives for each of the above groups, the representatives of the public being chosen to represent, proportionately as far as practicable, the leading groups of users of railway service, the representatives of classified labor to include a representative of the technical and a representative of the administrative personnel, the representatives of the stockholders to include the leading groups of ownership and of control. This commission, having at its service the accumulated experience of the interstate commerce commission and the railway labor board, would not be obliged to investigate the entire situation de novo, but might be required to report to congress within a reasonable space of time, certainly within the present year. Its work would be further facilitated by the presentation of the plans of the railroad security holders and other organized interests concerned.

(1922, pp. 58-339-346-349) When the Esch-Cummins law was under consideration, labor opposed this legislation with all the power at its command. At the time of the enactment of this bill into law it was believed that this legislation to regulate the operation of the railroads and to fix the wages and conditions of employment of labor by a governmental institution would prove unsatisfactory, if not disastrous. Despite all predictions to the contrary, this law has proven a failure and has been the cause of more unrest, disturbance and dissatisfaction than have ever been experienced by either railroad workers or the users of our transportation system. This fact is recognized alike by the railroad owners, managers and security holders who constantly find cause for complaint. Of course the grievances of the railroads are centered solely on the effort to maintain high transportation charges, to reduce the wages of the railroad workers and to use our railroad system as a means of exploitation for dividends and profits. Thus we find the railroads constantly clamoring for further and further reductions in wages of the railroad employes in order to place, as is alleged, the railroads on a sound financial basis and to permit the lowering of transportation rates. In that manner the center of attack is made on labor and the whole failure of our transportation system is sought to be shifted on to the shoulders of the wage earners. Consequently the railroad workers have been compelled to fight not only against the further lowering of their inadequate wages, but they also have been compelled to use every effort and ingenuity at their command to maintain their effective trade union organization. Under these circumstances, the railroad workers have been required to study every phase of the railroad problems and the astounding fact has been disclosed that our transportation system is not in the control of men who are interested in the operation of the railroads for service to the public, but that it is dominated and controlled by a small group of bankers and industrial interests who are interested solely in dividends and profits. It has been revealed that the control of the supply companies which furnish the railroads with the necessary equipment and do the "outside" labor work at excessive costs and profits are the same interests that own and control the railroads themselves. It has been demonstrated that members of the board of directors of New York banks controlled 270 directorships of 93 class one railroads; that the boards of the principal railroad systems do not often number more than 15 directors; that on an average 45 members on the boards of the principal railroad systems are directors of New York banks and that among these is included the U. S. Steel Corporation, one of the most powerful forces in the railroad and mining industry. Practically 25 Wall Street men control 103 railroad directorships and through this concentrated power, bear a great influence upon practically every large industry throughout the country. In summing up the situation last October before the railroad labor board, the railroad unions presented the following significant statement: 1. That the control of the transportation system of the country, including nearly every important system today, centers in New York City, and that the main lines of policy for the industry are determined on a national basis by a comparatively small group of New York banks. 2. That this group of New York banks is closely knit together into a single unit through a maze of interlocking director rates and that leadership in this combine has been maintained through credit cont ol by the house of Morgan. 3. That this control extends not only to the various railroad systems, but also to the chief industries of the country which furnish the railroads with fuel, material for maintenance of way and equipment, new equipment and other supplies. 4. That certain members of this financial group are primarily railway directors and that they constitute what might be termed the railway department or committee of this unified financial combination. 5. That Thomas DeWitt Cuyler and W. W. Atterbury (of the Pennsylvania Railroad, handmaiden of the U. S. Steel) who are at present leading the attack upon the organized employes of the road, both before the country and the railroad labor board, are members of this railway committee of the combine. 6. That the spread of control of this New York railway department extends to every section of the country, thereby accounting for the fact that the present policies are being followed on a national basis. Under the Esch-Cummins act the railroads were guaranteed for a certain period by the government five and one-half per cent (5½%) to six per cent (6%) on a capitalization to be fixed by the interstate commerce commission. Under this act the interstate commerce commission has endeavored to determine the capitalization, but by the same act the method of determining the capitalization was so outlined as to require it to secure its conclusions from the book accounts rather than from the actual values of the properties engaged in the service. Under this method of estimating the capitalization of the railroads and the fixing of their rates, high costs need not disturb the railroads because they are insured their financial return no matter what the cost may be. Under this arrangement the railroads have impressed the country with the belief that the only method of reducing railroad rates is by reducing the wage cost. The railroads, however, have used this cost-plus basis arrangement not only to depress the wages of labor, but also to swell their dividends and profits through "outside" and equipment concerns which are practically dominated by them. The railroad organizations have constantly indicated that these contracts for outside repairs and equipments were excessive in nature and that this practice

was being indulged in to keep up the cost of operation and to enlarge the profits and dividends of those who control and dominate the railroads. It remained, however, for the interstate commerce commission to look into these charges and to find that in the case of the Pennsylvania Railroad that upon the resumption of corporate control and operation by the Pennsylvania Railroad Company this company awarded to the Baldwin Locomotive Works a contract for the repair of 200 locomotives while maintaining shops of its own for such work and that the cost to the Pennsylvania Railroad Company was over $3,000,000 in excess of the cost at which the same work might have been done in its own shops. It also found that there was work paid for twice in some instances, which the company could have done in its own shops within a reasonable time, by an appropriate co-ordination of effort and with reasonable exertion. The interstate commerce commission also found that in the case of the New York Central Railroad Company under contracts negotiated in the early months and in the summer of 1920, certain locomotive construction companies, 195 locomotives of the New York Central Railroad Company were sent to "contract" shops for classified repairs and that the cost to the New York Central Railroad Company was in the neighborhood of $3,000 000, in excess of the cost of similar work in its own shops. The interstate commerce commission likewise found that the New York Central Railroad Company could have repaired at least a greater number of locomotives in its own shops within the time in which the contract work was done. These findings of the interstate commerce commission and the railroad labor board give added validity and present demonstrative evidence to the statement made by the railroad unions that approximately $2,000,000,000 a year is wasted by methods of this kind, by improper financing and a useless duplication of effort. These decisions, as well as the cost-plus principle itself give added value to the conviction that it is not wages that should be reduced, but that these methods of exploitation, permissible and encouraged under the Esch-Cummins law, should be wiped out. In the case of the Indiana Harbor Belt Railroad Company and the Burnham Car Repair Company, the railroad labor board, in decision, ruled that any railroad "farming out" its shop and maintenance work for the alleged purpose of removing its employes from the operation and application of the transportation act or the jurisdiction of the railroad labor board is in direct violation of the provisions of this act, although official contracts involved in such transactions are at the same time held legal by the railroad labor board. It is said this decision will serve as an "example" to be followed in 36 other similar cases involving 17 railroads now on the docket for decision. Immediately upon the announcement of this decision the surmise was made in railroad circles that the railroad labor board will again find itself restrained in the enforcement of its decisions by an injunction and if this prediction becomes a reality and if the case of the Pennsylvania Railroad Company is a fair criterion of the attitude of our courts upon the powers of the railroad labor board, this ruling of the railroad labor board will prove as impotent as its former decision against the railroads. Indeed, it would seem that the only legal decisions that the railroad labor board is permitted to make are such as affect the railroad workers adversely and as benefit the railroad magnates alone, directly or indirectly. A review of the decisions of the railroad labor board for the past year confirms the conviction expressed a year ago that its operation shows nothing of a constructive statesmanship and that its decisions are not in the direction of justice, uniformity and economy. However we may characterize the decisions, the important fact emphasized is that the decisions of the railroad labor board have given satisfaction neither to the workers nor to management and have tended toward a more general demoralization of the morale of the mechanical forces upon whom the successful operation of the railroads depend. Indeed, it is inconceivable that there could be designed a court or tribunal which would bring to all concerned that same degree of satisfaction that arises out of collective agreements, mutually entered into. The Esch-Cummins law, through the railroad labor board, has practically destroyed the conception of voluntary agreements between employers and workers and the subject of compensation for services rendered has become a constant source of litigation and irritation. How to meet this vicious circle of control and how to establish the principles of democracy in the labor relationship on our transportation systems is the direct problem of the railroad workers. Indirectly the solution of this problem affects every other group of workers. The mine workers are are now engaged in a death struggle against this same powerful combine and the weapon used by those workers is the economic power with which they are endowed, their freedom to cease mining coal and thereby to compel these financial interests to deal fairly with them. Under the Esch-Cummins law it is intended to deny the railroad workers this natural and economic power with which nature has endowed them and by arbitrary legislation to enslave them to the properties of the railroads as effectively as were the workers enslaved to the land under the old feudal system. It is of immediate importance that the rights of the railroad workers to cease work, whenever the pressure becomes too great and whenever they deem themselves justified in so doing must be fully protected. It is well enough to urge the need of continued transportation facilities in the interests of the general public, but it can not be in the interest of the general public to continue further and further the enslavement of free workers under the devious methods employed by the railroads, to earn dividends and profits for a few at the sacrifice of the very existence of the railroad workers. Under the directions of the Denver convention, the Executive Council has been helpful in every way within its power to the Railway Employes Department of the A. F. of L. conforming to the Denver convention instruction and in cooperation with the department. As evidence of the appreciation of the Railway Employes Department, we quote from a letter from the president under date of February 24, the following: "The department sincerely appreciates the support and cooperation which they have received from the A. F. of L. and its officers during the past year in connection with controversies which have affected the organizations representing railroad employes." (Pp. 110-340) Bills introduced in congress having for their purpose the penalizing of railroad officials by fine or imprisonment do not get very far along the legislative road. H. R. 8958 prohibits the giving of railroad repair work or contracts for new equipment by any manager or purchasing agent who has stocks, shares or any other such interest in any firm or corporation to which the contract is let, except that it be the lowest bidder after fair competitive bidding. H. R. 10798 provides that it shall be unlawful for any railroad having facilities for construction, repairing or rebuilding of equipment or doing maintenance work of any kind to award contracts to outsiders without first obtaining the consent of the interstate commerce commission. (P. 345) The railroad industry of the U. S., upon which the progress and prosperity of the nation so largely depends, is waging a campaign to break down organizations of employes and reduce wages below the subsistence level, through the U. S. railroad labor board, a tribunal created by the Cummins-Esch law; known as the transportation act of 1920, which act was passed by congress over the strong protest of the A. F. of L. and the 16 standard railroad labor organizations. After more than two years of operation under this act there is recorded not a single deliberate violation of the law by employes, while continued flagrant and cunningly devised violations have been publicly known and are now chargeable to railroad management, and said managements continue to defy the law, thus creating a situation inimical to the public peace and stability of the industry. Recent decisions of the railroad labor board, charged with the duty and responsibility of establishing "just and reasonable" wage schedules, have made effective on July 1 standards of wages for certain classes of employes which will not permit of the purchase of the barest essentials of a normal living, a wage which, measured in food, clothing, housing, etc., will place hundreds of thousands of American workers below the level which now obtains in the poverty-stricken regions of Europe. Therefore, the A. F. of L. again reiterates its opposition to the iniquitous Cummins-Esch law and calls upon congress for its repeal; that the railroad labor board has in the overwhelming majority of decisions functioned in the interest of railroad management and against the employes; that it has placed the dollar sign over and above the human needs of the workers, serving as an instrument to shackle and coerce 2,000,000 wage workers in the industry, a policy which is hurtful not alone to the railroads, but to every branch of American industry. (P. 346) Almost the first act of the railroad labor board was to take from the railway employes an agreement which has been given to them by the railroad administration, or rather had been negotiated with these railroad employes by representatives of the railroad adminsitration, and applied to all the railroads and covered practically all the various classes of employes. Prior to the time the railroad labor board annulled the so-called national agreement, the president of the U. S. called a representative of one of the largest groups to Washington, and without giving him an opportunity to say one word to the president as to the merits of that agreement or explain the contents of that agreement, he said: "Jewell, your national agreement has got to go." Now, we do not believe the president of the U. S. knew what that national agreement contained; we do not believe he knew whether it was fair and equitable to both sides, but the statement was made without qualification that the agreement must go.

(1923, pp. 73-274) The transportation act—otherwise known as the Esch-Cummins act—has proved, as was prophesied by representatives of labor, to be a great benefit to the railroad exploiters and a great detriment to railroad employes. The valuation and guaranteed income provisions provide a basis for supporting the most extravagant claims of the banker managements of the railroads for high freight rates and parsimonious demands for reduced wages. Meanwhile the act purports to give to the employes remedies in wage disputes which are more likely to work to their injury than to their benefit. If the employes obtain favorable decisions from the labor board after long and extensive hearings, the employers are free to reject the findings as did the railroads in over a hundred instances prior to the shop trade strike. If, on the other hand, the decisions are favorable to the railroads and the men reject the decision, then the drums will be beaten, the trumpets blown and public opinion stirred against the workers who are accused of defying the government. Despite all claims to the contrary, the Esch-Cummins law has proven an utter failure and has been the cause of unrest, disturbance and dissatisfaction, manifested by wage earners, farmers and the people in general. It has never served a single useful purpose and its immediate repeal will be but a belated act of justice. The dominant fact is, that it has well served the Wall Street interests but it is time that consideration be given to the people's common interests.

Railroad Officials, Salaries of—(1921, p. 374) Executive Council directed to secure a statement of the complete salaries paid to railroad officials and attorneys and then take such steps as the facts warranted.

Railroads—(1919, pp. 124-328) This report of the committee on resolutions was adopted by the convention: "With reference to the subject matter contained in the Executive Council's report and in the resolution submitted, your committee, in submitting a declaration in favor of ownership or control of railroads by the U. S. government, recommends that inasmuch as the details connected with the same are at present in a formative stage, the subject matter be referred to the Executive Council with instructions to cooperate with the organizations representing the railroad employes.

(1920, pp. 399-420) The Executive Council is hereby instructed to use every effort to have the transportation act of 1920 repealed and legislation enacted providing for government ownership and democratic operation of the railroad systems and necessary inland waterways.

(1921, p. 361) The Executive Council of the A. F. of L. is directed to assist the recognized railroad labor organizations by every effort within its power to have proper legislation enacted providing for government ownership and democratic operation of the railroad systems of the U. S.

Railroad Shopmen's Strike—(1923, p. 100) Report of Railway Department of the A. F. of L.: At the time of our report to the Cincinnati convention the railroad shop trade organizations, affiliated with the railway employes department, were soon to become involved in a nation-wide strike as a protest against the intolerable conditions being imposed on them and having no avenue of redress. Every means was used to avert the impending strike, but it was self-evident from the attitude assumed by the railroad general managers' committee that they were unitedly determined to force the strike of the shop trade organizations, evidently having the full assurance of support from the administration in Washington in an attempt to annihilate them. How well this compact was carried out is borne out by facts in the subsequent developments. In their bill of grievances the railroad shop trade organizations cited the instance of more than 90 railroads which had flagrantly violated the transportation act and the decisions of the labor board, without penalty, while in the few instances where the employes declined to accept the decision of the board, or suspended work to force the railroad to carry out the provisions of the labor board rulings, they were immediately classed as outlaws and publicly condemned for their action. Carrying out the instructions of the department convention held in April, 1922, three ballots were spread to the membership of the six shop trade organizations, to be returnable to department headquarters not later than midnight, June 30, 1922. The propositions to be voted on were first, on the acceptance or rejection of the further reduction of wages ordered by the labor board in its decision No. 1036, docket No. 1300; second, on the acceptance or rejection of amended rules 6, 10, 12, 14, 15, 46, and 177, as contained in labor board's decision No. 222 and addendum No. 6 thereto; third, on the acceptance of piece work and conceding to railroad managements the right to contract out their repair work to contractors, thereby depriving employes of their seniority rights, past privileges, rates of pay and working conditions established by negotiations and agreements and by decisions of the U. S. labor board. Following is the result of the vote of the six shop trades in favor of striking against each of the three propositions: First, 94.5 per cent; second, 97 per cent; third, 96 per cent. It will be noted that the larger per cent of vote was cast in rejection of the labor board's amended rules. In the modification of these rules, the labor board took away from the shop employes the punitive time and one-half pay for Sunday and holiday work, which had been in force on a large number of railroads for many years, it permitted the railroad to use the physical examination as a means of excluding applicants from employment for no other reason than their activity in the organization. But for the fact that many thousands of union members, principally car department employes, had been placed on furlough for nearly one year prior to taking the strike vote, by reason of the railroads contracting out their work and their refusal to accept the reduced wages and unfair conditions imposed upon them, the number voting would have been greatly increased. On the date of the strike, the organizations were still waiting action by the labor board on the farming out policy of the railroads, on which the shop trade unions had protested to the board some 18 month previous, these long delays in handling grievances through this governmental tribunal, while extremely aggravating to say the least, inasmuch as the railroads were permitted to administer the unemployment cure to thousands of union members who had given their best years of service to the railroads, was further aggravated by the fact that the chairman of the labor board had used the prestige of his office in public articles and public addresses to individually and collectively attack the policies and purposes of the union organizations, prejudging the grievances as set forth by the employes and thereby encouraging the railroad managements to maintain their arbitrary attitude. Promptly on the hour of 10.00 a. m., July 1, the members of all shop trade organizations suspended work.

The response was fully 96 per cent and also included large numbers of unorganized men together with a large per cent of general foremen and subordinate foremen, whom the railroads had succeeded in placing in a preferred class and were exempted in the wage cut, undoubtedly, with the expectation that they would remain on the job. The almost unanimous response involving such a large number of men, far exceeded the expectations of the chief executives of the organizations. In many instances the vote was more than sustained, not one man remaining on the job. While the vote of the firemen and oilers had not been completed in time to take action on July 1, the great majority of these men walked out with the shop trades and were later followed by the others. A considerable number of members of the U. B. M. of W. E. also swelled the ranks of the strikers smarting under many grievances of long standing, although the strike of this organization was held in abeyance by their executive board after conference with certain members of the labor board. Under date of July 3, 1922, Chairman Hooper of the railroad labor board by majority vote of the board members succeeded in putting through a resolution, outlawing the striking shopmen and calling upon the railroads to form their own organization of the strike breakers employed, so that the board could function in the interests of these men. In order that President Harding might have the full facts of the controversy a lengthy telegram incorporating the railroad unions' bill of complaints was transmitted to the White House on July 12, 1922, by the railway employes' department. This resulted in the president calling together the representatives of both parties at issue. A series of conferences were held in the White House. Under date of July 31, 1922, President Harding submitted a proposition to the railroads and to the employes' representatives outlining terms under which the strike should be called off: First: That railway managers and workers are to agree to recognize validity of all decisions of the railroad labor board and to faithfully carry out such decisions as contemplated by law. Second: The carriers will withdraw all law suits growing out of the strike and labor board decisions, which have been involved in strike may be taken in exercise of recognized rights by either party to labor board for rehearing. Third: All employes now on strike to be returned to work and to their former positions with seniority and other rights unimpaired. The representatives of the carriers and the representatives of organizations, especially agree that there will be no discrimination by either party against employes who did or did not strike." The representatives of the employes accepted President Harding's proposition, advising him that under the pressure of the responsibility the organization representatives had voted by requisite constitutional majority to accept the terms of agreement submitted, and that the terms of settlement as proposed would be carried out in good faith. If the proposals failed to bring about the desired results, they set forth, the responsibility of failure would not rest upon the representatives of the organized employes. The railway executives balked on the question of granting seniority rights to the strikers, using as an argument their pledge to the strike breakers and to the men who remained at work. In accepting the first proposed plan submitted by President Harding, the union representatives were assured that the power of the

government would be utilized to enforce its acceptance by the railroads, the unions were therefore the more surprised when a second proposal was offered in line with the recommendations of the railroad managers, providing on the settlement of the main question, that of seniority, to be decided by the U. S. labor board. President Harding was promptly notified that a settlement could not be entertained on any such terms as surrendering the right of seniority for the striking employes. The strike had run its course but a short time when the railroad managements proceeded through the courts to serve restraining orders of the most far-reaching nature against any and all of the employes involved in the strike, the primary object and use to which these injunctions were applied, together with the enrollment of thousands of guards and thugs, was to intimidate the strikers and create disturbances to discredit the striker in the eyes of the public, to break the spirit of the men and involve them in costly legal entanglements thereby depriving the needy members of financial assistance. Hundreds of the strikers were arrested on the pretext of violation of injunctions for no more serious offense than applying the term "scab" to the strike breakers who flocked into the shops. Following the conferences in the White House and the refusal of the railroad managers to accept the president's first proposal to settle the strike, using the words as expressed by President Harding that the striking shopmen had kept the faith, but the railroads had double-crossed him after having assured him the terms would be acceptable, the unions little anticipated that the willingness of the organizations to accept these terms in good faith and in the interest of the public welfare, would be rewarded by the full power and influence of the government being used to crush their ranks. It is unnecessary to recite in detail the incidents in connection with Attorney General Daugherty's secret trip to Chicago and his appearance before Federal Judge Wilkerson seeking an injunction against the railway employes' department of the A. F. of L. and others. The "turn about face" on the part of the administration in our opinion was brought about by the flood of propaganda from the railroad executives, big business interests and chambers of commerce throughout the country protesting against any consideration being given the strikers, the underlying thought being, as stated by Attorney General Daugherty in his presentation to the court—"that the administration would not permit labor unions to destroy the open shop." The shopmen were charged with having engaged in an unlawful conspiracy and in addition to being blamed with an impending fuel and food shortage, were charged with creating a reign of terror by the use of bombs, dynamiting bridges, placing obstructions on tracks and impeding and hindering the transporation of passengers and freight. The injunction was the most sweeping and drastic ever issued extending over the entire U. S. and permitting the use of the federal troops in the enforcement thereof. We are advised that immediately following the reading of the complaint and without hesitation on the part of Judge Wilkerson, even though none of the defendants were in evidence, nor had the organizations been advised of the contemplated action, the judge announced that the restraining order would be issued at once. The reply of the organizations to this high-handed action is set forth in the following press statement, issued by the railroad shop trades September 2, 1922: "Enforcement of the injunction obtained by the attorney general against lawlessness and violence in connection with the shop crafts' strike will be aided by every power of the shop crafts' organizations. The officials of these organizations have done everything possible since the beginning of the strike to maintain a peaceful suspension of work. Considering the difficulty of preserving perfect order in any group of four hundred thousand men engaged in a struggle for a decent livelihood, it must be admitted that the strike has been a remarkable demonstration of the law-abiding character of the workers involved. It is unfortunate that in a suit for the announced purpose of preventing lawlessness the attorney general's office has prepared and a court on hasty consideration has entered an order which, unless carefully interpreted might be read as a flagrant violation of constitutional rights of American citizens as repeatedly affirmed by the supreme court of the U. S. Apparently either haste of failure to use the English language with precision has led to the drafting of an order which read too literally would deny the right of free speech or communication of any sort or just payment of debts or mutual aid in lawful association, to men engaged in the peaceful legal conduct of their business. It can hardly be assumed that the federal court has intended to restrain, or has restrained, those lawful acts necessarily involved in carrying on the legitimate work of labor organizations, some or all of whose members are engaged in a legally conducted strike to accomplish lawful purposes. Such acts, including peaceful picketing, as have been repeatedly and recently held to be lawful by the supreme court of the U. S. can not be assumed to come within the provisions of the restraining order entered by Judge Wilkerson. If a strike of railway employes and its peaceful conduct were unlawful proceeding it can not be assumed that the attorney general of the U. S. would have waited two months to proceed against the strikers or that the president of the U. S. would have held conferences with law breakers and proposed that the law breakers whom they represented should return to work under terms which they afterwards accepted and which the railway executives rejected. Therefore we assume that the right of the railway employes is acknowledged to continue a lawful strike in a lawful manner until a satisfactory settlement is made. At least until advised that the constitution of the U. S. and the decisions of the supreme court are no longer to be relied upon as the law of the land, the officials of the organizations of railway employes will continue to perform their legitimate duties to their members, to aid them in the lawful pursuit of their lawful purposes; and to do all in their power in conjunction with officers of the government to restrain and to punish every unlawful act of those who are rightfully involved, or who without right involved themselves, in the operation of the railroads." The general conference committee composed of the executive boards of divisions 1, 2, and 3, general chairmen of the Stationary Firemen and Oilers and the executive council of the railway employes' department met in Chicago, September 11, 12 and 13. A basis of settlement of the present controversy between the railways of the U. S. and their employes was carefully considered and, in accordance with the authority vested in the general conference committee by the laws of the railway employes' de-

partment and the strike vote of the membership, action was taken adopting this memorandum of agreement for the railroads as present parties thereto and directing that the memorandum of agreement be the settlement which the system federations, representing employes on railroads not as present parties thereto, shall secure prior to returning the men they represent to work. As a result of the "outlaw" resolution adopted by the U. S. labor board, the bona fide organizations are in most cases confronted with the company organizations aided and abetted by the railroad companies as a means of preventing the federated shop trades from securing the right of representation by majority vote. The antagonism of these men who entered as strike breakers is very pronounced and aided by the subordinate officials insisting in many instances that all men entering the service join the company organization. This situation will require considerable time and effort to overcome. After 13 months of strike during which time many of the members and their families endured all manner of hardship and suffering, there is a most remarkable spirit of determination to continue the fight until the railroads are forced to capitulate to reasonable terms of settlement. When considering the fact that the strike had been conducted throughout without strike benefits, because of the inability of any of the organizations to meet such expense involving such a large number of men, we feel safe in saying that such a demonstration of united spirit is unsurpassed in the history of the labor movement. The continued arbitrary attitude of the "die hard" railroad managements can well be traced to the lack of public interest permitting the railroads to lull them to sleep with false propaganda and the amazing and inexcusable laxity of the administration in permitting the railroads to openly violate the safety appliance and other laws. Just how long these conditions will be tolerated is a matter of conjecture. These railroads on which the strike continues, while employing many hundreds of additional men above their normal force, are still unable to secure one-half of the former output of work and in addition are in most cases having the bulk of repairs done at contract shops under heavy expense. The workers are keenly alert to the situation and realize that no good business institution can continue long under such conditions. Fortunately, owing to the increased business in other industries practically all of the strikers have secured employment either at their trade or other work, and many thousands have also entered the service of the railroads where settlements have been reached and are assured of reasonably steady employment for some time. During the early part of the strike, the Executive Council of the A. F. of L. called upon the president and secretary of the A. F. of L. and requested that an appeal be issued to the membership of the organizations affiliated with the A. F. of L. through the respective organizations. This request was complied with. Every cent of moneys contributed to the railway employes through the A. F. of L. as well as from other sources, was distributed to the membership through a special finance committee created by the railway employes' department. All remittances were made direct to responsible local officers elected by the men themselves, and it would be extremely encouraging to all those who contributed if it were possible to convey to them the thankful, appreciative outburst of feeling which has come to us direct from those whose sufferings have been in any manner relieved. (P. 273) The railway shopmen's unions are to be commended for the decision made by them to resist the constant encroachments made upon them, and the conditions of employment of their respective members. Arrayed against them were all the power and influence of wealth, of business, of political government. The wonderment is not that they fared so well but that they survived at all. As a direct outcome of this conflict there will develop among the railway shopmen's unions greater and stronger trade unions than ever before and that having demonstrated their power of resistance a more respectful hearing and more considerate treatment will hereafter be accorded to their representatives.

Railroad Training Act—(1920, p. 114) Senator Thomas, of Colorado, has been unusually active in developing ideas which he believes if enacted into law will hamper the normal activities of the trade union movement. He has been particularly persistent in hammering away at organized wage earners and their officials. He presented a bill making strikes a conspiracy in restraint of trade and also evolved a plan whereby a trained army of railroad men could be established to be used as strike breakers in times of strikes on the transportation systems. S. 3450, of which he is the author, provides for the organization and training of a railroad army reserve force to aid in the operation of the railroads in times of emergency and for other purposes. Among the "other purposes" it is evident that this army reserve force could be used to break strikes. It provides that the reserve force will constitute members of the military forces of the U. S. under the direction of the secretary of war. Men between the ages of 18 and 30 would be recruited as reservists from time to time, all of whom shall be citizens possessing at least complete grade or grammar school education. Preference would be given those of railroad experience, the term of enlistmet to be 10 years. Each reservist is to receive $1 a day, rations and living quarters. No reservist shall join any trade or labor union or brotherhood composed of railroad operatives or work on a railroad except at the call of the secretary of war. It is proposed that the colleges for teaching strike-breaking be conducted by the states, which will be compensated by the government. The object of the bill is to furnish strike breakers to private employers at government expense. (P. 361) Executive Council directed to continue opposition.

(1921, p. 117) S. 3450, presented in the last congress to aid unfair employers to establish autocracy in industry, was not considered by the committee on military affairs to which it was referred. The bill was for propaganda purposes alone, as it would be impossible to pass such an un-American measure.

Reclassification—(1919, pp. 132-313) Approved of the appointment of a commission by congress to investigate wages and working conditions of government employes because of the difficulty in securing and holding competent employes at wages paid. (P. 322) Directed the Executive Council to aid federal employes to procure the extension of the duties of the reclassification commission, which was appointed by act of congress to reclassify the federal civil service in the District of Columbia.

(1920, p. 114) The study of the wages and conditions of public employes reiterated the charge so often made that large numbers of them are greatly undepaid. Men and women were found working for wages fixed by law in the early part of the last century. The only change was the addition of the war bonus of, first, $120 a year and then $240 a year. The commission recommended increases, in salaries aggregating $33,000,000 per annum. About 100,000 persons are affected. The commission provided for equal pay for men and women and promotion by merit. The employes are divided into 1,700 classes. While most of them will receive an increase a few will have their wages reduced. By what method of reasoning anyone in this day and time of high cost of living could figure out why a person working for the government should receive a decrease in wages it is impossible to conceive. This is especially true where it is notoriously known that no government employe ever received sufficient wages. (P. 396) The A. F. of L. calls upon congress to reclassify immediately the civil service and adopt a wage scale commensurate with the work performed.

(1921, p. 111) The joint commission on reclassification reported a bill to congress providing for reclassification of the federal civil service. No headway was made in the 66th congress and it was reintroduced in the 67th. Two other bills also were introduced by opponents of true reclassification. No action was taken.

(1921, p. 380) Called upon congress to immediately reclassify the civil service and adopt a wage scale commensurate with the skill, training and responsibility involved in the work performed, with just relation to the increased cost of living and without discrimination on grounds of sex. (P. 414) Executive Council directed to cooperate with the legislative representatives of the postal employes' organizations in securing the early passage of legislation to correct inequalities in the postal reclassification act of June 5, 1920.

(1922, pp. 109-485) Aside from the mechanics in the navy yards and arsenals and employes in the postal service, who are covered by an existing satisfactory wage classification law, there is a demand on the part of the organized government employes for a systematic, definite method of fixing wage scales under which opportunities for favoritism or reprisal would be minimized. The reclassification legislation, now pending in the senate would accomplish this object.

(1923, p. 91) The classification act of 1923, passed by congress in the last hours of the session which ended March 4, represents the culmination of a legislative campaign on the part of the National Federation of Federal Employes which had lasted for more than five years, the A. F. of L. co-operating. The classification act is regarded as the most important piece of civil service legislation since the original civil service act. It writes into law principles and definitions designed to set up a genuine merit system of appointment, promotion and dismissal. Salary rates are revised on the basis of equal pay for equal work, irrespective of sex, and in accordance with the skill, training and responsibility of the job, instead of the inconsistent, unequal, hit-or-miss wage scale that has prevailed. For the District of Columbia new rates are provided in the bill, these to absorb the current "bonus," so-called, of $240 a year, and in most instances afford an increase besides more nearly proportionate to the cost of living and the scale in private industry.

The new salary schedules, the law provides, shall become operative July 1, 1924. Before that date a complete survey of the field services shall have been made, and all employes allocated to their appropriate grade in time for approval by congress at its next session. A central classifying agency is created, to coordinate salary scales and establish or revise the efficiency ratings upon which salaries depend.

Reconstruction of Industry—(1921, pp. 128-311) "It requires bold and audacious reconstruction of method and process in the conduct of basic industries." Something of the true import and value of this sentence will be found in a vision of industry so arranged and coordinated that the periods of spasmodic, hectic employment and of deadening, destructive idleness, which now alternate in the great basic industries, and which radiate from them throughout all the ramifications of our industrial life, can be superceded by a rational system which will secure to the whole body of workers the full opportunity for productive employment under conditions that make for security and comfort, and thus contribute to the progress and solid worthy advancement of humanity at large. Those who are familiar with employment in seasonable industries need no explanation, and the student will very easily grasp the truth contained in this and quickly realize the tremendous meaning of the language of the declaration quoted.

Reconstruction Program—(1919, p. 70) The St. Paul convention instructed the Executive Council to appoint a committee on reconstruction, this committee to thoroughly investigate the problem of reconstruction and to take such steps as might be found possible to safeguard the interest of the soldiers and sailors and workers during the period of reconstruction. The report of this committee was rendered to the Executive Council at its meeting in New York on December 28, 1918, and was there endorsed by the Executive Council. We desire to say that the reconstruction program drafted by this special committee is not only the most complete and most constructive proposal yet made in this country for the reconstruction period, but constitutes practically the only program in existence having to do with the period of rebuilding the national life on a peace basis. The measures proposed in the report are measures which the nation can ill afford to ignore. They are measures also for the realization of which organized labor throughout the country should exert every possible influence. The proposals are fundamentally the proposals of democracy designed to make for a richer and freer human life. We call not only upon the organized workers, but upon the whole people of America to bring into a state of active operation the splendid humanitarian and democratic reconstruction program. (P. 373) The dislocations in our social, industrial and political relations by reason of the necessities of war have been as varied in nature as they have been grave in character. One of the most pronounced and most far-reaching results is the realization of the workers rights, duties and responsibilities in the structure of society, industry, and of government. Conscious as never heretofore of its power, labor will no longer rest content under a system which treats the workers as a commodity or an article of commerce. The workers have reached that status and have come to that determination which demands treatment of equality with all other men and women in

modern society. They now insist on the full observance of their rights of free men to the opportunity of a full value and a full compensation for services rendered on a basis that will enable all to enjoy the higher things in life rather than merely exist near the line beyond which we find human misery and which spells human bankruptcy. The great value of the report of the special committe on reconstruction, which has received the unanimous approval of the Executive Council, lies in its compilation in consecutive order of the fundamental, the most important and most urgent subjects and relations to which organized labor must apply itself diligently and unswervingly if the workers are to make permanent progress and gain in the struggle between democracy and autocracy in our industrial life. We approve of this program, not because we believe it all comprehensive, but fundamental; not because of its idealism, but because of its practicability; not because of its novelty, but because it is founded on experience and justice. We believe the program highly constructive in character and excellently designed to benefit not only a part of society, but to bring to all the people greater hope for a better day, a brighter life, greater liberty, and a larger degree of prosperity and happiness.

Reconstruction Program, A. F. of L.— (1919, pp. 70-373) The world war has forced all free peoples to a fuller and deeper realization of the menace to civilization contained in autocratic control of the activities and destinies of mankind. It has caused a worldwide determination to overthrow and eradicate all autocratic institutions, so that a full measure of freedom and justice can be established between man and man and nation and nation. It has awakened more fully the consciousness that the principles of democracy should regulate the relationship of men in all their activities. It has opened the doors of opportunity through which more sound and progressive policies may enter. New conceptions of human liberty, justice and opportunity are to be applied. The A. F. of L., the one organization representing labor in America, conscious that its responsibilities are now greater than before, presents a program for the guidance of labor, based upon experience and formulated with a full consciousness of the principles and policies which have successfully guided American trade unionism in the past.

Democracy in Industry.—Two codes of rules and regulations affect the workers; the law upon the statute books, and the rules within industry. The first determines their relationship as citizens to all other citizens and to property. The second largely determines the relationship of employer and employe, the terms of employment, the conditions of labor, and the rules and regulations affecting the workers as employes. The first is secured through the application of the methods of democracy in the enactment of legislation, and is based upon the principle that the laws which govern a free people should exist only with their consent. The second, except where effective trade unionism exists, is established by the arbitrary or autocratic whim, desire or opinion of the employer and is based upon the principle that industry and commerce can not be successfully conducted unless the employer exercises the unquestioned right to establish such rules, regulations and provisions affecting the employes as self-interest prompts. Both forms of law vitally affect the workers' opportunities in life and determine their standard of living. The rules, regulations and conditions within industry in many instandes affect them more than legislative enactments. It is, therefore, essential that the workers should have a voice in determining the laws within industry and commerce which affect them, equivalent to the voice which they have as citizens in determining the legislative enactments which shall govern them. It is as inconceivable that the workers as free citizens should remain under autocratically made law within industry and commerce as it is that the nation could remain a democracy while certain individuals or groups exercise autocratic powers. It is, therefore, essential that the workers everywhere should insist upon their right to organize into trade unions, and that effective legislation should be enacted which would make it a criminal offense for any employer to interfere with or hamper the exercise of this right or to interfere with the legitimate activities of trade unions.

Unemployment.—Political economy of the old school, conceived by doctrinaires, was based upon unsound and false doctrines, and has since been used to blindfold, deceive and defeat the workers' demands for adequate wages, better living and working conditions, and a just share of the fruits of their labor. We hold strictly to the trade union philosophy and its developed political economy based upon demonstrated facts. Unemployment is due to underconsumption. Underconsumption is caused by low or insufficient wages. Just wages will prevent industrial stagnation and lessen periodical unemployment. Give the workers just wages and their consuming capacity is correspondingly increased. A man's ability to consume is controlled by the wages received. Just wages will create a market at home which will far surpass any market that may exist elsewhere and will lessen unemployment. The employment of idle workmen on public work will not permanently remove the cause of unemployment. It is an expedient at best. There is no basis in fact for the claim that the so-called law of supply and demand is natural in its operations and impossible of control or regulation. The trade union movement has maintained standards, wages, hours and life in periods of industrial depression and idleness. These in themselves are a refutation of the declared immutability of the law of supply and demand. There is in fact no such condition as an iron law of wages based upon a natural law of supply and demand. Conditions in commerce and industry, methods of production, storing of commodities, regulation of the volume of production, banking systems, the flow and direction of enterprise influenced by combinations and trusts have effectively destroyed the theory of a natural law of supply and demand as had been formulated by doctrinaire economists.

Wages.—There are no means whereby the workers can obtain and maintain fair wages except through trade union effort. Therefore, organization is paramount to all their other activities. Organization of the workers leads to better wages, fewer working hours, improved working conditions; it develops independence, manhood and character; it fosters tolerance and real justice and makes for a constantly growing better economic, social and political life for the burden-bearing masses. In countries where wages are best, the greatest progress has been made in economic, social and political advancement, in science, art, literature, education and in

the wealth of the people generally. Although wage paying countries contrasted with America is proof for this statement. The American standard of life must be maintained and improved. The value of wages is determined by the purchasing power of the dollar. There is no such thing as good wages when the cost of living in decency and comfort equals or exceeds the wages received. There must be no reduction in wages; in many instances wages must be increased. The workers of the nation demand a living wage for all wage earners, skilled or unskilled—a wage which will enable the worker and his family to live in health and comfort, provide a competence for illness and old age, and afford to all the opportunity of cultivating the best that is within mankind.

Hours of Labor.—Reasonable hours of labor promote the economic and social well being of the toiling masses. Their attainment should be one of labor's principle and essential activities. The shorter workday and a shorter work week make for a constantly growing, higher and better standard of productivity, health, longevity, morals and citizenship. The right of labor to fix its hours of work must not be abrogated, abridged or interfered with. The day's working time should be limited to not more than eight hours, with overtime prohibited, except under the most extraordinary emergencies. The week's working time should be limited to not more than five and one-half days.

Women as Wage Earners.—Women should receive the same pay as men for equal work performed. Women workers must not be permitted to perform tasks disproportionate to their physical strength or which tend to impair their potential motherhood and prevent the continuation of a nation of strong, healthy, sturdy and intelligent men and women.

Child Labor.—The children constitute the nation's most valuable asset. The full responsibility of the government should be recognized by such measures as will protect the health of every child at birth and during its immature years. It must be one of the chief functions of the nation through effective legislation to put an immediate end to the exploitation of children under 16 years of age. State legislatures should protect children of immature years by prohibiting their employment, for gain, under 16 years of age and restricting the employment of children of less than 18 years of age to not more than 20 hours within any one week and with not less than 20 hours at school during the same period. Exploitation of child life for private gain must not be permitted.

Status of Public Employes.—The fixing of wages, hours and conditions of labor for public employes by legislation hampers the necessary exercise of organization and collective bargaining. Public employes must not be denied the right of organization, free activities and collective bargaining and must not be limited in the exercise of their rights as citizens.

Cooperation.—To attain the greatest possible development of civilization, it is essential, among other things, that the people should never delegate to others those activities and responsibilities which they are capable of assuming for themselves. Democracy can function best with the least interference by the state compatible with due protection to the rights of all citizens. There are many problems arising from production, transportation and distribution, which would be readilly solved by applying the methods of cooperation. Unnecessary middlemen who exact a tax from the community without rendering any useful service can be eliminated. The farmers, through cooperative dairies, canneries, packing houses, grain elevators, distributing houses, and other cooperative enterprises, can secure higher prices for their products and yet place these in the consumer's hands at lower prices than would otherwise be paid. There is an almost limitless field for the consumers in which to establish cooperative buying and selling, and in this most necessary development, the trade unionist should take an immediate and active part. Trade unions secure fair wages. Cooperation protects the wage earner from the profiteer. Participation in these cooperative agencies must of necessity prepare the mass of the people to participate more effectively in the solution of the industrial, commercial, social and political problems which continually arise.

The People's Final Voice in Legislation.— It is manifestly evident that a people are not self-governing unless they enjoy the unquestioned power to determine the form and substance of the laws which shall govern them. Self-government can not adequately function if there exists within the nation a superior power or authority which can finally determine what legislation enacted by the people, or their duly elected representatives, shall be placed upon the statute books and what shall be declared null and void. An insuperable obstacle of self-government in the U. S. exists in the power which has been gradually assumed by the supreme courts of the federal and state governments to declare legislation null and void upon the ground that, in the court's opinion, it is unconstitutional. It is essential that the people, acting directly or through congress or state legislatures, should have final authority in determining which laws shall be enacted. Adequate steps must be taken, therefore, which will provide that in the event of a supreme court declaring an act of congress or of a state legislature unconstitutional and the people acting directly or through congress or a state legislature should re-enact the measure, it shall then become the law without being subject to annulment by any court.

Political Policy.—In the political efforts, arising from the workers' necessity to secure legislation covering those conditions and provisions of life not subject to collective bargaining with employers, organized labor has followed two methods; one by organizing political parties, the other by the determination to place in public office representatives from their ranks; to elect those who favor and champion the legislation desired and to defeat those whose policy is opposed to labor's legislative demands, regardless of partisan politics. The disastrous experience of organized labor in America with political parties of its own, amply justified the A. F. of L.'s non-partisan political policy. The results secured by labor parties in other countries never have been such as to warrant any deviation from this position. The rules and regulations of trade unionism should not be extended so that the action of a majority could force a minority to vote for or give financial support to any political candidate or party to whom they are opposed. Trade union activities can not receive the undivided attention of members and officers if the exigencies, burdens and responsibilities of a political party are bound up with their economic and industrial organizations. The experiences and results attained through the non-partisan political policy of the A. F. of L.

cover a generation. They indicate that through its application the workers of America have secured a much larger measure of fundamental legislation, establishing their rights safeguarding their interests, protecting their welfare and opening the doors of opportunity than have been secured by the workers of any other country. The vital legislation now required can be more readily secured through education of the public mind and the appeal to its conscience, supplemented by energetic independent political activity on the part of trade unionists, than by any other method. This is and will continue to be the political policy of the A. F. of L. if the lessons which labor has learned in the bitter but practical school of experience are to be respected and applied. It is, therefore, most essential that the officers of the A. F. of L., the officers of the affiliated organizations, state federations and central labor bodies and the entire membership of the trade union movement should give the most vigorous application possible to the political policy of the A. F. of L. so that labor's friends and opponents may be more widely known, and the legislation most required readily secured. This phase of our movement is still in its infancy. It should be continued and developed to its logical conclusion.

Government Ownership.—Public and semi-public utilities should be owned, operated or regulated by the government in the interest of the public. Whatever final disposition shall be made of the railways of the country in ownership, management or regulation, we insist upon the right of the workers to organize for their common and mutual protection and the full exercise of the normal activities which come with organization. Any attempt at the denial by governmental authority of the rights of the workers to organize, to petition, to representation and to collective bargaining, or the denial of the exercise of their political rights is repugnant to the fundamental principles of free citizenship in a republic and is destructive of their best interest and welfare. The government should own and operate all wharves and docks connected with public harbors which are used for commerce or transportation. The American merchant marine should be encouraged and developed under governmental control and so manned as to insure successful operation and protect in full the beneficent laws now on the statute books for the rights and welfare of seamen. The seamen must be accorded the same rights and privileges rightfully exercised by the workers in all other employments, public and private.

Waterways and Water Power.—The lack of a practical development of our waterways and the inadequate extension of canals have seriously handicapped water traffic and created unnecessarily high cost of transportation. In many instances it has established artificial restrictions which have worked to the serious injury of communities, owing to the schemes of those controlling a monopoly of land transportation. Our navigable rivers and our great inland lakes should be connected with the sea by an adequate system of canals, so that inland production can be more effectively fostered, the costs of transportation reduced, the private monopoly of transportation overcome and imports and exports shipped at lower costs. The nation is possessed of enormous water power. Legislation should be enacted providing that the governments, federal and state, should own, develop and operate all water power over which they have jurisdiction. The power thus generated should be supplied to all citizens at rates based upon cost. The water power of the nation, created by nature, must not be permitted to pass into private hands for private exploitation.

Regulation of Land Ownership.—Agriculture and stock-raising are essential to national safety and well-being. The history of all countries, at all times, indicates that the conditions which create a tenant class of agriculturists work increasing injury to the tillers of the soil. While increasing the price of the product to the consumer these conditions at the same time develop a class of large land owners who contribute little, if anything, to the welfare of the community but who exact a continually increasng share of the wealth produced by the tenant. The private ownership of large tracts of usable land is not conducive to the best interests of a democratic people. Legislation should be enacted placing a graduated tax upon all usable lands above the acreage which is cultivated by the owner. This should include provisions through which the tenant farmer, or others, may purchase land upon the lowest rate of interest and most favorable terms consistent with safety, and so safeguarded by governmental supervision and regulation as to give the fullest and freest opportunity for the development of land-owning agriculturists. Special assistance should be given in the direction of allotments of lands and the establishment of homes on the public domain. Establishment of government experimental farms, measures for stock-raising instruction, the irrigation of arid lands and reclamation of swamp and cut-over lands should be undertaken upon a larger scale under direction of the federal government. Municipali ies and states should be empowered to acquire lands for cultivation or the erection of residential buildings which they may use or dispose of under equitable terms.

Federal and State Regulation of Corporations.—The creation by legislative enactment of corporations, without sufficient definition of the powers and scope of activities conferred upon them and without provisions for their adequate supervision, regulation and control by the creative body, has led to the development of far-reaching abuses which have seriously affected commerce, industry and the masses of the people through their influence upon social, industrial, commercial and political development. Legislation is required which will so limit, define and regulate the powers, privileges and activities of corporations that their methods can not become detrimental to the welfare of the people. It is, therefore, essential that legislation should provide for the federal licensing of all corporations organized for profit. Furthermore, federal supervision and control should include the increasing of capital stock and the incurring of bonded indebtedness with the provision that the books of all corporations shall be open at all times to federal examiners.

Freedom of Expression and Association.—The verv life and perpetuity of free and democratic institutions are dependent upon freedom of speech, of the press and of assemblage and association. We insist that all restrictions of freedom of speech, press, public assembly, association and travel be completely removed, individuals and groups being responsible for their utterances. These fundamental rights must be set out with clearness and must not be denied or abridged in any manner.

Workmen's Compensation. — Workmen's compensation laws should be amended to provide more adequately for those incapacitated by industrial accidents or occupational diseases. To assure that the insurance fund derived from commerce and industry will be paid in full to injured workers, state insurance must supplant, and prohibit the existence of employers' liability insurance operated for profit.

Immigration.—Americanization of those coming from foreign lands as well as our standards of education and living, are vitally affected by the volume and character of the immigration. It is essential that additional legislation regulating immigration should be enacted based upon two fundamental propositions, namely, that the flow of immigration must not at any time exceed the nation's ability to a similate and Americanize the foreighers coming to our shores, and that at no time shall immigration be permitted when there exists an abnormal degree of unemplovment. By reason of existing conditions we urge that immigration into the United States should be prohibited for a period of at least two years after peace has been declared.

Taxation.—One of the nation's most valuable assets is the initiative, energetic, constructive, and inventive genius of its people. These qualities when properly applied should be fostered and protected instead of being hampered by legislation, for they constitute an invaluable element of progress and material development. Taxation should, therefore, rest as lightly as possible upon constructive enterprise. Taxation should provide for full contribution from wealth by a tax upon profits which will not discourage industrial or commercial enterprise. There should be provided a progressive increase in taxes upon incomes, inheritances, and upon land values of such a nature as to render it unprofitable to hold land without putting it to use, to afford a transition to greater economic quality and to supply means of liquidating the national indebtedness growing out of the war.

Education.—It is impossible to estimate the influence of educat on upon the world's civilizaticn. Education must not stifle thought and inquiry, but must awaken the mind concerning the application of natural laws and to a conception of independence and progress. Education must not be for a few but for all our people. While there is an advanced form of public education in many states, there still remains a lack of adequate educational facilities in several states and communities. The welfare of the republic demands that public education should be elevated to the highest degree possible. The government should exercise advisory supervision over public education and where necessary maintain adequate public education through subsidies without giving to the government power to hamper or interfere with the free development of public education by the several states. It is essential that our system of public education should offer the wage earners' children the opportunity for the fullest possible development. To attain this end state colleges and universities should be developed. It is also important that the industrial education which is being fostered and developed should have for its purpose not so much training for efficiency in industry as training for life in an industrial society. A full understanding must be had of those principles and activities that are the foundation of all productive efforts. Children should not only become familiar with tools and materials, but they should also receive a thorough knowledge of the principles of human control, of force and matter underlying our industrial relations and sciences. The danger that certain commercial and industrial interests may dominate the character of education must be averted by insisting that the workers shall have equal representation on all boards of education or committees having control over vocational studies and training. To elevate and advance the interests of the teaching profession and to promote popular and democratic education, the right of the teachers to organize and to affiliate with the movement of the organized workers must be recognized.

Private Employment Agencies.—Essentials in industry and commerce are employe and employer, labor and capital. No one questions the right of organized capital to supply capital to employers. No one should question the right of organized labor to furnish workers. Private employment agencies abridge this right of organized labor. Where federal, state and municipal employment agencies are maintained they should operate under the supervision of joint committees of trade unionists and employers, equally represented. Private employment agencies operated for profit should not be permitted to exist.

Housing.—Child life, the workers' physical condition and public health demand that the wage earner and his family shall be given a full opportunity to live under wholesome conditions. It is not only necessary that there shall be sanitary and appropriate houses to live in, but that a sufficient number of dwellings shall be available to free the people from high rents and overcrowding. The ownership of homes, free from the grasp of exploitative and speculative interests, will make for more efficient workers, more contented families, and better citizens. The government should, therefore, inaugurate a plan to build model homes and establish a system of credits whereby the workers may borrow money at a low rate of interest and under favorable terms to build their own homes. Credit should also be extended to voluntary nonprofit making housing and joint tenancy associations. States and municipalities should be freed from the restrictions preventing their undertaking proper housing projects and should be permitted to engage in other necessary enterprises relating thereto. The erection and maintenance of dwellings where migratory workers may find lodging and nourishing food during periods of unemployment should be encouraged and supported by municipalities. If need should arise to expend public funds to relieve unemployment the building of wholesome houses would best serve the public interests.

Militarism.—The trade union movement is unalterably and emphatically opposed to "militarism" or a large standing army. "Militarism" is a system fostered and developed by tyrants in the hope of supporting their arbitrary authority. It is utilized by those whose selfish ambitions for power and worldly glory lead them to invade and subdue other peoples and nations, to destroy their liberties, to acquire their wealth and to fasten the yoke of bondage upon them. The trade union movement is convinced by the experience of mankind that "militarism" brutalizes those influenced by the spirit of the institution. The finer elements of humanity are strangled. Under "militarism" a deceptive patriotism is established in the people's minds, where men believe that there is nobility of spirit and heroism in dying for the glory of a dynasty or the maintenance of institutions which are inimical to human progress and democracy. "Militarism" is the application of arbitrary and irresponsible forces as opposed to reason and justice. Resistance to injustice and tyranny is that virile quality which has given purpose and effect to ennobling causes in all countries and at all times. The free institutions of our country and the liberties won by its founders would have been impossible had they been unwilling to take arms and if necessary die in the defense of their liberties. Only a people willing to maintain their rights and defend their liberties are guaranteed free institutions. Conditions foreign to the institutions of our country have prevented the entire abolition of organized bodies of men trained to carry arms. A voluntary citizen soldiery supplies what would otherwise take its place, a large standing army. To the latter we are unalterably opposed as tending to establish the evils of "militarism." Large standing armies threaten the existence of civil liberty. The history of every nation demonstrates that as standing armies are enlarged the rule of democracy is lessened or extinguished. Our experience has been that even this citizen soldiery, the militia of our states, has given cause at times for grave apprehension. Their ranks have not always been free from undesirable elements, particularly the tools of corporations involved in industrial disputes. During industrial disputes the militia has at times been called upon to support the authority of those who through selfish interests desired to enforce martial law while the courts were open and the civil authorities competent to maintain supremacy of civil law. We insist that the militia of our several states should be wholly organized and controlled by democratic principles so that this voluntary force of soldiery may never be diverted from its true purpose and used to jeopardize or infringe upon the rights and liberties of our people. The right to bear arms is a fundamental principle of our government, a principle accepted at all times by free people as essential to the maintenance of their liberties and institutions. We demand that this right shall remain inviolate.

Soldiers and Sailors.—Soldiers and sailors, those who entered the service in the nation's defense, are entitled to the generous reward of a grateful republic. The necessities of war called upon millions of workmen to leave their positions in industry and commerce to defend, upon the battlefields, the nation's safety and its free institutions. These defenders are now returning. It is advisable that they should be discharged from military service at the earliest possible moment; that as civilians they may return to their respective homes and families and take up their peacetime pursuits. The nation stands morally obligated to assist them in securing employment. Industry has undergone great changes due to the dislocation caused by war production and transportation. Further readjustments in industry and commerce must follow the rehabilitation of business under peaceful conditions. Many positions which our citizen soldiers and sailors filled previous to enlistment do not exist today. It would be manifestly unjust for the government after having removed the worker from his position in industry and placed him in military service to discharge him from the army or navy without having made adequate provision to assist him in procuring employment and providing sustenance until employment has been secured. The returned citizen soldier or sailor should not be forced by the bitter urgent necessity of securing food and clothing to place himself at a disadvantage when seeking employment. Upon their discharge, transportation and meals should be supplied to their places of residence. The monthly salary previously paid should be continued for a period not to exceed twelve months if employment is not secured within that period. The federal and state employment bureaus should be directed to cooperate with trade union agencies in securing employment for discharged soldiers and sailors. In assisting the discharged soldier and sailor to secure employment, government agencies should not expect them to accept employment for less than the prevailing rate of wages being paid in the industry. Neither should any government agency request or require such discharged men to accept employment where a trade dispute exists or is threatened. Nor should the refusal on the part of any of these discharged soldiers or sailors to accept employment where trade disputes exist or are threatened or when less than the prevailing wage rate is offered, deprive them of a continuance of their monthly pay. Legislation also should be enacted which will give the nation's defenders the opportunity for easy and ready access to the land. Favorable inducements should be provided for them to enter agriculture and husbandry. The government should assume the responsibility for the allotment of such lands, and supply the necessary capital for its development and cultivation, with such safeguards as will protect both the government and the discharged soldier and sailor.

Conclusion.—No element in our nation is more vitally concerned with the problems of making for a permanent peace between all nations than the working people. The opportunities now before us are without precedent. It is of paramount importance that labor shall be free and unhampered in shaping the principles and agencies affecting the wage earners' condition of life and work. By the light that has been given to it the A. F. of L. has attracted to its fold over three millions of wage earners and its sphere of influence and helpfulness is growing by leaps and bounds. By having followed safe and sound fundamental principles and policies, founded on freedom, justice and democracy, the American trade union movement has achieved successes of an inestimable value to the masses of toilers of our country. By adhering to these principles and policies we can meet all problems of readjustment, however grave in importance and difficult of solution, with a feeling of assurance that our efforts will be rewarded by a still greater success than that achieved in the past. Given the whole-hearted support of all men and women of labor our organized labor movement with its copstructive program, its love for freedom, justice and democracy will prove the most potent factor in protecting, safeguarding and promoting the general welfare of the great mass of our people during this trying period of resonstruction and all times thereafter. The A. F. of L. has attained its present position of dignity and splendid influence because of its adherence to one common cause and purpose; that purpose is to protect the rights and interests of the masses of the workers and to secure for them a better and a brighter day. Let us therefore strive on and on to bring into our organizations the yet unorganized. Let us concentrate our efforts to organize all the forces of wage earners. Let the nation hear the united demand from the laboring voice. Now is the time for the workers of America to come to the stand of their unions and to organize as

thoroughly and completely and compactly as is possible. Let each worker bear in mind the words of Longfellow·

"In the world's broad field of battle,
 In the bivouac of life,
 Be not like dumb, driven cattle!
 Be a hero in the strife!"

Red Cross—(1923, p. 309) The A. F. of L., acknowledging the effective work accomplished by the American Red Cross in all its various services, commends the unselfish activities of this national organization as deserving of unselfish support, and bespeaks for it full and hearty cooperation in its purpose to extend to the remotest community its healing ministrations to humanity.

Referendum and Recall for A. F. of L.—(1919, p. 432) Proposals to amend the constitution to provide for the election and recall of officers of the A. F. of L. were defeated, the convention declaring: "In view of the fact that this entire subject matter was dealt with at the convention of the A. F. of L. held in Rochester, N. Y., in 1912, and that a thorough investigation was made at that time by the Executive Council and submitted to the convention, and that it was decided at that convention that the election of officers of the A. F. of L. by referendum was impracticable, that action is hereby reaffirmed." (P. 436) The system of voting in the conventions of the A. F. of L. is satisfactory and any change at this time would not be to the best interests of the organizations affiliated. (1921, p. 330) Reaffirmed.

Rehabilitation of Civilians—(1919, p. 113) A bill to promote the rehabilitation of persons injured in industry or commerce was introduced in the 66th congress. (P. 327) Executive Council directed to continue its efforts to have the bill enacted into law.

(1920, pp. 113-360; 1921, p. 117) Public 236, providing for the promotion of vocational rehabilitation of persons disabled in industry or in any legitimate occupation and their return to civil employment, was approved June 2, 1920. It provides for an appropriation of $750,000 for the fiscal year ending June 30, 1921, and $1,000,000 annually for a period of two years after June 30, 1922. These sums are allotted to the states in the proportion which their population bears to the total population of the U. S., according to the last preceding U. S. census. The federal board for vocational education is cooperating with the various state boards for vocational education in carrying out the provisions of the act.

(1921, p. 318) The A. F. of L. urges upon the state federations of labor the necessity of calling to the attention of their legislatures the advantages of the industrial rehabilitation act and that the state federations of labor request their legislatures to accept the federal act for industrial rehabilitation. We commend the work of industrial rehabilitation now carried on by those states that have accepted the industrial rehabilitation act.

Relief for Suffering Peoples—(1921, pp. 149-374) During the year the A. F. of L., its affiliated bodies and its individual members have continued to assist in the relief of the suffering peoples throughout the world. They have contributed their time, effort and money to relieve and assuage their distress. The president of the A. F. of L. on December 9, 1920, was appointed by President Wilson to be a member of the famine relief committee for China. He has also served as a member of the near east relief committee, the committe for relief of the distressed people of Ireland, American central committee for Russian relief, and the committee for the reconstruction of the devastated areas of France. These committees have been instrumental in saving the lives of thousands of starving people in the near and far east. In contributing to these relief funds, the trade union movement has given generously and will continue to do so while the suffering continues. The action of our president in serving on relief committees and in assisting, so far as possible, in securing funds for relief, has the hearty approval of the convention.

Rents, Excessive—(1919, p. 346) Executive Council directed to take such action as may be necessary to protest against the policy of the emergency fleet corporation charging excessive rents for the property built by them with public money.

Research, Scientific—(1919, p. 319) The productivity of industry is greatly increased by the technical application of the results of scientific research in physics, chemistry, biology, and geology, in engineering and agriculture, and in the related sciences; and the health and well-being not only of the workers but of the whole population as well are dependent upon advances in medicine and sanitation; so that the value of scientific advancement to the welfare of the nation is many times greater than the cost of the necessary research. The war has brought home to all the nations engaged in it the overwhelming importance of science and technology to national welfare, whether in war or in peace, and not only is private initiative attempting to organize far-reaching research in these fields on a national scale, but in several countries governmental participation and support of such undertakings are already active. The A. F. of L. therefore urges that a broad program of scientific and technical research is of major importance to the national welfare and should be fostered in every way by the federal government, and that the activities of the government itself in such research should be adequately and generously supported in order that the work may be greatly strengthened and extended.

Resolutions Expunged—(1919, p. 389) In all cases where resolutions have been withdrawn at the request of the introducers, the introduction of the resolutions, the requests for their withdrawal, the reports of the committees, and all reference to these resolutions shall be expunged from the record.

Retirement Act—(1919, pp. 119-327, 352) An earnest and persistent effort to secure the passage of a retirement system for federal employes was made in the three sessions of the 65th congress, but without success.

(1920, pp. 120-362) The retirement bill became a law. The retirement age was fixed at 70 years, but optional retirement was fixed at 62 for railroad mail clerks and 65 for others. For the first 10 years of its operation all clerks are allowed to continue at work if their immediate chief certifies that they are capable of performing their duties in a satisfactory way, but after the 10 years, retirement is immediate upon reaching the age provided for.

(1921, p. 114) The civil service retirement act, despite some obvious defects and maladministration in certain departments, has been of great benefit to thousands of aged government employes who might otherwise have been forced out of employment without the protection of a service annuity. The act provides for the appointment of a board of actuaries to report to congress when the law has been in operation one year. This report

will not be forthcoming for several months. It is unlikely that congress will change the law in any important respect until this report is available. The organized government employes are desirous that the annuities be made more liberal and that the scope of the act be extended to include unclassified civil service workers. There are a number of other features of the present law shown to be inadequate by actual operation and appropriate legislation will be sought when congress begins consideration of the recommendations anticipated from the board of actuaries. (P. 382) Executive Council directed to aid the organizations of government employes to secure from congress the legislation desired to liberalize the retirement laws.

(1922, pp. 110-324) Companion bills were introduced in the senate and house to protect employes of the government who may be discharged after becoming 50 years of age and having served 15 years or more in the classified civil service. When let out such persons are to be given a certificate which will entitle them upon reaching the retirement age to an annuity as provided in the retirement act. This annuity is paid whether the discharged employe is working for the government or for a private employer.

(1923, pp. 87-358) The efforts of the organized and affiliated government employes are now centered upon three major improvements in the retirement law: First, that length of service, preferably 30 years, and not age shall be the retirement requisite; second, that the present inadequate annuities shall be increased; third, that the present 70-year age requirement be reduced to at least 65 years. As in the past the officers of the A. F. of L. have extended all possible assistance in the perfection of this humane law, which is so important to government employes.

Retirement, Joint Conferences on—(1923, p. 306) The A. F. of L. directs the Executive Council to notify all national and international organizations which either directly or through local action participate in the joint conference on retirement to purge such conference of any non-union or dual taint, and to reorganize it along bona fide trades union lines.

Russia—(1919, p. 333) This convention expresses its well-considered conviction that the U. S. government should withdraw all its troops from Russian soil at the earliest possible moment. This convention refuses its endorsement of the soviet government of Russia, or any other form of government in that country, until the people of Russia, through a constituent or other form of national assembly, representing all of the people, through popular elections shall have reestablished a truly democratic form of government.

(1920, p. 210) Bolshevism has been a lure for some of our people and its doctrines have been propagated with vigor. This hideous doctrine has found converts among two classes of people principally—those intellectuals, so-called, who have no occupation save that of following one fad after another, and those so beaten in the game of life that they find no appeal in anything except the most desperate and illogical schemes. The rank and file of the organized labor movement, as was to have been expected, has given no countenance to the propaganda of bolshevism, but has, on the contrary, been its most effective opponent in America. (P. 368) The A. F. of L. is not justified in taking any action which could be construed as an assistance to, or approval of, the soviet government of Russia as long as that government is based upon authority which has not been vested in it by a popular representative national assemblage of the Russian people; or so long as it endeavors to create revolutions in the well-established, civilized nations of the world; or so long as it advocates and applies the militarization of labor and prevents the organizing and functioning of trade unions and the maintenance of a free press and free public assemblage. (P. 372) In reply to a question by the president of the A. F. of L. the secretary of state said: "There is no licensed or regular trading between the United States and Russia at present. . . . The soviet government is insistent upon political recognition as a condition precedent to a renewal of any commercial contact."

(1921, pp. 90-442) The Executive Council's report sets forth facts of vital interest from authentic and authoritative sources. Nearly all statements of facts are quoted from the official papers of the soviet government and acknowledged utterances of its leaders. We commend this report to the careful reading and thought of all people who are interested in this all-absorbing question. Much is said in the report concerning trade agitation, labor in soviet Russia, the absolute lack of democracy and substitution of autocracies. We find there are 604,000 members of the communists party of Russia, and that of this number 89 per cent are government or town officials, officers and soldiers, communist party employes, while only 11 per cent are workmen. The communist party and the soviet government of Russia have denounced and repudiated the International Federation of Trade Unions and have attempted to establish the Communists' International, which is known and generally referred to as the Third Internationale Federation, and points out the activity of the representatives of the soviet government in our own American trade union movement, as well as in England, France, Italy and many other countries. We particularly note the concluding paragraph of the report on this subject: "It should be understood clearly that between the people of the U. S. and the great masses of the people of Russia there has been, is and will continue to be the most earnest and sincere friendship and that the people of the U. S. express no sentiment to the contrary except toward those in Russia who are destroying the opportunities of the Russian people for democratic self-government, but, who, on the contrary, are imposing upon the Russian people a brutal, defenseless tyranny. This friendship is the friendship of the working people and of all the people of our country for a great people whose character and aspirations have ever justified the confidence, respect and friendship of all liberty-loving people, and the earnest hope that the situation in Russia may so change that freedom, justice, democracy and humanitarianism may be the guiding principles of their everyday lives. For that time and opportunity American labor fervently anticipates that the true bond of international fraternity may be established between the toilers of Russia and those of America."

(1922, pp. 111-326) When a bill appropriating $20,000,000 to purchase corn and seed grain for the relief of the people of Russia was before the house committee on foreign affairs the president of the A. F. of L. urged its passage. He said that the people of Russia were suffering from a most acute famine and that congress should come to their aid. The bill was passed. (P. 422) There has continued during the year a persistent propaganda in favor of some sort of recognition of the communist autocracy in Russia which has crushed and all but broken the Russian people. This propaganda has taken form under various heads as follows: 1. Propaganda for official American recognition of the soviet dictatorship as a government; 2. Propaganda among trade unions for relief for Russia to be forwarded for distribution in Russia under direction of the soviets; 3. Propaganda for so-called trade relations with Russia, which as a matter of fact have existed and now exist in so far as they can exist with a disorganized people ridden by a brutal tyranny; 4. Propaganda for communism in the abstract among American working people; 5. Propaganda having the definite purpose of destroying the A. F. of L. in obedience to the command of the chief of the Russian tyranny to the effect that the A. F. of L. must be destroyed as the first necessary step in the communist scheme to overthrow the republic of the U. S. All of this propaganda is based upon the desire of communists and communist central power to undermine and overthrow democratic institutions everywhere. We find in brief, the facts in the case to be: 1. The Russian Soviet authority, called a government, is a most rigorous, brutal, tyrannical autocracy in the absolute control of communists of whom there are among all of the millions of Russians less than 400,000, with no freedom of speech, no freedom of press (only authorized government contolled newspapers are permitted), no freedom of assemblage, no secret ballot, a system of plural voting which gives communists four votes to one for the peasant; there is a complete economic breakdown due to communist tyranny in theory and practice; there is thrust upon the people the burden of the largest standing army in the world; there are and have been persecution and execution of thousand of workers whose crime was their effort to be trade unionists and to express their opposition to the autocratic powers in control; there is a despotism which seems to grant concessions as a part of its propaganda when that is deemed wise, but which may withdraw at any moment the concessions it grants; there is absolutely no power residing in the people who have been stricken of everything material, political, industrial and ethical; there is the most brazen misrepresentation to the peoples of the world; 2. As to relief, which it is sought to gather from trade unionists, this is a deception of the most despicable kind, since it plays upon the heartstrings for the deliberate purpose of bolstering the despotism; the American Relief administration is putting into Russia regularly more food than Russian equipment can transport inland to the famine area; relief sought for propaganda purposes from trade unionists through special agencies can not even, if collected, be got to those who need it because the Russian transportation system is incapable of transporting that which is and has been available through the generosity of the American people and the American government; and the soviet powers, utterly lacking in human sensibilities and ready to practice any deception for a propaganda purpose, have deliberately sought to impose upon American workers the most heartless misrepresentation; 3. In relation to trade it can only be said that the accounts of riches awaiting Americans upon the establishment of trade relations are as false as other soviet propaganda and are calculated to serve soviet ends alone; there is now no bar to trade with Russia except the inability of Russia to pay for those things which she needs most sorely; the only end to be served by trade relations would be to extend a quasi recognition to a hateful tyranny and to make the American government in some measure a guarantor or collector for bills which the soviets unquestionably would seek to avoid paying; 4. Propaganda for communism in the abstract in America is too obvious to need fresh description. It is not effective, but it is in evidence and it appears to be well financed and well organized, all for the purpose of foisting upon Americans the nightmare that has ruined Russia; 5. Propaganda having for its definite purpose the destruction of the American labor movement is also declared; unfortunately some trade unionists, essentially sound and well meaning, are temporarily deceived by this propaganda, leading to sporadic outbursts here and there for such fantastic schemes as the "one big union," the "amalgamation" of unions which would mean the disintegration of unions, and even the complete abolishment of unions and their replacement by soviets; these various schemes having such variations as the propagandists think will win them the most support, their one aim being to destroy our trade unions in order that they may then destroy our government. (P. 423). We express again our great friendship for the Russian people, our distress because of their terrible misfortune, our compassion and our sympathy, our pledge of continued friendship and assistance, and that we further extend to Russian trade unionists our greeting and our hope that they may soon be free to act democratically as trade unionists, unfettered by any tyranny, and that in that way they may contribute mightily toward the rebuilding of a great nation by a people tried unto despair, victimized by adventurers, ridden and ruled by lust and avarice, denied the most elemental rights by the most audacious, unscrupulous and incongruous despotism in history. (P. 425) There can never be compiled any adequate statement concerning the number who have died of starvation as the result of soviet incompetence and blundering, but it is possible to present a partial tabulation of those who have been murdered by the soviets in pursuit of its policy of deliberate violence and extermination, because it is in the most convenient form we quote a compilation made by Archbishop Alexander, head of the Greek Orthodox church in North America, who drew his figures from soviet sources. Archbishop Alexander found that in the period from November 7, 1917, to July 1, 1921, the following executions were instigated by the soviets: "Clergymen, 1,215; bishops, 28; professors and school teachers, 6,775; physicians and their assistants, 8,800; army and navy officers, 54,650; soldiers, 260,000; policemen of higher ranks, 10,500; policemen of lower ranks, 48,500; land owners, 12,950; belonging to the intellectual class, 355,250; manual workers, 102,350; peasants, 815,100; total 1,766,118."

(1923, p. 296) Refused to endorse a resolution urging the government of the U. S. to take steps leading to the resumption of official trade relations with Russia and the eventual recognition of the Russian government. These reasons were given: "The A. F. of L. has at no time evidenced a feeling of indifference to those unfortunate people; to the contrary, the A. F. of L. has at all times manifested the kindliest of feeling toward the people of Russia: neither has the A. F. of L. attempted at any time to exact of Russia any particular form of government. To the contrary, the A.

F. of L., in the interest of the Russian people, has insisted that as a condition preceding recognition of any form or kind of government the people of Russia be given a full and free opportunity to determine the character of government that shall guide or control their destiny. If the people of that country are given the opportunity to vote, to elect, to endorse or to repudiate this system, this tyranny, this overlordship, and so decide their fate and destiny, the A. F. of L. shall offer no objection to whatever may be their choice.

Safety Laws—(1923, p. 230) The A. F. of L. urges the labor movement and the citizenship of California generally, notwithstanding the veto of the governor, to continue their efforts for better safety laws and greater protection for the workers employed in underground workings.

Salmon Industry Grievances—(1920, p. 468) There exists in the salmon packing industry, as applied to cannery employes, a condition that borders on slavery, the men being recruited throughout Western states, placed on sailing ships, under guard, and given quarters between decks which, in many cases, are poorly ventilated and insanitary, narcotics being freely sold in violation of the federal statutes. These cannery employes, many of whom are illiterate, are obliged to sign contracts agreeing to work any and all hours demanded by contractors and to be penalized for refusing to work if sick when the company's doctor so orders. Therefore the A. F. of L. requests the U. S. department of labor to investigate labor conditions maintaining in said industry and recommend legislation necessary to remedy existing conditions.

Saturday Half Holiday—(1919, p. 454) The A. F. of L. believes that eight hours should be a maximum workday so that with a five and one-half day week of 44 hours, the Saturday half holiday would be a most desirable achievement. In cases where the work week can be reduced to less than 44 hours the A. F. of L. believes it would be of advantage to the worker to so have these hours distributed as to provide for a full Saturday holiday, making the work week a 5-day week, still with a maximum eight-hour day. (1922, p. 350) Declared for the Saturday-half holiday observance in government establishments or a shorter work week and that it should be extended to benefit every possible worker. (1923, p. 230). Reaffirmed.

Schools, Trade Union—(1919, p. 135) The last convention directed the Executive Council to appoint a committee to investigate the educational system of the International Ladies' Garment Workers' Union and other similar schools with a view of reporting to this convention whether a feasible plan could be found which could be applied generally to the U. S. and Canada. The committee personally examined the classes conducted by the International Ladies' Garment Workers' Union in New York City and Philadelphia, and the system of classes organized in Chicago by the Women's Trade Union League, in cooperation with the Chicago Federation of Labor. Through correspondence we are also able to report on the Boston Trade Union College conducted by the Boston Central Labor Union, and the classes organized on the initiative of the Los Angeles Labor Union. In the judgment of your committee the most important differences in the systems described lie in the varying degrees of cooperation of the unions with the public schools and of the unions with each other. In New York City it is chiefly one large international, the Ladies' Garment

Workers, which has developed its own educational department and secured cooperation with the public schools to the extent of the use of four elementary school buildings for their unity centers, one high school for their central classes, and of the services of teachers of English. All of the educational work of the ladies' garment workers in Philadelphia is in cooperation with the public schools. In Boston, the Central Labor Union has organized a Trade Union College for advanced work, the public schools furnishing a high school building. In Chicago also, the Chicago Federation of Labor, in conjunction with the Women's Trade Union League, has organized the educational work, the public schools furnishing a large proportion of the teachers and meeting places. In Los Angeles, while the movement was initiated by the unions, the Board of Education now has full control, though utilizing the close cooperation of the unions in courses and methods. Your committee is instructed to formulate from its study of all these systems, recommendations applicable to the labor movement as a whole. We consider the subjects taught a matter of minor significance—you may feel that some should be added or omitted the main question at issue is the machinery, the basic principle on which the work is organized, its soundness from the standpoint of trade union and public policy, its effectiveness, and its adaptability to the varying conditions of different communities. It is unnecessary to emphasize labor's keen appreciation of the value of education. And it is unnecessary to more than mention organized labor's pride in the part it took in the establishment of our public schools, and the consistent and vigorous stand it has taken ever since, for the highest development of our system of public education. One of the things that impressed the committee in the classes of the Ladies' Garment Workers' Union in New York City was the feeling of the students that the classes belonged to them, that they were at home in them, and took a collective pride in them. That is high praise for those classes, but it is also an indication of a serious shortcoming in our public schools, and in the attitude of the public, that is not limited to New York City. For that sense of part-ownership should be in the minds of students in all public school classes whenever any citizen passes or enters a public school building he should feel, "Here is an institution which belongs to and is created to serve my fellow-citizens and me. It is an investment which should yield returns not merely during the five or six hours, five days a week, when the children use it, but during as many of the twenty-four hours as we may find uses for it." When that conception becomes general, the schools will be indeed a melting pot. That that conception is not more general is partly the fault of the public, and partly that of boards of education, which is again the fault of the public. Your committee believes that the educational facilities described in this report should be provided by boards of education whenever requested by a sufficient number, and should be open to the public. But this implies that the courses offered shall be selected in cooperation with the unions or other groups making the requests, that they shall meet the wishes of the citizens who are prospective students, rather than of the boards of education. And it also implies that the instruction and discussions must be unhampered. A teacher must not be open to the taunt, "Do you say that because you think it is true, or because if you said any thing else you would lose your job?" It is a sad commentary an American education that it is necessary to state these conditions. But it is necessary Boards of education in an alarming number of our communities are unresponsive to public opinion, forget that they and the teachers are simply fellow-servants of the public, and assume proprietorship over the schools, and the minds of the teachers. In such communities, before the goal of centering union educational activities in the public schools can be fully realized, labor and other liberal elements must secure effective representation on the boards of education. Meanwhile classes under union auspices will serve the additional purpose of demonstrating the existence of a demand which the schools are failing to meet. But such classes should be considered a stopgap. The sound solution is a progressive board of education, responsive to the public. Where the types of courses and instruction desired can not be obtained from the public schools, we believe that all interested unions, working through their central labor bodies, should cooperate in organizing their educatonal work. Not only would there be economy and efficiency in centralized effort, but it would make for better understanding among members of the various locals. In case sufficient interest can not be aroused in the central labor body, or a local has an educational problem peculiar to itself, an interested local would naturally take the initiative and work out its own solution. But it is a question to be worked out in each community according to its peculiar conditions and needs. We are not inclined to make invidious comparisons among the systems examined. We found in all of them an admirable idealism, a sincere and effective effort to enrich the lives of the workers. We believe that we are asked to present general conclusions, not to single out details for comment. But we would like to call attention to an activity of the Chicago public schools apart from the classes already described. One of the most important features of the work discussed in both New York and Chicago is the teaching of English to those unable to read and write the language of their adopted country. The Chicago school system is sending teachers of English to factories wherever there is an agreement of the employer to give fifteen minutes of the working time to match fifteen minutes which the employe gives from his lunch time, or other time of his own. This opportunity for a daily half hour lesson in English given at the places of employment is being eagerly seized by hundreds of workers in need of elementary English. Of course, many lunch periods are too short to stand further curtailment, but the general plan would seem to furnish possibilities of cooperation with the public schools and employers worth investigation by unions with non-English-speaking members. To summarize its general conclusions, your committee recommends that central labor bodies, through securing representation on boards of education, and through the presentation of a popular demand for increased facilities for adult education make every effort to obtain from the public schools liberally conducted classes in English, public speaking, parliamentary law, economics, industrial legislation, history of industry, and of the trade union movement, and any other subjects that may be requested by a sufficient number, such classes to be offered at times and places which would make them available to workers. If the public school system does not show willingness to cooperate in offering appropriate courses and type of instruction, the central labor body should organize such classes with as much co-operation from the public schools as may be obtained. Interested local unions should take the initiative when necessary. (P. 428) The secretary was instructed to transmit the recommendations, which were adopted, to all affiliated central bodies.

Schools, Social Studies in Public— (1922, p. 355) A survey of text books and social studies had been made and incorporated in a report entitled "Social Studies in the Public Schools." It is divided in six sections: Part I of the report reveals that a serious threat is menacing our public education system, which, however, is not working itself out so much against the means of education, such as the courses of study and the text books used, as against the human part of our educational system, namely, the great body of teachers. Responsibility for this threat devolves mainly upon a group of extra-educational associations, such as the National Association of Manufacturers, National Industrial Conference Board, "America First" Publicity Association, and others. Their influence, however, is being partially counteracted by public-spirited, progressive educational organizations. Safeguards and remedies are at the disposal of the organized labor movement individually and in co-operation with the progressive educational associations to reform the situation. This section concludes with a description of the many organizations active in the field of public education endeavoring to exert an influence upon it.

Part II brings out the true significance of the social studies in relation to the history, achievements, aims and ideals of the labor movement. It emphasizes, based upon scientific data, the place of the labor movement in the social sciences. Its great significance in modern society is thus clearly established. The opinions and judgments of our most eminent progressive educators are cited in support of these findings, having been secured by special inquiry. This section also reveals that the extent to which these studies which properly deal with the labor movement are being taught is entirely inadequate. Progress, however, has been made in recent years in the extension of the social sciences in our public schools. Nevertheless, very much still must be done. In fact, the whole public educational system, if the ideals of humanity as expressed by the labor movement are to receive adequate consideration in public education, will require reconstruction around the social studies.

Part III deals with the importance of the text book in teaching the social studies. It describes the basis upon which the tests were formulated by means of which the text books covered in this report were evaluated. The summary of these evaluations are then presented, together with a resume of the chief criticisms of the text scrutinized. In all, 123 text books—47 histories, 47 civics, 25 economics, and 4 sociologies—were evaluated. The tests bring out that one-half of the books (55 per cent) are of the newer type, dealing with the broader aspects of government and the social and industrial life of the people, rather than with forms of organization, military events and abstract theories. Still, a larger proprtion (60 per cent) recognized to a greater or less degree the power for growth in our institutions; are dynamic rather than static in their methods of treatment. In dealing with questions of particular interest to labor there is a great divergence in concept as well as in method of treatment. The older formal texts either omit these subjects entirely

or treat them so unsatisfactorily that for all practical purposes they might just as well be omitted. Some of the more modern ones deal with them briefly and perfunctorily, but on the whole the newer type of text does attempt to give the labor movement in the problem of industry adequate and just consideration. Failure to do so is apparently due to ignorance of the author or to a hesitancy to deal with this subject, rather than to a deliberate attempt to keep the facts of industry out of the schools. Although numerous cases of error, misleading statements, misplaced emphasis, discrimination against unions, and use of obsolete material, may be pointed out, the survey finds no evidence that text books are being used for propaganda purposes. The publishers, the report considers, are undoubtedly deserving of a great deal of credit for keeping school-books free from propaganda, and to this spirit of fair-play and desire for truth it considers that the organized labor movement may look for help in the correction of erroneous, misleading or unfair statements which mar the pages of otherwise excellent texts.

Concerning the text books in use, the report points out that not only is an increasing supply of the better books becoming available, but there is also a steadily increasing demand for them. The investigation made also reveals the fact that, especially in civics and history, the modern or more approved text is being used to a larger extent than the less satisfactory. Subjects discussed or investigated in supplementary courses of study such as Current Events, the report indicates, pay a great deal of attention to problems and matters of special interest to labor.

Seamen—(1919, p. 130) Two bills proposing to strike out sections 4 and 5 of the Seamen's Act were protested against by the A. F. of L. Both failed of passage. (Pp. 343–344–353) Called upon the committee on marine and fisheries of the house to investigate violations of the Seamen's act and take such steps as would compel its enforcement.

(1920, pp. 113–360) H. R. 9692, was submitted to the U. S. shipping board for an opinion by the committee on merchant marine and fisheries. Representatives of the vessel owners, seamen and the shipping board were appointed on a commission to inquire into the proposed changes; but the commission failed to agree. Notwithstanding this and while the commission was still in session the bill was presented to the house and passed. It is now before the senate. The bill reduces the number of able seamen on a vessel from 65 to 40 per cent, and the training period from three years to nine months. Vigorous protests have been made to the committee on fisheries of the senate.

(1921, p. 116) A law was enacted providing that all alien seamen afflicted with certain disabilities or diseases are to be placed in a hospital on arrival in ports of the U. S., the expense to be borne by the owner, agent, consignee or master of the vessel upon which the seamen shipped. If it is found that a cure can not be effected within a reasonable time the alien seamen shall be returned to the port from which they shipped at the expense of the vessel on which they came. A bill was introduced in the senate to provide compensation for seamen and the dependents of seamen killed in the course of employment and to create a federal seamen's compensation fund. It provides that immediately after injury sustained by a seamen he shall receive all necessary medical and surgical aid and hospital supplies. In the event of a total disability he shall receive a weekly compensation equal to 66⅔ per cent of his weekly earnings. If only temporarily disabled he shall receive a weekly compensation equal to 66⅔ per cent of his loss in earning capacity. The payment of compensation for injuries runs from 15 to 312 weeks. The weekly compensation for total disability shall not be more than $25 nor less than $10 unless the seamen's compensation shall be the full amount of his weekly earnings. The weekly compensation for any partial disability shall not be more than that proportion of $25 which the disability bears to total disability. No action was taken on the bill. (P. 177) We protest most emphatically against any lowering of the number of skilled men, and increase in the hours of labor or any extension of the season in which passenger vessels are permitted to operate in a condition in which 50 per cent of the persons on board have no means of safety except life preservers, the utility of which were shown in the loss of the Empress of Ireland, in the St. Lawrence river in May, 1914, where according to report, 1,027 persons drowned with life preservers on within less than three miles from shore and with assistance coming in less than two hours. (P. 263) Indorsed senate bill providing for investigation of the lockout of seamen by a combination of European and American shipowners aided by the United States shipping board. (P. 346) The A. F. of L. compliments the seamen upon their unchanged and undiminished patriotism, their self-sacrifice to America's interest and their loyalty to the principles of human freedom. This declaration was made after the seamen had reported that the U. S. shipping board had issued statements that it "would not give agents of the unions the privileges of visiting docks or ships" and that " no new agreement would be ratified for longer than six months." The seamen declared they would refuse to agree to this policy, accepting persecution and suffering instead.

(1922, pp. 105–327). H. R. 6754, passed the house but met with opposition in the senate. The bill seeks to amend sections 2, 13 and 14 of the seamen's act. It provides that the life-saving equipment on vessels during the summer months shall be reduced 25 per cent and that the number of able seamen provided for by the seamen's act should be reduced from 65 per cent to 50 per cent. The bill also provides for twelve-hour watches for firemen, water tenders and oilers. Representative John I. Nolan, of California, made a fight on these provisions and succeeded in amending the bill so that employes in these occupations. should work only eight hours, but they failed to prevent a reduction in the number of able seamen employed. The reduction in the life-saving equipment and the provision that it is not necessary that able seamen be employed in manning the life boats and life rafts gave the bill the title of "Drowning Made Easy." The original bill provided that there should be a sufficient number of boats and rafts on each vessel to save only 25 per cent instead of 50 per cent of the passengers in case of fire or shipwreck. The seamen in entering objection to this feature of the bill declared that the shipowners now have the legal right to drown 50 per cent of the persons they carry but want the legal right to drown 75 per cent. This argument compelled the house to reject the proposed reduction to 25 per cent, and retain the 50 per cent law.

(1923, p. 306) We enter our most emphatic protest against the policies now pursued by American shipowners whereby American sea-men are driven into other occupations. We call upon our federal government to enforce all laws enacted to provide greater safety of life at sea and do everything possible to develop a personnel that can compete in peace and defend our country in war.

Secession—(1920, p. 377) Officers of the various affiliated organizations are requested and urged to instruct their locals to refrain from giving moral or financial or assistance of any kind to any secessionist movement. Central bodies and state federations are advised of the laws relating to secession movements, and they are further informed that assistance, moral, financial or otherwise, to any secessionist movement will be considered a breach of the terms and conditions under which charters of organization and affilation are granted, and that the best interest of the trade union movement demands, that full power, influence and assistance should be given the recognized and affiliated trade union organization, to the end that secession and disruption may be put to an end speedily and effectively.

Sectarian and Captious Issues—(1893, p. 56) We deplore the introduction of any sectarian or captious side issues among the working people. Such movements are destined to divide labor's forces and produce bitter antagonisms, as they produce religious bigotry, provoke rancorous intolerance, and divert the working people from working out their own emancipation from the galling slavery of the present social and political conditions. We here and now reaffirm as one of the cardinal principles of the labor movement that the working people must unite and organize, irrespective of creed, color, sex, nationality or politics.

Sedition—(1920, p. 101) No more insidious conspiracy to abolish free speech, free press and free assembly could have been conceived than that contained in what is known as the Sterling-Graham peace time sedition bill. It went further. It would have made unlawful the normal activities of labor. The president of the A. F. of L. appeared before the committee on judiciary and pointed out the dangers of the bill to the people of the United States. He said: "It can be used to kill free speech and free assembly. It strikes a deadly blow at legitimate organizations of labor or any other progressive movement for the betterment of the masses which may be opposed by the advocates of privilege and reaction. We yield to no man, in public office or out, in our loyalty to the constitution and institutions of this republic. No self-respecting man has questioned or dare question that loyalty. We are for evolution, not revolution; for ballots, not bullets; for a majority rule, not class dictatorship of bolshevism, plutocracy or of the profiteer. We oppose this bill because every purpose for which it is framed is already covered by existing laws. Its legitimate features which compose two-thirds of the draft, are utterly autocratic, imperialistic and un-American." Section 5 of the bill could have been construed by a prejudiced federal judge to mean that a lapel button worn by any member of an organization whose purpose is to secure an amendment to the constitution of the U. S. or any existing federal law is sedition. Section 6 gave the postmaster general the power of censorship over any private correspondence This he could read and destroy. If a strike should occur and the business, the private property of an employer, should be indirectly injured, the strikers would be guilty of attempting to overthrow the government. Should the members of a union strike, a federal judge could decide it unlawful and the organization would have to be expelled from the A. F. of L. If this were not done the A. F. of L. itself would become unlawful, and in this event any person who gave or loaned it money for strike relief for starving men and women would be guilty of sedition. Organizing colored men would be considered as an attempt to overthrow the government on the ground that it would create racial prejudice which might result in riots. The rules committee, after President Gompers had condemned the bill, refused to grant a rule for its consideration by the house. (P. 385) We wish to congratulate the American labor movement, as well as the people of the U. S. that through the vigilance of the president of the A. F. of L. the insidious so-called Sterling-Graham peacetime sedition bill was brought to public notice. The storm of deserved condemnation and indignant disapproval aroused when the contents of this proposed statute was made public, shows how quickly the mind of the American people reacts in the presence of danger.

(1921, p. 116) Renewed efforts to enact what was known as a "peace-time sedition" law were defeated.

(1922 pp. 110–327) Due to the vigilance of the officers of the A. F. of L. the proponents of the so-called sedition bill have, not been able to make any progress in furthering this vicious legislation.

Sedition Law, Kentucky's—(1920, p. 115–386) Kentucky has a syndicalism-sedition law, owing to the lack of necessary courage by Governor Edwin P. Morrow of that state. Although he signed the bill making its provisions law, he attacked most viciously two sections. While these sections took away the inherent rights of the people of Kentucky he refused to veto the bill. Since the law was signed by him the governor has attempted to defend himself by saying that "the good in this bill is more than enough to offset whatever might be harmful." The facts are that the sections objected to by the governor constitute the real kernel in the bill. The enemies of labor desired to reach labor while engaged in its normal activities through some law that would force employees to remain at work no matter what the conditions. These sections were carefully prepared and then several other sections containing high-sounding phrases against the overthrow of the government by force were written into the bill. The latter sections were for the purpose of hiding the real intent of the proposed law. No stronger argument against the two sections mentioned could be made than that by the governor himself. Two of the sections to which he objected are sections 6 and 10. Section 10 provides: "It shall be unlawful for any person or persons, by speech, writing or otherwise, to arouse, incite or fix enmity, discord or strife or ill-feeling between classes of persons for the purpose of inducing tumult or disorder." Of this the Governor says: "This is a clear attempt to fix and prescribe the limits of speech and in my mind is a denial of the right of free speech or at least it presents a means by which that right may be seriously hampered. Speech arousing ill-feeling between classes of persons is a far different thing than advocating violent resistance to law or overthrow of the government by force. Speech which may arouse ill-feeling between classes may frequently induce public disorder and yet be in a cause as holy as the rights of man, or as sacred as the right

of womanhood or childhood. Under the provisions of section 10, every abolitionist, including Henry Ward Beecher and Theodore Parker could, and doubtless would have been convicted as felons because they gave utterance to speech calculated to arouse discord and ill-feeling between classes of persons. Every advocate of slavery in the northern state tried before a jury of the vicinage, would, under this law, have been found guilty. The terms 'public tumult' or 'disorder' are vague and uncertain. There is no limit placed upon them. Under the ordinary rule of law, that one intends the natural consequence of his act, a speech on a great moral issue against a class committing a great moral wrong might produce discord, ill-feeling and strife and tumult among the class denounced or among those who, holding a wrongful position or a wrongful privilege were determined to maintain same regardless of consequences. With section 10 as a law in their hands and entrenched by the power of a subservient court it would be no difficult matter for those rightfully denounced and rightfully excoriated to have a judgment of the court that their denouncer had a purpose when he made his denunciation of arousing discord and public tumult. A speech delivered in a community controlled by those who believe in child labor in mill and factory, which denounced such a practice and condemned it as inhuman and monstrous would doubtless create disorder and might cause tumult, and therefore though considered in a holy cause might be declared to be a speech calculated to arouse ill-feeling between classes for the purpose of promoting disorder. It is essential to the progress of humanity that wrong shall be denounced, and that the lips of truth shall not be sealed by the law of silence, and that a people may have the right to determine what is the truth from free discussion and through the agencies of free speech. Free speech is the guarantor of liberty—the avatar of progress. It is light, progress, hope—it is the dearest bought right of the sons of freedom. I believe that section 10 of this act presents a means and a possibility of stifling free speech; of preventing open discussion and that it may be so warped in its application as to produce injurious and tyrannical consequences. I do not believe that Kentucky needs such a law. I do not believe that there is necessity for it. I further believe that it violates the constitution of the United States and the constitution of Kentucky and that it will be so declared by the courts of the land." Of section 6 he says: "This act gives any peace officer (including constables, deputy sheriffs, police officers, etc.) the right upon mere notice to disperse any meeting of citizens, who, in their opinion are meeting for any of the purposes denounced in the bill. This provision makes of every constable in Kentucky, judge, court and jury, with the right to take persons and seize papers without a hearing of any sort upon his part, but who under this law can act upon mere notice. It gives to every peace officer a power greater than that of any court in the land and this power to be exercised without investigation and without any hearings. It would enable a constable or deputy sheriff, the creature of any group of men, to act in the most arbitrary way upon the mere statement of those who owned him, of those who had made him and of those to whom he gave ready obedience, and so acting would clothe him with the power of determining whether or not a meeting of persons being addressed by a public speaker was a meeting for the purpose of creating ill-feeling between classes for the purpose of promoting a breach of the peace by public disorder and forthwith to disperse the meeting; drive every one from the place of meeting and close the doors, seize papers, etc. I can not believe that such a section is anything but arbitrary, and I am conscientiously of the opinion that such a power should not exist in a government of free people."

Shipping Board, Training Service— (1919, p. 380) The recruiting and training service and the sea service bureau of the U. S. shipping board are asking congress for an appropriation under which those war institutions may continue during peace. Both of those institutions are useless for any practical purpose, and, if we really mean to build up a personnel for a merchant marine, we should return to the system of training men on board ships actually engaged in the ocean and coastwise service and under the direction of the ship officers, therefore the A. F. of L. 'enters an emphatic protest against any further appropriation being made for the continuance of the above-mentioned institution.

Ship Subsidy—(1922, pp. 98–327) It has been the general opinion that the idea of a ship subsidy would never again be broached in congress. But this belief was based on the contention that there never would be such a congress as is now in session. Furthermore never before have the same tactics been applied. Thirteen years ago when the last effort was made to foist such a scheme upon the country a great majority of the newspapers were opposed to it. Those who favor a ship subsidy now have seen to it that no such condition shall interfere with the present bill. Therefore, they had the head of the biggest advertising agency in the U. S. placed at the head of the shipping board. Through this advertising agency the chairman of the shipping board has free entry into every newspaper of the country. It has proved a most remarkable combination and the ship subsidy bill is now for sale to the people of the U. S. Its glories are set forth in most brilliant language. The chairman of the shipping board, who was selected to make the sale, is conducting a widespread campaign to secure the legislation. No sooner had the bill been introduced into congress on February 23, than the seamen discovered the menace to them in its provisions. It would repeal that section of the seaman's act, which guaranteed the right of seamen to leave ship in safe harbor. It also provides for a merchant marine naval reserve, which the seamen denounced as a proposed strike-breaking agency. As a bait for the seamen to become members of this merchant marine naval reserve they are to be given a retainer of a month's wages. So many protests about these two clauses were made that the chairman promised to eliminate them. He contended, however, that if this were done the seamen should support the bill. This, however, they refused to do. Two conferences were held between representatives of the A. F. of L. and the chairman of the shipping board, during which the latter submitted the same plan to secure the cooperation of labor in support of the bill. The chairman also used another argument to secure the support of labor. This was that as soon as the ship subsidy bill should have been passed, thousands of men now idle in the ship yards would be given employment. At the same time, he said that the ships owned by the shipping board were "junk" and ought to be sunk in the sea. There are a number of other dangerous provisions in the bill which affect every taxpayer in the U. S. It is

proposed to sell to private shipowners ships that cost from $200 to $250 a ton to build, for anything that can be obtained. These vessels may be sold for $20 a ton or less. The purchasers can then borrow from the shipping board two-thirds of the purchase prices and sufficient to motorize them at 2 per cent interest, all to be payable within fifteen years. During this period the purchasers can operate the vessels. They will depreciate as much as 75 per cent. At the end of fifteen years purchasers can tie them up at some dock and say to the shipping board: "You can keep them for what we owe you." The 1899 convention of the A. F. of L., by a practically unanimous vote condemned ship subsidies. Only one vote was cast in favor of the ship subsidy. This result came after a most persistent agitation by a lobby well-conditioned with arguments and funds which were used in an endeavor to secure the approval of the measure. (P. 169) The bill now pending in congress and which is purported to be "a bill to amend and supplement the merchant marine act of 1920 and for other purposes," is in reality a cunningly devised scheme to enrich certain classes of so-called American ship-owners at the expense of the truly American tax-payer and also to provide patronage which is certain to be used for purely political purposes." Said bill commonly known as the "ship subsidy bill" is being widely misrepresented as a measure intended for and necessary to the maintenance and upbuilding of the American merchant marine. The facts are that its enactment into law will bring about a condition under which all managers and operators of ships must regard politics as the prime factor in their business, and efficient management as a secondary consideration of comparatively little importance. The claim that ship subsidies are necessary to equalize the cost of operation between foreign and American vessels is deceptive, and cannot be substantiated except in cases where such inequality exists because American government officials have failed, and are failing, to properly enforce the existing American laws, intended to promote equalization, this being especially true of the law known as the seamen's act. The A. F. of L. hereby condemns the said ship subsidy bill as inimical to the public interest, and particularly destructive to the nation's hopes and aspirations for sea power.

(1923, p. 81) The greatest blow to the privileged few and a most beneficial outcome of congressional legislation was the defeat of the ship subsidy bill. The arguments in favor of a ship subsidy were all such flagrant misrepresentation that the number of opponents continued to grow until the members of the senate were convinced that they would meet political suicide if they voted for such a measure. As soon as the bill was introduced, the Executive Council at its session May 10, 1922, made a careful analysis of its provisions and found them so inimical to the interests of the people that a resolution of protest against such legislation was adopted and sent to the joint committee on commerce and marine and fisheries of the house and senate. The Cincinnati convention also condemned the bill. The representative of the largest advertising agency in the United States and also chairman of the U. S. shipping board was selected to push the bill through congress. He was so confident that it would pass that he told the members of congress that it was not necessary for them to know anything about the measure, that the president wanted it and that was sufficient. The support of labor was urged but this was emphatically refused because such a subsidy would be detrimental to labor and the people. Information as to the dangers in the bill was sent to all colleges, universities, state federations of labor, central bodies and local unions. All during the summer of 1922 efforts were made to have the house pass the bill, but the members refused to vote upon the measure before the November elections. In the November elections the ship subsidy bill was repudiated by the people, its most influential sponsors being recalled by their constituents. After the elections a special session of congress was called and President Harding on November 21, 1922, appeared before a joint session of the senate and house and urged the passage of the ship subsidy bill. Under the lash of the party whip, backed by the influence of certain interests that would benefit, the house passed the bill. It was for this bill that seventy-one lame ducks voted and it was passed by only twenty-four majority. As the 1922 convention had unanimously condemned the ship subsidy bill, the president of the A. F. of L. immediately notified all affiliated organizations of the action of the house and the danger of the passage of the bill in the senate. Members of the senate began to receive a flood of protests and the advocates of the bill began to weaken in numbers. Every trick known to practical politicians was used to convince the people that the bill should pass. The very arguments, however, were so full of false logic and chicanery that opposition continued rapidly to increase instead of receding as hoped. Finally, the leaders of the senate recognized that there was too much danger to their political future to pass the measure and they withdrew it from consideration. An outstanding fact in regard to the opposition to the ship subsidy bill was that labor was the only organization that openly fought against its passage. It can be said without fear of contradiction that had it not been for the A. F. of L. and its affiliated organizations this pernicious legislation would have been driven through congress under the whip and spur of party regularity and the fear of loss of patronage. The best evidence that American shipowners do not require a subsidy to be successful is contained in a dispatch from New York printed in the Washington Star of May 29 which states that the Japanese government has been petitioned by big shipping interests in that country to increase the subsidies granted Japanese shipping in order that the latter may be able to meet competition in Pacific waters. It was said that during the first five months of this year American shipping intra-transpacific trade has grown to such proportions that it exceeded the Japanese and British tonnage combined Furthermore, it was stated that freight and passenger capacities of American ships now plying the Pacific routes will be taxed to the limit within another year. (P. 277) Had it not been for the watchful attitude of the A. F. of L., the carefully planned raid on the U. S. treasury would apparently have been consummated with the greatest ease. In this connection the A. F. of L. wishes to call attention to the undisputed historical fact that sea power—the ability to successfully compete or fight at sea—depends upon the type, character and ability of a nation's seamen. Ships, guns, tools, etc., are all important, but the essential requirement for success is loyal and competent seamen. History teaches us that nations refusing to recognize this truth have slowly but inevitably lost power and control of the sea. America's policy for success upon the sea has been clearly defined in the seamen's act of 1915. Sympathetic enforcement of that law will bring greater results than the transfer of billions of dollars from the U. S. treasury to the private accounts of ship owners. Ship subsidies are like crutches—they lessen initiative and create a spirit of dependence. A man or an industry dependent upon crutches ultimately becomes a slave to the habit, i. e., the crutches.

Sims, Admiral—(1921, p. 375) Executive Council directed to request the president to discipline Admiral Sims if the published reports of a speech made by him in London were found to be true.

Six Hour Day, Eight Hours' Pay—(1921, p. 419) Refused to approve of a six hour day with eight hours pay, as it would be making more chaotic at this time an already mixed up industrial situation.

Six Hour Day, Unemployment—(1921, p. 420) Convention refused to indorse a maximum six hour day, declaring: "We agree that all the people of the earth who find it necessary to earn their subsistence by labor should have opportunity to labor. We also agree that through trades union organizations the working people have materially improved not only the standard of working conditions, but the standard of the lives of the workers. But to comply with the demand that the A. F. of L. seek to initiate 'and use all its resources to carry into effect' the introduction of a maximum six-hour day in all industries would involve something which we may all desire but which at this time is not feasible. The question of the shorter work day is referred to the different national and international unions affiliated with the A. F. of L. to put into effect when the opportunity presents itself, and the A. F. of L. will encourage all organizations undertaking such an effort." Explanation for recommending against a six hour day was thus given by the chairman of the resolution committee: "I can readily see by the discussion that has taken place on the report of the committee that there is a misunderstanding of what the committee has said and what the resolution proposes. The committee has said that it is not opposed to a shorter work day, but is in favor of a shorter work day. We recognize in our report the philosophy of lessening the hours of labor in order that the unemployed may be given work, but we say further that while we favor the idea, we regard the resolution as impracticable and that its adoption at this time would add confusion to an already chaotic condition. The miners of this country would be glad if they could work six hours a day, and we are battling for that principle. There is nothing in this report that prevents us from doing so, or any other organization from doing so, but we declare that for all industry to be required, by a declaration of this convention, to establish this as a maximum, with eight hours' pay, is impractical and impossible at this time. Surely we want to follow along practical lines now. That is the attitude of the committee; we are trying to proceed along rational and constructive lines, giving to every organization the widest latitude under their autonomy to put into effect their shorter work-day program, having in mind at the same time existing industrial conditions.

Social and Industrial Problems—(1920, p. 397) Official records show that of total expenditures of more than $5,500,000,000 by the U. S. government during the current fiscal year, 93 per cent was disbursed for expenses of recent and previous wars, and the maintenance of the war and navy departments; less than 6 per cent for the maintenance of the civil government and public works, and only 1 per cent for human welfare, educational and developmental purposes, including the study of labor problems, agriculture, mining, forestry, fisheries, markets, public roads, foreign commerce, general and vocational education, public health, and the needs of women and children. The progress and well-being of the people of America depend upon thorough understanding of the direct human needs and conditions of life, as well as upon military defence, and the promotion of property interests. Scientific research is necessary to increased production and better distribution of the necessities of life, as well as the physical protection of the workers at their jobs. Therefore the A. F. of L. calls upon the congress of the U. S. henceforth to provide liberally for the study of social and industrial problems and technical research in all branches of sciences, touching the welfare of the nation's people. (P. 397) The Executive Council is requested to consider the centralizing, analyzing and dissemination of information in connection with industrial conditions and problems.

(1921' p 121) Copies of a resolution adopted in the Montreal convention, which called upon congress to "provide liberally for the study of social and industrial problems and technical research in all branches of science," were sent to the president of the U. S., the president of the senate, the speaker of the house of representatives and candidates for president during the last election, as directed.

Soldiers' Adjusted Compensation— (1921, p. 115) Congress failed in the sixty-sixth session to enact any legislation for soldiers' relief. All such legislation was blocked in the senate. The influence behind the refusal to provide for a soldiers' bonus was said to be the federal reserve board. In reporting to the senate what it had done in the contraction of credits the federal reserve board recommended that congress practice most rigid economy. After reciting some of the legislation necessary to curb the inflation of currency and credits and consequent high prices the board in its report added: "These (policies of rigid economy) would of necessity preclude unwise appropriations, such as the proposed soldiers' bonus."

(1923, p. 85) Congress failed to enact legislation providing for adjusted compensation for former service men. A bill was passed by the house March 23, 1922, and by the senate September 15, 1922, but four days later was vetoed by the president. The house passed the bill over the president's veto, but the senate upheld the president. In November a bill was introduced containing practically the same provisions as that vetoed by the president. It failed of passage. It might be well to refer to a statement made by Senator Sterling in a discussion on the floor of the senate when the bonus bill was before that body: "He (the soldier) had the privilege of going and fighting for the grandest republic on God's footstool; and instead of claiming a bonus now he ought to consider himself, with all that he is and all that he has gained, the debtor of the nation rather than its creditor." It would not be difficult to imagine how the people would have taken this statement if it had been made while the boys were in the trenches in France. In those days the administration was doing its utmost to insure victory. June 1, 1917, congress doubled the wages of the soldiers, raising them from $15 to $30 a month. The committee on labor of the council of national defense was continually considering how to protect the interest of the men in the service. In the first meeting of the executive committee of the committee on labor compensation to be paid to soldiers and sailors and the platform of taking care of their families were discussed. Later, through the President of the A. F. of L., chairman of the committee on labor, the matter was presented to the council of national defense with the suggestion that the committee on labor be authorized to take up the entire subject matter and to draft appropriate legislation. The suggestion was approved. President Gompers appointed Judge Julian W. Mack, as chairman of the committee and the most comprehensive measure ever drafted was prepared. The committee also co-operated in the matter of insurance for soldiers and sailors. The law as enacted provided for generous contributions by the government to the wives and the children of all enlisted men as long as they were in the service. In case of death the widow and children were to receive sums ranging from $20 to $75 a month an no distinction was made between a private and the highest officer. A feature that marked it as the most progressive legislation of any country ever in war was the insurance provision. The government sold insurance to men of the service at less than private companies in [peace times to civilians. The government added nothing for expenses or profit. No such legislation was ever enacted by any country. The war is over but some of those who remained at home to legislate for those were offering the supreme sacrifice are now refusing adjusted compensation to the men who maintained the political freedom of our republic. (P. 279) The foregoing relates in clear and definite terms what may be well regarded the treachery to a grateful people by a small but rich minority who would freely shed the blood of the country's youth in times of stress, and in times of peace would throw them upon a pile of human wreckage to starve and rot and die, and would deny them the blessings and just rewards of a truly considerate and grateful people. The A. F. of L. is firmly convinced that the people as a whole desire that the nation's debt be speedily paid to all our service men. It is equally convinced that all attempts made to shift this obligation from the wealth of the nation to the backs of its wage earners is but a subtle means to deny. a just and long overdue compensation to our ex-service men and to prevent the grateful response of the whole of our people.

Soldiers and Sailor Help Our—(1919, pp. 94–428) More than twenty-eight thousand copies of a circular letter to trade unions urging them to establish employment committees for the benefit of our returning soldiers and sailors were issued. The circulars stated in part: "Technically, the war has not ended though hostilites have ceased. We are now passing through the initial stages of a process of readjustment and the peoples of most nations are rapidly turning their thoughts and attention to the solution of the many serious and complex problems which have developed out of the war. The world faces an infinitely more serious situation to-day than a year ago when the German superoffensive was at its height. At that time all our men were at work. If they were not fighting or training to fight, they were making shells or guns, or building ships or engines, or growing corn or wheat, or were engaged in the production of some of the other many things necessary to maintain the soldiers in the trenches and the sailors on the ships. Military defeat was then averted. With equal fervor and with the same vigor and determination we must now avoid a social and economic collapse, such as is now threatening many of the European nations. Without the long years of military training of the central powers and practically without preparation, our great Republic and its people entered the world struggle for the supremacy of righteousness, freedom, and democracy. We had the determined American will to win. We did win. With the signing of the armistice and the ending of hostilities, the American people find themselves practically unprepared for the immediate resumption of peace-time pursuits. The problems of readjustment in many instances are more difficult of solution than were those involved in the conduct of the war. Despite the difficulties and the obstacles, if the American will to win is again expressed, if our people will meet the requirements of readjustment with the determination which was shown in dealing with the demands of war, we should have no cause for fear or apprehension as to the final outcome. The matters which require our immediate attention relate to the demobilization of our military forces and the readjustment of our productive processes to peace-time pursuits. Necessarily readjustment involves sacrifices, but the sacrifices of reconstruction are insignificant when compared with the sacrifices which were entailed in the conduct of the war. Replacing the soldiers and sailors into the economic life of the nation is of the greatest importance to the wage-earners. This is a task in which the helpful co-operation of every individual worker and every group of workers is not only desirable but necessary. When a soldier or sailor returns to your community the employment committee of your organization should immediately get in touch with him and make sure that he is registered with the U. S. employment service or its bureau for returning soldiers and sailors. Then visit his former emloyer. In the vast majority of cases, his former employer will take him back. Should the effort to replace the returned soldier or sailor with his former employer fail, an endeavor should be made to secure him employment elsewhere. While finding employment, provision should be made for his immediate needs. Whenever a soldier or sailor is not content with his former job, or one that is open to him in his community, he should be persuaded to fill it until the industrial transition is over, the troops have returned, and another opening found. The employment committee you are urged to establish should at all times be made available to him for finding a place elsewhere. The employment committee should, with the help of all other agencies, get in touch with every nonresident soldier or sailor seeking employment in your city, find out where he belongs, and immediately communicate with the employment committee of the local union, city or state federation of labor, or other approved employment service in his home city. On receiving assurance that such employment bureau or agency will take care of him, arrange for his immediate return. In order that the soldiers and sailors may be helped to reabsorb themselves throughout the country in the ratio within which the man power was withdrawn for military purposes, the slogan should be established—'Local Jobs for Local Men.' By adopting this slogan and responding to this dictum we may bring into immediate operation the maximum reabsorbing capacity of the whole nation. It is fully recognized that the obligation to give employment to the soldiers and sailors rests primarily on the employers. The workers are not in a position to give employment. It is the workers' duty to see that every effort is made to secure suitable employment for the returned soldiers and sailors. It is also their duty to see that when the soldiers and sailors seek employment they are not dealt with unfairly or imposed upon by private employment agencies for profit or otherwise. It is the expressed hope and desire that the employment committees created by both employers and workers in your community may join hands and co-operate with each other in this patriotic and much needed work and thus prove helpful in the successful demobilization of our military forces and in reestablishing former peace-time activites with the least possible disturbance and a minimum of sacrifice." (P. 428) The committee on labor was granted an opportunity to continue its work for the co-ordination of resources and industries and for national security and welfare.

Soldiers and Unions—(1919, p. 347) The proper and adequate organizations to regulate the terms of employment and the conditions of labor for ex-soldiers, sailors and marines are the existing national and international unions, as recognized by the A. F. of L. Ex-soldiers, sailors and marines are hereby advised that the American trade unions which supported them so vigorously, patriotically and unanimously while they were in uniform are the organizations with which they should affiliate for the purpose of protecting their economic welfare and advancing their interests.

Soldiers as Policemen—(1919, p. 443) The A. F. of L. convention assembled denounces the action of the mayor of the city of Toledo in employing returned soldiers in the uniform of the U. S. army as citizen police in a labor controversy, which really means using the uniform of the United States as a protection for strike-breakers. (P. 469) The U. S. navy department has under consideration a plan to displace the civilian policemen stationed at the various navy yards and stations by detailing enlisted U. S. marines to perform these duties. The issuance of such an order would throw a large number of civilian organized employes out of employment, thus causing needless hardships to their families. The A. F. of L. hereby enters a most emphatic protest against the plan contemplated and demands that the present civilian force of policemen be retained.

Soldiers in Civilian Work—(1919, p. 357) The practice has grown up during the war of using men and women enlisted in the military and naval reserves of the U. S. in civilian positions. This practice is being continued now that the war emergency is over, with the result of introducing military standards into employment purely civilian in character. Therefore the A. F. of L. declares that temporary expedients of this nature necessary in time of war became a menace to shop standards if continued in time of peace and that the civilian employment by the government of men and women enlisted in the military service be discontinued upon the signing of the peace treaty.

Soldiers, Land and Work for—(1919, p. 117) Shortly after the signing of the armistice on November 11 unemployment began to be a factor in the industrial situation. The number of workers out of employment continued steadily to increase. Much dscussion was aroused in congress on the matter. The danger at this critical time of any considerable body of unemployed was recognized, excepting in the house commitee on appropriations, which refused the means necessary for the continuation of the U. S. employment service. Besides the needed work of bringing the "manless job" and the "jobless man" together, it was recognized that there was a possibility that there would not be enough jobs for all. In 1915 the secretary of labor in his annual report suggested the idea of making new opportunities of employment by acquiring land, fitting it for use, placing suitable buildings thereon and disposing of ready-made farms and homes to workers who desired that kind of employment. After our country entered the war this suggestion was taken up for more serious consideration and bills were introduced to provide for the emergency arising out of the demobilization of soldiers, sailors and marines, and the discharge of workers from war industries and other occupations by securing therefor permanent opportunities for profitable employment by means of a national construction service organized for the systematic extension of useful public works and the development of natural resources. The first thought in these measures was opening up new opportunties of employment. The preparation of these farms for habitation would involve a considerable expenditure and employ a large number of workers, and each farm would furnish permanent employment for one or more workers and thus relieve the labor market when over-crowded. None of the bills was passed. (P. 363) While the peoples in many European nations are thinking in terms of land as never heretofore, and while the apportionment of lands has proven one of the great, vexing problems of peace between nations, we here in our own country are permitting valuable lands to remain unused for the want of providing and a lack of determination to break the barrier of vested interests. While the problems of rents and housing are becoming more acute we are loath to demand of Congress to tax the wealth of the nation and in removing the artificial restrictions which prevent the further development of idle lands and encourage a greater distribution of our people on these lands. While we hear much of unemployment, we find no dearth of opportunity for the profitable employment of both men and women. Our country is yet young, our lands are not all fully developed, and there is much work yet to be performed in our country. Congress may well apply itself to this great and pressing task, if it sincerely desires to serve the well-being of the people. The A. F. of L. endorses the underlying principles of the bills introduced in congress which contemplate new principles of employment by acquiring the land, fitting it for use, placing suitable buildings thereon and disposing of ready-made farms under the most favorable terms and conditions and by providing for the systematic extension of public works and the development of natural resources. We urge the reintroduction of the bills and their early enactment into law. We also indorse the principles of the legislative proposals to survey, clarify and dispose to soldiers, sailors and workers all unentered and unused lands and aid in their development and settlement on a systematic and comprehensive, beneficial basis.

Soldiers Praise Labor—(1919, p. 299) Address in part of a representative of the Soldiers, Sailors and Marines Protective Association: "There are two bodies in the U. S. upon which the eyes of all the service men are cast, the congress of the U. S., at Washington, D. C., and the congress of the American labor at Atlantic City, N. J. You will all agree with me, ladies and gentlemen, that had it not been for these two bodies of great men supplying money and the necessary morale to us, German militarism and mediaeval autocracy would have triumphed. And furthermore, the abyss into which these relics of the old world have fallen was excavated by the soldiers, sailors, and marines, in conjunction with organized labor. And it is because of that we come to you once again for further consultation on matters of vital importance to the soldier, sailor, and marine, and to organized labor. With the signing of the armistice on November 11, 1918, 4,000,000 men became potential job-seekers. Our country was and is unprepared for the problems arising from the necessity of placing again in industry the men withdrawn by the war. Every city, town and village in the U. S. was full of men in uniform who are eagerly looking for jobs. And, to their sorrow, jobs were not to be found. In many instances men who fought for democracy on the other side were reduced to a state where they were compelled to retail their heroic achievements for a livelihood. The jobs that were open to us were either cheap or scab jobs, and that is what we object to. We believe that men who helped to preserve the institutions you cherish in the U. S. deserve better treatment at the hands of our fellow citizens. Employers of labor who had long sought an opportunity to break down the safeguards which had been built up by ceaseless and sacrificing toil grasped the occasion to attempt to put over their open-shop program. Where strikes occurred, men in uniform were hired at attractive wages to 'learn a trade'; all sorts of aluring promises were made, and through misrepresentation these men were to be used to break down the standards already established by you men. We come here to you, not because we demand too much, but because we understand that you as a body have the power to impress upon Congress that, first of all, we deserve $360, a year's pay, so that we can tide ourselves over the slack period and thus maintain the standards of livelihood, instead of breaking them down. We deserve a year's pay. At the present time we are getting only $60, and $60 is sufficient only to buy a civilian suit of clothes, a pair of shoes, a cup of coffee, and a doughnut. We also would like to see congress inaugurate a program of reconstruction whereby every man will be able legitimately to procure a position and thus maintain the American standard of living. We want to see public buildings constructed, so that men will not be compelled to walk the streets looking for a livelihood.   We believe that if we have a shorter work day the soldier will not have to worry about the job; that if we have six hours aday t o work every soldier will be able to get a job.

Soldiers, Protection for—(1919, p. 445) This convention gives its hearty approval of the efforts made by ex-soldiers, sailors and marines to protect themselves from the attempts made by unpatriotic employers to take advantage of their necessities to exploit them.

Soldiers, Rehabilitation of—(1919, pp. 113-327).   The bill for the rehabilitation and return to civil employment of disabled persons discharged from the military and naval forces of the U. S. became a law.   It provides that every disabled person who is discharged under circumstances entitling him to compensation after being discharged from the military or naval forces of the U. S., and who at the time of his discharge is unable to carry on a gainful occupation, to resume his former occupation, or to enter some other occupation, shall be furnished by the federal board for vocational education with such course of vocational rehabilitation as the board shall prescribe and provide.   Such person shall receive monthly compensation and allotments and family allowances so long as he follows the prescribed course of rehabilitation which he has elected to follow.

(1921, p. 319)   This is one of the most humanitarian pieces of legislation ever placed upon the statute books of the country.   Much organizing and preparation was necessary to carry out its purpose and intent.   At this time there are in training under the direction of the Federal board more than 80,000 persons who have been disabled through wounds or illness while in the service of the country.   They. are being trained in the widest variety of occupations.   The trainees are distributed over the whole field of human endeavor properly within the classification "vocational," therefore no disturbance of the ordinary distribution of labor is encountered, no danger of overcrowding any single occupation.   Trade unionists are deeply concerned in this great economic and humanitarian enterprise which they have been so influential in promoting.   All trade unions should appoint committees or representatives to cooperate wth the Federal Board for vocational education to the end that each disabled soldier, sailor or marine will have the active assistance of the trade union movement in regaining his economic independence.

(1923, p. 309)   The A. F. of L. is aware of complaints that have been made against so-called "trade schools" which developed out of the hope of support from the veterans' bureau and of existing trade schools that hoped to profit by the opportunity they believed to exist.   The A. F. of L. is pleased to be advised that the veterans' bureau is keenly alert to all these elements of exploitation and that measures to correct these evils and avoid their repetition, are under process of enforcement.   Therefore the Executive Council is requested to consider this subject and in co-operation with the director of the veterans' bureau endeavor to promote such policies and practices as will protect and ad-

vance the best interests of both workers and injured soldiers and prevent the exploitation of those injured in the service of our nation.

Soldiers, Relief for—(1920, pp. 110-360). Several bills for the relief of the soldiers were presented in the house in the 66th congress. After hearings had been held by various committees all were withdrawn and sent to the committee on ways and means of the house, which took the whole subject under advisement.   (P. 360)   The executive council was directed to give every assistance to the end that legislation giving adequate relief to former service men would be enacted.

Soldiers, Russian Railway—(1922, p. 322)   Endorsed legislation providing for honorable discharges to members of the Russian Railway Service Corps.

Soldiers' Uniforms for Strikebreakers —(1920, p. 394)   The A. F. of L. condemns the practice of clothing strike-breakers or strike guards, under control of private individuals or agencies, in the uniform of the U. S. army or navy.   The uniform of the great nation of freedom should be everywhere a badge and symbol of human rights and liberties, to which the A. F. of L. is traditionally devoted, and should never be permitted to become the insignia of tyranny or oppression.

Souvenir Condemned—(1919, p. 160) The Central Labor Union of Atlantic City was notified December 2, 1918 that the A. F. of L. prohibited central bodies from issuing so-called convention programs or souvenir publications, the proceeds of which were presumed to be used for entertaining the delegates of the A. F. of L. convention.   The central body promised to comply.   Later it was learned the central body and building trades council had made contracts with certain persons to solicit donations, alleging that they would be used to entertain the delegates to the 1919 convention in that city. The solicitors were notified by the officials of the A. F. of L. that they would "immediately prosecute any person or organization which used the name of the A. F. of L. or its officers for the purpose of soliciting funds of any character for the entertainment of delegates or its officers."   The central body held a special meeting and revoked its contracts with the professional solicitors.   Later the central body held another meeting and rescinded this action.   The charter of the central body was thereupon revoked by the executive council.   The U. S. post office department was asked to assist in preventing the contemplated fraud upon the public and it agreed to deliver all mail intended for those involved in the fraud to the mayor of Atlantic City, who would return all moneys enclosed to the senders.   (P. 459)   The mayor reported he had opened eighty-two letters, forty of which contained $3,250.   This money was returned to the contributors.   In his report the mayor stated that he had no' doubt that if the officers of the A. F. of L. had not taken such aggressive measures at least $50,000 would have been collected, as many of those who contributed believed they were giving the money to the A. F. of L.

Speed Tests, Government—(1919, p. 313)   The Post Office Department has in operation systems to measure the speed and efficiency of employes.   The A. F. of L condemns this policy as in practice the systems have resulted in unreasonable punishment and discrimination against the employes. (1920, p. 422) Reaffirmed condemnation of speed tests.

Strike, Boston Policemen's—(1920, p. 197) For many years the police force of Boston, recognized as one of the finest in the U. S., suffered from inadequate wages, unreasonable hours, unsatisfactory working conditions and unsanitary station houses, many of which were infested with vermin and rodents. In thirteen years the grievance committe of the policemen's social club could secure no improvements. When the present police commissioner came into office about two years ago he abolished the social club's grievance committee and established a "headquarters-controlled" grievance committee which failed to truly represent the men or to secure better conditions. In the meantime, through the instigation of Police Commissioner Curtis, the policemen of Boston were denied the benefits of the veterans' preference act and the right of redress for punishment or dismissal, a right enjoyed by every other police force in the state of Massachusetts. In fact, the police commissioner's entire record shows a studied design to repress and make all submissive to his supreme domination. Discontent among the men began to manifest itself. For years braving all manners of physical hardships and dangers in protecting life and property, a strong resentment crystallized against the perpetuation of their deplorable condition. Being unable to make themselves heard they naturally sought a spokesman and openly held meetings to discuss affiliation with the A. F. of L. The police commissioner objected but did not forbid it until after application had been made and the charter received. Application for a charter was made July 11, 1919, and it was received August 9. On August 11, Commissioner Curtis issued the following order which is so ambiguous and unreasonable as to be illegal. "Section 19. Rule 35. No member of the force shall join or belong to any organization, club or body composed of present or present and past members of the force which is affiliated with or a part of any organization, club or body outside the department, except that a post of the G. A. R., the United Spanish War Veterans and the American Legion of World War Veterans may be formed within the department." From the above it will be seen that the policemen were forbidden from joining or remaining a member of any outside organization fraternal, social, or even religious, except as noted. The situation became so critical that the mayor of Boston appointed a committee of thirty-four of Boston's leading citizens to investigate the entire situation and submit proposals for its amelioration. The men's substantiated and acknowledged grievances shocked Boston. In the meantime Police Commissioner Curtis had been prevailed upon to engage personal counsel and he submitted his willing submissive mind to the advice of one of the cleverest attorneys for "big business" and "the interests" in New England. Although the Boston Chamber of Commerce had urged Commissioner Curtis to employ personal counsel, on learning of his choice it sent a committee to him to suggest a change. The report of the mayor's committee was approved by the mayor, the Boston Chamber of Commerce, and, with the exception of one newspaper, was unanimously endorsed by the press of Boston. One of the proposals was that the charter of the A. F. of L. be surrendered with assurance from the attorneys for the policemen's union that they would accept that stipulation, thus eliminating the question of the policemen's affiliation with the A. F. of L. When the report of the mayor's committee was submitted by its chairman to the police commissioner he was abruptly dismissed with the statement: "This is my business and I will take care of it myself." This destroyed the last ray of hope for the policemen. Nineteen of their number who had been active in organization work were haledbefore the police commissioner and victimized by suspension from the force. These men did not strike. They were later "fired." The rank and file being guilty of every act committed by the victims could only expect like treatment at the hands of such a despot, especially as the police commissioner had several times publicly stated that he had the situation well in hand and could take care of any emergency with volunteer policemen who had been sworn in and were ready for duty. In this provoked frame of mind and driven to desperation, the police held a meeting and unanimously decided to cease work at 5.45 the following afternoon. With weeks of notice and ample men including 400 "loyal" policemen, Police Commissioner Curtis made absolutely no effort to protect the city from the lawless element between the hours of 5.45 p. m. and 8 a. m. the next morning. With the power and the force to prevent it, he either neglected his sworn duty or purposely permitted crimes, misdemeanors and outrages on the commonwealth. The following extract is quoted from the first report of the mayor's committee of thirty-four to the mayor dated October 3: "An endeavor had been made by your committee on Sunday, September 7, to obtain a second conference with the governor for the purpose of reporting upon the then critical situation and presenting for his consideration the committee's plan, but the governor was reported to be in the western part of the state and such a conference could not be arranged. On Monday, September 8, the mayor in cooperation with the members of your committee again endeavored to obtain a conference with the governor, and such a conference was arranged to take place early in the evening of that day. At that time the commissioner had taken final action in regard to the police officials. Your committee in collaboration with your honor thereupon advised the governor of the entire situation, presenting the plan and stating its status. Constructive action upon the principles proposed was urged. In the absence of such action your honor and the members of your committee emphasized the prospective seriousness of the situation which would result from the absence of the great majority of the patrolmen and expressed their strong conviction as to the necessity of troops to the number of not less than three to four thousand to be present in Boston on the day following at 5.45 p. m. either upon the streets or ready in the armories. On Tuesday, September 9, at about 1 o'clock, your honor visited the commissioner at his office in Pemberton square, and was assured by the commissioner that he had the situation well in hand and had ample means at his disposal for the protection of the city. Your honor asked him whether he did not think he ought to have the state guard ready for emergencies, and the commissioner replied that he did not need it and did not want it. Your honor then suggested to the commissioner that the governor's consideration of the question of protection of the city should be asked. The commissioner replied that it was not necessary, but consented to see the governor with the mayor. At this conference the same ground was gone over again. The police commissioner reiterated his assurances that he had the situation in hand and had made ample provision, and again stated that he did not need or want the state guard. No action was taken. The volunteer police were not called to duty until Wednesday morning. On Tuesday evening, September 9, riots, disorders and robbery occurred, and on Wednesday morning, September 10, your honor assumed temporary control of the police department, acting under the Statute of 1917, Ch. 327, Part 1, Sec. 26 which gives your honor the power to do so, "tumult" having then occurred. Your honor also immediately called out that part of the state guard located in Boston which you then had authority to do, and requested the governor to order out three additional regiments of infantry. By Thursday morning order had been generally restored in the city. On Thursday afternoon, September 11, the governor assumed control of the situation, as indicated by his proclamation of that day."

From the above it will be seen that "no action was taken" until the mayor took charge the next morning. The Boston public received a second shock when an affidavit sworn to and subscribed by a reputable newspaper correspondent was read at a public meeting in Boston. It was a sworn statement that the ex-superintendent of police who had been recalled some time before to recruit a new police force had stated to him on the afternoon of the strike that his orders from higher up were not to put any policemen on the street until 8 a. m. the next morning, thus deliberately turning the city over to the lawless element and permitting, if not actually inviting, all that happened. On September 10, Mayor Peters made the following statement:

"The committee of thirty-four appointed by me and myself, have made every human effort to avoid the strike of the policemen but received no co-operation from the police commissioner and no help or practical suggestions from the governor."

What other conclusions can be deducted from these facts except that it was a deliberately premediated plan to throw odium and cast a stigma upon the good name and work of the American labor movement, and discredit the rising power of organized labor? With this record the Massachusetts authorities go forth prostituting the slogan "law and order" in the greatest campaign of deceit and hypocrisy ever perpetrated upon the American public and Police Commissioner Curtis is still being protected by those who do not dare jeopardize political aspirations by the full flood light of truth and justice. To paraphrase a familiar quotation: "Oh, law and order, what crimes are committed in thy name." Although the cause of the Boston policemen led them to martyrdom they achieved not only for their successors but for hundreds of police forces throughout the U. S. thoughtful consideration and improved conditions that could not have been achieved in any other way. The narrative of the Boston police is but history repeating itself. It proved that in this year of grace, 1920, men will not submit to being "hog-tied and gagged." It proves that those, blinded by egotism, arrogance and autocracy, who strike against the laws of nature by constructing a human machine without a safety valve are not only unmindful of the welfare of the masses but are inviting disaster and are therefore especially unfit to be in charge of public safety, for it is only a matter of time before a machine, mechanical, or human, without a safety valve, will explode, and the man or men who advise, construct, or approve such a blunder are a menace and a danger to modern society. It proves that the rational, normal activities and natural aspirations of mankind for a just share of self-respect, decency and happiness can not be denied in spite of autocrats and despots benevolent or otherwise. It proves that only through organization, solidarity, and unity in thought, spirit and action are the rights and welfare of wage-earners to be protected and promoted. The Boston police situation is but one more sacrifice in the human struggle against autocracy, injustice and wrong out of which has grown a better and a brighter day for their successors and fellow-workers. (P. 363) Prior to the summer of 1919, the municipal authorities and police commissioners of a majority of American cities had failed to give any adequate consideration to the urgent necessity for higher wages to policemen· a cost of living which had practically doubled since 1914, had not met with any practical or satisfactory consideration by the majority of American municipalities. The policemen's efforts to have the serious problem of their wages given adequate consideration met with seeming indifference or incapacity on the part of a majority of local authorities. Immediately following the bureaucratic action of Police Commissioner Edwin U. Curtis, of Boston, which led policemen to doff their uniforms, police commissioners and municipal authorites not only throughout New England, but generally throughout America, seemingly awoke to the necessity of paying to policemen a wage which would enable them to maintain a decent standard of living for their families. Throughout the New England territory as well as in other sections, the police force within a few months after September, 1919, were given advances in salaries approximating the rates which had been requested by the police of Boston. That the Boston policemen's request was fully justified is indicated by the fact that the men employed to fill their places after the strike were given the wages and other improved conditions which the Boston policemen had requested in a respectful and proper manner. The responsibility for the conditions which arose in Boston should be placed squarely and completely upon the police commissioner, and his attitude and his methods should be condemned as tending to make loyal, active and vigilant police departments an impossibility in a democratic country. The policemen are and must be regarded as guardians of the peace and protectors to the citizens. In donning the uniform they assume a responsibility to the citizenship of the municipality. The citizens have a right to expect a constant and loyal service on the policemen's part; but the police cannot fulfil their full duty if they are forced to suffer rankling injustice through tyrannical or arbitrary over-officials, or are to be prevented from presenting their claims for higher wages when the welfare of their wives and children makes this an absolute necessity. The policemen owe a duty to the public, but the public owe an equivalent duty to those who are employed to wear the policemen's uniform; and the public owe it to themselves to see that no arbitrary, bureaucratic or tyrannical methods are allowed to develop on the part of those who are in direct administrative authority of the police forces.

Strike, Steel Industry—(1920, pp. 193-260-385) Because of the conditions existing in the steel industry of the country, and because of the great number of appeals which had come from the workers in that industry to the A. F. of L., asking for assistance, the convention of the A. F. of L., held in St. Paul in 1918, adopted the following resolution: "That the executive officers of the A. F. of L. stand instructed to call a conference, during this convention, of delegates of all international unions whose interests are involved in the steel industries, and of all the state federations and city central bodies in the steel districts, for the purpose of uniting all these organizations into one mighty drive to organize the steel plants of America." As a result of the action initiated by the St. Paul resolution, organization work was begun, and by the early spring of 1919 work had progressed to the point where unions existed in many of the large mills. The twenty-four international unions having members engaged in the steel industry from the outset cooperated in the work of organization. The steel corporation from the first viewed the work of organization with extreme dislike and during the spring of 1919, when it became apparent that the response to organization efforts was general, the corporations began the systematic discharge of men who became affiliated with the unions, or who were suspected of such affiliation. In May, 1919, it became apparent that serious danger existed of local strikes that might destroy the national character of the movement. Therefore, a general meeting of the representatives of all local unions of all the trades throughout the steel industry was called, to be held in Pittsburgh, May 25, in order that an expression of the rank and file might be had, and the national character of the movement emphasized by bringing together representatives of the workers from the different points. In this conference it developed that there was an insistent demand for relief and that summary action was necessary in order that it might be met. At this time the convention of the Amalgamated Association of Iron, Steel and Tin Workers was in session in Louisville, Ky., and in that convention a resolution was adopted instructing the president to undertake to secure a conference with the officials of the U. S. steel corporation. He undertook to carry out his instructions, but failed. In view of this failure, and having before it the correspondence between him and Judge Gary, the Pittsburgh conference adopted a resolution, asking the national committee, representing the twenty-four cooperating international unions, to take action. Two days later the national committee, meeting in Washington, adopted the resolution submitted by the Pittsburgh conference calling for a meeting with heads of the steel corporations. President Gompers was requested to write a letter to Judge Gary, asking for a conference. This was done. After waiting for several weeks for an answer from Judge Gary and receiving none, the national committee again met on July 20 to consider the situation. It was the judgment of the committee, expressed by vote, that a strike ballot of the steel workers should be taken, the voting to be under the laws of the respective organizations and the ballots

to be returned August 20. On August 20, the national committee met in Youngstown to canvass the votes. It was found that 98 per cent of the votes cast were in favor of a strike, provided no conference could be secured. The conference committee was instructed, therefore to make another attempt to secure a reply from Judge Gary and in the event of failure, to set a strike date. Thereafter the conference committee called upon Judge Gary at his office in New York. He refused to meet the committee, but asked that the proposition be submitted to him in writing. This was done and he made reply, refusing to meet the committee and outlining his well-known position toward the trade union movement. The committee, headed by the president of the A. F. of L., next called upon President Wilson in Washington and asked that he arrange a conference. The president agreed to make an effort to arrange such a conference. After a week had passed, the national committee again met and advised the president by telegraph of the situation in the steel industry, which, in the judgment of the committee, steadily had grown worse. Reports to the committee showed that hundreds of men were being discharged daily for union membership. At this time the meeting of the international presidents interested in the organization of workers in the steel industry, was set for September 9 to act upon the serious problems confronting the committee. When the meeting of international presidents was convened on September 9 a telegram was laid before the meeting from President Wilson, stating that the efforts of the president had been unavailing, but that he would continue them in the hope that a conference might still be arranged. Many of the delegates felt that this answer was final, but as a precautionary measure another telegram was sent to the president, which brought a reply on the following day, repeating the message contained in the first telegram. Thus, having exhausted every effort to secure a hearing for the steel workers, the organizations represented in the national committee for the organization of steel workers set September 22 as the date upon which a strike of all the trades would begin in all the mills of the U. S. Steel Corporation, and in the mills of all other steel companies not working under union agreements. Two days later the acting chairman of the A. F. of L. of the national committee, received a letter from the president of the A. F. of L., containing a copy of telegram from President Wilson, asking that the strike be postponed until after the president's industrial conference, which was to convene on October 6 in Washington. This was re-enforced by a request from President Gompers that the wishes of President Wilson be complied with, if it could be done without injury to the cause of the workers. On September 17-18 the national committee met to consider this request, but, after a thorough consideration of the situation, found it impossible to postpone the strike date. The condition in the industry was such, in their judgment, that with thousands of men on the streets and the rest of them prepared for the strike, any effort to postpone the strike date would have ruined whatever chance the workers might have had of success. Organizers reported to the committee that if the strike was postponed, they would not be able to return to their districts for they were certain that the men would strike in any event. They reported, also that emissaries of the steel corporations were circulating among the workers, telling them that the A. F. of L. was going to betray them. It was the opinion that postponement of the strike would be accepted as an abandonment of the men in their critical hour. On September 22, approximately 310,000 men in the steel industry ceased work. This number was added to during the following week, until finally it was estimated that 365,000 men had ceased work. This figure was never disputed by the steel corporations. The U. S. senate instructed its committee on labor and education to undertake an investigation of the steel strike and accordingly hearings were held in Washington, D. C., Pittsburgh and the steel centers in the Pittsburgh district. In this testimony before the committee, Judge Gary refused to consider arbitration looking toward a settlement of the controversy. The chairman, of the national committee, on the other hand, agreed in his testimony before the committee, to arbitration of the strike. On October 6 the president's industrial conference began its sessions in Washington. The labor delegations submitted a resolution at the outset, calling for the selection of two members from each of the three groups—labor, employers and the public—represented in the conference to undertake a settlement of the strike, and agreeing that the workers would abide by whatever settlement might be reached in that manner. The resolution met with no success. The Executive Council, at its meeting in Washington, October 5-22, declared its endorsement of the steel strike and recorded its determination to do everything possible to assist in winning the strike. It further denounced the attitude of the United States Steel Corporation toward its employes and instructed the president of the A. F. of L. to issue a public statement to that effect. It was further decided by the Executive Council that every organization be urged to give support to the strike to the fullest extent, and that an appeal be sent to national and international unions, state federations, central bodies and local unions, and that all contributions should be sent to the Secretary of the A. F. of L. The Inter-Church World Movement conducted an investigation of the strike, sending a committee of inquiry and a corps of skilled investigators into all the important strike centers to gather information. Because the attitude of the national committee seemed to be fair, the national committee proposed that the committee should undertake to mediate the strike. This the committee agreed to. The committee visited Judge Gary, but was met with a repetition of Mr. Gary's viewpoint about the strike, and a refusal of either mediation or arbitration. The strike continued until January 8, 1920, when in view of all the circumstances, it was decided that only unnecessary suffering could result from its continuance, and accordingly it was declared off. It was estimated that at the time the strike was declared off there were approximately 100,000 men still out. The international unions expressed their determination to continue with the work of organization and declared the firm intention to stand by the steel workers and not to leave them at the mercy of corporation blacklisting systems. In accordance with this decision, the work of education and organization is being continued. The total receipts and expenditures during the strike were: Receipts, $426,823.79; expenditures, $348,509.72.

(1921, p. 102) The executive council reported: "We have been helpful to the fullest extent of our power in the reorganization of the campaign for the organization of the iron and steel workers. The chairman and secretary of the former special committee resigned. Several conferences were held between the representatives of the various national and international unions having members employed in the iron and steel industry. A new committee was finally organized. The funds remaining in the hands of the former committee were turned over to the new committee. That committee is now functioning and in full cooperation with the officials of the Amalgamated Association of Iron, Steel and Tin Workers."

Steel Strike Investigation—(1920, p. 107-385) After the strike began the committee on education and labor of the senate held a number of hearings to investigate the causes of the controversy. The committee held sessions in Pittsburgh and afterward made a report to the senate in which the following recommendations were made to avert future strikes: "1. That a board or commission somewhat similar to the war labor board should be established. This board should have power of compulsory investigation; to have large powers in mediation and conciliation and recommendations; not to the extent of compulsory arbitration but before this board controversies could be heard, investigations made and decisions rendered. That pending said investigation and decision no strike should be declared provided no employes are discharged for taking part in the controversy and provided further that all opportunity for the employer to take advantage of the delay has been removed; that the principle of collective bargaining and an eight-hour day should be considered by said board and recommendations made to labor and industry in relation thereto; that the board should be in the nature of a federal industrial commission, seeking at all times not only to settle pending disputes but to help bring about a more harmonious condition between employer and employe. A just decision of said board would be indorsed by the public and public sentiment is powerful enough to enforce the findings of such a commission. 2. That an Americanization bill be passed by the congress which will provide for the effective education and Americanization of the illiterate foreigners and native illiterates in this country. 3. One real antidote for unrest in this country is home ownership. 4. Foreigners should be compelled to learn the English language and acquire some education within five years after they arrive with proper limitations on further immigration; giving to those here a certain period of time in which to become nautralized, and if this is not done then deportation should follow. 5. An effective law should be enacted dealing with anarchists, revolutionists and all who would destroy the American government." Objection was immediately entered to the compulsory features of adjusting labor disputes proposed by the committee on education and labor and no action was taken by the senate on the recommendations. (P. 385) Convention unanimously declared against the recommendations of the committee on education and labor.

Strikers Slain by Guards—(1921, p. 417) September 8, 1919, in Hammond, Ind., steel car workers (one of whom wore the uniform of an American overeas soldier and had just returned from patriotic service to this country), who were striving to better their condition in life economically, morally and physically through the agency of a strike, were shot down and killed by armed policemen employed by the city of Hammond and armed guards employed by the Standard Steel Car Company, and at the same time and place by the same parties many other workmen seeking to obtain the same ends were shot down and seriously wounded, a judicious, painstaking investigation of this transaction has established facts tending strongly to establish a conspiracy to bring about this dreadful result. The A. F. of L. condemns in unmeasured terms such conduct and places itself on record as requesting both individual and collective action upon the part of all interested in organized labor (because the victims in this case belonged to organized labor) to ascertain the actual facts in relation to the use of these barbarous weapons.

Strikes, Sympathetic—(1919, p. 342) The A. F. of L. is not in favor of all unions in the U. S.—except those industries in which the state of trade makes it more advantageous to make contracts at a different time—having their contracts with their employers made for only one year, and all to bear date of May 1, May 1 of each year to be observed by union labor as a holiday. Each international union must be free to determine at what season of the year it is most advantageous to its membership to enter into contracts with employers covering the terms of employment.

Suffrage, Canal Zone—(1919, pp. 319–359) The A. F. of L. favors universal suffrage for the citizens of the Canal Zone. (1920, p. 465) Reaffirmed. (P. 466) The A. F. of L. favors the representation in congress by a delegate elected by popular vote from among the electorate of the Canal Zone; this delegate to have the same powers and privileges enjoyed by delegates from other possessions of the United States.

Suffrage, District of Columbia—(1919, pp. 319–359) The A. F. of L. favors universal suffrage for the citizens of the district of Columbia either by legislation or a constitutional amendment. (1920, pp. 112–461) Congress failed to pass bills granting suffrage to the District of Columbia. The citizens of Washington, however, have kept up a continual agitation for the right of citizenship. It is a question that should interest every citizen in the U. S. It is evident that congress can not be prevailed upon to take any steps whatever toward freeing the people of the District of Columbia until the whole nation demands it. It is therefore necessary that agitation among the state federations and central bodies as well as local unions of the entire country be kept up for the purpose of waking members of congress to the great injury they are doing to nearly half a million people. (1921, p. 121) The many years struggle for the franchise by the people of the District of Columbia seems no nearer success than when it began. Every obstacle is being raised to defeat the agitation for the citizens of the district to govern themselves. Those who seem to be in control of the movement are urging bills providing for the election of delegates to the house of representatives. There are many associations, however, including the A. F. of L. which while favoring

these bills, are still insisting that the citizens of the district should be empowered to select their own public officials. They want a mayor, city council and other officials of the district elected by the people. But there is a strong and influential body of men in the district who although few in number have prevented this worthy outcome. They have managed to defeat the agitation by confining their efforts to the securing of a delegate or delegates to the house of representatives. (1923, p. 307) Reaffirmed declaration for suffrage in District of Columbia.

Suffrage in Rhode Island—(1919, p. 444) Rhode Island is the only state that has a law which deprives the citizens of the right of suffrage unless they own real estate. The A. F. of L. reaffirms its condemnation of this pernicious law and also those responsible for its continuance.

Suffrage, Woman—(1919, pp. 121–328–353) The A. F. of L. urges the ratification of the suffrage amendment by the several state legislatures, and shall do all in its power to aid in the speedy consummation of this last step in woman's enfranchisement, as it has ever aided throughout the long struggle. (1920, p. 119) Thirty-five states had ratified the amendment up to April 20.

Supreme Court—(1922, pp. 106–169) The "five to four" habit of the U. S. supreme court in making decisions has aroused the people of our country and undoubtedly has had the effect of lessening respect for the highest judicial tribunal in our republic. Demands are repeatedly made for better practitioners of the people. Representative McSwain introduced H. R. 9755, which does not go far enough. It provides that no state law can be held unconstitutional by the supreme court of the U. S. unless at least seven members concur in the opinion. The A. F. of L. has contended that the supreme court has no legal power vested in it and no right to decide unconstitutional any law passed by congress nor any law passed by any state within the U. S. which is not in itself in contravention of a republican form of government. (P. 371) The American people are facing a critical situation. Their very existence as a democracy and a government of law is at stake. A judicial oligarchy is threatening to set itself up above the elected legislatures, above the people themselves. Profiting by the unsettled industrial conditions of the country and the political apathy of the people, which have followed upon the conclusion of the World War, the forces of privilege and reaction have embarked upon a concerted and determined campaign to deprive the citizens of their constitutional liberties, to break down the standards of life which the American workers have laboriously built up in generations of suffering and struggle, and to emasculate or destroy their most effective weapon of resistance and defense—the labor unions. Side by side with the implacable anti-union drive conducted by powerful organizations of employers throughout the country, who exercise their own unquestioned right to organize and yet brazenly deny their employees the same right, the unblushing subservience of many public officials to the dictates of big business and their undisguised contempt for the interests of the workers, the courts of the country, and particularly the supreme court of the U. S., have within recent years undertaken to deprive American labor of fundamental rights and liberties which heretofore have been accepted as deeply and organically ingrained in our system of jurisprudence. Over a century ago Thomas Jefferson said: "It has long been my opinion, and I have never shrunk from its expression, that the germ of dissolution of our Federal Government is in the judiciary—the irresponsible body working like gravity, by day and by night, gaining a little today and gaining a little tomorrow, and advancing its noise-less step like a thief over the field of jurisdiction until all shall be usurped." The prophetic warning of the great champion of American democracy threatens to come true. What confronts the workers of America is not one or several casual court decisions favoring the interests of property as against the human rights of labor, but a series of adjudications of the highest tribunal of the land, successively destroying a basic right or cherished acquisition of organized labor, each forming a link in a fateful chain consciously designed to enslave the workers of America. Five years ago a severe blow was dealt by the supreme court decision in the notorious case of The Hitchman Coal and Coke Company vs. Mitchell, which seriously limited the right of organized labor to unionize establishments. The decision did not receive the condemnation it justly deserved because public attention was almost exclusively centered on the World War. On January 3, 1921, the Supreme Court in the case of Duplex Printing Press Company vs. Deering practically nullified the portions of the Clayton act which were intended to safeguard the rights of labor in industrial disputes and to limit the power of the courts to decide such disputes by summary injunctions, thus striking down with one fell stroke the result of unceasing agitation of organized labor which had extended over twenty years, and was designed to equalize before the law the position of workers and employers. In December, 1921, the supreme court, by its decision in the case of Truax vs. Corrigan set aside as unconstitutional a state law which limited the power of the courts to issue injunctions in labor disputes, thus frustrating the efforts of labor in all industrial states to secure relief from the arrogated authority of the courts. In the same month the court in the case of American Steel Foundries vs. Tri-City Central Trades Council virtually abolished the right of striking workers to picket, no matter how peaceably: authorized the courts arbitrarily to regulate the conduct of strikers, and set up a rule limiting strikers to the stationing of one "missionary" in front of each entrance to the struck establishment—one striking "missionary" to persuade hundreds or even thousands of strikebreakers of the iniquity of their course. What a mockery upon the acknowledged rights of workers on strike to win over would-be strike-breakers by pleading and persuasion. On May 15, 1922, the supreme court set aside as unconstitutional the child labor law, which had been enacted after years of agitation on the part of the most forward-looking and humane elements of our citizenship. On June 5, 1922, the supreme court handed down a unanimous opinion in the case of United Mine Workers of America vs. Coronado Coal Co., which in effect opens the way for a general raid upon union funds, by holding that labor unions are suable as such and liable for damages to employers if caused by unlawful acts on the part of any of their striking members, whether such acts are authorized or not, so long as the strike is sanctioned by the union. Thus by six

decisions the U. S. supreme court, composed of nine men without direct mandate from the people and without responsibility to the people, has set aside a congressional enactment which clearly expressed the will of the vast majority of the people, and all but outlawed the activities of organized labor, which alone can protect the workers from the oppression and aggression of the greedy and cruel interests. This despotic exercise of a unsurped power by nine men, or a bare majority of them, over the lives and liberties of millions of men, women and children, is intolerable. With the immortal Lincoln we believe that: "The people of these United States are the masters of both congress and courts, not to overthrow the constitution, but to overthrow the men who pervert the constitution." (Speech at Cincinnati, Sept. 17, 1859.) We are determined to preserve our rights as workers, citizens and freemen, and we call upon all fair-minded and liberty-loving citizens to unite with us in a determined effort to deprive the courts of the despotic powers which they have assumed, and to make our government in full measure a government of the people, for the people and by the people. To this end the A. F. of L. records itself in favor of, and promotes the adoption of, amendments to the constitution of the U. S. for the following purposes:

1. An amendment prohibiting the labor of children under the age of 16 years in any mine, mill, factory, work-shop or other industrial or mercantile establishment, and conferring upon congress the power to raise the minimum age below which children shall not be permitted to work, and to enforce the provisions of the proposed amendment by appropriate legislation.

2. An amendment prohibiting the enactment of any law or the making of any judicial determination which would deny the right of the workers of the U. S. and its territories and dependencies to organize for the betterment of their conditions: to deal collectively with employers: to collectively withold their labor and patronage and induce others to do so.

3. An amendment providing that if the U. S. supreme court decides that an act of congress is unconstitutional, or by interpretation asserts a public policy at variance with the statutory declaration of congress, then if congress by a two-thirds majority re-passes the law, it shall become the law of the land. In order to make the constitution of the U. S. more flexible to meet the needs of the people, an amendment providing for easier amendments of the same, that in conjunction with the campaign for the adoption of the suggested constitutional amendments, congress be urged to enact: a. A child labor law which will overcome the objections raised by the U. S. supreme court to the laws heretofore passed by congress and nullified by the court: b. A law which will make more definite and effective the intention of congress in enacting Sections 6, 19 and 20 of the Clayton act, which was manifestly ignored or overrideen by the court: c. An act repealing the Sherman anti-trust law, which was intended by congress to prevent illegal combinations in restraint of trade, commonly known as "trusts," but through judicial misinterpretation and perversion has been repeatedly and mainly invoked to deprive the toiling masses of their natural and normal rights. (P. 393) Executive Council directed to call conferences of persons and associations interested in any or all of the

above-specified recommendations, for the purpose of obtaining advice, assistance and co-operation in the preparation of the proposed laws and constitutional amendments, and in the education of public opinion for their support and adoption.

(1923, p. 35) The supreme court of the U. S. is a unique phenomenon in government. It is the only court in the world which exercises the power to nullify the laws enacted by the national law making body. There are two groups of interpolaters of the prerogatives of this court, one holding that the power to pass on the constitutionality of legislation has been usurped by the court, and the other that such authority is conferred. But regardless of the origin of the authority exercised many hold that the court must exercise this prerogative in order to maintain government in the U. S. in accord with principles outlined in our written constitution. It is indisputable that the supreme court of the U. S. has been a most powerful agency in determining our national policies. Not only by declaring laws invalid does it exercise veto power and forbid the adoption of certain policies, but by interpreting the law the court has definitely outlined and established general policies. Instances of this are the decisions upon federal income tax, first declaring it legal and a few weeks later reversing its own decision and declaring the income tax law unconstitutional, in both instances the court standing five to four. In this case, in the course of a few weeks, one of the nine justices of the supreme court changed his mind and his vote and that change declared a law of congress unconstitutional. The decision upon the anti-trust law when the court interpolated the word "unreasonable" and declared that only such combinations as unduly and "unreasonably" restrained trade were prohibited by the anti-trust act. Thus, the court arbitrarily set up two classifications of combinations, one good, the other bad: one illegal and the other legal. The decisions absolutely nullify the purpose of the original act. Irrespective as to the wisdom of the economic theory held by the court there existed a governmental situation under which an all-powerful court was negating the written intent of the law making body and establishing another version more in accord to its liking and judgment. In passing upon social and labor legislation the supreme court has frequently placed itself at complete variance and judgment with our national congress, with state legislatures and with the expressed will of the people. The court follows precedents as established by legal decisions and is far removed from the spirit and the methods of industrial undertakings. It has no conception of the radical difference between politics and industry but it has attempted to interpret economic situations from the legalistic point of view, whereas these situations respond to the forces and technique of science. Within the past year the U. S. supreme court has nullified the second child labor law, minimum wage law for women, and the labor provisions of the Clayton anti-trust law, thus overturning policies which have won public approval. These laws were enacted after years of patient educational work to convince public opinion of their validity and the struggle to overcome opposing forces. They were measures that were necessary to conserve human life and were designed to meet practical needs. The last convention directed that efforts be made to secure the

enactment of the following constitutional amendment: "That if the U. S. supreme court decides that an act of congress is unconstitutional or by interpretation asserts a public policy at variance with the statutory declaration of congress, then if congress by a two-thirds majority repasses the law, it shall become the law of the land." Why is there so much concern over vetoing the decisions of the supreme court? There are three branches of government, the legislative, the executive, and the judicial. Since the ratification of the constitution, by gradual encroachment the supreme court has assumed greater power than that exercised by either or both the legislative and executive branches of our government. The constitution provides that congress shall enact laws but they must be approved by the president. If he vetoes them congress can pass them over the veto by a two-thirds vote. Each house is a check on the other, the president is a check on both houses and congress itself is a check on the executive. But there is none now on the supreme court. It has assumed powers not given by the constitution. Why should not congress have the power to veto decisions of the supreme court? Is it more enlightened than the 531 representatives of the senate and house of representatives and the president? The supreme court is composed of nine men selected by the president, sometimes not alone for their judicial ability but for political or other reasons that are not given to the public. Five to four decisions are frequent. In a decision of the supreme court declaring the minimum wage law unconstitutional the following occurs· "This court, by an unbroken line of decisions from Chief Justice Marshall to the present day, has steadily adhered to the rule that every possible presumption is in favor of the validity of an act of congress until overcome beyond rational doubt." One of the justices did not act, as before his appointment he had fought for minimum wage laws. Therefore the decision was really five to four. On petit juries men are asked if they will find man guilty if the evidence shows beyond a "reasonable doubt" that he is guilty. Twelve men have to cast a unanimous vote. If one man has a "reasonable doubt" which undoubtedly is a rational doubt, the case results in a mistrial. Then there will be a disagreement. If four men out of nine declare a law is constitutional there certainly is a reasonable, rational doubt that the law is not unconstitutional. Therefore, the proposal of the A. F. of L. is that congress shall have power to reenact by a two-third's vote any law declared unconstitutional by the supreme court. (P. 265) A careful review of the development of the federal judiciary and the powers gradually but constantly assumed by the U. S. supreme court can lead to no other conclusion than that our legislative branch of government, because it is the most popular and responsive branch of government to the will of the people, is fast being undermined by those who distrust popular government and who find solace and relief in the ever-growing power of the judiciary, which is almost beyond the reach of the populace. It is because of this that we find so frequently corporation lawyers, and lawyers of rich and wealthy clients, through bar associations and the like, endeavoring to undertake what they choose to call the educating of the masses in the sacredness of the constitution and the divinity of the supreme court as at present selected and not elected. This very response to labor's demand that the assumed powers of the U. S. supreme court shall be limited and restrained, and that congress, as the expression of the people's will, shall be moved to assert its original powers, is perhaps the best demonstrated proof of the validity of labor's proposal. The Executive Council shall do all within the power and influence of the A. F. of L. to promote and to secure the enactment of constitutional amendment which will give congress final authority to express the people's will, but that efforts be made likewise to have all judges of our federal government, including the justices of the U. S. supreme court, elected by the people for fixed periods of time, rather than having them selected without the will of the people and for their lifetime.

Tariff on Crude Oil—(1921, p. 403) The A. F. of L. hereby urgently requests Congress to immediately enact an adequate import tariff on crude oil and its by-products to protect the independent petroleum and coal producing interests operating within the United States so as to afford fair return to such invested capital domestically engaged, and to assure a decent living wage to every industrial worker so employed.

Taxes, Sales and Profits—(1921, p. 107) After months of a publicity campaign, bills were presented in congress to repeal the excess profits tax and establish a sales tax. The true meaning of this shifting of taxation is that it is proposed to take $990,000,000 in taxes from those able to bear it and load them on the backs of the masses of our people. If the excess profits tax is repealed it will absolve those who pay it from a proper share of taxation. The turnover sales tax is a tax levied on "every pound of sugar, salt and starch that goes into the family use, from the growing of the sugar beets to its purchase at the store, on every pound of flour and other food, on evey pound of meat from the farm to the packer and back again, on every pound of tea or coal, on every garment from the hat down to shoes and stockings, or like an old-time description of a tariff bill, it is a tax "from the cradle to the grave." In other words, it is a tax on every turnover that may be had on practically all the necessary commodities of life. A sales tax, it is generally agreed, would have the most unfavorable consequences as it would fall with a force unequal to their ability to pay upon those least able to bear the burden. The rich would pay a less amount of tax for the same food, drink and wear than the poorest in the land, as they would purchase in large quantities. In addition a turnover sales tax would pyramid prices to the consumer. In other words, if the tax is on the turnover sale of everything, it would be most burdensome and most inequitable. The poor of necessity buy in small quantities. If they would purchase ten articles for 10 cents each they would have to pay at least 10 cents in taxes, as the vendor would charge 1 cent on every sale. This would be in addition to the turnover tax from previous sales. In fact, the purchaser would never know how much tax he was paying, as the dealer, as is generally the practice with those who sell, might add a larger amount to the selling price than is called for by the tax law. According to a statement made January 31, 1921, in the house of representatives, "there are practically nine turnovers in the case of cotton and woolen goods, eight turnovers in the case of leather goods, and seven or eight in the case of steel—that is, from the original ore

up to the time of the finished article. What applies to these articles applies with equal force to almost everything we use. In other words, this proposed tax of 1 cent on each turnover has to be applied from five, six and seven to nine times. But that is not the worst. You will find that in many cases where the present tax is imposed they have raised the price of goods sometimes 400 per cent during the different turnovers." We therefore declare· 1. That the excess profits taxes should be retained. 2. Every effort should be made to defeat proposals for new taxes, as all the money we need can be obtained from the present taxes under efficient administration. In fact, the best authorities declare that if we remodel our tax system on the basis of readjusting rates and improving the administration and assessment of taxes we can secure greater revenues than we do at present. 3. Nothing should be left undone to defeat the introduction of a turnover, consumption or sales tax. The excess profits tax carried us through the war and in time of peace it will be as valuable an aid when properly administered.   (P. 314) There can be little doubt that the outcry in interested quarters against the excess profit tax is primarily caused by the salutary fact that that tax is one of the few that cannot easily be shifted to the consumer, while the turnover sales tax is an amazingly brazen attempt to pile up on the consuming masses a share of the burden of taxation greatly disproportionate to their ability to pay. We also declare against the imposition of a retail or general sales tax or turnover tax, or any other tax on consumption, and oppose the repeal of the excess profits tax, and demand that the highest rate of taxation levied during the war upon incomes and excess profits be retained until the full money cost of the war has been paid, and further demand that the government promptly levy a rapidly progressive tax upon large estates and a moderate tax upon the value of land and other natural resources speculatively held in order that the national debt may be promptly retired.

(1922, p. 97) The campaign to relieve the well-to-do from excess profit taxes and surtaxes and business of corporation taxes and to make up the loss through the sales tax is well on its way. Excess profit taxes were repealed and the surtaxes reduced from 65 per cent to 50 per cent. Senator Smoot in the senate and Representative Longworth in the house are the leaders trying to bring about this legislation. Senator Smoot publicly declared last November: "While the manufacturers or sales tax is not embodied in the revenue laws of our country at this session of congress, it will be in the very near future, just as sure as God lives." The argument used to impress members of congress that they should vote for the sales tax, no matter how objectionable it would be to the mass of the people, is the following· "If you tax the people so they don't know it they can not object: but if they know they are paying a tax they will object." The scheme as outlined to representatives of the A. F. of L. is to first adopt a manufacturers tax of 3 per cent. The taxes on the well-to-do are to be gradually repealed and the sales tax extended until it becomes a tax on every sale, in other words, an overturn sales tax. A man with a million dollars net income under the present surtax rate of 50 per cent would pay $500,000 income tax. When the sales tax is loaded on the people he will not have to pay $500,000 but will simply pay a certain per cent on what he spends, less his exemptions. If he expended $250,000 a year to live and the sales tax was 3 per cent he would pay $7,500. Thus by grace of congress he would be able to save $492,500 that he has to pay now as income tax and $250,000 more, making $742,500 that he would have left to put in bank, speculate with or to do anything else he desired. The wage worker who earns $2,000 a year, if married, pays no income tax, but would pay the sales tax on every article he would buy. As it would be necessary for him to spend the entire $2,000 to support himself and dependents he would be compelled to pay $60 taxes. He would have nothing left to put in bank. The greater the net income the more desirable the sales tax would be. The most persistent advocates of the sales tax are individuals and those who represent great business and financial interests who have to pay large income taxes. The true inwardness of the agitation for the sales tax can best be explained by the statement made by one o Washington's largest department store owners, who said publicly; "I am not only in favor of the sales tax plan for raising funds for the soldiers' bonus, but would like to see it adopted as a permanent plan for raising government revenues to replace the present taxation system." Nothing can be plainer to prove the charges that the whole campaign for the sales tax is to relieve business and the well-to-do from taxation. The Executive Council has urged that the following declaration of the Denver convention on taxation be followed by congress; "The A. F. of L. declares against the imposition of a retail or general sales tax or turnover tax or any other tax on consumption and opposes the repeal of the excess profit tax and demands that the highest rate of taxation levied during the war upon incomes and excess profits be retained until the full money cost of the war has been paid: and further demands that the government promptly levy a rapidly progressive tax upon large estates and a moderate tax upon the value of land and other natural resources speculatively held in order that the national debt may be promptly retired." Much has been said about the sales tax being absorbed before it reaches the consumer. This claim is most effectually disproved in the brief presented to the Canadian government by the Canadian Manufacturers' Association. Representatives of the association on February 23, 1922, appeared before Canadian officials and submitted a program to repeal all taxes on business and extend the sales tax to make up the losses that would result. One clause in the brief submitted by the representatives of the association is as follows: "That as the sales tax is a tax payable by the purchaser, manufacturers and wholesalers should not be held liable for any taxes which they can not collect owing to the purchaser being insolvent or refusing to pay." Not many years ago there was a phrase used that accomplished its purpose, but in the years that have passed since the people have realized its untruth, and that is, that "the foreigners pays the tariff tax." This is on a parity with the claim that the "vendor pays the sales tax." (P. 325) Persistent efforts have been made during the past year to drive a sales tax through congress., Each time this effort has been frustrated by the vigilance of the spokesmen for labor. The danger is by no means past. It is expected that reactionary representatives of the large financial ɪnterests will endeavor to incorporate sales

tax legislation into the soldier bonus bill now awaiting senate action. Consequently the never-ceasing vigil of the representatives of the A. F. of L. must be continued to be exercised to prevent this objectionable tax system from being foisted upon the American people.

(1923, p. 82) Propagandists who sought to save the well-to-do from taxation and place the burden upon those least able to bear it were unable to carry out their scheme in the sixty-seventh congress. The effort to increase the burdens of the masses of the people was led in congress by Senator Smoot. He was supported by certain newspapers whose owners not only wished to be saved from taxation but who wished to bring about the same desirable result for their big advertisers. Representative Frear of Wisconsin led the fight against the sales tax. The A. F. of L. through its legislative and publicity departments made a vigorous onslaught on this vicious legislation, and the masses of the people are to be congratulated that it has been defeated. But those who are agitating for the sales tax have not given up hope of finally saddling it on the people. Secretary of the Treasury Mellon very adroitly claims that the increase in the income tax was caused by a reduction in the surtaxes. Everyone knows that approximately five million wage earners were out of employment in 1921. Therefore the income tax paid was much less than for 1922. It is through such misrepresentations as this that the profiteers and evaders of their just obligations are, through their representatives in congress, seeking to force through legislation inimical to the interests of the mass of the people and for the special benefit of a few. (P. 357) We urge the forces of labor to be on guard at the forthcoming session of congress to fight vigorously any attempts by the Smoots in congress to foist this discriminatory form of taxation upon the wage earners.

Taylor System—(1920, p. 119) The naval appropriation bill for 1921 was reported by the committee with the clause prohibiting the use of the funds appropriated for the conducting of stop-watch and other time measuring devices omitted. An amendment to restore the clause was adopted by a vote of 221 to 70.

Teachers—(1919, pp. 77–431) To elevate and advance the interests of the teaching profession and to promote popular and democratic education, the right of the teachers to organize and to affiliate with the movement of the organized workers must be recognized. (P. 311) The teachers, always wretchedly underpaid, have been unable to meet the doubled cost of living with the meagre salary increases which they have secured. The work of the teachers determines the quality of our future citizenship, and should receive financial compensation more nearly commensurate with its service to the community.

(1920, pp. 111–461) Retirement law was enacted for public school teachers in the District of Columbia when 62 years of age. The retirement fund is contributory, to be based on an annuity table such as the secretary of the treasury shall direct and vary yearly to correspond to changes in the salaries of the teachers. (P. 118) A senatorial investigation of District of Columbia schools ordered. Among the subjects to be investigated are the policy and influence of the teachers' unions in the conduct and management of the schools, and the extent to which said unions control teachers, members of the school board, and the selection of the teachers. (P. 462) The senatorial investigation of the schools of the District of Columbia has been completed, and the teachers' unions, of which there are ten in the district' including in their combined jurisdictions every type of teaching work, were only incidentally involved. Nothing derogatory of the teachers' unions was established, no union officials were summoned to testify, and the official report of the senatorial committee conducting the investigation contained no word of criticism of the union. However, a concerted attack upon the union movement among teachers has been made by the organized interests hostile to labor. In St. Louis the board of education has adopted the following rule; "No person shall be employed hereafter, in any capacity in the instruction department, who is a member of a trade or labor union or of an organization affiliated with a trade and labor union: and any person employed in the instruction department who becomes a member of any such organization shall be subject to immediate dismissal from the service." This rule was adopted, notwithstanding the fact that the Missouri law requires every member of the board of education to take oath "that he will not be influenced, during the term of office, by any consideration except that of merit and fitness in the appointment of officers and the engagement of employes." In Lancaster, Pa., eighty-six teachers were given the option by the Lancaster board of education, either of withdrawing from the American Federation of Teachers or of losing their positions: and upon their determined refusal to renounce their right as American citizens to maintain the religious, civic, or economic affiliations of their free choice, the board of education declared their positions vacant. This arbitrary action was taken in defiance not only of the rights of the teachers, but of overwhelming public opinion, as evidenced by the protests of the central labor union, business men, ministerial associations, mass meetings, and a petition demanding reinstatement, signed by thousands. Similar attempts are being made by autocratic boards of education in other communities. If the schools are to develop free, unafraid men and women, American citizens of the highest type, the teachers must live and work in an atmosphere of freedom and self-respect. The officers of the A. F. of L. are instructed to use every effort to protect teachers aganst intimidation and discrimination on account of affiliation with organized labor: and affiliated state and central labor bodies are urged to resist with all vigor any attempt to coerce the judgment and conscience of the teachers in the public schools. (P. 468) The history of the actions of many autocratic boards of education shows an urgent need for tenure of position for teachers based on efficiency. The A. F. of L. directly, and through its affiliated locals will use every effort to secure laws granting tenure of position for teachers along the following lines: (1) Tenure should be permanent during efficiency after the lapse of the probationary period, which should not exceed three years. (2) All dismissals, both during and after probation, to be for causes definitely embodied in the educational law, such as gross insubordination, inefficiency, conduct unbecoming a teacher, etc. (3) After period of probation, dismissal for any cause (including inefficiency) to be only by a trial board of seven chosen as follows: three by the school board, three by the teachers, the six to elect a

seventh, who is not to be either a member of the school board or of the teaching force. At all hearings teachers shall be represented by counsel. Appeal from the decision of the trial board may be made to the civil courts, whose decision shall be final. (P. 469) The New York legislature passed a bill, which was vetoed by the governor providing that all teachers of the state of New York should be required to be examined and to hold a certificate from the board of regents stating, "that the teacher holding the same is a person of good moral character, and that he has shown satisfactorily that he will support the constitutions of this state and of the United States, and that he is loyal to the institutions and laws thereof." The bill furthermore requires that, "the certificate authorizing a person to teach may be revoked by the commissioner of education on the ground that such person is not of good moral character, or for any act or utterance showing that he will not support the constitutions of this state and of the United States, or that he is not loyal to the institutions and laws thereof." In his veto message the governor said· "This bill must be judged by what can be done under its provisions. It permits one man to place upon any teacher the stigma of disloyalty, and this without even a hearing or a trial. No man is so omniscient or wise as to have entrusted to him such arbitrary and complete power, not only to condemn any individual teacher, but also to decree what belief or opinion he deems to be opposed to the institutions of the country. No teacher could continue to teach if he or she entertained any objection, however conscientious, to any existing institution. If this law had been in force prior to the abolition of slavery, opposition to that institution, which was protected by the constitution and the laws, would have been just cause for the disqualification of a teacher. Opposition to any present established institution, no matter how intelligent, conscientious or disinterested opposition might be, would be sufficient to disqualify the teacher. Every teacher would be at the mercy of his colleagues, his pupils and their parents, and any word or act of the teacher might be held by the commissioner to indicate an attitude hostile to some of 'the institutions of the United States or of the state.' The bill unjustly discriminates against teachers as a class. It deprives teachers of their right to freedom of thought: it limits the teaching staff of the public schools to those only who lack the courage or the mind to exercise their legal right to just criticism of existing institutions. The bill confers upon the commissioner of education a power of interference with freedom of opinion which strikes at the foundations of democratic education." (P. 471) In face of the existing national emergency in education caused by wretchedly inadequate teachers' salaries and the financial starving of the schools, and by the lack of self-respecting conditions under which teachers work, and the absence of any democratic voice of the teachers in the conduct of the schools the A. F. of L. particularly stresses Sections 17, 18 and 19 of the A. F. of L. declaration of educational principles.

(1921, pp. 105–326) There has been forcibly brought to our attention numerous flagrant attempts to intimidate teachers in the exercise of their rights and duties as citizens outside the school, and to compel them to serve the interests of propaganda within the classroom. In the light of the definite policy revealed by these attempts in all sections of the country, the frank boast of one of the leading advisory agencies of the business and employing interests, becomes even more sinister· "The war taught us the power of propaganda. Now when we have anything to sell to the American people, we know how to sell it. We have the school, the pulpit and the press." That boast may have been blatant and overconfident, but exceedingly powerful forces are working constantly to make it a reality. The Montreal convention approved the veto by former Governor Smith of New York of the so-called Lusk bill, designed to place the thinking of teachers under the control of a bureaucratic official. This year your committee regrets the necessity of reporting the incredible facts of the re-enactment of that measure by the New York state legislature and its signature by Governor Miller. Similar attempts have been defeated in other states, but organized labor must be on the alert everywhere and constantly against insidious efforts to pervert the schools.

(1923, p. 87) The age-old objection to those employed in educating the masses was found to be very effective in defeating a bill before congress providing for fixing the wages of teachers in the District of Columbia. It granted them a substantial increase and the teachers worked very hard for its passage. The bill was passed by the senate. When the bill reached the District of Columbia committee of the house the anti-educationists began their work to defeat the measure. Several amendments requested by the Teachers' Union and representatives of the A. F. of L. were made in committee and the bill was reported favorably to the house. Then the scheme to defeat it began to come to light. The leaders, or it might with justice be said the "misleaders" of the house, set out to defeat it. This bill could only come up on what is known as "district day," but for various reasons it was not permitted to come before the house although the "leaders" promised that before the session ended they would see that the bill was passed. The truth of the matter is that the bill as amended was opposed by the school administration forces for the reason that the amendments gave higher rates to the actual teachers while they cut the proposed excessive remuneration for the school administration. Representative Campbell of Kansas, chairman of the house rules committee, who was defeated in the last election, house leader Mondell and chairman Focht of the District of Columbia committee, both of whom also were defeated, juggled the measure in such a manner that they were able to prevent the bill coming to a vote. If it had come to a vote it would have been passed by an overwhelming majority. The scuttling of the teachers' pay bill was considered by the "leaders" to be an "administration victory." (P. 259) The A. F. of L. is deeply interested in the work of securing adequate compensation for school teachers. We have long recognized the fact that this class of wage earners is underpaid, consequently we have traditionally supported their movement which had for its purpose higher wages and a higher standard of life for the school teachers of our country.

Teachers, Open Shoppers Against— (1921, p. 269) The open shop and other reactionary interests are attacking organized labor and all progressive groups from every direction, making special efforts to secure control of the press, and even of the churches, and the schools, those most important public opinion forming agencies. Organized labor took the initiative in securing the establishment of tax-supported public schools, and has been a leading influence in the development and protection of public education. The American Federation of Teachers in cooperation with all organized labor is the most effective instrument in combating these un-American influences and maintaining the schools as the basis of democratic institutions, therefore the officers of the A. F. of L. are instructed to give substantially increased assistance to the American Federation of Teachers in this struggle.

Teachers, Organization of— (1922, p. 368) In a situation threatening the integrity of the public schools, the alert watchfulness of organized labor and other progressive groups is essential, but after all, the crux of the matter lies with the teachers themselves. Without steadfastness and tenacious idealism on the part of the teachers there would scarcely be a rallying point for liberal support: once the enemy succeeds in crushing them out there will be little left to salvage. The only adequate protection for the spiritual and professional independence of the teachers is effective organization. Primarily in the interests of the schools and of the community, the A. F. of L. recommends that the Executive Council of the A. F. of L. and all state and local central bodies give every assistance to the American Federation of Teachers in the organization of the teachers and the improvement of the schools. (1923, p. 217) Reaffirmed.

Telephone Investigation, Bell— (1923, p. 360) Executive Council directed to cooperate with the electrical workers in urging an investigation of the American Bell Telephone Company as the problems of the relation of telephone rates to telephone wages, the greatly increased cost of telephone service in recent years, the surtaxes devised in the way of installation and removal charges, the annual tribute paid by this company of several million dollars to the American Bell, the great salaries of executives enormously increased during the years in which wage increases have been arrogantly denied to the working employees, all challenge public concern.

Text Books— (1919, p. 467) Condemned the American Book Company's policy in its attitude toward Labor and urged upon all school authorities and purchasing agents for the public schools that they provide only such text-books and other material for the use of the school children of the country as are produced by union labor and under union conditions, to the end that the first inkling of general knowledge obtained by the children, and the first lessons they receive in the glorious history of a free people be not derived from sources tainted by the contamination of scab labor, to the profit of those who refuse to recognize the fundamental principles of justice and fair dealing on which the labor movement of America rests.

(1923, p. 249) The A. F. of L. urges upon the several States of the Union the use of free text books in the public schools where no such provision now exists.

Textile Workers— (1921, p. 268) Directed Executive Council to make every effort to bring about a congressional investigation of the conditions now existing in the cotton mills of the south where reductions in wages had been made of from 37½ to 40 per cent and the workweek increased from 55 to 60 and 65 hours.

(1922, p. 318) The United Textile Workers of America have, despite tremendous obstacles, succeeded in maintaining the eight-hour day in the textile industry of New England, which action has been of great value to the organized workers, unorganized workers and society as a whole. The A. F. of L. congratulates the United Textile Workers of America for their wonderful energy and fortitude, and we request all those interested in maintaining the eight-hour day to give to the officers and members of the United Textile Workers of America their full moral and financial support during this great struggle.

Textile Workers Slain—(1919, p. 312) On the night of May 21, 1919, while attending an open-air organizing meeting, seven innocent people, members of the United Textile Workers of America, were shot down in a cold-blooded manner by officials and paid hirelings connected with some of the textile mill corporations at Columbus, Georgia. As a result of this dastardly act, one of these innocent victims, Grady Tucker, a soldier who had just returned from service on the battlefields of France, paid the supreme sacrifice. We feel convinced that this cowardly act is a desperate attempt on the part of the mill owners to stem the tide of organization that is now sweeping over the textile districts of the southern states, to the end that they may maintain the long hours of labor, low wages, and the exploitation of child labor. The convention unanimously condemns this cowardly crime committed against peaceful, law-abiding American citizens.

Thrift and Protection For—(1921, p. 397) Huge sums of money were literally swindled from the public last year according to the best authorities, by the sale of fraudulent and worthless stocks and securities. The men and women in industry have neither the time, knowledge, nor experience to make a complete and thorough investigation and examination of stocks and securities that are offered to them in attractive ways to induce the investing of their small sums and savings accumulated through sacrifice, strictest economy, and thrift. The savings securities issued by the U. S. government, through the treasury department, in denominations of 25c, $1, $5, $25, $100 and $1,000, provide the means whereby the small investor and saver will have a safe and convenient investment increasing in value each month, returning a satisfactory rate of interest and free from speculative fluctuations. Therefore the A. F. of L. calls upon the U. S. government, through the treasury department, to adopt every necessary means of protecting small investors by calling their attention to the fraudulent and fake stocks and securities, and to adopt every possible method to rid the country and the people of these fraudulent schemers. The A. F. of L. strongly urges the U. S. government, through the treasury department to continue the issuance of treasury savings securities and to adopt every means to call to the attention of the great body of men, women, and children in the U. S. the splendid opportunity of practising thrift and investing their funds in government securities to the end that thrift, economy, and the accumulation of a savings fund may become a part of the everyday life of every American worker. The A. F. of L. offers to the U. S. government, through the treasury department, cooperation and assistance in bringing to the attention of the rank and file of all the local unions the advantages

to their members in placing their savings in government securities.

Thrift Stamps and Government Securities—(1919, p. 322) The A. F. of L. approves of the continuation and extension of the war savings and thrift stamp institution, or the substitution of a national savings institution akin in character and method which will prove helpful to safeguard the earnings of the toiling masses of our country.

1920, (p. 468) All national and international unions and local unions are urged to advocate thrift stamps, government savings stamps and treasury savings certificates as the best and safest method for saving and investment that their membership can adopt, as against the schemes of private corporations which are now attempting to take advantage of the government's savings program and the saving habit formed during the war by introducing thrift systems in industry through which they will make profit from the savings of the workers. Also in view of the current low market prices of liberty bonds and victory notes, advise all affiliated international and federal unions, as well as state federations of labor and central bodies, to urge their respective memberships to purchase government securities at current market prices, either for cash or in the instalment plan, and to hold their bonds until maturity. We also recommend that the various unions urge their employers and local banks to provide partial payment facilities for the purchase of government securities at market prices. (1921, p. 397) Reaffirmed.

Trade Autonomy—(1922, p. 135) During the past few years there has been a well studied effort by individuals here and there to create the impression that the A. F. of L. is not organized along proper lines. During 1920 and 1921, two or three central bodies were induced to adopt resolutions demanding that a new method of organization of the labor movement be devised. None contained a practical plan In fact, they all demonstrated clearly that their authors did not really understand the American labor movement. Nevertheless, the preambles to such resolutions generally arraigned the American labor movement on the lines upon which the A. F. of L. is founded and functions. While it was made to appear that there was a great demand for a change in the organization of our federation, yet this idea was effectually exploded by the fact there was not presented to the Denver convention one resolution containing any of the proposals of this character. During the past year there have been only isolated cases in central bodies of such resolutions intended to "revolutionize" the A. F. of L. In one case the secretary of a central body had a committee appointed to consider what could be done to bring about changes in the plan of organization of the A. F. of L. The committee reported a plan to re-organize the A. F. of L. upon a basis similar to that of the federal, state and municipal governments. The plan was practically that of the Federation as it is now organized, but it was so full of misrepresentation of the A. F. of L. that the central body refused to endorse it. Then the secretary on his own initiative without the knowledge, authority or sanction of the central body, sent a circular letter to all other central bodies, some of which were led to believe that the plan was the offering of the central body. Resolutions by another central labor union provided that all international unions should discharge their

organizers and give the work to state federations and central bodies, "thus guaranteeing
more effective work at a reduced cost."
Then state federations, district councils, city
central bodies and building trades councils
were "to be empowered to call strikes."
Another central body entered the arena with
a plan to industralize the labor movement
upon a plan which would eventually result in
"one big union." Due to lack of information
or because of misinformation, these are but
illustrations of the acceptance of supposedly
new thoughts and new beliefs, though in
reality ideas which, by reason of their utter
futility, have been discarded long years ago
by the labor movement. It is unnecessary
to comment on the statements contained in
these "declarations." It is only necessary
to state that but four central labor bodies
notified the A. F. of L. that they had approved them. Some of the central bodies sent
stinging letters to the offending central labor
unions. The officials of the A. F. of L.
explained to the central bodies the utter
futility of their proposals. There has also
been impressed upon them the fact that if
there be a member of the trade union
movement who has a really practical idea
that would benefit labor it would undoubtedly be received and favorably considered by
the conventions of the A. F. of L. The
efforts of those who would undermine or
destroy the trade union movement, either
because they would be personally benefitted
or are misguided, have met with defeat. This
demonstrates that the principles upon which
the A. F. of L. is founded are so appealing to
the sense of justice of the rank and file that
those who would create a cataclysm have
only failure to register for their work. There
is now less friction in the labor movement
regarding its form of organization than there
has been at any time in the past. Attention
is called to this matter simply to point out the
fact that the attempt to create dissension was
from a few individuals. The A. F. of L.
has accomplished so much in defense and
furtherance of the rights, the interests and
the welfare of the toiling masses of America
as to commend itself to the sincere respect,
affection and confidence of the wage earners.
(P. 337) The A. F. of L. calls attention to
certain facts relative to the trade union
movement. In one respect it differs from all
other movements of men organized for the
purpose of righting their wrongs, securing
their rights, protecting their welfare and
advancing their interests. The trade union
movement was not founded as a result of any
definite, preconceived industrial, economic,
social or political theory. It was born of
sheer necessity and developed through the
lessons it was compelled to learn in the stern
school of practical affairs. Its policies and
methods were forged white hot upon the
unyielding anvil of experience. Its development has been directed by applying the
principles and the methods of democracy.
The A. F. of L. from the beginning has held
that each group of organized wage-earners
should be left free and unhampered to
develop and apply that form of organization
which was most advantageous to them in
working out their own problems. From the
beginning it has favored amalgamation
between organizations when the majority of
these organizations believed such amalgamation to be advantageous. The A. F. of L.
has on many occasions given its kindly
assistance in bringing about such amalgama-
tions. Firmly in accord with the principles

and methods of democracy, the A. F. of L·
has opposed the spirit or methods of dictatorship, within or without the trade union
movement. We believe that only through
voluntary association, through voluntary
cooperation and federation, can the American
workingmen successfully and effectively
work out their industrial problems. Twenty-
one years ago the policy of the A. F. of L.
towards its affiliated organizations, their
jurisdiction, their right to self-government,
their freedom to develop and apply such form
of organization as seemed most advantgeous
to them was adopted. It is most advisable
that every trade unionist and every friend of
our movement should be thoroughly familiar
with this policy, and with this purpose in
mind, we now reaffirm and re-endorse the
decision relative to the rights of affiliated
organizations adopted by the Scranton
convention of 1901.

Trade Union, Bona Fide—(1921, p. 194)
Decision of president on meaning of "bona
fide" labor organization: "I do not think
there is any doubt as to what is meant by
bona fide—absolutely true, faithful, actual,
an organization that is not governed by
"bunko profundo."

Trade Union Evolution—(1923, p. 37)
During the year there has been developed a
propaganda of destructive criticism of the
trade union movement, the purpose of which
is to bring the movement under the control
of self-seekers who have their own personal
or revolutionary ends to serve. We are discussing the question at this time not because
there is anything to fear from the pernicious
propaganda but in order that certain facts
may be brought forward that may be helpful
to those who do not clearly understand the
character and the philosophy of the A. F. of
L. The propaganda to which we refer is
frankly revolutionary and has for its ultimate
purpose not only the destruction of the trade
union movement but the eventual overthrow
of the democratic government of the U. S.
Propaganda in the U. S. is carried on in accord with the tenets of the red international,
an organization which is completely under the
domination and dictation of the Russian communist oligarchy. The catchword of the
campaign in the U. S. has been "amalgamation." In accordance with the program of
the Russian communist leaders, an elaborate
program for the alleged "amalgamation" of
various international unions has been developed and secret or semi-secret organizations
have been formed within the international
unions for the carrying out of that program.
That these efforts will finally prove fruitless
we are sure, but confidence in their ultimate
failure is not an excuse for lack of effort to
prevent even moderate growth. Our trade
union movement must be maintained intact,
at the highest degree of efficiency and solidarity in order most to effectively deal with the
great problems with which we are confronted.
The natural amalgamation of organizations,
in accordance with the proven requirements
and in accordance with the desires of the organizations involved, is and has been urged
and aided by the A. F. of L. Amalgamation or
unification as a natural result of evolution is
strictly in accord with the policies and philosophy of the American trade union movement. So-called "amalgamation" against
the wishes of the organizations involved,
against their interests, and in accordance
with a plan evolved for the satisfaction of
personal or revolutionary ends, can be regarded only with the most unrelenting hos-

tility. The evolutionary progress through amalgamation that has gone on within the American trade union movement is a matter of recorded history. Some of the outstanding examples are as follows: Allied metal mechanics amalgamated with machinists; coremakers amalgamated with molders; amalgamated wood workers amalgamated with carpenters; steam fitters amalgamated with plumbers; lasters amalgamated with boot and shoe workers; the three leather workers unions amalgamated; print cutters and machine printers and color mixers amalgamated into United Wall Paper Crafts of North America; Amalgamated Glass Workers amalgamated with painters; Brotherhood of Railway Postal Clerks and National Post Office Clerks amalgamated; shingle weavers amalgamated with timber workers; Compressed Air and Foundation Workers amalgamated with hod carriers; cement workers amalgamated with plasterers; tin plate workers amalgamated with iron, steel and tin workers; slate and tile roofers amalgamated with composition roofers; tip printers amalgamated with bookbinders. It is important to recall that in its early history the International Typographical Union had jurisdiction over and encompassed within its membership all members of the various branches of the printing trade. By mutual consent and as the result of the demonstrated requirements of the workers in the industry there were subsequently organized the following separate international unions within the printing industry; International Typographical Union; International Printing Pressmen's and Assistants' Union of North America; International Photo Engravers' Union of North America; International Brotherhood of Bookbinders; International Stereotypers' and Electrotypers' Union of North America. At its last convention the International Typographical Union adopted a resolution urging that there be an amalgamation of all the unions in the printing trades. This was notwithstanding the early experience of the International Typographical Union which had led to separation of the various branches within the printing trade. The resolution adopted by the International Typographical Union convention has now been acted upon by the various international unions in the printing trade and in each case it has been rejected, the various international unions insisting that the present organizations, individually and in cooperation with each other, protect and promote the rights and interests of all the workers in the industry to the fullest possible extent. The trade union movement out of its experience and in accordance with the requirements of its membership will develop as it has in the past, along evolutionary lines, achieving results surely and steadily. It will resist to the utmost the designs of self-seekers and of the advocates of revolution. It should not be forgotten that the advocates of the revolutionary program who are seeking to bring about the destruction of the American trade union movement through their miscalled program of "amalgamation" are hostile to every guarantee of freedom which American labor holds fundamental. They are hostile to freedom of speech, freedom of press and freedom of assembly. They advocate the destruction, the abrogation of the entire bill of rights upon which modern freedom is based. They repudiate democracy and proclaim without shame or hesitation their desire for the establishment of a dictatorship over the wage earners. What is contemplated is not merely the amalgamation of various organizations which now function separately. Instead, the program is one for complete and thoroughly disastrous revolution, for the establishment of an autocracy to replace the democracy under which our present status has been achieved. If we entertained the slightest doubt as to the conviction of the great masses of the workers of our country on this point we should be unable to express our humiliation in the face of such a portentous tragedy. Modern democracy is not without its faults and under its protection and because of its remaining imperfections great and inexcusable injustices have been practiced. No movement has surpassed our own in warfare upon these injustices and in the effort to secure rectification of wrong. Be injustice no matter how serious, democracy does, however, leave opportunity for the application of remedy and for the achievement ultimately of every right and of every good thing. Workers throughout the world through all recorded time struggled to overthrow autocracy and bureaucracy as the first step toward the achievement of human rights. Anything that does not contemplate the preservation of democracy and a continuance of its opportunity and guarantees must be summarily rejected and defeated at all costs. We look with apprehension upon the treacherous and tragic untruths which are agitating workers in all lands and we feel that we can do no less than to call upon wage earners everywhere to have faith in democracy and to repudiate all that does not rest the cornerstone of its structure upon the human freedom and the human rights which are guaranteed and made effective only through democracy. We repudiate utterly and completely every suggestion and taint of autocratic character and we proclaim our purpose to defend the democratic institutions of our labor movement and of America against all incursions no matter from whence they come.

Trade Union Conference, Feb. 23-24, 1921, Declarations of—1921, pp. 59(307) "The Challenge Accepted—Labor will not be outlawed or enslaved." We ask the American people to give solemn consideration to this declaration. It is the pronouncement of a movement that is consecrated to the cause of freedom as Americans understand freedom. It is the message of men and women who will not desert the cause of freedom, no matter what the tide of the struggle. The American labor movement in this crucial hour here lays before the people the full story and asks them to rally with labor to the defense of our imperiled institutions. Labor speaks from no narrow or selfish point of view. It speaks from the standpoint of American citizenship. And the indictment it lays is an indictment of the enemies of freedom and progress. American labor battling for the preservation of American democracy and American institutions today stands between two converging destructive forces. Standing between two opposing forces, uncompromising toward both, the American trade union movement today finds itself and every American institution of freedom assailed and attacked by the conscienceless autocrats of industry and the followers of radical European fanaticism. If either of these wins, the doors of democratic freedom and opportunity can never be reopened in our time. Though inspired by vastly different motives, these two unrelenting forces work toward the destruction of the same ideals, each using the other as a tool in the struggle to overwhelm democracy and put an end to American progress, politically and industrially. On the one hand Labor is compelled to meet in a wide variety of manifestations the determination of reactionary industrial autocrats, autocrats who would destroy the organizations of labor and remove from the field of industry the only agencies through which the workers may protect themselves from aggression and the only agency through which they may offer to industry their co-operation in the improvement of industrial processes and the expansion of productive energy with that improvement of the product and lowering of prices justly demanded by the public.

Reaction Casts Off All Pretense—Reactionary employers have joined their might in a campaign which they are pleased to call a campaign for the "open shop," which they have been waging vigorously since the signing of the armistice. Compelled by the pressure of public opinion to accept labor's co-operation during the war, when the utmost conservation of productive energy was necessary to the life of the nation, they cast off all pretense immediately upon the passing of the emergency. This entire campaign on the part of the combined reactionary employers is in no sense a campaign for the "open shop," no matter what definition may be given to that term. The campaign is (distinctly and solely) one for a shop that shall be closed against union workmen. It is primarily, a campaign disguised under the name of an "open shop" campaign, designed to destroy trade unions and to break down and eliminate the whole principle of collective bargaining which has for years been accepted by the highest industrial authorites and by the American people as a principle based upon justice and established permanently in our industrial life. Not only during the war, but during every year since the labor movement has had a place in our industrial life, it has justified its existence and proved the necessity therefor, by making possible the necessary co-operation between employers and workers, on the one hand, and on the other hand by rescuing the workers from autocratic domination and developing for them a standard of living and of working conditions fitting to American citizenship. The American trade union movement is here because it is a necessity.

Unscrupulous Financial Speculation—The unscrupulous pirateers of finance, having squeezed the consumer throughout the period of the war, are now broadening their field and enriching themselves by squeezing both the producer and the consumer. Fortunes are being made to-day by commodity and financial speculation.

Flagrant Profiteering Continues—It is astounding, but true, that even after so great a lapse of time since the ending of hostilities there is, so far as the average family is concerned, practically no reduction in the high cost of living. It is admitted freely that in some commodities there has been a reduction of prices in the wholesale markets, but there has been no appreciable reduction in the retail prices at which the working people must make their purchases. Labor has time after time indicted the employers and the commercial interests of the country for wanton profiteering. We declare again that the government has been and continues impotent in the face of the criminal operations of profiteers and must therefore accept the responsibility for a great portion of the indignation and resentment of the people against those who have filched their pockets for no reason except that they have had the power to do so. Going hand in hand with profiteering there has been, and is, a shameful and undoubtedly unjustified overcapitalization of industrial and commercial projects, compelling the consuming public to pay interest in the form of inflated prices on vast sums of money back of which there is no foundation of intrinsic value or productive capacity.

Curtailing Consuming Power—Due to the maladministration of industry, and principally and primarily because of the studied and calculated arbitrary policies of reactionary employers, there has come upon us a state of unemployment which is depriving fully three and one-half million working people of the opportunity to earn a living. That there should be this tragic situation at a time when hardly any portion of the world has a sufficient supply of the necessaries of life is a commentary upon the methods of those responsible for the conduct of industry which they can not justify. It is a rebuke to their methods which only prompt and fundamental remedial action can remove. The condition of unemployment has been accentuated by keeping open the flood gates of immigration, which has added to the confusion and given employers an additional weapon in their efforts to reduce the American standard of living. One result is the effort to lower wages. The stupidity of such policies as these, whether or not apparent to employers inspired only by a desire for monetary gain, is, a matter which should give the most serious concern to the American people as a whole. Every reduction of wages is a reduction in the consuming power of the wage-earners and a direct blow at the prosperity and well-being of the country. Labor not only insists upon maintaining the present standard of wages and working conditions but declares its solemn purpose to continue its struggle to further improve those standards. Where the unorganized workers are concerned, while they benefit by the protests and progress of the organized workers, they find themselves unable to meet properly the present crucial situation. Their recourse is to join the organizations of their trades or callings, and we demand for them the right freely to follow such a course and to exercise all of the powers and privileges which that implies. Collective bargaining is one of the great stabilizing influences in industry in the relations between employers and workers. It is censurable that employes have in too many instances dissipated these friendly and mutually advantageous arrangements. We strongly urge upon both employers and unions to keep inviolate the instrumentality of collective bargaining.

Tragic Penalties of Maladministration—Another manifestation of the unscientific and inhumane policies of industrial autocracy is found in what is commonly known as "labor turnover," which means the repeated hiring and discharging of individual workers without any opportunity for an expression on the part of those workers in determining the terms or the conditions under which they shall give service. This endless movement of workers from shop to shop, with its inevitable burden of idleness and loss of production, is the individual protest of the unorganized against conditions of employment which they have no power to remedy. Where there is organi-

zation of labor and the opportunity for negotiation and agreement, labor turnover is
eliminated as a check and drain on industrial
life. Those manifestations of autocratic
policy in industry already cited are almost
entirely of a purely industrial character.
There remain other abuses equally serious, if
not more so, finding expression more often
through our political machinery. Through
reactionary decisions of courts, through the
unwarranted and reckless use of the writ of
injunction, through laws establishing industrial courts and boards, through compulsory
arbitration laws, and through the utter
failure of congress and of state legislative
bodies to attempt anything which might
serve as a stimulus to labor in these trying
times, the welfare of the entire country, and
in fact, the stability of many of our democratic institutions are most seriously menaced. These are matters of paramount
interest to every American.

Industrial Courts Destroy Freedom—
Through the establishment of industrial
courts, employers are seeking to inject into
American industrial life a device through
which they may annul constitutional guarantees and deprive workers of freedom and of
the right to function through their organizations. Aside from the denial of guaranteed
rights brought about by the establishment of
industrial courts, these instruments serve to
create in industry a disharmony which
inevitably must result in a chaotic industrial
condition and consequent loss of production.
The joint relationship between organized
workers and employers which exists when
these two industrial forces meet in voluntary
conference to reach voluntary agreements is a
relationship of negotiation; that which exists
when industrial courts are established to
determine the conditions in industry is a
relationship between litigants—litigants never
voluntarily yield a jot. Trade unionism
establishes a condition of harmony through
mutual effort toward a common purpose,
while the industrial court establishes a condition of antagonism, each party in hostile
suit against the other and each inevitably
hostile toward the court itself when the
decision is unfavorable. Industrial courts
and the like, created by law, are pernicious
devices, the fundamental error of which must
become more clear as time passes. The
paradox of the situation is that those
employers who look upon them as devices
for their benefit and who are propagating the
idea with the zeal of faddist will, in the long
run, suffer equally with labor as a penalty
for their short-sightedness.

Injunctions Restore Feudalism—The revival
of the unrestrained use of the injunction also
imperils the stability of our economic structure. For six years the Clayton act, accepted on all sides as the established law of
the land, to an appreciable degree checked
the abuse of the writ of injunction. A majority of the justices of the supreme court have
swept away this strong barrier against a
feudalistic legal concept and labor finds itself
again at the mercy of an unlimited use of
judge-made law. The injunction as it is
now used and abused in labor disputes is
without sanction either in the constitution
or in the fundamental law of the land. It is a
pure usurpation of power and authority. The
only possible and practical remedy in the
face of a power so usurped and so completely
unjustified lies in a flat refusal on the part of
labor to recognize or abide by the terms of injunctions which seek to prohibit the doing of

acts which the workers have a lawful and
guaranteed right to do, or which seek to compel workers to do those things which they
have a lawful and guaranteed right to refuse
to do. This is the only immediate course
through which labor can find relief and this
course it purposes to pursue. Labor realizes
fully the consequences of such a course but
in the defense of American freedom and of
American institutions it is compelled to adopt
this course, be the consequences what they
may. The workers maintain that the constitution of the United States is a living document, its provisions and guarantees as applicable today as when they were adopted.
The workers maintain that in their everyday
life and work rights which the constitution
declares to be inalienable should in practice,
as well as in theory, be inalienable. Among
these rights is the right to liberty—freedom
from involuntary servitude or compulsory
labor, except as punishment for crime. This
guarantee of the thirteenth amendment
lives, and the workers are determined that
it shall not be denied them. Nor shall this
guarantee of their freedom be so distorted as
to compel a group slavery in modern industry as reprehensible as was the individual
chattel slavery of old. Slavery, compulsory
labor, the tying of men to their jobs, will be
no more tolerated now than was chattel
slavery then. It has no more right to exist
and is just as repugnant under our democratic form of government as it would be
under a monarchical, bureaucratic or any
other form of government. The Clayton act
was made law by congress and by the signature of the president for the express purpose
of correcting a condition under which cases
such as the Danbury hatters' case were
possible. It was made law for the express
purpose of instructing judges in the limitation of their powers. Shortly after placing
his signature to the Clayton act with its
labor provisions the president of the U. S.
made the following declaration: "A man's
labor is not a commodity but a part of his
life. The courts must not treat it as if it
were a commodity, but must treat it as if it
were part of his life. I am sorry that there
were any judges who had to be told that.
It is so obvious that it seems to me as if section 6 of the Clayton act were a return to
the primer of human liberty; but if the
judges have to have the primer opened before
them, I am willing to open it."

Trade Unions Defend Liberty—The greatest
force in American life capable of restraining
predatory capital and to that extent capable
of maintaining the democratic institutions of
the country is the trade union movement.
The trade union movement would be false
to its trust, false to the ideals of our republic
and false to the great public whose confidence
it must have, as well as false to its own members, whose interests it is organized to protect, if it neglected any proper effort in behalf
of the liberty or well-being of the great
masses of our people. To that end this
movement of the organized workers sets its
face against all forms of compulsion, including such devices as so-called industrial courts,
the un-American and repugnant idea of compulsory arbitration and the vicious, tyrannical abuse of the writ of injunction. Through
such devices, in addition to the great danger
which they constitute to the general public
welfare, legislative enactments are set aside
so that the organizations of labor may be
mulcted, crippled or destroyed. Through
such devices voluntary, democratic and con-

structive organizations of labor are practically outlawed.

Labor Resists Reaction—However great may be the determination of the institutions of reaction to destroy the organizations of labor by these means, the resistance of labor will be uncompromising and unremitting. The organizations of labor must not and will not be destroyed. Trade unions foster education, uproot ignorance, shorten hours, lengthen life, raise wages, increase independence, develop manhood, balk tyranny, reduce prejudice, protect rights, abolish wrongs, and make the world better. It should be the purpose of government properly to stimulate our industrial processes. It should be the purpose of government to make voluntary negotiation more easily entered into. If, on the other hand, all of the safeguards set up in our constitutional and legal structure for the protection of the workers are to be destroyed by judicial construction, as the vitality of the Clayton act has been destroyed, then labor demands the immediate and sweeping repeal of all of that body of laws known as anticombination and conspiracy laws. Labor is anxious to serve. It has made this declaration repeatedly. It has lived and practiced that determination. It has done this in the face of most wanton and brutal opposition. Government has given little assistance. It has even destroyed the simplest and most obvious beginning of what might have been an effective employment service. Labor repeats it is time for the immediate and comprehensive restoration of this service.

Fanatical Propaganda and Intrigue—Converging upon labor from the extreme right is autocratic reaction, while from the opposite extreme is the insidious propaganda of radical European fanaticism, which is particularly and peculiarly deadly in its hatred of the American labor movement because of its democratic character and its steadfast refusal to adopt revolutionary destructive policies. It is a curious and startling fact that this propaganda of fanaticism has the sympathy and support of many of those in our country who style themselves as liberals, but who do not distinguish between that which is truly liberal and that which is destructive and fraudulent. Because of its opposition to the American labor movement, this overseas propaganda has even secured in the U. S. the support, at times secret, of some of the most reactionary American employers because of a common antagonism to the trade union movement. There is an unscrupulousness and a natural aptitude for intrigue in this fanatical propaganda which makes it a most subtle menace to every democratic ideal and institution in our country. This propaganda, this constant effort to undermine the constructive organizations of American labor, this constant poisoning of the very foundation of our democracy, finds its expression everywhere and through countless agencies. It is assisted in its work of destruction not only by the publications devoted to a perverted expression of "liberal" thought, but it is assisted as well by many of those who speak from our platforms and who write and edit our periodical publications and our daily newspapers. Much of this assistance is involuntary and unconscious, which testifies to the subtlety of the propaganda and to the need for constant study and alertness on the part of all those who have at heart the preservation of democratic life in America.

Labor's Purposeful Determination—In face of the situation here set forth, which is still further embittered by the activities of private detectives and agents provocateur paid by many employers, the American trade union movement, speaking through its duly authorized representatives, offers on the one hand constructive practical suggestions for relief and remedy, and on the other hand utters its uncompromising protest against the injustices and the autocratic policies which reaction seeks to impose. It declares in measured and emphatic tones its unalterable determination to resist at every point and with its entire strength the encroachments both of industrial tyranny and fanatical, revolutionary propaganda. The American labor movement is determined at all costs to maintain that freedom and those liberties which constitute American democracy. The labor movement believes this policy to be one embodying the highest statesmanship, as the only policy that can preserve and maintain and develop that harmonious relationship in industry without which our productive processes must be sacrificed to a reign of chaotic disorganization. The labor movement offers those voluntary and conciliatory methods of negotiation, arbitration and agreement through which it is possible to develop in our industrial life the highest degree of good will and the highest degree of productivity, in order that there may be for all of our people the fullest enjoyment of life and the loftiest standards of life.

Voluntary Principle Is Vital—The effort to crush the voluntary organizations of the workers may be designed by employers as an effort to secure their own immediate enrichment, but no such effort can stop at that point. Whether its sponsors will it or not, it is an effort to bring upon our whole national organization of society unprecedented disaster and retrogression. The principle of voluntary agreement is the kernel from which has grown the success of this country as a democracy. If that is destroyed in our industrial life, it can not exist in any other phase of our life, and the social organization that has made America must crumble and disappear. Neither the principle of state dictatorship nor the principle of private autocratic dictation in industry can be permitted to gain a foothold in America, for where either of these comes in freedom and democracy must cease to be. American trade unionists have long since made their choice of principles. Their movement is founded upon the principles laid down in the foundation stones of the republic. It is now for the American people as a people to make a choice. We are confronted with a supreme crisis. Not even in the days when the nation hovered on the brink of war was the situation more critical. The path of progress and constructive peaceful achievement and evolution is laid down by the trade union movement. The road to autocracy, unfreedom and chaos is laid down by its enemies. The choice is now before the country. This conference calls for public support and recognition of: The right of the working people of the U. S. to organize into trade unions for the protection of their rights and interests. The right to, and practice of, collective bargaining by trade unions through representatives of their own choosing. The right to work and to cease work collectively. The right collectively to bestow or withhold patronage. The right to the exercise of collective activities in furtherance of the welfare of labor. This conference purposes and urges public support for: Enactment by congress of legislation which shall protect the workers in their organized capacity against the concept that there is a property right in the labor of a human being. No application of the use of injunctions in industrial disputes where they would not apply in the absence of such disputes. Prohibition of immigration for a period of not less than two years. More general application of the initiative and referendum in the political affairs of the U. S. and of our several states. Removal by congress of the usurped power of courts to declare unconstitutional laws · enacted by congress. Election of judges. Immediate restoration of exemption from or the repeal of all anti-combination and so-called conspiracy laws. Restoration of an adequate federal employment service. Administration of credit as a public trust in the interest of·all the people. Repeal by the states of all industrial court laws and all restrictive and coercive laws, including the so-called open port law of Texas, and freedom from decisions of courts holding trade unions and individual members thereof liable in damages for the unlawful acts of others. Enactment by congress of a law declaring that labor organizations are not copartnerships and shall not be so treated in law or in equity. Investigation by congress of the activities of so-called private detective agencies in the field of industrial relations. We urge upon the unorganized workers the urgent necessity of joining the unions of their trades and callings, their haven of refuge and protection. We call upon the workers to resist the efforts to destroy trade unions, whether by the false pretense of the "open shop," the usurped authority of courts through writs of injunction, or otherwise. We call upon the trade unions for a closer banding together, a greater solidarity and unity of purpose. We call for united support in the protection of standards of wages and conditions already gained and we summon the workers to continued efforts to increase the consuming power, raise the standards and improve the conditions of life and work. We call upon the workers and all of our people to give their support, their effort and their combined strength of righteous purpose to this appeal for the preservation of the spirit and the letter of that great declaration which was written to guarantee to all Americans "the right to life, liberty and the pursuit of happiness" and freedom from involuntary servitude. To the above declaration and appeal we, the officers and other representatives of the national and international trade unions of America, assembled in the Executive Council Chamber of the A. F. of L., Washington, D. C., February 23, 1921, pledge ourselves and those whom we represent.

Trade Union Gains—(1920, p. 8) We have grown in numbers, we have grown in influence, we have grown in power in the same ratio that we shall grow, and grow, and still grow, providing we hold ourselves in leash, having power and influence and using them with moderation and determination that the ranks of labor, no matter how far advanced some may be, must keep time and step with those who are the most backward in order that they may keep on the firing line for labor's advancement and progress and disenthralment.

Trade Unionism, Message of—(1921, p. 16) The American trade union movement has just gone through a year of unexampled struggle and difficulty. A great part of the effort of our movement during that time has been defensive, but we may well say that labor has conducted a triumphant defense. The enemies of labor and of human progress have assailed from every side. The movement for the reduction of wages, the movement to crush our organizations masquerading under the fictitious "open shop" slogan, the wave of unemployment and, perhaps most sinister of all, the revival as a part of the general anti-labor campaign of the vicious, enslaving individual contract by which workers are bound to their employers in unwilling servitude, have been massed and concentrated against the most potential voluntary movement of the wage-earners of our country. Added to these have been legislative assaults and court decisions most destructive in character. Each of these manifestations will be treated as fully as essential in this report, together with a wide variety of subjects of vital interest to our movement. Against the whole field of opposition labor has conducted itself in accord with the best traditions of our country and our movement, holding the ranks intact everywhere. The coming year must be a year of progress. The blight of reactionary effort has bitten as deeply as possible. It has been checked. We must always expect and tolerate constructive criticism, but we can not and must not fold our arms under the fire of wantonly destructive movements directed by greed and avarice. Our movement everywhere must now rally to a militant offense against the powers that have sought our ruin. We call upon the workers everywhere to open our new year with an energy for constructive, progressive work, with a consecration to the ideals and purposes of our movement, to the end that there may be a more complete realization of those ideals and purposes in our time. We have checked the progress of those who have sought to destroy freedom through the annihilation of the organizations of labor. In the coming year we must make sure beyond all chance or doubt the stability and supremacy of the democratic ideals of the trade union movement. We call for a great rallying, a great unity, a great movement forward for humanity. The message of trade unionism must be carried to every corner. Our membership must be built beyond all records: our purpose must be to act in harmony and with supreme courage and energy. Ours is an inspiring movement, worthy of the devotion of all freedom-loving men and women. Like a mighty army of liberation let us go forward for the deliverance and enrichment of human life. Our faces must be set toward the future, undauntedly and with renewed courage and energy.

(1923, p. 14) Guided by basic principles whose correctness and adequacy can not be successfully questioned, the American trade union movement has successfully resisted the employers in their five-year war to destroy our labor organizations and establish an employer dictatorship based upon the non-union shop. Guided by these same principles our labor movement has defeated the anti-union employer wage reduction policy so thoroughly that wage increases have become the regular order everywhere, while labor's shorter work-day is becoming the policy of even the most notorious sections of anti-union-long-work-day industry. Organized labor's immigration restriction policy insisting that un-American employers shall not make use of cheap alien labor to beat down the living standards of American workers is now the accepted policy of all who love America and her institutions. Labor's policy for the adjustment of labor disputes by voluntary negotiation between representatives of the organized workers and employers directly concerned has become so thoroughly the national policy that the advocates of compulsory institutions and compulsory processes are limited to a few die-hard employers and employer economists still under the influence of the slave owner's and feudal lord's conception of industrial relations. During the prolonged period of unemployment the policy and thought of the labor movement became more and more the policy and thought of the nation. Today, with industry thriving, the conception of the labor movement must continue to be the leading force of national progress. This is inevitable. For the objective of the labor movement is to make the rights to life, liberty, and the pursuit of happiness material, moral and spiritual facts for every person.

Trade Unionist, What Is a—(*American Federationist, Nov.* 1914) Wage-workers, members in good standing of the union of the trade or calling at which they are employed, who realize as a fundamental principle the necessity of unity of all their fellows employed at the same trade or calling; who recognize the vital, logical extension, growth and development of all unions of all trades and callings and who strive for the unity, federation, cooperation, fraternity, and solidarity of all organized wage-earners: who can and do subordinate self for the common good and always strive for the common uplift: who decline to limit the sphere of their activity by any dogma, doctrine or ism. Finally, those organized wage-workers who fearlessly and insistently, maintain and contend that the trade unions, the trade union movement, are paramount to any other form of organization or movement of labor in the world.

Trade Unions, Attacks on—(1922, p. 51) The attempt made to stifle the growth of trade unions, to weaken their membership and to exhaust and dissipate their financial resources has not been confined to whatever social, industrial and financial influences could be directed against them. In addition, to the attacks made upon the trade unions by the courts, attacks have been made likewise in several of our state legislatures by the enactment of laws intended to destroy the trade union movement for all practical purposes and to leave it merely as a form of organization without substance or force. This attack has expressed itself in several forms of proposed as well as enacted legislation. The labor movement is obliged to be continually alert in opposition to encroachment upon its rights and freedom, because those who would build a legislative machine for the control of organizations of labor are so numerous and appear through so many channels. High sanction was given to all the proponents of restrictive legislation by the attorney general of the U. S. in an address to the "American Bar Association" at its 1921 convention. Undoubtedly he expressed the viewpoint of the administration. Upon that occasion Attorney General Daugherty said: "It is an undisputed fact that the public have a right to know what the quarrel is about in every actual or threatened strike or lockout and similar controversies." He said further that "there should be some definite agencies in government" for finding these facts and for

making an "impartial finding," and went on to conclude that "compulsory jurisdiction over these two factors to compel them to submit to an inquiry of this sort is not only desirable but just." Entirely in harmony with this suggestion by the attorney general, a bill was introduced in the senate by the then Senator Kenyon. This bill provided for the creation of a government board having powers to "decide" questions involving relations between workers and employers in mining industries. From these and from many other sources indications have come of the desire and the determination to secure the enactment, both in state legislatures and in the national congress, of laws creating government boards and commissions for the restriction of the exercise of the normal and natural rights of the workers.

Trade Unions Cannot Be Destroyed— (1920, p. 8) The trade union movement pure and simple is the most effective movement to protect and promote the interests and rights of labor and to bring about the disenthralment of labor from all forms of injustice and wrong. No one can hurt us, no one can injure our movement, no one can destroy it but ourselves. For unity, to obtain the best results, to maintain the spirit of unity of action on the part of our men and our women—that is the work. And for all the activity of ourselves and our fellows, let us spur them on and urge them on to duty, to right thinking and right action. Let us impress upon ourselves the voluntary discipline which is so essential to our unity, our progress and our success.

Trade Unions, Compulsory Incorporation of—(1922, pp. 51–486) One of the methods of legislative attack has been the attempt made to require the compulsory incorporation of trade unions and to make them responsible in damages as corporate bodies to all intents and purposes by permitting them to be sued as though they were incorporated entities. A careful analysis of these proposals indicates that they are but another snare advanced for labor's despoilment, intended to limit and restrict the rightful and justified activities of trade unions by involving them in extensive and expensive litigation so as to prevent them from accumulating the necessary funds to present an effective resistance whenever attacked. Under these proposals it is intended to make the injury to an employer and the ability to pay indemnities for such injury the test of legality of trade unions and of the workers' right of collective bargaining. To compel trade unions to incorporate is to compel the workers who desire to form a trade union to become members of a corporation. If they decline to do so, they are then prohibited from voluntarily associating themselves for their mutual advancement and for lofty purposes. To say that a labor union can not be formed unless it is incorporated is equivalent to saying that the worker daring to become a member of a labor union has to become a member of a corporation or cease to be a union worker. By such a governmental requirement the workers would be prevented from pursuing a lawful purpose and denied the right to assemble for their mutual protection and advancement. The proposal for compulsory incorporation is advanced not in the interests of the workers or of the public but is intended to limit the functions of trade unions, to check and curtail their growing power and influence and to regulate them not in the interests of the wage earners but in behalf of employing interests. All such proposals must receive our united opposition. The proposal to hold trade unions responsible as though they were incorporated bodies is subject to the same criticism. Under this proposal it is intended to accomplish indirectly that which is intended directly by compulsory incorporation laws. All such proposals are equally bad and should be opposed wherever and whenever advanced. In these attempts to weaken and destroy the trade union movement, we find a close parallel in the confiscation by the crown of England of the funds of the guilds when the government stepped in and robbed the workers of the funds they had accumulated to serve them in times of illness, or under the depressing circumstances of death, or for the burial of the wife, the husband or the children. The workers are not unmindful of the Taff-Vale decision of the house of lords, the highest judicial tribunal of Great Britain, which despite the acts of 1871 and 1875 which legalized trade unions and strikes in Great Britain, made the trade unions corporate bodies to all intents and purposes and subjected the whole of their funds, their death benefits, unemployment benefits, sick benefits and all to legal liabilities. Neither are the workers unmindful of the decision which followed the Taff-Vale decision which attempted to establish the principle that when a trade union seeks to compel an employer to deal fairly with his workmen and with trade unions and to that end urges others not to deal with such an employer, that the unions will be held liable in damages for any loss that the employer might suffer. This would have meant practically that even where no violation or intimidation was involved and where trade unions limited themselves to means strictly peaceful, yet where employers were inconvenienced or injured by a strike, they might obtain indemnities for such restrictions. To remedy the wrongs which followed the Taff-Vale decision, the British parliament enacted the trades dispute act in 1906, which denied further application of the conspiracy and anti-monopoly doctrines to trade unions and trades disputes and declared that any act done in pursuance of an agreement or combination by two or more persons, if done in contemplation or furtherance of a trade dispute, shall not be actionable unless the act if done without any such agreement or combination would be actionable. The wrongs inflicted upon the workers and the trade-unions by the Taff-Vale decision is precisely what is intended by those who would require trade unions to incorporate or to hold them responsible in damages as though they were incorporated bodies. All legislation of this character is unjustified and should not be permitted to gain a foothold in our land.

Trade Unions, President Harding's Proposal to—(1922, pp. 56-487) While all attempts made to enact similar legislation to that of the Kansas industrial law in several states were successfully defeated, a new source of danger has developed in this direction through reference to this subject by President Harding in his message to congress on December 6 of last year in which he said: "Just as it is not desirable that a corporation shall be allowed to impose undue exactions upon the public, so it is not desirable that a labor organization shall be permitted to exact unfair terms of employment or subject the public to actual distresses in order to

enforce its terms." There are two distinct implications involved in this statement. It implies that the employers acting in their corporate capacity are successfully restrained by law from imposing undue exactions upon the public and that they are not permitted to exact unfair terms of employment or to impose actual distresses on the public in order to enforce their terms. The other implication is that labor organizations do exact unfair terms of employment and do subject the public to actual distresses in order to enforce their terms. One could hardly conceive a statement of the president more at variance with the real facts as they exist in our industrial life. Unquestionably, it is this erroneous conception of actualities in our industrial life which led the president to express the following conclusions in the same report to congress· "In an industrial society such as ours the strike, the lockout, and the boycott are as much out of place and as disastrous in their results as is war or armed revolution in the domain of politics." Having advised congress that the strike and lockout and the boycott are as much out of place in our industrial society as armed revolution in the domain of politics he recommended that: "In the case of the corporation which enjoys the privilege of limited liability of stockholders particularly when engaged in the public service, it is recognized that the outside public has a large concern which must be protected; and so we provide regulations, restrictions and in some cases detailed supervision. Likewise in the case of labor organizations we might well apply similar and equally well-defined principles of regulation and supervision in order to conserve the public's interests as affected by their operations." It is difficult to understand what form of regulation the president had in mind in submitting this recommendation. It would seem that he did not contemplate mediation or voluntary arbitration. It is hardly conceivable that he should confuse voluntary organizations of workers, organized not for profit, with corporate enterprises organized for profit and to measure both forms of organizations with the same yard stick. It is almost inconceivable that the president should attempt to urge that human life should be regulated by the same rules and laws that regulate material things. If the concept of labor and capital implied relations now as in times of old we should now as then find children of 4 and 6 years of age going into mines and working underground for twelve, fourteen and sixteen hours a day. If the old concept of labor and of capital were still in vogue, we should still find women working in coal mines giving birth to children, the parentage of which they knew little. It is as absurd as well as it is inhumane that labor and capital should be regulated by the same rules and be measured by the same yardstick. Evidently what the president contemplated was a system of industrial laws similar to those which prevail in Kansas and which would place the workers again in a condition of "status" and deny them the right to freedom of contract. It is hardly believed possible that the president implied that the present administration intends to further a policy which will deny America's workers the right to cease working collectively and to determine for themselves the conditions under which they will give service. Yet the language used leaves little room for a different conclusion. When the people of the world have passed through the indescribable tortures and sacrifices of the greatest war humanity has ever experienced in order that reality might be given to the hopes and aspirations of the people and that autocracy and despotism might be ended for all time to come, it is astounding that principles should be promulgated having for their purpose the economic enslavement of the workers through a denial of equal rights, nullifying and destroying the effectiveness of the thirteenth amendment of the United States constitution which was enacted to abolish involuntary servitude and slavery for all time to come. Strikes and lockouts may cause slight inconveniences for the time being. Invariably they have marked a condition of progress in the lives of our people and in the improved conditions of employment among the wage earners of our land. Surely, if it was not in the interests of the public to continue longer the slavery of the black man it can not be in the interest of the public to deprive the wage earners of the rights guaranteed to them under the United States constitution; to bring the white man into a condition of involuntary servitude can not be in the public interest; to reduce the worker to a condition of "status" does not conform to constitutional conception of "freedom of contract." In this confused state of mind and disorder, surely, it can not be in the interest of democratic principles to appeal to public favor and commendation by advocating an autocracy of employers of labor made secure by depriving the workers of their democratic rights. Rather, indeed, organized labor must hold fast to the more humane, democratic, and rightful principles enunciated by that great statesmen and liberator, Abraham Lincoln, when as president of the U. S. he declared· "I am glad that a system of labor prevails under which laborers can strike when they want to, where they are not obliged to work under all circumstances and are not tied down to work whether you pay them for it or not. I like a system which lets a man 'quit' when he wants to and I wish it might prevail everywhere. I want a man to have a chance to better his condition; that is the true system. I am not ashamed to confess that twenty-five years ago I was a hired laborer."

Trial by Jury Unconstitutional— (1923, p. 71) A case has recently been decided by the United States circuit court of appeals, sitting at Chicago, which shows again the extent to which judges will go in over-riding the will of the people, as expressed through their legislative bodies. In this case the court held the guarantee of trial by jury provided in the Clayton act to be unconstitutional. Shop trade strikers of North Hudson, Wisconsin, were found guilty by the U. S. district court of violating its injunction issued in a suit by the Chicago, St. Paul, Minneapolis and Omaha Railway company. The defendants demanded a trial by jury in accordance with the requirements of the Clayton act. The court denied this demand and imposed fines on the strikers found guilty of contempt. They appealed to the U. S. circuit court of appeals. The opinion of that court written by Judge Baker (case entitled Michaelson et al. *vs.* United States ex rel, Railway Company) is a most amazing statement—or misstatement—of fact and law. In its opinion the court states that employes can not conduct lawful strikes against interstate railroads because the railroads "are bound hand and foot." According to the court the railroads "can not exert any sort o f economic pressure in any sort of industrial combat. They are powerless to use the lockout as a weapon against their employes." Therefore, the court holds that the interstate commerce act and the transportation act must "be interpreted and applied to forbid an assault upon a helplessly fettered opponent and to forbid the calling of such an act a combat." In support of the petition for rehearing filed in this case by counsel for the railway employes department, the argument is made that these statements of the court "startle the informed person as would a statement by the court that the world is flat and immobile." In this argument it is also pointed out that "in combating the shop craft employes, railroads have reduced forces repeatedly without any excuse in diminishment of work, but solely as a means of exerting economic pressure. Over and over again the shop craft organizations have seen hundreds and thousands of men deprived of their jobs as a means of coercion. Now they are asked to believe the statement of this court that the railroads can not exert any sort of economic pressure, and that they are powerless to use the lockout, in the face of economic pressure to which they have been subjected, and the numberless lockouts from which they have suffered." Also this printed argument includes the following statement· "It is respectfully submitted that the U. S. circuit court of appeals can not alter facts by judicial opinions. But it can disturb the confidence of men in the justice of the courts by utilizing assertions not supported by any evidence as the basis for expressions of judicial opinion." After going out of its way to condemn the railway unions and to express its opinion on legal questions not before the court, the circuit court of appeals then decided the Michaelson case on the basis that that part of the Clayton act requiring a trial by jury when men are accused of criminal acts, is unconstitutional. The court holds "Congress can not constitutionally deprive the parties in an equity court of the right of trial by the chancellor." It is hardly to be assumed the court will change this opinion upon the petition for rehearing. If the opinion is allowed to stand, it will serve as a justification for a denial of trial by jury as required by the Clayton act in every federal court. The district court judges have heretofore shown their animosity to this requirement. During the shop trade strike one Illinois judge threatened to send a lawyer to jail for contempt of court if he persisted in demanding trial by jury for his clients, in accordance with the statute. The constitution of the U. S. requires trial by jury in all criminal prosecutions. The Clayton act gives the right of trial by jury only where the defendant is accused of an act constituting a violation of a state or federal statute. In other words, the Clayton act attempts to insure to defendants the constitutionally guaranteed right of trial by jury. The U. S. circuit court of appeals holds in effect that it is unconstitutional to enforce the constitutional requirement of trial by jury because when congress creates a court it can not prevent that court from making law to suit itself. The Michaelson case involves a square conflict between legislative power and judicial power, a square conflict between the power of the legislature to make laws, in accordance with the constitution, and the power of the courts to veto these laws by "interpreting" the constitution. It is to be hoped that the Michaelson case will be fought through to a decision by the U. S. supreme court. If that court again exercises its usurped power of vetoing legislation a clear issue will be presented to the American people as to whether the supreme authority in their government shall rest in the legislature, elected by the people to make laws and responsive to the people, or in the courts consisting of judges appointed for life not responsive to the will of the people, either as expressed in their statutes, or in their constitution, but writing their individual, political, social and economic opinions into the law of the land. (P. 274) Emboldened by the ease with which our courts have been able to defy the legislative branch of government it is not surprising that the U. S. court of appeals sitting in Chicago should hold that that section of the Clayton law providing for jury trial in all cases of contempt arising out of injunctions declared permissible was unconstitutional. One can hardly conceive of a more tyrannical doctrine than that enunciated by the U. S. circuit court of appeals that "congress can not constitutionally deprive the parties in an equity court of trial by the chancellor." This is equal to saying, "I am the state," and such is not far from the truth. Our judiciary has indeed developed its powers to such an extent that it may be truly considered the state and the nation. Gradually, but surely, we shall find developing in our own land a sovietized judicial oligarchy unless the American people arouse themselves and assert themselves in unmistaken terms and action.

Triumph of Labor Panel—(1919, p. 92) The Executive Council reported to the 1916 convention that a panel entitled "The Triumph of Labor" had been presented to the A. F. of L. by the parliamentary committee of the British Trade Union congress. Because of the great war it could not be shipped to this country. The oak used for the mounting was taken from Lord Nelson's flagship Victory at the battle of Trafalgar. When the A. F. of L. delegation returned from the peace conference at Paris the panel was brought to Washington. (P. 417) This beautiful work of art symbolizes in a manner more striking than words can portray one of the fraternal links of solidarity and goodwill in the chain of international trade unionism which cements our economic interests with those of other countries. This panel was designed and executed by one of the finest sculptors in England and was presented by the British trade-union parliamentary committee to the A. F. of L. and merits the appreciation of the A. F. of L.

(1920, p. 298) Parliamentary Committee to the British Trade Union Congress reported that the panel had been presented to the A. F. of L.

Truax vs. Corrigan—(1921, pp. 76-373) The cause of Traux vs. Corrigan is on appeal to the U. S. supreme court from the state of Arizona. This case was argued last April and indirectly involves the constitutionality under the federal constitution of the labor provisions of the Clayton act, including particularly the right of picketing. After the adoption of the Clayton act, the state of Arizona passed an enactment similar in all respects. Its constitutionality under the federal constitution was challenged by the plaintiffs who failed in the lower court and on appeal in the supreme court of the state, but thereafter brought their appeal to the U. S. supreme court.

(1922, p. 45) This case was argued April, 1920, re-argued in October, 1921, and decided December 19, 1921, by the U. S. supreme court, the decision being announced by Mr. Chief Justice Taft who had given the decision in the preceding Granite City case. This case is notable for the difference of opinion arising between the members of the supreme court and to some degree because of the realignment illustrated by tendencies in other cases of the justices. In this case Corrigan and others are members of the Waiters' Union and of the District Trades Assembly at Bisbee, Ariz. A dispute arose as to the terms of employment between the Waiters' Union and William Truax. Because of alleged conduct on the part of the waiters in picketing, carrying banners announcing "Truax is unfair to labor" and the circulating of hand bills, Truax sought the aid of the court through the injunction process. In defense, the union relied upon the state statute which limited the use of injunctions in disputes between employers and workers and prohibited the issuance of injunctions in their appeal to the public to cease patronizing a party to an industrial dispute. This law was modeled after the labor sections of the Clayton act. The state supreme court upheld the constitutionality of this law. Truax then appealed to the supreme court of the U. S. claiming that this law was in conflict with the fourteenth amendment of the U. S. constitution in that it deprived him of property without due process of law and that it denied to him the full protection of the "equality" provision of this constitutional amendment. The supreme court, by a vote of six to three, sustained the viewpoint of Truax. Speaking through Chief Justice Taft, it held that Truax had a property right in the patronage of the public and that an intentional injury thereto by the trade union was unlawful; that an attempt by the state legislature to interfere with this property right was to deprive employers of property without due process of law and that to classify labor as a distinctive group to be favored by the state for protection in its rights was a violation of the "equality" provisions of the fourteenth amendment. This decision is remarkable in that it denies to the several state legislatures the right to define property and property rights. By this decision the power to define property or property rights has been placed within the keeping of the judiciary, and the voice of the people in determining through their legislative representatives where property rights and personal rights begin has been silenced completely. It is hardly conceivable that the American people, so well experienced and trained in a legislative form of government should permit themselves long to be ruled by such judicial bias and usurpation of power. In reaching the conclusion that the Arizona state law was unconstitutional in that it violated the "equality" section of the fourteenth amendment, the majority of the judges of the supreme court were compelled to draw an unjustified and strained distinction between employes on strike and all other workers. The supreme court evaded questioning the validity of the Clayton act itself but rested its decision upon the construction placed upon the Arizona statute by the supreme court of Arizona, evidently giving to it a meaning as if it were written in wholly different language from the Clayton act. It is difficult to conceive how the Clayton act can well pass the judgment of the U. S.

supreme court in this case unless so interpreted by the supreme court as to render the whole act subversive of the purpose for which the law was enacted. Mr. Justice Pitney filed a dissenting opinion in which Mr. Justice Clark especially concurred and in which they held that the use of the process of injunction in the case under consideration is essentially a measure of police regulation which the state had a direct discretionary right to modify or relinquish. They were unable to find that the "due process of law" clause of the fourteenth amendment of the constitution was in any degree affected. They likewise believed that the Arizona state law would not deprive Truax of "equal" protection of the law but that this law merely limited or restrained the injunction in industrial disputes. Two important points are involved in this decision. First, it regards business as property and which may not be infringed upon even by statutory law without a violation of the due process provision of the constitution. This decision confirms the point of view that good will is property. The legal fiction called "destroying business" whenever the workers seek to divert public patronage from one employer, deemed to be unfair, to one considered fair to labor, arises out of confusing physical property with the intangible something called "good will." Good will emanates from individuals not concerned in the particular business in consideration. It has a direct bearing upon business but is not business. Employers are not guaranteed the right to be protected against all hazards. Workmen can no more be charged with destroying business than can competitors who build up their business at the expense of others engaged in the same line. This new philosophic doctrine, if carried to its extreme, will spell disaster to our entire competitive system of industry. The other point is that the power of the legislature to classify labor as a proper subject for legislative action is denied for all practical purposes. Practically all legislation is group legislation or classified legislation. Specific laws deal with groups which are clearly differentiated from others and which possess common characteristics. Labor has always been accepted as a proper subject for legislative classification and legislative action. Upon that theory employer's liability laws have been sustained. On that theory the Clayton law was enacted. On that theory all factory legislation has been predicated. Under that theory, labor and the farmers have been exempted from the many state anti-monopoly laws. The supreme court of the U. S. now holds this is all wrong and rules that all state legislation to be constitutional must affect all alike and not a group similarly situated.

Tuberculosis Sanitarium—(1921, p. 417) We are in hearty sympathy with the humanitarian work of the Lung Sanitarium of Denver, Colo., and we hereby recommend it to all our affiliated organizations and to the American people in general as being worthy of cooperation and financial support.

Two-Platoon System, D. of C.—(1919, p. 126) The two-platoon system has been installed in Washington. In the district appropriation bill of 1918 was a clause allowing the fire force to be increased to 144. This increase would permit the commissioners to arrange for two platoons, and it was understood that this would be done. In the district appropriation bill of this year was a clause making the two-platoon system mandatory.

Notwithstanding the bill was among those which failed at the close of the session, the mandatory clause for the two-platoon system was acted upon by the commissioners and the system went into effect on February 8, 1919.

Tyranny a Result of War—(1920, p. 8) Declaration of the president of the A. F. of L.: "There is an international aspiration among the toiling masses of the whole world that the time has come when a further attempt at tyranny and injustice shall come to an end wherever it exists. During the war and before the war, that is, before the U. S. entered the war, we met in a conference to consider what the attitude of the labor movement of the U. S. should be if we made up our minds to enter the struggle. Nearly a month before the president of the U. S. appeared before the congress of the U. S. to lay his indictment against the murderous, autocratic policy of the German imperial government, organized labor through its official representatives declared that, come what may, whether we might enjoy the beneficence of peace and peaceful pursuits or we were dragged into the maelstrom of the European war, we would stand behind the Republic of the U. S. against all its enemies whomsoever they might be. That declaration was unanimously adopted nearly a month before the president appeared before congress and before congress passed the resolution declaring a state of war. We were even at that time mindful of the fact that after every war there was a feeling of reaction against the freedom and liberties of the people of nearly every country. I commend to the thoughtful trade unionist and the thoughtful student of the American labor movement the declaration of March 12, 1917, and I think you will find the predictions that were clearly foreseen and told and the warning given to the men of labor of the U. S. and the whole American continent were well founded."

Underwood, Oscar—(1923, p. 350) Following telegram from Alabama made part of the minutes: "Committee of allied labor organizations of Birmingham, Alabama, by motion adopted today, urge the convention to go on record as opposed to Senator Underwood for president of the U. S." The reason given for the opposition was that Senator Underwood had made this statement January 2, 1920, before the Birmingham Chamber of Commerce: "I am probably more responsible for the labor clause in the Cummins bill than any man in the Congress of the U. S., because I originated it."

Unemployment—(1921, p. 120) Congress failed to act on bill providing for investigation of the possibilities of furnishing work to the unemployed, which was stated in the proposed measure to cost the nation $20,000,000 a day. Legislation providing for public works in times of acute unemployment must be passed in good times to be effective. It has been the case in all periods of industrial depression that the question of supplying work for the unemployed has not arisen until unemployment was at its height. The delay following any constructive legislation would then extend until the depression was over and there was no need for it. Congress should appropriate money in peace times for necessary public works and when a panic develops there would be work for the unemployed. This has been urged repeatedly by A. F. of L. conventions. (P. 271) Executive Council directed to appoint a committee to make a thorough investigation of unemployment and take whatever action is necessary. (P. 375) It is apparent that a portion of this industrial depression is artificial and was manufactured for the purpose of lowering living and working standards, weakening the organized labor movement and breaking the morale and spirit of the workers. All state federations and city central bodies are instructed to request state, county and municipal governments to immediately make provision to carry on such public works as they now may have under consideration.

(1922, pp. 72–263) The period of depression attending post-war readjustment developed more slowly in the U. S. than in Europe, but nowhere were its consequences of such gigantic proportions. As the world creditor country we found it impossible to maintain sales to debtor countries and hence had to suspend partially or close down many great industries. Great disparities in exchange rates augmented difficulties. By the summer of 1921 we were faced with an unemployment problem of unprecedented proportions. The real dimensions of the problem we had no agencies for ascertaining. It is not a gratifying commentary upon the efficiency of our national government that there are not adequate agencies to supply the essential facts of industrial conditions. Without facts industrial policies can be based only on guess and indefinite information. Ill-advised "economy" of congress had so crippled the U. S. employment service that it was unable to function. Instead of having available continuous information on unemployment so that the problem could be known by industries or localities it was necessary to create emergency agencies and machinery so as to get information upon which to base remedial plans. Even despite that discreditable condition which emphasized the fact that the U. S. is the only important industrial country which has not maintained effective unemployment agencies, congress has yet taken no step to remedy that for which it alone is responsible. As a nation we were slow in perceiving the unemployment problem because the workers had had the wisdom to accumulate savings during the period of industrial expansion. Their thrift was manifest in liberty bonds, savings deposits, home purchases and ownership of other valuables. These possessions constituted the financial resources on which the unemployed maintained themselves. Their thrift helped them to tide over the period of industrial depression for which industry was responsible. When it was evident that a critical problem was developing because of unemployment there were a number of efforts made to determine the dimensions of the problem. The need for immediate assistance to workers without employment devolved at once on the trade union organizations in the various industries. A number of the labor unions provided unemployment benefits and tried to help fellow craftsmen to find employment. Although the A. F. of L. has neither the facts nor the facilities to make a nation-wide survey on unemployment, it attempted to get data that would indicate the proportions of the problem. A questionnaire was sent to a number of industrial centers from which returns could be received quickly. The U. S. department of labor from the survey it made estimated the number of unemployed at 5,000,000. The first move for finding a way to deal with the problem nationally came from Herbert Hoover, secretary of commerce. Acting upon the suggestion of Mr.

Hoover, President Harding called a national conference on unemployment. The members of the conference were representative of the various elements concerned in industry. Many members of the employing group were extremely reactionary. Since the conference was a deliberative and not a legislative body, only unanimous reports were considered and all decisions were the result of unanimous agreement. In this way the controversial issues and special propaganda were not permitted to enter into the recommendations of the conference. The conference deliberations were greatly facilitated under the plan which supplied each committee with a corps of experts and made available for the committee work all of the expert information that could be obtained on the various phases of the problems submitted to the different committees. During the general sessions reports on the following subjects were unanimously adopted by the conference: Statistics, reclamations, business cycles, public works and emergency measures in shipping, permanent measures in shipping, construction, agriculture, transportation. Reports on the following subjects were received but not acted upon by the conference: mining, railroads, permanent measures for manufacturers, taxation, tariff. The conference adopted recommendations for an emergency program to be carried out by states and municipalities. This emergency bureau has no power except that which it can develop through resourceful leadership and suggestion. The conference declared that manufacturers can contribute to relieve the unemployment situation by: a. Part-time work, through reduced time or rotation of jobs. b. As far as possible, manufacturing for stock. c. Taking advantage of the present opportunity to do as much plant construction, repairs, and cleaning up as is possible, with the consequent transfer of many employes to other than their regular work. d. Reduction of the number of hours of labor per day. e. The reduction of the work week to a lower number of days during the present period of industrial depression. f. That employes and employers cooperate in putting these recommendations into effect. A large number of employers have already, in whole or in part, inaugurated the recommendations herein set forth, and for this they are to be commended, and it is earnestly urged upon those employers who have not done so to put same into use, wherever practicable, at the earliest possible opportunity. g. Specific methods for solution of our economic problems will be effective only in so far as they are applied in a spirit of patriotic patience on the part of all our people. During the period of drastic economic readjustment, through which we are now passing, the continued efforts of anyone to profit beyond the requirements of safe business practice or economic consistency should be condemned. One of the important obstacles to a resumption of normal business activity will be removed as prices reach replacement values in terms of efficient producing and distributing cost plus reasonable profit. We, therefore, strongly urge all manufacturers and wholesalers who may not yet have adopted this policy to do so, but it is essential to the success of these measures when put into effect that retail prices shall promptly and fairly reflect the price adjustment of the producer, manufacturer, and the wholesaler. When these principles have been recognized and the recommendations complied with, we are confident that the public will increase their purchases, thereby increasing the operations of the mills, factories, and transportation companies, and consequently reducing the number of unemployed. In all its procedure the conference was guided by the fact that it was not authorized to attempt an overturn of existing theory and practice but was expected to meet the problem as far as possible through existing agencies. There were four achievements: 1. The conference established the idea that the fundamental cause of unemployment is waste in industry which becomes cumulative and periodically produces an industrial depression. Unemployment is not the result of chance but has been a constant accompaniment of industry in normal proportions. Abnormal unemployment has this time called attention to the cause of normal unemployment. The causes are essentially the same. 2. The responsibility for dealing with the unemployment problem was removed from the controversial field and placed squarely on industry because it can be solved only by management's employment of the involuntary idle. 3. A method of temporary relief was provided by an executive agency directed to get practical results in the present emergency through action by the states and municipalities. A definite program for the guidance of this executive agency was adopted by the conference. 4. Permanent solution of the unemployment problem.was not to be expected of the first sessions of the conference, but a foundation was laid for eventual steps toward this end. Constructive programs are possible when it is recognized that accurate information is the basis for intelligent action. The conference went as far as it could go under its restricted authority to insure collection of the required information and to insure its utilization to obtain constructive measures. It made provision for a continuing committee on which the executive secretary of the A. F. of L. committee serves, and he also serves on a special committee to investigate the business cycle. The national bureau of economic research has taken charge of the task of making a report on unemployment and the business cycle. This report in addition to making available a wealth of practical information and expert opinion, will furnish the committee on business cycle with facts that must be considered in framing a program for the mitigation of cyclical unemployment. The report of the bureau is to be completed by August 20. Final judgment of the work of the conference can not be made, of course, until it goes out of existence. It can be reconvened at any time to deal either with temporary or permanent relief of unemployment, and it may be reconvened when the time comes to concentrate its authority and influence for the purpose of giving to its recommendations permanent form and substance. This fact of its permanence might also be regarded as a practical achievement of the first sessions of the conference. The background helped to focus public attention upon the problem and undoubtedly averted the full development of the situation through planning to keep the wheels of industry moving and to provide work for the unemployed. Undoubtedly, the most important principle for which the unemployment conference declared is that unemployment is preventable and industry is responsible for developing a preventive program. The records of the A. F. of L. show that labor has repeatedly called

attention to the burdens of unemployment and has sought measures of relief for and prevention of various types of unemployment. Labor alone, is unable to deal with such problems because the major responsibility rests upon industries and upon the centers of financial control. The period of industrial depression through which we are passing comes as the aftermath of a world war which brought world-wide' industrial and commercial dislocations and readjustments and disclosed with revealing vividness how necessary it is that men and women whose livelihood depends upon opportunity to earn wages should not be the victims of avoidable stoppages in business and production. Stabilized employment must wait the finding of controls to eliminate business crises, "boom" expansions and depressions. In our industrial development there have been cycles of prosperity, expansions and contractions. From the labor point of view unemployment is an important human problem; from the business point of view it is waste, hence unnecessarily adds to production costs. During the past year the first important constructive effort in the world was made to disclose the nature of industrial waste and hence to indicate preventive measures. It was made by the committee on the elimination of waste in industry appointed by Herbert Hoover then president of the Federated American Engineering Societies. This study was an assay directed by a committee of fifteen distinguished engineers. Industrial waste was conceived as caused by failure to use time and energy of living men as well as failure to utilize properly materials and productive equipment resulting from the time and energy expended by past generations. The facts developed in the report ought to serve as a foundation for industrial progress. Since they are impartially set forth they equally are serviceable to all groups concerned in industry. According to the findings of this committee responsibility for industrial waste responds more than 50 per cent upon management and less than 25 per cent on labor. However, the important feature is not to allocate responsibility but to disclose the preventive measures. By eliminating waste production proceeds more economically and more regularly for the cumulation of the costs of waste undoubtedly have a bearing upon the business cycle and periods of business depression. Eliminating avoidable waste will do much to regularize industry and hence to stabilize employment. The findings of the committee in cyclical unemployment will supplement the data available through the waste report. This information will indicate the preventive policies for dealing with the two recurring types of unemployment—seasonal and cyclical unemployment. The latter has been an unvarying accompaniment of business depression which has followed periods of expansion. The casual forces are to be sought in rigorous study of past experience. Unemployment due to seasonal factors can be minimized by deliberate planning to adjust seasonal work with related projects and continuous work in such a way as to afford full time employment for as many as possible. We believe that the economic problem of stabilizing employment must be worked out in various industries by the groups associated together in production, each in organized capacity. Industrial order is impossible without organization. Wage earners through their trade unions are prepared to do their part in this undertaking. Stabilization of employment will be in part the outgrowth of efforts to improve the methods and policies of production and development of a spirit of cooperation for service in production. To accomplish this end the active cooperation of the group of producing workers is necessary. We can not hope to eliminate unemployment in the immediate future. It is necessary then that labor reaffirm its remedial program and put renewed energy into the effort to secure each separate measure of the program. 1. An initial objective in that program is a federal employment service, competently organized and adequately financed. Such an agency is necessary to bring job and workman together and to supply unemployment necessary for inteligent planning by management and labor. The U. S. is practically the only important industrial country that has not established such an extensive and efficient business and humanitarian service. The employment service developed during the war emergency ought to have been intelligently reorganized instead of being scrapped by a short-sighted congress. We should seek at once proper legislation and adequate appropriation for such a service. 2. We recognize that the only way to eliminate unemployment is to start the wheels of industry, and to provide employment for workers. The most desirable result is to provide employment for each person at his preferred trade or calling. This means to keep in motion the wheels of industry. Every industry must support its workers. If a given industry fails to support its workers, the industrial problem can not be solved by trying to find some other occupations for these workers. Public works can not help the unemployed in the needle trades, or the cigar trade or the printing shops. But each industry must care for its own workers including the reserve force it requires. This problem can be solved by those directly concerned. To this end there should be organized in each craft or calling a national conference board of an equal number of employers' representatives and representatives of international trade unions, assisted by such expert advice and counsel as the Department of Labor and the Department of Commerce may be able to give to these boards. Anyone who gives more than casual study to the determining factors in production, finds that the service motive is allowed a very restricted influence entirely out of proportion to its nature. Although things should be produced for use, the needs of society have not a final determining voice in deciding output, as disinterested consideration of the question of output would indicate that the needs of society ought to be made the basis for guiding production. Change in controlling policies can not be effected by law. It will be the result of developing intelligence and by the force of public opinion together with demonstrations of its practicability. 3. An indirect way to stimulate industry in periods of depression is to provide for the expansion of public works and public highways, with the development of such cycles. We recognize that public works and such productive public investments are not primarily expedients to relieve unemployment but should be an integral part of a definite national program for conservation and development. However execution of parts of such a program can very properly and with economic advantages parallel periods of economic depression.

Extension of credit to investment projects of such a character will be based upon absolutely sound security. The chief fields for the new extension of public credit for public public purposes are: 1. *Reclamation*— Development and extension of the reclamation of arid, swamp, and overflow lands. 2. *Waterpower development*—Development of such part of the 'undeveloped water power in this country as would find an immediate market. This development to include the powers at Muscle Shoals on the Tennessee and others in the Appalachians, the Rocky Mountains, and the Pacific Coast Ranges. We recommend careful consideration of the plan for the super-power for the region between Boston and Washington developed by W. S. Murray and others. 3. *Inland waterways (canals, rivers, harbors)*— Development of the Mississippi River and its tributaries for domestic supply, navigation, irrigation, waterpower. Development of inland and coast-wise canal systems along the Atlantic and Gulf Coasts, thus affording cheap transportation of bulky freight and giving protected passage to our coast-wise shipping. Further development of rivers and harbors of this country in accordance with the foregoing and with the report of the Chief of Engineers. 4. *Public highways (roads)*—The principle of the public roads bill enacted by congress several years ago, and now re-enacted by the recent congress appropriating $75,000,000 and calling for a like expenditure by the states is sound. 5. *Forestry*—Development in the national forests of roads, trails, telephone lines, fire towers, and other permanent equipment for preventing and putting out devastating forest fires in accord with the principles laid down by the U. S. forestry service. There are more than 150,000,000 acres of national forests. Reclamation of more than 80,000,-000 acres of man-made desert once rich forested land. Forest devastation is adding to this desert yearly some 3,000,000 acres— an area as large as the state of Connecticut. 6. *Housing*—The A. F. of L. went on record in 1919 as demanding the use of the credit of the federal government for housing purposes. This can be done through a federal home loan bank similar to the federal farm loan bank. 7. *Railroads*—In providing for the payment of sums due to railroads by by the federal government a condition should be attached that would make such funds immediately available in greater part only for labor and material for maintenance of way and structures and for the maintenance of equipment and that the maintenance of equipment be performed in the shops of the railroads to their capacity thus insuring the constructive expenditure of the money so appropriated. The following summarized procedure is approved: 1. That the president of the A. F. of L. arrange for the continuous study of the unemployment problem either through a committee or a designated agency or executive secretary. 2. That this official agency make continuously available to trade unions information that concerns regularization of industry and that relations be established so far as practical with studies and efforts to develop such information. 3. That the labor movement make special effort to secure the enactment of legislation providing for an adequate federal employment service and for the extension of public credit for the purposes above enumerated.

(1923, p. 40) It is a matter of no small satisfaction to the American labor movement that the U. S. led the world in attacking the unemployment problem from the approach of prevention. Our movement has helped to shape that policy by consistently opposing unemployment state insurance or doles. We have held that under voluntary institutions each separate vicinity must assume responsibility for its progress and its own problems. We were therefore in hearty accord with the findings of the unemployment conference of 1921 which placed squarely upon industries the responsibility of eliminating preventable unemployment. That disastrous slumps in American business are not unavoidable, and that they may in a measure be prevented or at least discounted by prudent timely foresight during periods of expansion, was the conclusion reached by the committee on unemployment and business cycles, appointed by the secretary of commerce. The conference on unemployment, called in September, 1921, saw that emergency and temporary measures of relief were not sufficient: the country needed assurance that such a catastrophe would not recur. We hope to control the business cycle instead of permitting it to control industry with attendant evil of unemployment. Accordingly the responsible business men, labor leaders, and economists of the conference desired an exhaustive investigation in the whole problem of unemployment and of methods of stabilizing business and industry so as to prevent the widespread suffering caused by recurrent depressions in the so-called business cycle. Investigation into the causes, characteristics and phenomena of these business booms and slumps, consideration of possible measures of commercial and industrial stabilization, attempted estimate of the losses, human as well as economic, due to prolonged forced unemployment of millions of the country's wage-earning men and women, suggestions leading toward the prevention of a similar disruption of the national economic fabric—these were the subjects upon which the special committee appointed by Secretary Hoover was asked to report. The conclusions of the committee have already been fruitful. They are concerned with prevention rather than cure. A period of industrial activity, like the present, is the time to consider and to lay plans against industrial crashes equally devastating to employer and employe. The general conclusion of the committee, as stated in the foreword by Herbert Hoover, is: "Broadly, the business cycle is a constant recurrence of irregularly separated booms and slumps. As the slumps are in the main due to wastes, extravagance, speculation, inflation, over-expansion, and inefficiency in production developed during the booms, the strategic point of attack therefore, is the reduction of these evils, mainly through the provision for such current economic information as will show the signs of danger and its more general understanding and use by producers, distributors, and banks, inducing more constructive and safer policies. Furthermore, the committee has developed some constructive suggestions as to the deferment of public work and construction work of large public service corporations to periods of depression and unemployment, which while in the nature of relief from evils already created, would tend both by their subtraction from production at the peak of the boom and addition of production in the valley of depression toward more even progress of business itself." Conditions within business itself rather than remote, outside considerations are the primary cause of the business cycle. Past cycles have shown certain common tendencies. During the up grade or period of business revival, we see a rise in the volume of manufacturing, in stock exchange prices, in commodity prices, and in demand for credit by business men and speculators. Then follow stiffening money rates, and the gradual straining of credit, with possible curtailment to speculators. At this point, we are just ready for the change. It is heralded by falling of stock exchange prices, while business wavers or continues to rise unevenly, and transportation facilities are overburdened and deliveries delayed and the apparent shortage of goods intensified by speculative buying and duplication of orders. Credit expansion nears its limit; public confidence is shaken; orders are cancelled ruthlessly; quick liquidation of inventories; sharp and irregular fall of prices; workers are laid off. The cycle ending in the depression of 1921 was unusual in the extent of the preceding expansion, in the severity of the depression, and in the amount of unemployment. During its deepest slump as many as four or five million of America's wage earners were unemployed. Consideration of past dangers and disasters is worth while principally for the knowledge it gives, enabling us to read and interpret future danger signals. Three of the ten recommendations of the committee are concerned with the need for knowledge as a guide to business policies. An increase in the facilities of the department of commerce is also recommended and a greater degree of cooperation with that department in co-ordinating and extending business information. The committee also underscores the need for expansion and standardization of statistics by the department of labor. It urges especially periodic and prompt publication of the facts about the following key industries: Raw wool and woolen textiles, raw cotton and cotton textiles, hides and leather and shoes, iron and steel and leading fabricated products of each: zinc, lead and copper and leading products of each, and bituminous coal. A section of great practical values discusses the use of construction work as a balance wheel for business. If all branches of our public works and the construction work of our utilities—the railways, telephones, and others—could systematically put aside financial reserves to be provided in times of prosperity for the deliberate purpose of improvement and expansion in times of depression, we should not only decrease the depth of depressions but we should at the same time diminish the height of booms. This utilization of government projects as an employment reserve, so far as possible, by which demand for labor and materials may be stimulated during depression, is now being made a part of the government's policy. To continue the investigations to find the principles and the information necessary to stabilize employment, studies will be made of some of the seasonal industries. The American construction council which includes representatives of the A. F. of L., bankers, railroad men, architects, engineers, contractors, material manufacturers and dealers, bond and insurance representatives, and municipal officials, now is seeking to control construction in order to avoid a later depression. (P. 208) We believe wage reductions should be opposed and resisted at all times. Such reductions curtail the purchasing power of the wage workers and where put into effect are detrimental to the entire community.

Unemployment, Cure for—(1923, p. 304) The A. F. of L. approves H. R. 10967 which provides that the government navy yards and arsenals, through their proper officials, should have the opportunity to bid upon all contracts being let by the government, provided such navy yards or arsenals are prepared to perform the work and have the necessary machinery and equipment to do such work, and if such navy yards and arsenals are the lowest bidders for such contracts, the same should be awarded them. The object of the bill is to relieve unemployment.

Unemployment Ignored by Congress— (1922, pp. 106–262) Instead of considering measures of a constructive nature that would relieve the acute unemployment evil, congress engaged in a wordy wrangle on how to "reduce expenses by limiting employment." The bureau of the budget has also given its aid to increasing the number of those out of work. Every branch, division and department of the government received orders to lay off as many employes as possible. When President Harding called his unemployment conference, he stated in his address at the opening session that the government would not do anything for the unemployed. This declaration unfortunately proved true. The conference was drifted away from any attempt to rely upon the government to relieve the situation and the responsibility was passed to the city, state and county governments. The whole intention was to prevent any demands being made upon congress to pass legislation that would aid in bettering business conditions.

Unemployment Insurance—(1921, p. 376) Remarks by President Gompers: "Prompted by the reference to unemployment insurance I feel it incumbent upon me to submit some thought to you upon this subject of unemployment insurance, or so-called unemployment insurance, for it is not insurance against unemployment but is compensation for lack of employment. No one will bring insurance against unemployment of an effective character but the working people themselves. Wherever there are payments to the unemployed in any country it has not reduced unemployment one iota—quite to the contrary. But that is not the most important objection to so-called unemployment insurance and I am waving aside even the important question of state rights. The fundamental objection that as soon as there is established a so-called unemployment insurance, or pay for unemployment, the working people place themselves under the guardianship of the government of the country. If we should establish the so-called unemployment insurance every action of our life, in so far as it refers to labor and employment, would be subject to the regulation and the discipline and the decision of government. If an employer or a combination of employers were to offer to reduce wages and the men or the women of labor who would refuse to accept that reduction, these men and these women would be unemployed, voluntarily unemployed, not unemployed under any concept which the law could define as involuntary. The unorganized workers often rise in protest against further tyranny, further imposition upon their life and work and condition; and even the unorganized, if they were to leave their employment by reason of another iniquity

upon them would not receive any payment for their unemployment. The whole of activity to organize, to assert and to live our own lives would be subject to every petty or high official of the government, intermeddling and guiding and commanding the activities, according to the government's conception of what is and what is not voluntary unemployment. It was contended also that unemployment insurance would compel the workers to carry industrial passports. A man who receives an unemployed benefit must necessarily carry a book to show where he worked last, and why he is out of work.

Unemployment, Social and Industrial Conditions—(1919, p. 115) The president of the A. F. of L. appeared before a senate committee to register the attitude of the A. F. of L. to a resolution instructing the committee on education and labor to investigate and recommend methods of promoting better social and industrial conditions, particularly as to a "national tribunal to review and adjust difficulties between employers and workmen; the development of the U. S. employment service into a national labor exchange; regularization of employment; prevention of employment; promotion of better living conditions; extension of soldiers' insurance to the civil population so that the workmen may insure at the lowest possible rates; the feasibility of a national insurance law against old age, disability, sickness and accident; national minimum wage law; extension of training and education of all disabled people." He said of government insurance against non-employment: "I should be opposed—I know that my associates would be opposed—to leaving it within the power of the government or its agent or agents to determine what was non-employment, whether it was justifiable or otherwise, and who would be entitled to the insurance or the benefits that would result from the provisions of the law—that is, insurance against non-employment. There was a resolution proposed by a member of the house some two or three years ago covering that feature. This member of the house was present at the committee hearing and finally stated that it is true that the govenment agent would have to depend, or on him would rest the obligation of determining what constituted non-employment so as to entitle an unemployed person to receive the benefits of the insurance. Now, that would mean, where there would be any controversy with the employer, that the man would be unemployed. Who would determine that question? Well, the answer would be, by the government agent, 'there is work for you, and so long as you can get work you are not entitled to this government insurance for non-employment.'" (P. 363) The subject of better social and industrial conditions is one which has attracted the attention of many theorists and faddists and has also received the serious consideration of men of a practical turn of mind. This subject relates to a number of activities and relations upon which the A. F. of L. has clearly and definitely expressed its attitude and determination. Any arrangement or device which leads to the involuntary submission of industrial issues to a national or state tribunal or compels the acquiescence in its findings, decisions or awards is contrary to the rights and privileges of a free people and violative of our constitutional guarantees. Any and all such proposals should receive our unswerving and determined opposition. The convention concurs in the need expressed by the executive council for the extension of the soldiers' and sailors' insurance system to include the civil population in order to assure workmen against the hazards of ill health, accident and death, at the lowest possible rate. We insist, however, that the first element of insurance is ample compensation for work performed which includes a wage sufficient to permit the laying aside of an adequate saving to meet all the adversities of life. Secondly, we insist on a system of government, as distinguished from private, insurance which is voluntary and not compulsory in character and which excludes the possibility of invading the rights and trespassing upon the homes of the workers by governmental agents or representatives of private concerns. We are of the opinion that inasmuch as the workers are alone required to labor under whatever legislative principles may be enacted into law and which affect only their lives, their conditions of service, their well-being and the welfare of those dependent on them that, therefore, this subject is one in which the workers alone should designate that legislation to which they shall subordinate their activities as free men and that they should not be made to suffer the consequences of the wishes or whims or fancies of so-called reformation agencies or societies or be made the object for amusement or notoriety of so-called parlor reformers with which our country abounds.

Union Aliens, Repression of—(1921, p. 121) A bill providing that aliens "shall not vote in the management of labor unions, industrial organizations, and for other purposes," was introduced in the house. The bill particularizes members of organizations employed in any occupation connected with interstate and foreign commerce or any public works of the U. S. Protests were entered and the bill was not considered.

Union Cards, Transfer—(1919, p. 301) Refused to concur in a resolution providing that free transfer cards should be issued to workers in the steel industry who have to transfer from one union to another. (P. 310) Refused to recommend to national and international unions that members of one union shall be admitted to any other union on the presentation of a paid-up working card and a certificate showing they had served the required apprenticeship.

(1922, p. 263) The A. F. of L. refuses to endorse the exchange of clearance cards by unions in lieu of an initiation fee for the reason that each international union has complete autonomy over its own membership, and the admission of members to the various international organizations is a matter for them to deal with.

Unions, Company—(1919, p. 302) We disapprove and condemn all company unions and advise our membership to have nothing to do with them. We demand the right to bargain collectively through the only kind of organization fitted for this purpose, the trade union, and that we stand loyally together until this right is conceded us. Extensive experience has shown that while the employers are busily carrying on propaganda lauding these company unions to the skies, as a great improvement over trade unions, they are at the same time just as actively enforcing a series of vicious practices that ham-string such organizations and render them useless to their employes. Of these practices the following are a few;

1. *Unfair Elections and Representation*—

The first essential for the proper working of a genuine collective bargaining committee is that it be composed entirely as the organized workers may elect and altogether free from the company's influence. Only then can it be truly representative of the men and responsive to their wishes. Upon such committees, bosses, representing as they do the antagonisms of the company, are so much poison. Not only is it impossible for them personally to represent the men, but they also negate the influence of the real workers' delegates. Knowing this very well, the steel companies, through campaigns of intimidation and election fraud, load their company union committees with bosses, usually to the point of a majority. So baneful is this practice that, were the company unions otherwise perfect, it alone would suffice to entirely destroy their usefulness to the workers.

2. *No Democratic Organization Permitted*— It is common knowledge that, in order for the workers to arrive at a uniform understanding through the systematization and formulation of their grievances and demands, it is necessary for them to enjoy and practice the rights of free speech, free assembly and free association. They must conduct an elaborate series of meetings under their own control, and generally carry on their business in a democratic, organized way. But with the company union system this is impossible. All independent organization and meetings are prohibited on pain of discharge. Consequently the workers are kept voiceless and destitute of a program. They are deliberately held down to the status of a mob. Under such circumstances, intelligent, aggressive action by them is out of the question.

3. *Intimidation of Committeemen*—As part of the general plan to keep their company unions from being of any possible service to their employes, it is customary for the companies to summarily discharge committeemen who dare to make a stand in behalf of the workers. The records show a multitude of such cases. Being unorganized, the men are powerless to defend their representatives. The natural consequences is that the committee soon degenerate into groups of men supinely subservient to the wishes of the company and deaf to those of the workers.

4. *Expert Assistance Prohibited*—When dealing with their employes in any manner, employers always thoroughly safeguard themselves by enlisting the aid of the very best brains procurable. The only way the workers can cope with this array of experts is to have the help of experienced labor leaders, but under the company union system this is impossible. All association with trade union officials is strictly prohibited. The company reserves to itself the right to expert assistance. As a result the green workers' committee, already weakened in a dozen ways is left practically helpless before the experts upon the company's side.

5. *Company Union Lacks Power*—In establishing wages, hours and working conditions in their plants, employers habitually use their great economic power to enforce their will. Therefore to secure just treatment, the only resource for the workers is to develop a power equally strong and to confront their employers with it. Unless they can do this their case is hopeless. In this vital respect, the company union is a complete failure. With hardly a pretense of organization, unaffiliated with other groups of workers in the same industry, destitute of funds, and unfitted to use the strike weapon, it is totally

unable to enforce its will, should it by a miracle have one favorable to the workers. Weak and helpless, all it can do is to submit to the dictation of the company. It can make no effective fight for the men.

6. *Company Diverts Aim*—As though the foregoing practices were not enough to thoroughly cripple the company unions, the employers make assurance doubly sure by seeing to it that their committees ignore the vital needs of the workers and confine themselves to minor and extraneous matters, such as fake safety-first movements, problems of efficiency, handing bouquets to high company officials, etc. Discussions of wages, hours and working conditions are taboo on pain of discharge for the committeeman who dares insist upon them. Thus the company unions complete their record of deceit and weakness by dodging the labor question altogether.

(1920, p. 479) Many employers of labor are on record as adopting the so-called "American plan" of organization thereby creating individual units of workers in each particular plant and, in many cases, a number of organizations in the same plant, each separate, distinct, free and independent of all the other workers in that industry, without any connection, federated or otherwise, with the workers in like industries outside of their particular plant. The officers of the A. F. of L. are directed to lend their full assistance to any organization in its efforts to resist the attempts of employers to disrupt the trades union movement by the introduction of this mis-named "American plan."

Union Labels—(1919, p. 471) The A. F. of L. realizes fully the many grave questions which must be considered and disposed of by this convention. Among those of paramount importance we hold that from its very nature the question of the union label, shop card and working button is of prime interest to every member of organized labor. Making the world safe for democracy and the right to organize and bargain collectively have been advocated and urged upon our people generally for the past four years; and rightfully so, as they are fundamentals upon which we all can agree. The first has been accomplished on the battlefields of France and Belgium in the great war which has just terminated, and because of the activities of the trade union movement the second is being more clearly and generally recognized. The trade union label is the embodiment of democracy, and the principle of the trade agreement is apparent when this insignia of labor appears in the shape of a union label on commodities, in a shop window or as a working button, and it is a guarantee that all of the principles of freedom are embodied therein, for the reason that each member of the organization at interest has had his full voice and vote in determining the conditions under which the article was produced. It also indicates to the general public that the principle of collective bargaining is carried to its full fruition, as otherwise the employer would not be permitted to display this emblem either on commodities or in shops. Since the cost in bringing democracy to the world was necessary to sacrifice so much blood and treasure, we feel that when industrial peace is guaranteed by the emblem of fair conditions, it is obligatory upon every member of a union to do his full share in perpetuating not only the principle of collective bargaining, but also to use his every effort to see that it is extended until all of the workers

participate in its benefits. In the declarations of its aims and purposes the A. F. of L. endorses as basic these economic principles: "That no trade or calling can long maintain wages, hours, and conditions above the common level; that to maintain high wages all trades and callings must be organized." Resolution No. 74, introduced by the Cigar Makers' delegation and endorsed by this convention, deals with the American Tobacco Trust and its subsidiary factories and the conditions of the unorganized workers in that craft. In relation to that subject we desire to submit some facts of the conditions that obtain in the cigar industry under the control of the American Tobacco Company. The American tobacco trust of the U. S. and Canada, has under its control sixty-five factories and is adding more to their number of operations. They also operate a chain of cigar stores throughout the country, and because of the very small wages paid in their factories they are able to undersell all competitors. They employ about 30,000 cigar makers, very few of whom are members of the Cigar Makers' International Union. They do not and will not bargain collectively with their employes or consent to operate the industries under unionized conditions. Owing to the low wages paid them a system of blacklisting, fines and punishments, etc., is operated against the employes, and the cigar makers who are employed by the trust factories are now in a rebellious mood and determined to obtain better working conditions and an increase of prices in a number of factories located in various parts of the country. The employes of the Porto Rico American Tobacco Company have been on strike for the past six months. The employes of the Havana-American Tobacco Company-located in Chicago, have been on strike for about the same period of time. The trust factory in New York City is out on strike, also other factories including the Lorrilard, New York City, factories in New Brunswick, Newark, Perth Amboy, and a half dozen more throughout the country are now engaged in strike. We most earnestly condemn the methods of the American tobacco trust for its treatment of its employes and the determined effort on the part of that gigantic corporation to prevent organization among the workers, and their nefarious system of exploiting the workers in that industry, and we, therefore, declare that one of the greatest assistances that can be rendered to the members of the Cigar Makers' Union and organized labor in general, which will assist in ameliorating those conditions and more speedily effect the work of organizing the members of that craft is for the members of trade unions to demand the cigar makers' international blue label on all goods that are purchased when buying cigars. Unionism is the only hope of the workers. Individuals may go up or down in our present social system, but the workers as a whole can progress upward only through the exercise of unionism. This is beyond dispute, yet few of us have even begun to grasp the great need and value, or the power of unity. Millions of men in America do not dream of the immense financial value to them of unionism; less than four million men realize the power of unity in the shops, and how few they are, compared with the rest of the workers in America, yet look at what unity has done for them. They have the shortest workday, the highest wages, the best treatment; they have hopes, confidence, self-respect. Could the organized workers of our country be made to realize the tremendous power that could be wielded through conservation or cooperation in their power of purchase, your committee is firmly convinced that a much more marked advance in the trade union movement would be bound to result. Statistics indicate that the organized toilers of our country earn more than three billion dollars per year, most of which has been secured through the efforts of their organization, and until such time as these workers refuse to spend their money earned under union conditions for anything except goods made under like conditions, we cannot hope for marked progress in this direction. The man or woman who enjoys a fair or a high rate of wages with a short workday, has no more right to dispense the money earned under these conditions for the products of non-union labor, the sweat shop, the labor of children, or the labor of convicts, than he would have to take the place of his fellowmen during a strike, for the reason that he is doing by indirection, by refusing to buy union-made goods, that which he would not do in the case of a strike. The A. F. of L. cannot overlook the fact that there is an apparent laxity on the part of members of organized labor in adhering to the principles of trade unionism in purchasing none but articles bearing the union label, and we desire to urge upon the members of organized labor when purchasing goods in the future to be more conscientious in discriminating in favor of union-made products. The complaint is often heard that it is hard to procure union-made goods. The theory on which union-made goods are sought is that it is similar to looking for a job—in either event it is your duty to search until you get it. This in no wise excuses the members of a trade union for this laxity in their duty. We feel that they are lax in another direction, that is, in failing to educate the women of the household as to the objects, aims, hopes and ideals of the labor movement. As is well known, the woman in the household of the average wage earner is the disbursing agent, and we cannot expect her to discriminate against goods made under unfair conditions except she be informed as to why this discrimination should be made, and we urge upon our members that they lose no opportunity to impress upon their women folks, the absolute need of spending money earned under union conditions only for union-made goods. Another way in which our women folks can be educated is through membership in the organization known as the Women's Union Label League and Trade Union Auxiliary, an organization composed of the wives, sisters, daughters and sweethearts of trade unionists, which is doing yeoman service in this field of our endeavors. This organization is giving considerable time, effort and money in the exploitation of and agitation for union-made goods, and any encouragement which can be rendered them by trade unionists should be given freely and unselfishly. National and international unions as well as state federations of labor and central labor unions can be of material aid in union label exploitation by aiding in the formation of union label leagues, whose sole duty it is to agitate among trade unionists and merchants for the sale of union-made goods, thus centralizing this work in a manner to secure the greatest results with the least efforts. We are pleased to learn of the progress made during the past year by the Union Label Trades Department of the A.

F. of L., and commend its officers for the great work they are doing. However, this work cannot be conducted on as broad lines and scope as it should be until every national and international union having a union label, shop card or working button to exploit is in affiliation to this department, and we urgently request that those organizations now now in affiliation take immediate steps to affiliate with the Union Label Trades Department. The A. F. of L. expresses appreciation for the aid rendered in the union label agitation and propaganda during the past year by the several international unions, state federations, central labor unions and organizers, and expresses the hope that this work will be extended considerably during the years to come.

(1920, p. 334) The executive council is directed to instruct organizers of the A. F. of L. that when visiting central bodies and local unions to devote on each such occasion a part of their talk to union labels, shop cards and working buttons: and to urge central bodies and local unions to appoint committees to secure information and keep it posted in meetings, designating where union label products can be purchased, and that such instructions be given at least every four months. There is no question but that active and progressive union label leagues are of great benefit, not only to trades having union labels, shop cards and working buttons to exploit, but to the general labor movement as well: and we earnestly recommend to national unions having union labels, shop cards and working buttons to exploit that they make provision in their laws which will tend to bring their local unions into label leagues where they exist, and to help in forming such central leagues in co-operation with the several bodies where they do not now exist, and advertise the same in the labor press. These label leagues can be utilized as an effective agency for the dissemination of information on this very important phase of work in the labor movement, and it should be the aim and object of international unions at interest to develop these agencies to the fullest extent. Representatives of the A. F. of L. and international unions, officials of central labor unions and label leagues should keep informed of all movements in the union label, card and button field, so that when they are addressing gatherings of workers or called upon by friends of the labor movement or merchants, they will be in a position to give such information as will aid in creating an increased demand for goods produced, sold or delivered by union labor. Conservation seems to be a popular topic at this time, and with this thought in mind all international or national unions should keep constantly before the organized workers the absolute necessity for spending money earned under union conditions only in channels where it will aid and assist the workers in crafts whose commodities are made under union conditions, thereby carrying to a practical conclusion our motto of aiding our friends whenever and wherever possible. Activity in the field of co-operation is developing very rapidly among trade unionists, and the committee on co-operation of the A. F. of L. should take such steps as are advisable to induce these several co-operative societies to give preference to union label goods whenever possible. As it is a well known fact that the women of the household spend the major portion of the money used to maintain the family, no effort should be spared to educate them as to the necessity of spending this money only for goods made and sold under union conditions. Attention is called to the existence of so-called union labels which have not been endorsed by the A. F. of L. this being especially true of the clothing trade, as no clothing should be purchased which does not bear a union label that is endorsed and recognized by the A. F. of L. There is now taking place in Tampa, Florida, one of the large industrial cigar centers of the United States, a conflict between the members of the Cigarmakers International Union and the combination of cigar manufacturers which form a part of the gigantic American tobacco trust, and an aggregation of citizens in that community who have allied themselves with the manufacturers for the purpose of exterminating the Cigarmakers' Union in that locality, and are waging a determined and relentless war to the end that they might destroy membership in the cigarmakers' organization. The conflict is on, the members of the Cigarmakers' Union are arrayed on the industrial battle front waging with equal determination to maintain the right to organization, the privilege of securing humane treatment, a living wage and better industrial conditions, yet struggling against great odds and a determined group of manufacturers who are wielding their political, economic and financial powers to defeat them. There are 5000 members of the Cigarmakers' Union who have been on strike since April 18 who are standing steadfastly against the tyranny and oppression of the manufacturers, with a determination to maintain their organization and secure humane conditions and other just treatments. The manufacturers of Tampa are using every method of coercion known to unscrupulous employers in trying to break the strike by preventing cigar box manufacturers from furnishing goods to independent manufacturers who have reached an agreement with the strikers and are willing to employ members of the union. They are using the force of the black list against all manufacturers who refuse to enter their combination and take sides with them against members of the union. The Cigarmakers' International Union has unqualifiedly endorsed the strike and commends the position taken by the employes, and are financing the struggle to the amount of $30,000 per week paid in benefits to the strikers, and will continue to lend aid and assistance both morally and financially until victory has been won.

(1921, p. 286) In order in a measure to offset the onslaughts being made on the labor movement by the National Chamber of Commerce, the manufacturers' associations and other organizations of employers hostile to the principles of our movement, delegates to all future conventions are urged to come there with union labels on all wearing apparel, and to urge upon the membership of their respective unions to conserve their purchasing power by withholding their patronage from hostile manufacturers of non-union goods, the money earned under union conditions, and to at all times give preference when making purchases to goods bearing the union label and to patronize only such shops or stores which display a union shop card or where the employes wear a union button. We also urge the adoption of this or a similar resolution by every state federation of labor and central body, thus furnishing practical proof of our loyalty to

the labor movement. All members of affiliated unions are requested to advocate, urge and insist upon the union label, shop card and button when making purchases. Reaffirmed indorsement of the Tobacco Workers union label. (P. 294) We cannot too strongly emphasize the great necessity for a more liberal, consistent and persistent demand for the union-made goods, as it must be acknowledged that by conserving our purchasing power and refusing to buy the products of non-union concerns we have a moral and financial force which is bound to have beneficial results. No manufacturer that we know of is in business for philanthropic purposes. Profit and still more profit being not only the underlying but the paramount object for his being in business, and this being true, whatever inroads can be made into the profit column by refusal to purchase his goods which are made under non-union conditions, there is bound to be beneficial results if this attitude is assumed by all trade unionists. If brotherhood and fraternity in the labor movement stand for anything at all, they stand for mutual helpfulness and co-operation, and the more acute and determined this co-operation and helpfulness becomes will the proportion of benefit resulting be. Complaint is often heard of the unfairness of employers because of their refusal to permit their employes to organize and, when either organized or unorganized, to negotiate with them as to the conditions under which the industry is carried on. While we heartily agree in the condemnation of employers who assume this attitude, we have still greater condemnation for the great mass of workers who, after all, are the real employers, they being the consuming public who fail to see to it that the money they earn under union conditions is expended only through channels where it will help to advance the interests, working conditions and general welfare of their fellow-workers in other trades or industries. To offset the campaign for the so-called "American plan" now being conducted by our enemies, it should be made clear to our membership by the officers of the affiliated unions just what this proposed plan is. In addition to this circular letters could be issued or the official journals used to inform the membership of the great good that will ensue when money earned under union conditions is spent only for goods produced under union conditions. The union label, shop card or working button as a means of identifying union goods and union conditions, is a distinctively American idea, and the sooner we have our members boosting an "American plan" based upon the trade agreement as exemplified by the union label, shop card and working button, just so much sooner will our enemies be routed. Complaint is sometimes made that the only demand for union-made goods is before they are placed in stock by the merchants. This is an intolerable situation which no one, least of all a trades unionist, can justify. Surely it is incumbent upon us to buy the goods we have asked to be placed in stock, and if we fail to do this, then the full responsibility for conditions as they now exist rests with us. When it is realized that the members of the trade union movement receive in wages during the year approximately five billions of dollars, and that so little of it goes back into channels for the employment of fellow trade unionists, the indictment is so frightful to practical trade unionists as to be almost incomprehensible. While the union label, shop card and working button are not panaceas or cure-alls for our industrial difficulties, they are an excellent antidote for many of them, and we believe that we really would have no child labor problem nor would we have so much difficulty in solving many problems of women in industry if a more consistent and persistent demand were made for the insignia of honest toil than there now exists. We make the broad statement that more permanent benefits can be secured for not only the class of workers above referred to, but all workers, through the application of this program. One of the best mediums through which this propaganda can be forwarded is the formation of union label leagues. We note with interest the progress made in this particular direction by the Union Label Trades Department of the A. F. of L., which has conducted a continuous campaign of publicity and information during the past year. The old excuse that "We don't know where to get goods bearing the union label" has been eliminated to a great extent and can be entirely eliminated by those who really desire to wear and use only label commodities by the expenditure of time sufficient to write a letter and at a cost financially of two cents to make inquiry from the Union Label Trades Department, A. F. of L. Bldg., Washington, D. C., which department will gladly furnish all of this information desired. We call attention to the fact that there are some so-called union labels in existence which tend to confuse those desirous of purchasing union label goods, and with this thought in mind we urge upon all trade unionists and sympathizers the absolute necessity of patronizing only those union labels, shop cards and working buttons which are endorsed by the A. F. of L. `

Union Labels and Cards—(1923, p. 22) Fifty-one labels and cards are issued by the following organizations which have been indorsed by the A. F. of L.: American federation of labor, bakers and confectioners, bill posters and billers, boilermakers, blacksmiths, bookbinders, boot and shoe workers, brewery workmen, brickmakers, broommakers, carpenters and joiners brotherhood, carvers, wood, cigarmakers, coopers, draftsmen's unions, technical engineers, architects and, international federation of, electrical workers, garment workers, united, garment workers, ladies, glove workers, hatters, horseshoers, iron and steel workers, jewelry workers, lathers, laundry workers, leather workers, lithographers, machine printers and color mixers, machinists, marble workers, metal polishers, metal workers, sheet, molders, painters, papermakers, photo-engravers, piano and organ workers, plate printers, powder workers, pressmen, printing, print cutters, sawsmiths, slate workers, stove mounters, tailors, textile workers, timber workers, tobacco workers, typographical, upholsterers, and weavers, wire.

Organizations Using Cards—Actors, barbers, clerks, retail, engineers, steam, firemen, stationary, hotel and restaurant employes, meat cutters and butchers, workmen, musicians, stage employes, and teamsters.

The A. F. of L.—The following crafts and callings are using the A. F. of L. label: Badge and Lodge Paraphernalia Makers; Pearl Button Workers; Coffee, Spice, and Baking Powder Workers; Commercial Photographers; Nail (Horseshoe) Workers; Neckwear Cutters and Makers; Suspender Makers; Garter, Arm Band and Hose Supporter Makers; Soap Makers. (P. 234) Our movement can be materially advanced and permanent progress insured if the workers are fully informed that their power of purchase is a dominating factor in the economic and social life of the nation. When it is realized that more than six billion dollars come to the workers as a result of their labor annually, the significance of this fact in regulating and improving industrial conditions must be held before their view at all times in order that they may use this power, not so much in punishing hostile employers and associations of employers as in aiding fair employers to develop their various lines of business to the point where merited elimination will be the lot of those hostile to us. When five millions of our citizenship were forced into idleness by the campaign for the so-called "open shop" under the guise of what was termed an "American plan" we witnessed a demonstration of the power of money without a parallel in any civilized country in the world. Many unions were weakened; many families were disrupted because of unemployment; hunger and sickness were prevalent and our industrial system was placed in a condition of chaos from which it has not yet fully emerged. This brief review of conditions during the past two or three years in our industrial and social life is made solely with the thought of bringing more forcibly to the minds of our fellows what can be done in a constructive way through the use of this same power of money. There can be no doubt that if the vast sum of money heretofore mentioned was used only to employ members of trade unions in the exclusive purchasing of union label goods, in the making of repairs in and about residences and halls owned or leased by trade unionists; if all our energies were directed to aiding our fellows by co-operating with them through the power of purchase, we would then be making a sure and unerring approach to that industrial democracy so much to be desired and for which the trade union movement has so long and so earnestly striven. Reference has been made to a so-called "American plan." There is but one "American plan" whereby all of our people, whether members of trade unions or not, can be assured that the goods they purchase are made in America, and that is when a union label is attached thereto. Ours is the only movement in the world which uses this system to identify the product of its members: and the only way the same can be popularized and made effective is through untiring advocacy by a united membership. As a means to the carrying out of the ideas herein expressed, we recommend that all national and international unions which utilize a union label, shop card or working button have the same printed on all letterheads, envelopes and other stationery, and that national or international unions which do not have such label insignia adopt some suggestive line, trite saying or epigram concerning the union label and have the same printed on their stationery and general printed matter as an educational feature in aiding this important work. In the past committees on union label have had their attention called to conditions existing in the convention city relative to restaurants, hotels, barber shops, etc., with the charge made of patronage being accorded by delegates to places which were not unionized. We recommend, therefore, that within a sufficient period preceding future conventions the Secretary of the A. F. of L. request the proper officials of the entertaining central labor union to have printed for distribution among the delegates a list of fair houses, as well as unfair, in the classes above outlined, and that included in the list shall be the names of mercantile establishments where wearing apparel and furnishing goods, bearing the union label, can be obtained. An agency in the union label propaganda field which is doing excellent work and which is worthy of the co-operation of all trade unionists is the Women's Union Label League and Trade Union Auxiliary, whose membership is recruited from among the wives and daughters of our members. Volunteer in character though it may be, the activities of these splendid women are not confined to mere verbal union label agitation, but they at all times may be found doing their utmost to aid by practical means the furtherance of the cause we represent. Their work is constructive, not merely theoretical, and is worthy of the widest approbation. Standing as they do for all the ideals and principles for which the trade unionist movement is contending, let us give to these women an undivided support and the rich fruitage of such united effort will be apparent in the coming years.

Union Membership (1923, p. 22) The average paid-up and reported membership for the year 1923 is 2,926,468. National and international organizations are required to pay only the per capita tax upon their full paid-up membership, and therefore the membership reported does not include all the members involved in strikes or lockouts or those who were unemployed during the fiscal year, for whom tax was not received. The following is the average membership reported or paid upon for the past twenty-seven years;

Year	Membership	Year	Membership
1897	264,825	1911	1,761,835
1898	278,016	1912	1,770,145
1899	349,422	1913	1,996,004
1900	548,321	1914	2,020,671
1901	787,537	1915	1,946,347
1902	1,024,399	1916	2,072,702
1903	1,465,800	1917	2,371,434
1904	1,676,200	1918	2,726,478
1905	1,494,300	1919	3,260,068
1906	1,454,200	1920	4,078,740
1907	1,538,970	1921	3,906,528
1908	1,586,885	1922	3,195,635
1909	1,482,872	1923	2,926,468
1910	1,562,112		

Venezuela—(1923, p. 366) It has been persistently alleged for the past ten years by workers, newspaper men and others, native and non-native, coming out of Venezuela, that the present government keeps possession of the power of the state in that country by violence and tyrannous oppression, that it has rendered null the right to suffrage, the freedom of speech, of assembly, and of organization, and denies to the workers the right to cease work (strike) in defense of their just aspiration for a higher standard of living. It is further alleged that the methods employed to prevent effective protests against that tyranny are in many cases more inhuman than those employed for similar purposes during the darkest centuries of the history of mankind, and include the confinement of free men, without any process of law whatever, in infected cells and dungeons for indefinite periods of time, with iron balls chained to their ankles; the use of the rack; hanging by the toes, the fingers, and by parts of the body unmentionable in a convention of decent American workmen, and other revolting tortures. It is further alleged that among those arbitrarily imprisoned by the present government of Venezuela there have been American citizens, inscribed, when at all, under foreign names and ascribed to nationalities other than that of the U. S. The A. F. of L. is a member of the Pan-American Federation of Labor, an organization founded to carry to the sister republics of the American hemisphere the fight for better economic and civil conditions for the workers that has been so conspicuously successful in the United States; and as the most powerful body in the P. A. F. of L., the A. F. of L., is depended upon by the oppressed masses of those republics for moral support in their nascent struggle against economic and civil disqualifications. The A. F. of L. denounces in the strongest terms the establishment and permanence of any sort of despotism in Venezuela or in any other country. The president of the A. F. of L. is directed to request the P.-A. F. of L. to make a thorough investigation of the allegations made; that, if the result of the investigation carried out by the P.-A. F. of L. confirms in a detailed manner the allegations generally the president of the A. F. of L. is instructed hereby to appear before the president of the U. S., and his Secretary of state, and place before them the facts, with the request that they, as constitutional executive powers of a christian nation, give consideration to the convenience of withdrawing diplomatic contact with the present government of Venezuela.

Virgin Islands—(1920, p. 119) Congress ordered an investigation of conditions in the Virgin Islands to determine whether the present government should be changed to a civil government.

(1923, p. 367) All national and international unons having organizers or local unions in Porto Rico are requested to send representatives to the Virgin Islands for the purpose of furthering trade union organization.

Volstead Act—(1919, pp. 263–445) The A. F. of L. expresses its disapproval of war time prohibition and directs that a strong protest from the delegates at this convention be forwarded to the government at Washington, setting forth in a most emphatic manner the opinion of the delegates to this convention that the present mild beers of 2¾ per cent. alcohol by weight should be exempted from the provisions of the eighteenth amendment to the Constitution and also from the provision of the war prohibition measure. (P. 268) The convention ordered an adjournment for Saturday, June 14, Flag Day, to permit the delegates to accompany the president of the A. F. of L. and executive council to Washington to present the resolutions to the judiciary committee of the house of representatives.

(1921, p. 360) The A. F. of L. is in favor of a modification of the Volstead act to permit the manufacture and sale as a national beverage of wholesome beer.

(1923, p. 323) The A. F. of L. has gone clearly on record as being in favor of such modification of the existing law as will permit the manufacture and vending of wholesome beer and light wines. That we may correct an impression which has sought to be created by the advocates of the Volstead act, that the action of the A.F. of L. was not a fair statement of the attitude of the organized labor bodies affiliated to the A. F. of L.

this convention votes its reaffirmation of the action of former conventions dealing with this subject, giving approval at the same time to the statements made in the circular sent out by the executive committee of the non-partisan political campaign committee, in order that there may be no misunderstanding as to the position of the A. F. of L. on this important and vital question. It is our belief that the efforts at enforcement of the Volstead act have produced results that in themselves are so far from being what was promised or reasonably expected might follow the adoption of the eighteenth amendment that we feel warranted in saying that the reasonable modification now asked for, and a rational enforcement of the eighteenth amendment, will bring relief greatly sought by the people. The fact that the open saloon has been supplanted by the "speak easy," and that instead of licensed venders of liquor, who carried on their business under strict surveillance and regulation by law, we now have an unnumbered multitude of bootleggers, who dispense their vile and poisonous liquors in secrecy, to the great detriment of the health and morality of the people; the presence of this nefarious traffic has brought with it a great host of so-called law enforcement officers, many of whom have not hesitated to set aside or ignore all other laws in their zeal to enforce the one law in which they have interest. Between the lawless vender of forbidden liquor on the one side, and the lawless enforcement officer on the other, the public has suffered irreparable damage because of the consequent and inestimable diminution of regard for any law. We believe that this condition may be remedied by giving a more reasonable interpretation of the eighteenth amendment to the constitution of the U. S. than is contained in the so-called Volstead act, and the Executive Council through its legislative committee is directed to use all reasonable efforts to bring about such modification of this statute as will have the effect of giving to the people wholesome beverage in lieu of the flood of "moonshine" that now poisons those who are foolish enough to consume it, and which encourages the illicit traffic and the irrational efforts to suppress that traffic, which has brought so much confusion into our national, political and social life.

Voting Privileges—(1919, p. 348) A. F. of L. refused to petition congress to so change the registration laws that every citizen can cast a vote at all elections, who has resided within the precinct where the vote is offered to be cast, for a period of twenty-four consecutive hours previous to the act of voting.

Voting, Unit—(1920, p. 420) President decided that delegations of international unions should determine among themselves how they should vote on any question before A. F. of L. conventions as the latter had no power to dictate to them. There was no appeal from the decision.

Wages and Cost of Living—(1921, pp. 68-314) The American trade union movement believes that the lives of the working people should be made better with each passing day and year. The practice of fixing wages solely on a basis of the cost of living is a violation of the whole philosophy or is a violation of sound economic theory and is utterly without logic or scientific support of any kind. What we find as a result of practice, so far as it has gone, is that there

is a constant tendency under it to classify human beings and to standardize classes, each class having a presumptive right to a given quantity of various commodities. It is not difficult to understand that the ultimate development of such a policy must be ridiculous and fantastic; in fact, it already has become so in many cases. We are not prepared at this time to lay down in definite form a policy which we believe proper as a basis of wage measurement, but we are firmly convinced of the necessity of research and study in order that a principle may be found which will be scientifically sound and to which, therefore, our industrial life wil naturally adjust itself. American industrial development has reached a point where it must give to the workers a consideration that goes beyond the bare essentials of sustaining life. Hunger of the workers for those things which satisfy the diversified needs of human beings has in the U. S. in the main been satisfied, so far as the elementals of physical existence are concerned. There is beyond that point, however, a hunger which can only be described as one which demands opportunity for a broadening sphere of mental and spiritual life. To measure the life possibilities of a highly civilized people in terms of yearly allowance, or so many pounds and yards of commodities, is a conception which the American labor movement can not tolerate and which it must remove from the realm of practice. We realize fully that to substitute the present unscientific, unsound and unjust practice with one which shall meet all tests, requires deep study and much consultation. There must be laid down a principle that will endure. We must face the facts as they are and carefully develop a scientific procedure in so far as that is humanly possible. Ultimately, we feel, there must be found some method of relating standards of living to social usefulness, or production service, though under present industrial management this has not yet been found possible on any just basis. Unquestionaly the welfare of any people as a whole is directly related to the productivity of that people. The difficulty is encountered when it is attempted to apportion returns on the basis of individual productivity. Some of the blame for this is because of the lack of control by individuals over their own life work and by the practice of employers of pitting workman against workman, as well as the advantage which employers take in imposing speed efforts which it is possible to maintain for short periods only. However, progress that has been made in some cases in the development of the science of industrial management shows that it is possible to look forward along this line with some hope of results that will afford justice to the workers and to society at the same time. There are but two avenues leading to permanent higher standards of living for our people as a whole. One of these is the elimination of waste, either in the form of mismanagement or of undue exploitation and profiteering. The other is increased productivity. Both must be traveled simultaneously. The necessity and desirability of constantly improving standards of life and living compel labor to manifest a deep and intelligent interest in management, to the end that the reward for more effective effort may not be diverted into non-productive channels, or in other words, into the pockets of those who contribute nothing toward production. We merely set down these fundamentals as an indication of what we believe to be a necessary avenue of thought leading to possibilities of greater justice for the workers and a sounder basis for our social life as a whole. And, looking in this direction, as we believe we must, we are driven to the conclusion that those who contend for the fixation of wages on the basis of the cost of living are wrong. In that direction lies death through the perpetuation of a static condition. We draw no further conclusions at this time, because we realize fully the magnitude of the problem and the complexities which it presents. The Executive Council is authorized to conduct an investigation, leaving to the judgment of the council whether it should name a special committee for that purpose or conduct the investigation itself. We recommend that this investigation be prosecuted with diligence in order that it may be possible to report to the next convention a policy to serve as a guide for the labor movement of America. (P. 314) The Executive Council or a committee selected by it is directed to conduct an investigation into the whole question of wages and cost of living.

(1922, p. 34) The A. F. of L. in 1921 directed that an inquiry be made into wage determination in order to develop a comprehensive, well-considered theory capable of real service in the practical problems of determining wages. The importance of the inquiry parallels the significance of wages. Wages in terms of life symbolize progress from a status of servitude to free labor that has rights and accompanying responsibilities. Wages in the material world represent power to command opportunities and material benefits. The development of a theory that will properly interpret wages and at the same time perform a functional service in the determination of specific wage rates and methods is a task of very considerable dimensions. It is obvious wage earners ought to have an agreement upon this important issue and it is equally obvious that formulation of any proposal must be based upon most careful study and consideration. Economic theory of classical economists was largely speculation. More modern thinkers have been turning from the mythical economic man to industrial conditions and men who work for wages. Even very casual consideration of wage theories set forth by economists and by those actively engaged in industry indicates the inadequacy of proposals thus far made. From the period of classical economy down to the present day, wages have generally been interpreted as a phase of the value problem. Theories have been worked out on the basis of labor gain, iron law of wages, labor costs, marginal utility, supply and demand, subsistence wages, costs of living wage, saving wage, productivity, service, etc. These theories dealt with static cross sections of the wage problem. No one attempted to take into effect all factors concerned in the determination of wage rates or methods of wage determination, The important step to be taken is to make wage theory explain industrial facts and to find a theoretical explanation that parallels the processes of wage determination and indicates methods to enable workers to increase productivity with equitable distribution of returns from production. Wage theory properly related to methods and bases of wage determination should take into consideration incentives for creative work as well as indicate equitable

wages for specific industries. The investigation thus far made confirms the point of view that the consequences of careless application of inadequate theory have attended popular usage of "cost of living basis" for wage fixation. Following the rapid expansion and inflation of war finances, came big increases in prices. When wages were exchanged for those articles of living which must be replaced constantly, the wage earner felt keenly the inadequacy of his prewar wages as measured against inflated prices. He naturally expressed the maladjustment between his wage rates and the inflation expressed in high prices, by asserting that the costs of living—or depreciation of purchasing power of wages—necessitated wage adjustments. This condition of affairs indicates that a wage based solely upon costs of living or subsistence or a saving wage, bears no direct relation to production or service rendered. However, a wage based upon productivity or service must accept as an initial standard a wage based upon human needs and aspirations—a minimum determined upon human requirements without reference to the other considerations that enter into a wage which compensates for productivity or service. In every industry and gainful occupation a wage based upon human needs and aspirations should be regarded as a business liability. Productivity, service rendered, specialized training, and trade skill, the nature of the work, special irksomeness, unusual hazards and physical strain and every other factor entering the value of the product or service, should form the basis for wage increments. A very considerable degree of fluctuation in prices is due to the factors that control the business cycle. When research has indicated ways to stabilize industry by decreasing the area within which financial fluctuation influences wages, wages will be less subject to fluctuations. However, industrial factors which affect prices would still operate. This is one of the points of overlapping of wages and the unemployment problem. Cost of living indices only serve to indicate the minimum of human requirements and are the measuring stick for real wages and not the basis for determining wage rates. The problem of determining rates remains after indices have been considered. The problem involved is concerned with theory and practical methods. Fundamental for this study is availability of production and cost and expenditure records so that both management and workers shall have an opportunity to know what is accomplished in the establishment in which they are producing. Records are the sources of industrial facts. A study of records will disclose changes needed for more effective results. Present appalling ignorance of industrial facts due to insufficient or inadequate records makes this wage study increasingly difficult and expensive. The task involved requires much research and study. When facts shall have been made available then it will be possible to consider whether results are justified from the standpoint of individual and collective equity and social welfare. The responsibility for our ignorance of the basic facts of industry rests upon government agencies as well as upon management in private industries, but primarily upon the latter. Every business involves financial, commercial and industrial policies. While the worker may not be so directly concerned with the commercial and financial aspects of business these affect him vitally nevertheless. The workers are greatly concerned with industrial policies of business—that is control of process, machinery, nature of product. Over-capitalization, under and poor equipment, inefficient management, failure to reflect economic changes in business accounts, failure to write off adequate depreciation, failure to charge losses, wastes and gains to the proper accounts—all have a direct bearing upon wages. It is not sufficient that the wage earner should have individual records of his production and production costs but the employes of the company or the industry must have access to accountancy data that give a comprehensive understanding of production, distribution and consumption. This information should be available for those who are concerned with industrial problems. Since the information is for statistical use, the uniformity of accountancy methods within the industry is indispensible. This principle of uniformity is also a cornerstone to industrial organization that is essential to order in each trade or industry. The information is prerequisite to a rational basis of distribution of proceeds of industry. The problem of wage determination in prison industries which arises under the recent New York law, providing for wage payments upon any basis approved by the superintendent, was brought to the attention of the A. F. of L. and the co-operation of the A. F. of L. is deemed essential in finding an equitable basis for determining the wage paid to prisoners. It is hoped that in the attempt to solve this question by experimentation and careful and continued observation invaluable information may be obtained which will prove helpful in reaching practical and intelligent conclusions on the subject of wage determination. We have only attempted to indicate the nature and scope of the problem. We have not made even a statement of the problem, for that can be done only after thorough investigation. This study involves consideration of whether the wage problem is a scientific one or one which science can aid in solving, whether a wage formula can be educed, or whether basic determining laws can be found. We submit that provision ought to be made for carrying forward the study of wage theory which is of such fundamental importance to the whole labor movement as well as to the establishment of a more equitable industrial order, and to this end the Executive Council through the president is hereby authorized to continue the investigation through such means as the council may approve and release from time to time such findings as may be determined. (P. 354) The A. F. of L. directs continuation of the investigation of wage theories.

Wages Fixed by Law—(1921, p. 122) In recent years there has been much agitation in favor of fixing prices by law. Every bill presented in congress for the purpose of regulating some industry provides that the commission empowered to carry out the purposes of the proposed act shall govern prices. This is most dangerous legislation. Where prices are determined by a commission, the commission assumes the power to regulate and fix wages. The A. F. of L. should take a firm stand on this question. The bill to regulate the meat packing monopoly contained such a hidden provision and it was impossible for the A. F. of L. to support it in its entirety. The first convention of the A. F. of L. declared; "We believe the gaining of higher wages and a shorter workday to be the preliminary steps

toward great and accompanying improvements in the condition of the working people." Therefore, the wages of the workers in the great industries are more important than any consideration of the prices that should be fixed for the products of those industries. If American standards are to be governed by laws enacted by a congress made up of men not alive to maintaining those standards the workers of the country will suffer irreparable injury by legislation governing their wages. (P. 325) We believe that the fixing by statute of the wages of adult male workers in private employment is unsound and dangerous. Legislation to be helpful along these lines should take the direction of securing publicity for such elements as ownership, capitalization, production, distribution, cost, profits, conditions of employment, efficiency of management and waste.

(1922, pp. 114-323-339) Bills were introduced in congress to provide for the collection of data on the cost and distribution of the production of coal. They also gave the president in case of an emergency power to take over the mines. It was believed that "an emergency" would be when the miners in order to protect their economic interests would have to cease work. In that event the government could decide the wages and conditions of employment for mine workers, fix the price of coal at the mines and to the consumers wherever they might be located. This would establish a principle of government through a commission which could arrogate to itself the right to determine the wages of employes or groups of employes in any or all industries. No hearings were held on the bill and the protests entered appeared to have had good effect.

(1923, pp. 86-280) Underlying the proposals of fixing wages by legislation or to require submission to compulsory adjudication of the rewards that shall come by labor is the line of demarcation which distinguishes the free man from the slave or serf. Fixing wages by legislative enactment, directly or indirectly, through boards or commissions, for employees not in the government service, is to deny such group or groups of wage earners freedom of contract and to make of them industrial and commercial serfs. Making compulsory the submission to an arbitration board, labor board or industrial court of the question of the consideration that shall govern the making of a contract for service is to deny the very fundamental principles upon which our government is founded and by which the liberties of our people are secured. All legislative proposals which have for their ultimate object compulsory submission to any governmental body or device questions which affect industrial relations, or which have for their object the fixing of wages other than by voluntary action, whether such proposals be clothed in terms of mediation, conciliation or arbitration, justly demand our condemnation.

Wage Reduction, Resist—(1919, p. 85) Turning from war to peace upon the signing of the armistice, a condition soon became apparent to everyone that had long been feared by organized labor. It was made apparent very early that there had been no adequate forethought and provision made for the transition from a war basis to a peace basis in industry and that as a result a period of industrial confusion and unemployment was at hand. In addition there were pro-

nouncements from high sources among employers that extensive reduction of wages
would be undertaken. The taunt also was
thrown at working people that they should
have been able during the war, because of
increased wages, to save enough to carry them
through the period of readjustment. These
statements betray either ignorance or a
desire to wilfully deceive because they completely ignored the fact that the rising cost
of living had absorbed whatever increase in
wages had been secured and in many cases
went much beyond the point of absorption
effecting an actual decrease in the purchasing
power of the individual. Declarations of a
policy of wage reduction came to our attention at Laredo, Texas. The president of the
A. F. of L. there introduced the subject in
open conference and declared that labor
would resist to the utmost any policy of wage
reduction. This position has been affirmed
since that date on many occasions and it is
due to this prompt and decisive answer to
this challenge fully sustained by labor that
there has not been a general assault on wages
by employers who can not comprehend the
trend of the times. The position of labor
must be maintained and advanced at all
hazards. It is the opinion of the A. F. of L.
that no wages paid to American workmen
to-day are too high, but that on the contrary
wages far too low still are paid in many
industries. Progress is the word to-day
and the progress worth most and best understood is the kind that reaches the individual
in the form of a better life, a freer and larger
opportunity, and more of the things by which
life is sustained and enriched. The progress
of our movement in realizing these things for
the workers is not to be denied by any
influence or obstacle.

War Emergency Labor—(1919, p. 96)
While an investigation of the operation of
schools for training emergency labor was in
progress the armistice was declared. This
terminated the need for war emergency labor.

War, Labor's Service in—(1920, p. 96)
The annual reports of the secretary of the
navy for the year 1919, contained a generous
acknowledgment of the service rendered by
labor to the U. S. during the war. It is
fitting that this acknowledgment of service
be made a part of the permanent record of
the A. F. of L. It follows; "Labor was the
rock upon which our preparation and supplies
depended. It was mobilized and efficient.
Acting with closest accord with the department of labor, it was the privilege of the navy
to aid in stabilizing labor and in proving that
the government is the best employer. The
day of giving to skill and toil a mere living
wage has passed. It is entitled, after a fair
day's work, to a fair day's wage, sufficient
for comforts and some luxuries as well as
necessities. Navy wages have never lagged.
They have generally led and for good pay it
has, from its patriotic workers, received a
good day's work. Without the greatly increased production due to the skill and
industry and fine spirit of patriots in over-
alls, our men in arms could not have been
furnished the required munitions and
supplies."

War Referendum—(1921, p. 386) Convention refused to adopt resolutions favoring
an amendment to the constitution of the
U. S. taking from congress the power to
declare war and requiring that it be submitted to a referendum by the people:
"that those voting in favor of war should be
compelled to take up the active prosecution

of the same before those who voted against
war." (370) Request that convention
endorse "No More War Day" referred to
Executive Council for such action as it may
deem advisable.

War Risk Insurance—(1920, pp. 111-
360) Public No. 104 enacted by the Sixty-
sixth Congress, provides for increases in
compensation. S. 3607 provides for the
abolition of the bureau of war risk insurance
and transfers the jurisdiction of allotments
and allowances of compensation for death or
disability and of war risk insurance on other
establishments to other departments of the
government. Protests have been made
against this bill by the A. F. of L. and no
report has been made upon it.

War Time Laws—(1919, p. 392) This
convention expresses its insistent demand
that immediately following the signing of the
peace treaty all laws in any way limiting
or infringing upon the right of free speech, of
a free press, and freedom of assembly which
were enacted as war measures, shall be
repealed. No recommendation is presented
for a general pardon of all those who have
been sentenced under the espionage act or in
connection with industrial crimes. There
are instances where commutations of sentences or pardons are warranted; there are
undoubtedly many instances where the
sentences imposed were fully justified.

(1920, pp. 102-385) Efforts to repeal the
espionage law failed.

(1921, p. 121) The espionage act, which
many influences sought to have made a
permanent statute, has been repealed. Its
repeal was included in the measure repealing
war-time legislation after persistent agitation
by representatives of the A. F. of L.

War Veterans Associations—(1920, pp.
210-392) Convention approved following
report of the Executive Council: "The officers
and the Executive Council have been in
receipt of numerous letters and telegrams
concerning the activities of organizations of
war veterans, and the attitude of the Federation toward them. In some cases central labor unions and members of organized
labor have complained that certain organizations of veterans had shown themselves
hostile to labor. In no such instance,
however, has it been shown that the veterans'
organizations had by official word or deed
shown themselves in conflict with the aims of
organized labor; rather has it been shown
that such instances could be traced to the
unauthorized and unwarranted actions of
individuals. On the contrary, also the A.
F. of L. has been assured by officials of various veterans' organizations, both orally and
in writing, that nothing hostile to labor's
interests was contemplated. Where the
letters have been simple requests for information as to the attitude of the federation
toward these groups, the writers have been
informed that the American trade union
movement has in the past taken no official
stand in relation to the organization of war
veterans, and that, failing such official action,
no member of organized labor had the right
either to endorse or condemn any such organization in the name of organized labor.
There is another feature, however, to which
attention should be called in connection with
the organization of the ex-service men: that
is, it is not only current report but actual
information that the ex-service men in the
organizations which have been instituted
purpose to utilize the political power of these
men as service men. The American citizen-

ship have a common policy and polity, and where the divergent groups of our citizenship may exercise their political power to serve their respective interests no political group is justified to separate itself from the common polity and policy of our country purely upon the ground of having given service to the United States during war.

Water Power—(1920, p. 121) Congress, after ten years of consideration enacted a law that gives over the development and utilization of the water power on navigable streams almost entirely to private corporations. The law provides everything necessary to give a great public utility to private ownership. Representatives of the A. F. of L. protested against the measure but the influence of the promoters, who would obtain hundreds of millions, if not billions, of dollars of profit was sufficient to carry the measure through congress.

(1923, p. 228) Private interests will not and can not solve the related water problems or assure an abundance of water and power at the lowest economic cost. The A. F. of L. recommends to all citizens in all states a program of state conservation through complete use and development and control of the waters of the state, as submitted by the state to California voters in the water and power act, and for the service of the people at cost, as opposed to corporation development and control of water resources for private profit.

Welfare Work, National Committee on —(1919, pp. 92–360–428) Up to the signing of the armistice the committee on labor of the council of national defense continued to function in a manner which proved so helpful in the successful prosecution of the war. With the signing of the armistice the war emergency work was discontinued and the work of readjustment undertaken. The national committee on welfare work which had distributed expert reports upon "Industrial Fatigue," "Adequate Sanitary Devices to Prevent Industrial Poisoning," and "Lighting Codes," has developed and had printed others upon subjects as important in their relation to the health of workers as the ones reported upon at the preceding convention. One dealt with "Requirements and Standards upon Heating and Ventilation for Industrial Establishments and Dwellings": another with "Rural Sanitation," having special reference to new industrial villages and construction camps and referring particularly to housing. All of these reports have been sought by officers of labor organizations, manufacturers and educators; and within the past six months over 13,076 requests have been received for these pamphlets. It also has had put in pamphlet form, under its section on industrial safety, minimum standards of safety, structural safety, fire prevention and accident prevention. These exhaustive codes were prepared by leading experts connected with the National Council of Safety, the American Institute of Architects, the National Fire Protection Association (including the National Board of Fire Underwriters), and the welfare department of the National Civic Federation. This pamphlet will be distributed widely among employers. It is as valuable under peace conditions as in war times, as in many states there are no safety requirements in the form of legislative enactments with regard to fire prevention or accident prevention. The Section on Industrial Training for the war emergency, which was composed of one-third labor, one-third employers and one-third practical educators, conducted an investigation which showed there was no shortage of labor during the war except in some of the skilled trades made urgent by the war, and to this end emergency training was installed. The section on industrial training issued an illustrated pamphlet upon "How to Overcome the Shortage of Skilled Mechanics by Training the Unskilled," and then another indicating what had been achieved by the committee on labor in connection with this, entitled "How the Shortage of Skilled Mechanics is Being Overcome by Training the Unskilled." These books had great weight with employers in inducing them to install practical war emergency training rooms. The section on recreation of the committee on welfare work issued a preliminary plan for shipbuilding, aeroplane making and munition making centers, providing a program of recreation for: (1) •The industrial plant itself; (2) The industrial community. One of the important activities of the committee on labor has been the maintaining of existing safeguards for the conservation and welfare of the workers and that no departure from such existing standards should be taken without a declaration by the council of national defense that such a departure was essential for the effective pursuit of the national defense. In September of last year, so many women having entered the industrial field to replace the men drafted into our army and navy, a meeting was held by the executive committee of the welfare committee on the subject of night work for women and steps were taken to secure a complete list of important war production plants in the leading industrial states asking for women to be placed on night work and that an investigation should be made as to the effect of night work upon the health; whether or not in night work it is profitable to use women, and if not, if it would be profitable upon three eight-hour shifts and when three should be used; whether or not it would be practicable to have men upon the third shift or the alternating shift; whether or not it is possible to avoid night shifts; whether, where night work exists, it is absolutely necessary to employ women in order to maintain production and to determine where such cases exist, and what are the operations upon which women can work more efficiently than men and, therefore, must be required to go upon night shifts. With the signing of the armistice this investigation was discontinued. The committee on women in industry advised on women's employment in such ways as to bring about the maximum effectiveness of the woman power of the country and this committee assisted in securing the enforcement of the labor laws. The committee on labor of the advisory commission of the council of national defense was not created merely as a war emergency body. By an act of congress in August, 1916, the secretaries of war, navy, interior, agriculture, commerce, and labor were charged with the "coordinating of industries and resources for national security and welfare" and "with the creation of all relations which will render possible in time of need the immediate concentration and utilization of the resources of the nation." The further duty was imposed that the council of national defense "should supervise, direct investigations, make recommendations and report on all inquiries or subjects appropriate to the national safety and welfare to the president and through him to congress, and that it might also report to the heads of executive departments upon special inquiries or subjects appripriate thereto." Everywhere men and women, employers and employes, placed themselves and their resources unsparingly at the service of our country. This committee, though not vested with executive authority or created for executive action, became an efficient and most helpful channel for centralizing and directing this voluntary effort in our industrial life during the time of national need. While the problems now pressing for solution have changed in form, there is involved in their solution fundamentally the same principles—that is, the coordination of industries and resources for national security and welfare. To the same degree that the committee on labor of the advisory commission of the council of national defense served to assist in the effective transformation of the country from a peace to a war basis, it can now assist in restoring the nation to normal life in peace with the least possible friction and disturbance. (P. 428) The investigations and publications of the national committees on welfare work and on women in industry, and of the sections on industrial training for the war emergency and on recreation, have proved their value. One of the most important achievements of the committee on labor has been the maintenance of labor standards under war conditions.

(1920, p. 95). The committee on labor of the advisory commission to the council of national defense, of which the president of the A. F. of L. is chairman, continued its efforts for the protection of the workers during the reconstruction period. Among the efforts vital to the protection of the workers continued by the committee on labor during the year, was one to aid discharged soldiers and sailors to secure employment in civil life. At the solicitation of the library war service, the committee on labor undertook to send to the workers, and to the trade unions appeals calculated to be of assistance in furnishing discharged soldiers and sailors with books on vocational subjects, for which a great demand was manifested by the men leaving the ranks. The appeal issued by the committee called attention to the fact that the public libraries offer to returned soldiers and sailors, as well as to all workers, splendid opportunities for study and mental development and that, in the more than 4,000 libraries of the country, there are books to be had containing information on practically all trades, books on all of the problems of life and living, and books on all past and present phases of social relationships. Appeals were made to the committee on labor to aid in the work of explaining to the returning soldiers, sailors and marines the advisability of retaining their insurance. This insurance, provided for under the war risk insurance act, and under rules formulated by the committee on labor in accordance with the best concepts and principles, was in many cases not fully understood or properly valued by the returning men of the army and navy. The committee exerted every effort to induce the men to continue their insurance and it is a fact that because of these efforts thousands of men continued this most beneficial and economical insurance who otherwise would have allowed it to lapse. In December, 1919, the committee on labor ceased to function and all of its subcommittees were dis-

solved. The president of the A. F. of L., as chairman of that committee, in dissolving the several sub-committees extended an earnest expression of thanks and obligation to all who had contributed their services patriotically without pay or hope of reward.

Wilson, Address of W. B—(1919, p. 294) It is a great pleasure to have the opportunity of being present, even though it may be at but one of the sessions of this historic victory and reconstruction convention of the A. F. of L. The wage-workers of our country have reason to be proud of the part which they played in the great world war for freedom and democracy. You have reason to be proud not only of the part you have taken in the struggle, but of the great part that has been played in the contest by your selected representative, the president of the A. F. of L. Upon him has devolved not only the direction of your forces and associated forces in the great struggle against the military autocracy of Germany, but there has also fallen upon his shoulders—and he has borne the burden manfully, he has directed the movement intelligently—the great burden of conducting the battle against the other insidious forces that would endeavor to utilize violence for the destruction of democracy, the powers of bolshevism as expressed in some of the countries of Eastern Europe. The part played by labor has been due in a great measure to the appreciation by labor of the development that has taken place in the progress of human democracies. I have a theory, and time alone will demonstrate whether the theory is sound, that every individual and every group of individuals becomes influential in the affairs of the government just in so far as the individual or the group of individuals is necessary for the defense of the state. I know my British friends will pardon me if I refer to what in my mind was the great starting point in the development of modern democracy. I don't look upon the battle of Bannockburn as being purely the heritage of the people of Scotland alone, but I look upon it as being the heritage of the masses of the people of all the world. Those of you who are familiar with the history of that struggle and the ones preceding it, realize that up until that time the only people who had been permitted to participate in the affairs of government were the monarchs and the nobility, the nobility comprising the flower of knighthood. The nobility were permitted to participate because the man on horseback and in armor was the man who at that time was necessary for the defense of the state. Nearly all of the nobility of Scotland had been brought up at the court of England and when the battle of Bannockburn took place very few of the men in armor were on the side of the Scottish monarch. He had to depend for his support in the conflict upon the yeomanry of his country and for the first time in the history of warfare the yoemanry, with pikes in their hands, were formed on the battlefield of Bannockburn in what has since come to be known as the "hollow square"—only in that case it was the hollow circle. The historians have failed to grasp the importance of that situation. They tell us of the pitfalls that had been made on the moor for the horses of the English monarch and his men and how some of these fell into the pits. There were a sufficient number who crossed over the moor to have crushed the

Scottish army if it had not been for the new military tactics which the necessity of the situation compelled Bruce to employ, and he formed his men into hollow circles to receive the men of the opposing forces on their pikes, and when the nobles came, they came on to the pikes of the yeomanry and were destroyed. The yeoman at that moment became a more important factor in the defense of his country. The British monarch was later compelled to follow the same tactics that Bruce had followed. And when the wars were carried by Edward over into the continent, with the yeomen as a fighting factor in his armies, the European military chiefs were compelled also to change their tactics. From that period dated the fall of knighthood and the beginning of manhood. Slowly the masses of the people represented in the yeomanry began to realize their importance, and before the reign of Bruce had passed, they had compelled him to yield concessions to the yeomanry of his country, and this was true also of Edward and true over all the continent. The individual, the man in the mass, the toiler of society, began to see the dawn of a new day. It took centuries before it began to crystallize, but those same people, coming over to our country, settling on our shores, carried with them the ideals of the importance of the workers of humanity. When our declaration of independence was proclaimed to the world, when it was being prepared before it was given to the world, there came down from the north those who insisted that there should be included in the document the statement that taxation without representation was tyranny, and there came up from the south workers who in the meantime had become imbued with a spirit of racial artistocracy but yet were imbued with the same thought that had developed on the other side of the water, who insisted that there should go into the declaration of independence that basic principle of all democracies—that every government derives its just powers from the consent of the governed. Modern warfare has still more thoroughly accentuated that thought. In the battles of ancient times it was frequently possible for large armies to support themselves upon the country in which they were operating, receiving but a small portion of their supplies from home. From the days when Joshua overcame the enemies of Israel until Sherman made his famous march to the sea, great armies supported themselves upon the country in which they were fighting. That is no longer possible. It has been variously estimated that it takes anywhere from six to ten workers in the rear to maintain one soldier in the trenches. Consequently, the workers of all the world have become more important factors in the defense of their respective countries, and they are insisting and will continue to insist that in the consideration of the problems of reconstruction, the laws shall be so constructed and social affairs so conducted that every individual in the community shall have the greatest possible opportunity for self-determination. The labor movement of this country is no exception to the rule in that respect. We have in our country our faddists—people, many of them who have never had experience in the practical problems of life. Some of them have been following after false gods. It is not those who are following after the false gods that will be the saviors of the

workers of our country. It is those who have persistently made and are continuing to make self-sacrifice for the common good who will achieve results. I recall, and I may have mentioned it to you on previous occasions, but it will bear repeating— I recall the conditions we found in the middle west when the president's mediation commission was sent out to investigate the conditions brought about by the activities of the Industrial Workers of the World some two years ago. The Industrial Workers of the World had almost gone out of existence prior to that time. Suddenly there was a renewal of activities. Industries that were essential for the success of the war were being tied up. There seemed to be no way of keeping them in operation. The president appointed a commission of which I had the honor of being chairman. We found some oddities and many crude theories that the average man in the labor movement would not stand for. We found that people were coming in on the rods to the mining camps of the mountain regions —coming in quite large numbers, and practically over night establishing locals of the I. W. W., and then, without submitting the question to the voice of the workers themselves, either through organization or otherwise, declaring strikes against the companies that were operating; declaring those strikes for a given wage and for a given number of hours, refusing to meet the employers in conference and insisting that it must be this rate which they published and no other, and that idleness would follow the employers' refusal to comply with their demands. But that was not all. We found that wherever the legitimate evolutionary aspirations of the workers were given an opportunity to develop, there the I. W. W. found no foothold; that it was only in the places where there was the iron hand of repression on the part of the employer used upon the workers themselves that this peculiarly revolutionary spirit found expression. It found expression in addition to the manner I have stated in the philosophy that was being taught. They announced as the basis of their movement the philosophy that every man is entitled to the full social value of what his labor produces. Now that philosophy is purely of socialistic origin. It had its first exponent in Marx. It is also a philosophy that every individualist can subscribe to with thoroughness and with complete acceptance of the principle. Every man is entitled to the full social value of what his labor produces. The great difficulty has been that human intelligence has not yet devised a method by which we can compute what the social value is of anyone's labor. No one can compute the value of your labor; no one can compute the value of my labor; no one can compute the value of the labor that has been performed by the president of this organization, or the labor that was performed by the man with a pick and shovel in the ditch. Our intelligence has not yet devised a method by which we can compute it, and so, in the years gone by, we have endeavored to make the computation by one of three processes: By the process of the employer using his economic power to arbitrarily fix the compensation of the workers; by the process of the worker using his collective power, arbitrarily fixing the compensation and imposing it upon the employer, and by the process of negotiation. It is the process of negotiation that the American labor movement has insisted upon for the bringing of the different elements together and endeavoring to work the problems out on as equitable a basis as the circumstances will permit. But there is a wide misapprehension of the scope of the labor movement of our country. There are those who assume that the negotiations that the American labor movement seeks with the employers only involve consideration of the question of wages, or the hours of labor. But the negotiations that the American wage-workers, the labor movement of America, stand for, include in their scope every industrial activity that affects the mental, the material or the spiritual welfare of mankind. They laid down as the second step in their philosophy that property is only valuable in so far as profits can be secured from the property, that if you eliminate the profits the property will become valueless and no one will want to retain it: and that, so far as it goes, is also sound. If there is nothing that can be produced from a piece of property that will be valuable to mankind, then no one wants to be bothered with the possession of that property. Then came what to my mind and to the minds of the great bulk of the trade unionists of this country that I have come in contact with, was the poison in their whole philosophy. They said that the way to destroy the value of the property was to strike upon the job, that is, to "soldier" as we say here in the East, to produce a stint, as they say in Great Britain, to put sand on the bearings, to break the machinery, to reduce production and to reduce the amount of returns from labor to as small a point as possible and enable the worker to retain his job, then in this way the profits would be destroyed, the value would be eliminated, the owner would no longer desire to retain the property and it could be taken over by the workers, operated collectively, and the workers secure the full social value of what their labor produced. Whatever there may be of value in the collective ownership and operation of property there is at least no value whatsoever in that method of bringing it about. All we had to do among those workers in the middle west was to point to the historical fact that prior to the rebirth of the inventive genius of man, prior to the building up of our modern factory system with its wonderful processes of machinery, when everything that was produced was produced by hand, there was a much smaller production per individual than could possibly result from any system of sabotage that could now be introduced: and yet in those days there were still profits for the employers and there was still value to the property. What did result was a very much lower standard of living for the workers, and the only thing that would result from such a scheme now would be a lower standard of living for the wage-workers of the present, and our wage-workers are not going to stand for any system that will lower their standards of living. The employers and the employees have a mutual interest in securing the largest possible production with a given amount of labor, having due regard to the health, the safety, the opportunities for rest, recreation and improvement of the workers. These being safeguarded, the larger will be the amount that is produced, the larger will be the amount that there is to provide. If there s nothing produced, there will be nothing

to divide. If there is a large amount produced, there will be a large amount to divide. Their interests diverge only when it comes to a division of what has been mutually produced, and if they are wise in their generation in these modern times, with labor realizing its importance in the defense of the country and the maintenance of the country, instead of solving the problem by the use of the economic power on the part of the employer, imposing this will upon the worker, or the use of collective power on the part of the employees imposing their will upon the employers, they will sit around the council table and endeavor to work out the problem on a democratic basis that will secure to each all that he is entitled to receive. Closely allied to the work of the I. W. W. during the past year, at least, there has been more or less bolshevist agitation in the United States. It has not been to any great extent prevalent among the real workers of the country. It has existed principally among the "parlor coal-diggers" of our greater cities. I have no fear of a political revolution in the United States. It may be possible that these "parlorites" may misguide a sufficient number of laboring men to cause local disturbances that will be annoying, but no one in the ranks of labor, whether he is classed as an extreme radical or an extreme conservative, or any of the elements between these two, will stand for bolshevism for a minute when he knows what bolshevism itself stands for. They talk a great deal about the dictatorship of the proletariat. We who have been more or less familiar with the theories that have been promulgated by Marx and his assertion of the dictatorship of the proletariat had interpreted the term to mean that a majority of the workers of the land would determine the policy of it and impose it upon the balance of our people. And our workers were not willing to accept even that kind of a principle. They realized the many centuries of struggle there had been to secure the franchise on the part of the workers in the face of the claims that had been made that they had no property to be taxed, and having no property to be taxed they should have no voice in imposing the taxes, and further, that they had not developed enough, that they had not sufficient intelligence to be permitted to participate in the affairs of state. During all the centuries there has been a struggle to remedy the wrong, and the basis of that struggle, the basis of the contention of the workers has been that every person who has to obey the laws of a country ought to have a voice in determining what those laws should be. Having fought all through the centuries for the accomplishment of that ideal, having accomplished this purpose, the American workingman was not disposed to impose the same kind of a disfranchisement upon other portions of the people that he did not want imposed upon himself. The bolshevists did not even take that interpretation of the dictatorship of the proletariat as their guide in the countries where they are just now supreme. In his long speech before the national soviet at Moscow a little more than a year ago, Lenine laid down the principle that the dictatorship of the proletariat meant the dictatorship of a self-selected, so-called "advance guard;" that the proletariat himself was not to be trusted because he would waver, and that this self-selected advance guard would impose its will upon the workers and the others must obey, and in that obedience was included obligatory labor. From the time that Moses led the Israelites out of bondage in Egypt until Lincoln issued the emancipation proclamation, the struggle of the masses has been to get away from slavery, to get away from compulsory labor, and yet it is proposed by this new form of government to re-introduce obligatory labor upon the workers of the world, imposed upon them by a small group of the "parlorites" of Russia. The great distinction between slavery and freedom is that under freedom every man shall have the right to cease work for any reason that may be sufficient to himself. We have protested to the extent of sacrificing our blood and our treasure against the military autocracy of Germany and yet the military autocracy of Germany was built upon the self-same idea, that the Kaiser and his group of advisers knew better what the workingman desired, what he needed and what was good for him than the workers knew themselves, and this new group is setting itself up as the advance guard, taking exactly the same position that they know better what is good for the workers than the workers know themselves, and that one of the things that is good for them is that they must be compelled to labor at any price that the advance guard may say, at any kind of work they may determine, for any number of hours the advance guard may decide upon, and the powers of government are to be used to enforce that will. That is their policy. The American workingman wants nothing of that kind of dictatorship of the proletariat. The American workingman wants nothing of that kind of obligatory labor. The American workingman wants nothing of the political, social or economic conditions that have existed and still exist in Russia. We have worked out our destiny far beyond that stage, and we are going to continue to work it out to the achievement of higher ideals, not by the will of an advanced guard no matter how right or just their position may be, but by the will of the majority themselves. The use of force, as some of these people are advocating, for the overthrow of our insitutions, we will not tolerate. Why, my friends, our institutions have been until recently the most completely democratic institutions in the world, and it is only recently that Great Britain has come up shoulder to shoulder with us. Our declaration of independence, while it declared, as I have stated, that governments derive their just powers from the consent of the governed, did not give to all of the people a voice in the affairs of state. The adoption of our constitution did not give that right, that privilege. It was not until after sixty or seventy years of struggle that there came to the workers of our country practically universal manhood suffrage and every element in our country had at least the right to a voice in determining how the affairs of state should be conducted. In Eastern Europe they had not reached that stage of development. The workers were not permitted to have a voice in determining the affairs. The only method by which they could bring about change was by the use of force. Force over there and force here are two different propositions. The use of force to overthrow an autocracy may be the highest kind of patriotism. But the use of force to overthrow a democracy is treason to the masses of the people. We

are proceeding by evolution, not by revolution. We have the power of the ballot to remedy our grievances. If we fail to use the ballot rightly the fault is our own. And those of us who cannot be depended upon to vote right cannot be depended upon to shoot right. And, may I add that in making that statement I am not advocating either the attachment to any political party or the creation of any new political party. Our conditions here are very much different from the conditions on the other side of the ocean. Over there there is a snug little island. The great majority of their people are engaged in industrial and commercial pursuits. A separate party over there can, without having an accession from the intellectuals, become a majority party. That is not the case in our country. There are just as many people engaged in agricultural pursuits, in pursuits that do not lend themselves to organizations, as there are engaged in industrial pursuits, and even if we were able to soldify all of the wage-workers of the country in a common mass, as the others would soldify against us, we could not become a majority party, and any progress we might attempt to make would be retarded as a result of the partisan feeling that would be engendered by virtue of these contests. And so we are in a position where we can, if we will, organize a separate party, or we can pursue the policy that has been pursued successfully so far, and that is to throw the weight of our support, of our influence, to the individuals or to the parties that, for the time being, are willing to go along with our program. May I, also, Mr. President, take this opportunity of giving a word of advice in connection with another situation that has been tense throughout the country? The advice is given freely, honestly and earnestly. You may accept it or leave it as your own judgment tells you is best. I have been very much interested in the Mooney case. I was requested by the president when his commission went west, to look into the Mooney case and report to him. We looked into the Mooney case and in doing so we came to this conclusion: That so far as the jury was concerned that passed upon the evidence presented to it, it could have come to no other conclusion under its sworn duty than to convict Mooney: that so far as the judge was concerned who tried the case, he tried it with absolute fairness. But there were some things existing in addition to that. At the time of the trial certain evidence had been given by certain individuals relative to the supposed activities of Mooney. It afterwards developed that one of the principal witnesses had written to a friend of his in Illinois asking him to come to San Francisco and be prepared to testify that he had seen Oxman, the witness, at a given point at a given time, so as to testify to the possibility of Oxman's being at the point where he claimed to have secured the evidence. The commission was of the opinion that in view of that change in the evidence, and in view of other changes that had taken place in the evidence from the date of trial, Mooney ought to be given a new trial, and his innocence or guilt decided upon the evidence as it existed when this new evidence was produced. At that time I had no fixed opinions as to either the guilt or the innocence of Mooney. With me it was not a question of whether Mooney was guilty or was innocent, but a question of securing a fair trial for him under the existing circumstances. Every effort that the national administration was able to put forth was put forth for the purpose of trying to secure that new trial, and we are not through with it yet. We are still working on it. But that is not the phase of the situation that I particularly wanted to advise you about. I am simply stating these facts as preliminary to what is to follow. There has been carried on throughout the country a nation-wide agitation for a universal strike as a protest against the conviction of Mooney. My friends, do you realize just what that action means to the masses of the people? Do you understand fully—most of you do—the struggle that has taken place in order that trials may take place by jury where people are accused, with the accused having the opportunity of meeting the witnesses and the jury face to face, and the jury having opportunity of witnessing the manner in which the witnesses give their testimony? That change, the establishment of the jury system, was not brought about for the purpose of protecting the monarch or protecting the nobility. It has not been principally essential for the protection of men of great wealth; they have usually been in a position to protect themselves. The jury system was brought into existence for the purpose of protecting poor fellows like you and me from the power and influence of the other fellow. It may occasionally miscarry; occasionally an injustice or a wrong may be done, but in the great bulk of cases justice is meted out through the jury system. Neither you nor I nor anyone in the labor movement, no one who belongs to the great masses of our people, can afford to undertake to try Mooney by the process of a strike. If he is to be tried he should be tried by a jury that can meet him face to face and meet the witnesses face to face and be able to digest the evidence as it comes out, bit by bit. Very few of us have had an opportunity of examining the evidence in the Mooney case, very few of us know anything more about the Mooney case than simply that which is connected with Oxman, one of the principal witnesses, and yet it is proposed that every workingman in the country, whether he has information concerning the Mooney case or not, shall become a juror in this case, and at the same time that he becomes a juror, shall enter into a strike to bring about a decision. What influence will it have? The man who under our laws can pardon him or liberate him from prison is not under the jurisdiction of the voters of any other part of the country than that of California. And I do not know but that, even though there may be a miscarriage of justice occasionally, it is a wise thing that that is the case. The further you get the responsible officers removed from the electorate, the less influence the electorate has with those responsible officers, and while the responsible officers may occasionally pursue a course that is not acceptable to the multitude, it is better that they should be close to the multitude, close to the electorate, than that they should be far removed, as would be the case if the responsibility rested with the federal official instead of with the state or local official. My friends, we in this country have been moving on by the evolutionary processes, taking hold of the problems that confront us, holding fast to that which experience demonstrates to be good, letting loose of those things which experience demonstrated to be bad. It is the safest method, the surest method. Revolutionary processes may move us forward rapidly for a brief period. On the other hand, the chances are that when a revolution takes place no one will be able to determine where it will end. That has been true of nearly all the revolutions of the world, and the policy that has been pursued by the American labor movement of going forward by evolutionary processes, making sure of each foothold with every step that it takes, so that there will be no step backward, is the surest and best process for the achievement of the highest ideals of mankind.

Wilson, William B.—(1921, p. 148) The A. F. of L. feels that it can not, consistent with the interests of the working people of our country, permit the occasion of this forty-first annual convention to pass by without in some manner recognizing and expressing its appreciation of the work, the ability, the faithfulness and the stalwart characteristics of Hon. William B. Wilson, Wilson the miner, Wilson the trade unionist, Wilson the faithful and efficient officer of the United Mine Workers of America, Wilson the many times delegate to the conventions of the A. F. of L., Wilson the statesman in congress, Wilson the patriot, Wilson, the first secretary of the department of labor, Wilson the first trade unionist to sit in the cabinet of the president of the U. S. In every sphere of his varied activities, whether in the ranks of labor or in the congress of the U. S. or in the great post in which he was placed in the organization to conduct the affairs of the new department of labor, in the councils around the cabinet table with his associates and the president, he has stood for labor, for the people, for the country, whether in peace or in war and his great, strong heart and mind acted in unison and sympathy for common humanity. It is not our purpose here more than to record these few sentiments as a tribute to a man of sterling qualities and to express the hope for his health and strength for many years to come to enable him to serve in the attainment of the highest aspirations of our great movement. (P. 310) Those who have enjoyed the pleasure of personal acquaintance with William B. Wilson know what a rare privilege it is to count such a man as a friend. His straightforward honesty, his contempt for sham, his unswerving devotion to right and his unquestioned loyalty to the cause which has absorbed his life's effort, are the outstanding characteristics of a man whose simple nature renders him incapable of duplicity or deceit in any degree. So long as the American labor movement is able to point to a man of the type of William B. Wilson as exemplars of its principles it need fear no assault from its foes, however powerful or however strongly intrenched in public opinion they may be. In whatever line of endeavor Mr. Wilson shall employ his great talent and ability, we feel certain that his achievements will shine because of the rugged, inflexible honesty and the unfailing gentleness of the man.

Wilson, Woodrow—(1919, p. 1) The following cablegram from Woodrow Wilson, who was in Paris, was read: "May I not send my warm greetings to the annual convention of the A. F. of L. and express my deep gratification that the international conferences which have grown out of the discussions of peace have led to a much fuller and more adequate comprehension of the questions of labor to which statesmen throughout the world must direct their most thoughtful attention? It has been a real happiness to me to be of a little service in these great matters. I cannot justly refrain when sending this message from expressing in very warm terms the appreciation felt by all who have been dealing with labor matters of the invaluable service rendered by Mr. Gompers. He has won universal confidence and has firmly established in international circles as well as at home the reputation of the A. F. of L. for sane and helpful counsel."

Women's Auxiliaries—(1923, p. 220) The organizing of women's auxiliaries of labor unions comes under the authority of the national and international unions.

Women's Bureau—(1920, pp. 113-461) Indorsed bill creating a women's bureau in the department of labor. (1921, p. 120). Public 259 created the women's bureau in the department of labor. The duty of the bureau is to formulate standards and policies which shall promote the welfare of wage earning women, improve their working conditions, increase their efficiency, and advance their opportunities for profitable employment. It has authority to investigate and report to the department of labor upon all matters pertaining to the welfare of women in industry. A member of the Boot and Shoe Workers' International Union was appointed chief of the bureau.

Women, Equal Rights for—(1921, p. 436) The A. F. of L. since its inception, has done everything in its power to organize the women workers of the country and to obtain for them equal rights, political as well as economical. We, therefore, now reiterate all the many previous declarations of the federation that we stand for equal rights for women in industry, as well as for equal rights of women in the political and industrial life of our nation. A large percentage of the international unions now admit to membership women workers of their trade or calling. There are, however, a few international unions that have not yet decided to admit to membership women workers, due largely to the nature of their work. Considerable progress is being continually made to reach a better understanding with international unions on this particular subject. We, therefore, recommend that those international and national organizations that do not admit women workers to membership give early consideration for such admission.

Women in Industry, School for—(1921, p. 327) In the exceedingly important field of adult education, the committee commends the growth and success of the schools under trade union auspices, and such promising plans for cooperation with educational institutions as those of the Bryn Mawr summer school for women in industry.

Women in Industry—(1922, pp. 101-456) During the past year agitation has been in progress to have congress adopt a resolution providing for an amendment to the constitution of the U. S. alleged to be in the interest of women. It provides: "No political, civil, or legal disabilities or inequalities on account of sex or on account of marriage unless applying equally to both sexes shall exist within the U. S. or any territory subject to the jurisdiction thereof." The constitutional amendment was being urged by the national woman's party. President Gompers protested against the amendment, as it would have had the effect of repealing all the protective laws for women in industry. He held several conferences with representatives of the national woman's party, who stated that they were willing to accept any amendment that would protect women in industry. But this was found to be impossible, as a constitutional amendment can not contain reservations. The opposition became so great that the sponsors for the amendment found that they could not secure its passage in congress, so they set out to have laws enacted in the various states embodying the alleged "equal rights" contained in the proposed amendment. Representatives of all state, city central bodies and local unions should carefully study such legislation as its passage would be of the greatest injury to wage earning women. Minimum wage laws would be repealed, laws limiting the hours of work for women would be repealed. Many other laws having for their purpose the protection of women in industry would be repealed. While those urging the enactment of the equal rights law may not be aware of the fact they are aiding unfair employers.

(1923, pp. 55-227) The decision of the U. S. supreme court invalidating the minimum wage law for the District of Columbia has weakened and perhaps eliminated the protection which wage earning women had received from legislation of that character. Minimum wage laws of various types for women workers have been enacted in twelve states which affected the wage standards of one million, five hundred thousand women. To take counsel on the serious situation resulting through the initiative of wage earning women a conference was called composed of representatives of organizations directly interested. The conference urged that earnest consideration be given to helping women to organize in trade unions for protection and for the development of their economic power in furtherance of constructive industrial ideals and authorized the appointment of a permanent committee to study the following legislative proposals; (1) Restriction of power of the U. S. supreme court. All proposed methods to be studied. (2) Amendment of the federal constitution for the broad purpose of insuring protection of social legislation and the rights of labor. (3) Amendment of the federal constitution which will give to the states and congress the power to enact minimum wage legislation. (4) Minimum wage statutes to come within the limits of the supreme court decision. The organization of the study committee is now in progress and the federation is participating in the undertaking. That part of the problem of women in industry which is exclusively a labor problem should have our most serious consideration. The A. F. of L. has consistently maintained that the only agency in which wage earning women could place absolute confidence is economic organization. Irrespective of any legislative program that may be endorsed, we feel that the fundamental problem at present time is a special undertaking to develop more thoroughly ways and means of organizing women workers. It is now a demonstrated fact that women are permanently in industry as wage earners. As a consequence of the development of factory production, homework has been revolutionized. Food and clothing that were formerly prepared or made in the home are now made in factories. In addition to highly organized industry as a causal factor, many women are under the necessity of earning a living for themselves and those dependent upon them. Women as a a group and as individuals have been broadening woman's sphere of activity until there are few callings which are not open to them generally or into which a few individuals have not entered. Our census figures show a large increase in the number of women wage earners. In 1910, 8,075,772 women were gainfully employed; in 1920, 8,549,511. The changing proportions in the groupings according to occupation is even more significant than the numerical increase as it indicates women's entrance into professions and industrial callings requiring high skill. Women workers are permanent members of our various industries and have been notably increasing in numbers. Unorganized they constitute a menace to standards established through collective action. Not only for their protection but for the protection of men in the industries there should be organization of all within the industry. Because there are special problems of procedure in this field as well as problems of method the president of the A. F. of L. is directed to call a conference of officials of such organizations as are particularly concerned with the problem of organizing women wage earners in order that a more thorough organizing campaign be planned and inaugurated.

Women, Organization of—(1922, p. 306) International and national organizations that do not admit women workers to membership are urged to give early consideration for such admission. Where women workers are refused admission to international unions having jurisdiction over the industry in which they are employed, the executive council of the A. F. of L. is directed to take up the subject with the international unions involved and endeavor to reach an understanding as to the issuance of federal charters.

Women, Protective Laws for—(1919, p. 450) It is the declared policy of the A. F. of L. that there should be no discrimination in the employment of women, and that where women are employed they shall receive the same wages and have the same conditions under which to work as are given to men. It is, however, realized that there is necessity for the protection of the health of women workers: that unless this protection is given them the race cannot continue to progress as it is desired that it should. It is therefore, necessary that laws for the protection of the health of the women in industry should be passed, and that one of the most potent laws to this end is that which provides for the shortening of the work-day and the work-week. .Your committee believes that if these points are kept in mind there will be no necessity for discussion as to the moral effect of any hours of work upon female employes.

Wooden Cars—(1922, p. 351) Directed executive council to secure legislation from congress prohibiting the use of wooden baggage and express cars.

Workday for Federal Employes, Longer —(1919, p. 132) At the time the the St. Paul convention was in' session, the annual agricultural appropriation bill was pending in the senate. This bill contained an hour-lengthening amendment which required the federal employes to work a full eight-hour day, without any provision for overtime. Although the clerks and other employes of the government work nominally a seven-hour day the head of the department is at

liberty to call upon them for overtime or Sunday or holiday work without extra pay. This is frequently done. The federal clerks declared that they had no objection to congress establishing by law the basic eight-hour workday, but that in doing so congress should provide for payment of time and one-half for all hours worked in excess of eight No such provision was made. Resolution No. 71, which was adopted by the convention, denounced this proposition to lengthen the workday without provision for overtime, and instructed the executive council of the A. F. of L. to take appropriate means for defeating the same. Urgent letters opposing this amendment were addressed by the president of the A. F. of L. by instructions of the executive council, to each member of both houses of congress. Nevertheless the obnoxious provision was incorporated in the agricultural appropriation bill as it finally passed congress and was transmitted to the president. A vigorous protest was then made to the president, in which it was respectfully and urgently submitted that unless the congress would exclude the so-ca led Borland amendment from the measure the president might see the justice and wisdom of returning the bill to congress without his approval. On July 1, President Wilson vetoed the bill and it was subsequently passed without the hour-lengthening amendment. The labor people in Congressman Borland's district, aided by the A. F. of L., made a vigorous opposition to his renomination and he was defeated by a large vote. This matter came up again on February 20, 1919, when Senator Thomas of Colorado offered a similar amendment to the last legislative, executive and judicial appropriation bill, which was then pending in the Senate. The amendment was rejected.

Workday, Hours of Labor—(1919, p. 452) Reasonable hours of labor promote the economic and social well-being of the toiling masses. Their attainment should be one of labor's principal and essential activities. The shorter workday and a shorter work-week made for a constantly growing, higher and better standard of productivity, health, longevity, morals and citizenship. The right of labor to fix its hours of work must not be abrogated, abridged or interfered with. The day's working time should be limited to not more than eight hours, with overtime prohibited, except under the most extraordinary emergencies. The week's working time should be limited to not more than five and one-half days. In giving consideration to a shorter work-day at this time there are many things to be taken into consideration. In the first place it must be realized that during the war five million of the most active young men in the country were taken from industries for war service. In spite of this the production of the country during the war period was greater than it had been at any other given period in history. Of course this great production was materially assisted by the introduction of women into the factories, and to a large extent the elimination of the liquor industry and taking over of people previously engaged in that work for war production. Labor organizations for many years have been fighting to secure the 8-hour day, once known as the shorter workday. This 8-hour day meant 48 hours of labor per week. Because of the changed conditions brought about by the war a number of the industries have been able already to introduce the 44-hour week, continuing the 8-hour day with a half holiday on Saturday. Only twelve years ago the International Typographical Union expended more than four million dollars in securing for its members the 48-hour week in the printing industry. At the present time that organization is négotiating for and will probably receive, the 44-hour week through conciliation and without the expenditure of any sum of money. The garment working trades have succeeded in securing the 44-hour week. Other industries have done or are doing likewise. The A. F. of L. believes it will be but a short time till the 8-hour day with a half holiday on Saturday, meaning a 44-hour week, will be the universal hours of labor and adopted in all industries. While this is most desirable and we recognize that the executive council has used all its available power for the purpose of assisting in bringing about a 44-hour work week in all of the crafts, this convention advises it to go even further than this. There is at the present time a large volume of unrest among the workingmen on this continent. There can be no doubt but that there are two reasons for this unusual condition—first, the high cost of the necessaries of life; second, unemployment. Until wages are so adjusted that the earnings of labor will buy the same amount of the necessaries of life that could be purchased by the earnings previous to the war, this unrestful exhibit by the working people has a foundation for its existence that cannot be set aside. Previous to the war the dollar earned by labor would buy a certain amount of a certain quality of food and clothing. The dollar earned at the present time will also buy a certain amount of a certain quality of food and clothing, but it will not buy the same amount that the dollar earned previous to the war would buy. Until this gap is bridged and the wages increased so that the same amount of the same quality of goods can be bought with the dollar of today as was possible before the war, the condition of the laborer will be less desirable than in the pre-war period. Manufacturers and employers of labor should recognize this fact and increase the wages to this point without any controversy. Regarding unemployment. It is almost impossible to peruse a daily paper without finding somewhere in its columns a statement that every effort should be put forth to secure employment for soldiers returning from across the sea or from the camps maintained in this country. This is a most laudable effort and meets with the approval of all classes of people. However, for the general good of the community work must also be provided for civilians as well as ex-soldiers. If there is not sufficient work in the country to give the returned soldiers steady employment and at the same time give continuous employment to all other people seeking work, then conditions must be so changed that all of these people can be taken care of. This can best be done by the shortening of the hours of labor. There is no doubt but that in the near future many organizations will determine that in order to take care of all of their members gaining a livelihood by employment at their trade it will be necessary to inaugurate a six-hour day. The executive council is directed to lend its assistance in the fullest degree to any organization seeking to establish a shorter workday that will provide

for the employment of all its members. The organization itself must necessarily be the judge of what should be the length of the workday in the industry over which it has jurisdiction. When it has decided and established its claim to shorter hours, no matter what they may be, then the A. F. of L. of will lend its fullest assistance.

Workday in Mail Service—(1919, p. 449) The A. F. of L. requests congress to repeal that part of section 1599 which requires that the entire time of railway mail clerks is subject to the control of the post office department, and to substitute in its stead a new section, establishing a standard day for railway mail clerks in which the hours to be required for them shall be clearly defined. That in fixing the standard consideration be given and all credit allowed for the work which these clerks are obliged to perform for the government in their own homes when off road duty; and also that a reasonable limit be set to the time that they may be detained between trips at the outward terminus of their runs, and that every minute which it shall be necessary to detain them beyond that reasonable limit shall be counted as a part of their working time whether or not they are actually performing service.

Workday, Shorter—(1919, p. 145) Executive council reported: In view of the several resolutions of the St. Paul Convention dealing with the subject of the eight-hour day and the directions of the convention that the Executive Council should continue its work along the line of the shorter workday activities, we feel it necessary to make further reference to the subject, for there is nothing in which labor is more vitally interested than in fewer hours of daily toil whereby are afforded leisure for rest and recuperation and opportunity for the things that make life worth living. In every way within its power the A. F. of L. through its executive officers and organizers has assisted the organizations that have made the struggle for the shorter workday. There is nothing spectacular in such work. It is the steady onward progress day by day. Particularly in the textile industry has progress been made. Many of the workers of that trade now enjoy the forty-four-hour week. Other organizations have conducted vigorous and fruitful campaigns for the eight-hour day or the forty-four-hour week. Few other years have shown a more satisfactory progress in the reduction of the length of the workday than the year just closed. It is significant that the practical value of the shorter workday was shown most emphatically during that period of the nation's life when the utmost in production was required to satisfy the demands of war. The satisfactory results, not only in health and comfort and the general well-being for the workers, but in volume of production as well were demon⌐strated during the war beyond all question. The rapid trend toward the general establishment of the shorter workday developed during the war must not be allowed to wane during the period of reconstruction. (P. 449) The A. F. of L. declares in favor of the eight hour-day as a maximum work day and the 44-hour week, and instructs the executive council to use its best efforts in assisting any organization that is endeavoring to inaugurate these working hours.

(1920, p. 336) Reaffirmed action of 1919 convention on the eight-hour day and 44-hour week.

(1921, p. 426) The A. F. of L. reiterates its former well-defined policy of supporting any organization affiliated with it in any effort it may make to shorten the working hours of its members to the point that will insure permanent and continued employment to all of its members.

(1922, p. 482) In dealing with the subject of the shorter workday, the A. F. of L. unhesitatingly declares this to be of paramount importance. We further assert that year by year it is becoming more and more the conviction of thinking men and women that herein is to be found the one solution for many of our industrial and economic ills; that only by universal establishment of the scientifically calculated shorter workday can we build a continuing and enduring condition of national and world prosperity; that by thus balancing production and consumption, and in that way only, can we solve the problems of unemployment and all its attendent social, political and economic ills which threaten the perpetuity of American standards and American institutions. The shorter workday is demanded in the interest of health, mental and moral development, and the general well-being of those who give service to the world. Where progress has been made toward its realization the result has to the fullest degree justified the soundness of the position of labor with regard to this great reform. We assert, with all the power at our command, that in many lines the shorter workday has become an absolute economic necessity. Aside from offering the only permanent relief from unemployment, the incontrovertible fact is that only by shortening the work period can the workers enjoy the share of increased production through the invention, development and use of labor-saving devices, to which they are justly entitled. Our nation suffers in this day from overproduction and underconsumption. With millions unemployed, and a vast amount of productive machinery in every line idle, we produce more than our people can secure the wherewithal to obtain and consume. Were it possible to secure full-time maximum production from our industries, operating upon the established basic workday, it is apparent to the most obtuse mind that the scale of production and consumption would be thrown more acutely out of balance and so-called depression from which our country has suffered would be many times multiplied. With the development of machines which multiply the productivity of the individual; with millions of women in industry because of their experiences during the war; with other millions who have been producing for the enormously destructive purposes of war, turned to normal productive action by disarmament, it must be plain to all that labor's only relief is in the establishment of the shorter workday. From bitter experiences the organized workers have learned they can expect no constructive and continuing relief from men in whose minds there is no thought of progress. The kings of finance who seek to autocratically determine every phase of the industrial and economic life of the nation are without vision or altruistic purpose. They rightly assume that with more workers than jobs wages can be forced to the lowest possible level. They wrongly assume that with minimum forces and maximum hours production costs are lowered and mass production increased. With no further

thought they know the greater the mass production and the smaller the portion accorded to labor the greater the residue which they can retain for themselves. But they fail to observe the inevitable consequences which follow from such conditions. Reduced consumption destroys the balance and without fail brings ever recurring periods of depression, chaos and ruin. The right of collective action is essential; protection of the rights of the individual and his organization is imperative; a living wage with proper standards is all important; but we are sure recognition of and protection of these rights must be predicated upon the concrete statement of fact that the opportunity to work is a supreme necessity. In full recognition of this the A. F. of L. most forcibly insists that the only solution is the universal enforcement of the shorter workday.

(1923, p. 346) In the shorter workday lies one solution of many of our industrial, social and economic ills; and we believe that only by universal establishment of a scientifically calculated shorter workday can we build a continuing and enduring condition of national and world prosperity; that by thus balancing production and consumption, and in that way only, can we solve the problem of unemployment and all its attendant social, industrial and economic ills. The shorter workday is demanded in the interest of health, mental and moral development, and the general well-being of the workers. In its practical application the results realized have justified the position of organized labor. In the present-day development and use of labor-saving devices, the application of the shorter workday has become a necessity if the worker is to enjoy a part of the increased production. We can expect no continuing relief from those employers who place profits above the health and well-being of their employes. They rightfully assume that with more workers than jobs, wages can be forced to the lowest possible level. They assume that by mass production and the smaller portion accorded to labor, the greater the residue for themselves. In its final analysis their position is untenable. Reduced consumption destroys the balance and without fail brings ever-recurring periods of industrial depression and thus those who oppose the shorter workday, thereby denying to others a richer and fuller life, bring chaos and industrial ruin upon themselves. Undoubtedly, unemployment is the greatest menace to established standards and the opportunity to raise those standards. In the coal mining industry and in the printing trades the fight for a shorter workday has been waged with commendable determination. They have paved the way and we feel that the fight must be pressed and the field of action broadened to a point where every worker of this country shall be guaranteed the opportunity of continuous employment. In the realization of a shorter workday the destructive effects of unemployment will be eliminated and the workers will thereby be enabled to enjoy that richer and fuller life to which all mankind is entitled. (P. 345) Indorsed struggle of textile workers for a forty-eight hour week in southern textile mills.

Workday, Six Hour—(1919, p. 453) There is no doubt but that in the near future many organizations will determine that in order to take care of all of their members gaining a livelihood by employment at their trade it will necessary to inaugurate a six-hour day. Therefore the Executive Council is directed to lend its assistance in the fullest degree to any organization seeking to establish a shorter workday that will provide for the employment of all its members. The organization itself must necessarily be the judge of what should be the length of the workday in the industry over which it has jurisdiction. When it has decided and established its claim to shorter hours, no matter what they may be, then the A. F. of L. will lend its fullest assistance.

Workmen's Compensation—(1920, p. 424) Indorsed the insurance feature of the Ohio Workmen's Compensation law and urged all state federations of labor to endeavor to have similar provisions enacted in their respective states.

(1921, p. 118). By direction of the Montreal convention a circular was sent to all state federations and city central bodies urging that all workmen's compensation laws be amended by the addition of the insurance feature similar to that in the Ohio workmen's compensation act. The Ohio act prohibits private casualty companies from operating. Reports show that there was much agitation for workmen's compensation laws in those states that do not have them and for amendments to those in force. (P. 392) Directed the Executive Council to aid the Missouri State Federation of Labor in defeating the enemies of workmen's compensation. (Pp. 393–395) Indorsed Ohio Law. Also urged all officers and members of unions to read Senate Document No. 419 on workmen's compensation, which was prepared by members of the Executive Council. Also recommended that rate of compensation be increased to not less than 66⅔ per cent of the wages paid and that the payments extend over a greater length of time where amputations are performed as the result of injuries. Declarations of the 1914 convention (P. 322) were reaffirmed. Approved of the Jones-Fitzgerald bill providing compensation for injured workmen in the District of Columbia.

(1922, pp. 104–326) Bill introduced in congress provides compensation for the injured in industry in the District of Columbia. Similar to Ohio Law. (P. 323) Directed Executive Council to aid government employes in securing legislation increasing the compensation paid to beneficiaries under the compensation for injury act. (P. 325) Reindorsed Ohio workmen's compensation act. (P. 478) Directed Executive Council to select a committee to study the question of workmen's compensation from a national aspect with a view to—1. To standardize the provisions of workmen's compensation through co-operation of the various state federations of labor. 2. To provide for an old age pension system for the infirm and handicapped who are unable on account of alleged extra hazard to obtain regular employment. 3. To extend the provisions of workmen compensation through federal amendment to all employees engaged in interstate commerce.

(1923, p. 76) Report of Committee on Workmen's compensation laws. Complying with instructions given by the A. F. of L. your committee was especially charged to inquire into the following subjects: (a) The activities of insurance companies in preventing the establishment of state insurance funds to carry the risks arising out of industrial employment. (b) Differences arising out of conflicting interpretations and con-structions of laws of state and federal governments. (c) Activities of employers in adopting and enforcing limits of age and standards of physical employment to lessen risks arising out of industrial employment and using workmen's compensation laws as a pretext to do this. (d) The wide difference in the administrative features, scheduled benefits and other allowances and provisions contained in the various state laws. We have endeavored to perform the work assigned us by making diligent inquiry, through all means available, into the very important subject matter referred to us for inquiry and investigation. We respectfully submit the following report:

(a) The activities of insurance companies in preventing the establishment of state insurance funds to carry the risks arising out of industrial employment; Workmen's compensation legislation is based upon the fixed principle that employers must be required to furnish adequate security guaranteeing the payment of compensation, as provided in the statutes, to injured workmen and the dependents of killed employes. Exclusive state insurance, mutual companies, private stock companies and self-insurance are the commonly accepted forms of insurance employed as security in the payment of workmen's compensation schedules of benefits. All but three states (Alabama, Arizona and Kansas) require the employer to secure his compensation payments either by insuring his risks in an authorized private insurance carrier or in a state fund where such fund is provided or, in the case of self-insurers, to deposit bonds or other collateral security and to furnish a financial statement showing assets and liabilities. Thirty-two states permit insurance in private carriers. Seven states have an exclusive state insurance fund in which the fund becomes the sole insurance carrier, no private company being allowed to operate. Nine states have a competitive state insurance fund in which the fund operates in competition with other forms of insurance. Of the forty-two compensation states, twelve are compulsory and thirty are elective. Many of the states enacted elective laws to overcome constitutional difficulties. Unquestionably private insurance companies are opposed to the establishment of state insurance funds. This is particularly true where the statutes creating state insurance funds are supplemented by the enactment of legislation which excludes private insurance companies from participation in the sale of workmen's compensation insurance. The private companies are active in their opposition to workmen's compensation state insurance fund legislation. They are powerfully organized and naturally seek to retain for themselves the business of selling workmen's compensation insurance. It is a question of business and profit to the liability insurance companies. As evidence of the power and influence of private insurance companies in the enactment of workmen's compensation legislation, only in seven states have exclusive state insurance funds been created by law, no private companies being allowed to operate, while in thirty-two states employers are permitted to insure with private carriers. Summarizing the situation which our inquiry disclosed, the private insurance companies are engaged in the work of preventing the enactment of exclusive state insurance workmen's compensation legislation. Their agents work both openly and secretly, as circumstances may require. They attempt to deceive the unwary and unthinking representatives of labor by misrepresentation and through insidious propaganda. Stories attacking the solvency of exclusive state insurance funds are surreptitiously circulated and criticism of the schedules provided in the laws are made by agents of the private companies. In some instances they succeed in preventing the passage of exclusive state insurance workmen's compensation legislation by encouraging labor representatives to oppose the enactment of such legislation because the legislation proposed does not carry with it the ideals and full demands of labor. They create opposition to this form of legislation, among labor representatives, not because of the exclusive state insurance fund feature but because, in some inconsequential, minor way the bill proposed does not measure up to the demands of labor. By this policy the agents of private companies have succeeded in preventing the passage of exclusive state insurance workmen's compensation legislation in some states. The U. S. department of labor made an investigation into the subject of workmen's compensation insurance. It reported and commented upon the relative types of insurance as follows: "There has been much discussion as to the relative merits of different types of insurance. The department of labor recently completed an investigation upon the subject. The result of this investigation showed that the state funds could operate cheaper than either the mutual or stock companies. In fact, the average exclusive state funds can do business about 25 to 30 per cent cheaper than the average private stock company. There is considerable variation in the quality of service furnished by the several state funds. However, comparing the state funds as a whole with the private companies as a whole it was found that the state fund furnished slightly better service than the private companies. As regards security state funds are on a par in this respect with private carriers. Thus far no injured workman has lost his compensation because of the insolvency of state funds nor has any large mutual company become insolvent. On the other hand there have been several disastrous failures of private stock companies during the last three or four years. These failures have resulted in hundreds of thousands of dollars in unpaid claims."

(b) Differences arising out of conflicting interpretations and constructions of laws of state and federal governments. It does not appear, from such information as we were able to secure, that any serious differences have arisen out of conflicting interpretations and constructions of law defining state from federal governments. No controversies of any serious consequence have arisen with regard to persons employed upon railroads and pipe-lines, but some differences have arisen affecting those employed in maritime work. This prevails in California, Oregon, and some other Pacific and Atlantic coast states where persons are employed in maritime labor connected with the ocean-going and coast-wise trade. State workmen's compensation laws can be made to apply only to employers and employes engaged in private industry and intrastate commerce. Legislation of this character can not be made to apply to persons employed on railroads and transportation lines engaged in interstate commerce. The higher courts have held, in decisions made sustaining the constitutionality of workmen's compensation legislation, that the states have a legal right to enact workmen's compensation legislation, and that the states may make such legislation compulsory in its application to private industries located in and coming within the jurisdiction of the respective states. However, the courts have held, in construing the interstate commerce section of the constitution of the U. S., that persons employed by common carriers, engaged in transporting interstate commerce can not come within the scope of or become subject to the operation of the state workmen's compensation laws. Obviously, the remedy for this state of affairs is the enactment of a federal workmen's compensation law applicable to those persons engaged in interstate commerce and who come wholly within the federal jurisdiction. We believe such legislation should define clearly the class of employers and employes who are subject thereto and should be similar to the Ohio workmen's compensation law which the A. F. of L. has officially accepted as the standard act in this character and kind of legislation.

(c) Activities of employers in adopting and enforcing limits of age and standards of physical employment to lessen risks arising out of industrial employment and using workmen's compensation laws as a pretext to do this. Our investigation discloses the fact that employers in some industries establish age limits and require physical examination on the part of persons seeking employment. This practice, however, is not generally followed by employers of labor. Age limits and physical examination are required of those seeking employment upon railroads and in some rubber factories, electrical manufacturing plants and in other miscellaneous trades and callings. While these requirements may be set up in order to reduce risks arising out of industrial employment and using workmen's compensation laws as a pretext to do it, there is no evidence which we could find in support of it. The practice itself seems to be followed as a matter of policy rather than to accomplish a purpose. It was put into effect in some industries before the enactment of workmen's compensation legislation. It would no doubt be carried on if there were no workmen's compensation legislation in effect. In our opinion the only effective safeguard upon which the worker may rely as protection against injustice and discrimination growing out of age limit and physical examination, as followed by some employers is thorough and effective organization. Imposition of wrong and injustice by selfish employers can be successfully resisted in industries, factories and establishments where the workers are thoroughly organized.

(d) The wide difference in the administrative features, scheduled benefits and other allowances and provisions contained in the various state laws. Our investigations into the principal provisions of existing state compensation laws, has disclosed the fact that there is a wide variation in these essential provisions of compensation legislation. The principal provisions requiring attention may be said to include: 1. The scope or coverage of existing laws. 2. Inquiries embraced. 3. Waiting period involved. 4. Medical service provided. 5. Percentage rate of compensation fixed. 6. Weekly maximum and minimum compensation requirements. 7. Compensation periods embraced. 8. Second injuries included. 9. Administrations. 10. Accident prevention. 11. Suits for damages. 12. Compulsory or elective compensation. 13. Insurance and other like features. It must be self-evident that a thorough inquiry into all these provisions and the formulation of concrete proposals suitable to all states and uniform in character involves a large task requiring the utmost care and most intelligent consideration possible. Your committee has made substantial progress in this work. However, the work done has not been advanced sufficiently to enable us to present a complete and comprehensive report at this time. Instead, it is recommended that the investigation made, compilation undertaken and formulation of a standard model workmen's compensation law at present under consideration, be continued by this or a like committee, with the understanding that the committee's final report be submitted to the Executive Council of the A. F. of L., and that the Executive Council be authorized to pass final judgment upon this report and publish and distribute it in pamphlet form and in such other manner as may be deemed most helpful, desirable and advisable by the Executive Council. Pending the final report of this committee and the conclusions reached by the Executive Council, it is recommended that the Ohio workmen's compensation law continue as the model law on this subject.

(P. 309) Private insurance companies have interfered with and seriously retarded progress in the field of workmen's compensation and employers' liability laws. Opposition to state insurance funds on the part of private insurance companies is easily understood, because whenever a state insurance fund is well established profits that are enjoyed by the private insurance companies are cut off from them and remain in the possession of the state, and thereby tend to reduce to that extent at least the cost to the employers of the maintenance of the fund required to take care of the victims of industrial mishaps. The solution for this serious phase of the general question that readily suggests itself is the rigid exclusion from the field of the private insurance company. Before this remedy can be effectively applied there must be a more general dissemination of information concerning the exact nature of the work that is undertaken by the state in the establishment of the insurance fund. Experience has shown that the workmen as well as the employers are not willing to entirely forego certain of their natural rights, even though it be made plain that by doing so and accepting the conditions of a properly safeguarded compensation law, with the accompanying state insurance fund, they really are accepting an advantage to themselves. The impersonal character of the state insurance is a guarantee to both employer and employee of justice rather than the unavoidable suspicion that attaches to transactions controlled by a privately managed concern that frankly exists solely for the profits that arise from the business it transacts. When those who are most vitally interested in this tremendously important feature of our modern industrial life come to realize that their interests are identical, and to trust one another in this as they do in other matters pertaining to their relations, and will accept the operations of an agency that is within their own control, because it is set up by a law which they have helped to make, and not allow themselves to be pulled apart by ambulance-chasing lawyers and profit-seeking insurance agents the true benefits of the workmen's compensation law will become apparent to all. The mutual distrust which has been created by interested persons or agencies for selfish purposes must be dispelled and for it must be substituted a confidence resting on the mutual understanding of the parties most directly concerned We feel that this is one of the most important subjects now being dealt with by organized labor bodies, by welfare groups, state boards, legislatures and the courts. The literature on the subject is increasing rapidly as experience determines the need for modification or extension, or the abandonment and substitution of new for existing practices. In addition to the suggestion contained in the Ohio law, the following eight points should be given full weight in the preparation of any compensation law or amendments to same; 1. Employees in all occupations to be protected. 2. Work accidents and occupational injuries and diseases to be compensated. 3. Benefits to be provided only by state insurance funds. 4. Such surgical care, hospital service, orthopedic appliances and artificial limbs as may be necessary to as complete physical restoration as is possible. 5. Compensation for widows for life or until remarriage. 6. Compensation for life for permanent and total disability. 7. No waiting period. 8. Vocational rehabilitation. The A. F. of L. approves the report of the committee.

Workmen's Compensation, District of Columbia—(1923, p. 83) Early in the sixty-seventh congress Senator Jones of Washington and Representative Fitzgerald of Ohio introduced bills providing for compensation for injured workmen in the District of Columbia. They were practically the same bills, both providing for an exclusive federal fund to cover the risk. The bills were approved by the Cincinnati convention of the A. F. of L. and there was every prospect of their passage. When it was considered certain that the Fitzgerald bill would pass the house, Representative Underhill of Massachusetts (who is pointed to as being the Blanton of New England) introduced a bill which would give the exclusive right to insurance companies to insure under the proposed act. His bill was supported by the insurance companies. When the Fitzgerald bill came up for action in the house all after the title was stricken out and the Underhill bill substituted. In this shape it passed the house. When the bill came before the senate committee on the District of Columbia the A. F. of L. opposed the measure as passed by the house. It was decided that it was better to have no legislation for workmen's compensation in the District of Columbia unless it prohibited insurance companies from getting a strangle hold on the compensation funds. It has been demonstrated that the insurance companies wherever they have been allowed to insure for workmen's compensation make enormous profits to the detriment of injured victims of industry. The best evidence of why insurance companies fight for the right to insure under compensation laws is given by the department of banking and insurance of the state of New Jersey. It reports that for the year ending December 31, 1920, the insurance companies in that state collected premiums of $7,157,248.27 and paid losses amounting to $3,001,407.18. This left as the insurance companies' share of the premiums paid $4,155,841.09, more than 100 per cent more than was paid to injured workmen or the dependents of workmen who have been killed. These figures staggered even the most reactionary of the members of the senate committee. It was clearly understood that should a workmen's compensation law for the District of Columbia be enacted which gave insurance companies the exclusive right to insure employers it would be used as propaganda in the various states to change the laws already enacted providing for exclusive state insurance. States that have not the state insurance feature would be influenced to legislate in favor of insurance companies. Therefore, it was considered better to have the Underhill bill defeated. This was accomplished.

Workmen's Compensation, Longshoremen—(1919, pp. 131–378) It was believed that the passage of an amendment to the judicial code, inserting in clause 3, section 24, the words, "and to claimants the rights and remedies under the workmen's compensation law of any state," approved October 6, 1917, relieved the hardships arising from the anomalous condition in which longshoremen and other water front workers were placed by the U. S. supreme court decision of May 21, 1917. That decision was to the effect that men engaged in loading vessels were maritime workers and came within the admiralty jurisdiction. Immediately upon the passage of this amendment to the judicial code, the commission having charge of the administration of the New York workmen's compensation act began paying claims presented by the longshoremen and other water front workers. It is said that the California compensation commission did the same. In the state of Washington, however, a different interpretation was placed upon the act amending the judicial code. The chairman of the Washington industrial insurance department, wrote: "Our supreme court has held in the case of Jarvis vs. Daggett, 87 Wash., 253, that this commission can not enforce against employers the payment of premiums upon payrolls in maritime employment, for the reason that we can not protect the employer against suits that may be brought for damages under the admiralty jurisdiction of the federal court." And further, that an employer who had paid contributions to the commission was sued under the admiralty law and recovery was sustained amounting to $3,000. This seemed to expose the employers of maritime workers to two liabilities,

one in the admiralty court and one to the state workmen's compensation fund. In the state of Washington the situation was such that if an accident occurred to a workman at one end of a gang plank, next the shore, he would be compensated, but if the same accident occurred at the other end of the gang plank, on the vessel, there would be no compensation. This condition would not obtain in states whose compensation laws were elective, but where the compensation law is compulsory it is difficult to determine whether the longshoremen were or were not under the state compensation act.

(1920, p. 377) Directed Executive Council to endeavor to bring about such changes in the compensation laws of the U. S. or of the several states under whose jurisdiction maritime laborers fall as will remedy the deplorable situation of workers engaged in longshore work. This was made necessary by a decision of the supreme court denying longshoremen the benefits of state laws.

(1921, pp. 116–373) Endorsed bills providing for the restoration of dock workers and repair men along shore to the protection of state accident compensation laws, which had been denied them by the supreme court in its decision in the Jensen case. The court held in 1917, that "under certain circumstances longshoremen were maritime workers and therefore outside of state jurisdiction."

(1923, p. 79) Congress enacted a law for the protection of longshoremen. It provides for a method of obtaining compensation by longshoremen injured or for their heirs if killed while at work. (The supreme court declared this unconstitutional.)

"Work or Fight"—(1919, pp. 119–328) The second draft bill, which required men between 18 and 45 years of age to enroll was introduced on August 5, 1918, both in the senate (S. 4856), and in the house (H. R. 12731). The senate committee on military affairs began consideration of the bill at once and on August 19 reported it to the senate with an amendment. "Provided, that, when any person shall have been placed in a deferred or exempted class for any of the reasons in this paragraph set forth, he shall not be entitled to remain therein unless he shall in good faith continue, while physically able to do so, to work at and follow such occupation, employment, or business, and if he fails to do so shall again become subject to the draft." Newspaper reports had before this date stated that such an amendment would be embodied in the bill as it came from the senate military committee. In view of those statements, on August 10, the president of the A. F. of L. addressed a strong protest against such legislation, setting forth that the workers in the U. S. were producing more per man, and in the aggregate than any man or group of men in any other country in the world, and that legislation of this kind would be interpreted as a reflection upon the loyalty and services of the whole body of workingmen for the sake of penalizing a few who might not be working up to the full measure of their powers. The amendment was at once construed by members of organized labor as a covert attempt to punish strikers by making them subject to the draft, regardless of the merits of their case or the nature of their grievance. It would enable unfair employers to impose upon their workmen such conditions as they saw fit, and if the workers resorted to their extreme remedy and ceased work they would be inducted into military service forthwith. The A. F. of L. immediately started a vigorous opposition to embodying this obnoxious clause in the bill. Its opposition was well supported by international and local bodies throughout the country. Numerous letters and telegrams of protest reached the senators from home. The opposition to the amendment pointed out that the president already had power to deal with such situations, but what the proponents sought was a law to deal summarily with strikers, not leaving action to the discretion of the president. On the same day that the senate committee on military affairs reported the draft bill to the senate with this "work or fight" amendment, the house committee on military affairs took up consideration of the draft bill. The secretary of the A. F. of L. appeared before the committee in opposition to the amendment. The house committee on military affairs reported the draft bill to the house without the "work or fight" amendment and it passed the house without that amendment on August 24, with 336 yeas, 2 nays and 92 not voting. The bill as it passed the house reached the senate and was substituted for the pending senate bill on August 26, but before the substitution the senate committee on military affairs had inserted the "work or fight" amendment into the house bill, so that the house bill came before the senate with that obnoxious clause. After the passage of the draft act by the senate, the bill was sent to conference between both houses in order to reach an agreement regarding amendments. The house conferees insisted upon the elimination of the "work or fight" clause and to this the senate conferees finally agreed. So the measure was enacted in each house without that clause.

"Yellow Dog" Contracts—(1923, p. 93) It is almost inconceivable that individual contracts of employment which breathe the very atmosphere of repression and which are not alone anti-social in character but specifically designed to deprive workers of their natural rights and constitutional guarantees to freedom should be upheld as legal and binding upon the individual and all others not concerned in its making. That the U. S. supreme court has added its weight of authority to such repressive measures does not lend dignity to this court but merely emphasizes how deep this germ of suppression has entered the mind of those presumed to judge all human affairs and relations in the spirit of justice and fairness. Surely a contract of employment between an individual workman and a gigantic corporate institution of immense resources, mental, physical and financial can not be said by any stretch of imagination to be possessed of the essential elements of mutuality. If there be added the further requirement that such workman can not associate or join with his fellow worker in the trade union of his calling to improve his power of bargaining, then, indeed, do our courts perpetrate the most grievous wrong and disregard the very fundamentals of justice in holding such repressive arrangements as legal and binding obligations. Such arrangements are not contracts in the true sense of the term and deserve to be treated with contempt and indifference and the public conscience should be aroused to this

gross miscarriage of justice so that all courts including the U. S. supreme court will be moved by the spark of justice. (P. 276) Individual contracts of employment, which breathe the very atmosphere of repression, are anti-social in character and should not receive the sanction of law to the exclusion of the right of the wage earner to be fully protected and safeguarded in his right to join with his fellow worker in the protection and improvement of his conditions and for the rewards of toil. To exact as a condition of employment the waiver of the right to join with our fellow-workers in promoting a common welfare and to give such an exaction the sanction of law is to make a fetish of individualism in a life of corporate and organized industrial activities and wherein this dogma can only serve to perpetuate the mastery of the few over the many. It is urged that this unjust doctrine may not only be denied further legal sanction and that every possible legislative effort be made to that end, but that likewise consideration be given to the feasibility of denying corporate power to any industrial and commercial institution, unless the right to association, organization and combination is fully and freely accorded to all employed by such corporate enterprise.

Yeomen Competition—(1919, p. 330) The A. F. of L. protests against yeomen being retained in clerical positions unless the civil service register is exhausted and then only after competitive examinations, and urges congress to enact the legislation necessary to secure the results desired.

Zone System and Labor Press—(1919, p. 430) Many rules put in force by the post office department during the war and the arbitrariness of local postmasters caused labor papers to suffer great financial loss. Executive Council directed to urge the rescinding of the objectionable rules in order that the good work of the labor press would not be hampered.

Zone System, Mail—(1919, p. 430) The A. F. of L. again expresses its disapproval of the zone-rate method of charging for the delivery of second-class mail and it petitions Congress to annul this obnoxious legislation enacted under pretense of a war revenue measure and that it request a thorough investigation of the entire postal service and postal rates, and that pending such investigation that all former rates be reestablished. (1921, p. 322) Reaffirmed.

CONSTITUTION

OF THE

AMERICAN FEDERATION OF LABOR

1923-1924

PREAMBLE.

WHEREAS, A struggle is going on in all the nations of the civilized world between the oppressors and the oppressed of all countries, a struggle between the capitalist and the laborer, which grows in intensity from year to year, and will work disastrous results to the toiling millions if they are not combined for mutual protection and benefit.

It, therefore, behooves the representatives of the Trade and Labor Unions of America, in Convention assembled, to adopt such measures and disseminate such principles among the mechanics and laborers of our country as will permanently unite them to secure the recognition of rights to which they are justly entitled.

We, therefore, declare ourselves in favor of the formation of a thorough Federation, embracing every Trade and Labor Organization in America, organized under the Trade Union system.

CONSTITUTION.

ARTICLE I.—NAME.

This Association shall be known as THE AMERICAN FEDERATION OF LABOR, and shall consist of such Trade and Labor Unions as shall conform to its rules and regulations.

ARTICLE II.—OBJECTS.

SECTION 1.—The object of this Federation shall be the encouragement and formation of local Trade and Labor Unions, and the closer federation of such societies through the organization of Central Trade and Labor Unions in every city, and the further combination of such bodies into State, Territorial, or Provincial organizations to secure legislation in the interest of the working masses.

SEC. 2. The establishment of National and International Trade Unions, based upon a strict recognition of the autonomy of each trade, and the promotion and advancement of such bodies.

SEC. 3. The establishment of Departments composed of National or International Unions affiliated with the American Federation of Labor, of the same industry, and which Departments shall be governed in conformity with the laws of the American Federation of Labor.

SEC. 4. An American Federation of all National and International Trade Unions, to aid and assist each other; to aid and encourage the sale of union label goods, and to secure legislation in the interest of the working people, and influence public opinion, by peaceful and legal methods, in favor of organized labor.

SEC. 5. To aid and encourage the labor press of America.

ARTICLE III.—CONVENTION.

SECTION 1. The Convention of the Federation shall meet annually at 10 A. M., on the first Monday in October, at such place as the delegates have selected at the preceding Convention, except during the years when a presidential election occurs, when the Convention in those years shall be held beginning the third Monday of November. If the proper Convention arrangements or reasonable hotel accommodations can not be secured in that city, the Executive Council may change the place of meeting.

SEC. 2. At the opening of the Convention the President shall take the chair and call the Convention to order, and preside during its sessions.

SEC. 3. The following committees, consisting of fifteen members each, shall be appointed by the President: First, Rules and Order of Business; second, Report of Executive Council; third, Resolutions; fourth, Laws; fifth, Organization; sixth, Labels; seventh, Adjustment; eighth, Local and Federated Bodies; ninth, Education; tenth, State Organizations; eleventh, Boycotts; twelfth, Building Trades (to which shall be referred all grievances and other matters pertaining exclusively to the building trades); thirteenth, Legislation.

SEC. 4. The President shall direct the chief executive officers of three National or International Unions, at least ten days previous to the holding of the Annual Convention, to appoint one delegate each from their respective delegations-elect, who shall compose an Auditing Committee. The committee shall meet at such place as the President of the American Federation of Labor may direct, and at such time prior to the Convention as the President may determine is necessary for the proper performance of their duty; and they shall audit the accounts of the Federation for the preceding twelve months, and report upon credentials immediately upon the opening of the Convention. The expense of said committee shall be paid out of the funds of the Federation.

SEC. 5. Resolutions of any character or proposition for changes in this Constitution can not be introduced after the second day's session, except by unanimous consent.

SEC. 6. The Convention shall have power to order an executive session at any time.

SEC. 7. None other than members of a bona fide Trade Union shall be permitted to address the Convention or read papers therein, except by a two-thirds vote of the Convention.

SEC. 8. Party politics, whether they be Democratic, Republican Socialistic, Populistic, Prohibition, or any other, shall have no place in the Conventions of the American Federation of Labor.

SEC. 9. The rules and order of business governing the preceding Convention shall be in force from the opening of any Convention of the American Federation of Labor until new rules have been adopted by action of the Convention.

SEC. 10. A quorum for the transaction of business shall consist of not less than one-fourth of the delegates attending a Convention.

SEC. 11. No grievance shall be considered by any Convention that has been decided by a previous Convention, except upon the recommendation of the Executive Council, nor shall any grievance be considered where the parties thereto have not previously held a conference and attempted to adjust the same themselves.

ARTICLE IV.—REPRESENTATION.

SECTION 1. The basis of representation in the Convention shall be: From National and International Unions, for less than four thousand members, one delegate; four thousand or more, two delegates; eight thousand or more, three delegates; sixteen thousand or more, four delegates; thirty-two thousand or more, five delegates, and so on. From Central Bodies, State Federations, National Departments, Federal Labor Unions, and Local Unions having no National or International Union, one delegate; provided, however, that Local Unions and Federal Labor Unions herein referred to, located in one city, shall have the right to unite in sending a delegate to represent them unitedly. Only bona fide wage workers who are not members of, or eligible to membership in, other Trade Unions, shall be eligible as delegates from Federal Labor Unions.

SEC. 2. The delegates shall be elected at least two weeks previous to the Annual Convention of the American Federation of Labor, and the names of such delegates shall be forwarded to the Secretary of this body immediately after their election.

SEC. 3. Questions may be decided by division or a show of hands, but if a call of the roll is demanded by one-tenth of the delegates present, each delegate shall cast one vote for every one hundred members or major fraction thereof which he represents, provided that the delegate's union has been affiliated with the Federation for the full fiscal year preceding the Convention. When affiliated for a period of less than one year, each delegate shall cast one-twelfth of one vote for each one hundred members or major fraction thereof which he represents for each month for which per capita tax has been paid upon the members of his union. No City or State Federation shall be allowed more than one vote.

SEC. 4. The Secretary shall prepare for use of the Convention printed poll lists, containing the number of votes the delegates from National and International Unions are entitled to, based upon the average membership during the year, from reports made to the office of the Federation not later than August 31 preceding the Annual Convention.

SEC. 5. No organization or person that has seceded, or has been suspended, or expelled, by the American Federation of Labor, or by any National or International organization connected with the Federation, shall, while under such penalty, be allowed representation or recognition in this Federation, or in any Central Body or National or International Union connected with the American Federation of Labor, under the penalty of the suspension of the body violating this section.

SEC. 6. No organization shall be entitled to representation unless such organization has applied for and obtained a certificate of affiliation at least one month prior to the Convention, and no person shall be recognized as a delegate who is not a member in good standing of the organization he is elected to represent.

ARTICLE V.—OFFICERS.

SECTION 1. The officers of the Federation shall consist of a President, eight Vice-Presidents, a Secretary, and a Treasurer, to be elected by the Convention on the last day of the session, and these officers shall be the Executive Council.

SEC. 2. The President and Secretary shall be members of the succeeding Convention in case they are not delegates, but without vote.

SEC. 3. All elective officers shall be members of a local organization connected with the American Federation of Labor.

SEC. 4. The terms of the officers of the American Federation of Labor shall expire on the thirty-first day of December succeeding the Convention.

SEC. 5. The President and Secretary shall engage suitable offices in the same building at Washington, D. C., for the transaction of the business of the organization.

SEC. 6. All books and financial accounts shall at all times be open to the inspection of the President and Executive Council.

ARTICLE VI.—DUTIES OF PRESIDENT.

SECTION 1. It shall be the duty of the President to preside at the Annual Convention; to exercise supervision of the Federation throughout its jurisdiction; to sign all official documents, and to travel, with the consent of the Executive Council, whenever required, in the interest of the Federation.

SEC. 2. The President shall submit to the Secretary, at the end of each month, an itemized account of all moneys, traveling and incidental, expended by him in the interest of the Federation; and shall report to the Annual Convention of the Federation through the report of the Executive Council.

SEC. 3. The President, if not a delegate, shall have the casting vote in case of a tie, but shall not vote at other times. He shall be required to devote all his time to the interest of the Federation.

SEC. 4. The President shall call meetings of the Executive Council, when necessary; and shall preside over their deliberations, and shall receive for his services $12,000 per annum, payable weekly.

SEC. 5. In case of a vacancy in the office of President by death, resignation, or other cause, the Secretary shall perform the duties of the President until his successor is elected. In that event it shall be the duty of the Secretary to issue, within six days from the date of vacancy, a call for a meeting of the Executive Council at headquarters for the purpose of electing a President to fill said vacancy.

ARTICLE VII.—DUTIES OF SECRETARY.

SECTION 1. The duties of the Secretary shall be to take charge of all books, papers, and effects of the general office; to conduct the correspondence pertaining to his office; to furnish the elective officers with the necessary stationery; to convene and act as Secretary at the Annual Convention, and to furnish the Committee on Credentials at the Convention a statement of the financial standing of each affiliated body; to forward on March 1st and September 1st of each year to the secretaries of all affiliated organizations a list of the names and addresses of secretaries and organizers.

Sec. 2. The Secretary shall keep all letters, documents, accounts, etc., in such manner as the Annual Convention may direct; he shall receive and collect all moneys due the Federation and pay them to the Treasurer, taking his receipt therefor; provided, that he may retain in his hands a sum not exceeding $2,000 for current expenses, which money shall be paid out only on the approval of the President.

Sec. 3. The Secretary shall submit to the Auditing Committee, for their inspection, vouchers for all moneys expended; close all accounts of the Federation on August 31 of each year, and all moneys received or disbursed after such date shall not be reported in the general balance account of the ensuing Convention. He shall print the financial statement quarterly as a separate document and forward copy to all affiliated National and International Unions, State Federations of Labor, City Central Bodies and directly affiliated local unions.

Sec. 4. The Secretary shall give a bond of $2000 for the faithful performance of his duties, and shall report to the Annual Convention of the Federation, through the report of the Executive Council, and for his services he shall receive $10,000 per annum, payable weekly.

Sec. 5. The Secretary shall issue stamps to Local and Federal Labor Unions, which shall be used by such unions with which to receipt for members dues.

Sec. 6. It shall be the duty of each International, National, Local Trade and Federal Labor Union affiliated with the American Federation of Labor to furnish to the Secretary of the American Federation of Labor a copy of all official reports issued by such affiliated organizations, containing a statement of their membership in good standing, and to furnish such additional statistical data as may be called for by the Secretary of the American Federation of Labor as may be in the possession of the respective unions.

ARTICLE VIII.—Duties of Treasurer

Section 1. The Treasurer shall receive and take charge of all moneys, property, and securities of the Federation delivered to him by the Secretary or other officers of the American Federation of Labor. All funds of the American Federation of Labor exceeding fifteen thousand dollars shall be deposited by the Treasurer in bank, or banks, on interest-bearing certificates of deposit in the name of the American Federation of Labor, and in order to be cashed shall required the signatures of the Treasurer, the President, and Secretary of the Federation. The Treasurer shall collect the interest on all such certificates or other deposit at the expiration of each six months and pay the same over to the Secretary. The Treasurer shall deposit in open account in bank or banks, in the name of the American Federation of Labor as Treasurer, all amounts in his possession not on certificates of deposit, and before any money thus deposited can be drawn each check shall be signed by him as Treasurer. A copy of this section shall be forwarded by the President of the Federation to each bank upon which the Federation holds certificates of deposit.

Sec. 2. The Treasurer shall pay, through the Secretary, all warrants regularly drawn on him, signed by the President and countersigned by the Secretary, as required by this Constitution, and none others.

Sec. 3. The Treasurer shall submit to the Annual Convention, through the report of the Executive Council, a complete statement of all receipts and disbursements during his term of office, and at the expiration of his term of office he shall deliver up to his successor all moneys, securities, books, and papers of the Federation under his control; and for the faithful performance of his duties he shall give a bond in such sum as the Executive Council may determine. The annualy salary of the Treasurer shall be $500.

ARTICLE IX.—Executive Council.

Section 1. It shall be the duty of the Executive Council to watch legislative measures directly affecting the interests of working people, and to initiate, whenever necessary, such legislative action as the Convention may direct.

Sec. 2. The Executive Council shall use every possible means to organize new National or International Trade or Labor Unions, and to organize Local Trade and Labor Unions, and connect them with the Federation until such time as there is a sufficient number to form a National or International Union, when it shall be the duty of the President of the Federation to see that such organization is formed.

Sec. 3. When a National or International Union has been formed, the President shall notify all Local Unions of that trade to affiliate with such National or International Union, and unless said notification be complied with, within three months, their charters shall be revoked.

Sec. 4. The Executive Council shall also prepare and present to the Convention, in printed form, a concise statement of the details leading up to approved and pending boycotts (and all matters of interest to the convention), and no indorsement for a boycott shall be considered by the Convention except it has been so reported by the Executive Council.

Sec. 5. While we recognize the right of each trade to manage its own affairs, it shall be the duty of the Executive Council to secure the unification of all labor organizations, so far as to assist each other in any trade dispute.

Sec. 6. Whenever the revenue of the Federation shall warrant such action, the Executive Council shall authorize the sending out of Trade Union speakers from place to place in the interests of the Federation.

Sec. 7. The remuneration for organizers of the American Federation of Labor shall be $10.00 per day as salary, actual railroad fare, and hotel expenses of $8.00 per day when traveling away from their home city. The remuneration for services of members of the Executive Council, fraternal delegates, interpreters and speakers, or other persons temporarily employed by the American Federation of Labor shall be determined by the Executive Council.

Sec. 8. The Executive Council shall have power to make the rules to govern matters not in conflict with this Constitution, or the constitution of affiliated unions, and shall report accordingly to the Federation.

Sec. 9. In the event of a vacancy of any member of the Executive Council, other than that of the President, by reason of death, resignation, or other cause, the President shall make such vacancy known to the Executive Council, and shall call for nominations. The names of all nominees shall be submitted to the Executive Council, and it shall require a majority vote of the Executive Council to elect. Upon each unsuccessful balloting the name of the candidate receiving the lowest number of votes shall be dropped.

Sec. 10. All Local Trade Unions and Federal Labor Unions holding charters direct from the American Federation of Labor, desiring the assistance of the American Federation of Labor in trade disputes, shall submit to the President of the American Federation of Labor for approval by the Executive Council the full statement of the grievance, and shall receive within twenty (20) days from the President an answer as to whether they will be sustained or not, and no benefits shall be paid where a strike takes place before the Local Union has received the approval of the Executive Council.

Sec. 11. No charter shall be granted by the American Federation of Labor to any National, International, Trade, or Federal Labor Union without a positive and clear definition of the trade jurisdiction claimed by the applicant, and the charter shall not be granted if the jurisdiction claimed is a trespass on the jurisdiction of existing affiliated unions, without the written consent of such unions; no affiliated International, National, or Local Union shall be permitted to change its title or name, if any trespass is made thereby on the jurisdiction of an affiliated organization, without having first obtained the consent and approval of a Convention of the American Federation of Labor; and it is further provided, that should any of the members of such National, Internationl, Trade, or Federal Labor Union work at any other vocation, trade, or profession, they shall join the union of such vocation, trade, or profession, provided such are organized and affiliated with the American Federation of Labor.

Sec. 12. The Executive Council of the American Federation of Labor shall only have power to revoke the charter of an affiliated National or International Union when the revocation has been ordered by a two-thirds majority of a regular Convention of the American Federation of Labor, by a roll-call vote.

ARTICLE X.—Revenue.

Section 1. The revenue of the Federation shall be derived from a per capita tax to be paid upon the full paid-up membership of all affiliated bodies, as follows: From International or National Trade Unions, a per capita tax of one cent per member per month; from Local Trade Unions and Federal Labor Unions, twenty-five cents per member per month, twelve and one-half cents of which must be set aside to be used only in case of strike or lockout; Local Unions, the majority of whose members are less than eighteen (18) years of age, five cents per member per month; the amount received by the American Federation of Labor on each initiation fee from all directly affiliated local unions shall be 25 per cent of the total initiation fee received by the local union from the individual, but in no case shall the amount received by the American Federation of Labor be less than $1; from Central and state bodies, $10 per year, payable quarterly.

Sec. 2. Delegates shall not be entitled to a seat in the Annual Convention unless the tax of their organization, as provided for in section 1, Article X, has been paid in full to August 31 preceding the Convention.

Sec. 3. Any organization affiliated with this Federation not paying its per capita tax on or before the 15th of each month shall be notified of the fact by the Secretary of the Federation, and if at the end of three months it is still in arrears it shall be come suspended from membership by the Federation, and can be reinstated only by a vote of the Convention when such arrearages are paid in full, as provided in section 2 of this Article.

ARTICLE XI.—Local Central Bodies.

Section 1. No Central Labor Union, or any other central body of delegates, shall admit to or retain in their councils delegates from any local organization that owes its allegiance to any other body, National or International, hostile to any affiliated organization, or that has been suspended or expelled by, or not connected with a National or International organization of their trade herein affiliated; nor are delegates to be seated from locals of National or International organizations which are not affiliated to the American Federation of Labor, under penalty of having their charter revoked for violation of their charter, subject to appeal to the next Convention.

Sec. 2. It shall be the duty of all National and International Unions affiliated with the American Federation of Labor to instruct their Local Unions to join chartered Central Labor Bodies, Departments, and State Federations in their vicinity where such exists. Similar instructions shall be given by the American Federation of Labor to all Trade and Federal Labor Unions under its jurisdiction.

Sec. 3. Where there are five or more Local Unions in any city belonging to any National or International Union affiliated with this Federation they may organize a Central Labor Union, or shall join such body if already in existence.

Sec. 4. The Executive Council and Local Central Labor Unions shall use all possible means to organize and connect as Local Unions to National or International Unions the organizations in their vicinity; to aid the formation of National or International Unions where none exist, and to organize Federal Labor Unions where the number of craftsmen precludes any other form of organization.

Sec. 5. No Central Labor Union, or other central body of delegates, shall have the authority or power to order any organization, affiliated with such Central Labor Union, or other central labor body, on strike, or take a strike vote, where such organization has a national organization, until the proper authorities of such National or International organizations have been consulted and agreed to such action. A violation of this law shall be sufficient cause for the Executive Council to revoke the charter.

Sec. 6. Separate charters may be issued to Central Labor Unions, Local Unions, or Federal Labor Unions, composed exclusively of colored members, where, in the judgment of the Executive Council, it appears advisable and to the best interest of the Trade Union movement to do so.

Sec. 7. No Central Labor Union, or other central body of delegates, shall have authority or power to originate a boycott, nor shall such bodies indorse and order the placing of the name of any person, firm or corporation on an unfair list until the Local Union desiring the same has before declaring the boycott, submitted the matter in dispute to the Central body for investigation, and the best endeavors on its part to effect an amicable settlement. Violation of this section shall forfeit charter.

Sec. 8. No Central Body or Department affiliated with the American Federation of Labor shall reject credentials presented by a duly elected or appointed delegation of a Local Union chartered by a National or an International Union having affiliation with the American Federation of Labor; provided, however, that upon written charges, signed by at least three delegates, any delegate of an affiliated Union may, upon conviction after a fair trial, be expelled or suspended. Action of the Central Body under this section shall be subject to appeal to the Executive Council of the American Federation of Labor, and no delegation representing Local Unions affiliated, as herein described, shall be suspended or expelled until like action is taken.

Sec. 9. No Central Body shall take part in the adjustment of wage contracts, wage disputes or working rules of Local Unions, affiliated with a National or International Union, unless the laws of the National or International Union permit, except upon the request or consent of the executive officer of the National or International Union affected.

Sec. 10. Local Unions of National or International Unions affiliated with the Departments attached to the American Federation of Labor, in any city where a Local Department exists, shall not be eligible to membership in any Local Department unless they are connected with the chartered Central Body, nor shall they be eligible to membership in the Central Body unless they are affiliated with the Local Department.

Sec. 11. The representation of local unions entitled to affiliation in Central Labor Unions shall be as follows; Local unions having 50 members or less, 2 delegates; 100 members or less, 3 delegates; 250 members or less, 4 delegates; 500 members or less, 5 delegates; 1 additional delegate to be allowed for each additional 500 members or majority fraction thereof.

ARTICLE XII.—Assessment in Defense of National and International Unions.

Section 1. The Executive Council shall have power to declare a levy of one cent per member per week on all affiliated unions for a period not exceeding ten weeks in any one year, to assist in the support of an affiliated National or International Union engaged in a protracted strike or lockout.

Sec. 2. Any Union, International, National, or Local, failing to pay within sixty days the levies declared in accordance with Section 1 shall be deprived of representation in Convention of the American Federation of Labor and in City Central Bodies affiliated with the American Federation of Labor.

ARTICLE XIII.—Defense Fund for Local Trade and Federal Labor Unions.

Section 1. The moneys of the defense fund shall be drawn only to sustain strikes or lockouts of Local Trade and Federal Labor Unions when such strikes or lockouts are authorized, indorsed, and conducted in conformity with the following provisions of this Article;

Sec. 2. In the event of a disagreement between a Local Union and an employer which, in the opinion of the Local Union, may result in a strike, such Union shall notify the President of the American Federation of Labor, who shall investigate, or cause an investigation to be made of the disagreement,

and endeavor to adjust the difficulty. If his efforts should prove futile, he shall take such steps as he may deem necessary in notifying the Executive Council, and if the majority of said Council shall decide that a strike is necessary such Union shall be authorized to order a strike, but that under no circumstances shall a strike or lockout be deemed legal, or moneys expended from the defense fund on that account, unless the strike or lockout shall have been first authorized and approved by the President and Executive Council.

Sec. 3. When a strike has been authorized and approved by the President and Executive Council, the President of the Local Union interested shall, within twenty-four hours, call a meeting of said Union, of which every member shall be regularly notified, to take action thereon, and no member shall vote on such question unless he is in good standing. Should three-fourths of the members present decide, by secret ballot, on a strike, the president of the Local Union shall immediately notify the President of the American Federation of Labor of the cause of the matter in dispute; what the wages, hours, and conditions of labor then are; what advances, if any, are sought; what reductions are offered, if any; state the number employed and unemployed; the state of trade generally in the locality, and the number of persons involved, union and non-union; also the number of members who would become entitled to the benefits herein provided should the application be authorized and approved.

Sec. 4. No Local shall be entitled to benefit from the defense fund unless it has been in continuous good standing for one year; and no member shall be entitled to benefit from said defense fund unless he has been a member in good standing in the American Federation of Labor for at least one year.

Sec. 5. When a strike has been inaugurated under the provisions of Sections 2 and 3, the American Federation of Labor shall pay to the bonded officer of the Union involved, or his order, for a period of six weeks, an amount equal to seven ($7) dollars per week for each member. Each Local Union shall require its treasurer to give proper bond for the safekeeping and disbursement of all funds of the Local. No benefit shall be paid for the first two weeks of the strike. The Executive Council shall have the power to authorize the payment of strike benefits for an additional period.

Sec. 6. No member of a Local Union on strike shall be entitled to weekly benefits unless he reports daily to the proper officer of the Local Union while the strike continues, and no member who shall receive a week's work, three days to be a week, shall receive benefits. Any member refusing other work while on strike (providing said work is not in conflict with labor's interests) shall not be entitled to any benefits.

Sec. 7. Any Union inaugurating a strike without the approval of the Executive Council shall not receive benefits on account of said strike.

Sec. 8. In case of lockout or the victimization of members, the Executive Council shall have power to pay benefits if, upon investigation, it is found that the Local Union whose members are involved did not by their actions or demands provoke the lockout by their employer.

Sec. 9. During the continuance of a strike the executive board of the Local Union shall make weekly reports to the Secretary of het

American Federation of Labor, showing the amount of money distributed for benefits, and to whom paid, furnishing individual receipts to the Secretary of the American Federation of Labor from all members to whom such benefits have been paid, and all other facts that may be required.

SEC. 10. Before a strike shall be declared off a special meeting of the Union shall be called for that purpose, and it shall require a majority vote of all members present to decide the question either way.

SEC. 11. In the event of the defense fund becoming dangerously low through protracted strike or lockout, the Executive Council of the American Federation of Labor shall have the power to levy an assessment of ten cents on each member of Local Trade and Federal Labor Unions, assessments to be restricted to not more than five per year; and further, that there shall always be a surplus of five thousand ($5,000) dollars in the defense fund.

SEC. 12. No Local shall be entitled to any of the benefits of the defense fund unless it requires its members to pay not less than seventy-five (75) cents per month. The financial secretaries and the treasurers of each Local Trade or Federal Labor Union directly affiliated to the American Federation of Labor shall, through the Secretary of the Federation, bond said financial officers in such sum as shall be adquate to protect its funds.

SEC. 13. Local Trade and Federal Labor Unions shall set aside for the maintenance of a local defense fund not less than five cents a month from each member.

SEC. 14. That imitation fees charged by directly affiliated Local · Trade or Federal Labor Unions shall be not less than $2.00 or more than $10.00, and that 25 per cent of the total initiation fee received by such Local Trade or Federal Labor Union from each individual shall be forwarded to the Secretary of the American Federation of Labor, but in no case shall the amount received by the American Federation of Labor be less than one ($1.00) dollar, together with the per capita tax, accompanied by a monthly report giving the numper of members paid for, and names of those initiated, reinstated, suspended and expelled, and number of members upon whom back per capita tax is being paid and months paid for, on blanks to be furnished by the Secretary of the Federation. When dues are paid, the Financial Secretary of the Local Union shall place a per capita tax stamp in the member's due book. These stamps must be used. Suspended members can be reinstated only by the payment of three months' back per capita tax, in addition to the tax for the current month, and a fee of 25 cents for reinstatement stamps.

SEC. 15. That traveling cards issued to members by Local Trade or Federal Labor Unions shall admit members presenting the same to membership in Local Trade or Federal Labor Unions directly affiliated to the American Federation of Labor.

SEC. 16. That Local Trade and Federal Labor Unions shall be prohibited from assessing their members or appropriating their funds for any purpose other than union or American Federation of Labor purposes. That each directly affiliated union shall forward monthly to the Secretary of the American Federation of Labor a complete statement of all funds received and expended.

SEC. 17. No Local Trade or Federal Labor Union shall disband so long as seven members desire to retain the charter. Upon the dissolution of any Local Trade or Federal Labor Union all funds and property of any charter shall revert to the American Federation of Labor.

ARTICLE XIV.—MISCELLANEOUS.

SECTION 1. Certificates of affiliation shall be granted by the President of the Federation, by and with the consent of the Executive Council, to all National and International Unions and local bodies affiliated with this Federation.

SEC. 2. Seven wage-workers of good character, following any trade or calling, who are favorable to Trade Unions, whose trade or calling is not organized, and are not members of any body affiliated with this Federation, who will subscribe to this Constitution, shall have the power to form a local body to be known as a "Federal Labor Union," and they shall hold regular meetings for the purpose of strengthening and advancing the Trade Union movement, and shall have power to make tneir own rules in conformity with this Constitution, and shall be granted a local certificate by the President of this Federation; provided, the request for a certificate be indorsed by the nearest Local or National Trade Union officials connected with this Federation, but not more than three Federal Labor Unions shall be chartered in any one city. Employers who are working for wages, may, upon regular ballot, be admitted to membership in Federal Labor or Local Unions, directly affiliated with the American Federation of Labor, subject to the approval of the President of the American Federation of Labor. Such members shall not attend meetings of the unions or have a vote in controlling the affairs of the unions; they must comply with the scale of wages and rules adopted by the union of which they are members. The President of the American Federation of Labor shall have authority to appoint any person who is a member of any affiliated union to audit the accounts of such Federal Labor or Local Trade Unions as the President of the American Federation of Labor may direct and report the result thereof to the President of the American Federation of Labor. The books and accounts of each Federal Labor and Local Trade Union shall be at all times open to the inspection of auditors appointed under this section.

SEC. 3. The certificate fee for affiliated bodies shall be five ($5) dollars, payable to the Secretary of the Federation, and the fee shall accompany the application.

SEC. 4. The American Federation of Labor shall refer all applications for certificates of affiliation from Local Unions or Federal Labor Unions from a vicinity where a chartered Central Labor Union exists to that body for investigation and approval.

SEC. 5. Certificates of affiliation shall not be granted by State Federations of Labor. That power is vested solely in the Executive Council of the American Federation of Labor and the executive officers of National and International Unions affiliated therewith.

SEC. 6. Fraternal delegates attending the Convention of the American Federation of Labor shall be entitled to all the rights of delegates from Central Bodies.

ARTICLE XV.—GENERAL RULES GOVERNING DEPARTMENTS OF THE AMERICAN FEDERATION OF LABOR.

SECTION 1. For the greater development of the labor movement, departments subordinate to the American Federation of Labor are to be established from time to time as in the judgment of the American Federation of Labor, or of its Executive Council, may be deemed advisable. Each department is to manage and finance its own affairs.

SEC. 2. To be entitled to representation in any department, organizations eligible to join it must first be and remain in affiliation to the American Federation of Labor.

SEC. 3. To be entitled to representation in Local Councils, or Railway System Federations of departments, Local Unions are required to be part of affiliated National or International Unions affiliated to departments, or directly affiliated to the American Federation of Labor. Said Local Unions shall first be and remain in affiliation to Central Labor Unions chartered by the American Federation of Labor.

SEC. 4. The fundamental laws and procedure of each department are to conform to, and be administered in the same manner as the laws and procedure governing the American Federation of Labor. No Department, Local Council or Railway System Federation of same shall enact laws, rules, or regulations in conflict with the laws and procedure of the American Federation of Labor, and in the event of change of laws and procedure of the latter, Department, Local Councils, and Railway System Federations are to change their laws and procedure to conform thereto.

SEC. 5. Each department to be considered the official method of the American Federation of Labor for transacting the portion of its business indicated by the name of the department in consequence of which affiliated and eligible organizations should be part of their respective departments and should comply with their actions and decisions, subject to appeal therefrom to the Executive Council and the conventions of the American Federation of Labor. When an organization has interests in departments other than the one of its principal affiliation, in which it shall pay per capita tax upon its entire membership, it is to be represented in and pay per capita tax to the other departments upon the number of members whose occupations come under such other departments, but this in no instance shall be less than 20 per cent of the membership upon which it pays per capita tax to the American Federation of Labor.

SEC. 6. Departments of the American Federation of Labor are to have their headquarters located in the city of Washington, D. C., and if possible in the same building with the headquarters of the American Federation of Labor, unless there are reasons to the contrary satisfactory to the Executive Council of the American Federation of Labor.

SEC. 7. Departments of the American Federation of Labor shall hold their conventions immediately before or after the Convention of the American Federation of Labor and in the same city where the Convention of the American Federation of Labor is held, at which time and place their laws and procedure shall be made to conform to the laws and procedure of the American Federation of Labor and to go into effect the first day of January immediately following, to conform to the date when the laws and procedure of the American Federation of Labor go into effect. For reasons of transportation, expediency and the methods of representation the Railway, Metal Trades and Mining Departments may hold conventions at other dates and places, and in that event said departments shall authorize their executive boards to have said departments laws conform to the preceding portion of this section.

SEC. 8. The Executive Council of each department shall consist of not more than seven members, including the executive officer or officers thereof. This not to apply to or interfere with the procedure on this subject found to be essential in the Railway Department.

SEC. 9. The officers of each department shall report to the Executive Council of the American Federation of Labor that the department has conformed to the laws, procedure and actions of the American Federation of Labor as they affect each department.

SEC. 10. In the Building Trades Department (on the basis of its law of 1913), organizations having seven or more delegates, each such delegate shall on roll-call be entitled to two votes. A roll-call shall be held upon the demand of one-fourth of all delegates whose credentials have been accepted and who have been seated in the conventions.

SEC. 11. The officers of the various departments shall submit a quarterly report to the Executive Council of the American Federation of Labor of the work done by their department, and its general conditions.

SEC. 12. At all regular meetings of the Executive Council of the American Federation of Labor, there shall be present, during some period of the Council meeting, the executive officer or officers of each department, to take up with the Council matters that may be of mutual interest.

SEC. 13. A page of each issue of the *American Federationist* to be available to and to be used by each department for official report or for publication of some subject identified with the department, each department to designate its officer to submit the report.

ARTICLE XVI.—AMENDMENTS.

This Constitution can be amended or altered only at a regular session of the Convention and to do so it shall require a two-thirds vote.

OFFICERS OF AMERICAN FEDERATION OF LABOR
1881-1924

In the first five years the presiding officer or chairman was chosen by each convention. All authority between conventions was vested in the Legislative Committee, now known as the Executive Council. Officers for each year:

PITTSBURGH, 1881.

Chairman Convention—John Jarrett.
Secretaries—Mark L. Crawford, H. H. Bengough, William C. Pollner.
President Legislative Committee—Richard Powers.
First Vice President—Samuel Gompers.
Second Vice President—Charles F. Burgman.
Treasurer—Alexander C. Rankin.
Secretary—W. H. Foster.

CLEVELAND, 1882.

Chairman Convention—Samuel L. Leffingwell.
Vice Chairman—Samuel Gompers.
Secretary—Thompson H. Murch.
President Legislative Committee—Samuel Gompers.
First Vice President—Richard Powers.
Second Vice President—Gabriel Edmonston.
Treasurer—Robert Howard.
Secretary—W. H. Foster.

NEW YORK CITY, 1883.

Chairman Convention—Samuel Gompers.
Vice Chairman—Richard Powers.
Secretary—William C. Pollner.
President Legislative Committee—P. H. McLogan.
First Vice President—Samuel Gompers.
Second Vice President—Gabriel Edmonston.
Third Vice President—M. D. Connolly.
Fourth Vice President—Richard Powers.
Fifth Vice President—W. H. McClelland.
Sixth Vice President—E. M. Slack.
Treasurer—Robert Howard.
Secretary—Frank K. Foster.

CHICAGO, 1884.

Chairman Convention—W. J. Hammond.
Vice Chairman—Richard Powers.
Secretaries—M. D. Connolly, Emil Levy.
President Legislative Committee—W. M. McClelland.
First Vice President—J. W. Smith.
Second Vice President—Richard Powers.
Third Vice President—James O'Sullivan.
Fourth Vice President—Frederick Blend.
Fifth Vice President—W. B. Ogden.
Sixth Vice President—James Bernard.
Treasurer—Robert Howard.
Secretary—Gabriel Edmonston.

WASHINGTON, D. C., 1885.

Chairman Convention—M. D. Connolly.
Vice Chairman—John S. Kirschner.
Secretaries—Gabriel Edmonston, W. H. Foster.
Auditors—Charles H. Sharp, Samuel Gompers.
President Legislative Committee—Samuel Gompers.
First Vice President—Samuel S. Green.
Second Vice President—W. E. Tomson.
Third Vice President—P. F. McAuliffe.
Fourth Vice President—Hugo A. Miller.
Fifth Vice President—George G. King.
Sixth Vice President—Henry Emerich.
Treasurer—Gabriel Edmonston.
Secretary—W. H. Foster.

COLUMBUS, 1886.

Chairman Convention—J. W. Smith.
Vice Chairman—J. L. Wright.
Secretary—J. S. Kirchner.
Assistant Secretary—Henry Emerich.

AMERICAN FEDERATION OF LABOR.

President—Samuel Gompers.
First Vice President—George Harris.
Second Vice President—J. W. Smith.
Secretary—P. J. McGuire.
Treasurer—Gabriel Edmonston.

BALTIMORE, 1887

President—Samuel Gompers.
First Vice President—Dan McLaughlin.
Second Vice President—William Martin.
Secretary—P. J. McGuire.
Treasurer—Gabriel Edmonston.

ST. LOUIS, 1888.

President—Samuel Gompers.
First Vice President—Daniel McLaughlin.
Second Vice President—William Martin.
Secretary—P. J. McGuire.
Treasurer—Henry Emerich.

BOSTON, 1889.

President—Samuel Gompers.
First Vice President—William Martin.
Second Vice President—P. J. McGuire.
Secretary—Chris Evans.
Treasurer—Henry Emerich.

DETROIT, 1890.

President—Samuel Gompers.
First Vice President—P. J. McGuire.
Second Vice President—W. A. Carney.
Treasurer—John B. Lennon.
Secretary—Chris Evans.

BIRMINGHAM, 1891.

President—Samuel Gompers.
First Vice President—P. J. McGuire.
Second Vice President—W. A. Carney.
Secretary—Chris Evans.
Treasurer—John B. Lennon.

PHILADELPHIA, 1892.

President—Samuel Gompers.
First Vice President—P. J. McGuire.
Second Vice President—W. A. Carney.
Secretary—Chris Evans.
Treasurer—John B. Lennon.

CHICAGO, 1893.

President—Samuel Gompers.
First Vice President—P. J. McGuire.
Second Vice President—C. L. Drummond.
Third Vice President—James Brettell.
Fourth Vice President—W. H. Marden
Secretary—Christopher Evans.
Treasurer—John B. Lennon.

DENVER, 1894.

President—John McBride.
First Vice President—P. J. McGuire.
Second Vice President—James Duncan.
Third Vice President—Roady Kenehan.
Fourth Vice President—Thomas J. Elderkin.
Treasurer—John B. Lennon.
Secretary—August McCraith.

NEW YORK, 1895.

President—Samuel Gompers.
First Vice President—P. J. McGuire.
Second Vice President—James Duncan.
Third Vice President—James O'Connell.
Fourth Vice President—Mahlon M. Garland.
Treasurer—John B. Lennon.
Secretary—August McCraith.

CINCINNATI, 1896.

President—Samuel Gompers.
First Vice President—P. J. McGuire.
Second Vice President—James Duncan.
Third Vice President—James O'Connell.
Fourth Vice President—Mahlon M. Garland.
Treasurer—John B. Lennon.
Secretary—Frank Morrison.

NASHVILLE, 1897.

President—Samuel Gompers.
First Vice President—P. J. McGuire.
Second Vice President—James Duncan.
Third Vice President—James O'Connell.
Fourth Vice President—Mahlon M. Garland.
Treasurer—John B. Lennon.
Secretary—Frank Morrison.

KANSAS CITY, 1898.

President—Samuel Gompers.
First Vice President—P. J. McGuire.
Second Vice President—James Duncan.
Third Vice President—James O'Connell.
Fourth Vice President—John Mitchell.
Fifth Vice President—Max Morris.
Sixth Vice President—Thomas I. Kidd.
Treasurer—John B. Lennon.
Secretary—Frank Morrison.

DETROIT, 1899.

President—Samuel Gompers.
First Vice President—P. J. McGuire.
Second Vice President—James Duncan.
Third Vice President—James O'Connell.
Fourth Vice President—John Mitchell.
Fifth Vice President—Max Morris.
Sixth Vice President—Thomas I. Kidd.
Treasurer—John B. Lennon.
Secretary—Frank Morrison.

LOUISVILLE, 1900.

President—Samuel Gompers.
First Vice President—James Duncan.
Second Vice President—John Mitchell.
Third Vice President—James O'Connell.
Fourth Vice President—Max Morris.
Fifth Vice President—Thomas I. Kidd.
Sixth Vice President—Dennis A. Hayes.
Treasurer—John B. Lennon.
Secretary—Frank Morrison.

SCRANTON, 1901.

President—Samuel Gompers.
First Vice President—James Duncan.
Second Vice President—John Mitchell.
Third Vice President—James O'Connell.
Fourth Vice President—Max Morris.
Fifth Vice President—Thomas I. Kidd.
Sixth Vice President—Dennis A. Hayes.
Treasurer—John B. Lennon.
Secretary—Frank Morrison.

NEW ORLEANS, 1902.

President—Samuel Gompers.
First Vice President—James Duncan.
Second Vice President—John Mitchell.
Third Vice President—James O'Connell.
Fourth Vice President—Max Morris.
Fifth Vice President—Thomas I. Kidd.
Sixth Vice President—Dennis A. Hayes.
Treasurer—John B. Lennon.
Secretary—Frank Morrison.

BOSTON, 1903.

President—Samuel Gompers.
First Vice President—James Duncan.
Second Vice President—John Mitchell.
Third Vice President—James O'Connell.
Fourth Vice President—Max Morris.
Fifth Vice President—Thomas I. Kidd.
Sixth Vice President—Dennis A. Hayes.
Seventh Vice President—Daniel J. Keefe.
Eighth Vice President—William J. Spencer.
Treasurer—John B. Lennon.
Secretary—Frank Morrison.

SAN FRANCISCO, 1904.

President—Samuel Gompers.
First Vice President—James Duncan.
Second Vice President—John Mitchell.
Third Vice President—James O'Connell.
Fourth Vice President—Max Morris.
Fifth Vice President—Thomas I. Kidd.
Sixth Vice President—Dennis A. Hayes.
Seventh Vice President—Daniel J. Keefe.
Eighth Vice President—William J. Spencer.
Treasurer—John B. Lennon.
Secretary—Frank Morrison.

PITTSBURGH, 1905.

President—Samuel Gompers.
First Vice President—James Duncan.
Second Vice President—John Mitchell.
Third Vice President—James O'Connell.
Fourth Vice President—Max Morris.
Fifth Vice President—Dennis A. Hayes.
Sixth Vice President—Daniel J. Keefe.
Seventh Vice President—William D. Huber.
Eighth Vice President—Joseph F. Valentine.
Treasurer—John B. Lennon.
Secretary—Frank Morrison.

MINNEAPOLIS, 1906.

President—Samuel Gompers.
First Vice President—James Duncan.
Second Vice President—John Mitchell.
Third Vice President—James O'Connell.
Fourth Vice President—Max Morris.
Fifth Vice President—Dennis A. Hayes.
Sixth Vice President—Daniel J. Keefe.
Seventh Vice President—William D. Huber.
Eighth Vice President—Joseph F. Valentine.
Treasurer—John B. Lennon.
Secretary—Frank Morrison.

NORFOLK, 1907.

President—Samuel Gompers.
First Vice President—James Duncan.
Second Vice President—John Mitchell.
Third Vice President—James O'Connell.
Fourth Vice President—Max Morris.
Fifth Vice President—Dennis A. Hayes.
Sixth Vice President—Daniel J. Keefe.
Seventh Vice President—William D. Huber.
Eighth Vice President—Joseph F. Valentine.
Treasurer—John B. Lennon.
Secretary—Frank Morrison.

DENVER, 1908.

President—Samuel Gompers.
First Vice President—James Duncan.
Second Vice President—John Mitchell.
Third Vice President—James O'Connell.
Fourth Vice President—Max Morris.
Fifth Vice President—Dennis A. Hayes.
Sixth Vice President—William D. Huber.
Seventh Vice President—Joseph F. Valentine.
Eighth Vice President—John R. Alpine.
Treasurer—John B. Lennon.
Secretary—Frank Morrison.

TORONTO, 1909.

President—Samuel Gompers.
First Vice President—James Duncan.
Second Vice President—John Mitchell.
Third Vice President—James O'Connell.
Fourth Vice President—Dennis A. Hayes.
Fifth Vice President—William D. Huber.
Sixth Vice President—Joseph F. Valentine.
Seventh Vice President—John R. Alpine.
Eighth Vice President—Henry B. Perham.
Treasurer—John B. Lennon.
Secretary—Frank Morrison.

ST. LOUIS, 1910.

President—Samuel Gompers.
First Vice President—James Duncan.
Second Vice President—John Mitchell.
Third Vice President—James O'Connell.
Fourth Vice President—Dennis A. Hayes.
Fifth Vice President—William D. Huber.
Sixth Vice President—Joseph F. Valentine.
Seventh Vice President—John R. Alpine.
Eighth Vice President—Henry B. Perham.
Treasurer—John B. Lennon.
Secretary—Frank Morrison.

ATLANTA, 1911.

President—Samuel Gompers.
First Vice President—James Duncan.
Second Vice President—John Mitchell.
Third Vice President—James O'Connell.
Fourth Vice President—Dennis A. Hayes.
Fifth Vice President—William D. Huber.
Sixth Vice President—Joseph F. Valentine.
Seventh Vice President—John R. Alpine.
Eighth Vice President—Henry B. Perham.
Treasurer—John B. Lennon.
Secretary—Frank Morrison.

ROCHESTER, 1912.

President—Samuel Gompers.
First Vice President—James Duncan.
Second Vice President—John Mitchell.
Third Vice President—James O'Connell.
Fourth Vice President—Dennis A. Hayes.
Fifth Vice President—William D. Huber.
Sixth Vice President—Joseph F. Valentine.
Seventh Vice President—John R. Alpine.
Eighth Vice President—Henry B. Perham.
Treasurer—John B. Lennon.
Secretary—Frank Morrison.

SEATTLE, 1913.

President—Samuel Gompers.
First Vice President—James Duncan.
Second Vice President—James O'Connell.
Third Vice President—Dennis A. Hayes.
Fourth Vice President—Joseph F. Valentine.
Fifth Vice President—John R. Alpine.
Sixth Vice President—Henry B. Perham.
Seventh Vice President—John P. White.
Eighth Vice President—Frank Duffy.
Treasurer—John B. Lennon.
Secretary—Frank Morrison.

PHILADELPHIA, 1914.

President—Samuel Gompers.
First Vice President—James Duncan.
Second Vice President—James O'Connell.
Third Vice President—Dennis A. Hayes.
Fourth Vice President—Joseph F. Valentine.
Fifth Vice President—John R. Alpine.
Sixth Vice President—Henry B. Perham.
Seventh Vice President—Frank Duffy.
Eighth Vice President—William Green.
Treasurer—John B. Lennon.
Secretary—Frank Morrison.

SAN FRANCISCO, 1915.

President—Samuel Gompers.
First Vice President—James Duncan.
Second Vice President—James O'Connell.
Third Vice President—Dennis A. Hayes.
Fourth Vice President—Joseph F. Valentine.
Fifth Vice President—John R. Alpine.
Sixth Vice President—Henry B. Perham.
Seventh Vice President—Frank Duffy.
Eighth Vice President—William Green.
Treasurer—John B. Lennon.
Secretary—Frank Morrison.

BALTIMORE, 1916.

President—Samuel Gompers.
First Vice President—James Duncan.
Second Vice President—James O'Connell.
Third Vice President—Dennis A. Hayes.
Fourth Vice President—Joseph F. Valentine.
Fifth Vice President—John R. Alpine.
Sixth Vice President—Henry B. Perham.
Seventh Vice President—Frank Duffy.
Eighth Vice President—William Green.
Treasurer—John B. Lennon.
Secretary—Frank Morrison.

BUFFALO, 1917.

President—Samuel Gompers.
First Vice President—James Duncan.
Second Vice President—James O'Connell.
Third Vice President—Joseph F. Valentine.
Fourth Vice President—John R. Alpine.
Fifth Vice President—Henry B. Perham.
Sixth Vice President—Frank Duffy.
Seventh Vice President—William Green.
Eighth Vice President—William D. Mahon.
Treasurer—Daniel J. Tobin.
Secretary—Frank Morrison.

ST. PAUL, 1918.

President—Samuel Gompers.
First Vice President—James Duncan.
Second Vice President—Joseph F. Valentine.
Third Vice President—John R. Alpine.
Fourth Vice President—Frank Duffy.
Fifth Vice President—William Green.
Sixth Vice President—William D. Mahon.
Seventh Vice President—Thomas A. Rickert.
Eighth Vice President—Jacob Fischer.
Treasurer—Daniel J. Tobin.
Secretary—Frank Morrison.

ATLANTIC CITY, 1919.

President—Samuel Gompers.
First Vice President—James Duncan.
Second Vice President—Joseph F. Valentine.
Third Vice President—Frank Duffy.
Fourth Vice President—William Green.
Fifth Vice President—W. D. Mahon.
Sixth Vice President—T. A. Rickert.
Seventh Vice President—Jacob Fischer.
Eighth Vice President—Matthew Woll.
Treasurer—Daniel J. Tobin.
Secretary—Frank Morrison.

MONTREAL, 1920.

President—Samuel Gompers.
First Vice President—James Duncan.
Second Vice President—Joseph F. Valentine.
Third Vice President—Frank Duffy.
Fourth Vice President—William Green.
Fifth Vice President—W. D. Mahon.
Sixth Vice President—T. A. Rickert.
Seventh Vice President—Jacob Fischer.
Eighth Vice President—Matthew Woll.
Treasurer—Daniel J. Tobin.
Secretary—Frank Morrison.

DENVER, 1921.

President—Samuel Gompers.
First Vice President—James Duncan.
Second Vice President—Joseph F. Valentine.
Third Vice President—Frank Duffy.

Fourth Vice President—William Green.
Fifth Vice President—W. D. Mahon.
Sixth Vice President—T. A. Rickert.
Seventh Vice President—Jacob Fischer.
Eighth Vice President—Matthew Woll.
Treasurer—Daniel J. Tobin.
Secretary—Frank Morrison.

CINCINNATI, 1922.

President—Samuel Gompers.
First Vice President—James Duncan.
Second Vice President—Joseph F. Valentine.
Third Vice President—Frank Duffy.
Fourth Vice President—William Green.
Fifth Vice President—W. D. Mahon.
Sixth Vice President—T. A. Rickert.
Seventh Vice President—Jacob Fischer.
Eighth Vice President—Matthew Woll.
Treasurer—Daniel J. Tobin.
Secretary—Frank Morrison.

PORTLAND, 1923.

President—Samuel Gompers.
First Vice President—James Duncan.
Second Vice President—Joseph F. Valentine.
Third Vice President—Frank Duffy.
Fourth Vice President—William Green.
Fifth Vice President—T. A. Rickert.
Sixth Vice President—Jacob Fischer.
Seventh Vice President—Matthew Woll.
Eight Vice President—Martin F. Ryan.
Treasurer—Daniel J. Tobin.
Secretary—Frank Morrison.

LEGISLATIVE COMMITTEEMEN.

1895—Andrew Furuseth, Adolph Strasser.
1896—Andrew Furuseth.
1897—Andrew Furuseth.
Appointed by the Executive Council:
1898—Andrew Furuseth, George Chance.
1899—Andrew Furuseth, George Chance.
1900—Andrew Furuseth, George Chance
(Died), Thomas F. Tracy.
1901—Andrew Furuseth, Thomas F. Tracy.
1902—Andrew Furuseth, Thomas F. Tracy,
E. L. Tucker, Herman Gudstadt.
1903—Thomas F. Tracy, John A. Moffitt
(appointed but did not serve).
1904—James F. Grimes, Charles L Nelson.
1905—James F. Grimes.
1906—James F. Grimes (resigned), J. D.
Pierce.
1907—Thomas F. Tracy, Arthur E. Holder.
1908—Thomas F. Tracy, Arthur E. Holder,
M. Grant Hamilton, Jacob Tazelaar, J.
D. Pierce, James E. Roach, E. N. Nockels.
1909—Thomas F. Tracy (resigned), Arthur
E. Holder.
1910—Arthur E. Holder.
1911—Arthur E. Holder.
1912 Arthur E. Holder, John A. Moffitt.
1913—Arthur E. Holder, John A. Moffitt,
M. Grant Hamilton.
1915—Arthur E. Holder, M. Grant Hamilton.
1916—Arthur E. Holder, M. Grant Hamilton.
1917—Arthur E. Holder (resigned), M. Grant
Hamilton.
1918—M. Grant Hamilton (resigned), Rollo
S. Sexton, Henry Sterling.
1919—Henry Sterling, Rollo S. Sexton,
William C. Roberts.
1920—William C. Roberts, Edward F. Mc-
Grady, Edgar Wallace.
1921—William C. Roberts, Edward F. Mc-
Grady, Edgar Wallace.
1922—William C. Roberts, Edward F. Mc-
Grady, Edgar Wallace.
1923—William C. Roberts, Edward F. Mc-
Grady, Edgar Wallace.
1924—William C. Roberts, Edward F. Mc-
Grady, Edgar Wallace.

CONVENTION CITIES.

1881	Pittsburgh, Pa.	Dec. 15-18
1882	Cleveland, Ohio.	Nov. 21-24
1883	New York, N. Y.	Aug. 21-24
1884	Chicago, Ill.	Oct. 7-10
1885	Washington, D. C.	Dec. 8-11
1886	Columbus, Ohio.	Dec. 8-12
1887	Baltimore, Md.	Dec. 13-17
1888	St. Louis, Mo.	Dec. 11-15
1889	Boston, Mass.	Dec. 10-14
1890	Detroit, Mich.	Dec. 8-13
1891	Birmingham, Ala.	Dec. 14-19
1892	Philadelphia, Pa.	Dec. 12-17
1893	Chicago, Ill.	Dec. 11-19
1894	Denver, Colo.	Dec. 10-18
1895	New York, N. Y.	Dec. 9-17
1896	Cincinnati, Ohio.	Dec. 14-21
1897	Nashville, Tenn.	Dec. 13-21
1898	Kansas City, Mo.	Dec. 12-20
1899	Detroit, Mich.	Dec. 11-20
1900	Louisville, Ky.	Dec. 6-15
1901	Scranton, Pa.	Dec. 5-14
1902	New Orleans, La.	Nov. 13-22
1903	Boston, Mass.	Nov. 9-23
1904	San Francisco, Calif.	Nov. 14-26
1905	Pittsburgh, Pa.	Nov. 13-25
1906	Minneapolis, Minn.	Nov. 12-24
1907	Norfolk, Va.	Nov. 11-23
1908	Denver, Colo.	Nov. 9-21
1909	Toronto, Ont., Can.	Nov. 8-20
1910	St. Louis, Mo.	Nov. 14-26
1911	Atlanta, Ga.	Nov. 13-25
1912	Rochester, N. Y.	Nov. 11-25
1913	Seattle, Wash.	Nov. 10-22
1914	Philadelphia, Pa.	Nov. 9-21
1915	San Francisco, Calif.	Nov. 8-22
1916	Baltimore, Md.	Nov. 13-25
1917	Buffalo, N. Y.	Nov. 12-24
1918	St. Paul, Minn.	June 10-20
1919	Atlantic City, N. J.	June 9-23
1920	Montreal, Can.	June 7-19
1921	Denver, Colo.	June 13-25
1922	Cincinnati, Ohio.	June 12-24
1923	Portland, Oreg.	Oct. 1-12
1924	El Paso, Tex.	Nov. 17-30

VOTING STRENGTH OF FEDERATION 1897 TO 1923, INCLUSIVE.

Year.	No. Votes.
1897	2,747
1898	2,881
1899	3,632
1900	5,737
1901	8,240
1902	10,705
1903	15,238
1904	17,363
1905	16,338
1906	15,621
1907	16,425
1908	16,892
1909	15,880
1910	16,737
1911	18,693
1912	18,499
1913	20,976
1914	21,185
1915	20,433
1916	21,906
1917	24,973
1918	28,375
1919	33,850
1920	41,307
1921	40,410
1922	33,336
1923	30,486

VOTING STRENGTH

The following table shows the voting strength of the affiliated unions of the American Federation of Labor for the years 1919 up to and including 1923. This table is based upon the average membership reported or paid upon to the American Federation of Labor:

ORGANIZATIONS.	1919.	1920.	1921.	1922.	1923.
Actors, Associated, & Artistes of A	30	69	118	94	77
Asbestos Workers' Intl. Asso. of Heat and Frost Insulators	18	22	26	20	20
Bakery & Confectionery Wkrs. I. U. of A	210	275	280	248	229
Barbers' International Union, Jour	359	442	470	452	432
Bill Posters	16	16	16	16	16
Blacksmiths, Intl. Brotherhood of	283	483	500	367	50
Boilermakers and Iron Shipbuilders	849	1,030	845	417	194
Boot and Shoe Workers' Union	368	467	410	402	399
Bookbinders, Intl. Brotherhood of	164	207	247	163	129
Brewery Workmen, International Union	400	341	273	190	166
Brick and Clay Workers, etc	27	52	54	41	48
Bricklayers, Masons & Plasterers' I. U. A	700	700	700	700	700
Bridge & Struc. Iron Wkrs., Intl. Asso	170	242	199	140	146
Broom and Whisk Makers' Union, Intl	10	14	12	8	7
Building Service Employes' Intl. Union			8	94	78
Carpenters and Joiners, United Bro. of	3,079	3,315	3,521	3,138	3,150
Carmen of A., Bro. Railway	1,004	1,821	2,000	1,717	1,600
Carvers' Union, International Wood	10	12	12	11	9
Cigarmakers' International Union	363	388	342	320	309
Clerks, Bro. of Railway	714	1,860	1,696	1,378	961
Clerks, Intl. Protective Assn. Retail	150	208	212	167	103
Conductors, Order of Sleeping Car		12	25	26	23
Coopers' International Union	40	43	44	28	17
Cutting Die & Cuttermakers, Intl. Union	2	2	3	3	††
Diamond Workers' Prot. Union of A	5	6	6	5	5
Draftsmen's Union, Intl	18	35	22	10	6
Electrical Workers, International Bro	1,312	1,392	1,420	1,420	1,420
Elevator Constructors	30	31	38	38	52
Engineers, B'n. Asso. of U. S. & C., Nat. Mar	128	170	211	190	u
Engineers, Intl. Union of Steam	250	320	320	320	271
Engravers, Steel and Copper Plate	1	2	4	3	2
Engravers Intl. Union, Metal				1	1
Engravers' Union of N. A., Intl. Photo	50	59	65	65	65
Federal Employes, National Fed. of	204	385	330	250	212
Fire Fighters, International Assn. of	154	221	180	161	160
Firemen, Intl. Bro. of Stationary	205	296	350	250	125
Fruit & Vegetable Workers of N. A., Intl. Union of				19	††
Foundry Employes, Intl. Bro. of	54	91	52	40	40
Fur Workers' Union of U. S. & C., Intl	108	121	45	47	92
Garment Workers of America, United	460	459	472	475	476
Glass Bottle Blowers' Assn. of U. S. & C	100	100	100	97	70
Glass Workers, American Flint	95	99	97	87	81
Glass Workers, National Window	50	48	50	50	50
Glove Workers	7	10	7	4	2
Granite Cutters' Intl. Asso. of A., The	107	105	105	100	95
Hatters of North America, United	100	105	115	115	115
Hodcarriers and Common Laborers	400	420	460	460	475
Horseshoers of United States and Canada	54	54	54	25	20
Hotel and Restaurant Employes, etc	608	604	572	465	384
Iron, Steel and Tin Workers' Amal. Asso	197	315	254	159	117
Jewelry Workers' International	51	81	s	s	22
Lace Operatives, Amal	9	q	q	q	q
Ladies' Garment Workers. International	905	1,054	941	939	912
Lathers, Intl. Union of W. W. & Metal	60	59	80	80	80
Laundry Workers, International Union	60	67	70	65	55
Leather Workers' Intl. Union, United	67	117	80	34	20
Letter Carriers, National Asso. of	307	325	325	325	325
Letter Carriers, Nat. Fed. of Rural		3	16	10	6
Lithographers' Intl. P. & B. Asso	56	61	72	76	63
Longshoremen's Association, Intl	313	740	641	463	343
Machinists, International Association of	2,546	3,308	2,736	1,809	973
Maintenace of Way Employes, I. B. of	542	q	q	q	377
Marble, etc., International Asso. of	10	12	12	17	23
Masters, Mates and Pilots	62	71	91	55	41
Meat Cutters and Butcher Workmen	663	653	439	196	104
Metal Workers' Intl. Alliance, Amal. Sheet	202	218	242	250	250
Mine Workers of America, United	3,938	3,936	4,257	3,729	4,049
Mine, Mill and Smelter Wkrs., I. U. of	178	211	162	46	81
Molders' Union of North America, Intl	516	573	585	265	321
Musicians, American Federation of	654	700	746	750	750

VOTING STRENGTH—Continued

ORGANIZATIONS.	1919.	1920.	1921.	1922.	1923.
Oil Field, etc., Workers	45	209	248	61	25
Painters of America, Brotherhood of	827	1,031	1,133	978	928
Papermakers, United Brotherhood of	57	74	107	83	70
Patrolmen, Brotherhood of Railroad		26	16	9	†
Patternmakers' League of N. A	90	90	90	80	80
Pavers & Rammermen, Intl. Union of	18	19	20	20	20
Paving Cutters' Union of U. S. of A. & C	26	26	24	24	24
Piano & Organ Wkrs. Union of A., Intl	20	32	27	9	7
Plasterers' Intl. Asso. of U. S. & C., Oper	190	194	239	246	252
Plumbers, Steamfitters, etc	320	320	319	350	350
Polishers, Intl. Union Metal	100	100	100	82	67
Post Office Clerks, Natl. Federation of	145	162	170	178	180
Potters, National Bro. of Operative	74	80	91	92	91
Powder and High Explosive Workers	3	3	2	2	3
Printing Pressmen, International	340	350	370	370	370
Printers' Union of N. A., I. S. & C. Plate	13	14	15	15	12
Printers and Color Mixers, Machine	5	5	5	5	t
Print Cutters' Asso. of A., Natl	4	4	4	3	t
Pulp, Sulphite, and Paper Mill Wkrs	84	95	113	68	46
Quarry Workers, International	30	30	30	30	24
Railway Employes' Amal. Asso., S. & E	897	987	1,000	1,000	1,000
Railway Mail Association	134	144	150	166	167
Roofers, Damp & Waterproof Wkrs. Assn. United Slate, Tile and Composition	10	18	28	30	30
Sawsmiths' National Union	1	1	1	1	1
Seamen's Union of America, Intl	427	659	1,033	492	179
Sideographers, Intl. Assn. of	1	1	1	1	1
Signalmen, Bro. R. R.	62	123	113	105	89
Slate and Tile Roofers	6	r	r	r	r
Spinners' Intl. Union	22	r	r	r	r
Stage Employes, Intl. Alliance Theatrical	185	196	194	195	196
Steam Shovel and Dredge Men	d	d	d	d	d
Stereotypers & Electrotypers' U. of A	54	59	61	60	62
Stonecutters' Association, Journeymen	39	40	44	46	49
Stove Mounters' International Union	19	19	20	20	18
Switchmen's Union of North America	118	140	101	88	87
Tailors' Union of America, Journeymen	120	120	120	120	119
Teachers, Am. Fed. of	28	93	93	70	46
Teamsters, Chauffeurs, etc., Intl. Bro. of	756	1,108	1,057	764	727
Telegraphers, Commercial	20	22	32	34	26
Telegraphers, Order of Railroad	446	487	500	500	500
Textile Workers of America, United	558	1,049	829	300	300
Tile Layers and Helpers, Intl. Union	d	d	d	d	d
Timber Workers, Intl. Union of	32	101	58	8	††
Tip Printers	p	p	p	p	p
Tobacco Workers' Intl. Union of America	42	152	123	34	19
Tunnel & Subway Constructors, I. U	20	30	30	30	30
Typographical Union, International	647	705	748	689	681
Upholsterers, International Union of	55	56	60	67	73
United Wall Paper Craft of N. A					7
Weavers, Elastic Goring	1	1	1	1	1
Wire Weavers' Protective, American	3	4	4	4	4
Centrals	816	926	973	905	901
State Branches	46	46	49	49	49
Directly affiliated local unions	1,091	1,498	1,027	747	581
Total vote of Unions	33,849	41,307	40.410	33,336	30,486

†Suspended for non-payment of per capita tax.   ††Disbanded.   d Not recognized.
p Merged with Bookbinders.   q Suspended for failure to comply with decision of the Atlantic
City Convention.   r Merged with Composition Roofers, etc.   t Amalgamation of National
Association of Machine Printers and Color Mixers of the U. S., with National Print Cutters'
Association of America, and change of title to United Wall Paper Crafts of N. A.   u With-
drawn from Affiliation.

LIST OF DELEGATES AND FRATERNAL DELEGATES.

Delegates from the American Federation of Labor to the International Federation of Trade Unions

1909 Samuel Gompers.	1911. James Duncan.	1913. George W. Perkins
*1915.		*1917.

To British Trades Union Congress.

1895	Samuel Gompers. P. J. McGuire.	1905	John A. Moffitt. James Wood.	***1915	W. D. Mahon. Matthew Woll.
1896	J. W. Sullivan. Adolph Strasser.	1906	Frank K. Foster. James Wilson.	1916	W. D. Mahon. Matthew Woll.
1897	Martin Fox. Geo. E. McNeill.	1907	John T. Dempsey. W. E. Klapetzky.	1917	John Golden. James Lord.
1898	James Duncan. Harry Lloyd.	1908	Andrew Furuseth. James J. Creamer.	1918	J. A. Franklin. Wm. J. Bowen.
1899	James O'Connell. Thomas F. Tracy.	1909	John P. Frey. B. A. Larger.	1919	Wm. L. Hutcheson. John J. Hynes.
1900	J. M. Hunter. Sidney J. Kent.	1910	W. B. Wilson. T. V. O'Connor.	1920	Timothy Healy. Mrs. Sarah Conboy.
1901	Daniel J. Keefe. Eugene F. O'Rourke.	1911	Wm. B. Macfarlane. Daniel J. Tobin.	1921	Wm. J. Spencer. James J. Forrester.
1902	Patrick Dolan. Henry Blackmore.	1912	George L. Berry. John H. Walker	1922	Benjamin Schlesinger. E. J. McGivern.
1903	Max S. Hayes. Martin Lawlor.	1913	Chas. L. Baine. Louis Kemper.	1923	Peter Shaughnessy. Anthony J. Chlopek.
1904	W. D. Ryan. D. D. Driscoll.	*1914	W. D. Mahon. Matthew Woll.	1924	Peter J. Brady. Edward J. Gainor

From British Trades Union Congress.

1894	John Burns. David Holmes.	1905	William Mosses. David Gilmour.	1916	H. Gosling. W. Whitefield.
1895	Edward Cowey. James Mawdsley.	1906	Allen Gee. J. N. Bell.	1917	John Hill. Arthur Hayday.
1896	Sam Woods. John Mallinson.	1907	David J. Shackleton. John Hodge.	***1918	F. Hall. Miss Margaret Bondfield.
1897	Edward Harford. J. Havelock Wilson.	1908	John Wadsworth. H. Skinner.	1919	S. Finney. Miss Margaret Bondfield.
1898	William Inskip. William Thorne.	1909	A. H. Gill. J. R. Clynes.	1920	J. W. Ogden. J. Jones.
1899	James Haslam. Alexander Wilkie.	1910	W. Brace. Ben. Turner.	1921	J. H. Thomas. James Walker.
1900	John Weir. Pete Curran.	1911	G. H. Roberts. J. Crinion.	1922	E. L. Poulton. H. Smith.
1901	Frank Chandler. Ben Tillett.	1912	J. A. Seddon. R. Smillie.	1923	R. B. Walker W. C. Robinson.
1902	M. Arrandale. E. Edwards	1913	I. H. Gwynne. T. Greenall.	1924	C. T. Cramp. A. B. Swales.
1903	William Mullin. James O'Grady.	**1914			
1904	William Abraham. James Wignall.	1915	C. G. Ammon. E. Bevin.		

To Canadian Trades and Labor Congress.

1898 Thomas I. Kidd.	1907 Robert S. Maloney.	1916 Harry P. Corcoran.
1899 James H. Sullivan.	1908 Hugh Frayne.	1917 Emanuel Koveleski.
1900 W. D. Mahon.	1909 Jerome Jones.	1918 Stuart H. Hayward
1901 John R. O'Brien.	1910 John J. Manning.	1919 Sam Griggs.
1902 D. D. Driscoll.	1911 Wm. J. Tracy.	1920 W. G. Shea.
1903 John Coleman.	1912 John T. Smith.	1921 John O'Hara.
1904 John H. Richards.	1913 Wm. J. McSorley.	1922 William E. Hulsbeck.
1905 Frank Feeney.	1914 M. M. Donoghue.	1923 Walter N. Reddick.
1906 Thomas A. Rickert.	1915 H. J. Conway.	1924 Walter W. Britton

From Canadian Trades and Labor Congress.

1898 David A. Carey.	1907 W. R. Trotter.	1916 Thomas A. Stevenson
1899 David A. Carey.	1908 P. M. Draper.	1917 Wm. Lodge.
1900 David A. Carey.	1909 F. Bancroft.	1918 Thos. Moore.
1901 P. M. Draper.	1910 R. P. Pettipiece.	1919 J. M. Walsh.
1902 John H. Kennedy.	1911 Wm. Glockling.	1920 J. A. McClellan.
1903 James Simpson.	1912 John W. Bruce.	1921 U. M. F. Bush.
1904 John A. Flett.	1913 Gus Francq.	1922 Ernest Robinson.
1905 William V. Todd.	1914 R. A. Rigg.	1923 James A. Sullivan.
1906 Samuel L. Landers.	1915 Fred Bancroft.	1924 John Colbert

From German Federation of Labor.
1924 Peter Grassman

*No convention.	**No delegates.	***Delegates did not attend.

INDEX